International Political Economy Series

General Editor: **Timothy M. Shaw**, Professor of Commonwealth Governance and Development, and Director of the Institute of Commonwealth Studies, School of Advanced Study, University of London

Titles include:

Jomo K.S. and Shyamala Nagaraj (*editors*)
GLOBALIZATION VERSUS DEVELOPMENT

Dominic Kelly and Wyn Grant (*editors*)
THE POLITICS OF INTERNATIONAL TRADE IN THE TWENTY-FIRST CENTURY
Actors, Issues and Regional Dynamics

Craig N. Murphy (*editor*)
EGALITARIAN POLITICS IN THE AGE OF GLOBALIZATION

Michael Niemann
A SPATIAL APPROACH TO REGIONALISM IN THE GLOBAL ECONOMY

Morten Ougaard
THE GLOBALIZATION OF POLITICS
Power, Social Forces and Governance

Markus Perkmann and Ngai-Ling Sum
GLOBALIZATION, REGIONALIZATION AND CROSS-BORDER REGIONS

Leonard Seabrooke
US POWER IN INTERNATIONAL FINANCE
The Victory of Dividends

Timothy J. Sinclair and Kenneth P. Thomas (*editors*)
STRUCTURE AND AGENCY IN INTERNATIONAL CAPITAL MOBILITY

Fredrik Söderbaum and Timothy M. Shaw (*editors*)
THEORIES OF NEW REGIONALISM
A Palgrave Reader

Kendall Stiles (*editor*)
GLOBAL INSTITUTIONS AND LOCAL EMPOWERMENT
Competing Theoretical Perspectives

International Political Economy Series
Series Standing Order ISBN 0–333–71708–2 hardcover
Series Standing Order ISBN 0–333–71110–6 paperback
(*outside North America only*)

You can receive future titles in this series as they are published by placing a standing order. Please contact your bookseller or, in case of difficulty, write to us at the address below with your name and address, the title of the series and one of the ISBNs quoted above.

Customer Services Department, Macmillan Distribution Ltd, Houndmills, Basingstoke, Hampshire RG21 6XS, England

The Politics of International Trade in the Twenty-first Century

Actors, Issues and Regional Dynamics

Edited by

Dominic Kelly
Department of Politics & International Studies
University of Warwick, UK

and

Wyn Grant
Department of Politics & International Studies
University of Warwick, UK

First published in 2005 by
PALGRAVE MACMILLAN
Houndmills, Basingstoke, Hampshire RG21 6XS and
175 Fifth Avenue, New York, N.Y. 10010
Companies and representatives throughout the world.

PALGRAVE MACMILLAN is the global academic imprint of the Palgrave
Macmillan division of St. Martin's Press, LLC and of Palgrave Macmillan Ltd.
Macmillan® is a registered trademark in the United States, United Kingdom
and other countries. Palgrave is a registered trademark in the European
Union and other countries.

ISBN 1–4039–0483–9 (cloth)
ISBN 1–4039–0484–7 (paper)

This book is printed on paper suitable for recycling and made from fully
managed and sustained forest sources.

A catalogue record for this book is available from the British Library.

Library of Congress Cataloging-in-Publication Data
    The politics of international trade in the 21st century : actors, issues, and regional
dynamics / edited by Dominic Kelly & Wyn Grant.
        p. cm. – (International political economy series)
    Includes bibliographical references and index.
    ISBN 1–4039–0483–9 (cloth) – ISBN 1–4039–0484–7 (paper)
        1. International trade. 2. Commercial policy. 3. Foreign trade regulation.
    4. International agencies. 5. Regionalism. 6. International economic relations. I. Kelly,
Dominic, 1965– II. Grant, Wyn. III. International political economy series (Palgrave
Macmillan (Firm))

HF1379.P655 2005
382—dc22   2004051235

10 9 8 7 6 5 4 3 2 1
14 13 12 11 10 09 08 07 06 05

Printed and bound in Great Britain by
Antony Rowe Ltd, Chippenham and Eastbourne.

Contents

Part III Regional Dynamics

List of Illustrations

Figures

Tables

Notes on Contributors

Mark T. Berger is Senior Lecturer in the International Studies Program and the Department of Spanish and Latin American Studies at the University of New South Wales (Sydney, Australia). His most recent publications include, *The Battle for Asia: From Decolonization to Globalization* (Routledge, 2004).

Shaun Breslin is Professor of Politics and International Studies at the University of Warwick. He is author of *China in the 1980s: Centre–Province Relations in a Reforming Socialist State, Mao and co-author of Comparative Government and Politics: An Introduction.*

David Coen is Senior Lecturer in Public Policy and Director of the MSc in Public Policy in the School of Public Policy at University College London. Prior to joining UCL he was Fellow (1997–2001) at the London Business School, where he co-directed a study with the Max Planck Institute in Bonn on Business Perspectives to Utility Regulation. While at the LBS he held a visiting appointment as Lecturer in International Business at Warwick University. Previously he was Fellow at the Max Planck Institute in Cologne (1996–97) and completed his doctoral thesis at the European University Institute in Florence in 1996. He is currently editor of the UCL Public Policy Working Paper Series, serves on the editorial board of *Business strategy Review* and is Chair of the Business and Government Research Network of the International Political Studies Association.

Pedro da Motta Veiga is a partner at EcoStrat Consultores (Rio de Janeiro) and works on trade negotiations as well as trade and industrial policies issues. He is a permanent consultant to *Confederação Nacional da Indústria* (CNI) of Brazil and a member of the Advisory Board of the Working Group on Mercosur – EU Negotiations and of the Steering Committee of Latin American Trade Network – LATN. He has acted as consultant to many international institutions, such as UNCTAD, CEPAL, IADB, The World Bank, OECD and ALADI.

Andreas Falke is full professor and chairholder in International Studies (with emphasis on transatlantic relations and trade policy) at Business and Economics School of the University of Erlangen-Nürnberg (Nürnberg Campus). His research interests include the politics of globalization, trade policy, transatlantic economic relations and American politics. From 1992–2002 he worked as a senior analyst in the economics section of the American Embassy in Germany.

Wyn Grant is Professor of Politics at the University of Warwick and has written extensively on comparative public policy and political economy. His most recent book is (with William Coleman and Tim Josling) *Agriculture in the New Global Economy* (Edward Elgar, 2004).

Nigel Haworth is Professor of Human Resource Development at the University of Auckland, New Zealand. His research focuses on internationalization and the labour movement, particularly in relation to the contemporary debate around labour standards. He is also involved in research and policy matters related to regional integration and HRD, especially in the Asia–Pacific region.

Steve Hughes has long-standing research and teaching interests in International Organisations and International Political Economy with a particular emphasis on international regimes of regulation. Before taking up his current post at the University of Newcastle upon Tyne, he spent nine years at the University of Auckland. His research work is interdisciplinary in nature and he has consciously published in leading journals in the fields of International Political Economy, International Organisation and Industrial Relations. He continues to enjoy long-standing research collaborations with colleagues at the Universities of Auckland and Manchester and is a member of the British International Studies Association (BISA) and the BISA International Political Economy Group.

Dominic Kelly is Lecturer in International Political Economy at the University of Warwick and has written on comparative capitalisms, Japanese and east Asian Political economy, and the diplomacy of government–business relations. Publications include *Japan and the Reconstruction of East Asia* (Palgrave, 2002) and *Stakeholder Capitalism* (Macmillan, 1997), co-edited with Gavin Kelly and Andrew Gamble.

Christopher May is Reader in IPE at the University of the West of England, and a co-editor of the IPE Yearbook Series. He has published widely on intellectual property rights and is currently working on an international history of IPRs with Susan Sell. He co-edited a collection of Susan Strange's work, and has also recently written on the off-shoring of work, the ideology of the information society, AIDS and technical assistance. He is currently editing Global Corporate Power (IPE Yearbook 15) and is preparing work on open source software.

Peter Newell is a Research Fellow at the Institute of Development Studies. Prior to holding this position he was Lecturer in International Political Economy at the University of Warwick and worked with environmental NGOs in Brussels and London. He has published widely on the international politics of the environment, including the books *Climate for change: Non-State Actors and the Global Politics of the Greenhouse*, and *The Effectiveness of EU Environmental Policy* (co-authored). He currently works on the polities of crop biotechnology regulation and issues of corporate accountability and regulation.

Nicola Phillips is Hallsworth Research Fellow at the University of Manchester, UK. She is an editor of New Political Economy and Co-editor of the International Political Economy Yearbook series, and is author, most recently, of *The Southern Cone Model: The Political Economy of Regional Capitalist Development in Latin America*.

Tony Porter is Professor of Political Science at McMaster University, Hamilton, Canada. He is author of *States, Markets and Regimes in Global Finance* (Macmillan, 1993), *Technology, Governance and Political Conflict in International Industries*, (Routledge, 2002), *Globalization and Finance* (Polity, in press), and co-editor, with A. Claire Cutler and Virginia Haufler, of *Private Authority in International Affairs* (SUNY Press, 1999).

Mills Soko is currently completing doctoral research on the political economy of trade policy reform in post-apartheid South Africa at the University of Warwick (United Kingdom). From 1996 to 1997 he was a researcher to the Select Committee on Trade and Industry, Foreign Affairs, and Public Enterprises in the National Council of Provinces (NCOP), the upper house of the South African National Parliament. He subsequently served as Director of Policy and legislative research in the NCOP, where he oversaw and coordinated the work of committee researchers. His recent published articles on South African and African trade issues include: 'Championing African Trade Interests: The Africa Group within the WTO', co-authored with Mzukisi Qobo, in Peter Drapter and Steven Gruzd (eds) *Africa after Cancun – Trade Negotiations in Uncertain Times* (South African Institute of International Affairs, 2003); and 'US Trade Strategy after Cancun: Prospects and Implications for the SACU–US FTA', Co-authored with Peter Draper, SAIIA Trade Report No.4 (South African Institute of International Affairs, 2004).

Ian Taylor is a lecturer in the School of International Relations, University of St Andrews. He formely taught at the University of Botswana and holds a DPhil from the University of Stellenbosch, South Africa. He is the author of *Struck in Middle GEAR: South Africa's Post-Apartheid Foreign Relations* (2001), and co-editor of *Africa in International Politics: External Involvement on the Continent* (2004), *Regionalism and Uneven Development in Southern Africa: The Case of The Maputo Development Corridor* (2003), and *South Africa's Multilateral Diplomacy and Global Change: The Limits of Reform* (2001).

Jarrod Wiener is Senior Lecturer in International Relations at the University of Kent at Canterbury, England. He is Director of the University of Kent's Brussels School of International Studies, and Editor of *Global Society: Journal of Interdisciplinary International Relations*. He is author of *Making Rules in the Uruguay Round of the GATT* (Dartmouth, 1995), and *Globalization and the Harmonization of Law* (Pinter, 1999).

Rorden Wilkinson is Senior Lecturer in International Relations and International Political Economy at the University of Manchester, UK. He has held visiting positions at Brown University, Wellesley College and the Australian National University. He is author of *Multilateralism and the World Trade Organisation* (Routledge, 2000); editor of *Global Governance: Concepts and Issues* (Routledge, 2005); editor of *Global Governance: Critical Perspectives*, (Routledge, 2002); co-editor (with Louise Amoore and Randall Germain) of Routledge's RIPE series in Global Political Economy; and co-editor (with Thomas G. Weiss) of the Routledge Global Institutions Series. His work has been published in among others, *Third World Quarterly, Global Governance, Journal of World Trade, New Political Economy,*

Environmental Politics, Convergences, International Studies Perspectives, and the *British Journal of Politics and International Relations.* He is currently working on a book-length exploration of the tendency towards crisis in WTO negotiations.

Marc Williams is Professor of International Relations at the University of New South Wales. His publications include (with Robert O'Brien) *Global Political Economy: Evolution and Dynamics* (Palgrave Macmillan, 2004); (with Robert O'Brien, Anne Marie Goetz and Jan Aart Scholte) *Contesting Global Governance: Multitateral Economic Institutions and Global Social Movements* (Cambridge University Press, 2000).

Stephen Woolcock is a lecturer in International Relations at the London School of Economics, where he teaches international political economy, economic diplomacy and the politics of international trade. He is also head of the International Trade Policy Unit at the LSE, which conducts research on current trade issues and runs in-services programmes for trade negotiators. His research interests are centred on the regulation of integrating markets, both regionally within regional integration agreements and globally within the international trade and investment regimes. His recent other publications include *Regionalism, Multilateralism and Economic Integration: the recent experience,* with Gary Sampson (eds) (UNU Press, 2003), and *The New Economic Diplomacy* with Nicholas Bayne (eds), (Ashgate, 2002). Before joining the LSE in 1994 he had been a Senior Research Fellow at the Royal Institute of International Affairs (Chatham House), Deputy Director for International Affairs at the Confederation of British Industry and Paul Henri Spaak Fellow at the Centre for International Affairs, Harvard University.

Introduction: Trade Politics in Context

Dominic Kelly and Wyn Grant

Trade politics and global governance

We live in an era where global politics is dominated by a relatively small set of states, institutions and businesses supportive of market-led solutions to the world's ills, be these economic, social or strategic in nature. The key states are the United States, the European Union (in both its aggregated and disaggregated modes), Japan and, arguably, Canada.[1] The key institutions are the World Bank, the IMF and the World Trade Organisation underpinned by the military might of the United States, the NATO alliance and a host of regional and bilateral security agreements amongst the major powers. The key businesses are too numerous – and far-flung – to be individually named but appear regularly in the Fortune 500 and on the membership rosters of peak business associations such as the International Chamber of Commerce, the World Economic Forum, and the European Round Table as well as their national equivalents.

The specific goals of these actors are many and varied and therefore often cross-cutting and contradictory. Nevertheless, they share a vision of a peaceful, stable and prosperous world, and are in broad agreement as to how this might be brought about: that is, through the promotion of liberalism in both its political and economic forms on a global scale. Despite the apparent weakening of its appeal over recent years, liberalism remains the dominant ideological force in the global political economy. It continues to be intolerant of social, economic and political systems that do not conform to a particular template. This template, labelled 'good governance', requires the adoption or creation of social, economic and political institutions and processes reflective of the 'best practice' established in advanced industrial states. A system of benchmarking has evolved to chart progress toward this goal, and involves input from states, international organizations, non-governmental organizations, and even private bond-rating agencies (Wilkinson and Hughes 2002). Inducements come – often simultaneously – in the form of 'carrots' such as humanitarian assistance, aid, grants, investment, market access amongst others, and 'sticks' including military force, election monitors and accession procedures (Cox 2002; Duffield 2001; Thomas 2001).

The arena of trade politics has not been unaffected by this imposition of liberal ideas and ideology (Nadkarni 1999). The identification of new issues and their placement on the agenda of international trade talks is discussed below, as are the institutional changes that have been required as part of their incorporation. Underpinning these changes is a commitment to liberal assumptions that, rhetorically at least, has seen the debate over the relative merits of free trade and protectionism come to an end. The GATT allowed for a delicate balancing act between the perceived benefits for the global economy of an open and liberal trading order, on the one hand, and the requirements of domestic stability on the other. It was, in other words, a manifestation of the post-war compromise of 'embedded liberalism' (Ruggie 1982). The WTO, by contrast, is an institution devoted to a purer and less restrained version of liberalism. The biannual ministerial meetings ensure that pressure for liberalization is continually – rather than periodically – brought to bear. Even more significant, the disputes settlement mechanism is steadily eroding the policy autonomy of the member states through the slow accretion of case law regarding trade issues. The move from a power-based system to one grounded in the law constrains even the most powerful member states and threatens to tear down, piece by piece, the policy edifice constructed on the foundations of embedded liberalism.

What will be left of the embedded liberal compromise remains an open question. It remains an open question because the WTO is not free of power politics. What is not in doubt is that the WTO is no longer a forum in which to discuss the merits of free trade. Protectionism is tolerated but only under the strictest of conditions – these being determined by the strongest actors and therefore usually but not always in their own interests. Thus in the arena of trade politics the old maxim, that the strong do what they will and the weak do what they must, still applies.

The debate over free trade versus protectionism is, moreover, a debate that in its traditional form cannot any longer *fully* capture the complexity of trade politics. Trade now has a role and a significance that goes beyond traditional images of the exchange of goods across national borders. These images remain important but they have been overlain by others. At its simplest these images portray new actors in international trade, new processes through which trade and trade politics is conducted and new issues with which everyone must engage. In reality of course these images cannot simply be stacked atop one another but must be conceived as interlocking, cross-cutting and overflowing. It is a world with which Salvador Dali would be familiar. The next section outlines how this happened through a discussion of trade politics from the origins of the GATT to its replacement by the WTO and the launching of the 'Millennium Round'.

Trade politics in historical context

When the post-war international economic settlement was being constructed, it was proposed to create an international trade organization (ITO) that would work alongside the International Monetary Fund and the World Bank, forming a triumvirate of global governance agencies. Because of opposition within the United States and for other reasons, an ITO with an effective disputes settlement mechanism was not agreed. The Republican controlled Congress was suspicious of the ITO concept and the discussions about its establishment in Havana. President Truman and secretary of state Acheson gave a higher priority to building the North American alliance. When the Republicans won further gains in the November 1950 elections, Truman decided that the ITO treaty should not be resubmitted to Congress.

Instead what was put in its place as a second best solution was an already functioning international agreement, a General Agreement on Tariffs and Trade (GATT), serviced by a secretariat in Geneva. Initially, 23 countries were 'contracting parties', a number that had grown to 37 by 1960, still largely drawn from the developed countries. As Williams points out in Chapter 2, the GATT was a weak organization with limited power over its membership. It was a contractual arrangement that proceeded on an intergovernmental rather than a supranational basis. Its work was conducted through a series of 'rounds' or linked negotiations over a period of time, the first held in Geneva in 1947, that led to reductions in quantitative tariffs and hence to a step-by-step liberalization of international trade. 'Whatever limitations may have been inherent in this model were overshadowed by the unparalleled economic growth of the 1950s and 1960s as well as the dominant role of the United States which allowed Washington to set the agenda on international trade matters' (Warnecke 1978: 4).

Against the background of the Cold War, the United States was prepared to bear some of the costs of sustaining a more liberal international trading system. Indeed, the costs were not too evident in the 1950s and 1960s, while there were clear benefits for American multinational companies. Trade policy was not politically controversial in the United States and its formulation and implementation was chiefly in the hands of the executive branch with the legislature taking a largely passive role. As Porter notes in Chapter 11, one contested explanation of US trade policy is hegemonic stability theory that claimed that American support for a liberal trading order was a reflection of its emergence as a hegemon.

As growth slowed in the world economy in the 1970s, there was a swing back to protectionism. At least the GATT discipline restrained the use of tariff increases, although there was an increasing resort to anti-dumping actions. However, countries resorted to an increasing number of non-tariff barriers, often involving persuading exporting countries to restrict their exports through so-called 'voluntary' export restraints or orderly marketing agreements. As Kelly notes in Chapter 18 on Japan, this practice was a key characteristic of the US–Japan trading relationship. In the case of textiles, an important area of export activity for developing countries, an even more elaborate set of arrangements restricted the growth of exports in the form of the Long-Term Arrangement, later consolidated as the Multi-Fibre Arrangement in 1974. The Tokyo Round (1973–79) did little that curbed these new forms of protectionism.

Held against the background of a world recession which had seen trade actually shrink for the first time since the Second World War, the 1982 ministerial meetings in Geneva represented perhaps the lowest point in the history of GATT. Disaster in the form of a retreat from multilateral to regional or bilateral agreements was narrowly avoided. However, it also led to a realization that trade relations could not continue being handled through an unmodified GATT framework. Apart from anything else, a mandate limited to trade in goods was becoming less relevant as the world economy changed with an increasing role for trade in services. As the world economy recovered in 1983, a search was in progress 'for ways of putting international trade relations on a more secure and less divisive basis' (Croome 1995: 15).

The United States pushed hard for a new round of negotiations. The Reagan (and subsequently the Bush) administrations were ideologically in favour of free trade. Pressure for the liberalization of trade in services came from the financial services and telecommunications industries. Agri-business interests favoured greater liberalization in agricultural trade. Support for bringing agricultural trade into the negotiations came from the new Cairns Group of developed and developing nations led by Australia.

What was to be the longest and most radical of the GATT rounds, the Uruguay Round, was launched in Punta del Este in Uruguay in September 1986. 'The major issues of the Punta del Este meeting were agriculture and the three 'new issues', namely trade in services, protection of intellectual property and trade-related investment measures' (Preeg 1995: 4). The drafting of the ministerial declaration foresaw the controversies over agricultural trade that were to plague the whole round over the wording to be used and its meaning. The declaration contained relatively explicit language on services, but was more tentative on intellectual property and brief on trade-related investment measures. Intellectual property was a subject of increasing concern to the United States, prompted by key American industries such as the pharmaceutical industry. The United States wanted a much broader discussion than simply a focus on counterfeit goods. As Porter points out in Chapter 11, the new areas into which the Uruguay Round expanded rule-making are ones primarily of concern to leading US firms. Strengthening GATT institutions was also a theme of the declaration, and it became an issue of increasing importance as the negotiations developed. GATT had a disputes settlement mechanism, but it was largely discredited. 'The Dispute Settlement Group proceeded with low profile deliberations that steadily grew in importance during the course of the Uruguay Round' (Preeg 1995: 77).

The Uruguay Round was initially supposed to be completed in four years and a mid-term review meeting was scheduled for Montreal in 1988. This simply revealed the extent of the disagreement between the participants in the negotiations. In particular, it was evident that there were major difficulties over agriculture. It was agriculture that led to the suspension of what was supposed to be the final negotiating meeting in Brussels in December 1990 (see Chapter 5 by Grant). Meanwhile, however, there had been what were to turn out to be highly significant discussions in the informal but important 'Quad' group (the US, Canada, Japan and the EU) about replacing the GATT with a World Trade Organisation, although the United States was initially unenthusiastic. Nevertheless, Canada formally tabled this idea as a proposal in April 1990.

The issue of agriculture was eventually dealt with by bilateral agreements between the United States and the European Union (the so-called 'Blair House' accords) which provided the basis for a multilateral settlement. The final issue that had to be resolved was the question of European restrictions, prompted by France, on US audiovisual services that had to be left for further negotiations. The Uruguay Round negotiations were finally concluded, more than eight years after they had started, on 15 December 1994 and the final agreement was signed in Marrakech in April 1995.

The most important consequence of the Uruguay Round was the replacement of GATT by the WTO with 146 countries in membership in 2003, including the People's Republic of China. It was still handicapped by having a much more limited secretariat than the other global governance agencies, although its staff had grown to 550 by 2003. However, the centrepiece of the new WTO was an effective disputes settlement procedure. By the summer of 2003, 298 cases had been brought to the WTO for settlement. It was, of course, the very effectiveness of this procedure that led to concerns about an erosion of national sovereignty. As Williams points out in Chapter 2, the Uruguay Round extended coverage of the multilateral trading system to domestic policies, institutional practices and negotiations. For anti-globalization activists, the WTO was the 'World Terror Organisation' and its meetings in Seattle in 1999 were disrupted by violent demonstrations.

The outcomes of the Uruguay Round were not limited to changes in the institutional architecture. Although the substantive impact of the agreement on agriculture was limited, agricultural trade was fully integrated into the WTO system and made the subject of further discussions. Textiles and apparel was also integrated into the world trading system, even if there was a long transition period with substantial 'backloading' of its effects. Services were also integrated into regulated international trade and there was a wide-ranging agreement on trade-related aspects of intellectual property rights (TRIPs). Tariffs were cut further, although there was relatively little change in procedures for handling anti-dumping disputes. In sum, the Uruguay Round agreement could convincingly be portrayed as 'a major achievement in broadening and deepening the multilateral framework for world trade' (Preeg 1995: 210).

In the late 1990s, agreement was reached on a number of issues that had remained unresolved or only partially resolved in the Uruguay Round. Negotiations continued on telecommunications. In February 1997, 69 governments agreed further liberalization of the sector. The outcome was not entirely satisfactory from a US perspective with some issues left unresolved. Nevertheless, the agreement involved the opening of some key Asia Pacific markets and covered 90 per cent of the world telecommunications market by value (McDonald 1998: 237).

The Singapore ministerial meeting in 1996 set out a framework for liberalizing trade in information technology which was finalized in 1997. Forty governments successfully concluded negotiations for tariff-free trade in information technology products. Financial services were limited to a temporary agreement in the Uruguay Round, but in December 1997 it was agreed to include them on a permanent basis in the General Agreement on Trade in Services (GATS). Seventy countries made commitments that created a financial services deal that covered more than 95 per cent of the trade in financial services in areas such as banking, insurance and securities.

This success in concluding sectoral agreements contributed to a debate about whether the GATT structure of negotiating rounds was now redundant. The advantage of 'rounds' is, of course, that they permit 'trade offs' between various aspects of the negotiations. On the other hand, this may result in agreements that lack coherence or that fail to resolve difficult issues. It may also disadvantage those countries, particularly developing countries, that lack negotiating resources and skills.

Nevertheless, a momentum built for a 'Millennium Round' of trade negotiations. The Seattle ministerial conference of 1999 was unable to deliver such a round, not just because of the demonstrations on the streets, but because of a failure to take sufficient account of the concerns of developing countries. The old style of 'green room' negotiations with a few core participants mediated by the GATT secretariat was no longer seen as appropriate. (The 'green room' referred to a small conference room near the Director-General's office at the GATT building in Geneva, but the meetings also took place in the back rooms of restaurants around Geneva). There was a demand for a more transparent style of negotiating that was more inclusive of the developing countries.

A new Doha or 'development' round was eventually launched at the fourth WTO ministerial in Doha, Qatar, in November 2001, a location difficult for demonstrators to reach and well protected against them. This incorporated talks on agriculture and services that had begun in 2000. Other issues on the agenda included non-agricultural tariffs, investment, transparency in government procurement, intellectual property and anti-dumping and investment as well as newer issues such as competition policy and trade and the environment. Concerns were expressed by developing countries about difficulties they faced in implementing existing WTO agreements.

By the time of the Cancún ministerial review meeting in September 2003, it was clear that agricultural trade was once again a major, although not the only, stumbling block to progress. Scepticism was expressed about whether the round would really deliver benefits to the developing countries as promised or whether the United States and the European Union would still get most of what they wanted. Some of the ideological dynamic that had underpinned the Uruguay Round seemed to have dissipated, while as Williams points out in Chapter 2 non-governmental organizations have persistently challenged the liberalization project at the heart of the WTO. The sea change in the regulation of international trade represented by the formation of the WTO is not uncontested and may not necessarily prove to be durable.

The shape of the book

Against this background, the purpose of this book is to provide an introduction to the nature and characteristics of the politics of international trade in the twenty-first Century. The book examines the key structures and processes that underpin contemporary trade politics, paying particular attention to current debates and concerns within academic and policy circles as well as the concerns of civil society groups. These debates and concerns include the shifting identities and patterns of interaction between the key *actors* (states and firms, the WTO, civil society) now involved in the making of trade policy; the transformation of 'old' *issues* and the arrival of 'new' ones on the international agenda (agriculture, services, intellectual property, the environment amongst others); and the evolution of established *processes* in sometimes traditional and sometimes innovative forms (multilateralism, regionalism, bilateralism and unilateralism).

It is clear from the direction and tenor of these debates that thinking about trade politics and policymaking is moving in several directions at once both within and across the three broad groups identified above. These debates are thus more often than not bitter and polemical. Whilst this is nothing new in politics it does highlight the fact that while there is much that is fluid about the nature of contemporary trade politics there is also a great deal of resistance to change, and this resistance is manifest in the persistence of traditional structures, processes and ideas. Arguably, where trade politics is concerned the state still occupies centre stage and politicians, diplomats and civil servants play the major and supporting roles. Adaptation rather than 'retreat' captures most fully the changing position and role of the state.

Accordingly, this book considers the trade strategies of a number of key states lying on both sides of the 'North–South divide'. In their pursuit of the national interest each of these states has adopted strategies emerging from the interaction over time of historical, cultural, institutional and material forces, both global and 'local'. In unravelling the roots of these varying strategies therefore, a number of avenues of exploration are available. Thus, Porter's analysis (Chapter 11) of the United States introduces the hegemonic stability literature but also insists on the importance of the technological profile of various sectors and industries as a key variable in understanding apparent contradictions in US trade policy. In his analysis of trade politics in Brazil (Chapter 12), meanwhile, da Motta Veiga unpacks the changing patterns of domestic interests and forces set in motion by the liberal revision process undertaken in the 1990s. In contrast, in Chapter 18 on Japan Kelly adopts an historicist approach that bridges the structure-agency divide but in so doing requires analysis over a longer time frame. As other contributions make clear, these three approaches by no means exhaust the range of possibilities. What is striking, however, is that all these states, China included, have accepted to varying degrees the logic of the market and the agenda of neo-liberalism.

These various state strategies find expression not only at the national level but in international organizations as well. In one sense, therefore, the institutionalization of the GATT process in the form of the WTO can be seen as a reaffirmation of state power and a reconfirmation of diplomatic discourse and privilege. This suggests that modes of interaction in the WTO will continue to be dominated by alliance formation and the balance of power between states. As the disastrous

Seattle and Cancún ministerials confirm, there is no doubt that tensions, disagreements and shifts in power will continue to occur under such circumstances.

What is in doubt is whether the WTO can survive these pressures for much longer. What immediately threatens the organization is not issues of process. These are important of course but fail to make headlines except on the rarest of occasions. Rather, the WTO is being crippled by its manifest inability to facilitate progress in the liberalization of the agriculture and textile sectors of key 'states' – the European Union, United States and Japan. The inclusion of these sectors onto the agenda of the WTO was hailed as one of the triumphs of the Uruguay Round but came with a sting in its tail. As a 'single undertaking' the Final Act of the Uruguay Round required that members sign up to everything that had been agreed. In exchange for negotiations on agriculture and textiles Less Developed Countries (LDCs) had to agree to consider issues of importance to their developed counterparts such as Trade Related Aspects of Intellectual Property Rights (TRIPs), Trade Related Investment Measures (TRIMs) and GATS (see Chapters 8 and 9 by Wiener and May). Thus, the future of the WTO hangs in the balance between progress – or lack thereof – in liberalization of agriculture and textiles on the one hand and progress in TRIPs, TRIMs and GATS on the other. As the meeting in Cancun showed quite clearly, the perception is that no progress is being made in the former while great pressure is being brought to bear to speed up the very real advances already being made in the latter. How long developing countries will continue to tolerate this situation is now an open question.

As the Ministerial Meeting in Cancún – and Seattle before it – also demonstrated, the WTO has been targeted by the anti-globalization 'movement'. This rainbow coalition, and the broader civil society groups that surround it, has as its key concerns a number of issues surrounding democratisation, accountability, and empowerment of the weak, poor and the dispossessed. As such, as Williams suggests in Chapter 2, the WTO presents an almost perfect target since a direct and very visible line can be drawn between its decisions and deliberations and real impacts which manifest as unemployment, poverty, human rights abuses and damage to the biosphere amongst others. Coping with these criticisms, emerging from within and without, is a major task facing the WTO over the next few years.

Moreover, the shift to a rules-based system with the disputes settlement mechanism as its apotheosis has had, on the one hand, an unsettling impact on even the most powerful member states, raising fears of the interment of sovereignty beneath a thick covering of international law. On the other hand, some states such as Japan and South Africa and groups of states such as the developing countries, have welcomed the shift to a system built on rules since it helps to level the playing field and curb the power of the United States in particular and the 'Quad' in general. Clearly there are contradictory elements and currents here but at a time when regional processes appear more likely to secure results the WTO is in some danger of being the last great white elephant of the twentieth century.

Due to its association with the events of the 1930s the resurgence of regionalism in world politics has sent ripples of alarm throughout the global political economy. That this alarm may be based on poor evidence and bad theory is not the key question (Strange 1985). The key question is, rather, the identification and analysis of the series of dynamics underpinning both regionalism as a state strategy and regionalization as the outcome of private decisions made by individuals, firms and other actors and groups. As the chapters by Phillips, Berger, Woolcock and Soko demonstrate, these dynamics are not only unevenly experienced but are interlocking, cross-cutting and overflowing.

Again the United States is at the forefront, and is blazing a number of trails. One of these is unilateral and features recourse to a number of weapons, the most famous of which – historically at least – is the 'Super 301' legislation. Another is bilateral and manifests as a host of established or nascent agreements between the United States and its trading partners on a state-by-state basis. In both cases the United States is not so much gently parting the jungle fronds as it is blasting and chopping its way through to its ultimate goal. A third path, one only slightly less red in tooth and claw, is the regional route as – evidenced by US efforts to establish a Free Trade Area of the Americas (FTAA) on the foundation provided by the North American Free Trade Agreement (NAFTA), by the widening and deepening of European integration and by Asia Pacific Economic Cooperation (APEC) and its 'Asian' variant ASEAN +3 .[2] Germany, Japan and Brazil meanwhile, continue to play the multilateral game while developing regional and subregional initiatives of their own.

Notes

1. There is no doubt of course that other countries – including but not restricted to Australia and India – and other coalitions of countries – such as the G20/21 – also exercise power and influence in global politics in general and in international trade negotiations in particular. Quite how much power is exercised, and over what duration and in which issue-areas is another matter (see Narlikar 2003).
2. See Chapters 10, 13 and 17 by Phillips, Woolcock and Berger. The acronym ASEAN stands for the Association of Southeast Asian Nations. ASEAN +3 refers to the ongoing process of negotiation and consultation over economic and, increasingly, political and strategic concerns between ASEAN, China, Japan and South Korea.

References

Cox, R.W. with Schechter, M. (2002) *The Political Economy of a Plural World: Critical Reflections on Power, Morals and Civilization*, London: Routledge.

Croome, J. (1995) *Reshaping the World Trading System: A History of the Uruguay Round*, Geneva: World Trade Organization.

Duffield, M. (2001) *Global Governance and the New Wars: The Merging of Development and Security*, London: Zed Books.

McDonald, B. (1998) *The World Trading System: The Uruguay Round and Beyond*, Basingstoke: Macmillan.

Nadkarni, A. (1999) 'World Trade Liberalisation: National Autonomy and Global Regulation', in Michie, J. and Grieve Smith, J. (eds) *Global Instability: The Political Economy of World Economic Governance*, London: Routledge, pp. 113–50.

Narlikar, A. (2003) *International Trade and Developing Countries: Bargaining Coalitions in the WTO*, London: Routledge.

Preeg, E.H. (1995) *Traders in a Brave New World*, Chicago: University of Chicago Press.

Ruggie, J.G. (1982) 'International Regimes, Transactions and Change: Embedded Liberalism in the Postwar Economic Order', *International Organization*, 36: 379–415.

Strange, S. (1985) 'Protectionism and World Politics', *International Organization*, 39, 2: 233–59.

Thomas, C. (2001) 'Global Governance, Development and Human Security: Exploring the Links', *Third World Quarterly*, 22, 2: 159–75.

Warnecke, S.J. (1978) 'Government Intervention and an Open Global Trading System', in Warnecke, S.J. (ed.) *International Trade and Industrial Policies*, London: Macmillan.

Wilkinson, R. and Hughes, S. (eds) (2002) *Global Governance: Critical Perspectives*, London: Routledge.

Part I
Actors

1
The World Trade Organization and the Regulation of International Trade

Rorden Wilkinson

Introduction

The World Trade Organization (WTO) has been the subject of much media attention since its launch on 1 January 1995, though not always for favourable reasons. Launched out of a much protracted and politically awkward Uruguay Round of trade negotiations (1986–94) the WTO was intended to inject additional vigour into a recovering world economy, contribute to a significant expansion in the volume and value of world trade, and be a calming influence in the often turbulent political waters of international commerce. In some respects, the WTO did prove to be a panacea. Not only did the Organization overcome the difficulties that had afflicted two prior attempts to create a formal international trade body (the International Trade Organization (ITO) and the Organization for Trade Co-operation (OTC) – to which I return below), the WTO managed to oversee the resolution of a potentially awkward dispute between the United States and Japan over the latter's importation regime for cars and car components; world trade grew at a rate of 8 per cent in the WTO's first year of operations (*WTO Focus* May 1996: 1); the Organization's first ministerial meeting in Singapore in December 1996 was largely successful (in spite of some tense discussions on the issue of trade and labour standards – see Chapter 7 by Nigel Haworth and Steve Hughes in this volume); and the newly created dispute settlement mechanism seemed to be providing the stabiliser that had for so long been absent from international trade.

The WTO's honeymoon period was, however, short-lived. (See Figure 1.1.) In April 1997 the WTO announced that the annual growth in world trade for 1996 had fallen by 50 per cent on the previous year to 4 per cent (*WTO Focus* April 1997: 1). By the end of 1997 the turmoil from the Asian Financial Crisis had begun to have an effect on the world economy generating, among other things, much economic uncertainty. The WTO's second ministerial meeting in Geneva in May 1998 saw the Organization for the first time exposed to public demonstrations. Reports began to emerge of problems with the implementation of the Uruguay Round agreements, particularly among developing countries. A marked upsurge in political tension had begun to threaten the functioning of the dispute settlement body (DSB) as disputes broke out among the principal trading powers over alcoholic beverages, bananas,

13

Place	Date
SINGAPORE	9–13 DECEMBER 1996
GENEVA	18–20 MAY 1998
SEATTLE	30 NOVEMBER–3 DECEMBER 1999
DOHA	9–13 NOVEMBER 2001
CANCUN	10–14 SEPTEMBER 2003

Figure 1.1   WTO ministerial meetings up to September 2003

beef, aircraft 'hush-kits', foreign sales corporations and steel. And, more generally, signs were beginning to emerge of an over-burdened dispute settlement process. Yet, little prepared the Organization for what was to happen during the WTO's third ministerial meeting in Seattle in late November, early December 1999. The meeting was hampered by mass demonstrations as a vast coalition of civil society organizations gathered to protest at the alleged consequences of WTO-sanctioned activity on worker rights, the global environment and economic development. Concerns were also raised about the lack of transparency and demo-cratic accountability in WTO procedures. But the demonstrations were only part of the problem. Inside the meeting developing countries staged a revolt in response to a series of events which appeared to reveal a continuing Organizational bias towards the interests of industrial states. The consequence was a failure of the meeting to result in the launch of the much-hyped 'Millennium Round' of trade negotiations.

Seattle was a low point for the WTO. The post-mortem that followed witnessed the Organization embark on a two-pronged strategy designed to reconstruct its image. The first dimension of this strategy saw the WTO engage in a courtship of civil society organizations; the second dimension saw the WTO give issues of development a new emphasis – most obviously culminating in the re-branding of the current trade round as the 'Development Round' (see Wilkinson 2001, 2002a, 2002b). One consequence of this dual strategy has been an increased awareness of the function and workings of the WTO among its opponents; another has been a better understanding within the WTO of some of the concerns raised by the pro-testors and a greater appreciation of the difficulties faced by developing countries (though, in spite of this, there remains a marked deficit in understanding on all sides). That said, the WTO's efforts have not fully stemmed the tide of criticism. The WTO remains high on the anti-globalization's 'most-wanted' hit list; and Pascal Lamy, EU trade commissioner, has characterized the WTO's internal proce-dures as 'medieval' (*Financial Times*, 5 October 2001).

So what is the WTO? What is its role in international trade? How does it fulfil that role? And what are the key challenges currently facing the Organization? This chapter seeks to answer these questions. It begins with an account of the WTO's historical antecedence – an antecedence that has been central to shaping the character of contemporary international trade regulation. Second, it explores the way in which the Organization and its legal framework are structured and examines the WTO's role in contemporary global economic governance. Third, it explores the issues currently facing the Organization focusing on the post-Seattle process. And fourth, the chapter draws to a close by offering some concluding comments.

The post-war settlement and the creation of an international trade body

The WTO's roots lie not in the Uruguay Round of trade negotiations out of which the Organization was created, but in wartime and post-Second World War efforts to create an International Trade Organization (ITO) (see Figure 1.2). The purpose of the ITO was to administer a series of rules governing the conduct of international trade and its related areas as part of a wider effort to reconstruct a war-ravaged and relatively fragmented (the result of the depression of the interwar years) world economy. The ITO was itself intended to be one part of a wider plan to create a series of global economic institutions designed to manage the world economy. These institutions were themselves intended to form part of an even

	From ITO to WTO
1941	Foundations laid for the post-war economic order in the Atlantic Charter
1942	Commitment to centrality of trade to post-war reconstruction reiterated in the Lend-Lease Agreement
1943	UK and US delegates hold exploratory talks on post-war international commerce
1944	Bretton Woods Conference takes place in New Hampshire, USA. The International Monetary Fund (IMF) and the International Bank for Reconstruction and Development (IBRD) are established as a consequence
1945	Draft charter for an International Trade Organisation (ITO) prepared
1946	The Economic and Social Council of the United Nations (UN) calls for an international conference to be convened on trade and employment and establishes a Preparatory Committee to discuss the draft charter
1946	Preparatory Committee meets in London to discuss the proposed charter
1947	Preparatory Committee meets in Geneva for a second session
1947	General Agreement on Tariffs and Trade signed by 23 states
1947–48	Havana Conference on Trade and Employment takes place and results in the completion of the Havana Charter proposing the creation of the International Trade Organisation (ITO)
1948	GATT comes into force as a provisional and limited agreement seeking to kick-start the process of trade liberalization
1950	Havana Charter fails to secure US ratification and is pronounced dead
1955	Organisation for Trade Co-operation (OTC) proposed, but fails to come to fruition
1986	Uruguay Round commences
1990	Canada puts forward a suggestion to establish a World Trade Organisation (WTO)
1994	Uruguay Round concludes
1995	WTO begins operations

Figure 1.2   Key events in the evolution of the international trade regime

broader institutional framework designed to govern large tracts of global social, economic, political and cultural life under the auspices of the United Nations Organization (UNO).

Under this broad UNO umbrella, three institutions were intended to manage the global economy: the International Bank for Reconstruction and Development (IBRD or World Bank), the International Monetary Fund (IMF), and the ITO. Each institution was to have jurisdiction over its own field of operations, though all were to work together as a coherent ensemble. The underwriting of private capital was to provide the wherewithal to promote reconstruction (World Bank), in turn, nurturing a revitalisation of production; the flow of trade arising from this revitalisation was to be assisted by a process of liberalization (the lowering and removal of barriers to trade) (the ITO); and producer confidence was to be nurtured through a system of fixed exchange rates (the IMF).

Although comprising three distinct organizations, the principal aim of this system was to be the reconstruction of international trade. In recognition of this, the legal framework of the ITO contained a series of commitments that not only outlined its relationship with, and role within the UNO, but also detailed the substance of its cooperation with its siblings: the IMF and World Bank (UN Conference on Trade and Employment, 1948: Articles 3, 11, 24 and *Ad* 24). The ITO's legal framework also attributed a central, though second-order, role to the International Labour Organization (ILO) (UN Conference on Trade and Employment, 1948: Articles 2, 7 and the *Resolution to the Economic and Social Council Relating to Employment of the Final Act and Related Documents*). The ILO's inclusion was, in part, a function of the ITO's commitment to full employment, and, in part, the consequence of a national settlement reached between government, business and organized labour in western Europe (the so-called 'social contract' (Cox 1987: 373–4)).

As an addendum to the post-war efforts to create the ITO, the General Agreement on Tariffs and Trade (GATT) was negotiated to begin the process of trade liberalisation. The GATT was originally intended to be a provisional agreement that would, once the ITO had been established, be subsumed into the latter's legal framework. It lacked the elaborate provisions of its more formal relative; it sought only to regulate trade in goods; and it comprised a much watered-down version of the ITO's dispute settlement provisions. The GATT, nevertheless, embodied the ITO's core principles of most-favoured-nation (MFN), reciprocity, and a commitment to dispute settlement.

However, the ITO negotiations proved unable to overcome residual doubts over the content of the Organization's legal framework (Diebold 1952; Fawcett 1951; Feis 1948; Gardner 1956; Viner 1947; Wilcox 1949). Of the 53 states that signed the Havana Charter (the ITO's founding document), only 2 sought its ratification. Ultimately it was the absence of US ratification that resulted in the stillbirth of the Organization.

With the stillbirth of the ITO, the hopes of the wartime planners for a liberal trading regime came to rest with the fledgling GATT. Originally intended to lock into place the initial progress made in tariff liberalization, as well as to act as the

Year	Place
1947	GENEVA, SWITZERLAND
1949	ANNECY, FRANCE
1951	TORQUAY, UNITED KINGDOM
1956	GENEVA
1960–61	THE DILLON ROUND (GENEVA)
1964–67	THE KENNEDY ROUND (GENEVA)
1973–79	THE TOKYO ROUND (GENEVA)
1986–94	THE URUGUAY ROUND (GENEVA)
2001–05	THE DOHA DEVELOPMENT ROUND (GENEVA)

Figure 1.3   Trade negotiation 'rounds' under the GATT and WTO

bridge between the old order and that to be established around the disciplines of the ITO, the GATT comprised a series of provisions directed at liberalizing international trade in goods by putting into place a mechanism for conducting that liberalization through periodic negotiations (see Figure 1.3). The rise of the GATT was not, however, unproblematic – something that was to profoundly influence the character of international trade regulation in the post-war era. Not only was the GATT without a more elaborate set of commercial provisions, it also omitted the ITO's detailed inter-institutional linkages with the IMF and World Bank. Moreover, aside from a commitment to the pursuit of full employment in the GATT's preamble, there was little reference to the social contract upon which the post-Second World War global institutional structure was to be built, and, correspondingly, no mention of the ILO. Instead, the absence of any linkage between the GATT and the ILO ensured that this *de facto* form of trade regulation was to evolve in such a way that an institutional culture developed wherein the idea and reality of a formal linkage between trade and international labour regulation had little place.

There were, however, several areas that required attention if the GATT was to continue successfully. The GATT's main problem was its lack of an organizational structure. Its role as a bridging agreement to the ITO meant that in its drafting, provisions had not been made for the creation of a formal institutional and administrative structure. That said, the *General Agreement*'s body of rules did prove sufficient to give it an operational framework (through the utilization of Article XXV of the GATT on 'Joint Action by the Contracting Parties' (Curzon and Curzon 1974: 300)). From this evolved a quasi-organizational structure, which added to its ranks a permanent secretariat (that was to occupy the old ILO building in Geneva), a council to oversee GATT activities between the meetings of the contracting parties, and the development of a series of committees and working groups concerned with various aspects of international commerce.

Perhaps unsurprisingly, the decision to persevere with the GATT, and the *ad hoc* nature with which it operationalized its functions led to renewed calls in the mid-1950s for the establishment of a formal organization. This came in the form of a discussion on the relative merits of creating an Organization for Trade Co-operation (OTC). The idea of an OTC mirrored, in many ways, the designs that had been put forward for the ITO – though the Organization was only intended to regulate trade in goods, and not the elaborate and much more extensive provisions of the ITO. In reality, the proposed OTC differed little from the GATT. It was, for some, merely a case of semantics (*The Economist* 1955: 1101–2). Nevertheless, it was to experience the same fate as the ITO, leaving the GATT as the principal regulator of international trade (Curzon and Curzon 1974: 300; Gardner 1969: xxxiv; Goodwin 1956: 248).

During the early years of the GATT, trade liberalization appeared to thrive. Up to the mid-1970s progressive Rounds of trade negotiations enjoyed a certain degree of success. Between 1950 and 1975 the merchandise trade of the industrial countries grew at an average rate of 8 per cent (Cline 1980: 188). During the Dillon Round over four thousand concessions were exchanged; and at the Kennedy Round barriers to trade fell at an unprecedented rate – 35 per cent over a total of 60,000 products (Gilpin 1987: 192). Yet, relatively early on into the life of the GATT, the broad overview of tariff reductions obscured a more negative trend. Up until the 1956 Geneva Round, much headway *had* been made in lowering the general incidence of tariffs. However, beyond this the ability of the contracting parties to agree on mutually acceptable tariff cuts became increasingly difficult. This, in large part, resulted from the degree to which tariffs were cut in the early Rounds. The relatively high base from which tariffs were cut exaggerated the degree by which barriers to trade had been eroded. As the general level of tariffs decreased, so too did the ability of the contracting parties to agree to further reductions.

Beyond the mid-1970s, the general level of tariff cuts began to stagnate. The severity of this stagnation was worsened by the increasing use of non-tariff barriers (NTBs). Many of the industrial countries implemented elements of overt and covert protectionism (such as the adoption of quotas, licences, over-zealous health and safety checks, lengthy administration procedures, and voluntary export restraints on supplier countries) in an attempt to find substitutes to replace the loss of protection that had occurred as a result of tariff reductions (Cline 1983: 5–7). This ensured that, rather than liberalizing trade, those gains that had been made by tariff reductions were offset by the growth of NTBs. The impact of NTBs was not, however, system-wide. Much of the growth in NTBs disproportionately affected developing countries.

The principle of reciprocity around which GATT negotiations were conducted also became the source of some tension. Bickering broke out among the contracting parties as to the relative value of concessions exchanged. As negotiations became increasingly tense, the time it took to complete trade Rounds extended, and the outcome was often perceived to be inadequate. The external economic climate also began to have a negative impact on the GATT. The movement away from the exchange rate stability of the Bretton Woods regime in the late 1960s and early 1970s (formalized at the 1976 meeting of the IMF in Jamaica) exerted a large degree of pressure on the GATT's balance of payments rules – rules designed for a commercial system underpinned by fixed, rather than floating, exchange rates (van Whitman 1977: 33–4).

That said, one issue above all was to prove most troublesome for the GATT. As early as 1954, a sense that the provisions of the GATT were of disproportionately greater benefit to the industrial states than their developing counterparts had emerged. The 1958 Haberler Report added weight to this, albeit it was reasonably ambiguous in its findings. The Report concluded that although there was no evidence of specific discrimination, the terms of trade of many developing countries were hindered by the disproportionately higher incidence of tariff barriers that they faced. This exposure, coupled with certain unfavourable price trends, was deemed to have adversely affected the trade performance of developing countries (GATT 1958). In light of these findings, the Report recommended that in the first instance a programme of 'maintaining and expanding the export earnings of the less developed countries' should be undertaken (Evans 1968: 84).

The perception of a bias against developing countries was consolidated by a process of decolonization that saw few of the newly independent states manage to achieve anything other than a sharp decline in economic performance. It was against this background that criticism of the GATT accelerated during the early 1960s. By 1964 developing contracting parties grew to outnumber their industrial counterparts by two to one (Williams 1991: 24). The ill feeling directed towards the GATT was heightened further by the growing confidence of the non-aligned states. This was expressed most prominently in the convening of the first UN Conference on Trade and Development (UNCTAD) in Geneva between March and June 1964 – one outcome of which was the UN's declaration that the 1960s be a 'development' decade. The Conference, attended by 122 nations, resulted in the emergence of a coherent bloc of developing nations seeking to utilize their collective capabilities to change the trading fortunes of their number – the Group of 77 (G77).

These events culminated in 1966 with the annexation of 'Part IV' to the GATT (Gosovic 1972: 57; Williams 1991: 26) – a series of provisions designed to elevate some of the concerns of the developing countries.[1] Part IV, however, was unsuccessful. Part of the problem lay in its failure to alter to any significant degree the perceived industrial bias in GATT rules. Instead, it merely requested that the industrial states *consider* adopting certain measures to assist developing countries in their commercial activities. There was little compunction.

Two further events consolidated the perception that the GATT favoured the interests of the industrial states over their developing counterparts. In response to competition from overseas textile and clothing producers in the newly independent world, the industrial countries, most notably the United Kingdom and the United States, sought to introduce a means of protecting domestic producers. This involved, in the first instance at least, extracting a series of voluntary quotas limiting imports from Japan, Hong Kong, Pakistan and India. However, as such measures ran contrary to GATT rules, codification of these restrictions was sought. This involved, during the Dillon Round (1960–61), the negotiation of the *Short-Term Agreement on Cotton Textiles* which, in turn, evolved into the 1962 *Long-Term Agreement Regarding Trade in Cotton Textiles*, and subsequently the 1974 MultiFibre Agreement (MFA – of which there were four incarnations) (Hoekman and Kostecki

1995: 207). At their root, these Agreements enabled industrial states to offset a decline in competitiveness in the production of textiles and clothing *vis à vis* their developing counterparts by putting into place a system of regulation predicated on contracting parties negotiating bilateral quantitative restrictions or by unilaterally imposing import constraints (Jackson 1998: 207–9).

Allied to the *de facto* way in which the MFA and its predecessors removed textiles and clothing from the purview of GATT rules, was a comparable withdrawal of agriculture as a legitimate target for liberalization. On the insistence of first the United States and then the European Economic Community (EEC), agriculture became exempt from GATT rules on domestic support systems (Josling 1990: 157). This exemption was consolidated further by the failure of discussions during the Kennedy (1964–67) and Tokyo (1973–79) Rounds to bring agriculture back into the fray. After its initial insistence that agriculture be exempt from GATT rules, the United States increasingly came to view the EEC's Common Agricultural Policy (CAP) with some irritation. Yet, it was not until the Uruguay Round that the *Agreement on Agriculture* was negotiated. Even then, however, tensions between the United States and the European Community (EC), as it had become, resulted in a momentary and infamous hiatus in the Round. The result was that up until the completion of the Uruguay Round (and its subsequent implementation), agricultural and textile produce was subjected to discriminatory action by the industrial states – areas of principal economic importance for the developing world.

By the mid-1980s, it had become apparent that the inadequacies of the GATT required some kind of attention. Though the subject of some initial resistance (from the then EC, but also from a number of developing countries irritated at what they saw as the GATT's inability to address their needs), and after much politicking, the contracting parties agreed to launch the eighth (and final under the auspices of the GATT) Round of trade negotiations at Punta Del Este, Uruguay, in September 1986. The Uruguay Round proved to be qualitatively different from previous GATT negotiations. Whereas previous Rounds had concentrated on negotiating commercial concessions, for the first time since the ITO discussions Uruguay witnessed negotiations on the more fundamental issue of trade rules (Finger 1991: 22). Yet, in contrast to the ITO negotiations, the Uruguay Round proved more successful, ultimately culminating in the creation of the WTO.

The creation of a formal organization to oversee the conduct of world trade was not, however, the intended outcome of the Uruguay Round. The idea of a formal organization arose four years into the Round, when in 1990 Canada put forward a suggestion for a World Trade Organization to consolidate and supersede the GATT (Jackson 1990a, 1990b, 1993). The proposed Organization was not, however, without opposition. The US Congress voiced strong concerns about the proposed Organization, asserting that any relinquishment of its sovereign authority to such an organization was inconceivable. After further negotiation these concerns were abated and Congress announced that it was satisfied that the establishment of a World Trade Organization would not challenge US sovereignty as most of the institutional aspects of the Organization already existed under the GATT (Hoekman and Kostecki 1995: 36). The *Final Act Establishing the World Trade*

Organization (hereafter the *Establishing Agreement*) was agreed in Marrakech on 15 April 1994; and the WTO formally commenced operations on 1 January 1995.

The World Trade Organization

Given its history, the creation of the WTO marks a significant moment in the history of international trade regulation. Importantly, however, the WTO does not represent a clear departure from the GATT, or the two failed attempts at establishing a formal organization to oversee the conduct of international trade. Rather, there exists a strong 'family resemblance' between the WTO and its predecessors. This resemblance is most obviously expressed in the core principles – what I have called elsewhere its 'architectural principles' (Wilkinson 2000: 43–51) – around which the WTO's legal framework organizes international trade.[2] These principles are:

1. most-favoured nation (the extension of the preferential commercial treatment given to one party to all third parties) and its corollary national treatment;
2. reciprocity (the commitment to respond to any preferential treatment received in a like manner); and
3. dispute settlement (an agreement to abide by the workings of a commonly accepted dispute settlement mechanism).

The key difference between the WTO and previous incarnations of trade regulation lies in the extent of the arena of international trade subject to its rules. Under the GATT only trade in goods (and even then only trade in non-agricultural and textile and clothing goods) was regulated. Under the WTO, however, this has been both deepened and widened. In addition to the inclusion of the GATT (now one of the commercial agreements administered by the WTO) the arena of trade regulation has been deepened by the negotiation and inclusion of disciplines relating to trade in agriculture and trade in textiles and clothing under the Agreements on *Agriculture*, and *Textiles and Clothing* respectively (on agriculture see Chapter 5 by Grant in this volume). Moreover, the conclusion of the *General Agreement on Trade in Services* has deepened the arena of activity subject to the WTO's core architectural principles by drawing in trade in services (see Chapter 8 by Wiener in this volume).

This is not, however, the full extent to which the arena of trade regulation has been expanded with the creation of the WTO. The WTO also administers two agreements which have widened the arena of trade regulation to include certain trade-related areas – areas which, though not bearing tradable commodities, are deemed essential to the production process. This is the case with intellectual property rights under the *Agreement on Trade-Related Aspects of Intellectual Property Rights* (TRIPs) and with trade-related investment measures under the *Agreement on Trade-Related Investment Measures* (TRIMs). The nature of these Agreements differs from that of the GATT as well as the other Agreements administered by the WTO. The TRIPs seeks to endorse and safeguard intellectual property ownership (see Chapter 9 by May in this volume); and the TRIMs aims to go some way towards liberalizing global investment flows. As a result, neither Agreement seeks to bring about a direct expansion in commercial activity. Rather, their aim is to contribute to the creation of an environment that is perceived to be conducive to an expansion in the volume and value of trade. That said, both encapsulate the WTO's core architectural principles and serve to further consolidate the all-encompassing rules-based nature of the trade regime.

Global economic governance and the WTO

Although much of the legal framework of the WTO deals with the detail of trade regulation, it also contains important provisions which locate the Organization at the heart of the system of global economic governance. The stillbirth of the ITO not only put paid to the first attempt at formalizing international trade regulation, it also inhibited the establishment and functioning of a system of global economic governance. The GATT's contribution to the development of such a system was relatively small, providing for co-operation with the IMF in instances relating to 'exchange questions within the jurisdiction of the Fund and questions of quantitative restrictions and other trade measures within the jurisdiction of the Contracting Parties' (GATT 1947: Article XV, Paragraph 1) – though of course behind the scenes coordination took place with other organizations. In this respect, the creation of the WTO is more than just about the regulation of international trade through a complex set of rules governing specific areas of commercial activity centred around a set of core architectural principles. It also has a major role in the governance of the global economy, and, in many ways, is the most significant world economic organization. In this sense, it fulfils as well as expands upon the role envisaged for the ITO.

The WTO sets out its blueprint for this system of governance in the *Declaration on the Contribution of the World Trade Organization to Achieving Greater Coherence in Global Economic Policy Making* annexed to the *Establishing Agreement*, though the full extent of the system is only realized when provisions scattered throughout the Agreements administered by the Organization are drawn together. The central and primary feature of this blueprint is the development of mutually supportive polices and the removal of 'cross-conditionality' among the WTO, IMF and World Bank. The purpose of this cooperation is to harmonize the conditions under which (prospective) members deal with each Organization, as well as to consolidate the character of global economic governance.

The drawing together of the work of these organizations is supplemented by other provisions in the WTO's legal framework establishing linkages with particular bodies deemed intrinsic to the general goal of achieving greater coherence in global economic policymaking, but which relate to specific aspects of the WTO's remit. For instance, the TRIPs empowers the WTO to nurture a closer relationship with the World Intellectual Property Organization (WIPO). Similarly, the GATS contains a set of provisions enabling the WTO to strengthen links with two organizations deemed important to the development of a liberal services regime: the

International Telecommunications Union (ITU) and the International Organization of Standards (IOS). Moreover, since commencing operations the WTO has begun to develop limited relationships with the United Nations Environment Programme (UNEP), the Office International des Epizooties (The World Organization for Animal Health), and the United Nations Conference on Trade and Development (UNCTAD). The development of these more limited relationships has been made possible by a set of provisions empowering the WTO to establish relations with unspecified organizations. It should be noted, however, that the WTO's legal framework, unlike that of the ITO, does not contain provisions for the development of a cooperative and meaningful relationship with the ILO. Indeed, the WTO's official comment on its relationship with the ILO – the 1996 Singapore Ministerial Declaration – committed the two organizations to continue their 'existing collaboration'. This was, however, merely a 'throw away line' (Stigliani 2000: 188) intended to quell criticism of the WTO's refusal to incorporate in its legal framework a commitment to maintain certain minimum standards of labour.

The result of these provisions has been to develop a formal system of global economic governance centred around a core of three institutions – the WTO, IMF and World Bank – supplemented by a supporting cast of the WIPO, ITU and IOS and a host of other organizations with which relations are established on an ad hoc basis. This is not, however, the extent to which the WTO's establishment has nurtured the development of a system of global economic governance. The WTO's legal framework requires that all regional free trade areas and customs unions in which its member states participate register with the Organization; it also requires that the rules of these regional arrangements do not contravene WTO rules, but rather that they are broadly complementary with the goal of trade liberalization. The result has been the emergence of a coherent set of relations among international and regional organizations structured into a multi-layered system of economic governance.

Organization and decision-making in the WTO

What we have so far is an appreciation of how the creation of the WTO has not only formalized a system of trade regulation, but also deepened and widened the arena of commercial activity subject to that regulation. We have also seen how the creation of the WTO has brought with it the formalisation of a system of global economic governance – albeit evolving in form. What we have yet to appreciate is the organizational and decision-making structure of the WTO. The WTO's organizational structure comprises (see Figure 1.4):

1. a Ministerial Conference consisting of representatives from each of the member states (normally at the level of trade minister or equivalent). The Ministerial Conference meets at least once every two years;
2. a General Council which oversees WTO activities (and which acts as the executive for the Ministerial Conference between sessions), including the functioning of the Dispute Settlement Body (DSB) and the Trade Policy Review

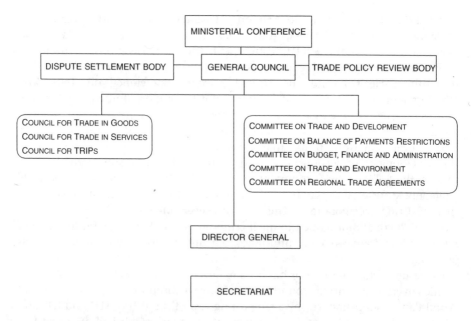

Figure 1.4   WTO organizational structure

Mechanism (TPRM). The General Council consists of representatives of member states, though normally at the level of trade official;

3. a series of Councils covering each of the three main commercial areas of the WTO's activities (trade in goods, trade in services, and trade-related aspects of intellectual property rights);

4. a series of Committees, responsible to the General Council, dealing with trade and development, trade and environment, regional trade agreements, balance of payments restrictions, and budget, finance and administration;

5. a Secretariat which handles the day-to-day running of the WTO; and

6. a Director-General who overseas the functioning of the WTO.

The majority of decisions made in the WTO are done so consensually, unless specified otherwise. Consensus is taken to mean agreement among all excluding those representatives of Members who are not present, or have abstained from participation (for a critical reading of WTO decision-making see McGrew 1999). Consensus is not understood to be unanimity, but rather agreement in the absence of major opposition. That said, there exist three other means by which decisions can be made. In those cases where changes to the core principles of the WTO are proposed, unanimity is required. In cases relating to the implementation of the provisions of the WTO Agreement, or in respect of a waiver of a member's obligations, a three-quarters majority is required. And a two-thirds majority is necessary for any amendment to the *Final Act* in cases relating to issues other than its core principles.

In cases where decisions are put to the vote, the WTO operates on the basis of one-member-one-vote. However, the *Establishing Agreement* specifies that Members are not bound by any amendment that passes a vote it has opposed (Article X). In such instances, the Ministerial Conference can decide whether to ask the member or members in question to leave the Organization, or whether to allow their continued participation within the WTO without adherence to the amendment in question.

Development, civil society and the new trade agenda

So far we have seen that the form the WTO has taken owes much to prior attempts to develop a system of trade regulation and efforts to construct a system of global economic governance. We have also seen how the establishment of the WTO has brought with it a deepening and widening of the arena of commercial activity subject to trade regulation; and we have explored briefly the WTO's organizational structure and decision-making processes. What of the key issues facing the Organization today? Given the tensions inside the Seattle Ministerial Meeting, the failure of the Meeting to launch the 'Millennium Round' of trade negotiations, a history of trade regulation perceived to have favoured industrial states over their developing counterparts, and the severity of the demonstrations that took place in Seattle, it is unsurprising that the WTO has channelled much of its recent energy into addressing issues of development as well as being seen to be more engaged with its critics.

Development

In the immediate aftermath of Seattle, the WTO embarked on a charm offensive directed at addressing the concerns of developing countries while at the same time caucusing support for the launch of a new round of trade negotiations (conveniently re-branded as the 'Development Round'). Four aspects of the WTO's strategy are noteworthy in this regard. First, Seattle was immediately followed by a marked upsurge in the language of developmentalism in official statements, press releases and speeches. Second, the WTO put into place a review mechanism directed at resolving the problems developing countries have faced over the implementation of the Uruguay Round accords. Third, an 'outreach' programme was implemented designed to enhance the participation of all members, but particularly the least developed. This programme comprised not only confidence-building measures and a comprehensive reassessment of technical cooperation, but also the installation of WTO reference centres in developing and least developed countries, as well as a commitment to closer coordination between the WTO, World Bank and IMF on development policy. Fourth, in order to nurture support for the launch of a new Round of trade negotiations, the WTO engaged in a concerted effort to highlight the 'benefits' of full participation in the multilateral trading system, while at the same time warning against the 'risks' of not participating in a new round by cautioning against the ills of protectionism.

The WTO's efforts proved successful in nurturing the necessary support for the launch of a new Round at its Doha Ministerial Meeting. In each of the priority areas identified for the negotiations (implementation, agriculture, services, and market access for non-agricultural products) development figured strongly. The proposed agenda for the Development Round was not, however, without considerable possibilities for the industrial members of the WTO. The Declaration also contains a series of provisions for a further deepening and widening of the arena of commercial activity subject to WTO rules. In addition to negotiations in the 'traditional' trade areas, the Declaration also points to an extension of the TRIPs and GATS agreements. More importantly, however, the Declaration sets out a desire to extend the WTO's remit into investment, competition policy, and government procurement; and it points to an intention to draw e-commerce under WTO rules. Traditionally, suggestions that the WTO's remit be extended into the realm of these so-called 'new issues' (investment, competition policy, government procurement and e-commerce) have been met with some hostility, largely because they are deemed to be of more value to industrial members than their developing counterparts. Reflecting the politics of the WTO post-Seattle, it is instructive to note that the Declaration states a decision on whether to extend the Organization's remit into these areas is only to be taken after the Cancun Ministerial meeting – far enough in advance of the start of the negotiations for the developmental aspects of the Round to be emphasized.

Civil society

Allied to the WTO's efforts to placate developing countries has been a concerted effort to improve the Organization's public image. Immediately following the Seattle Meeting, the WTO sought to improve public awareness of its functions. This involved the publication of two documents intended to quell popular misconceptions: '10 benefits of the WTO trading system' and '10 common misunderstandings about the WTO' (available at www.wto.org). The WTO has also speeded up the process of derestriction of documents, and made these more readily available via its website. In addition, the WTO has attempted to increase the level of public involvement through the development of various electronic forums. These have included, for instance, month-long on-line forums on key issues (such as trade and development) as well as a chat room and notice board.

In addition to improved access to information, the WTO has also intensified its courtship of non-governmental organizations (NGOs). NGOs have been able to attend the Ministerial Meetings of the WTO since Singapore, on the understanding that a process of registration and accreditation is first completed. The possibility of attending successive WTO Ministerial Meetings has been enthusiastically received by the NGO community, and applications have increased steadily. WTO figures put the number of NGOs that applied for accreditation for the Doha Ministerial Meeting at 673, of which 647 were deemed to be eligible (albeit for Doha NGO representation was limited to one per organization). Yet, although the WTO has intensified its courtship of NGOs, the substance of their interaction remains tightly controlled by a series of guidelines enacted in the run-up to the Singapore Meeting that prevent any meaningful involvement in the Organization's workings.

In addition to the involvement of NGOs at Ministerial Meetings, the WTO has put into place other measures. First, the WTO has committed itself to engaging in a number of 'dialogues and briefings'. These range from 'lunchtime dialogues' wherein NGO representatives have the opportunity (at the WTO's discretion) to attend an informal discussion of their work with interested delegations and sec-retariat officials, through 'open dialogue' discussions on specific issues, to NGO briefing sessions after key WTO meetings. Second, the WTO has committed itself to exploring 'opportunities' to allow NGO representatives to attend technical sem-inars on particular issues or aspects of the WTO's remit. Third, the possibility exists for 'stand alone' workshops to be organized on specific issues of interest to NGOs. And fourth, the WTO has developed an NGO outreach section on its website comprising chat rooms, NGO position papers, an NGO bulletin, and a dedicated NGO website during Ministerial Meetings. That said, and in spite of a more con-structive relationship emerging between the WTO and particular NGOs such as Oxfam, the Organization continues to be far removed from more critical quarters of civil society.

Conclusion

What can we conclude from this all-too-brief account of the WTO? What we have seen in the evolution of post-war trade regulation are elements of continuity and change. Each attempt at creating a formal system of trade regulation has been cen-tred around three core architectural principles, in spite of variations in organiza-tional form. It is safe to say, then, that any future extension in the WTO's remit resulting from the Development Round will also embody those core principles. However, the future of the WTO will depend on how successfully it continues to placate the concerns of developing countries as well as critical, though influential civil society organizations. In this regard, the Development Round promises to be a critical moment in the WTO's evolution. Beyond this, it is likely that the WTO's remit will be extended into the fields of investment, competition policy, govern-ment procurement and, albeit much later, e-commerce. Similarly, it is likely that relations between the IMF, World Bank and WTO will be strengthened further, thereby consolidating the character and functioning of the system of global eco-nomic governance. Any extension in the WTO's activities, however, is likely to ensure that the WTO remains the subject of media attention, and with it a key tar-get of the anti-globalization movement.

Notes

1. Prior to the introduction of Part IV only one provision existed that was in any way sen-sitive to issues of development – Article XVIII, empowering contracting parties to sus-pend, in part or whole, their procurement of MFN by imposing quantitative restrictions to rectify an adverse balance of payments situation. Even this was acutely problematic. See Wells 1969: 65.
2. These principles are not uniformly applied. Rather there exist a number of qualifications and procedural practices in their application which distorts the ability of certain mem-bers, particularly newly acceded and small, less able, developing and transitional states to benefit fully from the utilization of these principles (see Wilkinson 2000: 80–136).

References

Cline, W.R. (1980) 'Long Term Change in Foreign Trade Policy', in US Congress Joint Committee, Special Study on Economic Change, Volume 9, *The International Economy: US Role in a World Market*, Washington: US Government Printing Office.

Cline, W.R. (1983) *Trade Policy in the 1980s*, Washington: Institute for International Economics.

Cox, R.W. (1987) *Production, Power and Word Order: Social Forces in the Making of History*, New York: Columbia University Press.

Curzon, G. and Curzon, V. (1974) 'GATT: Trader's Club', in Cox, R.W. and Jacobson, H.K. (eds) *The Anatomy of Influence: Decision Making in International Organization*, London: Yale University Press, 2nd printing.

Diebold, W. Jr. (1952) 'The End of the ITO', *Essays in International Finance*, 16, International Finance Section, Department of Economics, Princeton University.

Evans, J.W. (1968) 'The General Agreement on Tariffs and Trade', *International Organization*, 22: 1.

Fawcett, J.E.S. (1951) 'The Havana Charter', *The Yearbook of World Affairs*, 5.

Feis, H. (1948) 'The Geneva Proposal for an International Trade Charter', *International Organization*, 2: 1 (February).

Finger, M.J. (1991) 'That Old GATT Magic No More Casts Its Spell (How the Uruguay Round Failed)', *Journal of World Trade*, 25: 1 (February).

Gardner, R.N. (1956) *Sterling–Dollar Diplomacy: Anglo-American Collaboration in the Reconstruction of Multilateral Trade*, Oxford: Clarendon Press.

Gardner, R.N. (1969) *Sterling-Dollar Diplomacy: The Origins and Prospects of our International Economic Order*, London: McGraw-Hill, 2nd edition.

GATT (1947) *General Agreement on Tariffs and Trade*, Geneva: GATT Publications.

GATT (1958) *Trends in International Trade: A Report by a Panel of Experts*, Geneva: GATT Publications.

Gilpin, R. (1987) *The Political Economy of International Relations*, Princeton: Princeton University Press.

Goodwin, G.L. (1956) 'The GATT and the Organisation for Trade Co-operation', *The Yearbook of World Affairs*, 10.

Gosovic, B. (1972) *UNCTAD Conflict and Compromise*, Leiden: A.W. Sijthoff.

Hoekman, B. and Kostecki, M. (1995) *The Political Economy of the World Trading System: From GATT to WTO*, Oxford: Oxford University Press.

Jackson, J.H. (1990a) *Restructuring the GATT System*, London: Pinter.

Jackson, J.H. (1990b) 'Reflections on Restructuring the GATT', in Jeffrey J. Scott (ed.) *Completing the Uruguay Round*, Washington: Institute for International Economics.

Jackson, J.H. (1993) 'A New Constitution for World Trade? Reforming the GATT System', in Stern, R.M. (ed.) *The Multilateral Trading System*, Michigan: Michigan University Press.

Jackson, J.H. (1998) *The World Trading System: Law and Policy of International Economic Relations*, London: MIT Press, 2nd edition.

Josling, T. (1990) 'The GATT: Its Historical Role and Importance to Agricultural Policy and Trade', in Hans J. Michelmann *et al.* (eds) *The Political Economy of Agricultural Trade and Policy*, Boulder: Westview Press.

McGrew, T. (1999) 'The World Trade Organization: Technocracy or Banana Republic?', in Annie Taylor and Caroline Thomas (eds) *Global Trade and Global Social Issues*, London: Routledge.

Stigliani, N.A. (2000) 'Labor Diplomacy: A Revitalised Aspect of US Foreign Policy in the Era of Globalization', *International Studies Perspectives*, 1: 2 (August).

United Nations Conference on Trade and Employment (1948) *Final Act and Related Documents*, 21 November 1947 to 24 March 1948, Havana, Cuba.

van Whitman, M. (1977) 'Sustaining the International Economic System: Issues for US Policy', *Essays in International Finance*, 121, International Finance Section, Department of Economics, Princeton University.

Viner, J. (1947) 'Conflicts of Principle in Drafting a Trade Charter', *Foreign Affairs*, 25: 4 (July).

Wells, S. (1969) 'Developing Countries, GATT and UNCTAD', *International Affairs*, 45: 1.

Wilcox, C. (1949) 'The Promise of the World Trade Charter', *Foreign Affairs*, 27: 3 (April).

Wilkinson, R. (2000) *Multilateralism and the World Trade Organisation: The Architecture and Extension of International Trade Regulation*, London: Routledge.

Wilkinson, R. (2001) 'The WTO in Crisis: Exploring the Dimensions of Institutional Inertia', *Journal of World Trade*, 35: 3 (June).

Wilkinson, R. (2002a) 'The World Trade Organisation', *New Political Economy*, 7: 1 (March).

Wilkinson, R. (2002b) 'The Contours of Courtship: the WTO and Civil Society', in Rorden Wilkinson and Steve Hughes (eds), *Global Governance: Critical Perspectives*, London: Routledge.

Williams, M. (1991) *Third World Co-operation: The Group of 77 in UNCTAD*, London: Pinter.

2
Civil Society and the World Trading System

Marc Williams

Introduction

International trade is an inherently political process with various actors contesting trade theory and practice. Until recently scholarly attention focused on the roles of states, firms and international organizations in the politics of international trade. The protests during the WTO's Ministerial Meeting in Seattle (November–December 1999) brought to the fore civil society engagement with the world trading system. While the Seattle protest captured media attention it is but a single instance of a more complex process. The Seattle protests were a highly visible but distorted image of the attempts by civil society actors to influence developments in the world trading system. This chapter explores the role of civil society actors in international trade politics through a focus on the tensions created by the multiple linkages between a globalizing world political economy and the expansion of the multilateral trading system.

Civil society actors have risen to prominence in the global political economy as a result of the impact of globalization on the interstate system. It is not necessary to subscribe to the 'retreat of the state' thesis to note that the process of globalization has disrupted traditional notions of sovereignty. The state remains a central actor in world politics with its control over territorial space and as a source of legitimacy. Nevertheless, there has been a transformation in regulatory activities with national forms of regulation increasingly supplemented with governing arrangements at the sub-state, supranational and private spheres (Scholte 2000: 132–58). This evolving framework has created a political space for civil society actors to influence global political and economic relations. Civil society actors critique constitutive practices of the international system and in particular expose their potential for offering alternatives and for instigating extensive social change. Recent research on civil society, social movements and world politics has shown that these groups are increasingly organized and impact the decisions of states, firms and intergovernmental organizations (Keck and Sikkink 1998; O'Brien *et al.* 2000).

The expansion of the multilateral trading system provides another key framework for understanding the activities of civil society actors. The expansion of trade rules into new areas has given increased prominence to the historical conflict between protectionists and free traders. In this context civil society groups have been active participants either through supporting initiatives aimed at trade liberalization or in resisting further economic liberalization through support for arrangements designed to protect national and sectional interests. Moreover, the strengthening of the international trade regime has provided the political space in which some civil society activists have sought to challenge the liberal ideology of the hegemonic discourse on trade policy.

The first part of the chapter explores transformations in the global trading system and the impact of these changes for the actors in international trade. It focuses on the impact of globalization on trade policy and the responses of civil society actors to these changes. The second section of the chapter is concerned with the relationship between civil society actors and the WTO. The WTO is the central institutional framework for the management of international trade and the chapter therefore focuses on efforts by various civil society groups to influence the WTO. Attention will be given to two issues in the discussion below. The politics of trade liberalization and debates over governance arrangements provide the framework for discussion. The third part of the chapter provides a brief assessment of the impact of civil society actors in the world trading system.

Globalization and the world trading system

The increasing politicization of world trade is one result of some of the underlying tensions generated by the process of globalization. Within the global political economy globalization has generated conflict between state and non-state actors, and instigated a search for regulatory frameworks to lessen the impact of globalizing processes. The literature on globalization is vast, contentious and suffused with a proliferation of definitions. Scholars differ concerning the scope and delineation of these linkages but most agree that these widespread changes cover economic, ideological, technological and cultural dimensions of social life. Nevertheless, in the absence of a consensus and despite the variety of meanings attached to the term popular conceptions of globalization generally indicate a 'widening, deepening and speeding up of worldwide interconnectedness' (Held *et al.* 1999: 2).

As used in this chapter globalization refers to a material and normative process. It consists of both a deepening of global economic integration, and a reconstruction of ideological frameworks of normalization and resistance. The political contest over world trade thus arises in the context of an evolving global political economy understood as a set of material and ideational practices. That is, the politics of international trade result from tensions created by global processes of production, distribution, consumption and the social arrangements made to organize these processes.

Trade liberalization

A dynamic and multifaceted connection exists between trade and globalization. The massive expansion of trade across frontiers, greatly exceeding the growth of world output, has been a powerful globalizing force in the world economy. International trade is a significant contributor to globalizing processes, a salient feature of globalization, and the impact of globalization on trade practices is a crucial factor in the contemporary global political economy. Since the end of the second World War international trade has increased more rapidly than global production thus providing a clear indicator of the increased internationalization of economic activities and of the greater interconnectedness which has come to characterize the world economy. In material terms, therefore, developments in trade signify deeper economic integration between national societies. In ideational terms, trade liberalization has become a key element in strategies designed to pursue economic growth and development. Globalization thus presents a structural context in which trade liberalization is taking place. It is within this framework that the activities of civil society actors have to be analysed.

Given the importance of trade as a sector in the contemporary global economy and its role in promoting economic growth many civil society groups have developed an interest in the activities of firms, states and international organizations in the promotion and management of international trade. Civil society actors attempt to influence trade policy and practice through lobbying and advocacy activities. Their attention is focused on the state as the primary regulators of economic activities in the global trading system;[1] firms as direct agents engaged in production and trade who also either directly or through industry associations exert influence on governing arrangements; and international organizations (regional or universal) that provide legal and normative frameworks for the conduct of trade.

The relationship between trade and growth and the benefits and costs of further trade liberalization lie at the center of civil society engagement with the world trading system. Three main features of post-war trade liberalization provide the material context for this engagement. First, significant trade liberalization has taken place initially under the auspices of the General Agreement on Tariffs and Trade (GATT) and latterly within the framework of the WTO. Second, the process of trade liberalization has been uneven with most of the benefits confined to producers of manufactured products. Third, the negotiating agenda has expanded to include new products and sectors. Civil society actors have been involved in debates on each of these issues.

Civil society actors have been involved in the exploration and contestation of the benefits of trade liberalization. Increased liberalization has given rise to a debate concerning the relationship between trade and growth especially since trade is recognized as vital for countries trying to promote economic development. The consensus among neoclassical economists is that trade promotes growth. That is, the evidence amassed by conventional economics demonstrates that countries with an open economy engaging in international trade have performed better than countries where policy has restricted domestic markets to foreign products. Trade theorists argue that international trade stimulates domestic producers to manufacture goods to world market standards thus increasing productivity. Furthermore, it acts as a stimulus to the local economy providing it with resources cheaper than it would cost to produce the same resources domestically and in so doing trade leads to a more efficient use of resources not only on a national level but also internationally. Trade is beneficial for states in raising the production possibility frontier enabling countries to consume more than they would have done in the absence of trade, and it is good for individual consumers through the provision of a wider array of products at lower cost. The politics of trade liberalization develops in a context where the theoretical benefits of free trade collide with the losses incurred by various sectional interests as the result of trade liberalization. Some civil society actors have been promoters of liberalization in general, others have supported particular liberalization initiatives and others have attempted to counter liberalization measures.

The uneven nature of globalizing tendencies has been another site of civil society activism. Not only has overall trade growth been uneven it is also so in respect of different countries and regions. The majority of transactions in world trade are restricted to the advanced industrial countries, and the fastest growth in trade has taken place among these countries. The share of the developed countries in world trade has consistently remained around the 80 per cent mark. Development and human rights activists have been prominent in attempts to counter the uneven impacts of trade liberalization.

One of the major issues for civil society actors has been the social impact of trade and these concerns have been heightened by the expansion of the trade agenda. This expansion is two-fold. On one hand it refers to the inclusion of issues that until the 1970s were seen as non-trade issues such as services, investment and intellectual property. On the other hand, it refers to the changing scope of international trade regulation from a focus almost exclusively on tariff reduction to one involving policy harmonization. Until the Uruguay Round (1986–94) trade negotiations were based on tariff concessions but the negotiations during that Round extended coverage of the multilateral trading system to domestic policies, institutional practices and regulations.

Governance

One of the crucial issues in the debate on the impact of globalization on the global political economy concerns the relationship between state power and sovereignty, and the changing contours of governance. Governance will be taken to mean the sum of the many ways that individuals and institutions, public and private, manage their common affairs (Commission on Global Governance 1995). The nature of governance and authority in the fields of international economic institutions (Woods 2000) and trade policymaking is going through a transitional phase. While it is not clear where the transition is going it is evident that actors other than states, whether they are private firms or civil society organizations have an increasingly significant role in multilateral negotiations. Developments in the world trading system have effected a transformation from a system in which national actors were the predominant decision-makers and exercised governance with a weak intergovernmental institution (GATT) to one in which national governments increasingly share control with an intergovernmental organization (WTO).

The architects of the post-war multilateral trade regime designed a system of embedded liberalism in which the pursuit of free trade was tempered by the necessity to protect national economic objectives. The institutional embodiment of this managed trade regime was the GATT. From its inception in 1947 until its demise in 1994 GATT faced a number of critical issues as it attempted to provide a regulatory framework for world trade. Key issues included protectionism, regional arrangements, and the interests of developing countries. GATT was a weak organization with limited power over its membership. It was a contractual arrangement with no supranational powers. Under this system civil society actors focused their attention at the national level and attempted to influence national policymakers. The most successful civil society organizations in this period were business associations. Representatives of these organizations were frequently included in national negotiating delegations. Another reason for limited civil society participation at the international level arose from the institutional framework of the GATT. GATT maintained a strict intergovernmental character and never established any formal linkages with civil society organizations.

For most of its 47-year history GATT retained a relatively low profile for civil society organizations. Occasionally an agricultural lobby group protested outside the headquarters of the GATT in Geneva. However, in the early 1990s two events brought increased civil society scrutiny of the organization. As the Uruguay Round of trade negotiations progressed civil society groups increasingly became aware of its wide-ranging mandate and the likely impact of trade rules on an array of issues. Negotiations on the future of the trading system drew attention to the possible transformation in regulation from the national to the international level. As they focused attention on world trade civil society representatives became increasingly aware of the limited influence they exerted on decision-making processes related to trade issues at the national and international levels. Second, a GATT dispute panel ruling in 1991 on the tuna–dolphin dispute between the United States and Mexico brought to prominence the conflict between representatives of the environmental social movement and supporters of trade liberalization. The environmentalist critique of the world trading system sparked an intense political conflict and further drew the attention of other civil society groups to the impact of trade rules on distributional and social justice issues.

If civil society interest in the multilateral trading system was awakened in the early 1990s the establishment of the WTO in 1995 has provided a focus for the organizational energies of many civil society groups. The creation of the WTO, reflecting as it does an important shift in the organization of the global trade regime, has brought governance issues to the forefront of public debate and scrutiny. As a successor to the GATT the WTO widens and deepens global regulation of international trade and payments. It extends GATT disciplines into areas previously governed by protectionist devices in the post-war global trade regime, that is, agriculture, and textiles, and brings 'new' issues such as intellectual property rights and investment measures under regulatory control. Moreover, the increased scope, permanence, and rule-making authority of the WTO have alarmed civil society groups which fear that trade decisions gradually and irretrievably have been displaced from the national realm, where civil society actors can exercise some influence, to a supranational organization shrouded in secrecy. The creation of the WTO thus increased insecurities concerning the impact of globalization through the further liberalization of trade and the apparent shift of regulation from the national to international level. The WTO's mandate has brought it into conflict with a range of civil society activists representing consumer, development, labour and environmental interests.

Civil society and the WTO

The WTO: institutional venue and trade politics

Prior to an examination of the attitudes and behaviour of civil society organizations towards the WTO it is necessary to analyse the role played by the WTO in the world trading system, and the institutional context of the WTO as a specific framework that conditions civil society participation in the global trading system. As the legal and institutional foundation of the world trading system the WTO makes three key contributions to global governance. First, it provides a framework of rules, norms and principles to govern the multilateral trading system. Second, the WTO provides a forum for multilateral trade negotiations. The principal contractual obligations determining trade negotiations and trade legislation are determined through multilateral trade agreements. Furthermore, the Trade Policy Review Mechanism facilitates the evolution of trade relations and trade policy through its surveillance of the policies of WTO member states. Third, the WTO also performs the vital function of dispute resolution. The Dispute Settlement Understanding (DSU) provides the machinery for settling members' differences on their rights and obligations.

Although the WTO is based on the same four key principles that underpinned the GATT namely, viz. non-discrimination, reciprocity, transparency and multilateral cooperation, nevertheless it effected a critical transformation in the world trading system. The trade regime constructed under GATT was a mixture of bilateralism wherein a compromise was struck 'between global economic integration, multilateralism, and a reliance on market forces on the one hand, and a quest for domestic stability, economic expediency and bilateralism on the other' (Williams 1994: 150). This compromise has been disrupted by the process of globalization and the quest for post-sovereign governance. Whereas GATT was essentially an enabling institution the WTO is both an enabling and regulatory institution (Williams 2001: 45). This is evidenced in both approaches to liberalization and governance.

While trade liberalization under GATT was a negative process of restricting barriers to trade through tariff cutting exercises, under the WTO this shallow or negative integration has been supplemented by deep or positive integration with emphasis on discussions of domestic policies, institutional practices and regulations. Furthermore, the WTO has expanded the scope (through the inclusion of services, trade-related intellectual property rights, and domestic [non-trade] policies), and altered the character of negotiations from a focus on bargaining over products to negotiations over policies that shape the conditions of competition.

The WTO not only extends the mandate of the GATT into new areas it redefines the relationship between national governments and the world trading system through the creation of an effective dispute settlement mechanism, the provision of a trade policy review mechanism, and the development of a set of mandatory codes. It has also initiated a movement towards policy harmonization, for example in the areas of subsidies, trade-related investment measures, and services. These changes essentially redefine the relationship between national authorities and the multilateral trading system, and herald a shift from embedded liberalism to neo-liberalism.

The WTO thus provides a higher and sharper profile for trade issues, and as such attracts the attention of a range of actors. Compared with the GATT, the increased scope, permanence and rule-making authority of the WTO has brought governance issues more sharply into focus and as such has become a focal point for civil society actors. Many of these actors express the view that the WTO represents an erosion of national decision-making in trade policy.

The ability of civil society actors to influence the world trade agenda through the WTO is constrained by the WTO's organizational characteristics. Like its predecessor, the GATT, the WTO is principally a forum for intergovernmental negotiations and is not formally open to civil society representatives. The sole members of the WTO are states and negotiations on international trade remain the exclusive responsibility of governments. Furthermore, the multilateral trading system resides on a system of legal rules and this contractual character of the system reinforces the centrality of states within WTO. Although civil society actors are prohibited from participating in its decision-making activities, as we have seen above, participation in global trade politics is not restricted to membership of formal international organizations. As previously mentioned, although governments are the legitimate representatives within the bargaining process trade policy is a political process in which special interest groups attempt to influence national policy. Depending on the policy process of specific states, national (and transnational) civil society groups will contribute to national policy formulation. Civil society groups representative of the interests of, for example, producers, consumers and workers participate in domestic debates on the formation of national trade policy. The resulting policy-mix within various states reflects the differential strengths of interest groups and the efforts of lobbyists. Moreover, some national delegations include representatives from civil society in an effort to gain consensus for any decisions reached, thus making it easier to gain domestic support for the trade agreement.

Increased attention to global trade rules has resulted in attempts by some civil society groups to influence the WTO more directly through participation in its activities. Unlike its predecessor organization the WTO has provided a space for direct contact with civil society organizations. Article V (2) of the Marrakech Agreement establishing the WTO noted that the new organization should make 'appropriate arrangements for consultation and cooperation with non-governmental organizations'.

While initially this stipulation was ignored, in response to pressure from civil society activists (with support from some Western governments) the WTO has initiated a number of measures to facilitate greater access for civil society groups. In July 1996 the General Council of the WTO adopted two decisions aimed at increasing civil society–WTO interactions. The first decision (WTO 1996a) provided for liaison between the Secretariat and civil society, and the second (WTO 1996b) provided for the derestriction of WTO documents. Continuing problems with the derestriction of documents led to a further decision in May 2002 (WTO 2002) to enhance the speed with which documents will be made publicly available.

The main decision-making body of the WTO is the Ministerial Conference which meets every two years. Ministerial Conferences have been held in Singapore (1996), Geneva (1998), Seattle (1999), Doha (2001) and Cancún in September 2003. The official participants are governments but civil society representatives have been permitted to attend all the Ministerial Conferences. There were 108 NGOs at the Singapore Ministerial, 128 at the Second Ministerial, 737 at the Seattle Meeting, and 366 at the Doha Ministerial Meeting. Civil society groups use these opportunities to lobby delegates, organize public meetings and to present their analyses of trade issues.

In the interval between Ministerial Conferences the substantive work of the organization is conducted in the General Council. The General Council also acts as the dispute settlement body and the trade policies review body. Civil society groups have no representation in these bodies. Civil society groups with offices in Geneva lobby delegates to the General Council. The formal work of the WTO is overseen by its Secretariat. Contact between the WTO Secretariat and civil society has expanded since the July 1996 decision. The WTO Secretariat maintains informal relations with non-governmental organizations (NGOs). It provides briefings on its work programme, receives representations from NGOs, organizes symposia and workshops with civil society representatives, distributes all position papers submitted by NGOs/civil society to WTO delegations and maintains a website with informational sources for NGOs and from NGOs. The Secretariat also provides briefings during the Ministerial conferences.

The arrangements outlined above provide civil society organizations with some access to the WTO. This access is limited and in some respects could be described as shallow. The organization remains one in which states exercise decision-making power. The WTO has not developed a formal consultative process with civil society organizations. It has increased its openness through the publication of documents and its excellent website but access to documents, while important, is not a full substitute for access to the policy process.

Civil society access to the WTO and participation in trade politics is also related to the sets of values embedded within the WTO. The normative structure of the WTO further shapes the access and influence potential of various civil society groups. Through its commitment to trade liberalization the WTO is a powerful instrument in the construction of global norms. We have argued above that the WTO is a managed trade organization in so far as it represents a specific mixture of national interests (protectionism) and international interests (free trade). While managed trade rather than free trade is the political outcome of the governing arrangements the organizational ideology of the WTO is one of liberal trade. The WTO is committed to the promotion of a liberal trading order. Its policies are predicated on an assumption that trade is better than no-trade and that barriers to trade are harmful to national and international welfare. This normative bias privileges trade over non-trade issues, and economic issues over non-economic issues.

The values embedded within the WTO support those groups with a similar commitment to trade liberalization and marginalize those groups critical of such strategies. Thus groups representing consumer rights, environmental protection, development, human rights and labour who demand attention to social and distributional issues face a harder task in exercising influence than, for example, business associations seeking to further trade liberalization. For example, business interests are well represented at symposia and workshops held in Geneva and, compared with other civil society actors, associations representing corporate interests have been the largest grouping.

Civil society actors: conformers, reformers and radicals

As should be evident from the above, there is no single global civil society perspective on the WTO. On the contrary the starting point for analysis is recognition of this diversity in civil society activism engagement with the WTO. Civil society actors with an interest in the world trading system comprise a diversity of organizational forms and attitudes. Some organizations are primarily based at the local level and are concerned with impacts of trade on local communities. Other organizations are oriented towards the national level and attempt to influence national policies and priorities on trade issues. And some organizations are of a trans-border type with strategies designed to influence national governments, international organizations, and transnational corporations. Furthermore, there is no single organizational type and among the diversity of organizational forms are grassroots organizations, non-governmental organizations, think tanks, business lobbies and academic networks. Given this diversity of organizational form it follows that civil society actors also differ in terms of their access to resources. Some groups can command large amounts of financial and technical resources while other groups lack both finance and technical expertise. This resource issue is a major constraint on the effective participation of many civil society groups in the world trading system. For example, effective participation depends heavily on the ability to engage in analyses of trade patterns and trade flows. Geographical location is also a further aspect of differentiation between civil society organizations. The North/South divide in the global political economy is replicated at the level of civil society with southern organizations on the whole being less well financed than their northern counterparts.

In terms of attitudes three broad types of civil society approaches have been identified (Scholte *et al.* 1999). Conformers (conservatives) are sympathetic to the goal of trade liberalization and the expansion of the regulatory activities of the WTO. Reformers (moderates) in principle support liberal trade rules but on either social justice or democratic principles campaign for changes to WTO rules and procedures. Reformist critics of the WTO seek to change the policies and procedures of the WTO. In terms of policies reformers have mounted specific 'issue' campaigns, and in relation to procedural change they have campaigned for the transformation of the WTO from what they term a secretive and unrepresentative organization into one reflecting general democratic principles. Both conformers and reformers adopt engagement strategies. The third main approach to the WTO is taken by those civil society organizations that adopt a radical (rejectionist) stance. These groups criticize the WTO and campaign to limit its powers or to replace the organization.

Agenda-setting and issue politics

The growth in concern with and collective action to address the international trade regime is indicated by enhanced civil society action over certain specific issues. Increased participation in the world trading system reflects the growing recognition by civil society actors that world trade rules have an impact on core concerns such as growth, development, environmental sustainability, health, gender equity and working conditions. Civil society actors have attempted to influence the outcome of world trade negotiations through lobbying efforts at national and international levels. At the forefront of these efforts have been reformist civil society groups that represent environmental, development, labour, human rights, consumer and women's groups. At the centre of world trade politics, however, is the issue of trade liberalization and it is to this that we now turn.

The liberalization of international trade

Civil society actors have been participants in the politics of trade liberalization. Competing civil society perspectives and lobbying on the issue of trade liberalization provides a convincing demonstration of the diversity of civil society participation in the world trading system. Discussion of the trade liberalization agenda and the politics of international trade can be divided into general perspectives on liberalization and the reduction of barriers in specific sectors.

Support for further liberalization has generally emerged from the business sector. In the debates on global trade regulation a variety of civil society organizations promote free trade policies and support current institutional arrangements. This does not mean, of course, that these organizations are in agreement on all major issues. It cannot be inferred, for example, that such organizations may not on occasion support protectionism for specific industries.[2] However, in broad terms representatives of these groups support the conventional neo-classical economic paradigm. They tend to reject the extension of the trade agenda to other issues arguing that trade is not an efficient mechanism with which to address the social justice concerns of reformers and rejectionists. These conformist civil society organizations are not simply supporters of the status quo. Indeed, it could be argued that some conformist groups are critical of certain aspects of the transformation of the trade agenda. In the forefront of such efforts are peak organizations representing business interests such as the Business Council on Sustainable Development, and the International Chamber of Commerce.

In direct contrast to civil society actors who lobby in support of further liberalization are those groups opposed in principle to the liberalization project. These rejectionist groups share some agreement with more radical reformist groups but they believe that it is not possible to reform the WTO. Many radical critiques of the WTO arise from a more general critique of global capitalism. The critics of further trade liberalization portray the WTO as a rich man's club, and argue that the WTO promotes free trade at the expense of local and national communities. It has been argued that trade liberalization is responsible for creating environmental degradation, increasing global poverty, supporting human rights abuses and undermining the power of democratic scrutiny of trade policies (Wallach 1999). Many of these critics adopt an anti-globalization posture, and call not only for an end to further liberalization but also for rollback of certain measures. Many of the demonstrators at Seattle and other WTO meetings are sympathetic to this rejectionist critique. The People's Global Action (PGA) a loose coalition of anti-WTO activists is the best-known anti-liberalization network (Williams and Ford 1999: 282–86).

Business groups have not only been at the forefront of general liberalization but also sector specific liberalization in attempts to gain commercial advantage. An important example of the role of business groups in the promotion of trade liberalization is that of intellectual property rights. The Trade-related Aspects of Intellectual Property (TRIPS) agreement was actively promoted by a coalition of American transnational companies that campaigned at national and international levels (Sell 2000; Chapter 9 by May in this volume). But caution should be exercised in linking peak business organizations with the promotion of trade liberalization. For example, agricultural interest groups in the European Union (EU) have traditionally opposed further agricultural liberalization whereas the agricultural lobby in Australia has recently supported agricultural liberalization. The agricultural lobby in Europe comprising a number of civil society organizations has targeted individual national governments and the EU Commission in Brussels (Keeler 1996). In Australia, the shift in trade policy towards greater liberalization made by the Hawke and Keating governments in the 1980s found support from agricultural interests (Capling 2001).

Support for or opposition to further trade liberalization arises from ideological preference and special interest. In terms of civil society we can identify five broad areas in which actors have been attempting to influence the world trade agenda and to insert reform proposals into the liberalization project. The best-known civil society grouping is represented by environmentalists but other important groups are those actors with interests in consumer issues, labour rights, development and women's rights. Civil society actors within each issue area are diverse and lobbying activities are targeted at national, regional and international levels. The following sketch provides an overview of the participation of reformist civil society actors in the world trading system.

Environmental issues first came to prominence in the world trading system at the beginning of the 1990s and arose from the opposition of many American environmental groups to the proposal to conclude a free trade agreement between the United States, Canada and Mexico, and the ruling by a GATT dispute panel on the tuna–dolphin dispute between the United States and Mexico. Environmental civil society organizations have been campaigning since the early 1990s for a mainstreaming of sustainable development throughout the WTO. NGOs such as the World Wide Fund for Nature (WWF), World Conservation Union (IUCN), Center for International Environmental Law (CIEL) and the International Institute for Sustainable Development (IISD) have been at the forefront of the trade–environment debate. At the centre of the environmentalist critique is the assertion that the current multilateral trading system privileges trade liberalization over environmental protection. Environmentalists claim that an inherent conflict exists between trade and environmental protection in the current formulation of trade policies (see Chapter 6 by Newell, this volume). They argue that this need not be the case and that the rules of the multilateral trading system can be altered so that global environmental problems are effectively addressed. Environmental groups have been successful in placing the environment on the agenda of world trade talks. They have been less successful in securing agreement on their demands. They have met strong opposition from supporters of the status quo who contend first that WTO regulations do promote sustainable development, and second that environmental standards beyond those already agreed are not a legitimate goal of the multilateral trading system. Trade rules should not be designed to combat environmental destruction. The opposition to the environmentalist critique includes business civil society groups (Williams 2001).

Labour issues have been placed on the agenda of the WTO by labour unions and human rights groups. The interest of the labour movement in trade issues was stimulated by the creation of the WTO which was viewed as an element in a strategy to further the interest of capital at the expense of workers' rights. Peak labour groups such as the World Confederation of Labour (WCL) and the International Confederation of Free Trade Unions (ICFTU) have lobbied national governments and taken part in WTO processes, for example ministerial meetings, in an attempt to promote the adoption of a social clause incorporating core labour rights into the WTO (O'Brien *et al.* 2000: 82–4). The campaign for a social clause has been opposed by developing country governments and civil society organizations with a commitment to free trade. Human rights NGOs and labour unions have been particularly concerned with the issue of child labour and have campaigned against the continued exploitation of child workers in developing countries. A variety of children rights organizations and leading unions such as the ICFTU have been lobbying for an end to child labour.

One of the main reasons for the failure to launch a new trade round at the Seattle Ministerial Meeting was the disillusionment of developing countries with the limited progress in the implementation of the Uruguay Round decisions. The campaign by representatives of the developing countries for a WTO more responsive to the needs of its poorer members is supported by many development organizations in the North and South. These groups contribute to the process through the provision of analyses and reports and some groups such as the International Center for Trade and Sustainable Development (ICTSD) based in Geneva contributes to the technical capacity of some developing countries. Some civil society organizations, for example, Oxfam and the Third World Network, have mounted forceful critiques of the world trading system. The agenda for development reform is broad, encompassing a range of objectives. Some groups promote a fair trade agenda while others concentrate on more limited issues around access and autonomy.

It was apparent after Seattle that further progress in trade liberalization is dependent on meeting the needs of developing countries. The Doha Ministerial Meeting adopted the Doha Declaration providing a mandate for trade talks and developing an agenda for the implementation of existing agreements. At the centre of the Doha Declaration is a concern with development. Civil society organizations cannot claim responsibility for the current high profile given to development issues but they have played a role through monitoring, analysis and lobbying activities in supporting the efforts of developing countries.

From the inception of the WTO, consumer groups have targeted the organization. Consumer activists argue that the WTO is biased in favour of the interests of transnational companies with the result that producer interests are given greater prominence than those of the consumer. They therefore propose reforms to trade rules to constrain the power of corporations. Prominent consumer advocate groups include Public Interest (in the US), Consumers International and the International Organization of Consumer Unions (IOCU).

In the 1990s women's groups began to study the gender implications of trade and trade policies. Civil society groups such as Women's EDGE, Women in Development Europe (WIDE) and the Women's Environment and Development Organization (WEDO) have recently begun articulating a campaign for greater attention to be given to the gendered nature of trade and the impact of trade policies on gender relations.

Issues

Civil society groups have been equally concerned with governance issues as they have been with the liberalization agenda. Indeed, as argued above, these two issues are inextricably linked. While rejectionist groups campaign for the abolition of the WTO reformist civil society groups have initiated a debate on the democratic credentials of the organization. The reformist critique of the WTO consists of two interrelated parts. A negative critique focuses on the absence of transparency, accountability and representation. The critics contend that the WTO lacks transparency and accountability, and is not sufficiently representative in so far as its operations are shrouded in secrecy, its decisions are removed from effective scrutiny by national legislatures, and it fails to provide participation for a wide range of stakeholders affected by its decisions (WWF 1999; Wallach 1999; Stichele 1998). The critics allege that transparency is lacking in two respects. First, negotiations are conducted, dispute panels are convened and decisions are taken solely in the presence of member states. Civil society groups are thus effectively disbarred from providing a valuable watchdog function for the wider public. Second, although the WTO Secretariat provides extensive information though its website and document derestriction, this does not guarantee full transparency. Reformists argue that the WTO is not sufficiently accountable or representative because states are the sole formal participants in its deliberations. Diverse communities around the world directly affected by trade liberalization are marginalized in WTO decision-making processes while the interests of groups most likely to profit from further liberalization are advanced since they are more likely to have access to elite national decision-makers. Instead of limiting participation to states, the WTO should provide a greater role for civil society groups since representatives from these groups can assist in making the world trading system more transparent. (Bellman and Gerster 1996: 31–74; Enders 1996; WWF 1999).

In addition to the negative critique, reformist groups claim that increased participation by civil society groups in WTO policymaking would automatically improve the representativeness and responsiveness of the organization. Three broad claims have been made for the increased participation of civil society groups in the WTO. The first claim is that increased input from civil society will provide decision-makers with more ideas and views and improve the results of policy deliberations (Esty 1999: 97–118). This claim has been made explicitly by Bullen and Van Dyke (1996) who contend that administrative structures that integrate public input will consistently produce better results than those where information input is restricted. The second claim is that the specialized knowledge possessed by civil society actors can make a constructive contribution to trade politics since these groups can provide information and technical expertise not necessarily available in inter-governmental deliberations (Esty 1999: 100). The third claim concerns the necessity for broad public support for further trade liberalization. It is argued that civil society participation in the WTO enhances credibility, ensures a better-educated public, and secures wider support for increased trade liberalization. The broad-based support fostered by public participation ensures that policies are likely to be implemented (Bullen and Van Dyke 1996).

Civil society and trade politics

We have argued that civil society actors have attempted to influence the trade liberalization and governance dimensions of the world trade agenda. Of course the activities of civil society groups do not in themselves suggest that they are important actors in the politics of global trade. It remains to assess the extent to which the participation of civil society actors has affected the decision-making of major WTO members and elicited a response from the WTO.

For some observers the protests at the Seattle Ministerial Meeting precipitated the failure of the WTO's Third Ministerial Meeting. Such a conclusion is, we have argued, too simplistic and fails to acknowledge the many conflicts among the WTO membership that contributed to the impasse in Seattle. But even though the Seattle protesters were not the main reason for the failure of the conference their activities brought to public prominence objections to further trade liberalization. Between the Seattle and Doha meetings the WTO Secretariat embarked on a series of activities designed to bolster support for further trade liberalization and the WTO itself. Central to this campaign was the recognition that there was wide-spread public disquiet with the operation of the world trading system. Even though some sections of the protesters could be dismissed as a disorganized rabble with a poor understanding of the economic and legal aspects of world trade, there was nevertheless the perception that the distributional and social impacts of world trade were politically significant issues that had to be addressed. Thus development became the major goal of the Doha Ministerial and the Doha Round is focused on providing maximum benefits for developing countries. This approach is required in order to placate developing countries and to foster consensus in the WTO but it is also spurred by the opposition of critical civil society actors.

As the WTO prepared for its fifth Ministerial Meeting in Cancún in September 2003 it remained unclear whether the political conditions necessary for a successful outcome had been established. It is widely acknowledged that one of the main reasons for the current malaise of the WTO arises from continued questioning of its liberalization project, and scrutiny of its decision-making procedures. The successful implementation of agreements reached at Doha is primarily dependent on governments but civil society actors are politically important in so far as public support is required for further trade liberalization. As Gary Sampson (1999: 3) has argued, 'Improving understanding of the WTO is important to securing the necessary support for future trade negotiations from environmentalists and other civil society representatives.' In the absence of such understanding the legitimacy of the rules and norms of the multilateral trading system will be called into question.

Civil society actors thus have a role to play in the legitimacy politics of the WTO. On one hand, conformist groups can bolster support for the organization and further reform. This support has been recognized by successive WTO Directors-General. Renato Ruggiero the first Director-General made overtures to civil society in 1998 (WTO 1998), and his successor Mike Moore was initially welcoming of interactions with civil society and embarked on a dialogue with selected groups prior to the Seattle conference. He was less inclined to maintain dialogue after Seattle and concentrated his attention following the failure of the Seattle meeting to improving relations with developing countries. But the offensive to demonstrate the virtues of trade liberalization for all sectors of the global economy had resonance for civil society actors. In June 2003 the current Director-General, Supachai Panitchpakdi, established a Consultative Board to prepare a report on the future of the WTO in the context of a changing global economy. The Consultative Board is not an intergovernmental forum but is instead composed of individuals selected in their private capacity.[3] Furthermore, major governments, especially the United States, have shown awareness of the necessity for wide public support of further trade liberalization, and of the WTO.

But in the search for legitimacy the importance of reformist critics and rejectionists have also been recognized by the trade community. Both supporters and opponents of the WTO recognize that public confidence is a necessary ingredient for trade reform (Esty 1999: 98). On one hand, governments are unlikely to create the necessary domestic coalitions required to support further trade liberalization in the absence of a domestic consensus in favour of such change. On the other hand, violent protests against trade liberalization in developed and developing countries in the absence of an informed public debate is likely to assist protectionist elements. Thus defenders of the liberal trade order and supporters of increased trade liberalization need to ensure domestic and global constituencies in favour of the liberalization project. In such circumstances criticism of the WTO that focuses on its shortcomings as a democratic institution and cast doubt on the wisdom of its policies is politically significant. Although it is debatable whether contestation by civil society activists over WTO policies has undermined the legitimacy of the organization, the evidence suggests that the debates outlined above have raised doubts concerning the legitimacy of the WTO and world trading system.

Conclusion

The formal process of the WTO excludes civil society actors from participating in its deliberations. Nevertheless, civil society actors have indirect access to trade politics through two sources. Civil society actors participate in domestic political processes, and through pressure group activities may influence national priorities in the formation of trade policy. And the globalization of economic activity and the emergence of the WTO have shifted the attention of civil society actors to the global level. Civil society actors have tried to engage with the WTO but such engagement is constrained by the intergovernmental character of the organization. Nevertheless civil society actors remain important constituents for further reform processes. Civil society actors are actively engaged in supporting or opposing various proposals for further reform and the debate on governance is promoted by an array of civic associations.

As demonstrated above the WTO has been the target of environmentalists, human rights activists, trade unionists, and supporters of international development among others. These critics have persistently challenged the liberalization project at the heart of the WTO, and its democratic credentials. They have pursued their critique through lobbying governments, the WTO itself and the dissemination of information to journalists and the wider public. These separate (and at times explicitly linked) campaigns have not, on their own, created the current malaise in the multilateral trading system but their efforts, especially their rejection of unfettered trade liberalization and promotion of a reform agenda centred on making the WTO more transparent and accountable, are important in assessing the likely success of the Doha agenda.

Notes

1. Some states have at various times acted as direct agents through state trading companies.
2. See, for example the arguments in support of strategic trade theory.
3. These individuals would broadly fit within the conformers category as discussed in this chapter.

References

Bellman, C. and Gerster, R. (1996) 'Accountability in the World Trade Organisation', *Journal of World Trade Law* 30, 6: 31–74.

Bullen, S. and Van Dyke, B. (1996) *In Search of Sound Environment and Trade Policy: A Critique of Public Participation in the WTO*, Geneva: Center for International Environmental Law.

Capling, A. (2001) *Australia and the Global Trade System*, Cambridge: Cambridge University Press.

Commission on Global Governance (1995) *Our Global Neigbourhood: The Report of the Commission on Global Governance*, Oxford: Oxford University Press.

Enders, A. (1996) *Openness and the WTO*, Winnipeg: A Draft IISD Working Paper.

Esty, D.C. (1999) 'Environmental Governance at the WTO: Outreach to Civil Society', in Sampson, G. P. and Chambers W. B. (eds) *Trade, Environment and the Millennium*, Tokyo: United Nations Press.

Held, D. *et al.* (1999) *Global Transformations*, Cambridge: Polity Press.

Keck, M. and Sikkink, K. (1998) *Activists Beyond Borders*, Ithaca: Cornell University Press.

Keeler, John (1996) 'Agricultural Power in the European Community; Explaining the Fate of CAP and GATT Negotiations', *Comparative Politics* 28, 2: 127–49.

O'Brien, R. *et al.* (2000) *Contesting Global Governance: Multilateral Economic Institutions and Global Social Movements*, Cambridge: Cambridge University Press.

Sampson, G.P. (1999) *Trade, Environment and the WTO: A Framework for Moving Forward*, Washington, DC: ODC Policy Paper.

Scholte, J.A., O'Brien, R., Williams, R. and Williams, M. (1999) 'The World Trade Organization and Civil Society', *Journal of World Trade* (February): 107–24.

Scholte, J.A. (2000) *Globalization: A Critical Introduction*, Basingstoke: Macmillan.

Sell, S. (2000) 'Structures, Agents and Institutions: Private Corporate Power and the Globalization of Intellectual Property Rights', in Higgott, R. A. Underhill, G. R. D. and Bieler, A. (eds) *Non-State Actors and Authority in the Global System*, London: Routledge, pp. 91–106.

Stichele, M.V. (1998) *Towards a World Transnational Organisation?* Amsterdam: Transnational Institute, WTO Booklet Series Vol. 3.

Wallach, L. (1999) *Whose Trade Organization: Corporate Globalization and the Erosion of Democracy* Washington: D.C. Public Citizen.

Williams, M. (1994) *International Economic Organisations and the Third World* London: Harvester Wheatsheaf.

Williams, M. (2001) 'In Search of Global Standards: The Political Economy of Trade and the Environment', in Stevis, D. and Assetto, V. (eds) *The International Political Economy of the Environment: Critical Perspectives*, Boulder: Lynne Rienner, pp. 73–107.

Williams, M. and Ford, L. (1999) 'The WTO, the Environmental Social Movement and Global Environmental Management', *Environmental Politics*, 8, 1: 268–89.

Woods, N. (2000) 'The Challenge to International Institutions', in Woods, N. (ed.) *The Political Economy of Globalization*, London: Macmillan, 2000, pp. 202–23.

WTO (1996a) *Guidelines for the Circulation and De-Restriction of WTO Documents* [WT/L/160/Rev.1; 22 July].

WTO (1996b) *Guidelines for Arrangements on Relations with Non-Governmental Procedures* [WT/L/162; 23 July].

WTO (1998) *Ruggiero Announces Enhanced WTO Plan for Cooperation with NGOs* WTO Press Release 107, 17 July.

WTO (2002) [WT/L/452 14 May].

WWF (1999) *A Reform Agenda for the WTO Ministerial Conference* Gland: WWF Position Paper.

3

Business and Government in International Policymaking: The Transatlantic Business Dialogue as An Emerging Business Style?

David Coen and Wyn Grant

The study of trade politics primarily focuses on the state and intergovernmental negotiations at organizations such as the World Trade Organisation (WTO) and UNCTAD, yet business, and increasingly NGOs, are active players in trade discussions at the national and global level. Traditionally, business involvement has been justified in terms of the growth of foreign direct investment and the international nature of supply chains, changing the domestic nature of trade flows (Stopford and Strange 1991; Strange 1994, 1996; Willets 2002). Yet business has broadened its political activities in recent years, as international organizations have encroached into wider public and economic debates such as the Environment, Health and Safety, Competition Policy, Standard Setting and Taxation (Hocking and McGuire 2002; Levy and Newell 2002). As such, big business has learned to create wider political alliances outside of traditional political allies in the market and to establish direct links with national and international organizations. In parallel, governments have learned to accept the recommendations of business and have encouraged business cooperation via industrial policy forums such as the Transatlantic Business Dialogue (Coen and Grant 2001; Cowles 2001). Hence, the questions to address in studying the role of business in trade politics are: are international business fora a trend towards internationalization of business–government relations, how far do these new collective groupings represent the privatization of trade policy and what are the political consequences of such business–government relationships?

To address these questions, this chapter briefly describes what business seeks from trade negotiations and how business mobilized at the European and US level to create complex advocacy coalitions with governments, agencies, civic and consumer groups. Having observed the emergence of business advocacy coalitions on both sides of the Atlantic, we assess how far these alliances have converged at the international level via their dealings with international agencies and the emergence of new business–government forums. Finally, we explore the degree to which we see international business–governmental norms evolving via a short case study of the Transatlantic Business Dialogue (TABD) and address questions of legitimacy and accountability of business involvement in policy.

The TABD represents a significant subject for a business–government trade policy study as it evolved directly out of business and government experiences of the early WTO rounds, has a credible membership size and recognizes that the European Union and United States share the largest bilateral trading relationship in the world and are the key players in international trade negotiations. Set up in 1995, as a joint initiative of the European Commission and US State Department, the TABD has evolved into a practical framework for cooperation between the business community and governments. The TABD brings together 112 top American and European chief executives to coordinate business responses to international trade, standards and regulation questions. The TABD's ability to coordinate quick and focused policy responses and its removal of the need for potential intergovernmental bargaining has been an appealing feature for CEOs and government officials. However, for all its policymaking advantages, questions can be raised about the accountability, representativeness, and legitimacy of big-business trade forums.

Business–government relations

In accepting that the business community is not homogenous and that firm preferences will vary depending on the nature of the industry, issue, origin and competitive advantages, some general objectives of lobbying can be specified. Traditionally business has lobbied for protection or free trade through the introduction or removal of tariffs and quotas (Caves 1976; Magee *et al.* 1989). The aim of such policy was to push up domestic prices and produce economic rents at the expense of the welfare of the consumers. Such claims were usually justified under infant industry arguments, a desire to attract foreign investment or employment policies (Frey 1989; Milner 1988). However, while occasional cases continue to be made for protection of developing economies at the WTO as seen in the efforts of the G-21 at Cancún, the trend in bilateral trade talks between the European Union and the United States has been for liberalization of markets. This is demonstrated by the fact that in the seven rounds prior to the Uruguay Round of the GATT tariffs for the major industrial world fell from 40 per cent to 4.7 per cent (Jones 2001).

Under these increasingly neo-liberal conditions, firms have sought out local privileges and exclusive rights, such as airline landing, government procurement contracts, tax exceptions and subsidies. However, increasingly, firms have seen these non-tariff barriers eroded and have sought international competitive advantages via the export of product standards and intellectual property rights. It is here that the business forums have the greatest potential for influencing the trade debates – as standards that have the majority of an industry's backing can be fast tracked by all governments and international agencies and avoid the potential political gaming of international negotiations. Hence, the 1990s have seen the growth of mutual recognition agreements (MRAs) which allow firms to have their products assessed for conformity with the import regulation of other countries

(Egan 2001). The potential savings of such recognition and the knock on effect towards standardization of related regulatory policy in health and safety and the environment have encouraged the birth of international standards-setting collective organizations like the TABD.

In seeking to access these new forums or in fact in seeking to counter their agenda-setting regulatory influence, firms have looked to develop complex alliances with national governments, NGOs, legislators, national and international regulatory agencies and the media. Thus, by adapting Sabatier's notion of advocacy coalitions, we see new international advocacy coalitions (IAC) evolving in response to the internationalization of policymaking and the birth of business forums. Advocacy coalitions were originally defined by Sabatier as being made up of people from various governmental and private organizations such as interest groups, legislators, researchers and even a few journalists that 'share a set of normative and causal beliefs and engage in a nontrivial degree of co-ordinated activity over time' (Sabatier 1998: 103). An IAC theoretical perspective shows that changes in business opportunity structures and representation have occurred in response to government willingness to use private interests in public policy (Haufler 1993; Ronit and Schneider 1999), and with the rise of social movements like the Greens (Levy and Newell 2002). Thus, as sections 4 and 5 illustrate, such IACs facilitate access of traditional outsider groups such as the environmental groups and small firms, and help to legitimate big business in the policy process.

Accepting that there are significant economic and strategic advantages for business of such action, why do states and international organizations accept this lobbying behaviour? A recent UNCTAD/WTO report stated 'Business advocacy is perceived ... as part of the democratic process and is regarded as a useful tool for obtaining information and reaching balanced trade policy decisions' (UNCTAD/WTO 2002). Moreover, in the increasingly technical areas of standard-setting and property rights debates, it is not surprising that the under-resourced international civil servants turn to business alliances and forums for credible information and a constituency. Recognizing that business input into the policy process has become the accepted norm and that there is a resource dependency in information supply, we need to understand how firms embedded themselves at the national and transpose themselves to the international levels.

European business–government relations

The European Union in establishing a single market has developed a common commercial policy that embraces a common tariff regime, common trade agreements with third parties and uniform application of trade policy instruments. In line with article 133 the European Commission proposes and negotiates trade policy in consultation with the European Council and European Parliament, with final decision by qualified majority voting at the European Council. What is more, in addition to formulating EU trade policy, the European Commission is also the agenda-setter with regard to standard-setting and mutual recognition within the single market (Pollack and Shaffer 2001; Egan 2001). That said, member states must not be underestimated as they continue to input directly into trade negotiations via export promotion policies and applications for deviations from the common commercial policy and exert an influence in the formulation and implementation of EU directives. Hence, any firm wishing to influence EU trade policy must develop a multi-level strategy that puts pressure on a number of national and European institutions and organizations (Coen 1997).

In addition to the multi-institutional aspects to EU trade policy formulation, the European Commission cannot be seen as uniform in its goals, with several directorate generals (DGs) involved in negotiations ranging from External Relations, Agriculture, Enterprise and Competition, to Development and Environment. Under these conditions, business has been encouraged at the European level to develop complex and shifting political alliances that follow the policy process from the agenda-setting of the Commission to the formulation debates in member states and ratification at the European Council (Coen 1997; Coen and Dannreuther 2002; Richardson 2000). This desire for a more European interest representation was formalized in the recent European Commission Green Paper on Governance that explicitly called for horizontal business interest alliances with consumers and European societal interests (COM 2001). In such a complex environment, no industrial or societal group can lobby in a political vacuum and firms wishing to lobby directly on trade issues have had to incorporate consumer demands and civic lobbies' views into their political strategies (Coen 1998; Grant 2000; Young and Wallace 2000).

Why the change in business–government relations in Europe? In policymaking terms, EU institutions faced with a boom in public interest lobbying, in the 1990s, recognized a need for some form of regulated representation, if information flows were to be managed. The Commission's informal solution has been to create policymaking forums and select committees (Coen 1997; Richardson 2001) based around policy insiders and policy outsiders (Broscheid and Coen 2003). Business in turn has recognized that if it is to access these restricted entry policy forums it must broaden its political and information legitimacy by being more representative of economic and societal interests. The result has been the explosion in the late 1990s of short-life, issue-specific political alliances and business forums (Coen 1997, 1998; Greenwood 2003, Richardson 2001; Webster 2002).

The creation of these new forums and alliances, which included many of the original European Round Table (ERT) committee members and active members of the EU Committee of the American Chambers of Commerce (Amcham), suggested an inner core of industrial policymakers and the institutionalization of big business in the policy process. Amcham, drawing on its US lobbying experience, illustrated the importance of focused policy committees that could provide early and detailed information to the policymakers (Cowles 1996). The ERT, representing 36 of Europe's top CEOs, demonstrated in the run up to the creation of the single market the importance of having high level decision-makers involved in the policy process, as a means of providing credibility to the debate and speed of action and implementation (Cowles 1995). Moreover, the case of the ERT illustrates that business and the Commission (international bodies) have found common ground in the liberalization agenda (Van Apeldoorn 2002). Under these favourable conditions big business has embedded itself in the formal and informal policy networks.

However, while the above business groups have formalized their role in the policy process, established secretariats and have a clear and focused membership, we are also seeing a growth in 'short life' alliances that form around the formulation of technical issues such as environmental standards in packaging directives and vehicle emissions, or seek competitive regulatory advantage in areas like computer software patents and genetically modified foods (Earnshaw and Wood 1999; Grant *et al.* 2002; Pijenburg 1997). Here we see complex and changing alliances with actors outside of the sector, civic and social groupings and various member states. For example, in the case of the 'End of Life' automobile directives we saw oil and car companies working with NGOs and a cross section of countries such as the Spanish, German and British governments at various stages of the directive (Tenbucken 2002; Young and Wallace 2000). This action has many similarities with the advocacy coalitions observed in the United States and would tend to confirm the hypothesis that governance in the European Union is no longer simply a process of intergovernmentalism, but rather part of a broader international trend towards private government (Egan 2001; Ronit and Schiender 1999).

US business–government relations

The dominant US position in international trade negotiations is first and foremost a function of its economic primacy in the global economy. However US economic leadership has been facilitated by recent changes in institutional arrangements that are at odds with its traditional principle of sharing power between the different institutions of congress, president and courts (Wilson 2003). In trade policy the president has developed 'fast-track' authority to negotiate reciprocal agreements at NAFTA and recent WTO rounds, with the congress voting 'yes' or 'no' without amendments. This fast-track policymaking was introduced to avoid the potential log rolling and local vested interests that have characterized much of US trade policymaking history at the congressional level (Magee *et al.* 1989). However, the congress and national regulatory agencies like the Food and Drug Administration (FDA) continued to exert a strong influence over trade debates via their market creation, gate-keeping functions and standard-setting functions (Vogel 1995).

Like their European cousins, American business lobbies have developed numerous political channels at the local, agency, congressional and presidential levels. To manage this complex process there has been an expansion of specialist government affairs offices in the 1990s (Smith 2000). The exact scale of business lobbying in Washington is hard to determine if we consider, that in addition to the Fortune 500 companies and most European and Japanese multinational operating offices in Washington, there are thousands of registered lobbyists, civic groups, foreign governments, religious organizations and environmental groups, and the numbers continues to grow (Mitchell 1997). While business lobbying in the United States was widely catalogued as a consequence of the growth of federal government regulation, without the comparable increase in bureaucratic resources in the 1970s (Vogel 1989; Wilson 2003), today's expansion in political activity can be explained more as a response to complex lobbying games that must be managed at a centralized level to maintain a constant voice. For example, firms have recognized that in this crowded political arena collective arrangements like the Roundtable of Industrialist debating normative issues like market liberalization have to run parallel with specialist 'issues networks' for regulatory issues.

Direct comparisons of issue networks and industrial forums in Washington and Brussels are complicated by the existence in the United States of a politicized bureaucratic administration and political campaign contributions. Political Action Committees (PACs) have been seen as an indispensable tool for gaining access to decision-makers, as this is transparent means by which firm and stakeholders can make financial contributions to its favoured candidates (Wright 1996). This direct funding gave a large structural advantage to business vis-à-vis civic interests in the Washington trade lobby. However, while disadvantaged in terms of funds, the fact that in the United States regulatory policy areas have been pushed out of the traditional power centres of federal government and into the congressional hearings and agencies has strengthened the role played by focused and specialist lobbyists, and has created a need for business to work with a much wider group of interests in ad hoc alliances (Martin 1991).

Thus, the logic of political action in Washington has come to focus on information exchange and credibility as much as monetary support. In this regulatory political environment firms have had to seek out advocacy coalitions with civic and social groups that are supportive of their political goals (Sabatier 1998). In such conditions it is fair to say that business lobbying is more decentralized and fragmented than the European business–government arrangements in member states, but that these new political cleavages based around issues, as opposed to sector or capital versus labour, do show many similarities with lobbying observed at the EU level (Coen 1999). Moreover the United States, like the European Union, has a division of powers, between agencies, congress and president that provides an opportunity for political 'venue shopping' and requires that firms realign and assess their coalitions and forums regularly, as opposed to unthinkingly utilizing traditional peak associations (Wilson 2003).

Evolution of an international business–government model

While acknowledging that lobbying the national government is important in terms of setting the trade policy agenda and in implementing and ratifying policy, business has recognized the importance of participating directly in the policy formulation and negotiation process at the global level. Thus, we have to assess how the successful forum and advocacy politics of the US and EU markets have transposed to the international level and what are the feedback loops and opportunity structures available in the international public policy environment.

Globalization is a highly contested concept, but most analysts would agree that there has been at least an acceleration of internationalization, reflected in the structure of international financial markets and the growth of foreign direct investment. However, despite the transformation of GATT into the WTO and the associated development of an authoritative disputes settlement mechanism, governance mechanisms at the international level remain relatively weak, particularly in terms of any arrangements that might be described as democratically accountable (Grant 2002: ch. 2). This mismatch between growing economic interdependence and much less coherent and authoritative political structures at the global level leaves something of a vacuum, although regional arrangements like the European Union could be construed as a partial attempt to fill it. This therefore creates an opportunity for business-based private governance arrangements like the TABD, as governments are continually seeking for new mechanisms that have sufficient influence on key issues to contribute to the settlement of international disputes in areas like trade.

With the success of organizations like the ERT in Brussels and the Roundtable of Industrialists in Washington, and the growth of policy networks in both public policy arenas, international business forums were seen as logical actors in high level global negotiations. In fact, groups like the TABD were no longer just industry driven but were actually encouraged and nurtured by national governments. As Al Gore noted when discussing the Third Generation wireless framework, 'A trade group seems to have succeeded in hammering out a basic 3G framework. Because of its make-up, the TABD appears to be a good place for the rest of the industry to bring pressure to bear on the combatants.' At the European end Sir Leon Brittan, former Vice-President of the European Commission observed, 'The ITA is the biggest success in multilateral trade negotiations since the Uruguay Round. The fact that such a positive and far reaching Agreement was reached so rapidly is due in large part to the inspiration and effective contribution of the TABD.'

But why were forums encouraged at the extraterritorial level? From a Commission perspective the TABD was seen as a government-led process that rapidly evolved into one where firms set the agenda. As a Commission official commented in interview, 'It's now industry led and industry driven ... US Government and Commission participate, but mainly as respondents.' What are the benefits to the Commission of participating in such a business-led process? These were succinctly summarized in interview by an official from the Enterprise DG. First, there was a strategic benefit. The TABD was invented after the end of the Cold War. It was a means of ensuring continued transatlantic ties by replacing military links with people to people links. Second, it facilitated the intensification of cooperation between the 'governments' on both sides. For example, it could be used as a means for preventing the development of trade barriers. Third, it was a means of creating international pressure to get things done in the European Union. Fourth, it was a means of bringing the European business community together and hence of facilitating the overall integration process.

The presence of these advantages did not mean that the Commission would necessarily follow the business line. As the DG Market official made clear: '[We are] always prepared to look very seriously into TABD recommendations, but we have to take action in the best public interest which is broader than TABD. ... Governments are always facing diverging views from different parts of civil society and have to take the best public interest option.' This statement meant listening seriously to what business had to say, but balancing it against broader public interest considerations, particularly where government had a clear policy line on an issue.

Even a relatively successful business policy process like the TABD can run up against frictions which occur in business–government relationships, particularly over the timescale within which decisions can be made and implemented. Governments have to answer to a variety of clienteles, while companies are principally accountable to their shareholders. These difficulties are understood on both sides of the process. A senior businessperson with extensive experience of the process commented, 'One is mixing fire and water. Business companies are not essentially democratic, decisions by board have to be implemented, happen within months. We have a political negotiating process, which has to be oriented on democratic issues.' This tension could be resolved by offering the Commission 'subject [s] with clear defined priorities that are politically realistic'.

In similar vein, a Commission official commented, 'It takes quite a while for the business community to understand policy concepts and law. It takes some education in some areas. These things are incredibly complicated.' It was not simply a matter of recommendations flowing into policy. Many regulatory matters were being worked on in a multilateral context. Hence, securing radical change in policy concepts might take over 20 years. The official concluded, 'we don't want to discourage them, but we don't want to encourage expectations that can't be realised'.

However, in such a joint process account also has to be taken of the US perspective, at least as seen by European actors. One business respondent described TABD as a 'typical American approach, hands on, selective, early harvest'. Tensions between Europeans and Americans had to some extent to be managed by business, a process which was helped by a realization on both sides of the Atlantic that ultimately the process could be seen as a win-win one. As a TABD official noted 'The Commission wants support from TABD for European views, Department of Commerce wants it for American views, have to keep balance. It forces them to do something they are not fundamentally opposed to but where for several reasons they have to take a different stance. Silently they do not mind getting pushed as long as it does not cause a negative problem.'

In the above TABD case, governments have had cause to use business for public purposes, so as to incorporate market incentive, norms and practices into the provision of public goods. That is, governments and international agencies gain in speeding up policymaking by gaining access to information and resources and delivery is improved as business can implement. At a more abstract level international bodies and governments also develop a constituency vis-à-vis other nations and, it is hoped, some policy legitimacy. Business on the other side reduces its political uncertainty by again speeding up the policymaking process, facilitating mutual recognition and creating a level playing field. There are, as we will see in the following sections, potential consequences of international business diplomacy, in that national governments find themselves distanced from the economic actors in their markets and national regimes become regulatory takers rather than makers. Such extraterritoriality raises a number of questions of legitimacy, and internationalizes even traditional politics and regulatory debates.

The TABD and privatization of international trade negotiations and MRAs

Organization and goals

The TABD is an informal process where European and American Companies and business associations develop joint policy recommendations to discuss with the EC and US administrations. Encouraged initially by Commerce Department Secretary Ron Brown and European Commissioners Leon Brittan and Martin Bangemann, it brings together top American and European CEOs to coordinate responses on international trade and regulation issues.

The criterion for membership is theoretically straightforward and requires that the CEO is pro-liberalization and trade, represents a transatlantic company and is deemed constructive to the policy process. However such definitions provide the TABD with a high degree of discretion as to who is admitted. Unsurprisingly there is a big overlap both with the ERT membership (including ABB, Bayer, Bertelsmann, Ericsson, ICI, Olivetti, Pirelli, Phillips, Siemens, Solvay, SKB and Unilever) and with American firms active in Amcham (Ford, IBM, Procter and Gamble, Time Warner and Xerox). Hence the TADB can be seen as a large industrial club of insider players. Such a grouping raises important questions as to the representativeness of the TABD and the role that SMEs (Small and Medium Enterprises) and other specific sectors have in the new business–government relationship.

The TABD, like the ERT, relies upon the personal involvement of the CEO. The organization, or framework, draws on the resources of the participating firms and has a very small secretariat in Washington and Brussels. In 2002 it organized its work around five priority themes: capital markets, networked economy and regulatory economy, plus two themes with a specific trade link, dispute management and WTO agenda. The latter theme was expected to produce specific proposals on industry's input to the Doha Round. Working under these broad themes are up to 40 working groups covering a number of different sectors and issues with each sub-issue group coordinated by a joint EU/US company chair.

Meeting once a year, the CEOs and senior executives' come together to discuss and make recommendations that foster transatlantic trade and investment opportunities. Focusing on the removal of costly inefficiencies caused by excess regulation, duplication and deficiencies, the TABD attempts to identify areas of consensus for EU and US business and government. In recent years it has achieved notable success in the areas of mutual recognition and harmonization of standards, active leadership of e-commerce and standardization of 'Third Generation' wireless telecommunications systems.

The CEOs, having agreed to the broad agenda, delegate the operationalization of the policy process to specialist working groups, which are coordinated by the secretariat. The secretariat operates as a central spoke for the CEOs by organizing the scope of contact with European Commission, US government officials, Members of European Parliament (MEPs) and US Congress. It takes responsibility for organizing the annual conferences of the CEOs and on a day-to-day basis acts as a contact point for the US/EU working group chairs. The two secretariat offices total five people (three in Brussels and two in Washington) and operate jointly as far as this is possible. Numbers in the secretariat have been limited to minimize overhead costs, reduce the bureaucracy and facilitate speed of action, as there is no chain of command. This skeleton secretariat works by drawing on resources of the companies of the various working groups' chairmen. However, conversely, the annual changes in company chairs and the policymaking lag restrict progress in January and February as individuals are brought up to speed on issues.

The goal of the TABD is to get government talking to business. It must therefore provide concrete and actionable recommendations and reliable information. There was some scepticism at the first conference in Seville 1995, but as the numbers and involvement of CEOs increased, so too has the credibility of the TABD to deliver operational policy. Significantly, CEOs have recognized that the TABD is not a single-issue conference, but a policymaking organization that needs to be nurtured if it is to maximize its influence with government. As one TABD official observed, 'CEOs see that it is not an organization just to promote itself, it's there to get results. We're not there banging the drum, we're here to have a forum for CEOs to sit down and talk with the relevant government players.'

Recognizing that the political relationship is not a one shot game with government, but an iterative process where trust must be established if influence is to be achieved, CEOs have become active participants in the TABD. However, while the CEOs set the working group issues at the annual conference and establish issue profiles with senior Commission and State Department figures, it is important that the TABD working groups deliver on implementation and policy initiatives or funding and enthusiasm will dry up. For this reason the secretariat has been keen to limit the numbers of actors at the working group table and has attempted to maintain a homogenous membership. This strategy however has come under pressure from EU and American administrations, excluded business and countervailing public interest groups.

By remaining primarily a policy-oriented process the TABD hopes to keep itself flexible and reactive to focused and topical needs of a limited number of CEOs as opposed to a more rigid but representative association. As one TABD official observed, 'We have got a bit cumbersome, we need to focus on hotter items, low hanging fruit (like product liability). Three years ago we had 115 recommendations all equal priority and it seemed a lot. Today we have 130–140. You can do more, but the secretariat gets behind and people don't necessarily want it, you become an infrastructure.' However, a core of 20 issues exist that the TABD secretariat attempts to move forward and on which it bases its credibility with the CEOs.

Process management

Issues can be identified simply by a chief executive officer calling the secretariat. However, if there is no joint (US–EU business) consensus on an issue, it will not develop further. Issues are not run through any formal checking process. However, as a TABD staffer put it, 'there is an implicit belief and trust that they need to be vetted, we cast as wide a net as possible'. This process has been facilitated by the development of information technology. As a TABD staffer put it, 'It couldn't be done six or seven years ago in terms of making a consensual working recommendation, technology has been crucial'.

It is clearly important to limit the demands that are made on the time of CEOs. The main participation of the CEOs comes in the two weeks leading up to the annual conference when the broad issues are discussed. The technical issue managers in the respective working groups produce a briefing book that includes draft outline recommendations on each issue.

This is very much a company driven process and one of the difficult issues has been how to involve associations. This is not a straightforward procedural question as the TABD is very much based on a 'company state' model as defined by Grant (2000). The assumption is that chief executive officers and other senior managers in firms are the key decision-makers. The TABD is consistent with developments in Brussels that have seen an increasing emphasis on direct representation of firms in federations. As one of our respondents commented, 'Classic business associations [that] have been in Brussels for thirty years are now facing a challenge just as traditional political parties are facing a challenge from organizations of civil society.' It is therefore not surprising that when associations 'see a forum dedicated to CEOs, there is a defensiveness'.

A businessperson involved in TABD acknowledged that there was 'a certain tension with associations like UNICE. We want to benefit from their knowledge, but we don't want to be held up by their democratic process.' Nevertheless, a series of informal links have been set up. The ERT acts as an adviser at steering committee level through its chair along with the president of UNICE. At the executive level of group leaders, the secretary-general of UNICE and his counterpart at ERT act as advisers.

At group level, a number of association executives act as issue managers. This is particularly apparent in the area of standards and regulatory policy where 14 association executives (eight from the United States, six from Europe) serve in this capacity. This is in an area where the technical expertise possessed by associations is of particular value. It is noticeable that no association executives are issue managers in the business facilitation area, although four serve in that way in the global issues area.

One sectoral association stated that although its director-general was not invited to the annual conference as such, each chief executive was allowed to bring one person with him and the director-general attended in that capacity. The respondent argued, 'It's a good combination of action between the federation and the firm. Company alone could lead to some kind of problem, we have more experience in political delivery.'

This respondent stated, 'I don't see why TABD could be an alternative to the work of the federation'. In a strict sense, this is true. The day-to-day processing of directives through the increasingly complex procedures of the European Union is likely to remain the bread-and-butter work of associations. As has been noted above, TABD and the associations do cooperate and in many respects their role is complementary. Nevertheless, TABD is based on a 'company state' model while the associations are part of an 'associative state' model that is increasingly being supplanted. As one company respondent commented, 'Industry associations played a very useful role in the past decades, they are not vehicles for lobbying the European Commission for the next ten years'.

The processes of TABD itself are well set up to focus on key issues and to minimize the demands on the time of chief executives. However, the process is not an end in itself. Its purpose is to influence public policy, to produce policy outputs that are different or occur on an accelerated timescale from those that would have resulted in its absence. This perspective was confirmed by a DG Market official who stated, 'It can deliver things that cannot be delivered by any other process'. This was evident during negotiations for MRAs which were concluded in June 1997. They reduced the costs of testing and certification in seven key industrial sectors.

Although the Commission stresses that it does not give the TABD 'a blank cheque', it does all it can to facilitate the TABD's work. A list of Commission contact points is made available for TABD sector groups. There is an attempt to pull matters together before and after the annual conferences. However, the TABD does not rely on systematic contacts with Commission officials, but on the fact that it is taken seriously by the college of Commissioners. The Prodi Commission has renewed its commitment to TABD.

European Voice perhaps used journalistic hyperbole in its account of the TABD (21/27 October 1999) before the TABD Berlin conference but the broad picture it presents is confirmed by our interviews:

> Captains of industry in the EU and US are preparing, once more, to remind politicians who really holds the power ... Hanging on their every word will be government ministers from both sides of the Atlantic including US Commerce Secretary Bill Daley and top officials such as new European Trade Commissioner Pascal Lamy ... When the big guns of industry speak with one voice, only the bravest of governments ignores their demands.

Nevertheless, there are some imperfections in the process. In organizational terms, the changing of chairs each year produces continuity problems and there is also an absence of long-term thinking about where TABD is going. At least one respondent was uncertain whether TABD would still be here in five years' time. Moreover, as the case study of the business alliances below demonstrates, as numbers involved in the grouping increase the policy focus will dissipate and potentially undermine the role of the forum.

TABD political alliances for business insiders and outsiders: the case of intellectual property rights in the pharmaceuticals sector

In 1992 the European Generic Drug Association (EGA) was formed, primarily as a single-issue group focused on intellectual property rights and patent expiry times. Reacting to the Bolar agreement, which allowed generic drug firms to build up capacity in the period prior to the expiry of a patent, the EGA brought together some 400 SMEs in a sector that had traditionally created ad hoc lobbying alliances.

The larger research-based pharmaceutical firms had, since the early days of the single market, found themselves at the forefront of Commissioner Bangemann's industrial forums and were against any reduction in their European patent times. Hence, with the creation of the TABD, companies like SmithKline and Beechams and Glaxo were keen to use the new forum to put pressure on national drug agencies and governments to lengthen or maintain patents. Generic drug firms' voices were excluded from the debate. As an EGA official noted: 'They (Commission and European federation) didn't know us or didn't want to know the generic drug firms as they were seen as the killers of research.'

Hence with the creation of the TABD in 1995, the European Commission, big business and the European Federation of Pharmaceutical Industries and Associations (EFPIA) did not seek to incorporate what they considered the generic producers' marginal position – as they noted 'the EGA is only 1.5% of the EU market'. Faced with outsider status with the Commission at DG Market, and the insider position of research-based rivals and the established trade association, EGA looked for a wider constituency at the European Parliament (EP). The EGA's break through came in 1996 with the EP 'Single Market Report' which favoured the Bolar provisions and lower drug prices. Armed with this document the EGA lobbied other DGs, such as the Food and Drink Unit, but found that it was resisted all the way by the EFPIA as the quote below illustrates: 'Generics problem lies basically in their hands. This is the pharmaceutical world, research, innovation is the future. In practice member companies (of EGA) are purely copying companies which are not interested in any kind of balanced approach, their interest is to be on the market with copied products as soon as possible.'

At the same time that the generic drug lobby attempted to embed itself within the EU consultation process, it also attempted to mobilize the American generic sector, and lobbied actively at state government and agency level. It was through this US lobbying that EGA became aware of the growing importance of the TABD in 1997. Significantly, DG Market had failed to ask them to join or even inform them of its developments. EGA approached the Commission to sponsor its membership of the TABD and the International Committee of Harmonisation (ICH) at the International Federation of Pharmaceutical and Medical Associations (IFPMA), and also approached the TABD directly. Bangemann and TABD rejected them initially because their members did not have transatlantic business activities and CEOs of stature. When EGA demonstrated its transatlantic membership, the TABD said that they could not join, as generics did not meet the TABD rules with respect to intellectual property rights. The EGA appealed to the Commission arguing that it fitted with the ideal of liberalization of trade regimes and that the membership criterion was not transparent or fair. It soon became apparent however, that the TABD was not accountable for its membership, regardless of its favoured position in the EU/US policy process. 'It just seemed to make up its own rules' as the EGA official noted. The TABD was thus seen to be an elite business club by the SMEs in the generic sector. Alternatively, the EFPIA saw the TADB as a 'Very global view, we are a big church, EGA a very minor segment of the generic market that does not make any concessions or compromises, their life is easy to some extent'. Thus we observed problems of collective action, where the TABD wished to maintain a focused and homogeneous membership to help it reach a consensus position at the expense of being representative of the whole sector's position.

Change only occurred when the European generic firms working with the US National Pharmaceutical Association (NPA) convinced the US Food and Drug Administration (FDA) not to attend any TABD discussions on MRAs. Thus while the FDA called for generic firm membership of the ICH and TABD, it also pushed the State Department to tone down its links with the TABD. In parallel with this alliance-building strategy, the NPA implied that it would take anti-trust proceedings against the TABD on the grounds of collusion and the EGA threatened the European Commission with the EU ombudsman in Strasbourg. These lobbying strategies were high profile and intentionally loud as the generic sector wanted to demonstrate to government and public that a single unified sector position was not being presented. By undermining the reputation of the TADB in the courts, its use as a fast and credible forum for big business and government would be reduced. Moreover, the strategy was also aimed at influencing the sectors within the TABD that had a consensus position and did not want the negotiation process slowed down with a return to intergovernmental negotiations or, worse, totally discredited. Significantly, Bangemann continued to resist the enlargement of the TABD to allow SMEs and generic drug producers even with internal unrest within the wider organization of the TABD (interviews with large pharmaceutical firm and EGA).

Finally, with additional pressure now being placed on the Commission and American administration by the World Health Organization, consumer groups, FDA and the risk of legal action the EGA was allowed to participate in the ICH in 1998, but only as single representative for the US/EU generic drug sector. The large research-based firms argued successfully that aggregation was required, as individual SMEs would not have the expertise to deal with all the technical issues. The above experience illustrated the importance of developing complex institutional and public interest alliances to create a lobbying critical mass, expertise and ultimate credibility to participate in the new global business policy process. Conversely, the experience shows how the large firms did not wish to see the decision-making function of the newly formed international organizations slowed by a large membership.

In succeeding at the ICH, the EGA legitimized itself within the international business–government policy process. Hence by 1998, the TABD was coming under huge political pressure – the FDA was losing patience with the TADB and the European Commission under new management at Commissioner and Unit level were more open to the EGA after its success at the ICH. The above changes also corresponded with changes in the TABD management and recognition that the bad press from the generic lobby was undermining the organization. The introduction of Xerox as the 1999 TABD chair in 1999 was the final turning point as a generic drug official noted: 'we now had a sympathetic chairman from a company thats business had always been to make copies'. Thus in late 1999 the generic drugs firms were allowed to attend the Berlin CEOs meeting as non-voting members. The EGA submitted a list of CEOs that it wished to attend, but the EFPIA fought to reduce their actual influence and voting rights within the TABD on the grounds of working efficiency of the group. Hence the EGA, acting as a focal point for the generic CEOs, has had to take a lead as a policy shaper for the generic voice within the TABD. The EFPIA still attempted to set the agenda, but now as an insider the EGA can veto if still not initiate policy. Improved legitimacy of the TABD was demonstrated by the *European Voice* (27 October 1999) quote from TABD delegates talking about the Berlin summit which 'argued that the limited scope of the existing MRAs should be widened to include more controversial areas such as drug and vehicle testing. There is progress being made, says Echenschwiller (a TABD official), pointing out that top officials from the US Food and Drug Administration – which has so far opposed such moves – will attend the TABD meeting for the first time to listen to the industry's views.'

In sum, the above lobbying case demonstrates that new global public policy is increasingly complex with actors attempting to establish multiple identities and alliances to access multiple organizations. While some issues may remain embedded in nation states with traditional association arrangements, others will require more disaggregated 'issue focused' responses. In both cases Coen (1998) observed that lobbying is mutually reinforcing with action at one level providing credibility and reputation at another. In the case of new forum structures and policy processes, like the TABD, recognition is vitally important and can act as a positive constraint – forcing it to become more open and transparent. The success of the FDA to change the membership of the TABD through its absences from the table can in part be explained by the fact that it is the dominant regulatory agency in the sector. Hence a Vogel (1995) style 'regulatory California effect' can be seen to be in operation where access to the largest market area dictates the rules and standards of international lobbying behaviour. In this case it was less significant that the research-based firms had favoured access at the European Drugs and Medicine Agency in London than they had the ear of the FDA and harmonization with the US market. Hence, the advantages for a small and focused policy group are undermined if the credibility and legitimacy of the organization are called into question. This leaves us with the question, can the TABD continue to find enough common ground policies or will it slowly congeal as its membership continues to grow? With scale may come legitimacy but it may lose its comparative advantage of speed and focus and with it its favoured access to governments.

Legitimacy of international business representation

Discussions of the role of international business interests in society have proceeded with little attention being paid to questions of legitimacy which have increasingly arisen in discussions of international trade. Perhaps the one exception has been some corporatist theorists who have sought a normative justification of corporatist relationships to justify their departure from traditional models of parliamentary democracy. The existence of a particular interest in organized form has led to an assumption that the association can be assumed to be representative, both in terms of membership density and the effective articulation and aggregation of the views of the membership. These questions are never probed very deeply: decision-makers seem happy with the repeated assurance that a particular association represents 80 per cent of its domain.

With the growing role of non-governmental organizations, there has been some concern about a frequent lack of internal democracy and their assertion that they speak on behalf of a particular cause or deprived group. This has led to calls for codes of conduct which would set basic standards of transparency and accountability which such organizations would have to meet before they were allowed to enter into a dialogue with decision-makers.

The problems posed by traditional sector associations and the organizations of 'civil society' are intractable enough. However, even greater difficulties arise from the notion of chief executive officers of leading firms getting together to pronounce on issues of public policy. The notion of an impersonal order is at the heart of Weberian conceptions of legitimacy, but this is a highly individualistic form of political activity which makes its own rules rather than being governed by a predetermined system of abstract rules. There are criteria for membership, but they are sufficiently elastic to be open to a variety of interpretations.

Further discussion of these problems requires the exploration of three key terms: accountability, transparency and credibility. Discussion of accountability has been confused by what is now a rather dated and tired debate about ministerial accountability in Britain. Central to this debate was the notion of answerability. A minister was obliged to give answers to Parliament about matters which fell within his or her sphere of responsibility. In practice, of course, the answers were intended to conceal as much as they revealed and this notion of answerability to an elected assembly is of little direct help when considering new types of political formation such as the TABD. Nevertheless, one might argue that the core idea that has to be pursued here is the notion of giving an account of what has been done and why it has been done to actors outside the process itself.

In fact, the lines of accountability from this process are tenuous and uncertain. First, there is the issue of who is allowed to join in the first place. Although there are instances of smaller firm participation, this is primarily a process open to very large firms. Indeed, that is one of the principal sources of its influence with governmental authorities. Firms are also required to sign up to a particular set of principles such as free trade. These might seem to be relatively uncontentious for large companies, but they can be used as a basis to exclude certain types of company as is evident from our discussion of the case of generic pharmaceuticals.

Even if the discussion is restricted to those firms that have been allowed to join, who are the chief executives themselves accountable to? Presumably, they are ultimately accountable to their shareholders and more specifically to their boards; however, their participation in the TABD is hardly likely to be an issue on which they are pressed at annual general meetings. Provided they stay within the broad lines of company policy, it is hardly likely to be the subject of discussion at board level. It is not the kind of subject that has been addressed in the development of standards of corporate governance.

Any recommendations they make require the endorsement of decision-makers on both sides of the Atlantic before they can be translated into action. It might be thought that this is where democratic accountability comes into play. The American political system certainly offers a number of veto points, as is evident from the difficulties that the MRA has run into with regulatory agencies. However, its very fragmentation also means that there are a number of entry points for the positions taken by the TABD and it is difficult to mount a coherent challenge to them across a range of institutions.

In the case of the European Union, the existence of a 'democratic deficit' is not accidental. It was built into the original design of the institutions which were seen as being driven by a technocratic elite inspired by a European vision. Attempts to give a greater role to the European Parliament in the decision-making process cannot obscure the fact that many important decisions are taken elsewhere in locations that are more permeable to business interests. There are a number of actors that might seek to hold to account decisions taken on the basis of a TABD recommendation, not least member states, but again it is the lack of a possibility of a coherent response that is at the heart of the problem. More fundamentally, there is an issue about the extent to which any private body can be called to account by a public institution, particularly if it is operating within the law. What this suggests is that our traditional notions of accountability are of little value in relation to new processes of the kind represented by the TABD.

This in turn raises the issue of the transparency of the interactions between the TABD and governmental authorities. This term is widely used but rarely defined, but it covers such notions as openness, disclosure and freedom of access. It is evident from our interviews that TABD are sensitive about the accusation that they are some kind of shadowy, secretive body exerting influence behind the scenes. Their immediate answer is that they have a web site in which their activities are openly discussed. Indeed, Scholte recommends (2000: 305–6), 'Regional and trans-world governance agencies could produce more publications, issue more press releases, maintain more extensive websites and so on ... The public could then be better equipped to judge whether a given multilateral organization was acting competently and in their interest.' If we treat the TABD as a multilateral organization, then the problem that is immediately encountered is that presumably it is primarily designed to serve the interests of the large firms that participate in it rather than the public interest. The objection that non-governmental organizations might make is that a web site or other forms of disclosure do not reveal the deals that are made between companies or between companies and governmental authorities.

The TABD might be more comfortable with the notion of credibility. A credible organization or process is one that can address a range of issues authoritatively and shows awareness of the constraints that restrict the freedom of choice of governmental decision-makers. The internal processes of the TABD ensure that the issues pursued are ones on which there is a consensus among chief executives of large businesses. There is ample opportunity for technical input into the discussions through the various working groups. There is also a conscious attempt to make recommendations that are feasible in the sense that they do not create too many political problems for governmental decision-makers. Nevertheless, this does not prevent the emergence of tensions. Business executives are used to operating within much tighter time frames in their companies than is customary in government. They may become impatient with a process where a number of formal decision points have to be cleared and where implementation can be frustrated by a variety of agencies (as happened with regulatory agencies in the United States in the case of the MRA). Government decision-makers may thus lose credibility with business executives, but the government decision-makers may in turn downgrade their appraisal of the credibility of the executives in the TABD because they think that they take insufficient account of the way in which political and business decision-making processes differ.

It might be argued that the legitimacy of the TABD is enhanced by the existence of institutionalized 'countervailing' interests in the form of the Transatlantic Consumer Dialogue (TACD) and the Transatlantic Labour Dialogue. However, these bodies are in a very embryonic form compared to the TABD. The TACD has nevertheless become increasingly active and has a secretariat located at Consumers International in London. As described by TACD, its aims seem to be aspirational: to 'explore ways of strengthening the EU and US consumer view at the international level' (http://www.tacd.org). Even if these groups did reach a higher state of organizational development in the future, questions remain about how their views would be weighed by decision-makers compared with those of the TABD.

The TABD has clearly succeeded in establishing credibility with decision-makers on both sides of the Atlantic. This is because of both who is involved in TABD (CEOs from major companies) and their ability to produce feasible solutions to policy problems. Questions of legitimacy and accountability remain largely unexplored and unresolved.

Conclusions

Critics of the way in which contemporary international trade policy is made often see it as driven by the interests of large multinational companies of the kind represented in the TABD at the expense of least developed countries or the environment. There is no doubt that trade is a priority issue for the TABD and one on which it expends considerable effort. However, the failure of the trade talks at Cancún, in large part as a result of the efforts of the G-21 emerging countries led by Brazil, shows that business can neither set the agenda nor determine its outcome. Of course, taking a longer-term perspective, trade has become increasingly liberalized in accordance with the wishes of business. However, the question of whether managed trade and high levels of protection are necessarily in the interests of poorer countries is a controversial one.

What is beyond question is that governments are increasingly dependent on large firms for fast and effective information and are willing to delegate public decision-making to private business forums. Perhaps then, the new corporate political strategy and global policymaking can be characterized as a company–state relationship as we have observed in the United States and United Kingdom

(Grant 2000). However, while this policy regime has given business a favoured place at the table, due in part to the nature of the issues, it does not mean that governments are not aware of the risks of capture.

Our TABD findings have shown that before industrial forums are legitimized within the political process and given favoured access, they must be seen to be representative of the sectors' views and capture a wider constituency of public interests. Business, however, has to weigh the advantages of fast access and focused goals (a short-run business time frame) against the long-run political considerations of the administrations. But in accepting that the new business forums must provide information and fit certain transparency and openness criteria, who are they accountable to? It is clear from the study that the TABD was set up to facilitate intergovernmental negotiations between the EU and US administrations and as such was given favoured access to both the State Department and the European Commission. We have seen that the domestic regulatory agencies that regulate access and standards in the market place exert a large influence on forum membership, by potentially withholding recognition of the body or refusing to enter negotiations. In our study we observed a policy style 'California Effect' where the FDA determined the nature of the issues and the type of membership of the TABD pharmaceuticals committees. Hence, any successful business lobby must play multi-level advocacy coalitions with civic and political groupings.

What is evident is that there are serious issues about the legitimacy of organizations like TABD and their participation in trade policymaking. In the real world, governments must broker the tensions between policy legitimacy (i.e. policy output), which are facilitated by technical, fast and effective decision-making processes, against political legitimacy that requires private business forums to be seen to be accountable and transparent decision-making organizations. At present the TABD would appear to have established credibility on the political legitimacy side of the equation, but must continue to improve its consultation procedures if its MRAs are to be recognized by national regulatory agencies and civic groups.

Conversely, accepting that many of the new private business forums are results driven organizations, business could conceivably become quickly dissatisfied with this new governance structure, if they fail to influence the policy process. Hence, advocates of these new public–private business forums do not want to see the dynamic policy process ossify into organizations that are all encompassing and rule-based. Thus it may be that the state–corporate interface of twenty-first century trade politics will be less characterized by long-life organizations, but will be a more loosely organized advocacy coalition or processes which achieve a set of limited goals and disappear or mutate into something new.

References

Broschied, A. and Coen, D. (2003) 'Insider and Outsider Lobbying of the European Commission: An Informational Model of Forum Politics', *European Union Politics*, 3, 2: 7–32.

Caves, R. (1976) 'Economic Models of Political Choice: Tariff Structures', *Canadian Journal of Economics*, 9: 278–300.

Coen, D. (1997) 'The Evolution of The Large Firm as a Political Actor in the European Union', *Journal of European Public Policy*, 4, 1: 91–108.

Coen, D. (1998) 'The European Business Interest and the Nation State: Large-firm Lobbying in the European Union and Member States', *Journal of Public Policy*, 18, 1: 75–100.

Coen, D. (1999) 'The Impact of US Lobbying Practice on the European Business-Government Relationship', *California Management Review*, 41, 4: 27–44.

Coen, D. and Dannreuther, C. (2002) 'When Size Matters. Europeanisation of Large and SME Business-Government Relations', *Politique Europeene*, 7, 1: 116–38.

Coen, D. and Grant, W. (2001) 'Corporate Political Strategy and Global Public Policy: a Case Study of the Transatlantic Business Dialogue', *European Business Journal*, 13, 1: 37–44.

Commission (2001) European Governance: White Paper, *Com 2001*: 428: Final.

Cowles, G.M. (1995) 'Setting the agenda for a new Europe: the ERT and EC 1992', *Journal of Common Market Studies*, 13: 501–20.

Cowles, G.M. (1996) 'The EU Committee of Amcham: the powerful voice of American firms in Brussels', *Journal of European Public Policy*, 3: 339–58.

Cowles, G.M. (2001) 'The TADB and Domestic Business-government Relations' in Cowles, G.M. *et al.* (eds) *Transforming Europe: Europeanisation and Domestic Change*, Ithaca: Cornell University Press.

Earnshaw, D. and Wood, J. (1999) 'The European Parliament and Biotechnology Patenting: Harbinger of the Future?' *Journal of Commercial Biotech.*

Egan, M. (2001) *Constructing a European Market*, Oxford: Oxford University Press.

Frey, B. (1989) *International Political Economics*, Oxford: Blackwell.

Grant, W. (2000) *Pressure Groups and British Politics*, London: Palgrave Macmillan.

Grant, W. (2002) *Economic Policy in Britain*, London: Palgrave Macmillan.

Grant, W., Matthews, D. and Newell, P. (2002) *The Effectiveness of European Union Public Policy*, London: Palgrave Macmillan.

Greenwood, J. (2003) *Interest Representation in the European Union*, London: Palgrave Macmillan.

Haufler, V. (1993) 'Crossing the Boundary between Public and Private: International Regimes and Non-state Actors' in Rittberger, V. (ed.) *Regime Theory and International Relations*, Oxford: Clarendon Press.

Hocking, B. and McGuire, S. (eds) (2002) *Trade Politics*, 2nd edition, London: Routledge.

Jones, R. (2001) *The Politics and Economics of the European Union*, Edward Elgar: London.

Levy, D. and Newell, P. (2002) 'Business Strategy and International Environmental Governance: Toward a Neo-Gramscian Synthesis', *Global Environmental Politics*, 2, 4: 84–101.

Magee, S.W., Brock, A. and Young, L. (1989) *Black Hole Tariffs and Endogenous Policy Theory*, London: Cambridge University Press.

Martin, C. (1991) *Shifting the Burden: The Struggle Over Growth and Corporate taxation*, Chicago: University of Chicago Press

Milner, H. (1988) *Resisting Protectionism: Global Industries and the Politics of International Trade*, Princeton: Princeton University Press.

Mitchell, N. (1997) *The Conspicuous Corporation: Business, Public Policy and Representative*, Ann Arbor: University Press.

Pijenburg, R. (1997) 'EU-lobbying by ad-hoc coalitions: An Exploratory Case Study', *Journal of European Public Policy*, 5, 2: 303–21.

Pollock, M. and Shaffer, G. (2001) *Transatlantic Governance in the Global Economy*, Lanham, MD: Rowman and Littlefield.

Richardson, J. (2000) 'Government, Interest Groups and Policy Change', *Political Studies* 48, 1: 1006–25.

Richardson, J. (2001) 'Interest Groups and EU Policy Making: Organizational Logic and Venue Shopping' in Richardson, J. (ed.) *European Union: Power and Policy Making*, London: Routledge.

Ronit, K. and Schneider, V. (1999) 'Global Governance through Private Organisations', *Governance* 12, 3: 243–66.

Sabatier, P. (1998) 'The Advocacy Coalition Framework: Revisions and Relevance for Europe', *Journal of European Public Policy*, 5, 1: 98–130.

Scholte, J.A. (2000) *Globalisation: A Critical Introduction*, Basingstoke: Macmillan.

Smith, M. (2000) *American Business and Power: Public Opinion, Elections and Democracy*, Chicago: University of Chicago Press.

Stopford, J. and Strange, S. (1991) *Rival States, Rival Firms: Competition for World Markets Share*, Cambridge: Cambridge University Press.

Strange, S. (1994) *States and Markets*, London: Pinter.

Strange, S. (1996) *The Retreat of the State: The Diffusion of Power in the World Economy*, Cambridge: Cambridge University Press.

Tenbucken, Marc. (2002) *Corporate Lobbying in the European Union: Strategies of Multinational Companies*, Frankfurt: Peter Lang.

UNCTAD/WTO (2002) Business advocacy and Trade Policy making: How the business Community in Developing Countries Can benefit from the Doha Development Round. Technical Paper ITC, April 2002.

Van Apeldoorn, B. (2002) 'The European Round Table of Industrialists: Still a Unique Player?', in Greenwood, J. (ed.) *The Effectiveness of EU Business Associations*, Basingstoke: Palgrave.

Vogel, D. (1989) *Fluctuating Fortunes: The Political Power of Business in America*, New York: Basic Books.

Vogel, D. (1995) *Trading Up: Consumer and Environmental Regulation in a Global Economy*, Cambridge, MA: Harvard University Press.

Webster, R. (2002) 'The Nature and context of Public Interest Coalitions in The European Union', *Politique Europeene*, 7, 1: 138–59.

Willetts, P. (2002) 'Transnational Actors and International Organizations in Global Politics' in Baylis, J. and Smith, S. (eds) *The Globalization of World Politics*, 2nd edition, Oxford: Oxford University Press.

Wilson, G. (2003) *Business and Politics A Comparative Introduction*, Basingstoke: Palgrave.

Wright, J. (1996) *Interest Groups and Congress: Lobbying, Contributions, and Influence*, Boston: Allyn & Bacon.

Young, A. and Wallace, H. (2000) *Regulatory Politics in the Enlarging European Union: Weighing Civic and Producer Interests*, Manchester: Manchester University Press.

Part II
Issues

4
Trade, Security and Globalization

Dominic Kelly

An analysis of the multifaceted relationship between international trade and security is pertinent for a number of reasons. First the security implications of the trade in goods, services, people and even ideas have raced to the top of the international political agenda following the hijacking of a number of civilian planes and their subsequent use as weapons in the attacks on the Pentagon and the World Trade Centre in September 2001. In both its planning and mode of execution the attack on the World Trade Centre demonstrated awareness on behalf of the perpetrators of the key material role of trade in the functioning of the capitalist mode of production as well as the important role played by the twin towers as symbols of the enduring strength of capitalism as an ideology. It also demonstrated the ability of the perpetrators to use trade flows in furtherance of their aims. The US-led response, similarly informed and enabled, has targeted the perpetrators of international terrorism (chiefly al-Qaeda and other such groups), their supporters (chiefly regimes in Afghanistan, Iraq, Iran, Libya and Syria but also North Korea) and the networks they employ. Thus the 'war on terror' is being conducted through both conventional military and economic means – the toppling of regimes in Afghanistan and Iraq, sanctions against Iraq and Libya – and through diplomatic and other pressures including the interdiction of flows (both legal and illegal) of money, arms, commodities and people.

A second reason why the relationship between international trade and security is pertinent is because it provides a convenient point of entry into wider debates concerning the actors, issues and processes involved in trade politics under 'globalization'. As already noted, one front of the war on terror is being waged as much against flows of money as it is against flows of arms. Thus, in addition to diplomats and national and international security services, banks and financial services agencies are becoming involved. Moreover, it is not just terrorist organizations that are being targeted. Mafia's, people smugglers and traffickers of all kinds of goods – from weapons to diamonds to drugs to coffee – are being singled out. The simple but inescapable conclusion to all this, confirmed by other contributions to this book, is that in a world arguably characterized by the globalization of economic activity states are no longer the only actors involved in the making of trade policy, and that the issues with which trade policy is either concerned or contingent upon are becoming more numerous, varied and complex. This is true also of the processes by or through which trade policy is made. A deeper reading of this, on the other hand, starts from the understanding that states are not 'victims' of globalization but the authors of it. As such, trade becomes one of many pathways through which the state itself is being transformed and security re-defined as a consequence of globalization.

One of the ways in which security is being re-defined is through a broadening of its focus beyond a narrow concern with military matters. If it is indeed the case that 'Job security, income security, health security, environmental security [and] security from crime [are] the emerging concerns of human security all over the world' (UNDP 1994: 2), then a Pandora's Box of issues is immediately opened. These issues – such as the trade in hormone treated beef, the compulsory licensing of AIDS drugs, violations of human rights, inadequate labour and environmental standards amongst others – emerge as equal in importance to, for example, the trade in arms on the agenda of trade politics (see Taylor and Thomas 1999, and various contributions to the present volume). Dealing with these so-called 'trade-and' issues may stretch the capacities of the institutional structures and processes already in place to breaking point and beyond (Wilkinson, Chapter 1 of this volume; Henderson 2002; Jones 2002). Even if they do not, it is increasingly clear that international organizations such as the World Trade Organisation (WTO) are moving away from their original purposes (in this case reducing visible barriers to trade in goods) and becoming instead 'global risk regulators' (King and Narlikar 2003) with oversight of everything from consumer health and choice to issues of government procurement and competition policy. As such, the workings of these organizations become simultaneously more intrusive and opaque and, therefore, more contested (O'Brien *et al.* 2000).

As a corollary of this, a third reason why the relationship between international trade and security is pertinent is the woeful lack of progress currently being made in international trade negotiations. The failure of Seattle was not balanced by success at Doha (see *inter alia* Bhagwati 2001; Laird 2002; Panagariya 2002; Hart and Dymond 2003). The collapse of Cancún amply demonstrates that the majority membership of the WTO have not been fooled by the re-branding exercise that saw the 'Millennium Round' transformed into the 'Development Round' (DR). Meanwhile the inability of the 'Quad' countries in general, and the United States and European Union in particular, to reach consensus on how best to move forward threatens to de-rail the DR completely. If the DR does fail, or even if it is concluded but fails to live up to expectations, then one of a range of possible outcomes might be a retreat behind protectionist trade barriers erected at national or regional boundaries (see Gordon 2003). Another might be a significant drop in (or lost opportunity for) gains from trade.[1] In both cases, neither of which is mutually exclusive, the outcome would be a potential loss of security whether measured as power or wealth and/or conceived of in terms of relative or absolute gains.[2]

The argument set out in the preceding paragraph points to a fourth reason why a discussion of the relationship between international trade and security is pertinent. That is, that the core theoretical arguments underpinning liberal, mercantile and Marxist positions on trade and trade politics make the link – albeit in different ways – between trade and security (Barry Jones 1986; Crane and Amawi 1997).[3] As such, it is incumbent upon us to interrogate their core assumptions, concepts and propositions in order to determine whether or not they are still relevant to discussions of trade, trade politics and security. This is particularly the case in an era where public policy, popular perceptions and academic discourse alike have been so profoundly affected by the globalization of economic activity. If liberal and mercantile arguments retain much – if not all – of their relevance, we can conclude that new issues bearing on the trade–security nexus can be dealt with under existing political frameworks although only with great difficulty and at increasing political, economic, social and military risk. Whether these issues *should* be dealt with under existing political frameworks is another matter entirely. If, on the other hand, liberal and mercantile arguments retain little of their relevance in a globalized world, then we need first to explain their continued appeal and, second, to begin to search for alternative theoretical frameworks and, subsequently, alternative policy prescriptions.

Concepts and parameters

In undertaking such a task it is necessary first to introduce limits to both the breadth and depth of the analysis. In its empirical coverage this chapter cannot hope to consider fully all aspects of the relationship between trade and security expressed in traditional nation-state terms through a focus on military security and/or economic statecraft. Amongst other things, such a discussion could range from the trade in basic commodities to the development and exchange of existing and new weapons and technology, including 'dual use' technology, to the imposition of sanctions and other barriers to trade, to the freezing and/or expropriation of assets and to government policy in general in both the domestic and international arenas (see Baldwin 1985; Haass and O'Sullivan 2000). Still less could the chapter hope to discuss fully the myriad of 'new' security issues that have arisen seemingly as a consequence of globalization – be these economic, ecological, psychological, cultural or otherwise – and the links between these and trade, trade politics and the trade regime.

In regard to theories and concepts the chapter does not engage in discussion of the contemporary condition of security studies (see Krause and Williams 1996; Terriff *et al.* 1999). Nor does it engage in extended discussion of the concept of security, albeit this has come under renewed scrutiny as a consequence of globalization and the events of 11 September 2001 (for a range of views see Scholte 2000, chapter 9; Baylis 2001; Hughes 2002; Lawson 2003, chapter 5). Rather, while acknowledging the debate surrounding the appropriate definition of the concept, the chapter follows Baldwin (1997: 13) in suggesting that security can be defined in its most general sense 'in terms of two specifications: security for whom? And security for which values?' Also accepted is his contention that for policy purposes 'one could' – but not necessarily always *should* – 'specify security with respect to the actor whose values are to be secured, the values concerned, the degree of security, the kinds of threats, the means for coping with such threats, the costs of doing so, and the relevant time period' (Baldwin 1997: 17).

Using this general definition of security, the chapter considers the implications for trade and trade theory of the broad impact of globalization and the 'securitization' of globalization following the events of '9/11' leading to the identification of an 'axis of evil' and the subsequent launching of the war against terror. Before moving to that discussion, however, we turn next to an analysis of traditional approaches to and conceptions of the relationship between trade and security.

Trade and security in theory

For the purposes of this chapter the key theoretical approaches concerned with analyses of the relationship between trade and security are economic realism or (neo)mercantilism on the one hand, and liberalism on the other. Both have deep historical roots that do not always point in the same direction (Barry Jones 1988a and b; Moon 2000; Zacher and Matthew 1995). Of the two, the liberal approach has been dominant in both theory and practice at least since 1945, although it has been clear since the 1970s that the commitment to open markets, free trade and laissez faire has been waning (Strange 1985). Tariff and non-tariff barriers are rife in certain sectors such as agriculture, textiles and steel for example, while other neo-mercantilist strategies such as bilateral negotiations, export promotion, fiscal and monetary policy, exchange rate policy, and industrial policy are becoming the norm even in the United States – the post-war champion of free trade – under the fig leaf of 'strategic trade theory' (Krugman 1995).[4]

So much so in fact that it is fair to say that while the rhetoric of free trade continues to ring out across the world the reality of political practice is very much closer to 'freer' trade or, in other words, a pragmatic mix of free trade and protectionism that can best be characterized as 'managed trade'. If this is in fact the case, then asymmetries of power – and wealth – remain at the heart of the politics of international trade. How these asymmetries of power and wealth come about and become embedded or 'structural' features of the global political economy is a major concern of both liberalism and economic realism, as are the consequences and the management of those consequences.

Economic realism

Drawing upon an eclectic mix of theory and commentary but most closely associated with Friedrich List's *The National System of Political Economy*, economic realists confront a world in which the key actor is the sovereign state the central concern of which is survival through the maximization of power. In a world of perpetual anarchy, the struggle for survival is an open-ended one and in this sense the nature of international relations is an unvarying struggle for power between states. Open conflict is always likely, and can only be put off – rather than prevented – through the skilful maintenance of a fluid balance of power.

In this context, trade is significant for the security of the state in two ways; it can both increase security and reduce it. The first of these claims turns around the understanding that the military and political power of the state is underpinned by the wealth of its economy. Thus, in the era of 'classical mercantilism' a positive trade balance implied a net inflow of bullion upon which the monarch could draw in order to pay for the services of mercenaries. This same logic underpinned the 'race to empire' and the protection of trade routes. In the modern era a more sophisticated understanding of the various ways and means by which one state can use economic instruments to affect changes in the behaviour of other states has developed. Sanctions, embargoes and blockades have become standard – if undiscriminating (McGee 1998) – weapons in the policy arsenals of states. So too have other instruments as noted above – and still others (foreign aid, international broadcasting, educational assistance) alluded to in the Bush speech cited below (see Baldwin 1985 and Barry Jones 1986 for detailed analyses). Despite the increasing number and sophistication of these techniques, however, the underlying logic is the same: trade remains a zero-sum game.

The significance of trade in these new circumstances lies in the relationship itself – where the more powerful state enjoys an asymmetric interdependence that simultaneously constrains the autonomy of its weaker partners and lessens the likelihood of war between them (the classic study is Hirschman 1945). The policy implications of this are, of course, that powerful states should endeavour to establish an extensive array of trading relationships. Paradoxically, however, this same logic has also led to a second and almost entirely opposed set of policy prescriptions regarding trade: that is, that states should avoid trade wherever possible. This is so for two reasons. First, the economic benefits that trade brings are addictive and therefore dangerous, and, second, that any contact or connectedness let alone interdependence between power-maximizing sovereign states is a recipe for conflict and war (Knorr 1973; Waltz 1979). If this is the case for states of nearly equal power it is doubly so where one state is far weaker – and therefore more 'vulnerable' – than the other (Keohane and Nye 1977). The acknowledgement of degrees of (in)security has engendered two strands of thinking and policy prescription here: one an outright rejection of trade, and the concomitant insistence on self-reliance and autarchy; the other a cautious acceptance of the benefits of trade measured in terms of its contribution to state power, and the concomitant insistence that limited trading links are a risk worth taking.

Liberalism

The origins of liberalism must be understood to lie in an explicit rejection of mercantilist ideas and policies that were the prevailing wisdom at the time that Smith and Ricardo sat down to write, respectively, *An Inquiry into the Nature and Causes of the Wealth of Nations* and *The Principles of Political Economy and Taxation*. In the context of a rising middle class and against a backdrop of imperial rivalry Smith, Ricardo and others such as Richard Cobden rejected the political power of the aristocracy, their war-mongering, and their penchant for secret diplomacy in pursuit of a balance of power. Liberals argued instead for democratic institutions, free trade and collective security (Burchill 1996).

Liberalism is, therefore, a normative theory of both domestic and international relations, and can be separated further (artificially of course) into a series of 'strands' such as 'republican', 'commercial' and 'regulatory' amongst others

(Keohane 1990; Nye 1988; Zacher and Matthew 1995). All of these various strands have as their starting point the assumption that a harmony of interests prevails between rational, self-interested individuals concerned with maximizing their well-being; a well-being, moreover, that can be expressed and understood in both political and economic terms. All of these various strands also recognize that a minimal framework of rules is necessary to ensure that the pursuit of one individual's interests does not detract from the freedom of any other individual to pursue his or her interests. Thus there is a tension at the heart of liberal thinking between freedom on the one hand and rules on the other.

Republican liberalism is concerned with the pacifying effects of democracy. In this variant, the freedom of individuals to maximize their well-being is guaranteed by a framework of rules arrived at through (mass) participation in democratic institutions. Since a key interest of every individual is the preservation of personal security from attack or war then this interest will be communicated through democratic mechanisms and become the general, or 'national', interest and will act as a guide to government policy. An enormous 'democratic peace' literature has evolved in order either to defend or attack the arguments contained within this strand (see *inter alia* Cohen 1994; Doyle 1983; Franceschet 2000; Owen 1994).

Commercial liberalism is concerned with the pacifying effects of commerce and, more specifically, trade. Since a key interest of every individual is the preservation of personal security from poverty and 'want' then this interest will be communicated through the spontaneous creation of a 'market' in which individuals truck and barter the goods and services which are the products of their labour. Underpinned by a legal framework of property rights, the differential skills and interests of individuals coalesce in a 'natural' division of labour and the productive potential thus unleashed serves to provide wealth and freedom from 'want'. Aided by advances in production, transport and communication technologies this same process produces an expansive 'market' that gradually but ineluctably creates an international division of labour – through the exploitation of 'comparative advantage' – where the dense network of commercial contacts (and contracts) combines with the more important exchange of goods and services to create even more wealth and to produce an international harmony of interests in peaceful commercial activity and exchange. Thus commercial liberalism contains within it both a negative principle (the threat war poses to wealth) and a positive principle (the contribution that commerce and trade make toward peace). Again, an enormous literature has evolved in order either to defend or attack the argument that international trade is a force for peace (see *inter alia* Buzan 1984; Hirschman 1982; McMillan 1997; Richardson 1995).

Regulatory liberalism is concerned with the pacifying effects of institutions. This strand has two main elements. On the one hand it is concerned with the harmonizing and pacifying effects of institutions in the context of imperfections leading to 'market failure'. The origins of these imperfections lie, of course, in the pursuit of one individuals' interests *at the expense of* the freedom of other individuals, and may be political (the 'capture' of the democratic state by narrow selfish interests) or economic (for example, the emergence of monopoly and/or oligopoly power) but in either case they lead to diminished security manifest as a reduction in or diversion of the gains from trade and therefore a reduction in the general welfare.

On the other hand, regulatory liberalism is also concerned with the operation and dissemination of 'norms and rules to realize common values that go beyond self-preservation and sovereignty' (Zacher and Matthew 1995: 134). In other words, like-minded liberal states recognize that the principle of sovereignty creates an enduring tension that threatens to undermine completely the security of individual interests and the state (conceived of as individual interests 'writ large'). The possession of sovereign authority enables the state to reconcile individual interests with the general interest within its own borders. However, since no such authority exists at the international level individuals and states are free to act there as they will. The international level is thus characterized by anarchy and made dangerous by the unchecked workings of power politics in all its forms.

Liberal states attempt to overcome this problem in two ways. First, they create institutions in which they 'pool' sovereignty in order to resolve 'collective action problems'. The European Union (EU) and the WTO are very different yet classic examples of this. Second, they attempt actively to spread the benefits of both republican liberalism and commercial liberalism. In other words, regulatory liberalism recognizes the existence of a significant 'other' existing beyond the confines of liberal space and seeks to preserve the security of those within its confines by subsuming that 'other' through a process of incorporation. This process of incorporation involves the elucidation and transmission of core liberal norms and values – democracy, free trade and peace – and their acceptance by the 'other'. This acceptance is manifest most clearly by admission of these 'other' – illiberal – states as members of the international institutions in which these values are inscribed. This is exemplified in the expansion in the memberships of the European Union and the WTO. It is important, nevertheless, to note that incorporation of the 'other' can be conducted peaceably or forcibly, which explains why whilst democracies may not go to war with one another they quite frequently go to war with illiberal or 'rogue' states. This is manifest in the US occupation and (attempted) pacification of Iraq. Either way, regulatory liberalism can be seen as an attempt to domesticate international relations and, as such, 'multilateralism matters' (Ruggie 1993).

Having introduced some of the key elements of both economic realism and liberalism we turn next to a brief examination of the historical record, laying particular emphasis on the opportunities this affords us to highlight some of the major strengths and weaknesses of each body of theory in the context of the Westphalian order.

Trade, security and the state–market nexus

As previously noted, of the two major strands of thinking introduced above it has been the liberal approach to political economy that has formed the orthodoxy amongst the leading industrial states. Indeed, the argument is that these states, beginning with Great Britain, achieved their status as leading industrial (and post-industrial) powers by virtue of the fact that they turned away from mercantilism and adopted liberal policies in their stead. Part of the continued appeal of liberalism is, therefore, its self-evident 'truth': liberal states become wealthy, democratic and peaceful. As Chang (2002), following List, has pointed out this is self-serving in the extreme.

Even a cursory look at the historical record will reveal, moreover, some disturbing anomalies that seriously weaken the liberal case.[5] Considered thematically rather than chronologically the major propositions of each of the 'strands' of liberalism introduced above can be called into question. First, democracy is not a guarantor of peace. Britain and the United States went to war in 1812, as did the United States and Spain in 1898, and Turkey and Cyprus in 1974. All these states were, to varying degrees, democracies.[6] Moreover, the continuation of imperial competition in the face of exhortations to embrace 'Wilsonian Liberalism' led to protectionism, global economic depression and eventually the collapse of the League of Nations and the Second World War. Second, free trade and open markets do not guarantee wealth and therefore do not always produce peace. For evidence of this one need look no further than the contemporary condition of much of continental Africa (see Chapter 15, by Soko, in this volume). Third, international organization does not always produce either wealth, peace, or democracy as the failure of the League of Nations clearly attests (on the general point see Murphy 1994).

What, then, can account for these anomalies? Barry Jones (1988b: 27) points to a series of fundamental flaws in the theory emerging from 'prior value preferences, simplifying assumptions, ... and the exclusion of unmanageable aspects of reality'. For his part, Waltz (1962) points to the tendency amongst 'modern' liberals to be selective in their reading of classical liberal theory, arguing that 'Montesquieu, Adam Smith, and Kant made no easy assumptions about the rationality and goodness of man'. Rather, 'Among men in nature and states in a world of states, they found not harmony and peace but hostility and war to be the natural condition.' In a similar vein, both Buzan (1984) and Tooze (1988) highlight the tendency amongst liberals to neglect power as a consequence of their vision of the world as an undifferentiated market. Finally, Mearsheimer (1994–95: 7) argues that 'institutions have minimal influence on state behavior, and thus hold little promise for promoting stability ... '

In the light of these anomalies and criticisms how can we account for the continuing appeal of liberalism as both a political and economic project? How can we account for the continued calls for open markets, free trade and their regulation through the WTO? Paradoxically, the assumptions, omissions and misreadings outlined above can, almost on their own, provide the answer. A surface understanding of liberalism and liberal ideals (such as that achieved by most politicians) accords with and affirms all that is best about human nature and the possibilities for community. It is, in this sense, a manifesto of and for hope. Another possible answer is the continued formulation of sophisticated liberal arguments that contribute to the continuing evolution of the theory (for an example see Moravcsik 1997; for analyses see Merquior 1993, and Zacher and Matthew 1995). A third answer perhaps lies in the dominance of the United States in world affairs and in the knee-jerk rejection by most Americans of the assumptions, concepts and propositions of (economic) realism. As Mearsheimer (1994–95: 47) insists, realism 'stands opposed to how most Americans prefer to think about themselves and the wider world'. This leads to a fourth possible answer, which is that liberal theorists have colonized economic realism just as surely as economic realists have colonized liberalism. Nowhere is this clearer than in the extensive literatures on hegemonic stability theory (see Chapter 11 by Porter, this volume; Kelly 2002) and neo-liberal institutionalism (see Baldwin 1993).

The origins of this mutual theoretical colonization can be found on the one hand in efforts to overcome the tension within liberalism between freedom and rules and, on the other, in the pragmatic recognition by economic realists of the very real benefits that have accrued as a consequence of freer trade and relatively open markets. Taking economic realists first: GATT did succeed, after all, in reducing average tariff levels to such an extent that – excepting agriculture and some other key sectors – they are no longer seen as the key issue in trade politics. Global welfare has been significantly raised by increased trade between states on the basis of comparative advantage. Where significant barriers to trade do still exist, as in agriculture, the welfare of those cut out of the circuit has been severely compromised. Moreover, and with due respect to all those who fought and died, it is a fact that there has been no *major* war between leading industrial democracies in the post-war period. Finally, those few states that have steadfastly kept to the path of autarchy, such as North Korea, have reaped the whirlwind, while those who have abandoned it, such as Russia and China, have begun to reap the economic rewards. The voices of those economic realists (and, it should not be forgotten, Marxists) who argued for autarchy and reduced trade links have been everywhere silenced.

Liberals, on the other hand, have been faced with a need to acknowledge explicitly the tension between (individual) freedom and (collective) rules. This tension has always been present, of course, but became particularly evident during the post-1945 period for two reasons. At first glance the first of these highlights the primacy of politics over economics and the 'international' over the 'domestic' level. The argument is that the 'long peace' of the Cold War was not a consequence of the pacifying effects of commerce, trade, democracy or institutions as liberals would have it but a consequence of the bi-polarity that lay at the heart of the post-war political order (Buzan 1984). It was not trade that kept the peace, but power politics. Similarly it was not liberalism that conquered or 'incorporated' the Soviet bloc but raw power.

At first glance the second instance illustrates exactly the reverse: the primacy of economics over politics and the 'domestic' over the 'international'.[7] Here the identification of a post-war compromise of 'embedded liberalism' (Ruggie 1982) serves to underscore the fact that in most, if not all, of the leading western industrial states classical liberal prescriptions gave way to a pragmatic acceptance of a mixed economy or 'welfare state'. The significance of this pragmatic acceptance is heightened by its proximity to the turbulence of the interwar era and the 'lessons' drawn from it: that even small protectionist steps may lead to war, and quickly. Be that as it may, in this case narrow domestic concerns over welfare distribution triumphed over US demands that European states adopt liberal economic policies – in line with its own values and practices and in accordance with the dictates of the Cold War struggle between capitalism and communism.

What these two examples point to is both the strength and the weakness of the liberal case. In the first instance the liberal position is undermined and in the second it is affirmed. A second reading of both cases is possible however. If a longer historical perspective is adopted then the bi-polar system and the Cold War that resulted represent not the triumph of economic realism and power politics – or of politics over economics and the international over the domestic – but an anomalous holdover, or throwback, to a time when mercantilism held sway. In this sense the Cold War represents the death rattle of mercantilism, and the post-Cold War era the triumph of liberalism (for different interpretations see Hawthorn 1999; Wallerstein 1992). However, a second reading of the embedded liberal compromise is also possible. In this reading, which is conducted through the theoretical lens of economic realism, the re-distributive policies associated with European welfare states were slowly worn away not by the operation of market forces but by the persistent *persuasive* efforts of the hegemon. Likewise the collapse of communism and the Soviet bloc can be attributed to the *coercive* use by the hegemon of its unrivalled military and economic power. In both cases the power of the hegemon prevailed.

What is clear from this is that individuals and individual states are not entirely free to maximize their well-being or power. States impose rules on individuals, and individual states are constrained both by the actions of other powerful states and, arguably, by the structure of the states-system itself. In other words, politics matters and no amount of wishful thinking on behalf of liberals can avoid this fact. Meanwhile, of course, sovereign states are 'penetrated' by the 'market' and 'market forces' in all sorts of ways and, because of this, are never entirely in control of their own destinies.[8] In other words, economics matters and no amount of wishful thinking on behalf of economic realists can avoid this fact.

Trade, security and globalization

In the preceding section we conducted a broad empirical overview of the relationship between trade and security within the state–market nexus in order to demonstrate the case for and against the two dominant theoretical perspectives – (economic) realism and liberalism – that seek to explain that relationship within that nexus. In the process we established a relationship between theory and practice that has resulted in the co-evolution of these theoretical perspectives such that certain elements of both have fallen into a loose and, for the most part, uncomfortable embrace. Largely unpopular policymaking has been both the cause and the consequence of this.

Building upon what has gone before, this section sets out to establish whether and to what extent 'globalization' has upset this applecart and with what consequences for the theory and practice of international trade. It accomplishes this in two moves. First it examines the impact of globalization on the state–market nexus as this manifests in trade and trade politics. In this reading globalization is conceptualized – rather awkwardly, it must be said – as external to and/or in some way 'above' or 'separate' from the state–market nexus, which becomes the 'victim' of it. Nevertheless, globalization is a phenomenon that can be 'managed' by the state–market nexus and, while this might entail processes of adjustment that significantly reduce security for some while increasing security for others, the existing logic of the state–market nexus remains.[9]

Second, and by way of a conclusion, it explores the possibility that the state–market nexus is being dissolved as a consequence of globalization. In this reading the state–market nexus itself is the 'author' of globalization and is fundamentally transformed by it. In other words the state–market nexus is sowing – or has already sown – the seeds of its own destruction; liberalism is, quite literally, 'an enemy to itself' (Hawthorn 1999). In this second reading the dissolution of the state–market nexus calls for a fundamental reappraisal of the boundaries of all communities, identities and relationships, including those associated with trade (on the wider point see Linklater 1998). In such circumstances, what is demanded is a thorough reappraisal of all social scientific concepts, including security, and the theoretical frameworks from which these derive their proximate meaning.

The state–market nexus as a 'victim' of globalization

If we accept that there is an uncomfortable set of relationships between states on the one hand and markets on the other (the state–market nexus) then it is fairly easy to see why globalization – defined here as 'the process of increasing interconnectedness between societies such that events in one part of the world more and more have effects on peoples and societies far away' (Smith and Baylis 2001: 7) – might make the overall relationship even more uncomfortable (see Kobrin 1997, for example). In short, 'increasing interconnectedness' implies less sovereignty for states and more rules for markets. Thus, in the aggregate, the security of both 'parties' is undermined. However, it also suggests that some individuals and states will become more 'secure' and other individuals and states less so. Further, it suggests that not all individuals within states will be affected similarly: insecurity will be experienced within even the most secure states, and security within the most insecure states.[10] Finally, (in)security will be experienced in many different ways, as noted in the introduction to this chapter. Management of (in)security is a delicate balancing act between state-led solutions and market-led solutions, with civil society playing a monitoring role that can both facilitate and retard the process.

In the contemporary global political economy the dominant approach to the 'management' of problems associated with globalization is one of neo-liberalism. This is not the place for a lengthy discussion of its key policy prescriptions.[11] What is important here is that global neo-liberal policy prescriptions reflect the concentration of geo-political and economic power in the United States. This sets up a key tension or ambivalence since the United States 'is the champion of globalization, yet its role as military enforcer is territorially based' (Cox 1996: 292).[12]

In terms of trade and trade politics this tension manifests in a number of ways and in a number of venues. First, the context is one in which the United States is seen to be profiting most from increasing interconnectedness in general and from increasing trade flows in particular. Second, the regulation of trade often appears to be guided more by US interests (domestic and foreign) than it is by a concern with raising the level of global welfare. Third, the United States can, and quite frequently does, ignore the rules whenever these interfere with the satisfaction of its interests. Other powerful states are implicated in this as well, of course (the other Quad members, for example), but the United States is unique to the extent that it is the only global military power.

A brief survey of the contemporary foreign (economic) policy of the United States will help to clarify these points. The conclusion of the Cold War put an end to the subservience of economic to security concerns within US foreign policy. Having 'won' the Cold War the general feeling in political and popular – not to mention academic – circles in the United States was that the country should reap the economic benefits. These benefits lay not only in reduced military spending and lower taxes but also in a reduction of the wider costs associated with maintaining the anti-communist alliance – expressed chiefly but not exclusively as unfair trading practices and a lack of access for US goods in foreign markets. In the words of one commentator of the time: 'In the distance you can almost hear beleaguered officials whispering the words "Smoot-Hawley" with something approaching nostalgia' (Mahini 1990: 42). Thus, in the 1990s economic issues returned to the top of the political agenda in the US and therefore in the world as a whole. When this sort of shift happens, as it did, for example, during the 1970s when the Carter administration reoriented US foreign policy from an East–West to a North–South focus following the oil crises, academic discussion and analysis quickly follow suit. International Relations is an 'American' social science (Hoffmann 1977; Mastanduno 1998; Smith 1987). This is confirmed by the rash of books and articles on 'geo-economics' and 'strategic trade theory' that appeared – chiefly but not exclusively – in the United States in the early to mid-1990s (see *inter alia* Krugman 1995; Moran 1990–91; Thurow 1993).[13]

This re-orientation of US policy was a major shot in the arm for the Uruguay Round (UR) of trade talks. However, this must be seen in the light of the 'competition in liberalization' that characterizes US trade policy resulting in pressures on 'multiple fronts – globally, regionally and bilaterally – [that] enhances our [i.e. US] leverage and best promotes open markets' (Robert Zoellick, the current USTR, cited in Gordon 2003: 105). Moreover, as many other contributions to this book demonstrate, on balance the result of the UR was a favourable one for the leading industrial countries in general and for the United States in particular.

The United States offered 'concessions' on some key issues such as agriculture, but these were motivated by its own interest in expanding opportunities for US exporters (Grant, Chapter 5, this volume). The subsequent passage of the Farm Security and Rural Investment Act in 2002 demonstrates that when the security of US farmers is threatened global rules are ignored. Moreover, 'concessions' on agriculture and textiles were balanced by agreements on TRIPs, TRIMs and a GATS, and followed by the opening of discussions on investment, competition, public procurement and trade facilitation (the 'Singapore' issues). This has left the US (and others) open to the accusation that since these issues are not strictly about trade they have been brought within the remit of the WTO 'to take advantage of the enforcement capability (the dispute settlement system) of the WTO, so that disciplines can be effectively put on developing countries to open their economies to the goods, services and companies of the developed countries' (Khor 2001: 49). Finally, in regard to the debate over the 'trade-and' issues – environmental, social and labour standards – that the United States has on occasion championed, these are seen either as the moral expression of liberal values on the one hand or as 'protectionist devices against the products and services of developing countries' (Khor 2001: 50) on the other.

US foreign and military policy has broadly followed this same mix of persuasion, coercion and intervention exercised through a range of multilateral, regional and bilateral regimes as well as by unilateral means.[14] This is evident in the fighting of the first Gulf War as well as in the use of 'soft' power resources in regard to China (MFN status and WTO membership). The reluctance to deploy troops in the former Yugoslavia and the failure to halt the Rwandan genocide, however, is evidence of the 'halfhearted liberalism' that has been a characteristic of post-Cold War US foreign policy in general and a feature of the Clinton Presidency in particular.[15]

However, by the late 1990s a series of financial crises had combined with the disastrous US intervention in Somalia, the unfolding of events in the Middle East and a host of other anti-US, anti-western terror attacks to shake the confidence of those championing not only liberalism but liberal globalization (see *inter alia* Kiely 1998; Naim 2000; Johnson 2002; Hellmann 2003; Prestowitz 2003). Following these events, and '9/11' in particular, what was once seen as an unalloyed good, a source of prosperity, liberty and peace is increasingly being seen as dangerous (Stiglitz 2002). Dangerous not in the sense that unfettered globalization threatens – for example – the biosphere, as many protestors and non-governmental organizations claim (see Chapter 6 by Newell, in this volume), but in the sense that it threatens the lives and well-being of Americans, and of citizens of other core industrial states, as well as the values – consumption (capitalism), freedom (democracy) and order (peace) – they hold most dear (see *inter alia* Duffield 2001).

This is the unambiguous, and rather chilling, message of a speech delivered by President George W. Bush (2002) on the occasion of the graduation exercise at the US Military Academy at West Point. After establishing that '[Americans] wish for others only what we wish for ourselves – safety from violence, the rewards of liberty, and the hope for a better life' and that 'Moral truth is the same in every culture, in every time, and in every place', he goes on to declare that:

Our security will require the best intelligence, to reveal threats hidden in caves and growing in laboratories. Our security will require modernizing domestic agencies such as the FBI, so they're prepared to act, and act quickly, against danger. Our security will require transforming the military ... – a military that must be ready to strike at a moment's notice in any dark corner of the world. And our security will require all Americans to be forward-looking and resolute, to be ready for preemptive action when necessary to defend our liberty and to defend our lives.

In other words: 'The right of self-defence, authorised by the UN Charter, has been replaced in US strategic thinking by a potentially unlimited doctrine of "preemptive action." This means that the UN Charter is no longer binding on its most powerful member' (Skidelsky 2003: 31). Thus President Bush appears to be saying that 'preemptive action' may be taken not only against 'mad terrorists and tyrants' and 'evil and lawless regimes', but is also to operate as a general principle underpinning US foreign policy, which is to be guided by a singular 'vision' of human progress that all right-minded governments should seek to uphold. To whit:

> The 20th century ended with a single surviving model of human progress, based on non-negotiable demands of human dignity, the rule of law, limits on the power of the state, respect for women and private property and free speech and equal justice and religious tolerance. America cannot impose this vision – yet we can support and reward governments that make the right choices for their own people. In our development aid, in our diplomatic efforts, in our international broadcasting, and in our educational assistance, the United States will promote moderation and tolerance and human rights. And we will defend the peace that makes all progress possible.

What is clear from this is that US foreign economic policy and public diplomacy has become, or is in the process of becoming, more closely attuned to US security policy and military strategy which is in turn being geared towards insulating the country from the 'negative' effects of globalization. So much so, in fact, that some see this as the 'securitization' of globalization leading to a fundamental shift in the meaning of sovereignty. In this new era the United States looks set to use its enormous economic and military power to guarantee its own sovereignty while undermining the sovereignty of every other state, including its closest allies (Higgott 2003). Whether this happens or not is an open question and one beyond the scope of this chapter (for a pre-'9/11' discussion see Guéhenno 1998–99). What is certain in this reading of trade, security and globalization, however, is that the relationship between trade and security will be increasingly under the microscope in the years to come. Wrapped in the cloak of liberalism, this examination will encompass a range of issues – from the trade in commodities to the issue of transgenic foods to the trade in nuclear materials (see *inter alia* Bahgat 2003; Buchan 2002; Kerr 1999) – and be conducted by the United States in its own interests and, to the extent that they can be reconciled, the interests of its major allies. This is bound to leave everyone else, liberals and 'illiberals' alike, feeling less secure.

The state–market nexus as the 'author' of globalization

By way of a conclusion, let us consider briefly the implications of the second 'reading' of the impact that globalization may be having on trade and, subsequently, on security. The broad argument here is that the state–market nexus is the 'author' of globalization and therefore in some way instrumental in its own demise. It is an argument that must remain partial and essentially incomplete since it is based on observation of events that are still unfolding and, therefore, on speculation as to where they might be leading and with what consequences. As a corollary of this it is also heavily reliant on evidence drawn from observation of events and patterns in play in the state–market nexus.[16] It is, therefore, both unsatisfactory as it stands and open to attack on a variety of grounds and from a variety of directions, of which economic realism is only one. Nevertheless, the general argument has been made and can help illuminate some key issues in trade politics. It deserves serious consideration.

In this reading trade and trade politics are contributing to the dissolution of the state–market nexus to the extent that they (partially) embody the 'substance' of globalization, act as a mechanism for its transmission, and constitute its physical, legal and moral framework. The introduction of a more complex definition of globalization than the one given earlier may help to clarify the point. Globalization can (also) be conceived as:

> a process (or set of processes) which embodies a transformation in the spatial organization of social relations and transactions – assessed in terms of their extensity, intensity, velocity and impact – generating transcontinental or inter-regional flows and networks of activity, interaction, and the exercise of power (Held *et al.* 1999: 16).

For our purposes we may take this to mean that under globalization the trade in goods, services and ideas will be more widely spread, more frequent, faster and have more profound consequences for political, economic, social, religious and cultural institutions, identities and values than ever before. Cherished values will be threatened and, often, denied; identities will shift and be re-drawn; institutions will be overturned; power will be up for grabs. In short, all boundaries will be called into question (see MacMillan and Linklater 1995).

A few examples may show how trade and trade politics contribute to the dissolution of boundaries of all types. First, liberalization of the trade in rice has been vehemently opposed by the Japanese government on largely cultural grounds. Rice cultivation is seen as an important – indeed defining – activity in the cultural life of the nation. The same is true of French opposition to the liberalisation of trade in services on the grounds that this threatens to undermine the French language and culture through removal of its strict controls on foreign content in the media and entertainment industries. Second, strict control over the internet and other communications technologies has been justified by the Chinese government – and others – on the grounds that exposure to 'foreign' ideas and influences threatens to corrupt its young people and 'destabilise' the country as a whole (including, presumably, its governing structures). Third, trade liberalization has been opposed by environmental groups on the grounds that more trade uses up the earth's scarce resources even faster, threatens biodiversity and the ozone layer and may thus lead to the collapse of the biosphere itself. Fourth, trade liberalization has been opposed by a range of governments and other actors (industrial groups and trade unions for example) on the grounds that it leads to unemployment.

This same argument, that trade liberalization has negative impacts that are simultaneously widely and unevenly spread and yet often highly concentrated, has been used in condemnation of, and resistance to, the abuse of human rights, poor labour standards, the exploitation of women, the exploitation of children, and the marginalization of ethnic, racial and religious groups. We could, therefore, go on and on in this vein. The key point here, however, is that individuals and communities are exposed to the forces of globalization by the state–market nexus itself. This undermines its legitimacy and leads to the assertion of other values. Individuals and groups turn inward (or outward), seeking security in the assertion of other values which may lead to the creation of other forms of community divided along racial, cultural, ethnic and economic lines.[17]

Indeed, since this is an open process some other formulation of the state–market nexus may appear, perhaps along traditional geographic lines but arranged on a scale and in a pattern that is wholly unrecognizable. Likewise, communities might appear based on values that we do not yet know and in patterns and on scales that we cannot know or even imagine. What is clear is that on the ground in the Middle East, the former Yugoslavia and on every continent and in every country of the world the (re)assertion of values that are at odds with the prevailing orthodoxy (and yet intimately wrapped up in it) is clearly undermining the security of individuals everywhere. In this regard the threat or use of weapons of mass destruction (nuclear, chemical or biological) on a global, regional national or local scale threatens to destroy all boundaries, networks and identities. Meanwhile, the prevalence of civil wars (see Cerny 1998) simultaneously dislodges the assumption that trade leads to peace *between* states and opens up the possibility that trade leads to war *within* states. In response, the state–market nexus wages war on many 'fronts' – domestic and international, political, social and economic – and in so doing further threatens the smooth functioning of networks of exchange and interaction and as a consequence further undermine its own legitimacy and authority. If this is the case it gives trade, and the politics of international trade, a vital place and role in the shift from the state–market nexus to a world where everything is unknown and nothing is certain. In such a world there would be no such thing as 'security' as we know it today.

Notes

1. For a more optimistic view see Bhagwati (2001).
2. For extended discussions of absolute and relative gains see a number of the chapters in Baldwin (1993).
3. For reasons of space – and of their marginalization especially since the end of the Cold War – we do not consider Marxist approaches here. See Brewer (1990).
4. The steady decline in the value of the US dollar in recent years is noteworthy in this regard.

5. This is not the place for detailed history. See *inter alia* Buzan (1984), Carr (1939/1946), Hinsley (1963), Mastanduno (1998) and Polanyi (1944/2001).
6. All examples cited in Cohen (1994: 213).
7. This points to an unresolved theoretical tension between structure and agency that will not be discussed here. See Wendt (1987).
8. In this regard Devetak's argument (1995: 20) that 'no state is complete and all states are struggling against failure' is particularly pertinent, as is his claim that as a consequence 'there is statecraft, but there is no completed state' (ibid: 19). This resonates very strongly with arguments made in the conclusion to this chapter.
9. This partly explains the linguistic shift from sanctions to 'smart' sanctions, bombs to 'smart' bombs and so on, indicating that globalization enhances the possibilities for statecraft by making it possible to more accurately 'target' the intended victims (geographically, demographically, politically and so forth).
10. The latter sometimes categorized as 'quasi' and even 'failed' states. See Helman and Ratner (1992–93) and Jackson (1990).
11. Encapsulated within the idea of a 'Washington Consensus' on economic reform (originally targeted at developing countries but increasingly being applied as a general principle), these include: fiscal discipline; redirection of public expenditure; tax reform; financial liberalization; a unified, competitive exchange rate; trade liberalization; eliminating barriers to foreign direct investment; privatization of state-owned enterprises; deregulating market entry and competition; and guaranteeing property rights. The original formulation was proposed by John Williamson in 1990. See Williamson (1993) and Naim (2000).
12. This point is made by Clark (1999: 115).
13. For a critique of this literature see Cable (1995).
14. Again, this is not the place for detailed history. See amongst others Baldwin (1985), Dodge (2003), Haass and O'Sullivan (2000), Klare (1992), Mastanduno (1998) and Robinson (1996).
15. The phrase 'halfhearted liberalism' is drawn from a review essay on humanitarian intervention by Barnett (2003: 410).
16. To borrow from mainstream IPE, the state-market nexus is both a 'dependent' and 'independent' variable in this strong globalization argument.
17. I owe the broad argument to my reading of Guéhenno (1998–99) and Clark (1999).

References

Bahgat, G. (2003) 'The New Geopolitics of Oil: The United States, Saudi Arabia, and Russia', *Orbis*, 47, 3: 447–61.
Baldwin, D. (1985) *Economic Statecraft*, Princeton: Princeton University Press.
Baldwin, D. (ed.) (1993) *Neorealism and Neoliberalism: The Contemporary Debate*, New York: Columbia University Press.
Baldwin, D. (1997) 'The Concept of Security', *Review of International Studies*, 23, 1: 5–26.
Barnett, M. (2003) 'What is the Future of Humanitarianism?', *Global Governance*, 9: 401–16.
Barry Jones, R.J. (1986) *Conflict and Control in the World Economy: Contemporary Economic Realism and Neo-Mercantilism*, Brighton: Wheatsheaf.
Barry Jones, R.J. (1988a) 'Economic Realism, Neo-Ricardian Structuralism and the Political Economy of Contemporary Neo-Mercantilism', in Barry Jones, R.J. (ed.) *The Worlds of Political Economy*, London: Pinter: pp. 142–68.
Barry Jones, R.J. (1988b) 'Liberal Political Economy', in Barry Jones, R.J. (ed.) *The Worlds of Political Economy*, London: Pinter: pp. 27–56.
Baylis, J. (2001) 'International and Global Security in the Post-Cold War Era', in Baylis, J. and Smith, S. (eds) *The Globalization of World Politics: An Introduction to International Relations*, Oxford: Oxford University Press: pp. 253–76.

Bhagwati, J. (2001) 'After Seattle: Free Trade and the WTO', *International Affairs*, 77, 1: 15–29.

Brewer, A. (1990) *Marxist Theories of Imperialism: A Critical Survey*, 2nd edition, London: Routledge.

Buchan, D. (2002) 'The Threat Within: Deregulation and Energy Security', *Survival*, 44, 3: 105–16.

Burchill, S. (1996) 'Liberal Internationalism', in Burchill, S., Linklater, A., Devetak, R., Paterson, M. and True, J., (eds) *Theories of International Relations*, Basingstoke: Macmillan: pp. 28–66.

Bush, G.W. (2002) 'Remarks by the President at [the] 2002 Graduation Exercise of the United States Military Academy West Point, New York', at www.whitehouse.gov/news/releases/2002/06/20020601-3.html

Buzan, B. (1984) 'Economic Structure and International Security: The Limits of the Liberal Case', *International Organization*, 38, 4: 597–624.

Cable, V. (1995) 'What is International Economic Security?', *International Affairs*, 71, 2: 305–24.

Carr, E.H. (1939/1946) *The Twenty Years' Crisis 1919–1939: An Introduction to the Study of International Relations*, London: Macmillan.

Cerny, P.G. (1998) 'Neomedievalism, Civil War and the New Security Dilemma: Globalization as Durable Disorder', *Civil Wars*, 1, 1: 36–64.

Chang, Ha-Joon (2002) *Kicking Away the Ladder: Development Strategy in Historical Perspective*, London: Anthem Press.

Clark, I. (1999) *Globalization and International Relations Theory*, Oxford: Oxford University Press.

Cohen, R. (1994) 'Pacific Unions: A Reappraisal of the Theory that "Democracies do not go to War with each other" ', *Review of International Studies*, 20: 207–23.

Cox, R.W. (1996) 'Production and Security', in Cox, R.W. with Sinclair, T.J. (eds) *Approaches to World Order*, Cambridge: Cambridge University Press: pp. 276–95.

Crane, G.T. and Amawi, A. (eds) (1997) *The Theoretical Evolution of International Political Economy*, Oxford: Oxford University Press, Second Edition.

Devetak, R. (1995) 'Incomplete States: Theories and Practices of Statecraft', in MacMillan, J. and Linklater, A. (eds) (1995) *Boundaries in Question: New Directions in International Relations*, London: Pinter pp: 19–39.

Dodge, T. (2003) 'US Interventions and Possible Iraqi Futures', *Survival*, 45, 3: 103–22.

Doyle, M.W. (1983) 'Kant, Liberal Legacies and Foreign Affairs', *Philosophy and Public Affairs*, 12, 3: 205–35.

Duffield, M. (2001) *Global Governance and the New Wars: The Merging of Development and Security*, London: Zed Books.

Franceschet, A. (2000) 'Popular Sovereignty or Cosmopolitan Democracy? Liberalism, Kant and International Reform', *European Journal of International Relations*, 6, 2: 277–302.

Gordon, B.K. (2003) 'A High-Risk Trade Policy', *Foreign Affairs*, 82, 4: 105–18.

Guéhenno, J-M. (1998–99) 'The Impact of Globalization on Strategy', *Survival*, 40, 4: 5–19.

Haass, R.N. and O'Sullivan, M.L. (eds) (2000) *Honey and Vinegar: Incentives, Sanctions and Foreign Policy*, Washington, DC: Brookings.

Hart, M. and Dymond, B. (2003) 'Special and Differential Treatment and the Doha "Development" Round', *Journal of World Trade*, 37, 2: 395–415.

Hawthorn, G. (1999) 'Liberalism Since the Cold War: An Enemy to Itself?', *Review of International Studies*, 25 (Special Issue), 145–60.

Held, D., McGrew, A., Goldblatt, D. and Perraton, J. (1999) *Global Transformations: Politics, Economics and Culture*, Cambridge: Polity Press.

Hellmann, D.C. (2003) 'The Asian Financial Crisis: A Preface to the Post-Cold War Global Political Economy', *Cambridge Review of International Affairs*, 16, 1: 13–15.

Helman, G. and Ratner, S. (1992–93) 'Saving Failed States', *Foreign Policy*, 89 (Winter): 3–20.

Henderson, D. (2002) 'WTO 2002: Imaginary Crisis, Real Problems', *World Trade Review*, 1, 3: 277–96.

Higgott, R. (2003) 'American Unilateralism, Foreign Economic Policy and the "Securitisation" of Globalization', Centre for the Study of Globalisation and Regionalisation, Working Paper no. 124/03.

Hinsley, F.H. (1963) *Power and the Pursuit of Peace: Theory and Practice in the History of Relations between States*, Cambridge: Cambridge University Press.

Hirschman, A.O. (1945) *National Power and the Structure of Foreign Trade*, Berkeley: University of California Press.

Hirschman, A.O. (1982) 'Rival Interpretations of Market Society: Civilizing, Destructive, or Feeble?', *Journal of Economic Literature*, 20, 4: 1463–84.

Hoffman, S. (1977) 'An American Social Science: International Relations', *Daedalus*, 106, 3: 41–60.

Hughes, C.W. (2002) 'Reflections on Globalization, Security and 9/11', *Cambridge Review of International Affairs*, 15, 3: 421–33.

Jackson, R.H. (1990) *Quasi-States: Sovereignty, International Relations and the Third World*, Cambridge: Cambridge University Press.

Johnson, C. (2002) *Blowback: The Costs and Consequences of American Empire*, London: Time Warner.

Jones, K. (2002) 'The WTO Core Agreement, Non-Trade Issues and Institutional Integrity', *World Trade Review*, 1, 3: 257–76.

Keohane, R.O. and Nye, J.S. Jr. (1977) *Power and Interdependence: World Politics in Transition*, Boston: Little Brown.

Keohane, R.O. (1990) 'International Liberalism Reconsidered', in Dunn, J. (ed.) *The Economic Limits to Modern Politics*, Cambridge: Cambridge University Press: pp. 165–94.

Kelly, D. (2002) *Japan and the Reconstruction of East Asia*, Basingstoke: Palgrave.

Kerr, W.A. (1999) 'International Trade in Transgenic Food Products: A New Focus for Agricultural Trade Disputes', *The World Economy*, 22, 2: 245–59.

Khor, M. (2001) *Rethinking Globalization: Critical Issues and Policy Choices*, London and New York: Zed Books.

Kiely, R. (1998) 'Neoliberalism Revised? A Critical Account of World Bank Concepts of Good Governance and Market Friendly Intervention', *Capital and Class*, 64: 63–88.

King, D. and Narlikar, A. (2003) 'The New Risk Regulators? International Organisations and Globalization', *The Political Quarterly*, 74, 3: 337–48.

Klare, M.T. (1992) 'US Military Policy in the Post-Cold War Era', in Miliband, R. and Panitch, L. (eds) *The Socialist Register, 1992*, London: The Merlin Press: pp. 131–42.

Knorr, K. (1973) *Power and Wealth: The Political Economy of International Power*, New York: Basic Books.

Kobrin, S.J. (1997) 'The Architecture of Globalization: State Sovereignty in a Networked Global Economy', in Dunning, J.H. (ed.) *Governments, Globalization, and International Business*, Oxford: Oxford University Press: pp. 147–71.

Krause, K. and Williams, M.C. (1996) 'Broadening the Agenda of Security Studies: Politics and Methods', *Mershon International Studies Review*, 40, 2: 229–54.

Krugman, P.R. (ed.) (1995) *Strategic Trade Policy and the New International Economics*, Cambridge, MA: MIT Press.

Laird, S. (2002) 'A Round by Any other Name: The WTO Agenda after Doha', *Development Policy Review*, 20, 1: 41–62.

Lawson, S. (2003) *International Relations*, Cambridge: Polity.

Linklater, A. (1998) *The Transformation of Political Community: Ethical Foundations of the Post-Westphalian Era*, Cambridge: Polity.

McGee, R.W. (1998) 'Trade Embargoes, Sanctions and Blockades: Some Overlooked Human Rights Issues', *Journal of World Trade*, 32, 4: 139–44.

MacMillan, J. and Linklater, A. (1995) *Boundaries in Question: New Directions in International Relations*, London: Pinter.

McMillan, S.M. (1997) 'Interdependence and Conflict', *Mershon International Studies Review*, 41, 1: 33–58.

Mahini, A. (1990) 'A New Look at Trade', *The McKinsey Quarterly*, Winter: 42–53.

Mastanduno, M. (1998) 'Economics and Security in Statecraft and Scholarship', *International Organization*, 52, 4: 825–54.

Mearsheimer, J.J. (1994–95) 'The False Promise of International Institutions', *International Security*, 19, 3: 5–49.

Merquior, J.G. (1993) 'A Panoramic View of the Rebirth of Liberalisms', *World Development*, 21, 8: 1263–69.

Moon, B.E. (2000) *Dilemmas of International Trade*, Boulder, CO: Westview Press, Second Edition.

Moran, T.H. (1990–91) 'International Economics and National Security', *Foreign Affairs*, 69, 5: 74–90.

Moravcsik, A. (1997) 'Taking Preferences Seriously: A Liberal Theory of International Politics', *International Organization*, 51, 4: 513–53.

Murphy, C.N. (1994) *International Organization and Industrial Change: Global Governance since 1850*, Cambridge: Polity Press.

Naim, M. (2000) 'Fads and Fashions in Economic Reforms: Washington Consensus or Washington Confusion?', *Third World Quarterly*, 21, 3: 505–28.

Nye, J.S., Jr. (1988) 'Neorealism and Neoliberalism', *World Politics*, 40: 235–51.

O'Brien, R., Goetz, A.M., Scholte, J.A. and Williams, M. (2000) *Contesting Global Governance: Multilateral Economic Institutions and Global Social Movements*, Cambridge: Cambridge University Press.

Owen, J.M. (1994) 'How Liberalism Produces Democratic Peace', *International Security*, 19, 2: 87–125.

Panagariya, A. (2002) 'Developing Countries at Doha: A Political Economy Analysis', *The World Economy*, 25, 9: 1205–33.

Polanyi, K. (1944/2001) *The Great Transformation: The Political and Economic Origins of Our Time*, Boston, MA: Beacon Press.

Prestowitz, C. (2003) *Rogue Nation: American Unilateralism and the Failure of Good Intentions*, New York: Basic Books.

Richardson, N.R. (1995) 'International Trade as a Force for Peace', in Kegley, C.W., Jr. (ed.) *Controversies in International Relations Theory: Realism and the Neoliberal Challenge*, New York: St. Martin's Press: pp. 281–94.

Robinson, W. (1996) *Promoting Polyarchy: Globalization, US Intervention, and Hegemony*, Cambridge: Polity.

Ruggie, J.G. (1982) 'International Regimes, Transactions and Change: Embedded Liberalism in the Postwar Economic Order', *International Organization*, 36, 2: 379–415.

Ruggie, J.G. (ed.) (1993) *Multilateralism Matters: The Theory and Praxis of an Institutional Form*, New York: Columbia University Press.

Scholte, J.A. (2000) *Globalization: A Critical Introduction*, Basingstoke: Macmillan.

Skidelsky, R. (2003) 'The American Contract', *Prospect*, July: 30–35.

Smith, S. (1987) 'Paradigm Dominance in International Relations: The Development of International Relations as a Social Science', *Millennium: Journal of International Studies*, 16: 189–206.

Smith, S. and Baylis, J. (2001) 'Introduction', in Baylis, J. and Smith, S. (eds) *The Globalization of World Politics: An Introduction to International Relations*, Oxford: Oxford University Press: pp. 1–12.

Stiglitz, J. (2002) *Globalization and its Discontents*, London: Penguin.

Strange, S. (1985) 'Protectionism and World Politics', *International Organization*, 39, 2: 233–59.

Taylor, A. and Thomas, C. (eds) (1999) *Global Trade and Global Social Issues*, London: Routledge.

Terriff, T., Croft, S., James, L. and Morgan, P.M. (1999) *Security Studies Today*, Cambridge: Polity.

Thurow, L. (1993) *Head to Head: The Coming Economic Battle Among Japan, Europe and America*, London: Nicholas Brealey.

Tooze, R. (1988) 'Liberal International Political Economy', in Barry Jones, R.J. (ed.), *The Worlds of Political Economy*, London: Pinter: pp. 108–21.

UNDP (1994) *Human Development Report 1994*, New York and London: Oxford University Press.

Wallerstein, I. (1992) 'The Collapse of Liberalism', in Miliband, R. and Panitch, L. (eds) *The Socialist Register, 1992*, London: The Merlin Press: pp. 96–110.

Waltz, K.N. (1962) 'Kant, Liberalism, and War', *The American Political Science Review*, 56, 2: 331–40.

Waltz, K.N. (1979) *Theory of International Politics*, Reading, MA: Addison-Wesley.

Wendt, A. (1987) 'The Agent-Structure Problem in International Relations Theory', *International Organization*, 41, 3: 335–70.

Williamson, J. (1993) 'Democracy and the "Washington Consensus" ', *World Development*, 21, 8: 1329–36.

Zacher, M.W. and Matthew, R.A. (1995) 'Liberal International Theory: Common Threads, Divergent Strands', in Kegley, C.W., Jr. (ed.) *Controversies in International Relations: Realism and the Neoliberal Challenge*, New York: St. Martin's Press: pp. 107–50.

5
Agricultural Trade

Wyn Grant

Agriculture was effectively excluded from the GATT regime until the Uruguay Round. The main achievement of the consequent Agreement on Agriculture was that agriculture was brought back within the process of international trade negotiations. The process of negotiation proved to be highly controversial and agreement was only finally reached after a complex bilateral deal between the United States and the European Union. The impact of liberalization was relatively limited and least developed countries in particular made few gains despite their reliance on exports of agricultural produce. By the time that the Doha Round was under way, some non-governmental organizations were arguing that it would be better for developing countries if agriculture was once again excluded from the international trade regime.

Agriculture under the GATT

In domestic politics in Europe and in North America agriculture has been sharply delineated from other areas of policymaking. Policy was generally formulated within an agricultural policy community made up of farmers' organizations, agricultural departments and their legislative allies. It was difficult for outside actors, such as trade ministries, to penetrate this policy community, a difficulty compounded by the complexity of the policies that developed. It was accepted as axiomatic that agriculture should be subsidized and protected for a variety of reasons such as food security, the perceived significance of farmers as a voting bloc in elections and the ideological halo attached to the 'family farmer'.

These features of domestic policymaking spilled over into the international arena so that agriculture was exempted from the new disciplines in international trade. 'A major reason for the failure of the United States to ratify the ITO Charter was that it was incompatible with US agricultural policy at the time' (Swinbank and Tanner 1996: 7). When the GATT became a second best substitute for the ITO the United States insisted that 'only parts of the elaborate system for regulating subsidies, particularly export subsidies, were carried over from the drafts of the Havana Charter into the General Agreement (Josling *et al.* 1996: 16). In particular,

'The GATT had been explicitly written to accommodate the agricultural import controls and export subsidies of the United States' (Josling *et al.* 1996: 21).

Difficulties arose in the early 1950s over quantitative restrictions imposed by the United States for protectionist reasons on dairy imports in particular. The actions of the United States were clearly illegal and attracted complaints from dairy exporting countries, with the Netherlands being given permission to retaliate in 1952. Under pressure from domestic farm interests, the United States used its political influence, and the implicit threat of a withdrawal from GATT that would have wrecked the agreement, to obtain a broadly based waiver on agricultural products. 'This waiver extended broad discretion to the United States to insulate its domestic agricultural market from foreign competition' (Avery 1993: 2). It was not limited to the dairy products that had provoked the original dispute and 'It was open-ended in that it applied not only to existing programmes but also to any that might subsequently be introduced' (Josling *et al.* 1996: 28).

As events developed, the waiver suited European countries as well because it allowed them to construct the Common Agricultural Policy (CAP) free from any international challenge that it represented a serious distortion of trade. 'The United States was hoist on its own petard when the special treatment for agriculture under the GATT rules formed the basis for the development, in the 1960s, of the [CAP] by the EC' (Swinbank and Tanner 1996: 10). Rather than pressing for a consideration of the special treatment of agriculture under GATT rules, the United States gave priority to other objectives. Although agricultural issues were raised, with increasing emphasis, in the Dillon, Kennedy and Tokyo Rounds, no progress was made. What happened was that a pattern of bilateral accommodation of mutual interests on agriculture between the United States and Europe to the exclusion of others was started, that persisted through to the Uruguay Round.

Why was the United States not prepared to push harder on agricultural issues? One reason was that sustaining the emerging European Community (EC) was a more important objective, in the context of the Cold War, than freeing up agricultural trade. The CAP was the one real policy that the Community had been able to put in place. Placing it under pressure might jeopardize the future of the European project. Decision-makers were also influenced by a widespread perception that the major problems in agricultural trade 'were not over-subsidization, but global food scarcity and unreliable access to supplies' (Josling *et al.* 1996: 101). This preoccupation with food shortages served to perpetuate the food security paradigm that had shaped agricultural policy in the immediate post-war period.

It should also be noted that, in spite of all the protectionist arrangements, farm trade 'expanded briskly during the 1960s' (Wolfe 1998: 61). This trend continued during the 1970s as food production was outstripped by increases in demand in some countries, reinforced by the emergence of the Soviet Union and other centrally planned economies as major purchasers of grain on the world market so as to deal with domestic shortfalls in production. Trade in grains rose from 8.6 per cent of world consumption in 1960/61 to reach 14.7 per cent in 1980/81 (Hathaway 1987: 13). The increased share taken by trade might seem to be quite low in absolute terms, but relatively small fluctuations in the amount traded can have a disproportionate impact on short-run prices. Of course, simultaneously, the share of agricultural trade in overall world trade was declining, but this did not reduce the potential for disputes given that farm trade is conducted in a politicized environment heavily influenced by government policies.

How, then, can the outbreak of what Wolfe calls the 'Farm War' be explained? What happened quite simply was a massive crisis in world agriculture that led to substantial increases in farm support and enhanced competition, underwritten by subsidies, between the European Union and the United States in third country markets. The commodity price boom of the early 1970s had encouraged increases in production capacity. The surge in prices seen in the 1970s did not last. 'In the 1980s, economic conditions again changed fundamentally. World markets for agricultural products weakened, and international farm prices collapsed' (Josling *et al.* 1996: 101). 'Indeed, by 1986 prices in real terms were only one-third of their 1974 value' (Swinbank and Tanner 1996: 20).

The costs of government support of agriculture increased substantially. In the United States 'the annual cost to taxpayers of the US farm programs exploded from between $3–$5 billion in the early 1980s to $17 billion in 1985 and $30 billion in 1986' (Swinbank and Tanner 1996: 24). These levels of support became more transparent as the result of the development of a methodology to produce 'producer subsidy equivalents' and 'consumer subsidy equivalents' which summarized the various forms of support made available to farmers by governments in one simple percentage figure. The EC had to take emergency action to attempt to deal with the spiralling budgetary cost of farm support, first by the introduction of dairy quotas in an attempt to control supply in 1984 and then through a system of 'budgetary stabilizers' in 1988. However, it was evident that domestic measures driven by budgetary pressures were not going to be sufficient to control zero-sum forms of competition in international markets. There was a renewed interest in the possibility of finding solutions to some of these problems through the GATT.

At the important Ministerial Session in 1982 it was decided to form a new GATT body to look into agricultural questions, the Committee on Trade in Agriculture (CTA). This was more significant than a matter of bureaucratic institutionalization of a changing trade agenda. 'Indeed, work in the CTA was in effect the start of the negotiating process in agriculture which later was formally initiated in the Uruguay Round. The text on agriculture in the Punta del Este declaration launching the Uruguay Round relied very much on wording developed by the CTA' (Josling *et al.* 1996: 128). CTA members became the nucleus of the negotiating group on agriculture in the Uruguay Round. The formation of the CTA thus started a process that culminated in the permanent Agriculture Committee of the WTO. The significance of such bodies is that they permit discussion in a more internationally oriented context of issues that are otherwise locked in by entrenched domestic arrangements.

The United States took a prominent role in these developments. Apart from the desire of the Reagan administration to curb increases in spending on farm support, there was a growing exasperation with the impact of the CAP on the United States as the world's leading agricultural exporter. One practical response by the Americans was the Export Enhancement Program (EEP). 'Adopted during the second Reagan administration in 1985 in retaliation against the European Community's program of subsidizing agricultural exports, the EEP was meant to increase the financial burden of the [CAP] to a politically unacceptable level' (Libby 1992: 1).

Underlying these measures by the Reagan administration was a subtle change in the balance of power within the agricultural policy community in the United States. Historically, US policy has shown a particular concern with protecting potentially vulnerable groups of 'family farmers', for example, dairy farmers. This had required a combination of import protection and domestic support. However, agri-business interests whose main goal was the aggressive promotion of exports on the basis of price competition were becoming more prominent. Corporate agriculture was likely to see advantages in a more level international playing field with reduced levels of subsidy that would offer it greater opportunities because of the technological and managerial lead enjoyed by American agribusiness. This growing gap between more traditional forms of family farming and corporately organized and vertically integrated agribusiness was reinforced by the growing importance of 'the broader interests of upstream food investment, processing, packaging, marketing and transportation businesses of the "agro-food" sector. Most of these businesses are pro free trade and stand to profit from greater volumes of food in commercial channels' (Balaam 1999: 69).

The United States was the main instigator of the Uruguay Round and had a substantial influence on shaping its agenda. The EC had an interest in keeping the cost of the CAP under control, but also regarded it as the cornerstone of European integration. 'Within the EC, it was suspected that an unstated aim of the United States was to destroy the CAP' (Ingersent *et al.* 1994: 59). In fact what the United States was preoccupied with was the CAP's impact on its export markets, particularly for grains. The strategy of refusing to negotiate was not a feasible one for the EC as it would simply end in protectionist retaliation and the risk of a generally damaging 'trade war'. Hence, the EC 'attempted to limit the scope of the negotiations to the modification of existing agricultural policies rather than radical reform' (Ingersent *et al.* 1994: 60). As a strategy it led the EC to be reactive rather than proactive in the negotiations, but in the long run it was actually quite successful in achieving its objectives.

The Uruguay Round

It is arguable that the United States made a strategic error at the beginning of the Uruguay Round negotiations by advancing the 'zero option'. Using language borrowed from nuclear strategy, the agricultural proposals of the United States called for:

- The freezing and phasing out of export subsidies
- Reduction of trade barriers, including quantitative restrictions and non-tariff barriers
- Strengthening the dispute settlement and enforcement process

- The phasing out of all trade-distorting domestic subsidies and import barriers over a ten-year period (by far the most controversial of the objectives and the most difficult to achieve) (Hillman 1994: 35–6).

The Reagan administration had suffered a serious defeat in its attempt to create a market-oriented agricultural policy through the 1985 Farm Bill and 'officials sensed an opportunity to pursue their domestic objective of farm policy reform at home through an international negotiation abroad' (Paarlberg 1993: 41). If this was their objective, it was politically damaging internationally and had the impact of slowing down the process of reaching agreement in the negotiations. The United States had unrealistic expectations that a short study of the politics of the CAP would surely have corrected. As Swinbank and Tanner observe (1996: 73–4):

> The Europeans could not take the American proposal seriously: it had to be an outrageous bluff. The United States, for its part, failed to appreciate the limited room for manoeuvre that the EC policy-making framework allowed and continued to do so through December 1990. It is quite remarkable that two partners could have been so badly informed about each other's intentions.

The difficulties in agriculture started to tarnish the negotiations as a whole. At what was supposed to be a 'mid-term review' of progress at Montreal in 1988, 'the deadlock in agriculture spilled over into other sectors, even where progress had been good' (Josling *et al.* 1996: 147). The meeting failed when the Cairns Group of agricultural exporting countries withdrew. The Uruguay Round was supposed to come to a conclusion at talks in Brussels in December 1990, but these broke down amid mutual recrimination over the agricultural issue with bizarre scenes as delegates from the Argentine interrupted meetings to tell other delegates to pack their bags and leave (Grant 1991: 88).

The Uruguay Round and the whole future of the international trading system was being placed in jeopardy by the failure to reach agreement on agriculture, threatening a resurgence of protectionism and disruption to the world economy at a time of recession. Clearly, something had to be done to reach agreement and this was achieved in three ways. First, the United States retreated from its politically unrealistic position (marginalizing the Cairns Group which continued to take a hard line). Second, the European Union introduced a significant reform of the CAP that facilitated agreement on the trade negotiations. Third, new efforts were made at mediation by the GATT secretariat and the 'Quad' (the European Union, United States, Canada and Japan).

In preparation for the 1990 negotiations, the United States reduced its demand for the total elimination of domestic subsidies to a 75 per cent reduction in the 'red box' over ten years. It also called for a 90 per cent reduction of export subsidies in two years. It should be noted that the negotiations were framed in terms of a series of 'traffic light' boxes – red, amber and green. As will be discussed later, a blue box had to be added in order to reach agreement. This idea originated in the Tokyo Round to make a distinction between prohibited (red), actionable (amber) and non-actionable (green) subsidies. 'The "red light" category of banned domestic subsidies was dropped from active discussion in early 1990' (Josling *et al.* 1996: 267). The amber box contained trade-distorting policies to be reduced over time, 'defined as any policy that would tend to achieve its effects by increasing production, because that tends to increase the surplus' (Wolfe 1998: 129). Policies that are placed in the green box are regarded as acceptable from an international trade perspective as they are supposed to have no, or at most minimal, trade distortion effects or effects on production, although whether that has been the case in practice is open to question. Most interventions in the market have some impact on production and trade.

The positions taken by the United States in 1990 were not acceptable to the EC and it required a bilateral agreement between the EC and the United States through the Blair House accord of November 1992 to reach agreement. What was eventually agreed upon was a 20 per cent reduction over six years in domestic support measures (excluding 'green box' measures) expressed through an 'aggregate measure of support' (AMS). The choice of a base period from 1986 to 1990 when levels of support were relatively high weakened the effect of these measures. Moreover, as a consequence of Blair House, the AMS applied 'to the total support across all commodities, thus making it virtually useless as a constraint on individual commodity support programmes' (Josling *et al.* 1996: 167). What is evident is that the final agreement was much closer to the position of the European Union than that of the United States. The CAP was left somewhat changed but largely intact. This outcome was in part the result of the unrealistic starting point of the United States, but also the mixture of intransigence and skill in the negotiating position taken by the Europeans, its toughness reinforced by France.

Following the breakdown of the Brussels negotiations, the European Union put forward a reform package for the CAP known as the MacSharry reforms, after the agriculture commissioner of the time. These changes, enacted in 1992, were largely focused on the arable sector, although there were also changes in the beef and sheep regimes. As far as arable crops were concerned, the role of intervention buying of surplus crops was reduced with farmers being given a very generous annual payment based on the hectares farmed. It was not, however, necessary to produce a given quantity of crop to claim this payment, thus reducing the incentive to over produce. In this sense, the subsidy was 'partially decoupled'. There was still a partial link to production because the subsidy was based on the area farmed.

Views differ about how the MacSharry reforms came about and what their significance was. Some commentators argue that MacSharry was a shrewd political operator who engineered the collapse of the GATT talks to force through a CAP reform. Others argue that this would have been a too-high-risk strategy because there was no guarantee that the talks would be restarted. (A good summary of this debate can be found in Ackrill 2000: 98–100.) Paarlberg (1997: 436) argues 'The MacSharry reforms were eventually instrumental in providing a foundation for the final US agreements with the EU at Blair House, but it is not easy to argue that they were designed with that goal uppermost in minds.' At the stage that the decision was made to partially decouple arable payments, there was no guarantee that these would eventually be protected by being placed in a new category of subsidies effectively exempted from the provisions of the Agreement on Agriculture, the 'blue box'. This contained payments that should have been placed in the amber box because they may have trade effects, but were excluded because of a political deal to trade off United States deficiency payments against European Union arable area aid. It can be argued that the European Union made a clever move by devising a policy 'that could act as an effective bargaining counter against US deficiency payments' (Ackrill 2000: 101).

Views differ about the significance of the 1992 CAP reforms. One view would be that they were not reforms at all because they did nothing to reduce the overall level of support to farmers, even increasing it, although it was provided in different ways that were claimed to be less trade distorting. However, as will be seen in the context of the discussion of the Doha Round, partial decoupling did open up the possibility of new reform options for the European Union. However, the 'blue box', although it represented a politically convenient solution for the US and the EU to the problems arising in the agricultural negotiations in the Uruguay Round, became an issue that had to be dealt with in the Doha Round.

Although the resolution of the problems relating to agriculture depended very much on US–EU bilaterals, a role was played by the GATT secretariat and by other countries. A useful ground clearing exercise was offered by what is often referred to as 'the Chairman's draft', produced in July 1990 by the Chairman of the Agricultural Negotiating Group, Art de Zeeuw. It provided the basis for the consolidated draft produced by the GATT Director-General, Arthur Dunkel, in December 1991. 'Countries generally accepted the Dunkel Draft as the basis for a final agreement, and proceeded to negotiate on the details' (Josling *et al.* 1996: 139). The 'Quad' countries also played an important mediating role in the final phase of the negotiations.

'What is clear is that the agreement is fairly modest when contrasted with the aspirations allegedly held by some of the participants in the early stages of the negotiations' (Swinbank and Tanner 1996: 141). A series of reports issued by the Organization for Economic Cooperation and Development (OECD) in 2001 concluded that the overall impact of the Agreement on Agriculture on trade in farm products had been 'modest'. This was not surprising when one considered that 'A high share, about 60 per cent, of total support to farmers is given outside reduction commitments in the blue or green boxes' (*Agra Europe* 2001a: EP/4). Overall subsidies to farmers in OECD countries had altered little over the 13 years since the commencement of negotiations. The impact of the agreement had been greatest in relation to export subsidies. However, tariff quotas remain unfilled and tariffs in agriculture average 40 per cent and peaked at more than 500 per cent, compared to less than four per cent for industrial goods.

Few gains for developing countries

No one was more disappointed by the practical impact of the Uruguay Round on agricultural trade than the developing countries. A Food and Agriculture

Organization review noted that 'few studies reported improvements in agricultural exports in the post-UR period – the typical finding was that there was little change in the volume exported or in diversification of products and destinations' (*Agra Europe* 2000: A/2).

The conversion of border protection into supposedly more transparent tariffs did very little to help them because tariff equivalents were often set at higher levels than the border protection they replaced. 'The choice of 1986–88 as the base period ensured that the gap between world and domestic support prices was captured at historically high levels ... it is clear that for many products very high tariffs were set' (Swinbank 1999: 396). Trade liberalization produced a surge in food imports in developing countries, especially of milk powder and poultry, but there was no compensatory increase in exports. The 'Like-Minded Group' of developing countries also complained that the special chapter of the Agreement on Agriculture dealing with Sanitary and Phytosanitary issues was increasingly used as a means to exclude them from developed country markets (*Agra Europe* 2000: A/2).

This is not just a question of sorting out the technicalities of the trade system such as 'dirty tariffication' in the conversion of non-tariff barriers into tariffs that produced tariffs as high as 350 per cent in some Quad countries. The underlying political reality is that there is considerable resistance in developed countries to opening up agricultural markets to low cost producers. This was evident when the EU proposed an 'Everything But Arms' agreement to open up its markets to least developed countries. There was considerable opposition to the proposal from agricultural lobbies and for a time it was referred to as the 'Everything But Agriculture' agreement. The implementation of the agreement in relation to key commodities such as sugar has been delayed.

For all the disappointments in terms of substantive policy change, the important achievement of the Uruguay Round was to bring agriculture back within the disciplines of the international trading system. Article 20 of the Agreement on Agriculture provides for negotiations on the continuation of the reform process to begin before the end of 1999. There is an incentive to resume negotiations because the Peace Clause (Article 13, technically known as 'Due Restraint') expires at the end of December 2003. The significance of the Peace Clause is that it effectively protects the CAP from challenge through the WTO Disputes Settlement Mechanism.

The launch of the Doha Round

In the run up to the launch of a new round of trade negotiations at the WTO ministerial meeting at Doha in Qatar in November 2001, the European Commission was seeking to emphasize that what united the United States and the European Union was more important than what divided them. In particular, both countries have displayed a reliance on domestic agricultural support, even if the level has been higher in the European Union than in the United States. The Bush administration also seemed to be less interested in pressing the cause of agricultural trade liberalization than the Clinton administration.

The real division was between the European Union and the United States and the agricultural exporting countries, some of them organized in the Cairns Group led by Australia. The Cairns Group includes both developed and developing countries, but developing countries as a whole were split over their stance towards a new round of trade negotiations. The net exporters had a clear preference for better access to developed country markets and therefore tended to align themselves with the Cairns Group. Other developing countries wanted to retain protection of their own producers, while retaining privileged access to EU markets.

It soon became evident that a major battle at Doha was going to be over export subsidies. The preliminary text drawn up by Stuart Harbinson of Hong Kong, the WTO General Council chairman, called for reductions of, with a view to phasing out, all forms of export subsidy in agriculture. Although the European Union declared that it was going to adopt a less defensive strategy than in the Uruguay Round, it was clear that the issue of export subsidies was a sticking point, not least for France. 'Although the EU is making much less use of export subsidies than it did ten years ago – notably in the grain sector, where domestic prices for wheat are now basically aligned with world market levels – the complete elimination of export subsidies would fatally undermine the whole basis of the EU dairy and sugar regimes' (*Agra Europe* 2001b: EP/2).

The work programme for agriculture agreed at Doha provided for negotiations on substantial improvements in market access and substantial reductions in trade-distorting domestic support. It was agreed without difficulty that in this 'Development Round' special and differential treatment for developing countries should be an integral part of all elements of the negotiations. The European Union's emphasis on the 'multifunctionality' of agriculture in terms of its contribution to such 'public goods' as landscape, a stance supported by Japan, was reflected in a sentence stating that non-trade concerns would be taken into account in the negotiations.

The inclusion of the original Harbinson phrase about export subsidies created real difficulties for the European Union. France, backed by Ireland, indicated that it was willing to see the whole meeting collapse rather than agree to the language on export restraints. Their objections were met by the insertion of a phrase that referred to 'without prejudging the outcome of the negotiations'. However, there is no doubt that export subsidies will be a key issue during the negotiations and the European Union would certainly be prepared to concede further reductions if it could obtain satisfaction on other points. These include the use of export credits by the United States, short-term loans to exporters that the Commission regards as just another form of export subsidy. They also argue that the United States uses food aid to dispose of surplus produce and create markets in developing countries.

For its part, the United States called in June 2002 for the elimination of export subsidies over a five-year period, while the Cairns Group called for a 50 per cent cut by developed countries in one year, followed by the elimination of the remaining 50 per cent over three years. A proposal by Switzerland called for more moderate cuts for some products in return for steeper cuts in others. The United States has also called for overall domestic farm subsidies to be limited to no more than five per cent of the total value of national production. Figures submitted to the WTO by the European Union on the scale of its 'amber box' domestic support suggest a subsidy-to-value ratio of around 17 per cent, over three times the proposed figure. The United States proposed that average agricultural import tariffs should be reduced from 62 per cent in 2002 to 35 per cent with targeting of the highest taxes known as 'tariff peaks'. No individual tariff would exceed 25 per cent after a five-year phase-in period. The United States has also proposed that tariff cuts should be based on the rates actually applied rather than the formal 'bound' rates that tend to be higher. It has also suggested that a date should be agreed for the eventual elimination of all agricultural tariffs.

The EU negotiating strategy in the Doha Round was built around four main components:

- Maintaining the 'blue box' in order to be able to continue subsidizing European agriculture
- The minimization of further reductions in tariffs, with strong resistance to any attempt to level off tariff peaks to 25 per cent as proposed by the United States and the Cairns Group (the European Union has more tariff 'peaks' than any of the other members of the Quad)
- To contain agreement on export subsidy with limits that can be achieved by changes in CAP commodity regimes through internal reforms
- To exploit acceptance of the 'non-trade concerns' and environmental consideration principles as a get-out clause wherever any proposals are unacceptable (*Agra Europe* 2001c: A/2).

These objectives were reflected in European Union's initial negotiating offer made in December 2002. The proposals called for a 55 per cent cut in levels of domestic support, a 45 per cent reduction in export subsidies and a 36 per cent cut in agricultural import tariffs. Superficially, these might appear to be radical offers, but in fact they are compatible with CAP reforms already planned or achieved. Tariff rates are so high for many products, that cutting them by more than a third would make very little difference. For example, the basic EU import tariff for butter would fall from €1896/t to €1213/t, still a prohibitive level.

The US Farm Bill

The landscape of the negotiations was changed by the passage in 2002 of new agricultural legislation in the United States, often referred to as the 'Farm Bill' but officially known as the Farm Security and Rural Investment Act. This measure has to be understood in the context of the 1997 Freedom to Farm (FAIR) Act, a measure that introduced a more market-oriented farm policy. It strengthened the hand of the United States in international trade negotiations so that it could say 'don't just do as we say, do as we do'. One of the main measures in the FAIR Act was the replacement of deficiency payments by decoupled forms of subsidy. The existence of deficiency payments had been a principal motive for the United States to agree to the creation of the 'blue box'.

Analysts were aware that the FAIR Act represented 'a precarious victory ... it leaves the traditional agricultural policy process establishment in place – ever ready to seek expanded benefits whenever circumstances offer the political opportunity' (Orden *et al.* 1999: 234). In particular the Act did 'not repeal the permanent legislation that will automatically trigger a reversion to high price supports and supply controls if Congress fails to take further action in 2002' (Orden *et al.* 1999: 169). Moreover, the Act did provide for 'supplementary assistance' payments to be made in 'emergencies'.

In 1997 the good times continued for America's farmers, but in 1998 prices for grain and many other farm products fell sharply. Farmers had also over-planted what were seen as profitable crops, creating surpluses that sent prices lower. In 1998 an agricultural appropriations bill signed by the President included $8.6 million in emergency assistance for farmers. As it turned out, emergency payments to farmers amounted to an average of $7.5 billion a year between 1996 and 2002. From an average expenditure of $8.8 million in the 1990–97 period government payments to farmers rose to more than $24 billion in 2001. 'Close to 40 per cent of these direct payments have taken the form of emergency assistance under three supplementary legislative packages enacted since October 1998, in response to pressure from farm interests alarmed by a continuing trend of low commodity prices' (*Agra Europe* 2002a: A/1). Despite all this additional help, US farm exports between 1996 and 2001 fell by almost 12 per cent while imports rose by more than 30 per cent (*Financial Times* 10 May 2002). As the 2002 Farm Bill was drafted, it was evident that talk of a more market-oriented agricultural policy had been swamped by the imperative to defend key US agricultural interests.

The 2002 Farm Bill, which covers the 2002–06 period 'not only reinforces the *ad hoc* measures introduced in the late 1990s, but also brings back into play all the market distorting measures which marked the farm programmes which preceded the 1996 FAIR Act' (*Agra Europe* 2002a: A/1). Neither the Democrats nor the Republicans wanted to provide their opponents with an opportunity to label them as the 'anti-farm' party in advance of the key Congressional elections in November 2002. One of the main provisions of the new legislation was the return of a counter-cyclical subsidy abandoned by FAIR – the target price/deficiency type payment. This is designed to provide additional top-up payments to farmers when commodity prices are low. However, in contrast to earlier programmes, deficiency payments are decoupled from production, so the United States still has a reduced incentive to defend the blue box. They will be based on 85 per cent of a fixed base acreage and a fixed historical yield. The 'blue box' covered in 2002 around three quarters of the European Union's budgetary expenditure on supporting agriculture or some $60 billion a year, compared with US payments within this category of $19 billion (*Agra Europe* 2002b: A/1).

The United States has defended the Bill on the grounds that it is compatible with its WTO obligations. Should there be a chance of breaking through WTO thresholds in any year, so-called 'circuit breakers' would come into effect. However, doubts have been expressed about whether it will be politically feasible to apply this aspect of the legislation. The United States has also claimed that the greater emphasis on channelling money into agri-environmental schemes is analogous to the growing emphasis on 'second pillar' measures within the European Union. Nevertheless, many analysts see the legislation as a repudiation of bipartisan US advocacy of agricultural trade reform. The United States will continue to press for measures such as the elimination of export subsidies within the Doha Round. However, its moral authority as a champion of liberalized agricultural trade has been severely undermined. This will make it easier for protectionist forces in the European Union to defend the status quo and reduce the chances of significant progress on agricultural issues in the Doha Round.

The Mid-Term Review

In July 2002 the European Commission put forward a radical set of proposals for the reform of the CAP under the guise of the Mid Term Review (MTR) referring to the mid-point of the implementation of the Agenda 2000 reforms agreed at Berlin in 1999. The proposals were driven by a number of considerations, including the need to cope with the impact of eastern enlargement of the CAP and public opinion which has become less supportive of the CAP in the wake of a series of food safety scandals. However, the reforms were also affected by the need to take account of the WTO negotiations. The Commission considered that it needed to avoid repeating the defensive stance it had taken in the Uruguay Round, but needed to gain the moral high ground. In particular the proposals aimed to replace aid payments to farmers by a single decoupled income payment per farm based on historical payments. It is hoped that it would be possible to place this new form of payment within the 'green box'. This would then remove the need for the European Union to defend the 'blue box' in its entirety, a difficult issue on which it is virtually without supporters in the WTO. Because its negotiating resources would not be absorbed in this issue, it would have more flexibility to negotiate on other issues, not least on non-trade related objectives such as environmental and landscape protection and animal welfare (another issue on which it is relatively isolated).

The principal difficulty with the strategy was that other countries might argue that a significant income payment to farmers could have an effect on production as it would enable farmers to grow crops or rear livestock that would otherwise be uneconomic. They would then be able to sell that produce at a lower price than if there was no subsidy. The term 'minimally trade distorting' is not defined in relation to the green box. 'On-going work in the OECD suggests that apparently non-trade-distorting measures, that is measures providing support that is not based on current production or factors of production may nonetheless have some production and trade effects' (*Agra Europe* 2002b: A/2).

A second element of the proposals that was related to the trade negotiations was the increased funding of rural development measures through 'dynamic modulation' whereby direct payments to farmers would be reduced and the savings redirected to the rural development budget which would be almost doubled. These would enable the European Union to support the 'public good' aspects of agriculture's contribution to the environment and landscape that it claims to value so highly. Agricultural exporting countries such as the Argentine are more sceptical, seeing the proposal as a means of redistributing subsidies that still have a distorting effect on production.

Following protracted negotiations, a watered down version of the MTR proposals was adopted in the summer of 2003. The revised proposals centred on a complex system of partial decoupling with considerable scope for national discretion. However, their significance as far as the Doha Round was concerned was that they gave the European Union more room for manoeuvre in the negotiations. The European Union submitted a revised offer following two days of informal talks among trade ministers in Montreal in July 2003. Following the reform package, it was possible for the European Union to offer a 60 per cent cut in trade-distorting domestic support covering both the amber and blue boxes. The European Union also indicated that it was prepared to eliminate some export subsidies, but it was not prepared to improve its import tariff reduction offer.

Collapse at Cancún

Following the agreement of the CAP reform package, the United States and the European Union began talks on a 'Blair House' style resolution of the differences between them. This led to fears on the part of the other participants in the trade round that an agreement would be made at their expense. The essence of the deal arrived at between the European Union and the United States in August 2003 was that European Union would give ground on trade-distorting domestic support, a move made possible by the partial reform of the CAP, while the United States would give ground on softening market access. On market access, a new 'blended formula' for tariff reduction was suggested which combined the approach of gradual, flat reductions on the Uruguay Round model favoured by the European Union with the US-support for the 'Swiss Formula' that would reduce tariff peaks quickly. However, the document was short on precise figures and products, although this was claimed to be a deliberate strategy to facilitate negotiation. There was no agreement on the future of the Peace Clause or on the vexed subject of geographical indications which the European Union wants to use to protect high value added products linked to particular regions.

The failure of this agreement to leverage a settlement at Cancún was seen by some commentators as marking the collapse of EU–US hegemony over the world trading system. As it happened, the Cancún talks largely collapsed because of disagreement over the so-called 'Singapore issues' such as investment and public procurement rather than over agriculture. The draft agricultural text that was tabled was little different from what had been under discussion in Geneva in the weeks preceding the Cancún meeting. However, the United States and European Union were alarmed at a proposal to cap 'blue box' payments at no more than five per cent of the total value of agricultural production.

What was significant at Cancún was the emergence of a new coalition of emerging countries led by Brazil and variously known as the G-20 or the G-21 (its membership fluctuated and six Latin American countries including Colombia and Peru subsequently left the grouping, it is thought in response to American pressure on them to do so). This grouping contained both agricultural exporters like the Argentine, net importers such as Egypt and countries with a protectionist orientation like India. However, the countries were united around an opposition to the protectionist agricultural stance of the European Union and United States. Indeed, most countries in the talks were involved in one grouping or another. In addition to the long-standing Cairns Group, the world's poorest countries came together in a 90-strong group. Agricultural importing countries such as Japan and Switzerland joined together in a Group of Nine.

With the expiry of the Peace Clause looming, the European Union suggested that the climate for further negotiations could be soured by an increased number of disputes referred to the WTO. One hopeful sign was that the European Union appeared to have moved closer than it had ever done before to accept the eventual abolition of export subsidies, although movement in that area would still leave the issues of market access and domestic support to be resolved. On the other hand, statements made by trade commissioner Pascal Lamy suggested that the European Union was calling into question its commitment to multilateralism, but they may have simply been a bargaining ploy. The Uruguay Round took eight years to complete and a similar time period might be required for the Doha Round.

Conclusions

Bringing agriculture within the ambit of the international trade regime has not so far realized the benefits hoped for, either by developed country advocates of liberalization or developing countries that rely on the export of agriculture produce. This is not surprising given the ability of agricultural policy communities in major developed countries to generate resistance to policy change.

Non-governmental organizations concerned with developing countries have developed their own discourse on the subject organized around the concept of 'food sovereignty'. This is viewed in terms of giving priority to peoples' and communities' right to food and to food production over trade concerns. For example, it entails the support and promotion of local markets and producers over production for exports and food imports.

There has been some discussion of whether agriculture should be removed once again from the international trade regime. However, it has been recognized that trade negotiations at least offer the potential of dealing with such issues as the dumping of food imports in developing countries, whether as food aid or heavily subsidized exports. What is needed from this perspective is a re-design of trade policies to allow more marginalized groups in rural areas to prosper. The call for 'food sovereignty' is not seen as one for autarchy or protectionism. With the developing countries displaying increasing capacity to influence the course of negotiations, greater attention will have to be given their concerns. The countries that provide large agricultural subsidies will have to give the greatest ground if agreement is to be reached. What is likely to eventually emerge is a further liberalization of agricultural trade with its greatest impact on export subsidies, some progress in border protection and much less in relation to domestic support. However, some of the momentum for liberalization that was created by the Uruguay Round has been dissipated. Further progress can be expected, but it remains an open question whether it will lead to fundamental change, particularly changes that would allow developing countries to take advantage of their potential strengths in world agricultural markets.

References

Ackrill, R. (2000) *The Common Agricultural Policy*, Sheffield: Sheffield Academic Press.

Agra Europe (2000) 'WTO Talks to Focus on Three Major Trade Issues', 13 October, pp. A/1–A/3.

Agra Europe (2001a) 'Uruguay Round Limited Trade Impact, Says OECD', *Agra Europe*, 12 April, pp. EP/4–5.

Agra Europe (2001b) 'CAP Under Pressure as New WTO Trade Round Launched', 16 November, pp. EP/1–3.

Agra Europe (2001c) 'Doha – A Qualified Success', 16 November, pp. A/1–2.

Agra Europe (2002a) 'US Abandons "Freedom to Farm" ', 3 May, pp. A1–A3.

Agra Europe (2002b) 'US WTO Plan Poses Major Policy Challenge to EU', 2 August, pp. A/1–2.

Avery, W.P. (1993) 'Agriculture and Free Trade', in Avery, W.P. (ed.) *World Agriculture and the GATT*, Boulder: Lynne Riener: pp. 1–16.

Balaam, D.N. (1999) 'Agricultural Trade Policy', in Hocking, B. and McGuire, S. (eds) *Trade Politics*, London: Routledge, pp. 52–66.

Grant, W. (1991) *The Dairy Industry: an International Comparison*, Aldershot: Dartmouth.

Hathaway, D.E. (1987) *Agriculture and the GATT: Rewriting the Rules*, Washington DC: Institute for International Economics.

Hillman, J.S. (1994) 'The US Perspective', in Ingersent, K.A., Rayner, A.J. and Hine, R.C. (eds) *Agriculture in the Uruguay Round*, Basingstoke: Macmillan, now Palgrave.

Ingersent, K.A., Rayner, A.J. and Hine, R.C. (1994) 'The EC Perspective' in Ingersent, K.A., Rayner, A.J. and Hine, R.C. (eds) *Agriculture in the Uruguay Round*, Basingstoke: Macmillan, now Palgrave, pp. 55–87.

Josling, T.E., Tangermann, S. and Warley, T.K. (1996) *Agriculture in the GATT*, Basingstoke: Macmillan, now Palgrave.

Libby, R.T. (1992) *Protecting Markets: US Policy and the World Grain Trade*, Ithaca: Cornell University Press.

Orden, D., Paarlberg, R. and Roe, T. (1999) *Policy Reform in American Agriculture: Analysis and Prognosis*, Chicago: University of Chicago Press.

Paarlberg, R.L. (1993) 'Why Agriculture Blocked the Uruguay Round: Evolving Strategies in a Two-Level Game', in Avery, W.P. (ed.) *World Agriculture and the GATT*, Boulder: Lynne Riener, pp. 39–54.

Paarlberg, R.L. (1997) 'Agricultural Policy Reform and the Uruguay Round: Synergistic Linkage in a Two-Level Game', *International Organisation*, 51: 413–44.

Swinbank, A. (1999) 'CAP Reform and the WTO: Compatibility and Developments', *European Review of Agricultural Economics*, 26: 389–407.

Swinbank, A. and Tanner, C. (1996) *Farm Policy and Trade Conflict: the Uruguay Round and CAP Reform*, Ann Arbor: University of Michigan Press.

Wolfe, R. (1998) *Farm Wars: the Political Economy of Agriculture and the International Trade Regime*, Basingstoke: Macmillan, now Palgrave.

6

The Political Economy of International Trade and the Environment

Peter Newell

This chapter provides a critical examination of the contemporary debate over the relationship between trade liberalization and environmental protection. It explores the relationship between trade and the environment at a number of levels that will provide the structure for the chapter. The first part of the chapter provides the historical context of this debate, reviewing the claims made by advocates of free trade and environmentalists alike. The second section reviews how the GATT and WTO have dealt with environmental issues in their agreements, including evidence from some of the cases that have come before these institutions. Debates about the appropriateness of negotiating environmental standards within the WTO are reviewed, as are the efforts of regional trade agreements to address environmental concerns including NAFTA, Mercosur and ASEAN. Part three offers an examination of the politics of the policy process around these issues. This includes a discussion of issues of access and transparency in decision-making and the question of the capacity of developing countries to effectively participate in WTO decision-making. It also provides a brief assessment of the evolving role of NGOs in WTO decision-making. Finally the chapter provides an assessment of proposals for reform, a review of debates about the need for a World Environment Organisation (WEO) and for reforms of the WTO.

Background and context of the debate

A number of factors and events have conspired to place the debate about the compatibility of trade liberalization with the goals of environmental protection centre stage. These include a number of high profile and controversial cases that have come before the dispute settlement panel of the WTO, perhaps most notoriously the dolphin–tuna case, discussed in section 2 below. More broadly social movement activism has increasingly targeted the WTO as the institutional embodiment of all that concerns people about globalization in general. Fears that the imperatives of accelerating trade liberalization are increasingly being allowed to take precedence over environmental regulations, have ensured that the relationship between trade and environment assumes central importance in the politics of international trade.

In many ways at the heart of this debate is the question of whether trade liberalization can be supportive of, or is necessarily detrimental to the goal of protecting the environment. Though there are clearly positions that can be held between these two polarities, there are broadly two conflicting perspectives that can be identified on this issue which Williams has described as liberal and ecological (Williams 1994). Some of the key differences and conflicts between these perspectives endure despite evidence of accommodation in the position of both perspectives (Williams 2001a).

The liberal view

Free trade advocates argue that environmental concerns can be accommodated within the basic paradigm of free trade. This is so for a number of reasons. Firstly, trade liberalization encourages the removal of wasteful activities damaging to the environment. Examples here include the removal of harmful subsidies, which encourage unsustainable industrial or agricultural practices. In this latter regard the EU is often criticized for encouraging surplus and wasteful production, creating market distortions and leading to the inefficient and over-intensive use of farmland. Though not embracing a trade liberalization agenda, many environmentalists have also been critical of the use of subsidies to prop up pollution-intensive activities when similar forms of support are not available for renewable energy development, for example. A Greenpeace study found that in Europe alone since 1990 close to $US 15 billion of taxpayers' money has been used in subsidies by the EU and Western European governments to support the fossil fuel and nuclear industries. In contrast renewable energy technologies received only one-tenth of the funding over the same period – $US 1.5 billion (Greenpeace 1997).

Second, and at a more fundamental level, advocates of free trade claim that competition promoted by open markets provides incentives for firms to use resources more efficiently. In order to reduce costs and to compete in global markets firms are increasingly recognizing that they have to minimize the through-put of resources and reduce waste in the production process which adds costs to the final product and in so doing reduces competitiveness (Schmidheiny 1992).

A third line of argument follows a 'logic' that assumes that trade generates the wealth and growth that funds environmental programmes. Jagdish Bhagwati (1993), for example, argues that growth enables governments to tax and raise resources for objectives which include the abatement of pollution and general protection of the environment. There are two assumptions behind this argument. One is that funding environmental programmes is a more effective way of tackling ecological degradation than tackling the causes of that degradation. For critics, however, trade liberalization is itself one of the key drivers of environmental degradation. This is the 'end-of-pipe' paradigm that environmentalists decry which focuses on clean up rather than prevention. The argument also makes a leap of faith in assuming that because trade creates potential resources for environmental protection those resources will necessarily be used towards that end.

The second broader assumption that often lies behind such arguments is that environmental consciousness follows development. Post-industrial values associated with environmentalism have to follow a process of industrialization. A more benign reading of this argument from a development perspective is that basic needs have to be met before demand for environmental protection can be generated and in so far as trade helps to meet those needs it may increase the demand for environmental protection. Support for this position would be found in the contested notion that demand for environmental quality rises with incomes. While using a willingness-to-pay argument might allow you to arrive at such a conclusion, it is worth noting that some of the largest and most vocal environmental movements in the world are in developing countries such as India.

Related to this is an argument that posits that measures that restrict trade and go against the thrust of trade liberalization are ineffective at bringing about the desired change in environmental practices. Eco-protectionism, economists argue, is both damaging to the environment and has negative economic impacts, particularly for developing countries. Not only do barriers relating to the way a product is produced potentially conflict with international trade law, but they also discriminate against exports from developing countries, in particular, where resource-intensive activities are more heavily concentrated. In many cases bans on particular products, labelling regimes and restrictions on imports also fail to promote the desired change. Sáez (2000: 21), for example, shows that since 'Indonesia introduced a ban on log exports in 1985, replacing it in 1992 with very high export taxes ... there has been an increase in domestic processing capacity, which has led to an increase in total demand for logs rather than a reduction'. In addition the transaction costs involved in trying to regulate such trade are high. This problem has plagued efforts to control the trade in endangered species, tracking rhino horn that can be ground into powder or tracing the source of elephant ivory to establish whether or not it has been illegally poached. In sum, therefore, even if restrictions on trade are desirable, they may often not be practicable. Behind this lies a broader concern that the gains of trade that have been built up over 50 years of negotiations 'should not be easily surrendered to new protectionism sanctioned by environmental concerns' (Whalley 1996: 6). There is caution not to set a new precedent such that special treatment for one issue will lead to claims for special treatment on a range of issues, subverting the generality of the rule regime in the trading system (ibid.).

This issue taps into a broader debate about the potential for countries to invoke trade-restrictive measures on environmental grounds as a cover for protectionist interventions. This has of course been the dilemma facing the dispute settlement panel of the WTO in determining whether barriers erected to trade on environmental grounds are being used to protect domestic industries. The suspicion in the dolphin–tuna case (discussed below) was that the United States was restricting access of imports of Mexican yellow-fin tuna in order to protect its own tuna industry from competition rather than for the reason publicly given; that the nets used to catch the tuna were inadvertently trapping and killing dolphins. Environmentalists and free traders may find common ground, however, in the idea that a more effective way of governing or regulating damaging trade and production processes is to address the demand for that trade. As long as there is a consumer demand for ivory or mahogany, then a trade will exist to meet that demand. Encouraging consumers to consider the environmental and social implications of their consumption choices may ultimately be a more effective way of controlling unsustainable forms of trade. This is leaving aside for the moment the bluntness of punitive boycotts or other more positive forms of consumer activism as tools for encouraging the upgrading of social and environmental standards (Kabeer 2000; Newell 2001b). There is a resonance here with neo-liberal orthodoxy, in that willingness to pay for environmental protection is the guide to action. In other words, people make choices about how much they value the environment through consumer preferences and therefore there is no need to interfere with markets.

A further increasingly popular argument in the armoury of those advocating free trade is that environmentalist concerns about the growth of pollution havens are over-stated. Contrary to narratives about a 'race to the bottom' in environmental standards, whereby mobile capital exploits reduced barriers to trade to relocate and invest in areas with poorer standards of environmental regulation, many assert that the overall effect of trade liberalization has actually been a 'trading up' of standards. David Vogel (1997) in his book 'Trading Up' supports this claim with reference to evidence from NAFTA, the WTO and EU. Upgrading is achieved because of the desire of traders to access the most profitable markets for their products, which, in many cases, will be the triad economies of North America, Europe and Japan where environmental standards are higher. To access these markets exporters have to conform to higher standards encouraging a global ratcheting up of standards rather than a competitive race to the bottom.

Related to this is the claim that the costs of meeting environmental standards constitute a small part of the overall costs faced by industry and certainly pale into insignificance compared alongside other factors such as labour costs, the skills-base of the workforce or the available infrastructure in an investment location, with costs to industry from domestic environmental regulation estimated to rarely exceed 1.5 per cent of overall production costs (Brack 1997: 5; Williams 2001a: 5). Whatever the actual costs of meeting standards, environmentalists contend that repeated threats of relocation in response to the proposed raising of environmental standards have the effect of creating a 'regulatory chill' effect where there are strong incentives not to upgrade standards of protection. Indeed the history of environmental regulation suggests that in many settings, the development of national environmental laws followed competitive deregulations to attract investors at state level (LeQuesne 1996: 69).

Beyond the formal process of regulation liberals argue, in any case, that trade liberalization and the internationalization of production have created the conditions for the transfer of clean technologies and improved production processes. In the World Development Report of 1992, the World Bank claimed 'Liberalised trade fosters greater efficiency and higher productivity and may actually reduce pollution by encouraging the growth of less polluting industries and the adoption and diffusion of cleaner technologies' (1992: 67). In many cases, investors 'export' environmental standards to new investment locations either because it is more costly to adapt a production process to a new site or because public and consumer expectations regarding a company's social and environmental conduct mean that it is politically inadvisable to exploit the existence of lower environmental standards (Garcia-Johnson 2000). On trade grounds too, it may be possible to argue that when governments relax environmental regulations for export-or import-competing industries, these preferences constitute a subsidy (Morici 2002).

The ecological view

An ecological view, as opposed to a more narrowly conceived environmentalist position, which might hold that under certain conditions trade liberalization can be made compatible with the goals of sustainable development (WWF 1991), challenges many of the assumptions and premises that form the starting point for the liberal position.

First, a key source of concern for ecologists is that trade externalizes environmental costs. The social and ecological impacts or costs associated with trade are not reflected in the price of goods. They are not, in the language of economists, 'internalized'. Instead they are passed on to the environment and society in the form of waste and pollution. Both the ecological costs of producing and transporting costs are rarely included in prices, hence the emphasis on ecological taxation as a means to internalize those costs. More fundamentally, however, critics point to the enormous environmental impact of trade which results from the intensive transportation of goods around the world over increasing distances. For example, it is estimated that one-tenth of world oil production is consumed by just moving goods around the world. In this reading potential efficiencies that might be produced by the liberalization of trade are offset by the net impact of increased trade on the environment. LeQuesne (1996: 73) cites the EC Task Force on the Single Market that concluded 'The favourable environmental effects of efficiency in the use of resources are likely to be outweighed by the growth in demand, with consequent increases in environmental pressures'.

Underpinning this concern is a broader questioning of the logic of comparative advantage from an ecological point of view. While economic orthodoxy dictates that producing a product from components sourced from all over the world to capitalize on the lowest possible costs and comparative economic advantages of countries makes perfect sense, ecologically it is a disaster. Critics suggest that the costs associated with the production across many sites are environmentally unacceptable. While economic logic dictates that transporting components across hundreds of miles, using extensive packaging and utilizing vast amounts of pesticides and preservatives in order to allow a product to endure large-scale transportation and enjoy a longer-shelf life are a price worth paying, ecologists insist that the same product can often be produced locally at greater benefit to the community and with much lower associated social and environmental costs.

Underpinning conventional economic assessments about the merits of free trade are certain assumptions about peoples' willingness to pay for environmental benefits and their willingness to accept environmental harm. This logic was exposed by former Chief Economist at the World Bank Lawrence Summers in a leaked internal memo in 1991 which he later dismissed as a joke to colleagues.

He claimed that 'the economic logic behind dumping a load of toxic waste in the lowest wage country is impeccable ... under-populated countries such as Africa are vastly under-polluted' (quoted in Elliott 1998: 46). Some economists have argued that allowing countries to achieve a comparative advantage through lower environmental standards is not necessarily a bad thing. Marc Williams quotes d'Arge and Kneese claiming that relocations to pollution havens 'are desirable from a global efficiency viewpoint, since comparative advantage and differences in preferences are reflected' (1994: 85).

A further implication of the rationale which underpins the theory of comparative advantage is an emphasis on specialization and export-oriented growth. Not only is this idea the driving ideology behind trade liberalization within the WTO, but also it is a key plank of the reforms required of developing countries by the World Bank and IMF. Alongside the concerns of social activists that this approach locks developing countries into inherently unfair and exploitative trade relations (Curtis 2001; LeQuesne 1996), Greens also raise objections to the environmental costs associated with resource-intensive export-led growth. Not only does processing goods for export require extra packaging, it also requires forms of production, in agriculture for example, which are polluting, damaging to health and use land so intensively that it often rapidly degrades (Madeley 2000). A food security perspective also suggests that being self-sufficient in foodstuffs and other goods is an essential part of sustainable livelihoods; protecting yourself from market and other forms of vulnerability and dependence. Diversifying what you produce spreads risk but goes against the logic of comparative advantage. A broader critique still is the idea that export-led growth is often at the expense of meeting basic needs. Cash crops are grown in countries where people are starving because they are said to generate more revenue, when it is argued that land could be better used to grow subsistence crops which the poor are more likely to benefit from directly. Icke argues

> the poorest countries in the world grow cash crops on land that could be growing food for their own people. That's why Ethiopia was still exporting food at the height of the famine ... in Ghana half their farming land is not growing food for the malnourished but cocoa for western chocolate bars ... 40 per cent of the food growing land in Senegal is growing peanuts for western margarine ... during the great drought in the Sahel the production of peanuts for export increased there while tens of thousands starved ... in Colombia where malnutrition is common, fertile land is used to grow cut flowers for the rich in the west. (1990: 63–4)

This perspective is, in part, informed by a broader Green critique of prevailing development paradigms which owes a lineage to the debates about the limits to growth derived from the Club of Rome report by that name published in the early 1970s. It also resonates, however, with more contemporary Green critiques of globalization and corresponding calls for 'localisation' and a reduction in the volume of international trade (Lang and Hines 1993). Lang and Hines call this the 'new protectionism' which attempts to re-legitimate active interventions in markets aimed at exercising social control over them (Lang and Hines 1993). Rather than being anti-capitalist per se, many Greens are in favour of forms of small-scale market activities, such as the increasingly popular LETs schemes (Local Exchange Trading Schemes) (Glover 1999). Self-sufficiency is seen to be important socially as well as ecologically, as it enhances peoples' control over their resources, closing the loop between the site of production and the site of consumption and reducing vulnerability to the whims and unpredictabilities of global markets; a form of disengagement from exploitative relations of exchange (Douthwaite 1996).

At a policy level, Greens are also concerned about the ways in which the use of policy instruments aimed at protecting the environment are increasingly undermined on the grounds that they are incompatible with trade rules and disciplines. Expressing this concern LeQuesne notes;

> current WTO rules provide an inadequate framework for sustainable development precisely because they do undermine governments' ability to legislate in favour of environmental sustainability ... current trade rules discourage governments from pursuing a strategy of internalising costs precisely because they prohibit governments from protecting their domestic industry from cheaper competition from countries who have not internalised costs to the same extent. (1996: 73–4)

In the past, for example, labelling schemes, bans, border taxes, subsidies and other trade restrictions have been used to explicitly discriminate between environmentally destructive and environmentally benign activities. While economists may approve of the use of carrots and sticks to create incentives and disincentives regarding behaviour towards the environment, they strongly disapprove of these forms of direct intervention in the market. As van Bergeijk argues (1991: 106) 'A solution on the basis of trade impediments will waste the potential contribution that international specialisation can make to global environmental efficiency ... liberalizing trade is probably a necessary (but not sufficient) condition for sustainable development' (ibid.: 109).

Most problematically for Greens is the fact that discrimination on grounds of production process is key, yet forbidden by trade rules as the dolphin–tuna and many subsequent cases have clearly demonstrated. This is the basis of their campaign for the incorporation of PPMs (Process and Production Methods) into trade rules. It is increasingly difficult to maintain a distinction between production processes and products in the light of increasing emphasis on life-cycle approaches, the popular use of eco-labelling and efforts to address the use of energy which are necessarily caused by the PPM and not the product. As LeQuesne notes (1996: 81) 'from an environmental point of view, there is no meaningful distinction to be drawn between environmental harm which is generated by a product, or the harm generated by its process and production methods'.

Some of the controversy has centred on the GATT panel's interpretation of 'like-products', which in a dispute between the United States and the European Union over whether vehicles with different fuel efficiency standards could be considered *not* to be like products, determined that factors relating to the manufacture of the product before its introduction into the market were irrelevant (Brack 1997). Writing in 1994, Lee describes the GATT's narrow recognition of the standards that apply to goods and services in trade and not the process by which goods and services are produced as a 'head-in-the-sand attitude that runs counter to the political reality that worldwide countries are moving to adopt product standards with related trade measures that affect both natural resources as well as manufactured goods' (Lee 1994: 322). *The Economist*, in slightly dramatic tones, adopts the opposing position that 'This distinction between products and processes may seem mere semantics; actually it is crucial if a liberal trading order is to be maintained. It is hard to see how GATT could sanction trade restrictions based on processes rather than products, without setting off a protectionist tide' (quoted in Lee 1994: 322).

A related concern in this regard is the use of trade-restricting measures in MEAs (Multilateral Environmental Agreements). Many such agreements, in different ways, employ restrictions on the trade in substances considered to be harmful to the environment. The Montreal Protocol on substances that deplete the ozone layer, for example, restricts the trade in CFCs to those that have signed up to the accord, thereby excluding non-parties from the trade in ozone depleting substances (ODS) and therefore violating the most-favoured nation principle (Brack 1996). The rationale behind this is to create positive incentives for countries to comply with the accord and reduce the potential for free riding by non-parties to the Protocol. The CITES (Convention on the International Trade in Endangered Species) agreement elaborates a list system which bans altogether the trade in certain endangered species of plants and animals and imposes restrictions on the trade in others, depending on the degree of perceived threat to their future. Similarly the Basel Convention on the trade in hazardous wastes outlaws certain forms of trade (Krueger 1999). The use of trade embargoes in these instruments violates WTO prohibitions against quantitative restrictions.

The CTE (Committee on Trade and Environment) of the WTO has identified 22 MEAs that require or cause governments to implement trade measures that may violate their WTO obligations, yet the use of TREMs (Trade-Related Environment Measures) in these MEAs has not been challenged to date (Morici 2002).[1] The 1996 Singapore Ministerial meeting endorsed the CTE finding that members may bring to the WTO disputes concerning MEA-related trade measures, but no conclusions have been reached on proposals to modify article XX of the GATT to incorporate MEAs explicitly (Williams 2001b). What is interesting is that their use in new legal instruments has been subject to significant contestation in ongoing negotiations, shaped by the need to anticipate and pre-empt conflicts with trade rules. The Cartagena Protocol on Biosafety provides a case in point in this regard (Newell and MacKenzie 2000). The preambular language to the Protocol reflects strong differences of opinion between the EU and US over what was known as the 'savings clause' determining the extent to which the provisions contained in the Protocol should be subordinate to the trade rules of the WTO. The result is a product of political compromise embodying the concern of the EU that the instrument should not be subordinate to trade disciplines and of the US that the Protocol should be consistent with WTO rules. Environmentalists resent, however, the way in which environmental agreements are assumed to be subservient to trade regimes. They feel that social and environmental protection should not be accorded less priority than the objective of trade liberalization. While some would like to see a general exception for environmental measures from WTO rules (Morici 2002), others endorse a more full frontal attack on the mentality of 'the market über alles' (Hines 1997: 5).

The lack of coherence at the international level on these issues is in many ways a product of the parallel and independent bodies of public international law that have emerged and the absence of a global forum to mediate the competing claims that each places on governments. Where the WTO has taken on the discourse of sustainable development it has done so for its own ends and consciously adopted a 'weak sustainability' agenda, rather than addressing many of the concerns that underpin the ecological view outlined above, with the preamble to the 1994 agreement calling for expanded production and trade in accordance with the objective of sustainable development.

GATT, WTO and the environment: the record to date

This section reviews some of the provisions within the trade agreements of the GATT and the WTO that impact on the environment, as well as some of the cases that have come before the dispute settlement panel of the WTO.

The word environment appears nowhere in the text of the GATT, though the term sustainable development is mentioned in the preamble to the agreement that brought the WTO into being. At the 2001 Ministerial meeting in Doha members of the WTO agreed to launch a new round of multilateral trade negotiations. The relationship between WTO rules and the trade obligations set out in international environmental agreements was included in the formal negotiating agenda and it was agreed that the Committee on Trade and Environment will continue its work on the broader effects of environmental measures on market access (Morici 2002). This is a significant move on from the conclusion of the Uruguay Round of the GATT where delegates failed to agree on the inclusion of the environment as a permanent feature of the trade agenda (Williams 2001a: 1). The CTE, initially established on a temporary basis, has been granted permanent status. Williams notes (2001b: 46), 'Although directed to explore whether modifications to the multilateral trading system were required, the CTE in fact restricted its recommendations to a number of technical issues relating to the impact of environmental policies on trade such as the creation of databases relating to trade–environment issues'. The CTE is mandated to take forward the work carried out by the former GATT Working Group on Environmental Measures and International Trade, created in 1971 but inactive until 1991 (Brack 1997).

There are in fact a number of provisions in the agreements of the WTO that can be used as a basis for validating actions in defence of the environment (see Box 6.1). GATT article XX provides exceptions for measures (b) 'necessary to protect human, animal or plant life or health' and (g) 'relating to the conservation of exhaustible resources ... made effective in conjunction with restrictions on domestic consumption and production'. Again emphasizing the distinction between product and process-based standards, dispute settlement panels have not permitted members to invoke exceptions for measures that regulate unincorporated PPMs to protect the environment (or other social policy objectives) (Lee 1994). Hence as Morici notes 'governments have been able to regulate how imports affect their domestic environment (e.g. emissions standards for cars) but not how imports are produced or how they may affect the environment beyond their jurisdiction' (2002: 4).

Box 6.1   WTO rules for environmental protection

Examples of provisions in the WTO agreements dealing with environmental issues include the following:

Rule of Exceptions (Article XX), which allows exceptions for measures 'necessary to protect human, animal or plant life or health', and 'relating to the conservation of exhaustible natural resources', if such measures are made effective in conjunction with restrictions on domestic production or consumption. The word 'environment' is not expressly found in Article XX, but the text has been interpreted as general environmental protection. However, 'measures must not constitute arbitrary or unjustifiable discrimination between countries where the same conditions prevail' nor be a 'disguised restriction to international trade'.

Technical Barriers to Trade (TBT) Agreement, which specifically covers environmental protection and recognizes the legitimacy of government policies to this end. Any tighter standards imposed in pursuance of this objective must be scientifically justified and necessary to achieve legitimate objectives. The Agreement provides that, in addition to the two conditions imposed by Article XX, environmental standards should not create unnecessary obstacles to trade, and countries can seek resolution of disputes that may arise.

The Sanitary and Phytosanitary Agreement negotiated in the Uruguay Round specifically mentions the environmental issue, in broadly the same terms as the TBT Agreement.

The Agreement on Subsidies and Countervailing Measures specifies that subsidies provided for the adaptation of existing facilities to new environmental requirements cannot be countervailed by a partner country. Subsidies are allowed for up to 20 per cent of firms' costs in adapting to new environmental laws.

The Agreement on Agriculture exempts payments made to farmers under government environmental or conservation programmes from the general requirement to reduce subsidies.

Intellectual property: governments can refuse to issue patents that threaten human, animal or plant life or health, or risk serious damage to the environment (TRIPS Article 27).

GATS Article 14: policies affecting trade in services for protecting human, animal or plant life or health are exempt from normal GATS disciplines under certain conditions.

Source: Adapted from Richardson (ud)

Trade and environment cases

Perhaps the most high-profile of the cases involving trade rules and environmental protection measures was that involving the United States and Mexico in a dispute over restrictions on the import of Mexican tuna on the grounds that it was caught with nets that were trapping dolphins. Under pressure from domestic environmental groups, in 1990 a US district court ordered the secretary of commerce to ban the import of canned, fresh and frozen tuna from Mexico, Venezuela and the Pacific Islands of Vanuatu because their methods of catching tuna violated the Marine Mammals Protection Act. As Vogel notes (1997: 108) 'For Mexico, the American tuna embargo was symptomatic of the efforts of developed nations to protect themselves from growing competition from third world countries'. The case marked the first time a GATT dispute panel had been requested to address the extra-jurisdictional scope of a national environmental regulation.

For many the outcome of the dolphin–tuna case confirmed the inevitable pro-trade bias of decisions taken within a trade body. The decision, made in 1991, was that the restriction of trade for protection of the environment outside a country's border contravened GATT rules and that production process standards are considered to be non-tariff barriers. The key issue is that while governments may impose regulations on imports comparable to those imposed on domestic goods regarding their physical characteristics and performance, they are not allowed to discriminate on the basis of how a product is produced if those methods have no effect on product characteristics or performance. In determining whether the US legislation was consistent with the exemption clause of Article XX, the panel concluded that this provision only applied to activities within the jurisdiction of the country adopting the measure and not to affect production and consumption outside that jurisdiction. US environmentalist Ralph Nader described the decision as a 'breathtaking attack on progress made in the last ten years' (quoted in Vogel 1997: 114).

A second case concerned a challenge by Venezuela and Brazil in 1996 to the implementation of the US Clean Air Act of 1990 which, they argued, discriminated against foreign refineries. The Dispute Panel ruled in favour of Venezuela and Mexico and the Appellate body confirmed this ruling. The decision served to entrench the view of environmentalists that the dispute settlement procedures in the world trading system were biased against environmental interests.

A third dispute arose from a challenge by India, Malaysia, Pakistan and Thailand to a US measure prohibiting the import of shrimp from countries that do not require the use of turtle exclusion devices on shrimp fishing nets in areas where sea turtles are found. Interestingly, the shrimp–turtle case established that, subject to certain conditions, a nation could take unilateral action to protect a resource in the global commons. The United States was permitted to embargo shrimp caught without sea turtle excluding devices. Despite disagreements of interpretation between the Dispute Panel and the Appellate body of the WTO, Morici claims the case 'represents a fundamental shift in how WTO jurisprudence may be expected to regard international environmental law and the impacts of environmental measures on trade' (2002: 4).

Relying on the language in the preamble to the agreement establishing the WTO, which recognizes sustainable development and incorporates into WTO jurisprudence provisions of international environmental law (such as the Rio declaration and Agenda 21), the Appellate body reasoned that members could invoke articles XX (b) or (g) (see above) to impose conditions on imports to accomplish environmental objectives both outside their jurisdiction and in the global commons. In this case support for this decision was found in the fact that through membership of CITES all parties to the dispute have adopted the policy that sea turtles should be protected; sea turtles are highly migratory; none of the parties may claim exclusive ownership of them and the United States has sought to negotiate agreements to protect sea turtles so the evidence against an instance of disguised protectionism was stronger (ibid.: 7). As Morici notes, through this decision, 'The Appellate body did not endorse unilateral action ... Rather, the decision opened the door to such measures when an international consensus has been achieved regarding a conservation goal, measures applied beyond national jurisdictions are necessary to accomplish these goals and the government taking action earnestly seeks an international agreement on these issues' (ibid.).

The standards debate

Partly as a result of the ad hoc case-by-case decision-making on these issues and a preference for commonly agreed standards rather than the unilateral use of environmental measures subject to political whim and protectionist abuse, there has developed a debate about the desirability of negotiating environmental standards within the WTO. For some such standards would provide important floors, if not ceilings, below which countries would not be expected to fall in the provision of basic standards of environmental protection. What many environmentalists are concerned to address, is the situation whereby countries seeking to advance environmental protection by internalizing environmental costs suffer a competitive disadvantage. To counter this and incentives that may exist to accelerate a race to the bottom in environmental standards, some have called for a floor of internationally agreed minimum environmental standards to which all countries must adhere; a minimum parity level for some of the most environmentally damaging production processes. The attraction of such an approach for some environmentalists is the use of the sanctioning mechanisms of the WTO to penalize those countries failing to meet their environmental obligations. This is also of course what concerns many developing countries that fear they would be the targets of such sanctions. It is worth noting, however, that many environmentalists are not demanding that the WTO set environmental standards. Instead they want to restrict the WTO's right to shape environmental policy at national level and in international environmental regimes.

Those opposed to having environmental standards within the WTO question the probable effectiveness of standards set by a body whose primary goal is the liberalization of trade and raise concerns about market access and the imposition of environmental conditionalities on trade measures, tying trade gains to environmental protection measures. Since the arrival of the WTO countries negotiating trade rounds have to accept all the terms of a round and not just pick and choose à la carte as they were able to do before (Jackson 1998). Therefore, in order to access trade gains that have been negotiated during a round they may also be forced to accept environmental commitments. Many are concerned about the potential of the trade–environment debate to re-ignite North–South divisions in the international trading system (Whalley 1996). Many developing countries argue that poverty is the cause of low standards among countries desperate to attract investors on terms that are not of their choosing and that access to Northern markets which has been denied to them is vital to raising environmental standards. At the same time environmentalists argue, the pursuit of trade expansion without environmental safeguards will only impoverish the resource-base upon which many developing countries depend for their wealth.

The debate that follows from this is over which institutional venue is the most appropriate for mediating these conflicts. LeQuesne suggests 'The setting of environmental standards should not be undertaken by the WTO itself, since it has neither mandate nor competence in this area, but by another mechanism or body with the appropriate expertise which would be transparent, democratic and accountable; possibly a body established under the auspices of the CSD or a new Intergovernmental Panel on Trade and Sustainable Development' (1996: 77). A combination of NGOs and developing country governments continue to oppose the idea that the WTO should set environmental standards. In so far as there is a need to strengthen the power of institutions dealing with environmental issues and to counter the power of the WTO, a disparate group of governments, academics and activists have begun to call for the creation of a World Environment Organisation. The prospects and limitations of such a venture are discussed briefly in the concluding section of the chapter.

Non-tariff barriers to trade

The uneven proliferation of health, safety and environmental regulations in recent years has created a further problem for the global trade regime in that unintended barriers to trade may be erected by requiring producers to meet different standards across jurisdictions. In this sense, as Lee notes, 'Environmental protection, therefore, constitutes an entirely new genre of non-tariff barriers that can eat away at the discipline of the GATT trading system' (1994: 323). To promote fair treatment between domestic and foreign producers and to both enhance transparency and reduce transaction costs, two agreements have been created. These are the Agreement on Sanitary and Phytosanitary Measures (SPS) and the Agreement on Technical Barriers to Trade (TBT) which require that measures adopted by states in these fields be based on 'sound science' risk assessments and are no more trade restrictive than necessary to accomplish their objectives. The issue of 'sound science' was key in the beef hormones case, when the WTO Appellate body found that the EU import ban on meat from hormone-treated cattle was inconsistent with SPS because proper risk assessment procedures had not been followed. The use of the precautionary principle in EU environmental law potentially runs counter to this, and the TBT could be used to challenge EU labelling rules for genetically modified foods. In 2003, the United States threatened to bring a case against the European Union before the WTO on the grounds that its *de facto* moratorium on the import of genetically modified organisms (GMOs) constituted an infringement of the European Union's obligations under the WTO. Often it is the case, however, that powerful states such as the United States use bilateral pressures to cajole countries into removing perceived trade barriers. Sri Lanka, Croatia and Bolivia are examples of countries whose regulations on GMOs have been targeted in this way.

The push towards the universalization and harmonization of rules relating to standard-setting in the areas of health and environment has had the effect of encouraging governments to employ standards created by international regulatory bodies such as the ISO (14001 for example) and the OECD (guidelines on risk assessment of GMOs for example) (Finger and Tamiotti 1999; Newell 2003). This approach is in many ways also consistent with principles enshrined in international environmental law such as the Rio declaration, principle 12 of which declares that 'Unilateral actions to deal with environmental challenges outside the jurisdiction of the importing country should be avoided. Environmental measures addressing transboundary or global environmental problems should, as far as possible, be based on international consensus'. Potential problems remain, however, in the adoption or recognition by public bodies of what are essentially private standards. Krut and Gleckman (1998) outline six areas of concern regarding the relationship between the ISO 14001 series and the TBT agreement of the WTO, for example. These include potential ambiguities in the scope of PPMs, differences in the treatment of developing countries and the reduced status of standards set by intergovernmental bodies. Fuelling environmentalist concerns about WTO rules constraining environmentally progressive governments, they note, 'standards set by international bodies are now ceilings which require a country to justify if its practices are more rigorous than an existing international standard. A country that may have higher standards is unlikely to prevail against a challenge on the grounds that the international ISO standard is too weak' (Krut and Gleckman 1998: 68). In so far as particular environmental management systems, as opposed to quantitative standards, will be preferred, it should be of concern that bodies such as the ISO poorly respond to the needs of SMEs (Small and Medium-Sized Enterprises) or regulators from the developing world that are under-represented in the body (Clapp 1998). The moves described here indicate the ISO's transition from a purely technical organisation to one 'at the forefront of world trade developments' (Krut and Gleckman 1998: 71), a transition that has simultaneously secured the political marginalization of standards set through intergovernmental processes.

Regional approaches to trade and environment

Despite attempts by the developing world to forge an agreed position on issues touching their common interests, such as broad opposition to the use of environmental standards by the WTO, they continue to express different preferences on how to handle the relationship between trade and environment in their regional trade arrangements.

The NAFTA agreement has perhaps generated the most interest because of its environmental clause and is the most high profile of the regional trade regimes because of the involvement of the United States and Canada. Critics envisaged a scenario in which 'increased trade would give way to greater movement of hazardous materials between the parties, that lower environmental standards in Mexico would attract polluting industries in the US and Canada towards Mexico and that harmonisation of standards would pull Canadian and US levels down to an inferior common denominator dictated by the less demanding nature of Mexican rules' (Schatan 2000: 167). The negotiations towards the agreement brought to the fore many of the conflicts and disagreements between trade advocates and ecologists described above. It also, however, produced some interesting new alliances between governments, unions, the business community and environmentalists. Audley (1997) and Hogenboom (1998) describe divisions within the environmental movement between those engaged in the process of trying to reconcile the trade provisions of the NAFTA accord with environmental imperatives, which included more conservative elements of the environmental movement such as Environmental Defense Fund, The National Audubon Society and Natural Resources Defense Council, and those opposed to the very basis of the agreement, such as Greenpeace, Friends of the Earth and the Sierra Club.

The NAFTA agreement did, however, include an environmental side agreement, one of the most sensitive issues in the NAFTA negotiations, aimed at countering the fears expressed by some environmentalists that pollution-intensive industries would relocate to the Maquiladora area on the Mexican side of the border. Indeed President Clinton made support for NAFTA conditional on the conclusion of an environmental side agreement.

The agreement is meant to ensure an upward harmonization of environmental standards so that a country can set the standard it considers most appropriate for achieving the level of protection it desires, even if these are stricter than those established internationally (Schatan 2000). Formally companies are also required to return production waste back to the country of origin but the NAFTA rule of national treatment meant companies could dispose of waste according to Mexican environment laws where there is concern that monitoring and enforcement is weak. In one survey more than a quarter of companies said stronger environmental provisions in the United States prompted them to relocate in Mexico (French 1993). According to Mexico's secretariat of Urban Planning and Ecology more than half the Macquiladora plants produce hazardous waste, and while waste is supposed to be transferred to the US 'compliance has been the exception rather than the rule' (LeQuesne 1996: 68).

Despite the fact that an environmental commission was established to provide periodic reporting on the state of the environment and the impact of the NAFTA agreement in particular, sanctions against persistent violators of legislation are seen as a last resort. Indeed at the end of 1995 the US Congress threatened to reject 'fast-track' authority for the incorporation of new countries into NAFTA unless sanctions were removed from the Side-Agreements. Instead the North American Commission for Environmental Cooperation is empowered to summon technical advisers, mediate and make recommendations to parties aimed at finding a mutually satisfactory solution to the dispute.

Where a party is not implementing its own environmental laws effectively it can be taken to dispute settlement through a complex process whereby the complainant (which can include communities threatened by a violation of environmental law) has to prove systematic non-implementation according to weakly defined criteria, after which the country is required to pay a fine where there is evidence of a 'persistent pattern of failure to effectively enforce its environmental law' (Article 22). Alongside this, however, is a provision which determines that standards can be challenged if it is felt that they negatively impact trade and do not employ recognized risk assessment and sound science criteria. Interestingly these provisions are more relaxed than those in the SPS agreement of the WTO. Finally, as a further sop to critics and to pacify concerns about the potential for environmental deregulation, there are guidelines for environmentally responsible business investment. Article 114 of the Environment Side Agreement (ESA) attempts to invalidate the relaxing of health, safety or environmental measures in order to attract investors and the NAFTA agreement also provides that international environmental agreements recognized by the three parties should take precedence over national rules. Where there is conflict between NAFTA and an MEA the latter prevails.

Limitations of environmental provisions within NAFTA from an environmental point of view include the fact that environmental concerns can only be raised with a party when a trade link exists; the scope of 'environmental' is restricted to traditional pollution control measures; the fact that lowering standards to attract foreign investment, though forbidden in the agreement, does not incur sanctions; key environmental principles such as polluter pays are not incorporated into the agreement and, like the WTO, standards cannot be process-based (Schatan 2000). Hogenboom (1998: 250) notes in this regard that 'the debate's narrow focus was partly caused by the strategy of the moderate wing of the US environmental movement in accepting the narrow environmental approach of the three governments and denouncing proposals by critical organizations for a North American development initiative which would comprehensively deal with environmental issues'.

By contrast, the debate on the relationship between trade liberalization and environmental protection within Mercosur in Latin America is less well advanced. The incorporation of environmental issues has been weak and sporadic at best (Onestini 1999). And while there is a technical sub-committee (REMA – Reunión Especializada de Medio Ambiente) which looks at non-tariff restrictions, international norms (ISO 14001), labelling (a possible Mercosur eco-label) and the provision of information about countries' environmental legislation and joint impact assessments, it focuses only on trade-related aspects of environmental policies. The aim has been to eliminate non-tariff barriers to trade applied for environmental reasons by harmonizing PPMs, expressed in the form of non-binding directives. A protocol to the Asunción Treaty establishing Mercsour is essentially an expanded re-articulation of these directives. In the case of ISO standards, the purpose has been to identify possible effects these might have on the international competitiveness of Mercosur products. There is no broader remit for its work, for example, with regard to the environmental impact of trade liberalization, and environmental standards are viewed as barriers to trade in potential conflict with the goals of trade liberalization that drive the Mercosur project. This may in part reflect that, as Tussie and Vásquez note, Mercosur's path 'is mainly drawn up by agreements between the government and the private sector with little input from other actors in the society' (2000: 188). It may also reflect the fact that none of the Mercosur countries has yet adopted domestic rules for industry location from an environmental policy perspective and common minimal environmental requirements may be difficult to develop given that attracting investment is the driving rationale for Mercosur. In addition, if the infrastructural developments proposed for the region in order to enhance integration are not managed responsibly, the environmental consequences could be devastating. For example, the Inter-American Development Bank has identified a mixture of transport, hydroelectric power projects and gas pipelines as essential foundations of an infrastructure for integration (Onestini 1999).

In many ways the environment remains a side issue in Mercosur despite early declarations professing a commitment to sustainable development and the desire to reconcile the goals of growth and efficiency with environmental protection. 'Piecemeal cooperation has developed on the definition of shared interests over jointly owned resources. The definition of a proactive agenda, however, is blurred' (Tussie and Vasquez 2000: 190). At best it should be regarded as a 'potential coordinating mechanism for environmental upgrading rather than as the up-grader itself' (ibid.: 202).

ASEAN provides a different context again. Within the ASEAN group there is an increasing acknowledgement that poor pollution control policies in one member country have negative spill-over effects for others in the region (Wiebe 2000). Wiebe suggests that the likely response to such problems will be 'coordinated independent action rather than cooperative joint action' (Wiebe 2000: 206) such as the bilateral memorandum of understanding governing the flow of hazardous waste between countries. But there is also a rising level of international pressure to address problems pertinent to the region such as logging but which carry global ramifications. This issue became manifest in a dispute over eco-labelling of tropical timber products between Austria and ASEAN over the former's law requiring all commercial tropical timber and products using that timber to carry a label. ASEAN members objected to the lack of consultation about the law and the way it discriminated only against tropical rather than temperate timber. Austria ultimately revoked the law and it has been replaced by a multilateral labelling scheme overseen by an advisory body consisting of representatives from other international environmental protection agencies (Wiebe 2000).

The preference among ASEAN members to date has been to deal with these issues in regional and international fora other than ASEAN. Importantly for ASEAN members this approach 'avoids the appearance of potentially divisive issues on the ASEAN agenda and allows the institution to retain a non-confrontation stance vis-à-vis the rest of the world' (Wiebe 2000). Actions that have been taken have focused on education and awareness-raising and problems of pressing relevance to the whole region such as urban air quality, though the body has also been reactive to events such as the forest fires that swept across Indonesia in 1994. In this latter regard while it has been difficult to create 'new regional mechanisms for responding to future problems' (ibid.: 213), several bilateral agreements were concluded and an ASEAN Cooperation Plan on Transboundary Pollution was created to try and anticipate and prevent future fires. The approach suggested by these events may shape the way in which ASEAN handles environmental problems in the future and it seems unlikely that ASEAN will produce side agreements to trade accords in the same vein as NAFTA because as Wiebe notes 'institutions for bilateral and multilateral enforcement simply do not exist in the region' (2000: 221).

The politics and processes of trade and environment

The Commission on Sustainable Development in a review of relationships between trade, environment and development found that 'there is considerable need for improvement in areas of transparency, openness and the active involvement of the public and experts in relation to its work on trade and environment' (CSD 1995). While there has been some progress in the level of cooperation between institutions active in this area, including the extension of observer status to a range of international bodies including the Commission on Sustainable Development (CSD), UNCTAD, UNEP and the World Bank, little progress has been made with regard to the involvement of NGOs (LeQuesne 1996).

Although the WTO's dispute settlement mechanism is more transparent than the GATT system it replaced and panel findings have been published more speedily than before (Brack 1997), it effectively remains closed to non-participants in the dispute. Although in the shrimp–turtle case the Appellate body allowed NGOs to submit amicus briefs to panels and appellate bodies, broader forms of participation from independent experts have not thus far been permitted. Moreover, panels and the appellate body continue to meet behind closed doors and submissions of parties are not automatically made available to non-participants (Williams 2001a). Williams notes elsewhere that while

> the earlier closure of the WTO process to non-corporate actors has been tempered ... the venue still privileges those who possess structural power, granting them superior instrumental access. While the WTO has progressively expanded access to non-governmental organisations, the fact that the organisation includes business groups in the NGO category reinforces the influence of the corporate sector in the policy process. (2001b: 46)

Without going into the intricacies of lobbying strategies at the national level and within the WTO, the work of writers such as Sell (1999, 2003) and May (Chapter 9 of this volume) suggests that business groups have played a key part in shaping and driving government positions on commercially sensitive agreements such as the TRIPs accord. Through these means according to Sell 'A small group of corporate executives of US-based multinational corporations succeed[ed] in making intellectual property policy for the rest of the world' (Sell 1999: 169).

Within the environmental movement, NGOs have adopted different positions on the best way of promoting environmental concerns within the WTO. For example, while Friends of the Earth have called for the closure of the CTE on the grounds that it has failed to promote sustainable development within the WTO, WWF, while critical, have called for the continuation of the Committee's work. Alongside this, the group has also established their own Expert Panel on Trade and Sustainable Development to generate policy recommendations to be circulated among WTO members (Williams 2001b). This difference in approach reflects a broader split within the environmental movement between those who view trade liberalization per se as antithetical to ecological sustainability and those who take the view that under certain conditions trade liberalization can contribute to sustainability. In a 1991 discussion paper on the GATT, for example, WWF claim that the agreement (GATT) 'does have the potential to promote sustainable management of the world's resources and protection of its fragile environment [but] to realize this potential, the narrow trade-focussed orientation of the agreement must be broadened to balance and integrate trade and environmental policy objectives' (1991: 4).

While debates about the democratic deficits associated with the way the WTO makes decisions have tended to focus on the exclusion of NGOs and Unions, fundamental questions remain about the capacity of many states to adequately represent their interests within the institution. Paradoxically this is despite the fact that developing countries outnumber their Northern counterparts by about four to one and have access to a one-country-one-vote system of representation (Das 2000). The discrepancy is explained by disparities in access, representation and capacity between developed and developing countries. There is a difference between 'equity in theory', whereby the WTO allows countries equal access and equal representation in decision-making, and 'equity in practice' where practices of exclusive 'green room' decision-making marginalize the input of many developing countries. Developing countries have repeatedly registered their dissatisfaction with the way in which the key elements of a proposed round are worked out in private between principally triad states and then developing countries are invited to sign up afterwards (TWN 2000).

This exclusionary practice, reflective of the power imbalances that exist within the organization is compounded by developing countries' lack of legal and technical expertise, which is increasingly crucial to tracking and shaping negotiations and outcomes within the WTO, particularly in areas of high science such as sanitary and phytosanitary measures which circumscribe action on health and environmental issues. Developing country delegations are also much more sparsely represented at WTO meetings than delegations from the United States and Europe, for example, that will often contain a spread of departmental interests, lawyers, experts and often representatives from the business community. The location of the WTO in Geneva further stretches the resources available to many poorer countries to attend meetings, leaving Northern countries better placed to influence the agenda. The fact that many meetings and rounds of discussions run in parallel underscores the importance of having a delegation of adequate size and capacity to be able to intervene effectively in debates. These issues remain a high priority for many developing countries and UN bodies such as UNCTAD have launched initiatives to strengthen their capacity to shape global decision-making.

Proposals for reform and future directions

The debates about the lack of scope to promote environmental measures within the framework of the WTO, concerns about negotiating environmental standards within the organization and the desire among many to see a strengthened global environmental architecture able to provide checks and balances on the extension of the WTO's authority into environmental policy areas, provide the context for contemporary debates about the desirability or otherwise of creating a World Environment Organisation.

The first thing to note is that there is a lack of consensus about the appropriate form or function of such an institution even where there is agreement on the need for institutional reform. Some impetus has come from the WTO itself. Renato Ruggerio, the former Director General of the WTO has endorsed the idea of creating a WEO on the grounds that environmental issues are more appropriately dealt with by an institution other than the WTO. For others the rationale is to see a centralization of resources and decision-making on environmental issues within one body with extended powers of oversight and sanction (Biermann 2001). The different versions of the organization that have been proposed in many ways reflect disagreement about what the problem is and therefore how likely it is that it would be addressed by a new body. For economists, the lack of progress in tackling environmental problems is due to a failure of internalization. The answer is therefore pricing mechanisms and explicit payment for environmental goods. These would have to be clearly defined by property rights and overseen by a global deal-brokering body managing the exchange of financial resources for environmental commitments (Whalley and Zissimos 2001). For others the problem is lack of coordination across regimes and the weakness of UNEP, though many resist the idea that centralizing decision-making within one body would improve the situation (von Moltke 2001).

Despite support for a WEO that has been expressed by the governments of France, Brazil and South Africa, as well as a range of academics (Biermann 2001; Whalley and Zisimos 2001), others remain sceptical about the ability of a WEO either to enhance the effectiveness of the existing system of environmental governance or to do anything to reconcile the trade regime with the effective use of trade-based policy interventions in MEAs (Newell 2001a; von Molkte 2001). In many ways, the debate about the desirability or otherwise of a WEO should be regarded as a distraction from the more pressing need to address, in the short term, the nature of the institutional arrangements that should mediate the relationship between trade liberalization and the environment, given that this would in any case be only one of the functions performed by a WEO. Neither does the current framing of this debate help to address the need to regulate the impacts of trade liberalization measures on the environment. Calls for social and environmental impact assessments of previous and proposed rounds of trade liberalization make clear that not everyone shares the WTO's view that the environmental impacts of trade are either neutral or insignificant. Nor does such an approach suggest ways in which possible conflicts between TREMs in MEAs and WTO disciplines can be pre-empted, managed and settled.

We clearly have some way to go in designing a workable architecture for mediating the relationship between trade liberalization and the environment, one that goes beyond the weak notions of sustainability employed by the WTO, but is sufficiently sensitive to the concerns of developing countries and smaller producers about the potential for trade restrictive environmental measures to be used discriminately and arbitrarily against them. The proliferation of private standard-setting bodies such as the ISO and the popularity amongst multinational firms in particular of certification regimes that certify responsible production practices add further to the institutional messiness that complicates the relationships between public and private bodies, international and national regulators. What is becoming clear is that future agreements on the environment and future rounds of trade liberalization will be more sensitive to potential conflicts with other institutions and policymaking processes than has previously been the case. This does not mean that the conflicts will become any easier to solve, especially in so far as the dialogue of the deaf between liberal trade advocates on the one hand and ecologists on the other, persists.

Note

1. Individual countries have contested particular provisions of MEAs however. Zimbabwe, for example, applied in 1997 for compensation in the WTO for loss of ivory markets when African elephants were listed as an endangered species by CITES.

References

Audley, J. (1997) 'Institutionalising environmental interests in NAFTA', in *Green Politics and Global Trade: NAFTA and the Future of Environmental Politics*, Washington DC: Georgetown University Press.

Bhagwati, J. (1993) The Case for Free Trade, *Scientific American*, 265(5), November.

Biermann, F. (2001) 'The Emerging Debate on the Need for a World Environment Organisation: A Commentary', *Global Environmental Politics*, 1, 1, February: 45–56.

Brack, D. (1996) *International Trade and the Montreal Protocol*, London: RIIA/Earthscan.

Brack, D. (1997) *Trade and Environment: An Update of the Issues*, RIIA Briefing Paper No. 35 February.

Clapp, J. (1998) 'The Privatisation of Global Environmental Governance: ISO 14001 and the Developing World', *Global Governance*, 4: 295–316.

Commission on Sustainable Development (1995) 'Trade, environment and sustainable development: Report of the General Secretary', 3rd session, 11–28 April 1995 (E/CN.17/1995/12), UN Economic and Social Council.

Curtis, M. (2001) *Trade for Life: Making Trade Work for Poor People*, London: Christian Aid.

Das, B. (2000) 'Why the WTO Decision-making System of "Consensus" Works Against the South', *Third World Resurgence*, Issue No. 108–109, January, Penang Malaysia: Third World Network.

Douthwaite, R. (1996) *Short Circuit: Strengthening Local Economies for Security in an Unstable World*, Devon: Green Books.

Elliott, L. (1998) *The Global Politics of the Environment*, Basingstoke: MacMillan.

Faber, G. (1996) 'International Trade and Environmental Policies', in Blowers, A. and Glasbergen, P. (eds) *Environmental Policy in an International Context* (Chapter 4), London: Arnold.

Finger, M. and Tamiotti, L. (1999) 'New Global Regulatory Mechanisms and the Environment: The emerging linkage between the WTO and the ISO', *IDS Bulletin*, 30, 3 July.

French, H. (1993) *Costly Trade-Offs: Reconciling Trade and Environment*, Worldwatch Paper 113, Washington, March.

Garcia-Johnson, R. (2000) *Exporting Environmentalism: U.S Chemical Corporations in Mexico and Brazil*, Cambridge MA: MIT Press.

Glover, D. (1999) 'Defending Communities: Local Exchange Trading Systems from an Environmental Perspective', *IDS Bulletin*, 30, 3 July: 75–81.

Greenpeace International (1997), *The Subsidy Scandal: The European Clash between Environmental Rhetoric and Public Spending*, Greenpeace International, http://www.greenpeace.org/~comms/97/climate/eusub.html.

Hines, C. (1997) 'Big Stick Politics', *The Guardian*, 8 October: 4–5.

Hogenboom, B. (1998) *Mexico and the NAFTA Environment Debate*, Utrecht: International Books.

Icke, D. (1990) *It Doesn't Have to be Like This: Green Politics Explained*, London: Green Print.

Jackson, J. (1998) *The World Trade Organisation: Constitution and Jurisprudence*, London: Pinter and RIIA.

Kabeer, N. (2000) *The Power to Choose*, London: Verso.

Krueger, J. (1999) *International Trade and the Basel Convention*, London: Earthscan/RIIA.

Krut, R. and Gleckman, H. (1998) *ISO 14001: A Missed Opportunity for Sustainable Global Industrial Development*, London: Earthscan.

Lang, T. and Hines, C. (1993) *The New Protectionism: Protecting the Future Against Free Trade*, London: Earthscan.

Lee, J. (1994) 'Process and Product: Making the Link between Trade and the Environment', *International Environmental Affairs*, 6, 4, Fall: 320–41.

LeQuesne, C. (1996) 'Profits and Pollution Havens' (Chapter 3), *Reforming World Trade: The Social and Environmental Priorities*, Oxford: Oxfam publishing.

Madeley, J. (2000) *Hungry for Trade: How the Poor Pay for Free Trade*, London: Zed Books.

Morici, P. (2002) 'Reconciling Trade and the Environment in the WTO', Economic Strategy Institute.

Newell, P. (2001a) 'New Environmental Architectures and the Search for Effectiveness', *Global Environmental Politics*, 1, 1, February: 35–45.

Newell, P. (2001b) 'Managing Multinationals: The Governance of Investment for the Environment', *Journal of International Development*, 13.

Newell, P. (2003) 'Globalisation and the Governance of Biotechnology', *Global Environmental Politics*, 3, 2 May: 56–72.

Newell, P. and MacKenzie, R. (2000) 'The 2000 Cartagena Protocol on Biosafety: Legal and Political Dimensions', *Global Environmental Change*, 10: 313–17.

Onestini, M. (1999) 'The Latin American Southern Common Market (MERCOSUR): Environment and Regionalisation', paper for CSGR conference on 'After the Global Crisis: What Next for Regionalism?, Warwick University, 16–18 September.

Richardson, J. (undated) 'Trade and Environmental Standards', in *Trade and Investment Background Briefing*, No. 8, Brighton: Institute of Development Studies.

Sáez, R. (2000) 'The Case of a Renewable Natural Resource: Timber Extraction and Trade', in Tussie, D. (ed.) *The Environment and International Trade Negotiations: Developing Country Stakes*, Basingstoke: MacMillan Press, pp. 13–33.

Schatan, C. (2000) 'Lessons from the Mexican Environmental Experience: First Results from NAFTA', in Tussie, D. (ed.) *The Environment and International Trade Negotiations: Developing Country Stakes*, Basingstoke: MacMillan Press, pp. 167–87.

Schmidheiny, S. (With the Business Council for Sustainable Development) (1992) 'The Business of Sustainable Development', in Schmidheiny, S. (ed.) *Changing Course: A Global Business Perspective on Development and the Environment*, Boston: MIT Press, pp. 1–13.

Sell, S.K. (1999) 'Multinational Corporations as Agents of Change: The Globalisation of Intellectual Property Rights', in Cutler, C., Haufler, V. and Porter, T. (eds) *Private Authority and International Affairs*, Albany: SUNY Press.

Sell, S.K. (2003) *Private Power, Public Law: The Globalization of Intellectual Property Rights*, Cambridge: Cambridge University Press.

Third World Network (2000) 'Transparency, Participation and Legitimacy of the WTO', *Third World Resurgence*, Issue No. 108–109, January, Penang Malaysia: Third World Network.

Tussie, D. and Vasquez, P. (2000) 'Regional Integration and Building Blocks: The Case of Mercosur', in Tussie, D. (ed.) *The Environment and International Trade Negotiations: Developing Country Stakes*, Basingstoke: MacMillan Press, pp. 187–205.

van Bergeijk, P. (1991) 'International Trade and the Environmental Challenge', *Journal of World Trade*, 25, 5 October: 37–55.

Vogel, D. (1997) *Trading Up: Consumer and Environmental Regulation in the Global Economy*, Cambridge MA: Harvard University Press, 2nd edition.

Von Molkte, K. (2001) 'The Organisation of the Impossible', *Global Environmental Politics*, 1, 1: 23–29.

Whalley, J. (1996) 'Trade and Environment beyond Singapore', Unpublished paper.

Whalley, J. and Zissimos, B. (2001) 'What Could a World Environment Organisation do?', *Global Environmental Politics*, 1, 1 February: 29–35.

Wiebe, F. (2000) 'Environmental Cooperation in ASEAN', in Tussie, D. (ed.) *The Environment and International Trade Negotiations: Developing Country Stakes*, Basingstoke: MacMillan Press, pp. 205–25.

Williams, M. (1994) 'International Trade and the Environment: Issues, perspectives and Challenges', *Environmental Politics*, 2, 4: 80–97.

Williams, M. (2001a) 'Trade and the Environment in the World Trading System: A Decade of Stalemate?', *Global Environmental Politics*, 1, 4, November: 1–10.

Williams, M. (2001b) 'In Search of Global Standards: The Political Economy of Trade and the Environment', in Stevis, D. and Assetto, V. (eds) *The International Political Economy of the Environment: Critical Perspectives*, Boulder Co: Lynne Rienner, pp. 39–63.

World Bank (1992) *World Development Report*, New York: Oxford University Press.

WWF (1991) *The General Agreement on Tariffs and Trade, Environmental Protection and Sustainable Development*, WWF Discussion Paper, November.

7

From Marrakech to Doha and Beyond: The Tortuous Progress of the Contemporary Trade and Labour Standards Debate

Nigel Haworth and Stephen Hughes

There is now an impasse in the contentious issue of a link between trade and labour standards. After a long controversy rooted in turn of the century trade concerns and evolving in the growth of intergovernmental organizations, contemporary debate has arrived at a stalemate over a social clause – that is, a sanctions-based clause attached to multilateral trade agreements requiring the recognition of defined labour rights. Attempts to anchor regulatory mechanisms within the World Trade Organisation (WTO) have been consistently, and effectively, resisted by the various WTO Ministerials that have taken place since the end of the Uruguay Round. A mix of developing country resistance, an increasingly complex trade agenda and contradictions in the support of industrialized economies has withered away the debate from the WTO agenda. However, there are more positive outcomes in relation to the international recognition of a set of core labour standards – those protecting freedom of association, collective bargaining, minimum age of employment, forced labour, discrimination and equal remuneration. The International Labour Organisation (ILO) has used the debate as an opportunity to emerge from its reluctant role in the geo-politics of the Cold War and position itself as the established model of social engagement in the system of global governance.

In this chapter we address the evolution of the debate over trade and labour standards by examining both the insitutional and analytical positions that have emerged since the conclusion of the GATT. We begin by briefly charting outcomes from successive post-Uruguay WTO Ministerials and their impact upon ILO activity. We follow this by offering a typology of the various analytical positions that have emerged in the course of the debate. Finally, drawing on these positions we identify and examine some of the political options the debate offers.

The social clause and the World Trade Organisation Ministerials

Singapore 1996

The WTO's Singapore Ministerial saw the developing world successfully block the establishment in the WTO of a social clause linking global trade arrangements with labour standards. The defeat of this linkage in Singapore signalled the fragility of the social clause push. The WTO supported the observance of core labour standards, but was not prepared to see observance backed by trade sanctions. The emerging consensus within WTO circles argued that labour standards were not part of the WTO remit, which was characterized narrowly in terms of trade issues. Some other location – the ILO, or a third location in which the WTO and the ILO might collaborate – was suggested as the appropriate location for the debate about international labour standards. The idea of a 'third location' echoed the commitment to the 'existing collaboration' between the WTO and ILO, made in the Singapore Declaration. It also allowed supporters of the labour standards push to hope that there would be further opportunity to engage with the WTO at a later date. Thus, whilst many thought the Singapore Ministerial had put paid to a trade–labour standards linkage involving the WTO, others felt that a small window of engagement remained open.

The Declaration represented a compromise squeezed from a conference, marked by high emotion and political intrigue, which brought into sharp relief international tensions underpinning the debate. The WTO Declaration committed WTO members to the observance of core labour standards without specifying how this commitment could be achieved. In consequence, it placed the issue firmly at the door of the ILO while indicating an end to the debate within the WTO itself.

Geneva 1998

The celebration of three years activity by the WTO was, on the surface at least, unlikely to offer significant opportunities for countries wishing to promote a trade–labour standards link. The widely held view was that the issue had been set aside in the Singapore meeting and that the Geneva Ministerial was primarily about confirming the WTO's single focus on trade issues and celebrating its successful formation. However, external factors came to bear on the WTO in unexpected fashion. The Asian crisis was in full swing, resulting in significant questioning of much received wisdom concerning economic openness. Moreover, the crisis had also shown that the implications of liberalization for social protection required major re-assessment. In particular, support for stable employment became a pressing issue. As the crisis threatened to spread into Russia and Latin America, social protection concerns were given added impetus. The WTO could not ignore this implicit challenge to a narrow 'technical' focus on trade liberalization. The legitimacy of liberalization became increasingly entangled with its wider social impacts and the need to provide adequate social protection. Civil society emphasized this relationship. Geneva saw an early case of civil mobilization against the WTO and globalization.

In terms of labour standards, the WTO reacted to these pressures by affirming the importance of core labour standards and accepting a US/EU proposal to convene a joint WTO–ILO forum. It is difficult to see these moves as anything other than placatory. Apart from a small group of countries with a hardcore commitment to a trade–labour standards link, the general view of WTO members was consistent with the Singapore outcomes. This view appeared to gain support from both the ILO and the wider UN process. Within the ILO, there was some concern that the ILO's traditional role might be compromised, even marginalized, by a serious uptake of the trade–labour standards question by the WTO. Thus, for some ILO staff, the WTO's wish to have little to do with labour standards guaranteed a continuing role for the ILO. Meanwhile, the UN's Global Compact initiative provided an alternative forum in which non-trade dimensions of economic liberalization could be raised, thus allowing the WTO graciously to cede responsibility for these issues to the UN and ILO and get on with its own technical trade work. Geneva, therefore, did not provide an opportunity for the trade–labour standards link to develop in the WTO. However, its relevance was reinforced in other contexts, suggesting that the WTO might expect the issue to arise in the future.

Seattle 2000

The Seattle Ministerial, a debacle for the WTO and the trade liberalization agenda, was notable for three key outcomes: massive civil mobilization against the WTO and globalization; the derailing of the WTO process as a result of developing country dissatisfaction and the United State's sustained voice on labour issues in the context of the US presidential elections. The United States and European Union continued their push from Geneva and argued for a joint working party between the WTO and the ILO on the trade–labour standards issue. In the context of developing country fury at the attempt by developed countries to impose trade outcomes, it is not surprising that developing countries' established opposition to a trade–labour standards link would be magnified. The US administration was accused of cynical support for the link as a way of winning protectionist sympathy amongst US voters, further exacerbating tensions in the meeting. More generally, positions on the link seemed to be defined along the divide between developed and developing countries. From a WTO perspective, the progress of the trade–labour standards discussion in WTO circles was set back considerably in Seattle. The diplomatic distancing of the WTO from locations in which the link might be discussed, a 'benign neglect' approach set in train in Singapore, was replaced by an angry 'in house' confrontation within the WTO meeting. Moreover, civil mobilization against the meeting gave high external prominence not only to the failure of the meeting in trade terms, but also the clash between developed and developing countries over labour standards.

Doha 2001

The Doha meeting sought to overcome a number of problems most notably the fissures that had emerged in dealing with an increasingly complex trade agenda and the growth in WTO membership. With these in mind, Doha was very carefully prepared to respond to developing country concerns that emerged in Seattle. Moreover, it also sought to address the WTO–civil society relationship by involving NGO participation, albeit in limited and strictly defined confines. Following the Seattle debacle and anxious to be seen responding to the 'new reality' of the trade agenda, the fresh cycle of trade negotiations was quickly christened 'The Doha Development Round'. Developing and transition economies now accounted for four-fifths of WTO membership. More significantly, this membership was increasing its participation in negotiation activities and with it challenging developed countries grip on WTO processes and outcomes that had been forged in earlier GATT rounds (see Chapter 1 by Wilkinson, this volume). Despite this, many developing countries questioned the value of a new trade round. Still struggling to implement a number of the agreements from the Uruguay Round, they were concerned that a new trade round would require more commitments and bring more problems over their implementation (Harbinson 2002).

Following Seattle, a chastened Mike Moore and the WTO staff worked hard to ensure that the Doha agenda acknowledged these concerns and remained focused on trade and access to developed countries markets undistracted by 'non-trade' issues such as labour standards. For many observers of the trade and labour standards debate then, it was no surprise when the Doha Declaration simply revisited ground originally covered in Singapore. It reaffirmed WTO member commitment to core labour standards but once again pointedly indicated the ILO's responsibility for labour standards. Whilst there is recognition that the issue will not disappear completely, WTO officials believe that any possibility of a trade–labour standards link within the multilateral agenda is ended.

The aftermath of Singapore in the ILO

The Singapore Ministerial, and the debate that followed in subsequent WTO ministerials discussed above, signalled a number of outcomes. First, for some, keeping labour standards off the WTO agenda represented a victory for developing countries, which construed proposals for a social clause as nothing less than disguised protectionism. Others however, construed support for the shift in institutional emphasis from the WTO to the ILO as part of a cynical containment strategy as developing countries later rejected proposals for strengthening ILO supervisory mechanisms (Lee 1997). Second, while the former ILO Director-General Michel Hansenne studiously avoided any reference to a social clause in his speeches and reports in the aftermath of the WTO Singapore Declaration, he was particularly energetic in promoting the ratification of core labour standards. In this respect, the ILO response has centred on two key mechanisms. The first concerns a campaign for the ratification of core standards. Each year since May 1995 a circular has been sent to those member states of the ILO who have yet to ratify the seven core standards requesting information on the obstacles to ratification. The campaign has been supplemented by the provision of technical assistance to help various countries overcome these obstacles. The second – complementary to the first – is the formulation and adoption of a 'solemn and binding' Declaration on Fundamental Principles and Rights at Work and its Follow-Up (1998) designed to emphasize the universalism of core standards, commit member countries to their recognition and stimulate the acceptance of a more proactive promotion mechanism additional to existing supervisory instruments. The Follow-Up is designed to compliment existing mechanisms for the monitoring of freedom of association and cover the remaining core standards related to non-discrimination and the abolition of child and forced labour. In essence, the Declaration remains rooted in the existing

Constitution of the ILO (Article 19(5)(e)) which requires member states to report on their law and practice in areas covered by ILO Conventions. For core standards the ILO requests reports to be submitted at more frequent intervals (every four years). However, the decision to ratify or not to ratify a convention remains the discretion of the country concerned. Notably, there is no reference to a link between core standards and multilateral trade.

Once the WTO finally rejected the inclusion of labour standards in its remit, the drive for a social clause, including a linkage between trade and labour standards, effectively died. It was left to the ILO to examine ways in which core labour standards could be recognized and applied, removed from the context of multilateral trade agreements. The wider political resistance to linking labour standards to trade and the divisions which have emerged over support for a social clause in the international union movement, lead us to conclude that the political context for linking labour standards to multilateral trade agreements no longer exists, if indeed it existed at all. Simultaneously, and in response to the political realities that now structure the debate, international labour has begun to channel its energies through more regional processes in an effort to mobilize support for the recognition and regulation of core labour standards. We now turn from the institutional developments surrounding the social clause to the underpinning analyses that informed discussion in the WTO and elsewhere.

Trade and labour standards: analytical approaches

The debate around trade and international labour standards has evolved into a number of well-defined positions. These we have classified as: Neo-liberal Critique; Institutional Corporatism; Labour Internationalism; Positive Sum Outcomes; Capital Logic Accounts.

Neo-liberal critique

The neo-liberal critique of international labour standards is in many ways the dominant analytical tradition in the field (Brown 2000). In recent years, as the prospect of a trade sanctions-based rights regime emerged around the Uruguay Round, neo-classical and neo-liberal economists have combined to launch a rigorous (and remarkably consistent) critique of such interventions (Bhagwati 1994, 1995, 1996, 2001; Srinivasan 1994, 1996, 1997, 1998). This critique has numerous elements which has informed much of the policy emanating from the established international financial architecture (Sengenberger 2002). This may be summarized as follows: the assertion of ambiguity about which labour standards should be enforced and at what levels; the argument that there are difficulties in universalizing labour standards, which even if achieved, may not respond to the neo-classical condition for such transnational intervention, that is, the existence of negative transnational externalities and the view that there exists a market-driven global diversity of labour standards and conditions which stands to be illegitimately and inefficiently ordered by the imposition of international labour standards. This is complemented by Field's view (1994), quoting approvingly Robert Reich and the ICFTU, that poverty in much of the world makes many proposed labour standards unachievable. Premature introduction of these standards, argues Fields, may preclude competitiveness in trade with adverse effects on labour. Fields also points to the difficulty of enforcing labour standards beyond the 'proper' limits of such enforcement, that is, national boundaries. Fields provides a detailed rationale for this conclusion – for example, unwarranted intrusions into nation states sovereign affairs, disguised protectionism, lack of effective enforcement mechanisms wherein even the ILO has avoided sanctions-based patrolling of its conventions.

Neo-liberals also focus on the possible adverse economic impacts of labour standards, including the impacts of a reduced supply of labour combined with increased production costs which may reduce an economy's total welfare. Conversely, argues Fields, encouragement of economic growth may produce circumstances where standards can be afforded and take on relevance. Fields presents the cases of Korea, Hong Kong, Taiwan and Singapore as examples where tremendous growth has created the circumstances in which real wages have risen dramatically in the context of growing labour scarcity, and a variety of social protections aimed particularly at people at the bottom end of the income distribution have been introduced. Neo-liberals also note that under certain conditions (particularly, the freedom of international income transfers), the achievement of Pareto efficiency with the socially desired labour standards requires free trade. In other words, labour standards imposed by means of trade-related sanctions are inefficient and welfare reducing.

These arguments are accompanied by a critique of the arguments for international labour standards. For example, neo-liberals suggest humanitarian arguments for labour standards are overstated. Furthermore, when accompanied by trade-related sanctions, they argue that such standards threaten free trade and consequently undermine welfare maximization whilst requiring someone other than the champion of labour standards to carry the costs of suboptimal efficiency. They support the view that the creation of a level playing field for workers in economies supposedly threatened by products from economies in which labour standards do not apply – avoiding the 'race to the bottom' – by means of the imposition of higher labour standards in the latter economies (or by means of explicit protectionism) is a flawed strategy. Neo-liberal analysis finds no evidence for the existence of a threat to jobs in the industrialized economies from developing economies and similarly denies that international investment decisions are generally driven by the search for lower labour standards. Rather, they suggest that technological differences and consequent productivity outcomes are far more apposite explanations of the emergence of low-paid work in the industrialised economies. From the other side of the equation, the imposition of higher standards on developing economies may well distort efficient modernization. Neo-liberals note that some agreement may be struck on the basis of a distinction between labour standards and rights. Perhaps all economies might agree on the undesirability of certain practices – slavery, indentured labour, child labour, unsafe working conditions – and the desirability of others – for example, freedom of association and the right to organize and bargain collectively.

Institutional regulation

A second analytical approach to international labour standards has an institutional basis in the ILO and the WTO. The ILO has been the international forum in which international labour standards have been defined since 1919 (Hughes 2002). Its tripartite structure is a tested mechanism for the creation of consensus around labour standards and its officials are in general terms wedded to the convention model of international standards. The intellectual basis for their support for labour standards is rooted in a combination of moral and humanitarian arguments and a classical adherence to pluralist bargaining traditions.

The outcome is a powerful technicist lobby within the ILO which finds itself in a contradictory position vis-à-vis a link between trade liberalization and the social clause. On the one hand, it is concerned that the ILO does not lose its pre-eminent position in the field of international labour standards. Such a concern emerged at the prospect that a trade sanctions-related standards regime might be built under the auspices of the WTO. On the other hand, it sees merit in the creation of a stronger international labour standards regime. The lobby is concerned that the haphazard ratification process and the difficulty of patrolling existing conventions may, in a period of deregulation which particularly affects bargaining regimes, weaken the impact of existing standards. They view this prospect against a background of budget threats in the ILO which further challenge its traditional role. As already noted, the emphasis on mechanisms such as the ratification of core standards and the introduction of a new Declaration form the main planks of the ILO response to the outcome of the WTO Singapore meeting in 1996. Thus, the energy and effort the ILO has invested in developing a strategy for core labour standards while avoiding explicit reference to a social clause has derived not only from the political sensitivities surrounding the issue but a recognition that the debate has had a significant bearing on the future of the ILO (Haworth and Hughes 1997).

For the WTO, the Singapore Declaration represents its considered (and final) position on the linkage between trade and labour standards. It prevents the incorporation of labour standards into the rules of the WTO and distances it from further work on the issue. Despite representations from some industrial powers such as the EU, the possibility of any significant change to the current WTO position remains remote (Wilkinson 2002).

Labour internationalism

The third analytical approach to international labour standards looks to their establishment as a combination of human rights concerns and responses to internationalization. Its chief protagonist is the international trade union movement, particularly the International Confederation of Free Trade Unions (ICFTU), and it is reflected in debates in numerous fora, including the ILO and the Organisation for Economic Co-operation and Development – the latter in the deliberations of the OECD's Trade Union Advisory Committee (TUAC).

The focus on labour standards by the international trade union movement is, of course, not new. Their role in the ILO's tripartism is well established as are other national and international campaigns around labour rights issue. However, since the 1980s, labour rights has taken on an added importance as unions came to recognize that internationalization of capital does not create in any automatic way conditions for the internationalization of labour's response. The strengthening of labour standards and their integration into a global trade regime offers to unions both organizational advantage (in terms of the extension of freedom of association and bargaining provisions) and a mechanism through which to address key human rights issues.

The ICFTU position in support of the social clause is based on three premises. First, as trade and productivity grows in previously poor economies, labour standards need to be in place which ensure wages and other conditions of work also rise as national conditions permit. Collective bargaining and freedom of association are the keys to this process. Second, a social clause would provide protection to vulnerable workers facing extreme working conditions. Third, adherence to core standards might prevent the most extreme forms of exploitation and cut-throat competition by focusing on productivity improvement and its consequences – growth of consumer markets, increased domestic and foreign investment and employment. Overall, a social clause would facilitate a smoother process of adjustment to changes in the global division of labour (ICFTU 1996).

In direct contrast to the neo-liberal model, the ICFTU sees in the social clause an anti-protectionist device which would strengthen the political authority of the WTO and thus the multilateral rule-driven framework for open world trade. It sees labour conditions as a potential source of conflict within the international trade regime and the probable source of future protectionist policies. The ICFTU also sees the social clause as a constraint on irresponsible Multinational Companies, thus promoting a more stable, and therefore more beneficial, international investment regime. In contradicting the neo-liberal account of labour standards, the ICFTU makes a case relating to the universality of standards. Mechanisms already exist for adapting ILO conventions to the particular conditions applying in a given economy. In other words, the issue of the universality of labour standards in circumstances where different levels of economic development have emerged has long been resolved. However, the ICFTU makes a strong case that cultural arguments for the non-application of standards are unacceptable, denying the arguments put forward by some leaders of developing economies (and some neo-liberals) that labour conditions are the sovereign concern of national regimes and may be determined solely by the economic development agendas of these economies.

Positive-sum outcomes

The ICFTU draws on a fourth analytical tradition confronting the issue of international labour standards. Most frequently associated with the work of Sengenberger, it seeks, in the words of the ICFTU, seeks to promote constructive rather than destructive competition by focusing on the positive impact on flexibility and growth of labour standards. It is a positive-sum argument – international labour standards will promote upward directed competition (a process whereby entrepreneurs are guided towards alternative products, new markets and better technology by the imposition of minimum standards) at the expense of downward directed labour market competition (an overemphasis on wage flexibility leading to low-wage strategies which eventually undermine competitiveness). Upward directed competition benefits both labour and capital (Sengenberger 1991).

The assumptions made in this analysis are important. Sengenberger assumes that the firm is committed to maintaining wages and other conditions whilst seeking to respond to changing market conditions. Furthermore, he argues that firms will recognize that the most effective way to respond to economic and technological change will be through negotiated cooperation. He also assumes that the firm will embrace collective (i.e., joint labour–capital) agreement as a basis for defining acceptable outcomes, thus positing a channelling of competition in socially desirable directions. Given these assumptions, he sees a clear positive interdependence between labour standards and flexibility emerging round three processes – participation, protection and promotion (the latter the mechanism whereby labour institutions promote positive development paths for the firm). He concludes from this model, 'Where labour organisations and labour market regulation have appeared to conflict with adjustment requirements or, more specifically, where labour market flexibility has been felt to be restricted by the existing labour code, this was not so much a function of the excessive development of labour institutions as of their insufficient development' (Sengenberger 1991: 238).

Sengenberger's argument – institutional and microeconomic – cuts at the heart of the neo-liberal model. It posits the need for institutional responses to imperfect market conditions – for example, imperfect information flows, labour market monopsony, imperfect signals about mechanisms for increased productivity and improvement of the human capital stock. Institutional cooperation between labour and capital creates conditions in which some of these imperfections may be nullified, to the mutual advantage of both parties. Also implicit in Sengenberger's argument, and a point made explicitly in the OECD Reports on Trade and Labour Standards (OECD 1996, 2000), is the suggestion that the collective interests of capital may require baseline core standards as protection against narrow, short-term and ultimately destructive views of education and training, up-skilling and the like held by advocates of downward-directed labour market competition.

Capital logic accounts

This argument is captured more explicitly in the fifth analytical tradition to be considered. We dub this the capital logic approach, as it seeks to explain the contemporary pressure for extended international labour standards in terms of the need to create the conditions of existence for capital accumulation on an international scale. The deliberations around protective legislation in nineteenth century England establish the nature of the debate. In the critique of humanitarian explanations for protective legislation, two alternative positions emerged. The first – broadly defined as a functionalist explanation – suggested that protective legislation emerged from the capitalist state responding to the need to discipline individual capitals which were unwilling to carry the long-term costs of reproduction of the labour force. In other words, the state created the conditions of existence for long-term accumulation over the protestations of particular firms and sectors manifesting a lack of long-term vision.

Critics of this functionalist explanation pointed out that protective legislation was a more complex enactment in which other social processes – gender, the family, independent working class organization – played a key role and in so doing, challenged the simple functionalist explanation. The contemporary debate around international labour standards has been drawn towards this discussion by Piore. He observes that '... the early labour standards can be thought of as both a substitute for capital insensitivity and a spur toward capital sensitive business strategies. The labour standards designed to foreclose sweating thus operated to promote economic development and industrialisation' (Piore 1994: 23).

Piore goes on to note the continued existence of sweating in the global economy but turns his attention to the contemporary choice facing the industrial world – between classic mass production and flexible production. A key element of this choice is the role of worker involvement. Flexible production – the desirable outcome – will require intensive consultation between labour and management, the point made also by the ICFTU and Sengenberger. A regime of international labour standards might, he argues, contribute to the environment in which sweating is marginalized internationally and flexible production is promoted.

The relationship drawn by Piore between the application of early labour standards and the contemporary debate on production possibilities merits further development. Extending his argument to encompass the debates around the nature of protective legislation, a complex picture emerges. For example, a functionalist account might argue that the extension of international labour standards is an essential, indeed, inevitable consequence of internationalization, not simply in terms of regulation of the international economic order, but also in terms of the broader conditions of existence of capital in an international environment. In other words, international labour standards may in the long term not be an option so much as a requirement.

However, drawing on the critique of functionalist accounts of protective legislation, were it to emerge as an internationally driven phenomenon, the complex process which would mark its enactment in each domestic economy should be noted. The capacity for protective legislation to mean different things to different sectors – large-scale capital versus SMEs, formal and informal sectors, children versus adults, women and men, unionized and non-unionized, rural versus urban and so on – would result in its enactment becoming the site of complex and often quite contradictory mobilization. By extension, therefore, Piore's comments take us substantially further down the track begun by the ICFTU and Sengenberger into the political economy of international labour standards and their political significance (a dimension studiously and, it may be assumed, quite deliberately avoided by neo-liberal commentaries).

The politics of labour standards

Drawing from these positions, the contemporary debate around international labour standards and trade may be reduced to two dominant strands. On the one hand, neo-liberal and neo-classical analyses are united in their distrust of the social clause. The most frequently cited commentators equate linkages between international labour standards and the WTO-patrolled trade regime with economic inefficiency, overt or covert protectionism and cultural insensitivity on the part of the industrialized economies. On the other hand, a common theme uniting the ICFTU, Sengenberger and Piore is the need to create an environment in which international economic integration takes place on the basis of high-wage, high-skill and advanced technological production. Far from seeing international labour standards as distortions of the pricing mechanism, this perspective believes that a standards regime will not only rectify some of the imperfections in market signals but will also establish higher and more effective levels of cooperation between labour and capital. This follows from the recognition that trade operates in imperfect markets. Neo-liberal and neo-classical thought assumes that markets will function efficiently if left to their own devices. Both Bhagwati and Srinivasan, for example, do not recognize imperfections in market transactions as a fundamental challenge to their view of the international trade regime.

The politics of international labour standards has been alluded to in relation to the complex outcomes of protective legislation. However, political mobilization around international labour standards confronts the theoretical and practical implications of the distinction made between rights and standards. We have described Field's argument that a distinction can be made between labour rights – relating to forms of forced labour, children's labour, health and safety, freedom of association and collective bargaining – and labour standards, which may be desirable but do not comprise universal rights basic to all people. This follows an established tradition within the ILO that puts conventions into three categories; those that protect basic human rights; those that underpin key aspects of social policy formation and those that establish basic labour standards. The emphasis on rights in the Declaration of Fundamental Principles and Rights at Work has particular relevance. Here the emphasis is 'rights at work' rather than 'worker rights', anchoring the protective coverage of the Declaration in rights that all people have by virtue of being human and not just workers (Bellace 2001). In this way, the 'rights at work' emphasis is given political credence by their establishment in other international instruments, most notable the United Nations Universal Declaration of Human Rights 1948.

These distinctions carry interesting political implications, especially for labour mobilization. In developing economies, for example, the distinction, if accepted in the first instance, permits the playing-off of rights against standards. A country establishing the rights may argue that they have fulfilled a reasonable commitment to universal values and can retreat into cultural relativism or level of economic development in relation to other standards. Such positions were deployed by a number of developing countries as the debate over linking labour standards to trade agreements took hold in the WTO and ILO. For labour mobilization the basic platform of rights may become the pinnacle of achievement particularly in countries where the State mobilizes to attract international capital via, among other things, the regulation of labour.

An alternative formulation might dispense with the notion of rights altogether on the basis that they may inhibit the achievement of wider standards. Rather, standards might be viewed as contingent and arbitrary, the outcome of some tripartite or consensual process of definition without reference to universal human rights. In this case, standards and their status might be left in the hands of agencies such as the ILO, much as is the case today. For the labour movement, however, this poses the interesting issue of where to focus energies. Where an agency such as the ILO exists and offers tripartite opportunity, the temptation to lodge resources and effort in such activities at the expense of political mobilization is great. Where also the experience of alternative modes of mobilization for international labour standards is not rewarding, the opportunities provided by such agencies become even more attractive.

A third approach to standards is that they are neither universal, as rights, nor consensual, as simple products of tripartism and legislation. Empirically, it is clear that, despite formal ratification, ILO conventions are flouted regularly as a broad agreement in a continuing emphasis on moral suasion re-establishes itself within the ILO (Weisband 2000). Reams of standards legislation do not obscure the failure to implement conventions in many economies. Furthermore, standards regimes can be seen as relative neither to levels of economic development nor to particular cultural traditions. In this approach, the standards and conditions applied to work are primarily the function of political mobilization – domestic and international – and the balance of forces between the mobilized, the employer and the state.

We make these distinctions in order to identify the political options that the international standards debate permits. For labour, the choice may be this – seek rights and accept that this may inhibit the implementation of other standards; remain in the tradition of consensual standards definition and accept that their implementation may well be partial or ineffective; build either of these alternatives on a base of independent political mobilization in which the goal is not defined by rights or conventions in a simple sense, but in the maximization of control over the circumstances and conditions of work. Such a view is ultimately at odds with the Positive-Sum and International Labour positions. Both, for different reasons, posit a positive-sum outcome from the implementation of international standards. They argue that reasonable employers and governments will recognize the advantages offered by upward-directed competition. Our third option views the world differently. It sees the international regulation of production by a standards regime as the site of a struggle for control. As the protective legislation debate shows, one set of outcomes may provide substantially improved conditions for profitable enterprise, possibly at the expense of labour; another might produce opportunities for labour-defined outcomes that re-order the priorities and nature of production.

On these terms, our third option extends labour's struggle to hitherto unorganized and largely unregulated areas of work in the informal sector. The mobilization of casual workers seeking protection within increasingly deregulated labour markets has led to new alliances among labour, women's groups and labour-oriented NGOs (Vosko 2002). Much of this has been advanced by the limitations of the international labour standards regime in protecting workers in the informal sector and the acknowledgement that 'rights at work' and the pursuit of social justice extend beyond established conceptions of work and employment. However, it also driven by a pragmatic recognition of a global decline in the power of organized labour and an expansion in the number of marginalized workers engaged in the informal sector. If, as we suggest, the standards regime provides a new frontier in labour's struggle with global capital then the nature and form of outcomes will be increasingly determined by the forging of new alliances that seek to extend the frontier beyond domestic boundries and into international institutions of regulation.

References

Bellace, J. (2001) 'The ILO Declaration of Fundamental Principles and Rights at Work', *The International Journal of Comparative Labour Law and Industrial Relations*, 17, 3.

Bhagwati, J. (1994) 'Policy Perspectives and Future Directions: A View from Academia', in Schoepfle, G. and Swinnerton, K. (eds) *International Labour Standards and Global Economic Integration*, Washington DC: Bureau of International Labor Affairs, US Department of Labor.

Bhagwati, J. (1995) 'Trade Liberalisation and "Fair Trade" Demands: Addressing the Environmental and Labour Standards Issues', *World Economy*, Vol. 18: 745–59, November.

Bhagwati, J. (1996) 'The Demands to Reduce Domestic Diversity Among Trading Nations', in Bhagwati, J. and Hudec, R. (eds) *Fair Trade and Harmonisation: Prerequisites for Free Trade?* (2 vols.) Cambridge, MA: MIT Press.

Bhagwati, J. (2001) 'After Seattle: Free Trade and the WTO', *International Affairs*, Vol. 77, 1: 15–29.

Brown, D. (2000) *International Trade and Core Labour Standards: A Survey of the Literature*, OECD Labour Market and Social Policy Occasional Papers, No 43, Paris: OECD.

Fields, G. (1994) *Trade and Labour Standards: A Review of Issues*, Paris: OECD.

Harbinson, S. (2002) *Lessons from the Launching of the Doha Round Negotiations*, Cordell Hull Institute Trade Policy Roundtable, 18 April.

Haworth, N. and Hughes, S. (1997) 'Trade and International Labour Standards: Issues and Debates over a Social Clause', *Journal of Industrial Relations*, 39, 2.

Hughes, S. (2002) 'Coming in from the Cold. The ILO, Tripartism and Global Governance', in Wilkinson, R. and Hughes, S. (eds) *Global Governance: Critical Perspectives*, London: Routledge.

Hughes, S. and Wilkinson, R. (1998) 'International Labour Standards and World Trade. No role for the World Trade Organisation?' *New Political Economy*, 3, 3.

ICFTU. (1996) 'Outcome of the WTO Ministerial Meeting Singapore'. Circular No 69, 20 December.

ILO. (1996) 'Employment. Combatting Unemployment and Exclusion: Issues and Policy'. Paper to the G7 Employment Conference, Lille, April.

Lee, E. (1997) 'Globalisation and Labour Standards: A Review of the Issues', *International Labour Review*, 136, 2, Summer, Geneva: ILO.

OECD. (1996) *Trade, Employment and Labour Standards: A Study of Core Workers' Rights and International Trade*, Paris: OECD.

OECD. (2000) *International Trade and Core Labour Standards*, Paris: OECD.

Piore, M. (1994) 'International Labor Standards and Business Strategies', in Schoepfle, G.K. and Swinnerton, K.A. (eds) *International Labour Standards and Global Economic Integration*, Washington DC: Bureau of International Labor Affairs, US Department of Labor.

Sengenberger, W. (1991) 'The Role of Labour Market Regulation in Industrial Restructuring', in Guy Standing, G. and Tokman, V. (eds) *Towards Social Adjustment. Labour Market Issues in Structural Adjustment*, Geneva: ILO.

Sengenberger, W. (2002) Economic Globalisation and Social Progress. What can be done to promote International Labour Standards? Geneva, January. Accessed at http://www.uta.fi/laitokset/sospol/opetus/kokemuksia/Sengenberger.

Srinivasan, T.N. (1994) 'International Labor Standards and International Trade: International Labor Standards Once Again!', in Swinnerton, K. and Schoepfle, G. (eds) *International Labor Standards and Global Economic Integration*: Proceedings of a Symposium. US Department of Labor, July.

Srinivasan, T.N. (1997) 'Trade and Human Rights', in Alan V., Deardorff, A.V. and Stern, R.M. (eds) *Representation of Constituent Interests in Design and Implementation of U.S. Trade Policies*, Ann Arbor: University of Michigan Press.

Srinivasan, T.N. (1998) *Developing Countries and the Multilateral Trading System: From the GATT to the Uruguay Round and the Future*, Boulder and Oxford: Harper Collins, Westview.

Srinivasan, T.N. (1996) 'International Trade and Labor Standards', in van Dyck, P. and Faber, G. (eds) *Challenges to the New World Trade Organization*, Amsterdam: Martinus Nijhoff/Kluwer.

Vosko, L. (2002) '"Decent Work". The Shifting Role of the ILO and the Struggle for Global Social Justice', *Global Social Policy*, 2, 1.

Weisband, E. (2000) 'Discursive Multilateralism: Global Benchmarks, Shame, and Learning in the ILO Labour Standards Monitoring Regime'. *International Studies Quarterly*, 44.

Wilkinson, R. (2002) 'Locked Out, Shut Down. Worker Rights and the World Trade Organisation'. Paper to the British Journal of Industrial Relations Conference 'Politics of Employment Relations', Windsor Great Park, September.

8
GATS and The Politics of 'Trade in Services'

Jarrod Wiener

Compared with the furore surrounding other aspects of the WTO in the media and among NGOs – especially calls for greater democracy in the organization, and the outcry over patents for pharmaceutical products – attention on the General Agreement on Trade in Services (GATS) has been comparatively low-key. This might owe to its name: it begins with 'General Agreement' and that might evoke images of the General Agreement on Tariffs and Trade (GATT) that for some 50 years was of interest mostly to trade lawyers, specialist lobbyists – and insomniacs. International negotiations on accounting and insurance simply do not stoke passions. Perhaps they should not. Perhaps free trade in services in principle is a quite legitimate complement to any economic system that seeks open commerce, and thus the issue of how to go about doing it is properly relegated to the technocrats of international relations.

There is a growing literature about the economic and welfare gains of liberalized services trade. However, the economic argument is not without difficulty, and perhaps the greatest difficulty, as with any mono-logic argument, is that it is self-encapsulated: there are equally persuasive criticisms on both political and normative grounds – to the extent the two meaningfully can be separated. As is the case with most debates in international political economy, the debate over liberalizing trade in services revolves around incommensurable definitions of 'welfare'.

While critics of the GATS have been low-key *in comparison* with other aspects of the WTO, this is by no means to say there is an absence of debate. Indeed, it appears to be gaining momentum – prompted in part from the WTO and OECD publishing papers in response to their critics (OECD 2001; WTO 2001), which appears only to have fuelled the debate (Sinclair and Greishaber-Otto 2002). The aim of this chapter is certainly not to settle the issue – it is a microcosm of all that is debated about 'globalization' more widely. However, this chapter does argue that if liberals are not to lose the argument, they must make their case by appealing to the *normative* defence of free markets. The difficulty with the liberal case in general is that it has been overtaken by the positivism of the dismal science, made all the more dismal by the fact that it is bureaucrats – in Geneva, Paris and elsewhere – who are making it. And, in doing so, their arguments about the benefits of trade in services appear to differ little from their traditional arguments about the economic and welfare gains from liberalizing trade in goods. Yet, as this chapter shows, the liberalization of trade in services by definition involves a much deeper degree of liberalization – among other things, adaptation of domestic policies, and liberalization of foreign direct investment – than simply border measures like tariffs and quotas, which are the traditional stuff of goods trade. While domestic policies are becoming internationalized important social issues are raised, and there is a *perception*, at least, that there remains little in the way of a protective bulkhead between international policy adaptation and domestic transformation. Yet, liberals continue to chant a litany of economic and welfare gains, as if standard arguments about the benefits of trade in goods will suffice. Throwing production function curves at social insecurities is unlikely to quell them.

In the context of the purposes of the present volume, this chapter details the contours of GATS. It begins with an examination of why the international liberalization of trade in services was deemed necessary, and illustrates alternative explanations of how 'trade in services' came onto the international trade agenda. Following that, the mechanisms of GATS are explained. That section shows how the GATS was a compromise – as are most international agreements – because of competing political and economic interests among the members themselves. Interestingly, the GATS is so much a compromise that little in it commits members to undertake liberalization measures that they wish not to take. If anything, some argue that it has not gone far enough (Footer 2002). The sectors covered to date, such as financial services and basic telecommunications, are not the kinds of sectors that inflame the passions of civil society. Indeed, the normative concerns over GATS and the further liberalization of services are highly irrational in that they are speculative and conjectural: they concern sectors – like education and health care – that *might* be covered by future agreements. Yet, it remains important for the liberal case to engage those concerns on their own terms: economists need to understand that politics is rarely rational.

Why include services in the trade agenda?

The genealogy of the idea that services *can* be traded internationally and therefore can be liberalized originates in the OECD in the early 1970s, at the behest of the United States (Drake and Nicolaïdis 1992). Prior to the activities of an 'epistemic community' concretizing the language and meaning of 'trade-in-services', a few economists spoke about 'invisibles', but with limited ideas about how these could be 'traded' (e.g., Griffiths 1975). Of course, it had long been realized that producer services, including transport, communications, finance, insurance and legal and accounting services, among a host of others, are all necessary institutions of a capitalist economy (Condliffe, 1951). However, the prevailing view was that the function of these services – in the literal sense of the term – is simply to 'service' the economy, and that services therefore are subordinate to production and trade of durable goods.

Certainly the classical liberal view, itself an intellectual product of industrial capitalism, is that 'the economy' is a national creature, and what happens in the space between states, the international economy, is primarily the trade in what those economies produce: goods. That thinking informed the creation of the GATT. The prevailing idea in the 1940s was that trade in goods would be the engine for economic growth, and especially for re-igniting economies recovering from the Second World War. The GATT therefore applied mainly to trade in industrial manufactures, though it is interesting to note that the failed project to create an International Trade Organization (ITO) was much broader in scope, and included competition and investment issues (Wilcox 1949; Wilkinson, Chapter 1, this volume). An important legacy of its failure was to reify liberal intellectual separations, most importantly between the international and the domestic – and ironically, this was reinforced by the Keynesian 'compromise of embedded liberalism' (Ruggie 1983) that sought to shelter national spaces of economic and social regulation from each other to preserve domestic governance autonomy.

It is not surprising, therefore, that when the United States introduced the idea of liberalizing services internationally in the Tokyo Round of the GATT (1973–79) this was met with both scepticism and confusion by most, and additionally with suspicion by some. There were several conceptual levels of confusion. One was very practical: how can services – invisible both to customs officials and in government accounting records – be counted, let alone traded? Other more cerebral sceptics had deeper philosophical constructs to overcome: not only the liberal legacy of separating goods from services, but the Keynesian legacy of separating domestic regulation from the international, with its important normative values. To liberalize a service can entail permitting a foreign supplier, such as a telecommunications operator or a financial services firm, to set up shop in the market to be serviced. This erases the traditional line that divides trade and foreign direct investment (FDI). And, the regulations that govern the service provider are traditionally conceived as purely domestic regulations, quite distinct from the border measures used to regulate trade, principally tariffs and quotas. Services regulations relate to domestic governance, and are executed by a range of government regulatory agencies, that is, telecommunications, financial services and so forth. Thus, international services liberalization leads to the internationalization of the state both to a greater degree, and to a greater extent. Yet to a Keynesian, or at least more *dirigiste* mindset of many European states at the time, the border serves a functional role as bulkhead separating, and sheltering, the domestic from the international. To overcome cerebral shock about trading services therefore meant overturning much of the traditional philosophy of the trade system itself.

It was not easy. Though the Tokyo Round was the first multilateral trade negotiation (MTN) to reach agreements in areas other than trade in industrial manufactures (c.f. Cline 1978; Krasner 1979), first real consideration of services in the trade forum came at the GATT Ministerial Meeting in 1982 when the then US Trade Representative (USTR) Bill Brock proposed the launching of a new MTN that would include services, among other 'new issues' such as trade-related investment measures (TRIMS) and trade-related aspects of intellectual property rights (TRIPS) (GATT 1982; *National Journal* 1982; *The Economist* 1982). That Ministerial failed to reach agreement for a number of reasons (Wiener 1995) among them the general perception, shared by developed and developing trade partners alike, that the US motives for negotiating services were suspect, and that there already existed forums with greater competence in the area, such as the OECD or UNCTAD.

There are a number of reasons why the United States wished to include services on the trade agenda, and all of them relate to different aspects of the failure of the Keynesian compromise. For purposes of exposition these can be separated according to both general motives for broadening the trade agenda in principle, and reasons specific to services, though in practice the separation is less meaningful. Each of these contains a domestic perspective and an international one.

The general reasons relate to system maintenance, and involve both a domestic public choice argument and the 'bicycle theory' of international institutional dynamics (Wiener 1996). The early 1980s were a time of considerable protectionist pressures in the states of the OECD, and in the United States in particular. As US trade deficits reached record levels, the number of protectionist lobbies seeking relief from Congress increased exponentially. Congress responded by passing increasingly protectionist legislation – including successive revisions strengthening the unilateral retaliation measures of Section 301 of the US Trade Acts – and Congress considered a number of other Bills that were even more protectionist (Bhagwati 1988, 1991). There were fears of a replay of the logrolling in Congress that had led to the 1930s Smoot-Hawley Act that had contributed in large part to the severity of the Great Depression. Mac Dessler and Mancur Olson eloquently explained the dilemma in public-choice terms: there was a lack of countervailing 'pro-export' lobbies in Congress (Dessler 1986; Olson 1965, 1982).

The domestic politics of international trade are such that success in achieving support for liberalization always depends on a careful balancing act of ensuring that more interests would benefit from a trade agreement than would lose from increased competition. The difficulty in the early 1980s was that the GATT had done its job exceedingly well: in its principal field of competence, industrial manufactures, tariffs had been cut from over 40 per cent in the 1940s to a low level of about 4 per cent on average after the implementation of the Tokyo Round agreements. Therefore, the many groups that *could* benefit from successive rounds of tariff liberalization were satisfied and had little compunction to do anything other than go about their business of making money. They certainly would have no incentive to run to their representatives proclaiming how happy they were. Yet, the losers – industries facing closure or painful restructuring as a result of foreign competition, and labour facing redundancy – combined to capture the ear of legislators.

Thus the public-choice explanation for the inclusion of new industries is that having satisfied its mandate, the trade system found itself a victim of its own success: the traditional pro-trade lobbies had been satisfied; all that was left were the protectionists. The choice of the words 'traditional pro-trade lobbies' here is quite deliberate, for this holds the reason why services industries 'needed' to be brought on board. Pro-trade interests to countervail the protectionist lobby had to be sought elsewhere – beyond the traditional mandate of GATT. Services in general, and financial services in particular, would be 'new' industries to the game of trade politics, and powerful forces indeed. The Reagan Administration wasted little time convening a special Advisory Group to the USTR, led by the chairman of American Express.

On this argument, these new industries 'needed' to be enfranchised because of the perceived desirability of maintaining the impetus of trade liberalization. This is explained by the well-rehearsed 'bicycle theory' of free trade: if the forward momentum of the project falters, the edifice falls down, risking a return to 1930s beggar-thy-neighbourism. Both the public-choice and bicycle theory explanations are the traditional stuff of the analysis of international trade politics, and rest on a normative foundation of some considerable conservatism: that systemic stability is valued because the alternatives are too horrible to contemplate, and preservation of the international trade regime is therefore a good thing. These traditional arguments are somewhat strained, however, since efforts to 'rescue' the system entail metamorphosing it into something quite different.

This argument is also the internationalist one: it focuses on the international regime consequences of domestic political configurations. That is, ensuring that the trade regime continues entails domestic adaptation, defined as the transfiguration of domestic trade politics. It also places agency in domestic governments, and makes success contingent on their adept leadership at structuring both the domestic and international agendas. The other set of arguments – those that are specific to including services on the trade agenda – reverse this logic. These arguments speak to the 'need' (again in inverted commas) for international institutions to keep pace with, and to reflect, domestic adaptation – and here domestic adaptation is defined as the economic transformation of industrialized states into post-industrial ones. Here, agency is the economy itself: it progresses relentlessly according to a logic of its own, and governments are relegated to a game of catch-up in adapting the mechanisms of domestic and international governance to it. This argument speaks to the more fundamental demise of the Keynesian compromise, since the economy that Keynes and fellow Bretton Woods architects had constructed had simply outlived the world it was created to serve.

Indeed, that the United States – and as Europe soon found, they as well – had these powerful service industry lobbies to enfranchise in the first place owes to the fact that the economy itself had undergone a considerable transformation. There are two aspects to this. The first is the putative growth of services in the domestic economy such that it came to account for the largest share of Gross Domestic Product (GDP) in all advanced industrial states, but the United States was the first to 'notice'. The second, related, aspect is the change in domestic governance of the economy that had taken place in the mid-to-late 1970s.

First, it had been estimated by the US General Accounting Office that a staggering 79 per cent of the US labour force was employed in service industries, and that services accounted for 60 per cent of US GDP (*National Journal* 1986a, b, 1990). According to the Office of the USTR, US trade in services accounted for $110 billion in foreign earnings in 1981. In that year, the US merchandise trade deficit was $27.8 billion, whereas there was a trade surplus in services of $38.9 billion (*New York Times* 1982). The growing importance of services to the status of a major force in the domestic economy therefore can explain why the

United States sought to create market access opportunities for it abroad. On purely economic terms, it is as understandable that the United States should seek to open foreign services markets in the 1980s as it is that it sought to build a regime for free trade in industrial manufactures in the 1940s.

Second, and related, the drive to include services in an international institution was driven by domestic regulatory reforms of service industries – particularly in the finance sector – that occurred as the result of liberalization following the reordering of the Bretton Woods financial agreements. The shift from sheltered and compartmentalized territories of finance bounded by the capital controls of the International Monetary Fund's (IMF) gold standard to a more classical system of free flowing private finance once the gold standard was abandoned between 1971 and 1976 is explained very well elsewhere (Cerny 1993; Helleiner 1995). A dramatic consequence of the change in the international ordering for finance was its transformation from a subordinate sector of the economy whose function during the era of the welfare state was to service trade, to a sector that not only became competitive internationally in its own right, but became one of the most important sectors of the economy (Strange 1986). This was accompanied by domestic deregulation of finance to permit greater international competition: the governance role of the state changed from the welfare state to what Phil Cerny called the 'competition state' (Cerny 1988). The domestic regulatory functions changed from public regulation to privatized regulations on financial services to ensure prudential regulation and safety and soundness (Wiener 1999).

One could argue with some considerable persuasiveness, therefore, that the drive to enhance market opportunities for service industries in general, and financial services in particular, owes the movement to an alternative form of economic governance, one that embedded the state more firmly into the global system. An international market-opening agreement would enhance market opportunities, encourage competition and all attendant efficiency gains promised by the neo-liberal agenda – and its international institutionalization would lock in domestic reform.

Of course, these alternative explanations are stylized for the purpose of exposition. Craig Murphy provides the balanced view that change in international economic institutions normally owes to 'the dialectic between capitalism and the alternative ways of organizing economic and political life' (Murphy 1994: 4). To believe otherwise is to accept some form of determinism of the alternative explanations presented here – either of interest group politics being animated by the puppet mastering of the government; or of domestic and international governance mechanisms being reconfigured by governments to follow slavishly structural changes of the economy. Indeed, Drake and Nicolaïdis identify a broad set of actors comprising the epistemic community that 'created' the issue of trade-in-services, including: '[t]rade officials seeking new turf and constituencies, politicians wanting to appear farsighted, industry analysis concerned with the operation consequences of competition, academics intrigued by the analytic challenges, [and] corporate lobbyists hoping to legitimate their private agendas' (Drake and Nicolaïdis 1992: 46). However, even that explanation, as the others, relegates ideologies of governance in the state–society complex to a subservient role as mechanisms of legitimation of other agency interests, not as the force driving the interests of agents. Nevertheless, it is within ideologies of governance that the normative justifications – the basis of legitimacy for the system – are found. The discussion will return to this issue, but it is necessary first to turn to an examination of how and why the issue of services finally was accepted onto the agenda, as the compromises that were made influenced directly its institutional structure.

Why GATS?

The explanation of how negotiators got from scepticism about services as an issue and hostility towards the US motives to an agreement is actually quite simple: it has to do with power and interest. The most important impediment was Europe, and to a lesser extent Japan. As Gilbert Winham aptly recognized, trade negotiations in the GATT always had been 'pyramidal' in structure, atop which are the bargains reached between the United States and European partners (Winham 1979). While civil society groups today criticize the 'Quad', neither the fact of great-power management of the trade system, nor its important functional mechanism in regime maintenance would come as any surprise to these groups had they taken an interest in trade issues prior to the establishment of WTO, or indeed if they were to read a little trade history. During the course of the pre-negotiations, Europe came to identify its own interests in liberalized services, which solidified the coextension of interests atop the 'pyramid' necessary for progress. Studies by the European Commission had shown that Europe as a whole had an equal and possibly larger services sector than the United States, and that many industries were very competitive. When the European Commission launched its agenda for 'Project 1992', it was mostly about liberalizing services within the Community, and an international agreement would complement domestic and regional reforms within Europe.

What remained as impediments were the developing countries. Indeed, negotiations at the San Rafael Hotel at Punta del Este in Uruguay in September 1986 that launched the Uruguay round MTN had to be extended from the 19 September to the 21 September, mainly due to a disagreement over services. Developing countries made a number of compelling arguments, but three in particular, and these were overcome through a mixture of compromise and coercion. The manner in which some of the issues were resolved influenced in some measure the final substance and institutional form of GATS.

The first issue was that GATS should be optional, not mandatory. This was the deal-clincher at Punta del Este. Brazil and India, as leaders of a developing country bloc known as the G77, insisted that the services negotiations be separate from the rest of the Uruguay round negotiations. The US and Europe agreed to the formula 'distinct but parallel' (Oxley 1990). Thus the Negotiating Group on Services (GNS) was placed formally outside of the GATT negotiations, though it would have to make progress in tandem with the other negotiating groups. That was meaningful at the time, but *only* at that time when the GATT was the only trade institution, that is, before consideration of an umbrella organization (originally the 'Multilateral Trade Organization', but later the WTO) under which would fall both the GATT and GATS, along with other agreements. In any case, the informal cross-issue linkages that emerged during the Uruguay Round negotiations *de facto* destroyed any practical significance to this separation. The clever move later to create the WTO in which to house the diverse agreements solidified the US insistence that the entire Uruguay Round was a 'single undertaking'. In consequence, members acceding to the WTO are required to adopt GATS along with the rest of the WTO agreements. However, as will be illustrated below, the way in which GATS operates means that members do not make commitments they wish not to make.

A second, substantive point made by developing countries was that the use of the word 'trade' to describe what could really be FDI for service industries was a thinly veiled attempt to permit northern multinational corporations (MNCs) to dominate their markets. They retorted that *their* most competitive 'services' export would be cheap labour – for instance, in construction – and in equity any services agreement should include the movement of workers. The final GATS agreement does include both the permanent establishment of service providers and the movement of temporary workers as two of four 'modes of delivery', as we will see. Hence, the principle of developing country workers having mobility was accepted, though in the context of developed states recognition that many of their own services – particularly professional services, such as legal, accounting, engineering, and so forth – also depend for their delivery on the temporary movement of natural persons. The final bargain was that each Member must schedule specifically not only which services it will liberalize in its national schedules, but also, crucially, through which modes of delivery. Thus, the liberalization of all modes of delivery is voluntary and subject to specific commitments. That concessions to developing country workers have not yet been forthcoming arguably is due to the fact that developing countries have not reciprocated sufficiently with commitments of their own (Srinivasan 1999).

The final objection, one could argue, is informed by quite deep philosophical arguments about development and the nature of the economy. Developing countries argued that competitiveness in services and finance could be reached only in stages of advanced capitalist development. That an economy progresses through stages of development – and that these can include ones dominated by agriculture, then industrialization, and finally to a service economy where finance dominates – is both crude and contentious, though the view has been elaborated (Gerschenkron 1962; Rostow 1960; Wallerstein 1974). What is interesting here is that it was developing countries themselves that were making it. From the logic of that argument, it follows that competitiveness in many if not most services is out of the reach of developing countries, for structural reasons – their ability to compete as equal partners is somewhere in the future, and in the meantime they should shelter their markets from more efficient foreign competition. Liberalization of trade in services *now* would not only result in those sectors of their economy being dominated by developed country MNCs, but more fundamentally, it would remove from their reach the last stages of economic development, and 'trap' them in a perpetual stage of agricultural and industrialized development – and even then, without many opportunities for export given developed country tariff structures.

Alternative understandings of development are perhaps no more persuasive than this one, but what the alternatives lacked in the force of intellect they made up in the force of the resources that backed them. The neo-liberal argument, in particular, was that developing countries' traditional approach to trade was very ill conceived, and crudely is as follows. The reason for developing countries' difficulties competing in international trade owe to the weaknesses of their domestic institutions. Yet, their position towards the GATT historically had been to seek greater concessions from developed country markets as a way of compensating for their perceived lack of market power against more established and efficient producers in the developed world. That strategy resulted among other things in developing countries obtaining 'Special and Differential' treatment of their exports. The effectiveness of that special treatment always has been questionable, and the principle itself quite strange: seeking special access to markets was to focus on the degree of openness of the barn door – exogenous conditions – without any regard to the anaemia of the horse trying to stumble through it – endogenous conditions. Trade in goods is not the beginning of an economy, but the endpoint. Liberalizing services is a precondition for competitive goods exports. Hence, competitiveness begins at home, and it depends on an appropriate – meaning, liberal – domestic regulatory and competitive framework. Thus a change in trade policy to a more 'enlightened' one could be achieved by liberalizing services trade: domestic competition among service providers creates greater efficiency in the economy, by decreasing transaction costs, which leads to more competitive exports. For instance, efficient transportation and communications infrastructures make transporting goods cheaper; and a competitive financial sector makes insurance cheaper, and access to varied, specialized, and efficient credit providers are crucial to underwrite the sale of goods.

Interestingly, these arguments were made before much of the empirical data from econometric studies that now exist was available, and it remains sketchy. Calculating precisely the efficiency gains of liberal services to an economy is difficult methodologically, because of the difficulty of holding other things constant (Melvin 1989; Hoekman and Primo Braga 1997). Nevertheless, studies have shown that the volume of a state's trade is correlated positively with the extent to which its services are liberalized, or 'tradable' (Djajic and Kierzkowski 1988; Harrington 1989). Liberalization creates efficient institutions. Thus, rationalization depends on an 'appropriate domestic regulatory framework' (Mattoo 2000: 472) that includes privatization, liberalization, non-discrimination, and transparency. Moreover, the same studies that show gains in trade from domestic services liberalization also highlight that foreign direct investment in service industries is more productive than domestic firms since the latter bring with them economies of scale and a wealth of experience (Mattoo 2000).

Thus, the neo-liberal argument was able to link intellectually domestic liberalization including liberalization of FDI to a traditional gains-from-trade argument. But that argument also had the force of money behind it. Many developing countries were grappling with a debt crisis throughout the 1980s, the resolution of which depended on funds from the IMF and the World Bank. These institutions did become involved, the *quid pro quo* being the acceptance by developing countries of a set of liberalizing restructuring measures ('conditionality') that included both open international trade policies *and* domestic privatization and liberalization – both of which would be served by accepting liberal trade in services.

This discussion provides a flavour of the ways in which the political economy arguments of 'linkage' were made: of linking the domestic and the international; of linking 'trade' to domestic liberalization reforms, and of both to FDI. The compromises to some of the arguments explain a few of the institutional features of the GATS – others of its institutional features are functional to the trade in services, while still others are compromises for different reasons. But what these arguments really point to is a growing conception of – or project to create, depending on one's point of view – an integrated 'global economy' as a system that incorporates in an undifferentiated way what had been held traditionally in the trade system – and in Keynesian and welfare-state ideas of economy more widely – to be discrete: the 'inside' of a state, and its 'outside'. Endogenous commercial policies and domestic configurations and exogenous factors meld into each other in one seamless enterprise: 'commerce'. The GATS is either informed by a burgeoning and highly sophisticated view that finally treats the international and domestic 'economy' as one and the same, and thus overcomes finally classical liberal binaries and intellectual limitations, or it is the beginning of a hegemonic ideological project of global proportions. It is probably both. In any case, the French name for the WTO as the *Organisation Mondiale du Commerce* – is thus much more appropriate than the English one that retains the word 'trade'.

What is GATS?

GATS is a compromise (see generally, Broadman 1994; Hoekman 1992). Stated simply, states do not have to liberalize any sectors that they chose not to, and if they choose to do so, they can determine the extent and mode of that liberalization by crafting stipulatively their national schedules, as well as to stipulate exemptions.

First, GATS differentiates according to 'General Obligations' (Part II of the Agreement) and 'Specific Obligations' (Part III), which itself is a compromise. General Obligations apply to all services, and include such things as Unconditional Most Favoured Nation (MFN), a commitment to transparency, and a set of disciplines. The GATS does not stipulate which services it covers. Rather, it states that 'trade in services is defined as a supply of a service' under four different modes of supply (GATS 1994: Article I: 2):

1 from the territory of one Member into the territory of any other Member;
2 in the territory of one Member to the service consumer of any other Member;
3 by a service supplier of one Member, through commercial presence in the territory of any other Member;
4 by a service supplier of one Member, through presence of natural persons of a Member in the territory of any other Member.

This is partly due to the fact that the mode for the 'trade' of a service is a function of the type of service. In Mode 1, the service itself crosses a border (that is, online distance education), or is embodied in goods that cross a border (that is, advertising in a publication). Mode 2 delivery occurs when consumers cross borders to enjoy a service (that is, tourism). Other services by nature require the provider to have a more permanent presence in the economy (Mode 3), referred to as 'establishment trade' (that is, hospitals and schools). Finally, Mode 4 recognizes that services can also be embodied in people (for example, engineers, lawyers, and accountants) who must cross borders to provide their services.

That services are not defined might be construed as being exceedingly broad, and indeed standard classification systems collate some 160 different kinds of services. This is broad, but it does not follow that states *must* liberalize all of their service sectors. This is because members undertake only to liberalize the services they stipulate in their national schedules, and also stipulate the modes of supply for those services, under Specific Obligations. This bifurcation between the General Obligations and Specific Obligations is partly functional, and partly normative.

It is functional for two reasons. First, not all states wish to liberalize trade in the same services, thus states 'opt in' to plurilateral – as opposed to multilateral – agreements in specific service sectors. Second, different services are regulated by different sets of rules; for instance, the market access restrictions that affect telecommunications are quite different from those relating to, say, financial services.

The normative reasons for carving out Specific Obligations relate to the sensitivity of domestic regulations, which are issue-specific. While trade negotiators approach a market access problem in terms of non-tariff barriers (NTBs), the line between a *bona fide* NTB (that is, a policy designed purposely to shelter a market) and a legitimate social policy is exceedingly difficult to establish, but it is even more difficult to establish as a general principle. While in finance regulations are designed to ensure safety and soundness of the system through minimum requirements for capital adequacy and protection for depositors, regulations on professional services might relate to public health and safety. Thus, these need to be considered in an issue-specific context.

Hence, it is necessary for both functional and normative reasons to establish an encompassing set of General Obligations and then to engage in issue-specific discussions on particular services. But there are compromises *within* both the General Obligations and the Specific Obligations. For instance, the GATS General Obligations of Unconditional MFN is defined in the traditional fashion to require members to accord to the services and service suppliers of any other WTO Member treatment that is no less favourable than it accords to any other. However, MFN applies unconditionally only to sectors that are stipulated in members schedules, and in stipulated modes of delivery. Moreover, members are free to restrict their obligations under this requirement (for a period of 10 years, as stipulated in the Annex on Article II Exemptions). In essence, Unconditional MFN in GATS means conditional MFN. Interestingly, in light of the developing country arguments made on the issue of FDI and mobility of natural persons – and shockingly to the European Union negotiators – this stipulation was at the insistence of the United States.

The reason is that the United States feared that if a state (namely, it) that had a relatively open domestic market enters into an agreement that includes a state whose market is relatively closed, it would be forced to give greater concessions than it receives. Thus, the ability to restrict MFN can serve as a functional tool to induce others to open their markets. However, it also can serve as a means to ensure fairness in treatment.

The Specific Obligations are another compromise. The GATS is comprised of sector-specific, plurilateral agreements, in which members make positive commitments. Agreements reached to date are in Financial Services (1996 and 1999) and Basic Telecommunications (1998). A 'positive list' approach to liberalization means a state specifies in its national schedule the sectors that it wishes to include, as opposed to a 'negative list' approach, which automatically includes all services *except* those that a state specifically excludes. This differs from other services agreements, such as the one in the North American Free Trade Agreement (NAFTA) that uses a negative list approach. It also deviates from the traditional GATT practice of a negative list approach to goods trade liberalization. Relatedly, that this creates a series of plurilateral agreements each with its own membership as well as with its own rules deviates from the traditional GATT practice of multilateralism.

Unlike the GATT, GATS is a continuous process of negotiation. It contains a 'built in agenda' that mandated negotiations to begin on 1 January 2000, irrespective of whether other negotiations would be launched at the Seattle Ministerial Meeting, which in the event failed to reach agreement. The services negotiations agreed principles of procedure, reached the end of the 'requests' phase on 30 June 2002, and the 'offer' stage is planned to conclude by the end of 2004. However, there is much other work of a technical nature that is ongoing, including further work on domestic regulations, subsidies, safeguards and government procurement. Arguably, the multilateral framework of the GATS is yet to be completed (for a comprehensive discussion, see Footer 2002).

In general, therefore, the GATS is a carefully crafted series of inter-locking compromises, and requires governments to do little beyond what they choose to do – however, the following section will subject this to closer scrutiny. One could reasonably argue that many of the potential criticisms – of states losing autonomy and economic self-determination – are misplaced. Indeed, the WTO Secretariat is at pains to point out at every opportunity that the WTO is a 'member-driven' organization. However, the GATS is not without critics. It is to these issues that the following section turns.

Normative issues

There are criticisms of the economic arguments themselves that underlay the GATS, but the majority of dissent comes from non-economic arguments that centre around the political and normative issues raised by the linkage of 'trade' policy to domestic policies.

As outlined above, the economic arguments about the 'necessity' for competitive producer services focus on their role in creating competitive exports, because domestic institutions become more efficient when exposed to competition. However, that privatization and liberalization of services *necessarily* leads to greater efficiency would not be an argument made forcefully by a commuter to London on the British rail system. On the other hand, governments continue to provide ammunition to the liberal argument by maintaining ailing public services that have *not* been privatized. For instance, liberals wonder how it is that the state-owned postal service in Britain has contrived only recently to realize that shedding a massive 30,000 jobs is necessary to ensure its solvency, and more to the point that it only now realized it is feasible (*The Guardian*, 21 June 2002). The point is this: it does not follow that liberalization *itself* causes either benefits or detriments. Government management of privatization and liberalization must be considered an important intervening variable.

In addition to the economic arguments of efficiency are those of welfare gains. A study by the World Bank concludes that developing countries can achieve additional income of US$6 trillion between 2005 and 2015 (World Bank 2001). This may or may not be accurate, and it is in any case conjectural, dependant not only on the commitments made in the current negotiations but on the manner in which the liberalization is managed. Moreover, revenue gains is not the same as welfare. Liberals argue that overall welfare will be increased by the liberalization of services in general, and that these global welfare gains are estimated at US$130 billion (Dee and Hanslow 2000). The central question is whether the traditional economic definition of 'welfare' is readily applicable to the issue of services. The classic definition of overall welfare gains is the amount of wealth generated in an economy such that the losers from liberalization can be compensated through assistance in reorienting in the economy while still maintaining that overall increase in wealth. The issue is whether economic 'wealth' is the only good that should be valued when considering services – or all services in a non-differentiated way – or whether unquantifiable non-economic values, social goods, are also to be valued.

Indeed, the logic that informs the liberal case itself might be suspect. The economic argument of efficiency and welfare gains is a structural one: it is assumed that there is a singular rationality to the market that operates according to exogenous principles – either one adapts to them and gains efficiency and welfare, or one does not. As such, it is a homogenizing rationale in an economic sense (that services are better if they are liberalized) and is quite distinct from, but carries with it, the issue of policy harmonization (i.e., that services should be provided in the same way). The counter argument does not accept that there is only one way to be efficient, and historicizes the market as a construct that is deeply embedded in social and cultural practices, and in the historical compromises made in the state–society nexus. To maintain legitimacy, therefore, the economy cannot be reduced to its economic fundamentals, for to do so abstracts it from its social context. Thus, international agreements to liberalize services that *of necessity* entail negotiation of domestic policies is seen by critics as more than simply an undemocratic exercise that happens in the far-flung reaches on Lake Geneva. It is nothing less than an assault on the social and cultural forces that lend legitimacy to the market – one that liberals repeatedly inflame by resorting to the efficiency argument in defending their cause. And it is perhaps understandable that fears – albeit yet unrealized – of GATS-mandated deterioration in a government's ability to provide essential public services, like education and health care, strike a raw nerve in an atmosphere in which neo-liberal agendas for privatization depend for their legitimacy on the support of those very commuters to London and elsewhere who endure daily the results of poorly managed privatization policies.

Negotiations aimed at market access for service industries necessarily involve domestic policies and regulations – or, as supporters of the WTO prefer to call them, policies that are 'ostensibly domestic' (Blackhurst 1997). On the other hand, as Dymond and Hart put it, '[t]he agendas on services ... are clearly not about trade liberalization. Rather, they are about the interface between the private economy and public regulation and the blurring of lines between the domestic and global economies' (Dymond and Hart 2000: 38). Locating the line that separates the 'ostensibly domestic' – those of little consequence if their national character is altered – from the 'purely domestic' – public services that are constitutive of the state–society nexus – is therefore the first issue. And, whether or not public services are excluded from the GATS is a matter for some considerable debate.

Formally, services provided by governments are exempt from the GATS. The agreement states that 'services includes any service in any sector except services supplied in the exercise of governmental authority' (Part I, Article I: 3b). Mike Moore, then Director-General of the WTO and Ambassador Alejandro Jara of Chile, Chairman of the Special Session of the WTO Services Council issued a statement rehearsing this stipulation (WTO 2002) – as if that would suffice to quell concern. It likely will not, because that Article is qualified: 'A service supplied in the exercise of governmental authority means any service which is supplied neither on a commercial basis, nor in competition with one or more service suppliers' (Part I, Article I: 3c). Thus, on a strict reading, to qualify as a sector outside the scope of GATS, a government service must be both free and managed wholly by the government. However, what is defined as 'free' and 'wholly managed by the government' both remain open to questions.

What is a 'free' service eventually might be clarified, because of the obligation to ensure transparency. Under GATS, members are required to ensure full transparency of their services regulations, *both* those that relate to specific services if they accede to a plurilateral agreement *and* those that are of general application (Article III). Effectively, this means that *all* domestic practices relating to services can potentially become subject to international scrutiny. To date, there have been very few issues raised in the WTO dispute settlement procedures relating to services policies for which specific commitments have not been made ('non-violation' complaints) (Zdouc 1999). However, it could be that in future governments will be required to ensure transparency in the ways in which they subsidize education, or health care.

What is meant by 'wholly managed by the government' is relatively straightforward, but what is unclear is how many such services are left, given that many are partly privatized to varying *degrees*. One example is health care. A WTO background paper put the issue in this way:

> The hospital sector in many countries ... is made up of government-owned and privately owned entities which both operate on a commercial basis, charging the patient or his insurance for the treatment provided. Supplementary subsidies may be granted for social, regional, and similar policy purposes. It seems unrealistic in such cases to argue for continued application of Article 1:3, and/or maintain that no competitive relationship exists between the two groups of suppliers of services. (Quoted in Price *et al.* 1999)

That a greater range of national policy in general now falls under international scrutiny is not misplaced (Wiener 2002), and in the specific domain of GATS it is possible that any government service that is *partly* privatized might become subject to international liberalization. The *domestic* neo-liberal agenda of privatization therefore could place all that is privatized or partly privatized onto the *international* agenda – and this is no less true of privatized services in the developed states than of IMF and World Bank-mandated privatization schemes in developing countries.

At issue is therefore not whether domestic policies are becoming internationalized; they are. It is whether the nationalist rejection of the phenomenon is misplaced that is a matter for debate. As explained above, the Keynesian legacy of economic governance is that deep normative value is attached to insulating states – as containers of differentiated domestic spaces of economic and social governance – from each other. This might be something of a peculiar perception of political cartography: that withdrawing tariffs and other economic border guards that stand at the 'edges' of a state's jurisdiction – the traditional means for regulating the cross-border flow of goods – is somehow less intrusive on sovereignty than negotiating other government policies that are perceived to be more 'deeply' ingrained into the state. Indeed, one might argue that the conceptual distinction between a 'domestic' regulation and an 'international' regulation has been just that – conceptual – rather than in any practical sense meaningful. After all, as noted above, the stillborn International Trade Organisation, included trade, development and employment in its remit, reflecting a mode of thinking about the economy that did not erect strict conceptual barriers between 'economy' and 'society'. Perhaps all the talk about 'spillovers' of the domestic into the international is simply a legacy of both classical liberal and Keynesian binary divisions. Perhaps the more enlightened view is that domestic and international regulations are constitutive of each other because they form part of an integrated global economy.

But perhaps there is something quite serious about which concern is most appropriate – and that is the continued ability of domestic societies to remain autonomous, to the extent that domestic autonomy serves the economic functional equivalent of established principles of self-determination in the states system. Autonomy and self-determination permit *difference*, based on non-economic values. Non-economic values can be quite inefficient. It is whether such non-economic values have any place in a hegemonic definition of the economy where the singular rational of efficiency prevails.

This issue touches on policy harmonization. Within the plurilateral agreements is a commitment to national treatment, defined in the traditional sense that a foreign service supplier must be treated no less favourably than a domestic provider of the same service. Importantly, this does not necessarily lead to harmonization of domestic practices – under the national treatment regime, a service provider that operates in a number of different jurisdictions can potentially be subject to as many different regulatory regimes. However, GATS can lead to harmonization of some domestic practices, as it is one mechanism through which to ensure that domestic regulations do not act as barriers to the free trade in services. The issue is this: a government should ensure that foreign professionals – accountants, lawyers and so forth – who operate in their market are trained or certified in the accountancy procedures and laws of that state so as to provide their services appropriately. However, governments should not use standards and certification as barriers that would frustrate the market access commitments they have made. Thus, the Council for Trade in Services has also drafted a set of 'Disciplines' – an interesting choice of term the use of which Michel Foucault certainly would agree – so that governments can balance market access with prudential concerns. This does not have to include harmonization of domestic legislation, which can be a particularly intrusive and homogenizing practice (Wiener 1999), though this has been the way in which accountant services have been organized (Chanda 2001); Mutual Recognition Agreements (MRAs) are another means through which to create disciplines. The point is that although national treatment is a principle that normally ensures national diversity, the creation of Disciplines might erode the substantive meaning of diversity. As Vincent Cable put it, 'convergence of standards makes cross-border business easier and products or services cheaper, while at the same time it erodes many of the things which make different societies distinctive' (Cable 1996: 238).

The same kind of argument can be made about the linkage of 'trade' to foreign direct investment. Foreign establishment is a crucial part of the international provision of services (Djajic and Kierzkowski 1988; Harrington 1989; Matoo 2000). The United Nations Conference on Trade and Development (UNCTAD) estimates that just over 50 per cent of the global stock of FDI is in service industries, the most important of which is finance (UNCTAD 2001). On one view, 'linkage has come to be protectionism through other means' (Srinivasan 1999). Indeed, it has been said that, 'the GATS contains the single largest number of investment-related provisions found in the Final Act of the Uruguay Round' (Sauvé 1994: 9. See also Brewer and Young 1998). GATS members must refrain from applying measures that might be considered trade-related-investment-measures (TRIMS) that would prejudice service providers, including quantitative restrictions on foreign capital, the number of providers of the same service, the number of people employed by the service, or the total value of transactions.

One criticism of this is that the GATS has managed to liberalize rules for FDI in a stealthy manner that avoids the conundrum over the failed OECD Multilateral

Agreement on Investment (MAI), the failure of which owed partly to outcries of international civil society. To critics, this smacks of democratic unaccountability. While that is hardly the case since democratic countries (as well as others) negotiated and ratified GATS, there is a case for highlighting a sleight of hand – indeed the arguments about democracy and the WTO are much more involved than can be detailed here (Howse 2002). That criticism is also the cosmopolitan-internationalist one that champions the cause of the underprivileged developing country against the market – and negotiating – power of the now much-disparaged 'Quad'. That is, a commitment to liberalize services is the Trojan horse for the global dominance of developed country multinational corporations (MNCs). This is an ancient – almost Mercantilist – criticism that liberal systems operate in the service of the large states and companies that are better able to take advantage of it (cf. Ruigrok 1991) and hence nothing peculiar to GATS, though the fact that the argument is made more forcefully by NGOs in developed countries than by the developed countries themselves is both peculiar and interesting. The WTO reports that in the current stage of GATS negotiations, 32 of the 55 governments that have tabled proposals are developing countries (wto.org). Indeed, it has been suggested that states might actually prefer establishment, since this locates the providers within the national law and makes them subject to the control of national authorities (Hoekman 1992: 714; Wiener 1999). Perhaps the real issue, again, that animates critics is that the boundary between 'inside' and 'outside' the state has become blurred.

Conclusion

Depending on one's point of view, the liberalization of international trade of services could be one of two things. It could be the greatest innovation in commercial regulation since the GATT, to be hailed for its technical eloquence and economic rationality, and credited with having modernized the international trade regime from a creature of mid twentieth century industrialism to a tool of twenty-first century global governance. On the other hand it could be a mistake on a colossal scale, and the comparatively low-key attention given to GATS to date could be nothing short of a ruthless complacency, one that international civil society is beginning to redress.

The debate revolves around easily identifiable issues – essentially the location of 'boundaries' in international political economy: the boundary between trade and FDI; expectations of the functional role of the national border as a boundary between a domestic policy and an international one; and the boundary of legitimacy between a welfare state and a competition state, revolving around which services can be privatized, liberalized and internationalized with little consequence to the legitimacy of the state, and which cannot.

What is less identifiable is how the incommensurable language of each side of the debate can be reconciled. At essence, the debate talks at cross purposes because of incommensurable definitions of 'welfare' – and as outlined earlier, this is not particular to trade in services but general to all that is debated about globalization more widely. The well-rehearsed argument about protecting non-market values is one that liberals always have had to contend with, yet they have not become much more adept at it than they were in the late 1800s. And the liberals are responsible for that. The essential cause of the incommensurable discourses is that liberalism depends on economists and bureaucrats to make its case. Economists frantically draw production functions to assuage the fears of those perceiving identity insecurity, and are staggered that their figures do not do the job. Rather, their strategy serves only to compound the problem by demonstrating to domestic societies that those at the helm of the domestic–international governance nexus do not speak their language. Possibly this is due to complacency: liberals depend on the marginalization of critics who founder in a retrenched position without the intellectual clout of a systematized counter-hegemonic ideology. Political economy does not help either: the mainstream depends on public choice and 'bicycle' theories to underscore the 'need' to widen and deepen the international trade discourse, and more sophisticated arguments adopt a structural view of progress of the economy to which mechanisms of global governance adapt. Determinism in either form hardly helps assuage concerns that are essentially normative and ethical.

The liberal argument has to return to its roots as a system of ethics to engage seriously the essential critiques of liberalism revolving around state–society legitimacy, cultural and identity security, and liberty. To do that they must disentangle the classical liberal confusions about the nature of the international economy as a space for the exchange of goods and its minimal relationship to the national one, while overcoming the Keynesian diktat that 'national means national'. Whereas wealth and welfare gains are important to the liberals, liberty is important to civil society – liberty defined as autonomy and difference in the face of perceived global homogenization to a singular rationality of economic efficiency. The liberal case needs a moral philosopher. Adam Smith was one, but he thought services too unimportant to consider. If the liberals do not want to lose their case, they have to invent what he might have said.

References

Bhagwati, J. (1988) *Protectionism*, London: MIT Press.

Bhagwati, J. (1991) *The World Trading System at Risk*, London: Harvester-Wheatsheaf.

Blackhurst, R. (1997) 'The WTO and the Global Economy', *World Economy*, 20, 5: pp. 527–44.

Brewer, T.L. and Young, S. (1998) 'Investment Measures at the WTO: The Architecture of Rules and the Settlement of Disputes', *Journal of International Economic Law*, 1, 3: pp. 457–70.

Broadman, H.G. (1994) 'GATS: The Uruguay Round Accord on International Trade and Investment in Services', *World Economy*, 17, 3: pp. 281–92.

Cable, V. (1996) 'The New Trade Agenda: Universal Rules and Cultural Diversity', *International Affairs*, 72, 2: pp. 227–46.

Cerny, P. (1988) *The Changing Architecture of Politics: Structure, Agency, and the Future of the State*, London: Sage.

Cerny, P., ed. (1993) *Finance and World Politics*, Aldershot: Edward Elgar.

Chanda, R. (2001) 'Movement of Natural Persons and the GATS', *The World Economy*, 24, 5: pp. 631–54.

Cline, W.R., Kawanabe, N., Kronsjö, T.O.M. and Williams, T. (1978) *Trade Negotiations in the Tokyo Round: A Quantitative Assessment*, Washington, DC: The Brookings Institution.

Condliffe, J. (1951) *The Commerce of Nations*, London: George Allen & Unwin Ltd.

Dee, P. and Hanslow, K. (2000) 'Multilateral Liberalisation of Services Trade', Productivity Commission Staff Research Paper, Ausinfo, Canberra. Available: http://www.cid.harvard.edu/cidtrade/issues/servicespaper.html

Dessler, I.M. (1986) *American Trade Politics: System Under Stress*, Washington, DC: Institute for International Economics, and New York: the Twentieth Century Fund.

Djajic, S. and Kierzkowski, H. (1988) 'Goods, Services and Trade', *Economica*, 56: pp. 83–95.

Drake, W.J. and Nicolaïdis, K. (1992) 'Ideas, Interests, and Institutionalization: "Trade in Services" and the Uruguay Round', *International Organization*, 46, 1: pp. 37–100.

Dymond, W.A. and Hart, M.M. (2000) 'Post-Modern Trade Policy: Reflections on the Challenges to Multilateral Trade Negotiations After Seattle', *Journal of World Trade*, 34, 3: pp. 21–38.

The Economist (1982) 'Protectionism Throws GATT's Free Trade Band out of Tune' (13 November), p. 83.

Footer, M.E. (2002) 'The General Agreement on Trade in Services: Taking Stock and Moving Forward', *Legal Issues of Economic Integration*, 29, 1: pp. 7–25.

GATT (1982) *GATT Activities in 1981*, Geneva, pp. 1–10.

General Agreement on Trade in Services (1994) *The Results of the Uruguay Round of Multilateral Trade Negotiations: The Legal Texts*, Geneva: GATT Secretariat. Available: http://www.wto.org

Gerschenkron, A. (1962) *Economic Backwardness in Historical Perspective*, Cambridge, MA: Harvard University Press.

Griffiths, B. (1975) *Invisible Barriers to Invisible Trade*, London: Macmillan for the Trade Policy Research Centre.

The Guardian, London (18 April 2002) 'A Privatiser's Hit List: European Commission Demands to Deregulate Services Spell Disaster for the Developing World'. Available: http://www.guardian.co.uk/Archive/

The Guardian, London (21 June 2002) 'PM Tries to Head Off Strike Threat'. Available: http://www.guardian.co.uk/Archive/

Harrington, J.W., Jr. (1989) 'Implications of the Canada-United States Free Trade Agreement For Regional Provision of Producer Services', *Economic Geography*, 65, 4: pp. 314–28.

Helleiner, E. (1995) 'Explaining the Globalization of Financial Markets: Bringing the State Back in', *Review of International Political Economy*, 2, 2.

Hoekman, B. (1992) Market Access Through Multilateral Agreement: From Goods to Services, *World Economy*, 15, 6: pp. 707–28.

Hoekman, B. and Primo Braga, C.A. (1997) 'Protection and Trade in Services: A Survey', *Open Economies Review*, 8, 3: pp. 285–308.

Howse, R. (2002) 'From Politics to Technocracy – and Back Again: The Fate of the Multilateral Trading Regime', *American Journal of International Law*, 96, 1: pp. 94–117.

Krasner, S.D. (1979) 'The Tokyo Round: Particularistic Interests and Prospects for Stability in the Global Trading System', *International Studies Quarterly*, 23, 4: pp. 491–531.

Mattoo, A. (2000) 'Developing Countries in the New Round of GATS Negotiations: Towards a pro-Active Role', *The World Economy*, 23, 4: pp. 471–89.

Melvin, J.R. (1989) 'Trade in Producer Services: A Heckscher-Ohlin Approach', *The Journal of Political Economy*, 97, 51: pp. 1180–96.

Murphy, C.N. (1994) *International Organization and Industrial Change: Global Governance Since 1850*, Cambridge: Polity Press.

National Journal (1982) 'Confrontation in Geneva' (4 December), p. 2080.

National Journal (1986a) 'Getting Services on the Agenda by Working the Washington Crowd', 30 August: pp. 2060–1.

National Journal (1986b) 'Services, Please', 6 December, p. 2967.

National Journal (1990) 'GATT Going', 12 May: pp. 1150–5.

New York Times (1982) 23 November: pp. D1 & D15.

Olson, M. (1965) *The Logic of Collective Action*, Harvard University Press.

Olson, M. (1982) *The Rise and Decline of Nations*, New Haven: Yale University Press.

Organization for Economic Cooperation and Development (2001) Working Party of the Trade Committee, *Open Services Markets Matter*, TD/TC/WP(2001)24/PART1/REV1.

Oxley, A. (1990) *The Challenge of Free Trade*, Harvester Wheatsheaf, London.

Price, D., Pollock, A.M. and Shaoul, J. (1999), 'How the World Trade Organisation is Shaping Domestic Policies on Health Care', *Lancet*, 354, 9190, 27 November: pp. 1889–992.

Rostow, W.W. (1960, 1991) *The Stages of Economic Growth: A Non-Communist Manifesto*, Cambridge: Cambridge University Press.

Ruggie, J.G. (1983) 'International Regimes, Transactions, and Change: Embedded Liberalism in the Postwar Economic Order', in Krasner, S.D. (ed.) *International Regimes*, Ithaca: Cornell University Press, pp. 195–232.

Ruigrok, W. (1991) 'Paradigm Crisis in International Trade Theory', *Journal of World Trade*, 25, 1.

Sauvé, P. (1994) 'A First Look at Investment in the Final Act of the Uruguay Round', *Journal of World Trade*, 28, 5: pp. 5–16.

Sinclair, S. and Greishaber-Otto, J. (2002) *Facing the Facts: A Guide to the GATS Debate*, Ottawa: Canadian Centre for Policy Alternatives.

Srinivasan, T.N. (1999) 'Developing Countries in the World Trading System: From GATT, 1949, to the Third Ministerial Meeting of WTO, 1999', *World Economy*, 22, 8: pp. 1047–64.

Strange, S. (1986) *Casino Capitalism*, London: Blackwell.

United Nations Conference on Trade and Development (2001) *World Investment Report 1999: Promoting Linkages*, Geneva: UNCTAD.

Wallerstein, I. (1974) *The Modern World System: Capitalist Agriculture and the Origins of the European World Economy in the Sixteenth Century*, New York: Academic Press.

Wiener, J. (1995) *Making Rules in the Uruguay Round of the GATT: A Study of International Leadership*, Aldershot: Dartmouth.

Wiener, J. (1996) 'Transatlantic Trade: Economic Security, Agriculture, and the Politics of Technology', in Wiener, J. (ed.) *The Transatlantic Relationship*, London: Macmillan: pp. 134–72.

Wiener, J. (1999) *Globalization and the Harmonization of Law*, London: Pinter.

Wiener, J. (2002) 'International Legal Harmonisation: Peace, Prosperity, and Democracy?', in Nagel, S. (ed.) *Multinational Policy Towards Peace, Prosperity, and Democracy*, Lanham, MD: Maryland Rowman Littlefield.

Wilcox, C. (1949) *A Charter for World Trade*, London: Macmillan.

Winham, G. (1979) 'Practitioners' Views of International Negotiation', *World Politics*, 32, 1: pp. 111–35.

World Bank (2001) *Global Economic Prospects for Developing Countries, 2001*, Washington, DC: World Bank.

World Trade Organization (2001) Trade in Services Secretariat, *GATS: Fact and Fiction*, Geneva. Available: http://www.wto.org

World Trade Organization (2002) 'Director-general of WTO and Chairman of WTO Services Negotiations Reject Misguided Claims that Public Services are Under Threat', WTO Press Release, Press/299, 28 June 2002. Available http://www.wto.org

Zdouc, W. (1999) 'WTO Dispute Settlement Practice Relating to the GATS', *Journal of International Economic Law*, 2, 2: pp. 295–346.

9

Intellectual Property Rights

Christopher May

Since 1995 intellectual property rights (IPRs) have been subject to the Trade Related Aspects of Intellectual Property Rights Agreement (TRIPs) which is overseen by the WTO) (see Chapter 1 by Wilkinson in this volume). While this agreement does not determine national legislation, for members of the WTO to be TRIPs-compliant their domestic law must support the protections and rights in the realm of intellectual property that are laid out in its 73 articles. The agreement covers not only general provisions and basic principles, but most importantly represents an agreement to uphold certain standards of protection for IPRs and to provide legal mechanisms for their enforcement. Furthermore, the robust dispute settlement mechanism, which is a central aspect of the WTO, now encompasses disputes about IPRs. Prior to 1995, while there were long-standing multilateral treaties in place regarding the international recognition and protection of IPRs (which were overseen by the World Intellectual Property Organization) these were regarded as essentially toothless in the face of widespread 'piracy' and disregard for the protection of non-nationals' intellectual property. Although there are still some members of the WTO who are in a transitional period, the TRIPs agreement establishes for the first time a potentially global settlement on the recognition and protection of IPRs.

Despite the frequent claim by policymakers and negotiators that the governance of the international trade in IPRs is a technical issue best left to the experts, the issues at the heart of the international recognition and enforcement of IPRs are profoundly political. The current global settlement, brokered during the Uruguay Round of trade talks (and still subject to continuing negotiations) is not a 'done deal' with only its implementation outstanding; rather it is the site of continuing and significant global contestation and political disagreement. To make this argument, I first briefly introduce IPRs and how their use is justified. I then lay out two short case studies to emphasize the political issue that is at the centre of any discussion of IPRs; the balance between private rights of 'ownership' and public rights of access to knowledge and information. This leads me to conclude that intellectual property remains not only contested but a subject central to any critical contemporary political economic analysis of global trade relations.

What is intellectual property?

When knowledge and/or information becomes subject to ownership, intellectual property rights express ownership's legal benefits: the ability to charge rent for use; to receive compensation for loss; and demand payment for transfer. Intellectual property rights are sub-divided into a number of groups, of which two generate most discussion: industrial intellectual property (patents) and literary or artistic intellectual property (copyrights). Conventionally the difference between patents and copyrights is presented as between a patent's protection of the idea itself, and copyright's protection of its expression. Laws of intellectual property attempt to support the rights of individuals over their creative endeavours, while at the same time recognizing that the extensive social benefits from the diffusion of innovation, in terms of economic and social advance, should be unlimited by cost. This important balance between private reward and public interest is at the heart of all intellectual property legislation and is expressed through time limits on IPRs. Unlike property rights in material things, IPRs are formally temporary: once their term has expired they return to the public realm where no price can be exacted.

For patents the knowledge which is to be registered and thus made property should be applicable in industry. To gain the rights attached to a grant of patent an idea must be:

- *new*, not already in the public domain or the subject of a previous patent;
- *non obvious*, it should not be common sense to any accomplished practitioner in the field who having been asked to solve a particular practical problem would see this solution immediately, it should not be self-evident using available skills or technologies and;
- *useful*, or *applicable in industry*, it must have a stated function, and could immediately be produced to fulfil this function.

Following the harmonization of national legislation across all members of the WTO through the TRIPs agreement, once these three conditions have been fulfilled then an idea can be patented within each member's territorial jurisdiction. The patent application (detailing the idea and all its relevant details or specification) is lodged at the national patent office (or with the European Patent Office). For an agreed fee national patent offices allow others access to the patent document, but perhaps more importantly the office supports legal action against unauthorized usage when infringement is reported. Essentially, patents are an institutionalized bargain between the state and the inventor: the state agrees to ensure the inventor is paid for his/her idea when others use it (for the term of the patent) while the inventor allows the state to lodge the idea in its public records, to ensure public dissemination of innovation.

Unlike patent, copyright is concerned with the form of knowledge and information that would normally be termed, 'literary and artistic works', and needs no formal initial registration. Among those forms of expression that are usually regarded as subject to copyright are: literary works (fiction and non-fiction); musical works (of all sorts); artistic works (of two *and* three dimensional form, and importantly, irrespective of content – from 'pure art' and advertising to amateur drawings and doodles); maps; technical drawings; photography; audio-visual works (including cinematic works, video and forms of multimedia); and audio recordings. However, the underlying ideas, the plot, the conjunction of colours, the musical key or chords, do not receive protection, only each specific creative expression attracts copyright.

Copyright is intended to ensure that creative expression should not be reproduced without the express permission of its author or producer. These rights can be legally transferred to another person or company who then exercises them in their own interest. In Anglo-Saxon countries (reflecting the common law tradition) these rights are limited to an economic right, where the creator (or copyright owner) is legally entitled to demand a share of earnings from the utilization or reproduction of the copyrighted work. In continental Europe (and in jurisdictions drawing from the Roman law tradition), there is an additional moral right not to have work tampered with or misrepresented. In all cases, failure to agree on terms prior to the act of reproduction or duplication may result in any income being awarded to the original copyright holder by the court if an infringement is deemed to have taken place. Unlike patents however, copyright resides in the work from the moment of creation; all that is required is for the creator to prove that any supposed infringement is a reproduction of the original work.

Trademarks are an important third form of IPRs. These distinguish the products of one company from another and can be made up of one or more distinctive words, letters, numbers, drawings or pictures, emblems or other graphic representations. Generally trademarks need to be registered to ensure the mark is not already in use. A particular trademark is unlikely to succeed in being registered if it is too similar to, or liable to cause confusion with, a trademark already registered by another company or if it is already in common use. Of all IPRs trademarks have perhaps the longest history, tracing their origins back to makers' marks on early pottery and before that to tribal animal branding. Foreshadowing contemporary problems by over two thousand years there is evidence of extensive piracy (or copying) of renowned makers' marks in the Roman Empire.[1] There are other sorts of intellectual property from process patents (which cover processes as opposed to actual machines) to geographical indicators (such as 'champagne' and 'Parma ham') but these share the key characteristics noted above; they construct a form of information or knowledge as ownable property.

The most important aspect of IPRs is their formal construction of scarcity where none necessarily exists. Knowledge and information, unlike material things, are not necessarily rivalrous, co-incident usage does not detract from utility. Take the example of a hammer (as material property); if I own a hammer and we would both like to use it simultaneously, our utility is compromised by sharing use. I cannot use the hammer while you are, you cannot while I am and our intended use is rival. Thus, for you to also use my hammer, either you have to accept a compromised utility (relying on my goodwill to allow you to use it when I am not) or you must also buy a hammer. The hammer is scarce. However, the idea of building something with hammer and nails is not scarce. If I instruct you in the art of simple construction, once that knowledge has been imparted, your use of that information has no effect on my own ability to use the knowledge at the same time, there is no compromise to my utility. We may be fighting over whose turn it is to use the hammer, but we do not have to argue over whose turn it is to use the idea of hammering a nail into a joint, our use of the idea of cabinet construction is non-rival. Ideas, knowledge and information are generally non-rivalrous.

To be sure, there are cases where knowledge may produce advantage for the holder (often called information asymmetries), by enabling a better price to be extracted, or by allowing a market advantage to be gained. Here information and knowledge *is* rivalrous, and wider availability of this knowledge would cause such advantage to evaporate. However, this is not necessarily of any wider social benefit: information asymmetries produce market choices that are not fully informed and which therefore can be inefficient, or even harmful. Thus, when information is 'naturally' rivalrous, the social good may be best served by ensuring that it is shared not hoarded. For instance, many problems for buyers in the second-hand car market could be ameliorated if all car dealers were required to reveal *all* they knew about the cars they were selling. This would likely reduce the price they could obtain for much of their stock, but would enhance the general satisfaction (and even safety) of second-hand car purchasers. Leaving aside this special case, generally speaking it is difficult to extract a price for the use of non-rival (knowledge) goods, so a legal form of scarcity (IPRs) is introduced to ensure a price can be obtained for use.

As this scarcity is far from natural or of self-evident benefit to all, significant time and effort is spent telling stories about intellectual property that are meant to justify its existence as a set of legal rights (May 2000: 22–9). These narratives revolve around three claims for the usefulness of making knowledge and information property. The first argument, frequently deployed in arguments about IPRs, is that effort deserves reward. This draws on a long line of political theory which sets out the idea that where man has improved nature he deserves to have propriety in the fruits of the effort that has been put in. This started as John Locke's argument about property rights in previously common land being awarded to the diligent cultivator, and has now become a more general argument that effort requires reward. In intellectual property this justification is expressed both as a reward and an incentive. Only by allowing innovators and creators ownership rights over their creations can we reward their efforts (and by doing so also encourage further effort). Thus the construction of scarcity serves the social need to encourage and reward effort and innovation. Second, IPRs also reflect the rights of individuals to own the products of their own efforts, in that these efforts reflect the expression of an individual's self-identity. Thus, individuals should be allowed to own intellectual property in the products of their mental activity, because it is *their* mental work that has produced that which might subsequently be made property. This argument is not as often utilized (although it is frequently alluded to in arguments about piracy), as it raises questions about the legitimacy of transferring ownership of IPRs to others.

The third narrative of intellectual property reflects the capitalist character of modern society. Here the argument is concerned with the benefits of introducing markets into any particular area of social existence. Markets, we are told promote efficiency of use, and therefore if we want to ensure that ideas and knowledge are used efficiently, for the maximum benefit of society, we need to introduce markets into the distribution of knowledge and ideas. This will ensure that those who value knowledge and information most highly will pay most for it (rewarding the innovators) and will be also forced by a competitive market to enhance their efficiency in using these knowledge resources. Here the imposition of scarcity promotes efficient use, because knowledge can be costly to produce, and the drive to enhance efficiency itself produces further surplus to spend on more knowledge. These three stories appear in various combinations and in various ways, but wherever IPRs are contested, disputed or merely discussed, these stories are (re)told and have become part of the 'commonsense' of treating knowledge as property.

However, what these stories hide and obscure is as important as what they reveal about why IPRs have become so important in contemporary global society. I have chosen two quite different case studies to demonstrate the politics of IPRs. Both reveal something about the general claims made by supporters of IPRs, as well as suggesting why there may be some problems with the real world balance between private rights and the public good in the international trading of intellectual property.

Public health, AIDS and 'Big Pharma'

Broadly speaking if property constructs scarcity and therefore requires a price to be paid for the use of information and knowledge resources, there will be a wealth effect on the patterns of use of this information or knowledge and the products derived from such use. Simply put: if something is relatively expensive, then poor people will find their use constricted by how much they can afford to purchase. One area where this is most evident is the use of AIDS-related drugs.[2] The yearly cost of keeping HIV + patients alive on the cocktail of drugs which are currently available in the developed countries is more than a thousand times the typical annual health expenditure per-capita of less developed countries (LDCs), many of whom under structural adjustment programmes (supported by both the World Bank and the International Monetary Fund) have seen health sector expenditure decline precipitously. Although estimates vary, sub-Saharan African states at the beginning of the new millennium are returning to foreign creditors (public and private) around four times the funds available for the health sector.

To ameliorate such problems, in recent years Ghana and Brazil have tried to import cheaper generic versions of the cocktail's component drugs manufactured by Indian companies. Indeed, despite a recent WTO ruling on India's transitional arrangements to full TRIPs compliance for pharmaceutical patents, which attempts to stem the flow of generic drugs, manufacturers are still active and export quite widely to LDCs. This reflects a long history of non-protection for foreign pharmaceutical patents in India, which has allowed a large generic manufacturing sector to develop since independence. This competition from generics has prompted some multinational pharmaceutical companies to offer discounts on their AIDS drug treatments (although large-scale importation remains beyond even Brazil which is relatively wealthy). The relative (non) availability of AIDS medicines in many LDCs also has been considered at some length during the discussions for the New Partnership for Africa's Development, leading GlaxoSmithKline to promise to 'relax' patents on some anti-retroviral treatments in the future.

However the use of generic substitutes for patented drugs also spurred legal action by the United States, on behalf of Merck and other companies, against Brazil at the WTO. The United States Trade Representative (USTR) argued that the production and use of generics was directly in contravention of the provisions of the TRIPs agreement, and there could be no justification for the appropriation of US companies (intellectual) property. To sidestep these companies' patents was theft, and the USTR vigorously protested that this helped no one. Despite being subsequently dropped due to political pressure, this action reveals much about the overall attitude of the office of the USTR: whatever the human costs IPRs must be upheld. However, this is not to say this was the position of all within the US government. In 1999, at hearings before a House subcommittee Congressman Henry Waxman suggested that the office of USTR treated the US pharmaceutical industry as a 'sister agency' (Bombach 2001: 281). This close connection between the government and a particular industrial sector somewhat undermines the office's claims for impartiality or independence on this issue. Although the USTR claims to be neutrally upholding the rule of law in their negotiations over drug patents, this close link suggests that arguments regarding continuing patent recognition might be given more weight than those regarding the likely benefits of relaxing (or even sidestepping) patent provisions for certain drugs.

While it is true that the TRIPs agreement, Under Article 8, does allow signatories to 'adopt measures necessary to protect public health', this is limited by the requirement that 'such measures are consistent with the provisions' of the agreement itself (TRIPs 1994, Section II A1C: 5). Usually patent law includes provisions for compulsory licence which allows a company to use (in this case) a drug compound developed and patented by another company, thereby infringing the latter's patent while only paying a small fee mandated by the government. Given patent law's traditional intent to balance private rewards with public benefits, compulsory licences in the past have been regarded as an action of last resort when companies holding important patents have either refused to produce (or licence) their innovative product, or have only made it available at such a high price that important social benefits of diffusion have been completely undermined. But even in extraordinary circumstances the assessment of the rights holder and the government may well diverge, and thus any award of compulsory licences is usually vigorously contested by the patent holder. Therefore, and reflecting much national legislation, TRIPs severely limits when such licences might be legitimately issued. After all, these licences wrest control of intellectual property from its owner, in direct tension with the avowed intent of IPR law. However, now that IPRs are effectively subject to a multilateral legal regime (with TRIPs' direct link to the WTO), the legal disputes that compulsory licences almost always prompt have moved from the domestic sphere to the global realm of international diplomacy.

While most of us might regard the AIDS crisis in Africa as clearly an exceptional public health emergency, this provision for compulsory licence in TRIPs until recently has been largely discounted, under pressure from the US government and specifically the USTR. Protecting the interests of their national companies, the USTR has argued that the continuing protection of the IPRs of the large pharmaceutical companies who produce many of the AIDS-related drugs used in treatments around the world is of paramount importance. Thus, for instance, despite its severe AIDS problem, Thailand not only acceded to the TRIPs agreement but specifically undertook not to implement Article 8 in regard of HIV/AIDS treatments. However, ignoring hostile interventions from the USTR, and responding to the continuing difficulty of obtaining sufficient AIDS-related (and other) drugs, the South African parliament passed the Medicines and Related Substances Control Amendment Act in November 1997 (Bombach 2001; Ostergard 1999).

The Act's two most controversial provisions, amending the 1965 Medicines Act, were measures to allow the substitution of generic drugs, and provide for the supply of cheaper alternative medicines in certain circumstances. Robert Ostergard points out that:

> Section 15(c) of the Bill gave the Health Minister extraordinary powers for increasing the conditions for the supply of affordable drugs, including abrogating patent rights to pharmaceuticals issued under South Africa's Patents Act of 1978, and the importation of identical pharmaceutical compounds from manufacturers other than the registered owner [of a specific patent]. (Ostergard 1999: 879)

Even before the bill was passed the American Ambassador had been instructed to make strong representations against these measures. While the South African parliament saw this as a public health issue, the American government, representing American pharmaceutical corporations regarded this as a clear case of expropriation of (intellectual) property. The choice faced by legislators and governments in both countries was clear if politically difficult to resolve: whose rights were to be protected, the owners of IPRs or those who could be saved by these drugs?

Given the provisions within the TRIPs agreement, if examined by the WTO's dispute settlement mechanism, it is likely that a panel would find in favour of compulsory licensing on the basis of a health emergency. AIDS is now the leading cause of death in Africa (fourth globally), with more than 20 per cent of the 15–49-year-old population HIV+ in the seven worst affected Southern African countries, rising to 36 per cent in Botswana (which has the highest rate of HIV prevalence in the world). This is leading to declining life expectancy in much of sub-Saharan Africa; in Botswana life expectancy has dropped from over 60 in 1980, to just above 40 now, in Mozambique it is already below 40. Around 28 million people are living with the virus in Africa, representing around three-quarters of all those infected. This makes a powerful public health case, despite the fact that

USTR Charlene Barshefsky in her communications with the South African government only ever discussed the IPR-related issue, scrupulously avoiding any mention of the underlying AIDS crisis which had prompted the government's action (Ostergard 1999: 880, 883).

Before the case could come before the WTO, the legislation needed to be challenged in its own jurisdiction. In March 2001 the South African government met a 39-company alliance in court to settle the legality of the amendment to the Medicines Act. After an adjournment for the companies to see documents filed by 'friends of the court' for the Government side, they withdrew their challenge. These documents revealed that the defence case was likely to be fought on the basis of the profits made on specific drugs relative to the costs of developing them. The alliance decided that whatever the costs in Africa this sort of information was unlikely to help their case at the global level. As *medicins sans frontieres* had already noted, combination cocktails are made up of drugs that were originally developed largely with the help of public funds in the United States (Boseley 2000). The case the companies were about to make was that without patent protection (and the inability to construct a scarcity of protected pharmaceuticals) there would be a dangerous decline in important medical research. However, the logic of this argument would have been seriously undermined by the revelation of the amount of public money received by these companies for conducting the research from which they were now profiting. Furthermore, estimates of the investment in the sector are often inflated by statistical sleight of hand, such as presuming all drugs developed involve no public funding for research (despite the fact that many do), and that the costs of investment should include the opportunity costs of not having invested in government bonds (which is hardly a legitimate inclusion for direct costs) (Mokhiber and Weissman 2002). Representatives of the companies decided their interests would not be served by having these issues discussed in court.

In a compromise deal, a joint working party was set up to re-examine the act. Nevertheless, South Africa's legal success prompted the Kenyan government to swiftly pass legislation that while formally complying with TRIPs explicitly laid out the terms by which the government could mobilize the agreement's public health provisions. This very public exploration of the balance of private rights to reward, and public welfare (the need to support the health of a country's population) has revealed the central problems with the uncritical acceptance of the expansion of an intellectual property dimension to the governance of international trade. The trade in patent-protected pharmaceuticals produces a potentially problematic privileging of the rights of large companies to continue to make a profit (and we should not forget that the industry is widely regarded as the most profitable in the world), against the rights of poor people to receive treatment for a fatal disease. However, an intra-TRIPs solution to this problem is starting to emerge with some form of compulsory licensing seen as a possible strategy for dealing with the widening epidemic in sub-Saharan Africa. But even utilizing the provisions of Article 8 (which form the basis of the Doha declaration on TRIPs and public health), many governments remain (rightly) cautious of the sorts of retaliation which could be mobilized through the WTO's dispute settlement mechanism if generic drugs from India and elsewhere are used to ameliorate the effects of the disease on their population.

Here Brazil led the world, being the first case related to AIDS patents to find its way to a WTO dispute settlement panel. However, before the case was formally heard by the panel the USTR withdrew the complaint halting any legal codification of Brazil's (successful) use of Article 8's provisions. Any formal precedent produced by this panel might have opened the floodgates to compulsory licensing by LDC members of the WTO suffering severe AIDS prevalence problems. Thus, rather than conceding a precedent, it is likely that the United States' government will for now prefer to tacitly accept infringements, while bringing political pressure to bear on governments to limit such 'theft'. This has already led to an expansion in the use of intellectual property clauses in bilateral trade agreements. These 'TRIPs-plus' provisions expand the protection of IPRs beyond those mandated by signatories of TRIPs, explicitly bypassing safeguards like Article 8. These agreements allow the USTR to use the very real need of many LDCs to secure entry to US markets for their exports to undermine the international agreements signed by the United States. Denying the explicit 'logic' of multilateralism that the US government publicly supports, and which is reflected in the WTO's constitution, the USTR uses selective market opening as a way to halt the use of agreed and ratified TRIPs provisions when they contradict the interests of US pharmaceutical companies. Thus, despite Brazil using its anti-patent stance to build one of the most successful responses to AIDS in the non-western world, an intra-TRIPs solution is firmly resisted by the US government and its developed country allies.

However, things are a little different when it is their own citizens under threat, as recent events revealed. Despite arguing for the sanctity of IPRs in the face of the AIDS crisis in Africa, when in November 2001 it seemed possible that the United States had been the target of a bio-terrorist attack using anthrax, suddenly compulsory licensing became a legitimate strategy in health emergencies. We should recall that five people died and a further 13 fell ill in this supposed terror action (which is not to devalue these deaths, only to note the comparison with the millions dying of AIDS). Nevertheless both the US and Canadian governments used the threat of compulsory licences to wring substantial discounts from Bayer for their anti-anthrax drug Cipro. *The Economist* was not the only newspaper to editorialize on this irony (*The Economist* 2001), but was perhaps most forthright in linking the situation to the then forthcoming multilateral trade negotiations. Conversely, Kavaljit Singh argues that what is really interesting here is that despite the threat, both governments quite swiftly backed down, suggesting that this was more posture than intended policy (Singh 2002). This suggests to Singh that both governments are so close to the big pharmaceutical companies that they are prepared to risk their own citizen's lives rather than resort to the compulsory licence of particular patented drugs, even in the face of a 'national emergency'.

The negotiations in Qatar (in the wake of September 11) were intended to initiate a new trade round (called by some a 'development round'). However, for many LDCs, the previous round, which had involved a substantial amount of horse trading to get the TRIPs agreement adopted (May 2000: chapter 3), had actually delivered very little. While the rich countries had been swift to demand implementation of TRIPs, other aspects of the deal relating to the opening of markets for LDC goods have been less than forthcoming. Indeed, as the continuing use of bilateral deals by the USTR to instigate an expansion of the TRIPs provisions indicates, the bargain struck over market opening has been systematically undermined in this area. In light of some obvious disquiet, and after considerable negotiation the Doha declaration on TRIPs and Public Health was agreed.

While hailed by some as proof that the WTO could respond to its poorer members perceived problems (for instance, Vandoren 2002), despite extensive and difficult negotiations the declaration only restated (in more lengthy terms) the provisions that were already included in Article 8 of TRIPs. Even with the declaration's contention that the signatories 'reaffirm the right of WTO Members to use, to the full, the provisions in the TRIPs agreement, which provide flexibility [to deal with health crises]' (quoted in Vandoren 2002: 13), a significant problem with the intra-TRIPs strategy remains. As Arvind Subramanian (2001) notes, while compulsory licensing can be enacted in the jurisdiction where the drugs are needed on the basis of national emergency, this will only be an effective method of reducing the price if the exporting country also enacts a temporary suspension of patent protection. But, unless the supplying country is also suffering similar problems, a compulsory licence is not mandated by the TRIPs agreement in such circumstances. This leaves the importing country dependent on generic suppliers outside the WTO-member countries; essentially the same legal position that they are currently in. While this is recognized in Article 6 of the declaration, all the article does is 'instruct the Council for TRIPs to find an expeditious solution to this problem and to report to the General Council before the end of 2002' (quoted in Vandoren 2002: 14). But this is the nub of the problem, and without action on this issue the declaration remains empty rhetoric.

Without domestic capacity, and reliant on international trade in pharmaceuticals, many developing countries with major AIDS problems are offered nothing directly helpful by the declaration. Those who do have domestic manufacturing ability are in the same position they were before the declaration. Where they have been encouraged to sign up to TRIPs-plus bilateral agreements, the declaration makes no difference. Where they have not, they still have to consider the possibility of the USTR discounting their health crises, as the office has done before, to bring economic pressures to bear on them. The key question is in essence a simple one: at what point do the rewards 'needed' by large pharmaceutical companies, justified on the basis of the narratives detailed above (most specifically in this case the 'reward for effort' story) no longer outweigh the social good of public health. At least part of the problem here is that the patent holders and the prospective users are only formally part of the same society. The social balance of private rewards and public good or benefit which IPRs construct has been promoted to the global level, while the notion of a global society (especially where the social costs of sub-Saharan incidence of AIDS is concerned) remains much less developed.

Piracy, the Internet and the end of the global music industry

In this section I turn to a more trivial issue (at least in respect of the life and death issues of the previous section), but one which is perhaps more familiar. There is probably no industry more reliant on IPRs than the music industry, and therefore it is unsurprising that much of the popular rhetoric about copyright 'piracy' and 'theft' is related to the copying and reproduction of music. This focus on rights is not a new development; as Simon Frith pointed out fifteen years ago, the recent history of the music industry has been a reorientation towards the notion of rights rather than products as the generator of profit (Frith 1987). However, recent technological changes have transformed the socio-technical context so significantly that the music industry may be unable to survive in a form that focuses on the reproduction and control of copyrighted material. (The problems I discuss below are also major concerns for the international software and film industries.)

The distribution of digitally reproduced music, alongside the deterritorialized character of the Internet, has become an issue of some importance for the four companies that have hitherto controlled the international trade in music. Whereas in the past the music industry was most concerned to limit the international 'grey' market for parallel imports (where non-domestic copyright holders undercut domestic rights holders by exporting cheaper copies of specific items), now their concern has moved to the legal protection of their property at the global level. This involves two relatively distinct issues: the continuing organized mass duplication of copyright materials for 'normal' distribution (on CDs or cassettes) in markets where copyright infringement is not treated seriously (and the 'flood' of these copies into the companies' main markets); and the increasingly widespread difficulty of ensuring copyrighted content remains formally scarce in the face of widely available new technologies of reproduction. This has led music industry representatives to worry incessantly and loudly about the abuse of their copyrights by individuals in their homes, and by organized crime, often trying to demonize the former by linking them to the latter. Organized pirates in China and elsewhere have certainly flooded some markets with CDs, but the real threat to the industry may be the advent of digital copying at home.

Compact discs are cheap to physically produce, with most of the final cost contributing to the artists' income and to the costs of the industry (including money lost on other unsuccessful recordings). Copyright is the mechanism that underpins this element of the CD's price, yet intuitively, many consumers recognize that while

> the intended effects of copyright are to create a flow of income for creative artists in order to encourage creative activities, the real effects are different. In reality, copyright essentially creates an environment where record companies and music publishers make large profits. (Dolfsma 2000: 6)

Thus, while unlikely to pass off home-made copies as our own creations, the re-recording of selected tracks onto recordable CDs (or cassettes in the past), or the recording of whole CDs for friends is seldom regarded as immoral or illegal. While possibly reducing the profitability of particular record companies, few see copying for one's own use as impacting on the artists' rewards. Reflecting this intuitive perception, 'fair use' doctrines, despite the best efforts of the music industry, have led courts in most jurisdictions to hold that individual re-recording does not contravene copyright. Under 'fair use' individuals must not market their copies for sale but otherwise are free to use them as they wish. Thus, while the music industry would like to forbid copying altogether, copyright law has usually only identified copying for sale as illegal, while copying for private use remains legitimate.

This used to be a mild irritant to the industry, but has been exacerbated by new technologies. Industries that develop and manufacture technologies enabling such actions operate in direct tension with intellectual property (content) companies (Avenell and Thompson 1994). Manufacturers of recordable CD technologies (now fitted as standard to many desktop computers) or those who have made MP3 players widely available, and before them the developers of audio cassette recorders, can only profit due to the disregard of copyright holders' self-perceived rights. The 'parasitic' product violates the commodity relationship established in the first instance by the intellectual property producer by allowing the dilution of the constructed scarcity through copying. But it also indicates that such behaviour is far from unacceptable: although the small print in advertisements for these technologies makes some reference to not violating copyright, the main (big print) text stresses exactly this use (or strongly implies such use through words like 'ripping', a hacker term for copying). It is difficult against this constant appeal to a 'hacker ethic' for copyright holders to present an unchallenged argument about theft and piracy.

The introduction of new re-recording technologies as consumer commodities has in each case (audio cassettes, digital audio tape and most recently recordable CDs) produced demands from the music industry to limit its capabilities. A similar problem beset the TV and film industries with the advent of the cheap domestic video-recorder, leading to the landmark case *Sony Corp. versus Universal Studios* in 1984 which settled the matter in favour of 'fair use'. Because the US Supreme Court accepted the argument that while copyright infringement was possible, most use would merely be for recording and watching programmes at a more favourable time ('timeshifting'), the technology should not be banned or technologically circumscribed as requested by copyright holders (Jeanneret 2002: 171–2). Subsequently similar definitions of fair use of video recorders were established worldwide. Ironically, of course, Sony now finds itself on both sides of theses debates, still a major manufacturer of innovative reproduction technologies, but now also owning one of the major record companies and a film studio. More recently the unauthorized reproduction of digital video discs (DVDs) has also become a major problem, with 'bootleg' files of new films often appearing on the Internet swiftly, if not before official release.

When mass-market DVDs were launched in the mid-1990s, the major copyright holders divided the world into six discrete sectors. In each geographic sector the copyright holder was able to market DVDs which could only be played on machines equipped with encryption which matched the area. The copyright holders had managed to ensure that licences were linked to specific territories through a technical fix, which itself took considerable negotiation with equipment manufacturers. Where a particular distributor was dominant in a particular territory they could be granted a licence without the fear that a 'grey market' of imports across the six sectors would emerge. This segmented international market, lasted until November 1999 when two computer programmers managed (due to one company's technical error) to crack the encryption and make the various algorithms public (CIPR 2000: 172). With the algorithms in the public domain 'all areas' DVD players could be legally produced and an international market for these players has emerged in the last two years, with machines manufactured by a number of mainstream companies. The attempt to segment the international market, to maximize the earnings from any particular film, failed. The short time that this technical fix lasted prompted a legal response in both Europe and America, which aims to ensure that copyright holders can 'manage' their rights in a digital environment in the future.

In the wake of the collapse of Napster, victim of a successful legal challenge by A&M records and others,[3] the music industry and other content companies have put their hopes for salvation in Digital Rights Management (DRM) software. To support *this* technical fix the music industry (as well as the film and software industries) lobbied hard for a new legal protection against the circumnavigation of technical protections for copyrighted material. This has been included as a major element in both the US Digital Millennium Copyright Act (DMCA) 1998, and in the EC Directive on Copyright 2001. In the EU and the US it is now illegal not only to use, or develop processes which might circumnavigate DRM software protection, but also to 'traffic' in these processes (to publicize them on the Internet or elsewhere) (Bygrave 2002). There are a number of legal issues that both these acts raise about fair use, not least of which is that to various degrees they make it illegal (except in narrowly defined circumstances) to distribute software or other tools for circumnavigation, even if the circumnavigation itself is covered by 'fair use' exceptions within the legislation. However, the key issue is that the control of copyrighted material which was to some extent lost after *Sony vs. Universal Studios* has been potentially regained (Brannan 2001). By making DRM software legally robust in the biggest markets in the world, any uncontrolled international trade becomes again subject to sanction.

The music industry is in some regards fighting a rearguard action against the successors to Napster. Non-centralized potentially global file-swapping (peer-to-peer) networks like Gnutella, Aimster and others will be much harder to close down as they have no central server. And like video recorders before them, as they can be used for many non-infringing file transfers, they may be less susceptible to legal challenge. However, as DRM software often acts to limit the number of copies that can be made to one (for personal use), and disallows further copies from the original or the copy, the hard-won concessions of 'fair use' seem likely to be compromised if such software becomes widely used. At present the sort of file-transfer which worries the industry so much is not only slow and time-consuming, for many it is beyond their technical capabilities. Therefore, despite this technological challenge, and the widespread availability of infringement capable hardware, the territorialization of music markets may have for the time being been partly reimposed. The anti-trafficking provisions in the DMCA and the EU Directive further ensure that in the major markets, even if encryption is cracked, the mere communication of the 'crack' to another user is punishable in law. Thus even if other markets are compromised, the major markets should be protected.

Whether this approach to 'piracy' in the home is any more successful than previous attempts remains to be seen, since widespread disregard of these provisions may make prosecution politically difficult. The potential extent of the problem is hinted at in figures released by the International Federation of the Phonographic Industry in 2001. These claimed that half of all writable CDs were purchased with the express intent of infringing copyright (although given the industry's difficulty in recognizing 'fair use', this is probably overstated). Nevertheless, such casual individual 'piracy' is now the major problem for the international industry, having largely supplanted the previous concern with organized crime.

While certainly a problem in their main markets, outside Europe and America it is generally recognized that the extent of organized piracy reached epidemic proportions in the mid-1990s. Estimated losses ran into billions of dollars, although any figures need to be treated with some scepticism; not only is it in the interests of the industry to inflate losses as a spur to action, they often assume all purchasers of cheap pirated copies would have paid the higher price for legitimate copies, which seems unlikely. Pirated, illegal copies of music content (as well as software and films) are widely available across Asia, and China has often been identified as a key source of this material. However, with China now a member of the WTO (and therefore a signatory to TRIPs), as well as other Asian countries being subject to stringent bilateral trade agreements with strong IPR provisions, this may now change. Certainly there has been a public crackdown on pirates in China, leading to the execution of five convicted bootleggers in 2001. But, as Donna Halbert (1999: chapter 4) has pointed out, the pirates served a useful rhetorical purpose for the industry. They have enabled the United States (and its content industries) to present themselves as the victims of organized crime, a narrative that dovetails well with the stories that have been traditionally used to underline copyright protection as a reward for effort.

During the Uruguay Round of trade negotiations that led to the establishment of the WTO and the TRIPs agreement, the content industries deployed their extensive resources to lobby the US negotiating team. What had originally started as an attempt to widen international anti-piracy agreements (in light of the piracy epidemic) became in the hands of industry lawyers an agreement to universalize a particularly strong reading of knowledge as property. Not only did the industry representatives successfully increase the scope of the multilateral agreement, they also (due to the lack of legal expertise in the USTR and elsewhere in the US negotiating team) largely wrote the US negotiating text. The bulk of this text was subsequently adopted as the TRIPs agreement (May 2000: 80–90). However, as the last few years have demonstrated the real threat to the industry was not necessarily from the organized pirates, but from you and me. Thus, in international forums, such as the World Intellectual Property Organization, the WTO and elsewhere, industry representatives are now arguing for yet more stringent protection of IPRs linked, as noted above, with the legal support for DRM technologies now targeting users, despite the continuing rhetoric of 'pirates' and crime gangs. Nevertheless, even with these efforts it is far from self-evident that the international music industry can survive in its current form.[4]

Rebalancing rights and needs

At the centre of the politics of intellectual property is the balance of private rewards for effort, creativity or ownership, and the public benefits of access or use of knowledge and information. The two cases I have briefly presented above demonstrate that the current political settlement regarding this balance is under severe pressure and remains contested, despite the best efforts of the multilateral governance regime to hold the line. The two challenges I have set out above are:

- a moral challenge, which concerns how competing rights are balanced when social costs are increasing, not least of all in light of the AIDS pandemic in sub-Saharan Africa;
- a technical challenge, which in some important areas of the international trade in IPRs has rendered the existing market potentially inoperable.

Let me take these two challenges in turn before linking them to a wider political problem.

The multinational pharmaceutical companies' claims regarding their need to be rewarded for the effort of developing marketable medicines are to some extent legitimate. However, the real question is whether the rights that these companies should enjoy (and which ensure their suitable rewards) can be justly universalized across an unevenly developed global system. Currently the international trade in IPRs is governed by a 'one-size-fits-all' regime, but this regime did not emerge naturally, it was the result of a political process. Prior to the establishment of the TRIPs agreement as part of the WTO, the protection of IPRs outside the most developed and richest countries was patchy and uneven. Indeed, TRIPs was explicitly intended to deal with this problem. Even before the conclusion of the negotiations there was some discussion of whether a universalized regime was most appropriate to the international system (e.g. Deardorff 1990). More recently, discussion around the AIDS crisis and the availability of medicines has led to a renewed debate about trade rules in this area. Given the wealth effect which greatly affects drug distribution in the world, and the ability of generic producers to ameliorate some (if not all) distributional effects, the idea of differential protection has been raised.

Prior to TRIPs differential protection was the *de facto* state of affairs whatever multilateral agreements might have indicated. Only with the application of the WTO's much more strident dispute settlement mechanism has this differential recognition of IPRs been brought under control. However, many researchers and activists (from UNCTAD to Oxfam) now argue that a return to the previous state of affairs would be preferable to the high human cost of upholding large pharmaceutical companies' patents in the less developed areas of the global system. While to some extent the TRIPs agreement allows solutions to health problems, there are many other areas where LDCs also need (or would like) access to patented technologies but are unable to afford them. A possible solution is to construct a new division between a core of wealthy fully-TRIPs compliant countries and those who have yet to reach the economic developmental level where they can afford full protection. This is not to suggest that no protection should be offered outside the core countries as there is a plausible argument that some form of IPR protection will help foster development. However, this should only be available to domestic companies, as it was when the now rich and developed countries were themselves developing.

When European countries and the United States were undergoing swift and prolonged economic development in the nineteenth and most of the twentieth centuries they did little to protect the IPRs of non-nationals, thriving on 'stolen' ideas and pirated technologies. Only now that these countries have matured do they wish to ensure that the international markets for their knowledge-related products and services are 'safe'. There needs to be a political move to highlight the injustice of forcing LDCs to develop with the exact opposite regime for IPRs that the now developed countries enjoyed when they were undergoing a similar stage of economic expansion. Thus, not only does the AIDS issue raise the question of what balance should be made between the lives of Africans and the rewards of rich shareholders, it also raises a more fundamental issue of the morality of development itself in the contemporary global system. In this sense, the politics of the international trade in IPRs needs to focus not only on the rights of owners, but also on the rights of (potential) users. A return to differential treatment might go some way to rebalancing the private and pubic rights across a diverse and uneven global system.

The second challenge is linked to technology. After the arrival of the Internet the international trade in IPRs (at least as related to the content industries) is in an odd position. While (even after TRIPs) the protection of IPRs is still reliant on national legislation, the notion of an international trade in IPRs, for these industries at least, has been rendered problematic. The Internet (although not as borderless as some might present it) has constructed a realm in which copyrighted goods are available which is increasingly non-territorial, if unevenly global. As I noted, the content industries are trying through DRM technologies to reimpose a more limited scope for reproduction in this realm. For other industries subject to similar problems, similar solutions may obtain, although like peer-to-peer networks, non-industry alternatives are also emerging. This is the case perhaps most famously in software: the emergence of a non-propriety alternative to the heavily protected products of Microsoft and others, in the expanding industry around the LINUX operating system, is starting to slowly but surely shift the parameters of software development and use.

What both these challenges reveal is that while the TRIPs agreement has produced a particular settlement, where all IPRs are treated similarly in all areas of the global system, there seems little justification of such a monolithic approach. In the past the balance between private rewards and public benefits has been constructed within national social contexts where political mediation of contending interests was possible. However, while TRIPs tries to assert that a similar politically robust balance can be substantiated at the global level, the political community which might be called on to legitimize such a balance is largely absent. Indeed, the socio-economic divisions in the global system preclude a singular settlement that might garner significant worldwide support. Without a more evenly developed global society, where a politics of IPRs could be meaningfully mediated and where competing needs were not so divergent, it is unlikely that any settlement for IPRs will remain uncontested if it remains as monolithic and undifferentiated as the current international governance regime.

The politics of the international trade in IPRs reached a watershed with the TRIPs agreement eight years ago, but this settlement itself has revealed the problem which remains at the heart of IPRs; the contested balance between private rights and public benefits. The TRIPs agreement was the internationalization of the Anglo-Saxon legal privileging of owners' rights. But in light of the moral and technical challenges which beset the governance of IPRs, a one-size-fits-all solution seems increasingly implausible. Critical political economic analysis of IPRs must, it seems to me seek to construct a more nuanced and variable understanding of the role of intellectual property in the global system, and help support a new pubic/private bargain which does more to recognize the social costs of knowledge ownership, as well as the changing manner in which certain sorts of information and knowledge will be distributed, and used. If we are entering the new millennium with a heightened regard for the economic importance of information and knowledge, then critical political economy must reveal and engage with the problems this brings in its wake.

Acknowledgement

I thank Susan Sell for reading the whole of this chapter and providing me with excellent advice regarding its improvement, as well as Richard Barbrook for giving me an opportunity to discuss the issues raised in the music industry section both at the Hypermedia Research Centre, University of Westminster and at Cybersonica 2002, Institute for Contemporary Arts. The remaining shortcomings are my own.

Notes

1. Intellectual property has a long and contested history, which I do not have space to discuss here, see Sell and May (2001) for an overview of this history, and May (2002b) for a discussion of the formal origins of IPR law in Venice in the fifteenth century.
2. This section draws in part on May (2002a).
3. Space precludes a full treatment of the Napster case; however, what seems clear is that a technological Pandora's box has been opened that the music industry and others will find very hard (if not impossible) to close.

4. There are widely contrasting speculations about the future of the global music industry but few see it surviving in its current form, now that its monopoly on the distribution of reproduction has been broken, see for instance Jones (2002), Kretschmer *et al.* (2001) and Ku (2002).

References

Avenell, S. and Thompson, H. (1994) 'Commodity Relations and the Forces of Production: The Theft and Defence of Intellectual Property', *Journal of Interdisciplinary Economics*, 5, 1: 23–35.

Bombach, K.M. (2001) 'Can South Africa Fight AIDS? Reconciling the South African Medicines and Related Substances Act with the TRIPs Agreement', *Boston University International Law Journal*, 19, 2: 273–306.

Boseley, S. (2000) 'Glaxo Stops Africans Buying Cheap Aids Drugs', *The Guardian*, 2 December: 25.

Brannan, A.C. (2001) 'Fair Use Doctrine and the Digital Millennium Copyright Act: Does Fair Use Exist on the Internet Under the DMCA', *Santa Clara Law Review*, 42, 1: 247–76.

Bygrave, L.A. (2002) 'The Technologisation of Copyright: Implications for Privacy and Related Interests', *European Intellectual Property Review*, 24, 2 (February): 51–7.

[CIPR] Committee on Intellectual Property Rights and the Emerging Information Infrastructure (2000) *The Digital Dilemma. Intellectual Property in the Information Age*, Washington, DC: National Academy Press.

Deardorff, A.V. (1990) 'Should Patent Protection be Extended to All Developing Countries', *The World Economy*, 13, 4: 497–507.

Dolfsma, W. (2000) 'How Will the Music Industry Weather the Globalisation Storm', *First Monday*, 5, 5 (May) [available at <http://firstmonday.org/issues/issue5_5/dolfsma/index.html> (3 May 2000)]

The Economist (2001) 'Patent Problems Pending', 27 October: 14.

Frith, S. (1987) 'Copyright and the Music Business', *Popular Music* 7, 1: 57–75.

Halbert, D.J. (1999) *Intellectual Property in the Information Age: The Politics of Expanding Ownership Rights*, Westport, CT: Quorum Books.

Jeanneret, C. (2002) 'The Digital Millennium Copyright Act: Preserving the Traditional Copyright Balance', *Fordham Intellectual Property, Media and Entertainment Law Journal*, 12, 1: 157–94.

Jones, S. (2002) 'Music that Moves: Popular Music, Distribution and Network Technologies', *Cultural Studies*, 16, 2: 213–32.

Kretschmer, M., Klimis, G.M. and Wallis, R. (2001) 'Music in Electronic Markets. An Empirical Study', *New Media and Society*, 3, 4: 417–41.

Ku, R.S.R. (2002) 'The Creative Destruction of Copyright: Napster and the New Economics of Digital Technology', *University of Chicago Law Review*, 69, 1: 263–324.

May, C. (2000) *A Global Political Economy of Intellectual Property Rights: The New Enclosures?* London: Routledge.

May, C. (2002a) 'Unacceptable Costs: The Consequences of Making Knowledge Property in a Global Society', *Global Society*, 16, 2 (April): 123–44.

May, C. (2002b) 'The Venetian Moment: New Technologies, Legal Innovation and the Institutional Origins of Intellectual Property', *Prometheus*, 20, 2 (June): 159–79.

Mokhiber, R. and Weissman, R. (2002) 'Stripping Away Big Pharma's Figleaf', *Focus on the Corporation*, 19 June [distributed on the corp-focus discussion list and available at <http://lists.essential.org/pipermail/corp-focus/2002/000118.html>]

Ostergard, R. (1999) 'The Political Economy of the South African–United States Patent Dispute', *Journal of World Intellectual Property*, 2, 6: 875–88.

Sell, S. and May, C. (2001) 'Moments in Law: Contestation and Settlement in the History of Intellectual Property', *Review of International Political Economy*, 8, 3 (Autumn): 467–500.

Singh, K. (2002) 'Anthrax, Drug Transnationals, and TRIPs' *Foreign Policy in Focus*, 29 April [available at <http://www.fpif.org/outside/commentary/2002/0204trips_body.html> (15 May 2002)]

Subramanian, A. (2001) 'The AIDS Crisis, Differential Pricing of Drugs, and the TRIPs Agreement: Two Proposals', *The Journal of World Intellectual Property*, 4, 3: 321–36.

[TRIPs] (1994) 'Agreement on Trade Related Aspects of Intellectual Property Rights, including Trade in Counterfeit Goods', in *Final Act Embodying the Results of the Uruguay Round of Multilateral Trade Negotiations*, Geneva: GATT Publication Services.

Vandoren, P. (2002) *'Médicaments sans Frontières?* Clarification of the Relationship between TRIPs and Public Health Resulting from the WTO Doha Ministerial Declaration', *Journal of World Intellectual Property*, 5, 1: 5–14.

Part III
Regional Dynamics

10
The New Politics of Trade in the Americas[1]

Nicola Phillips

There could be few more uncertain times at which to write a chapter on trade in the Americas. Patterns of commercial activity in the region in any case have long featured a very distinctive level of complexity, stemming not only from the diverse trading interests and strategies that the region accommodates, but also from the various overlapping levels at which trading arrangements in the region are articulated. For much of the 1990s, the politics of trade were dominated, on the one hand, by the often-uneasy coexistence of strong bilateral and equally strong subregionalist tendencies, and, on the other, by the complex relationship of these agendas with the multilateral agenda which overlaid and underpinned them. The study of contemporary trade in the Americas, in this sense, has needed to be conducted on at least three levels – the bilateral, the subregional and the multilateral. The introduction of a fourth, hemispheric, level in the form of the putative Free Trade Area of the Americas (FTAA) signals an intensification of this complexity, which carries important implications for the architecture and politics of trade within the region, and also outside it. In this context, I argue here that trade politics in the Americas are progressively about two sets of relationships. The first is the relationship between the hemispheric and multilateral agendas, in terms of both immediate negotiating issues and the interaction of the governance structures operative in these two arenas. The second is the relationship between hemispheric integration and subregionalism, with respect to the ways in which the hemispheric agenda is shaped by subregional dynamics, and to the implications of the hemispheric process for the evolution of existing subregionalist projects.[2] The dynamics of this overlap between the various processes are generating a reconfiguration of the architecture of trade in the Americas, and will be pivotal in determining the shape this new architecture will take.

At the present time, however, this likely shape is highly uncertain. First, the FTAA process remains to be concluded, is politically highly contentious, and seems, if anything, to be unravelling rather than solidifying in the run-up to the agreed deadline of 2005. It is thus not entirely clear whether an FTAA will come into being in the first place, and judgements on the likely form of an agreement remain speculative. Second, at the same time, the multilateral trading system is immersed in a deepening political and institutional crisis. Although the successful launching of the new WTO agenda at Doha in November 2001 was hailed by United States Trade Representative (USTR) Robert Zoellick as removing 'the stain of Seattle' (*Financial Times*, 14 November 2001), it still garnered significant opposition from developing countries, and the post-Doha agenda remained politically contested and ill-defined. The Cancún ministerial meetings collapsed unceremoniously in September 2003 under the weight of the long-standing tensions between the trade policies of the 'rich' countries and the demands of developing countries, and the political battle lines between these two groupings were shown to have become both stark and entrenched. And third, from the late 1990s the recurrence of economic crisis in parts of the Latin American region has carried notable destabilizing consequences for subregionalist projects, to the extent that there is some uncertainty surrounding both the prospects for these projects and the likely outcome of their current reconfiguration. This has been particularly the case in the Southern Cone, starting with the Brazilian devaluation of January 1999, moving to the thorough-going Argentine economic crisis triggered by the simultaneous currency devaluation and default on external debt payments in December 2001, and the consequent instability in Brazil and devaluation in Uruguay of 2002. The context is made yet more uncertain by the frequently contradictory trends evident in the trade policy of the George W. Bush administration in the United States, in both the hemispheric and the extra-hemispheric contexts.

In the light of this changing and uncertain environment, this chapter seeks to advance an understanding of the *evolving* dynamics of trade in the Americas, and to understand their significance rather than to offer definitive pronouncements on their likely outcomes. Specifically, its aim is to map out and explore the two relationships mentioned above, namely those unfolding between the hemispheric and multilateral agendas, on the one hand, and on the other between hemispheric and subregionalist projects. Its central questions are thus two-fold. The first concerns the extent to which the significance of hemispheric integration can be understood to lie in a process of 'regionalising multilateralism', by which I mean that the FTAA project is designed to further a floundering multilateral agenda by regionalist, rather than multilateral, means. The second concerns the extent to which the hemispheric integration process is propelling a reconfiguration of existing subregional projects in the Americas. The first part of the chapter offers a brief portrait of trade interests and strategies in the region, as a prelude to the discussions, in turn, of the contours of the two central relationships we have identified.

Patterns, interests and agendas

If there is a common thread in trade strategies in the Americas, it is the broad convergence over the 1980s and 1990s on trade liberalization as the centrepiece of the shift towards neo-liberalism. Early liberalizers such as Chile and Mexico set the pace for extensive processes of unilateral tariff liberalization across the region, as a result of which aggregate tariff levels were cut drastically from historically high post-war levels. These shifts in policy at the domestic level both reflected and generated key shifts in the participation of Latin American economies in the multilateral trading system. During the post-war period, the prevailing inward-looking development model and various nationalist ideological trends meant that trade issues became the heart of the North–South debate (Tussie 2003: 4), with the result that Latin American and Caribbean countries were both marginalized from the GATT process and resistant to participation in it. The broad shift to market economics in the region, however, went together with increased membership of the GATT/WTO and active engagement in the Uruguay Round, as central avenues by which Latin American and Caribbean governments sought to pursue both their commercial interests and broader international credibility for their domestic reform efforts.

These region-wide trends of unilateral liberalization and multilateral engagement were accompanied by a third common tendency – namely, the adoption of region-alist strategies as a means of pursuing and consolidating the new trade agenda. This is true not only of Latin America and the Caribbean, where the existing Andean, Caribbean and Central American blocs received new injections of vigour, and the newly established Mercosur[3] project in the Southern Cone emerged for a while as the most dynamic instance of regional integration among developing countries. It is also true of the north of the region, where the United States abandoned its previous reticence towards regionalism, instead initiating a web of regionalist projects both in its own region and outside it. North American regionalism specif-ically crystallized in the creation of the NAFTA[4] in 1994, but the regionalist drive in the United States took a more encompassing shape in 1990 with the proposal by President George Bush (senior) of the Enterprise for the Americas Initiative (EAI), which subsequently mutated into the current FTAA project.

Despite these three common threads, however, the most salient traits of the contemporary Americas are those of heterogeneity, diversity and divergence. These operate along a wide variety of axes, including population size, living standards, market size, per capita income, gross domestic product (GDP) and so on, but most relevant to our purposes here is that which derives from the widely divergent economic and trade structures of the economies of the region. As Table 10.1 demon-strates, it pulls together some of the most 'open' economies in the world along with significantly inward-looking ones. Trade openness indicators of imports/GDP and exports/GDP for the Central American Common Market (CACM[5]) in 1999 were 33.9 per cent and 20.9 per cent and 12.8 per cent and 15.7 per cent for the Andean Community of Nations (AC[6]). By contrast, in the Mercosur, and particularly for Brazil and Argentina, the internal market remains significantly more important than the external sector. The same openness indicators for the Mercosur in 1999 were respectively 9.6 per cent and 8.9 per cent. The preponderant weight of the United States – and, by extension, the North American region – does not require a great deal of illustration here, save to note that its principal relevance lies in the structures of dependence on the US market in various parts of the region. This dependence follows the same sort of geographical pattern as the openness indica-tors just mentioned. As detailed in Table 10.2, CACM and Caribbean Community (CARICOM[7]) manufactured exports, particularly, rarely break out of the regional

Table 10.1 Selected trade openness measures, 1990–99 (%)

	1990	1991	1992	1993	1994	1995	1996	1997	1998	1999
Imports / GDP										
W. Hemisphere	9.9	9.5	10.2	10.5	11.2	11.7	11.9	12.4	12.5	13.3
NAFTA	10.2	9.8	9.3	9.7	9.9	11.0	11.2	11.3	11.9	11.9
LAC	10.1	8.2	10.2	11.3	10.8	12.0	12.3	12.5	14.9	19.7
LAC excl. Mexico	8.0	7.4	10.2	10.7	10.4	11.0	10.8	11.9	11.7	13.8
Mercosur	4.7	4.2	6.3	6.9	7.5	7.6	7.7	8.7	8.6	9.6
Andean Community	12.5	13.7	16.4	16.9	15.3	15.8	15.2	15.8	15.4	12.8
CARICOM	36.3	40.2	41.3	35.9	40.5	45.3	39.5	45.5	n/a	n/a
CACM	24.2	24.6	23.6	26.6	25.8	24.6	27.6	25.4	27.7	33.9
Exports / GDP										
W. Hemisphere	8.5	8.3	8.5	8.5	9.4	10.3	10.5	10.8	10.2	10.6
NAFTA	8.1	8.2	8.3	8.2	9.2	10.3	10.5	10.9	10.3	10.3
LAC	12.3	9.9	11.3	11.2	11.6	13.2	13.8	14.0	13.4	19.7
LAC excl. Mexico	11.3	8.8	10.8	10.5	10.5	10.2	10.4	10.6	9.5	13.3
Mercosur	7.5	5.7	7.8	7.8	7.5	7.1	7.0	7.3	7.3	8.9
Andean Community	23.0	18.9	17.1	16.9	17.1	15.8	18.8	17.2	13.5	15.7
CARICOM	30.5	28.0	27.4	21.9	32.6	32.0	27.9	28.5	16.9	n/a
CACM	15.9	16.1	15.5	14.7	15.0	16.5	17.7	17.0	19.8	20.9

Source: IDB Integration and Regional Programs Dept / *Integration and Trade in the Americas*, December 2000.

Table 10.2 Direction of manufactured exports by subregional grouping, averages 1990–99, as per cent of total manufactured exports

	Western hemisphere	Respective subregion	European Union	Asia	Rest of world
Mercosur	66.0	26.7	17.5	6.8	9.7
AC	81.9	32.6	9.7	3.4	5.1
CACM	92.3	46.9	4.4	1.4	1.8
NAFTA*	49.0	43.2	16.1	14.9	10.0

Note: * Figures for NAFTA are 1990–98 averages.

Source: Elaborated on basis of data from IDB Integration and Regional Programs Dept / *Integration and Trade in the Americas*, December 2000.

marketplace, while the Mercosur is significantly less dependent on the North American market. In national terms, dependence on the United States is most striking in the cases of Canada, Mexico, Venezuela, and many of the individual economies that comprise the Caribbean and Central American subregions. Those economies most dependent on the US market, furthermore, encompass both exporters of primary products (Nicaragua, Honduras, Venezuela and Ecuador), and exporters of manufactured products, the latter dividing in turn between NAFTA members (Canada and Mexico) and those economies styled as export-processing zones (EPZs) based on intensive use of unskilled labour in manufacturing activities (Jamaica, the Dominican Republic, El Salvador, Haiti and many of the other countries of the English-speaking Caribbean) (Svarzman 1998: 46).

Similarly in the Southern Cone, considerable diversity exists between the economic profiles of Mercosur member countries and the extent of their reliance on regional markets. Along with the US, Brazil has a highly diversified trade structure – encompassing manufactured products and services (notably telecommunications, electricity and financial services in the latter category) – and for much of the 1990s around 60 per cent of Brazil's trade flows have been with the European Union (EU) and the rest of the world (Tavares de Araujo 1998). A comparatively diversified trade structure is also evident in the case of Chile, although to a lesser extent than in Brazil or the North American economies. A similar drive to distinguish the country as a 'global trader' has constituted the framework for Chilean governments' trade strategies since the mid-1980s, featuring an expansion of the range of both export markets and export products, although the much greater emphasis on non-traditional products remained located in many of the traditional sectors as opposed to newer manufacturing sectors. In addition, an increasingly important element of Chile's commercial profile lies in the area of trade in services. Indeed, over the 1990s, the sectoral profile of foreign direct investment in Chile shifted from a concentration in mining sectors (representing 58 per cent of the total in 1990–95) to a concentration in service sectors (64 per cent of the total in 1996–2000), particularly utilities and financial sectors (ECLAC 2001: 93). The trade profile has adapted as a result, with services having come to represent 7 per cent of total exports in 2000, a figure roughly similar to Argentina's (at 8 per cent) but still some way behind Brazil's (16 per cent) and Uruguay's (35 per cent) (ECLAC 2002: 50–4). The greater diversification in Brazil and Chile of both products and markets co-exists with the predominantly agricultural export profiles of Argentina and the smaller members of the Mercosur, although Uruguay enjoys the distinction, as noted, of having the highest ratio of services to total exports, and indeed services to GDP. This is largely the consequence of its position as the regional financial centre and thus accounted for largely by trade in financial services, along with some other sectors such as energy, telecommunications and tourism (INTAL 1999: appendix, 6).

In terms of specific trade policies, significant divergence is evident across the Americas in areas such as tariff levels and the use of commercial policy instruments. Table 10.3 gives an indication of tariff rates as they stood at the end of the 1990s, demonstrating the low average levels that prevail in the United States and Canada (4.5 per cent), the slightly higher levels in countries such as Chile, Bolivia and most of Central America (under 10 per cent), and the higher levels still across most of the rest of Latin America, reaching over 14 per cent in Brazil and over 16 per cent in Mexico. Taking simple tariff averages in this way, however, obscures a range of distorting factors, the most notable of which is the frequent resort to specific duties in the United States while their use in Latin America and the Caribbean remains negligible. The same applies to the availability in the United States of contingency measures such as Section 301 and the greater feasibility for the United States of resort to safeguards, anti-dumping (AD) and countervailing duties (CVDs) (de Paiva Abreu 2002: 9–11).

This thumbnail sketch flags up two key points. The first is that despite a broadly common commitment to trade liberalization, the nature of liberalization processes

Table 10.3   Tariff rates (selected countries)

Country	Year	Average rate	Min. rate	Max. rate
Argentina	1999	13.5	0.0	33.0
Belize	1998	11.2	0.0	70.0
Bolivia	1999	9.7	0.0	10.0
Brazil	1999	14.3	0.0	35.0
Canada	1999	4.5	0.0	245.0
Chile	1999	9.8	0.0	10.0
Colombia	1999	11.6	0.0	35.0
Costa Rica	1999	7.2	0.0	253.0
Ecuador	1999	11.5	0.0	99.0
El Salvador	1998	5.6	0.0	40.0
Guatemala	1998	7.6	0.0	28.0
Guyana	1998	10.6	0.0	100.0
Honduras	1997	7.8	0.0	70.0
Jamaica	1998	9.7	0.0	40.0
Mexico	1999	16.2	0.0	260.0
Panama	1998	9.0	0.0	50.0
Peru	1999	13.7	12.0	68.0
Paraguay	1999	11.4	0.0	30.0
Suriname	1998	9.7	0.0	50.0
Trinidad and Tobago	1999	9.1	0.0	45.0
Uruguay	1999	12.3	0.0	23.0
United States	1999	4.5	0.0	350.0
Venezuela	1999	12.0	0.0	35.0

Source: Inter-American Development Bank.

and their results have featured a considerable degree of national variation, including between members of trade blocs.[8] The second is that the trajectory and the politics of trade negotiations have borne the imprint of this diversity, in both regional and multilateral arenas. To an extent, it is possible to identify some common interests among Latin American and Caribbean countries, such as those relating to the obvious issues of market access and to key sectors such as agriculture, textiles and steel. Nevertheless, the much more notable feature of trade negotiations in the Americas has been the lack of common negotiating objectives, including among members of the same trade bloc and including in the sectors just mentioned. This is so despite a commitment by all of the subregional blocs, with the exception of the NAFTA, to approach trade negotiations from a platform of 'bloc bargaining'. This principle was established as the format for the hemispheric negotiations at the 1998 FTAA ministerial meeting in San José, Costa Rica, but extends to trade negotiations across the board. We turn, then, to the impact of this diversity on the hemispheric project, and its relationship with the multilateral process.

Multilateralism and hemispheric integration

The process of hemispheric integration represents one of the various dimensions of the neo-liberal ideological project, both within the Americas and in the wider global political economy. In this sense, it represents a device by which the globalizing neo-liberal project is further embedded in the region and by which the region is further embedded in the globalizing world economy, reflecting 'the triumph of economic liberalism, of faith in export-led growth and of belief in the centrality of the private sector to development processes' (Payne 1996: 106). While the initiative issued in the first instance from Washington, and relates in significant ways to the entrenchment of US hegemony (see Phillips 2003a), the propulsion of the EAI/FTAA agenda nevertheless came primarily from Latin American governments (see Feinberg 1997 for an account). Except for two Summits of the Americas in Miami in 1994 and Santiago in 1998, the agenda was largely neglected by the Clinton administration, and in any case hindered by its failure to secure re-approval of fast-track negotiating authority in 1998.[9] With the election of Bush in 2000, the Americas agenda received a new injection of vigour, but this dwindled with foreign policy shifts after 11 September 2001 and the consequently 'forgotten relationship' (Castañeda 2003) with the rest of the Americas has been widely lamented. It also remains far from clear that hemispheric free trade enjoys, or will enjoy, congressional and public support in the United States.

US interest in an FTAA is, in any case, perhaps not entirely self-explanatory. The importance of Latin America to US economic interests declines as one moves south through the continent, as we have seen, but more importantly the benefits of market access deriving from an FTAA would accrue predominantly to the Latin American region as barriers to trade and investment remain concentrated in the US economy. In the broadest terms, for this reason, Latin American and Caribbean interest in an FTAA and the attendant negotiating strategies have been dominated by market access issues, but these have little relevance for the United States. Rather, the US government's interest in hemispheric regionalism has lain resolutely in the possibilities it affords for pushing a 'new trade agenda', in the context of the slowing dynamism of the multilateral system, a progressive retraction of US compliance with multilateral rules (see Tussie 1998; Porter, Chapter 11 in this volume), and a growing disillusion among developing countries – including in Latin America and the Caribbean – with the conduct, agenda and implementation of WTO negotiations (see, *inter alia*, Finger and Nogués 2002; Laird 2002; Panagariya 2002).

For the United States, in this sense, the FTAA project has been less about trade *expansion* than about instilling a range of trade *disciplines* in the region, which reflect a set of wider 'global' interests (Phillips 2003a: 333). These relate to 'new' trade issues such as intellectual property, government procurement, competition policy, investment rules, and so on. There is, however, an important element of trade expansion which relates not to trade in goods but rather to trade in other areas, notably services, particularly in the growing services economies of the Southern Cone. The project for the United States has also been about the protection of US investments, for which reason the US government has favoured the application of the NAFTA's so-called 'investor-state' provision to a future FTAA agreement. This provision grants to corporations a legal status similar to that of states and expands their ability to use trade agreements to challenge local regulatory legislation. The USTR's commitment to 'investor-state'-type arrangements thus augurs an entrenchment of (US) investors' rights at the heart of the hemispheric project, whether or not the NAFTA pattern is directly replicated. Other hallmarks of US positions are found in the refusal to permit inclusion on the negotiating agenda of its domestic commercial defence laws (AD, CVDs, safeguards and so on), despite the centrality of these concerns to Latin American partners.

It is at this point, in any case, that we come to the key issue, namely the disparate visions of the FTAA project that characterize and shape the politics of the process. Given the above priorities, the vision of the FTAA favoured by the US government has consistently been of a 'WTO-plus' arrangement, in which the FTAA negotiations aim to exceed existing multilateral provisions in a range of key areas. The rationale has two dimensions. On the one hand, the negotiation of a range of trade disciplines in the hemispheric arena has been seen to offer greater potential for success than in the multilateral arena. Future WTO negotiations have widely been adjudged unlikely to deliver comprehensive results on market access issues, for instance – and the Cancún debacle can only have reinforced this scepticism – whereas the FTAA does indeed aim for the complete elimination of tariff barriers to trade in goods (albeit on a smaller list of goods than that addressed by the WTO). An FTAA has similarly been considered likely to make deeper inroads into such areas as the liberalization of trade in services, investment rules and competition policy, which have not yet been incorporated fully into the WTO agenda (see Salazar-Xirinachs 2000, 2002). On the other hand, this vision has been articulated not only as a means of advancing US commercial and investment interests within the region itself, but rather is also tied to the broader trade strategy articulated by USTR Zoellick based on 'sequential liberalisation' (see Feinberg 2003) – that is, to conduct trade negotiations simultaneously at multiple levels in order to establish what Craig VanGrasstek (1998: 169–70; also 2000) has called a 'spiral of precedents' to be deployed as the basis for subsequent negotiations. Concessions granted to partners in the Americas thus might well be matched or exceeded by concessions granted by the United States in subsequent trade agreements with other partners.

While a number of areas – notably agriculture and commercial defence policies – remain effectively excluded from the FTAA negotiations by the US, the rationale of 'WTO-plus' is thus that it facilitates both the entrenchment of rules in areas of strategic priority to the United States, and the development of a trading order consistent with its ideological and economic interests. Crucially, it is in this sequential strategy – in the prioritization of regional negotiations as a direct means to advancing the process of multilateral liberalization – that the FTAA process might be seen as an attempt to iron out some of the tensions between multilateralism and regionalism, that not only derive from the theoretical contradiction posited by neo-liberal economists (see, for example, Bergsten 1996) but also are reflected in the competing positions of key members of the Bush administration. In other words, it might be interpreted as representing an attempt, the success or failure of which is not yet apparent, to 'regionalise' multilateralism. We will return to this issue shortly.

The 'WTO-plus' principle has been accepted by Latin American and Caribbean negotiators, and was consecrated in the Ministerial Declaration which emanated from the Seventh FTAA ministerial meeting held in November 2002 in Quito, Ecuador. Their central concerns, however, have consistently been to ensure fuller implementation of the provisions agreed in the Uruguay Round, especially in the area of market access. In other words, the broad stance is one of 'WTO-compatibility', emphasizing at the same time that a 'WTO-plus' format must be *genuinely* WTO-plus, reaching across the full range of negotiating areas, including those areas excluded unilaterally from the negotiating agenda by the United States. The Brazilians, in particular, have been adamant that an FTAA would need to be 'comprehensive' if it is to be either meaningful or acceptable: in short, 'Brazil can only envisage the establishment of a free trade area if it is to obtain concrete and substantial access to highly protected sectors' (Barbosa 2001: 153). Without this, in the words of then presidential candidate Luiz Inácio Lula da Silva, an FTAA would represent little more than 'a process of the economic annexation of the continent by the United States, with extremely serious consequences for the productive structure of our countries' (*La Nación* / Argentina, 23 October 2002, my translation). Market access issues, furthermore, go hand in hand with issues of commercial defence mechanisms, in that any concessions forthcoming from the United States on market access might easily be eroded by the discretionary use of these instruments (de Paiva Abreu 2002: 20). This should not be taken to imply that there is no interest whatever in issues connected with the new trade agenda. Indeed, in a number of sectors – such as transport, construction, software and medical treatment – Latin American and Caribbean partners view hemispheric trade as a useful 'apprenticeship' for exporting such services to the rest of the world (Bulmer-Thomas 2001: 8). However, it does reflect the ongoing disenchantment among Latin American and other developing countries with the record of implementation of Uruguay Round provisions on market access, and with the perennially slow progress of agricultural liberalization.

The additional problem with WTO-plus, as mentioned earlier, is that even by the time of the Cancún ministerials the post-Doha agenda had not taken concrete shape, and indeed the negotiating programme has been thrown into disarray by the collapse of those meetings. Even before Cancún, negotiators in the WTO were reported increasingly to view the deadlines set at Doha as unrealistic (*Financial Times*, 13 December 2002). Especially given that both the FTAA and the WTO negotiations are scheduled for completion in 2005 (although it remains to be seen whether the events in Cancún will mean this is revised), it is thus not clear what WTO-plus might actually involve. What is clear, however, is that progress in the FTAA negotiations depends to a very significant extent on progress in the WTO arena, particularly in areas which specifically require multilateral agreement. This is especially the case with agriculture, in that FTAA provisions might easily be undercut if European and other countries are not constrained to observe the same obligations (Schott 2002: 31). Given the commitment to a 'single undertaking' in an FTAA agreement, the process is thus constrained by a dependence on continued progress at the multilateral level, even while it aims for 'WTO-plus' in the substance of a final agreement. In political terms, as well, Brazilian leadership (in conjunction with India and others) of the increasingly robust 'developing country' coalition in multilateral negotiations has been and will be reflected in its own strategies in the hemispheric context, and these global political dynamics can be expected to breathe further life into existing political resistance to hemispheric integration in many parts of Latin America and the Caribbean.

Progress towards the 2005 deadline is also faltering in the FTAA context, and the political debate across the region, as indicated earlier, has become noticeably less amenable to the successful conclusion of an agreement as originally projected. In Latin America and the Caribbean, political debate has long been characterized by a generalized lack of knowledge and information and by progressively organized forms of social resistance, but over the course of 2002/03 the positions of many governments have also shown signs of hardening into either scepticism or resistance, particularly among those larger countries with greatest influence in the region. Mercosur countries' interest in an FTAA has always been rather less pronounced than that of many others given that, of the countries of the region, they are the ones with most at stake in the multilateral system given their much more diversified trade structures and export destinations, and the marked Brazilian reticence has stemmed from the trade-off an FTAA would represent with its more significant multilateral interests (de Paiva Abreu 2003: 23–4). The US–Brazilian relationship in the FTAA context has been consistently tense – crystallizing largely around resistance to a US-dominated initiative and the consolidation of US hegemony in the region – and the Lula government since 2003 has hardened the already hard line taken by its predecessor. This is especially important given that the final stages of the FTAA process (from late 2002) are chaired jointly between the United States and Brazil. It has also ushered in an important redefinition of Brazilian negotiating strategies in the FTAA context, according to which the key issues of market access, services and investment will be negotiated in a bilateral 4 + 1 (Mercosur–US) format, leaving only 'basic elements' such as dispute settlement, trade facilitation and special and differential treatment on the hemispheric negotiating table (Amorim 2003). Mexico, already having an effectively bilateral agreement with the United States, has always been the most lukewarm about a putative hemispheric agreement, and there has been some coincidence with Brazilian concerns about a US-led hemispheric initiative. More recently, however, this reticence has shown signs of hardening into opposition in many quarters, including among many of the most influential figures in the political elite.

Crucially, however, political interest in an FTAA has also waned in the United States – from a much lower starting point in any case – in both public opinion and government circles. Consistent with the long-standing trends, an NBC News-*Wall Street Journal* poll conducted in April 2001 reported that 48 per cent of the US public considers foreign trade to be bad for the US economy, and labour unions have been particularly vocal in their rejection of hemispheric free trade. In government circles, more recently, the FTAA has taken largely second place to an alternative strategy – that of prioritizing bilateral agreements. One such agreement was signed with Chile in December 2002, the foundations have been laid for a similar agreement with Uruguay, Argentina has long been hoping to follow suit, and the United States has initiated 'bilateral' negotiations with both Central America and Mercosur (the latter in the 4 + 1 arrangement noted above). The logic propelling a more robust pursuit of bilateral rather than hemispheric arrangements rests on the apparently greater utility of bilateralism in serving key US negotiating priorities – that is, of obtaining access to services markets in the region in exchange for concessions on market access for a range of goods but, equally, the exclusion of significant concessions on agricultural liberalization or modification of domestic legislation on CDMs. This, indeed, was the substance of the agreement with Chile, which also went further to include provisions limiting Chilean governments' future ability to impose controls on capital flows. Yet the pursuit of bilateral agreements is also useful as a mechanism for increasing the incentives of other partners (notably Brazil) to engage in similar negotiations, or else for increasing their interests in the success of the FTAA negotiations and thus encouraging a softening of negotiating positions.

It is thus through the progressive prioritization of bilateral negotiations – mirrored in US negotiating strategies outside the Americas – that US influence over the architecture of the region has been most easily asserted, and indeed it augurs the sort of hub–spoke regional arrangements that the United States initially envisaged in the FTAA context. Moreover, it has come gradually to be favoured by a number of other governments in the region as the best means of pursuing their strategic priorities in trade negotiations given the apparent height of the hurdles facing the successful agreement of a comprehensive FTAA. The important point about bilateralism is that it has found most robust expression in the particular area of market access[10] – that is, in the defining pillar of Latin American and Caribbean interests in hemispheric trade negotiations – and in this sense has been moulded such that it has become apparently more consistent with the key negotiating priorities of Latin American and Caribbean governments than an FTAA itself. The bilateral bent thus adds a twist to the process of 'regionalising multilateralism'. While in one sense these agreements do not necessarily subvert such a notion, as they represent a strategy for establishing precedents within the Americas and thereby furthering the process of regional liberalization, they do mean that political interest in an FTAA had become by mid-2003 weaker than ever and, moreover, imply a fragmentation of the structure of the negotiations such that the 'single undertaking' principle holds increasingly little water.

One further stumbling block to the successful conclusion of the FTAA negotiations deserves mention – namely the ongoing ambivalence that has long been evident in US trade policy on matters of 'free' trade. Under Bush, this ambivalence is evident not only in the difficulty with which TPA was achieved, but also in the early spate of protectionist legislation in the areas of agriculture and steel. It stems both from divisions within the various concerned departments of the US state, but also, more importantly, from the persistence of strong protectionist sentiment in public views on free trade. Although passage of TPA was a triumph for the administration and various business interests, the nature of the final legislation compounds the ambivalence by granting Congress a much more significant input into the process than that which it enjoyed in the first incarnation of fast-track in the early 1990s. Congress retains the option of passing a 'resolution of disapproval', a provision described by House Ways and Means Committee Chairman Bill Thomas (R-Calif.) as 'the old shotgun behind the door' (*Washington Post*, 26 July 2002). Apart from diluting the fast-track principle, the implications are that any concessions that US negotiators might feel inclined to make on market access face complicated prospects once transferred to the arena of domestic legislation, and that labour and environmental standards are indeed likely to be incorporated into an FTAA agreement given the political climate in Congress, despite resistance across the region and within the Republican White House. The TPA bill also carries provisions on textiles that were widely received as disadvantageous to Latin American and Caribbean textiles producers,[11] signifying the incorporation of concessions to domestic protectionist pressures even within the framework for negotiations. These characteristics of both TPA and US trade policies have thus generated a distinctly uneven playing field in hemispheric negotiations, skewing the terrain unmistakeably towards US interests. Failure substantially to rectify these biases has entrenched tensions between negotiators from different parts of the region.

Hemispheric integration and subregionalism

Very often, the FTAA project is assumed to herald the weakening or redundancy of subregional arrangements. The well-known logic is that hemispheric free trade will erode the system of preferential treatment on which subregional projects are based, ultimately eliminating their rationale and utility. This vision of 'hemispheric globalisation' (SELA 1999: 36) informs much of the strategy of the US government, even while it concedes the principle of bloc bargaining in the negotiations. The alternative view, quite widely held in Latin America and the Caribbean, is that subregionalism and an FTAA can be – or should be made to be – compatible, and there is widespread resistance to the idea that subregional blocs would obsolesce with the advent of a hemispheric bloc. The maintenance of subregional dynamism, however, depends on a substantial reconfiguration of the nature of subregionalism, and evidence suggests that this process is already under-way in response to the demands of participation in the negotiating process, as well as in order to meet the challenges posed by an eventual agreement. This recon-figuration is premised on two sets of goals (see Phillips 2003a): the first relates to strategic and political objectives in trade negotiations, and the second relates to the processes of adjustment that participation in an FTAA requires. These goals are articulated differently in different subregions, but are broadly those that inform the contemporary evolution of subregionalist projects.

The strategic dimension of subregionalism is connected with the notion, men-tioned earlier, of bloc bargaining in trade negotiations. On the one hand, the attachment to collective negotiation that prevails in each of the subregions (with the exception of the NAFTA) derives from a very simple 'strength in numbers' rationale, as a means by which Latin American and Caribbean countries might more effectively press their demands in bargaining processes. On the other hand, it is envisaged as a means – particularly in the Mercosur, as noted, but also in other blocs – of resisting the unilateral dominance of the FTAA process by the United States, and of ensuring that an eventual FTAA agreement is consistent with the interests of all negotiating parties. The significance of this strategic agenda, however, lies primarily in its reinforcement of political commitment to subregionalism. Across the board, rhetoric and evidence suggest that strategic and political objectives are progressively the central pillar of subregional projects, and these objectives lend a form of political 'glue' to subregionalist endeavours. Especially in the Mercosur, Brazilian opposition to a US-dominated initiative has fostered the replacement of its previous lukewarm approach to the subregional project with the assumption of active leadership within it, and an insistence on approaching the FTAA negotiations from a Mercosur platform.

In some cases, the bloc bargaining principle has held relatively fast (see Phillips 2003a). The AC has displayed the most notable degree of cohesion, owing in part to the existence of fairly robust institutional structures and a certain devolution of authority to these institutions, but also to the degree of common ground between the interests (and economic profiles) of member countries. The pattern has been one in which different countries assume leadership on different issues and at different times: in the FTAA negotiations, for instance, Peru has taken the lead particularly on special and differential treatment for smaller countries and on indigenous peoples' rights. In other cases, bloc bargaining has been less successful. In CARICOM and CACM, the fact that negotiating positions cluster largely around a single issue – that of special and differential treatment for smaller and poorer economies – has facilitated the identification of common interests within the bloc and the articulation of common positions in negotiating forums on that basis.[12] In the case of CARICOM, the Regional Negotiating Machinery (RNM) constitutes a rare instance of an institutionalized mechanism for collective bargaining, and has been deployed to some effect in a range of negotiations. Nevertheless, the capacity for effective coordination is limited by the historically very tenuous linkages between the English-speaking Caribbean and other parts of the Basin, the pronounced weakness of institutional vehicles such as the Association of Caribbean States,[13] economic dependence on the United States and NAFTA, and of course their negligible weight in multilateral and hemispheric negotiations themselves.

In the Mercosur, it is the articulation of common interests in the first place which has proved problematic. Much of this stems from the peculiar position of Brazil that derives primarily from its highly diversified trade structure, for which reason its concern with hemispheric negotiations is significantly more qualified than its Mercosur partners', and its negotiating interests in all of the various forums is at times significantly at variance with theirs. It also stems from the striking level of internal political fragmentation that the Mercosur displayed from the mid-1990s, reflected in the inclination towards bilateral trade negotiations. The Chilean government has long been exceptional in the degree of autonomy it maintains from the rest of the Mercosur in its trade strategies, evident most notably in 2002 bilateral agreement with the United States, independent negotiation with the EU, and of course the maintenance of associate rather than full membership of the Mercosur itself.[14] Uruguayan – and, to an extent – Argentine preferences for bilateral negotiations with the United States, noted above, have generally been articulated as alternative rather than complementary to the subregionalist project, and indeed the bilateralist penchant of the United States and some Latin American countries does in important ways subvert the principles of collective negotiation and of a single undertaking in the FTAA negotiations. However, it also co-exists with a hardening commitment to bloc bargaining spurred by 'bilateral' strategies involving blocs rather than individual countries, such as that initiated by the United States with the Mercosur. In other forums as well, serious difficulties and lapses notwithstanding, evidence suggests that strategies in trade negotiations are increasingly – and in some cases increasingly effectively – articulated from subregional platforms, whether these are bilateral or hemispheric in their scope. Instances range from the agreement in the AC and the Mercosur on common external tariffs for presentation in the FTAA negotiations, to joint Mercosur declarations on agriculture in the Seattle WTO ministerials, increasingly routinized cooperation in the technical working groups of the FTAA, and collective 'inter-regional' negotiation between the Mercosur and the EU.

Moreover, this increasingly sticky political glue provides incentives for subregional cooperation in order to meet the demands posed by negotiated agreements. Specifically, coming to our second set of objectives, these relate to adjustment strategies. The root of these priorities lies largely in the need to manage the challenge posed by increased competition for Latin American and Caribbean industries, for the majority of which an FTAA represents a very sizeable threat. While also issues of domestic policy, the emphasis in these matters falls squarely on the ways in which subregional strategies might be elaborated for addressing adjustment costs, as well as for ensuring effective participation in the hemispheric project. Across the Latin American and Caribbean subregional blocs – which all broadly follow a 'customs union' (rather than free trade area) model of integration – the emphasis has fallen on the perfection of the incipient customs unions, and on the sorts of macroeconomic convergence necessary for the envisaged advance towards common markets. Policy harmonization, in this sense, is designed to overcome limitations on the capacities of individual states, but also to ensure the maximization of efficiency in order to build competitiveness in regional and global markets.

This competitiveness strategy, in turn, rests on twin pillars. On the one hand, it is designed to secure investment flows into the region by offering the prospect of investment in a regional economy of scale. This has been pivotal, for instance, in the automobile industry, and in this and other sectors has generated a process of operational rationalization designed to consolidate a genuinely subregional market. On the other hand, the construction of a subregional market is crucial to the increasingly assertive internationalization strategies of 'indigenous' firms, especially those in the larger economies of Mexico, Chile, Argentina and Brazil (see Chudnovsky *et al.* 1999). Especially in the NAFTA (for Mexico) and in the Mercosur, but also to varying degrees across the rest of the region, subregional arenas are styled as 'incubators' of industrial performance, and thus envisaged as 'stepping stones' to more global production strategies and more effective participation in a hemispheric marketplace.

Apart from questions of competitiveness and investment, the adjustment challenges of an FTAA lie in a range of socio-economic issues. The most obvious of these relates to special and differential treatment, and indeed this is especially contentious in the FTAA negotiations. In a number of blocs, such as the AC and the Mercosur, the emphasis has consequently fallen on subregional strategies in addressing these issues. The pattern is largely one in which the broad framework is pursued through collective negotiation at the hemispheric level, and consideration is then given within subregional blocs to how to manage the challenges and issues specific to the subregion in question. More broadly, subregional projects almost without exception are in the process of redefining their objectives to emphasize social and developmental imperatives, and not just commercial or investment priorities. The drift, in short, is towards a sort of 'multi-thematic regionalism' (Delgado Rojas 1999: 58), which privileges specifically subregional strategies in areas such as security, environmental protection, democracy promotion, and social policy, and goes hand in hand with a range of economic competitiveness strategies of the sort we have just discussed.

The reconfiguration of subregionalism that characterizes its relationship with the hemispheric integration process is thus a thoroughgoing one. It involves a movement away from the original strategy of 'open regionalism', which privileged unilateral trade liberalization as the cornerstone of subregionalist strategies, and from the emphasis on tariff liberalization as the central rationale for the various associated projects (Phillips 2003b). Rather, it coheres largely around a new set of strategic and political objectives oriented towards external trade negotiations; its economic dimensions revolve centrally around strategies for investment attraction and industrial competitiveness, and the construction of a viable subregional marketplace for both purposes. In the same way as bloc bargaining strategies remain imperfectly coordinated and frequently perforated, it must be noted that the prospects for achieving macroeconomic convergence and policy harmonization are complicated by a huge range of economic, political and institutional weaknesses, not to mention the impact of the Argentine economic crisis, and remain very much in their early phases. Nevertheless, the utilization of subregional blocs as arenas for the pursuit of subregionally appropriate strategies lies at the core of a refigured form of subregionalism, and at the core of its relationship with hemispheric processes.

Conclusion: the new architecture of trade in the Americas

The conjunction of these processes has ushered in not only a new politics of trade in the Americas, but also a changing architecture. This new architecture can best be depicted as an intricate and complex patchwork of agreements, institutions and processes, which pulls together four interlocking spheres of activity. The first is the plethora of bilateral relationships, pursued by a range of governments in both regional and extra-regional arenas. These currently constitute the most dynamic form of interaction in the area of market access, but it is notable that those agreements involving the United States have not made any significant dent in the most solid or contentious of the barriers to the US market. They also, at times, have been seen to run counter to the spirit of subregional cooperation, particularly since the adoption of bloc bargaining as the rule of thumb in trade negotiations. Recent proposals for a 4 + 1 agreement between the Mercosur and the US, however, indicate that bilateralism does not necessarily stand in contradiction with a collective bargaining approach, even while it might be designed to circumnavigate – and circumvent – the principle of a single undertaking in the FTAA process.

The second is the subregional sphere, which, I have argued, is undergoing a process of substantial reconfiguration. From the initial dynamism of an 'open regionalism' strategy across the subregional blocs, progress towards common markets over the 1990s was both ponderous and tortuous. The Mercosur, particularly, was beset by a combination of political fragmentation, institutional weakness and economic crisis; in Central America and the Caribbean, the picture of the 1990s was more one of stagnation. In part in response to this disappointing performance, and in part as a reaction to new strategic imperatives, the redefinition of the objectives of subregionalist projects indicates that they will continue to represent an integral part of the patchwork, particularly given the increasing salience of inter-bloc negotiations in the politics of regional and multilateral trade.

The third is the hemispheric sphere. There is as yet no concrete agreement, and indeed the shape of any future agreement remains highly uncertain. The term being bandied around in mid-2003 was 'FTAA-lite', and indeed, especially in view of efforts to limit the scope of hemispheric negotiations and dilute the 'single undertaking', this would seem to be the most realistic assessment of the likely substance of any agreement that does come into being in 2005. Yet it is important to recognize that there now exists a well-defined and robust hemispheric *arena* within which a range of trade and trade-related processes are conducted, whether or not an encompassing FTAA is called into being. In this sense, a substantive regional trade agenda is articulated at the hemispheric level in the Americas, entrenched progressively in both the strategies of national governments and the institutional structures that surround their negotiating agendas. Crucially also, this hemispheric trade arena is also a core component of the broader Summitry of the Americas process, and is central to the vision of an *integrated* hemispheric agenda for the pursuit of economic, security, social and democracy-related objectives.

The fourth is the multilateral sphere, which both underpins and shapes the politics of trade at the bilateral, subregional and hemispheric levels, and in turn is shaped by them. The major issues – and the major sticking points – in multilateral negotiations are mirrored in the FTAA negotiations, and progress in the FTAA negotiations and in the new WTO agenda are in important respects mutually dependent. Moreover, US approaches to the FTAA project have moulded it into an attempt to pursue the objectives of multilateral trade liberalization by other means – that is, to 'regionalise multilateralism' and, perhaps even more robustly, to 'bilateralise multilateralism' – with important implications for both the governance of world trade and the WTO as a mechanism of that governance.

Notes

1. Many of the arguments of this chapter were presented in a paper to the Annual Plenary Meeting of the Latin American Trade Network (LATN), Santiago, Chile, 12–13 December 2002, and this version has benefited greatly from the comments and insights of the participants.
2. I employ the terms 'hemispheric' and 'multilateral' here to connote distinct arenas of trade negotiations, although the term 'multilateral' has often been applied to the hemispheric project in the sense of 'multilateralism in the Americas'. In this chapter, 'multilateral' refers only to the multilateral trading system and process encapsulated in the WTO, and 'hemispheric' refers directly to the region of the Americas.
3. *Mercado Común del Sur* (Southern Common Market). Membership: Argentina, Brazil, Paraguay and Uruguay, with Chile and Bolivia as associate members. Established 1991, 're-launched' 2000.
4. North American Free Trade Agreement. Membership: Canada, Mexico, United states.
5. *Mercado Común de Centroamérica*. Membership: Costa Rica, El Salvador, Guatemala, Nicaragua, Honduras. Established 1960, 're-designed' 1993.
6. *Comunidad Andina de Naciones*. Membership: Bolivia, Colombia, Ecuador, Peru, Venezuela. Established 1969, 're-launched' and reorganized 1989.
7. Membership: Antigua and Barbuda, Bahamas, Barbados, Belize, Dominica, Grenada, Guyana, Haiti, Jamaica, Montserrat, St. Kitts and Nevis, St. Lucia, Suriname, St. Vincent and the Grenadines, Trinidad and Tobago. Established 1973.
8. For recent comparative studies of national trade policies, and the nature and results of national processes of trade liberalization, see IDB (2002); Wise (1999).
9. Fast-track negotiating authority limits Congress to either approving or rejecting trade bills negotiated by the executive branch in their entirety, without recourse to amendment. It expired in 1994, was not renewed in 1998, was re-styled as 'Trade Promotion Authority' (TPA) by George W. Bush and subsequently approved by Congress.
10. I am grateful to Pedro da Motta Veiga for highlighting this point.
11. These provisions stipulate that garments exported duty-free to the United States from Latin American, Caribbean and African countries be manufactured using cloth that has been dyed and finished in the United States.
12. For a fuller discussion of the issue of special treatment in the FTAA context, see Masi (2001).
13. Membership: all CARICOM members except Montserrat, all CACM members, Colombia, Mexico, Venezuela, Cuba, Dominican Republic and Panama.
14. For a fuller discussion of the Chilean strategy of 'going it alone' in this manner, see Grugel (1999).

References

Amorim, C. (2003) 'A Alca possível', *Folha de São Paulo*, 8 July.
Barbosa, R. (2001) 'A View from Brazil', *The Washington Quarterly*, Spring: pp. 149–57.
Bergsten, C.F. (1996) 'Globalizing Free Trade', *Foreign Affairs*, 75, 3: pp. 105–20.
Bulmer-Thomas, V. (2001) 'Introduction', in Bulmer-Thomas, V. (ed.) *Regional Integration in Latin America and the Caribbean: The Political Economy of Open Regionalism*, London: Institute of Latin American Studies: pp. 1–13.
Castañeda, J.G. (2003) 'The Forgotten Relationship', *Foreign Affairs*, May–June, online version: pp. 1–8.

Chudnovsky, D., Kosacoff, B. and López, A. (1999) *Las Multinacionales Latinoamericanas: Sus Estrategias en un Mundo Globalizado*, Buenos Aires: Fondo de Cultura Económica.

De Paiva Abreu, M. (2002) 'The political economy of economic integration in the Americas', paper for presentation at the IDB/INTAL Conference on Economic Integration in the Americas: Prospects and Policy Issues, Punta del Este, 15–16 December.

De Paiva Abreu, M. (2003) 'Latin American and Caribbean Interests in the WTO', in Tussie, D. (ed.) *Trade Negotiations in Latin America: Problems and Prospects*, Basingstoke: Palgrave, pp. 19–31.

Delgado Rojas, J.G. (1999) 'Los temas no comerciales del ALCA', *Contribuciones del CIEDLA* 1, 61.

ECLAC (2001) *Foreign Investment in Latin America and the Caribbean, 2000 Report*, Santiago: United Nations.

ECLAC (UN Economic Commission for Latin America and the Caribbean) (2002) *Latin America and the Caribbean in the World Economy, 2000–2001 Report*, Santiago: United Nations.

Feinberg, R.E. (1997) *Summitry in the Americas: A Progress Report*, Washington, DC: Institute of International Economics.

Feinberg, R.E. (2003) 'The Political Economy of United States' Free Trade Arrangements', *The World Economy*, 26, 7: pp. 1019–40.

Finger, J.M. and Nogués, J.J. (2002) 'The Unbalanced Uruguay Round Outcome: The New Areas in Future WTO Negotiations', *The World Economy*, 25, 3: pp. 321–40.

Grugel, J. (1999) 'Going it Alone? The Chilean Strategy for Subregional Integration', in Hook, G. and Kearns, I. (eds) *Subregionalism and World Order*, Basingstoke: Macmillan, pp. 139–61.

IDB (Inter-American Development Bank) (2002) *The Trade Policy-Making Process: Level One of the Two Level Game: Country Studies in the Western Hemisphere*, INTAL-ITD-STA Occasional Paper 13, Washington, DC: IDB, Institute for the Integration of Latin America and the Caribbean.

INTAL (Inter-American Development Bank, Institute for the Integration of Latin America and the Caribbean) (1999) *Informe Mercosur No. 5, 1998–1999*, Buenos Aires: BID-INTAL.

Laird, S. (2002) 'A Round By Any Other Name: The WTO Agenda After Doha', *Development Policy Review*, 20, 1: pp. 41–62.

Masi, Fernando (2001) 'Preferential Treatment in Trade: Is There Any Room Left in the Americas?', North-South Agenda Papers 49, Miami: North-South Center, University of Miami.

Panagariya, A. (2002) 'Developing Countries at Doha: A Political Economy Analysis', *The World Economy*, 25, 9: pp. 1205–33.

Payne, A. (1996) 'The United States and its Enterprise for the Americas', in Gamble, A. and Payne, A. (eds) *Regionalism and World Order*, Basingstoke: Macmillan, pp. 93–129.

Phillips, N. (2003a) 'Hemispheric Integration and Subregionalism in the Americas', *International Affairs*, 79, 2.

Phillips, N. (2003b) 'The Rise and Fall of Open Regionalism? Comparative Reflections on Regional Governance in the Southern Cone of Latin America', *Third World Quarterly*, 24, 2.

Salazar-Xirinachs, J.M. (2000) 'The Trade Agenda in the Context of the Inter-American System', Trade Unit, Organization of American States (March), http://www.sice.oas.org/tunit/STAFF_ARTICLE/jmsx_Agda_e.asp

Salazar-Xirinachs, J.M. (2002) 'Latin American Trade Policies in 2002 and Beyond: Diagnosis and Prognosis', Trade Unit, Organization of American States, http://www.sice.oas.org/tunit/STAFF_ARTICLE/jmsx_diagnosis_e.asp

Schott, J.J. (2002) 'Challenges to the Free Trade Area of the Americas', *Economic Perspectives: An Electronic Journal of the U.S. Department of State*, 7, 3: pp. 29–31.

SELA (Sistema Económico Latinoamericano) (1999) 'Reflexiones sobre la dinámica de las relaciones externas de América Latina y el Caribe', *Capítulos del SELA*, 55: pp. 7–57.

Svarzman, G. (1998) 'La Argentina y el Mercosur ante el proceso de integración hemisférica', *Boletín Informativo Techint*, 295, July–Sept.: pp. 27–60.

Tavares de Araujo, J. (1998) 'FTAA: Risks and Opportunities for Brazil', Organization of American States Trade Unit, March.

Tussie, D. (1998) 'Multilateralism Revisited in a Globalizing World Economy', *Mershon International Studies Review*, 42: pp. 183–93.

Tussie, D. (2003) 'On Shifting Ground: The Crossroads of Regional and Sectoral Associations', in Tussie, D. (ed.) *Trade Negotiations in Latin America: Promise and Problems*, Basingstoke: Palgrave, pp. 1–16.

VanGrasstek, C. (1998) 'What is the FTAA's role in the USA's global strategy?', *Capítulos del SELA*, 54.

VanGrasstek, C. (2000) 'US Plans for a New WTO Round: Negotiating More Agreements with Less Authority', *The World Economy*, 23, 5: pp. 673–700.

Wise, C. (1999) 'Latin American Trade Strategy at Century's End', North-South Agenda Papers 37, Miami: North-South Center, University of Miami, pp. 1–25.

11

The United States in International Trade Politics: Liberal Leader or Heavy-Handed Hegemon?

Tony Porter

United States trade policy can be puzzling. On the one hand the US government is often viewed as the most important supporter of the liberal international trading system, through the relatively open access it gives foreign firms to its markets; through throwing its enormous political and economic weight behind multilateral free trade initiatives in the Americas, at the World Trade Organization and elsewhere; and even in its unilateral use of trade policy to force open markets in countries such as Brazil, India or Japan – in which governments traditionally have sought to intervene to protect domestic industries. On the other hand the United States seems very quick to protect its own industries, as evident in duties on imports of steel and softwood lumber and in massive agricultural subsidies all of which grabbed headlines and angered US trading partners in 2002. Moreover the United States is frequently accused of undermining the multilateral trading system by its unilateral or bilateral arm-twisting of trade partners.

Most explanations of this schizophrenia in US trade policy look to a struggle between free traders and protectionists in the fractious US political system. Sometimes this is portrayed as taking place in the realm of ideas in which forward-looking free traders are periodically hindered by lingering backwards politically motivated attitudes of those who have not yet learned the basic truths of Economics 101. At other times it is viewed as clashes between political institutions, such as the conflict between a more free-trade-oriented Executive Branch and a more protectionist Congress, or between the smaller but more organized protectionists mobilized around specific pay-offs from protection versus the constituency for free trade whose capacity to organize is undermined by the diffuse character of the benefits of free trade. Sometimes it is portrayed as a conflict between more globally oriented industries and more nationally based ones. Yet other explanations look to the ambiguous demands of hegemony in which the United States is torn between its overall interest in a stable, rules-governed trading order, and its particular national interest (Cronin 2001), which may involve aggressive unilateral moves to protect its particular economic interests.

This chapter challenges these accounts that portray US trade policy as involving an ideological or political see-saw between a harmful, particularistic and political protectionism and a more universally beneficial market-oriented free trade and argues that US trade policy has consistently involved an aggressive use of political measures to promote US economic interests. What appear to be zigzags and contradictions in US trade policy are instead a variety of measures, consistent in the goal of promoting US economic interests, but tailored to technological variation across industries. Thus, for instance, while one might expect the steel and pharmaceutical industries both to have organized effectively for protection given the concentrated character of their industrial structure, in fact the US government has assisted the former through tariffs and the latter through an aggressive promotion of intellectual property rules at the global level. These differences are rooted not in the differing lobbying capacity of the two industries but rather in variations in their technological profiles. Even the more outwardly oriented character of the latter industry, while at first glance an alternative explanation to the technologically-based explanation of this chapter, is itself best explained by the industry's enduring technological profile rather than independently shedding much light on trade policy.

The chapter starts with a conceptual discussion of US trade policy, examining prevailing theories and developing the alternative I have introduced above. It then turns to the empirical record, examining key episodes in US trade policy in order to assess the relative merits of the differing theories.

Conceptualizing US trade policy

A useful way to distinguish among alternative conceptualizations of US trade policy is the distinction between systems-level, state-level and societal-level explanations (Ikenberry *et al.* 1988). In this section I begin by briefly reviewing each of these in turn. It will become apparent at each level that there is a tendency to artificially distinguish between market interactions, which are taken to be relatively free of institutions, and political interactions, which are seen as involving the use of state institutions, often to harmfully interfere in competitive markets. I challenge this tendency by arguing that markets involve institutions in which the struggle for power and resources is more like the political conflicts involving states than is often realized. I focus on one way to identify variations in institutions across industries, which I refer to as an industry's technological profile, and I propose that integrating this factor into explanations of trade policy will improve our ability to explain and reconcile apparent inconsistencies in US trade policy.

The best-known and most heavily criticized systems-level explanation of US trade policy is hegemonic stability theory (Lake 1993) which claimed that US post-Second World War support for a liberal trading order was a reflection of its emergence as a hegemon: as with nineteenth century British hegemony, the inordinate importance of the United States in the world economy gave it both the capability and the incentive to promote liberalized trade through support of multilateral trade negotiations associated with the GATT as well as opening its markets to imports from Japan, Europe, and other potential competitors. The US interest in free trade was both political (stabilizing alliances in the Cold War) and economic (given its share of world trade, the economic benefits of supporting free trade outweighed the costs). From this perspective the increased protectionism and unilateralism displayed by the United States in the 1970s and 1980s is a reflection of its declining relative power, while its support of the Uruguay Round agreement and the creation of the WTO in 1994 is perhaps a reflection of its resurgence following the collapse of the Soviet bloc. Although this theory has been criticized on both theoretical and empirical grounds it remains intuitively appealing. Other systems-level explanations focus on an apparent ongoing increase in international economic interdependence, which has an effect on the United States, as it does on other countries.

State-level explanations focus on the mechanisms in the US government designed to shift some of the control over trade policy away from Congress, with its vulnerability to protectionist lobbying, to the Executive Branch, which is seen to be more oriented to the overall welfare of the country, and therefore to free trade. The creation of the Office of the US Trade Representative at the White House, and of 'trade promotion authority' (TPA) (previously 'fast-track authority') in which Congress can only vote for or against an entire trade deal negotiated under the President's authority, rather than altering parts of it in response to protectionist measures, are the two major mechanisms for enhancing the prospects for free trade. Similarly the character of trade policy can be explained in part by differences among departments, with the State Department, with a broader perspective, including a willingness to make trade concessions in pursuit of non-trade diplomatic goals (Haggard 1988: 93), the Treasury Department focusing on broad macroeconomic concerns, and the Commerce Department being more attentive to the preferences and interests of industries (Cohen 2000: 47–57). In one variant of state-level explanation, institutional arrangements such as the USTR and TPA are due to the successful effort of the Executive Branch to enhance its own power rather than a consensus across the two branches that such arrangements are in the country's interest.

Societal-level explanations focus on the varying capacity and desire of different groups of citizens and firms to influence trade policy. For instance the contemporary Democratic Party has been seen as more protectionist than the Republicans, corresponding to the degree to which the former is supported by labour and the latter by business (Shoch 2001: 13). The prevailing liberal explanation for protectionism is that tariffs can create focused and easily identifiable pay-offs for protected industries that are able to effectively lobby because of the motivation that the pay-off creates and because the small size of the concerned group of firms and workers makes it easier to organize. In contrast, the benefits from free trade, it is claimed, are widely diffused and difficult to identify, reducing the political clout of supporters of free trade. As Krueger (1995: 3) puts it, in making this argument, 'if citizens could easily identify and vote on the magnitudes of gains and losses and the identities of winners and losers from trade restrictions, there is little doubt that American trade policy would be different'.

A common theme in all these explanations is an assumption that the main story to be told is about the ever-fragile successes of forward-looking supporters of free trade, promoting efficiencies that will increase the general welfare in the face of backward-looking special-interests, at home and abroad, who use trade protection to resist change and protect their own economic position at the expense of every-one else. Even in analysis where the pressure on the state of internationally ori-ented domestic interests is highlighted (Frieden 1988: 67) there is usually no discussion of the possibility that this can result in an outcome other than the expansion of mutually beneficial free trade.

There are serious problems with this story's excessive conceptual separation between markets, which are assumed to involve abstract, efficiency-promoting competitive pressures, and politics, which is assumed to involve wasteful zero-sum conflicts over how to expropriate and redistribute the wealth created by markets. Even the most internationalized markets involve highly structured arrangements in which private-sector rules and institutions have an enormous impact on deter-mining which people and firms can participate and prosper. The most dynamic and global industries are ones in which a few leading firms are dominant over long periods of time. For instance firms such as General Electric and Siemens in the electrical industry, Dupont and Bayer in the chemical industry, General Motors and Ford in the auto industry, and Motorola and Intel in the semiconductor indus-try have all been global leaders since their industries emerged, which, with the exception of the newer semiconductor industry, was a century or more ago (Porter 2002: 135). The free trade story discussed above is profoundly misleading since the efficiencies stimulated by arms-length trading contribute only a small part to the generation of wealth through the market. Of much greater importance is the capacity of firms to draw together resources, people and ideas to create new prod-ucts or production processes. This technological innovation, while stimulated by competitive pressures, is most importantly an organizational feat, both within the corporate structures of large leading firms, and in the networks that tie together these firms with customers, researchers, suppliers, and other allied firms within their industries.

In creating value these organizational features of markets are inherently ambiguous because they create exciting new products that can often satisfy all sorts of needs and desires, solve pressing problems, and stimulate economic growth, but at the same time create opportunities for leading firms to manipulate rules to their advantage and to intentionally or unintentionally arbitrarily exclude from an area of activity those who are not involved in producing the product or cannot afford it. Generally the private-sector institutions and rules that create these opportunities and exclusions are inseparably entangled with public-sector institutions, rules and laws. For instance, the Microsoft anti-trust case, in which the wonderful benefits of Microsoft's personal computing software were accom-panied by charges of ruthless anti-competitive behaviour towards its competitors, also involved a complex entanglement of Microsoft's proprietary standards, a form of private-sector rules, with the permissive and prohibitive features of US anti-trust and intellectual property laws.[1]

This complex entanglement in markets of welfare-enhancing wealth creation, new opportunities for arbitrary domination and exclusion, and both private- and public-sector institutions and rules means that the distinction between politics and markets that is at the heart of the free trade story discussed above is problematic. Expanding market opportunities through free trade does not just create new efficiency-enhancing competitive pressures: it also creates new organizational opportunities for leading firms with all the promise and dangers discussed above. If politics is thought of as involving conflicts over the allocation of resources through the creation and management of rules, then politics takes place within markets as well as within the state.

At the same time, the politics of protectionism involves much more than simply the backward and harmful extraction of revenues from the markets through a manipulation of the state. In addition to its condemnation of protectionism, liberal economic theory more approvingly holds out the possibility of compensation from the gains from trade for those who through no fault of their own lose from the changes it brings about. This too is seen as most appropriately carried out through the political system. Unfortunately economic losers are often politically weak, and they may be better able to offset this weakness by operating through market institutions, such as using an industry association to demand tariffs for threatened firms, than by more purely political negotiations over government-sponsored retraining or unemployment programmes.[2] States in other ways as well can potentially offset the arbitrary actions of leading firms, by for instance restricting the conduct of those firms or supporting firms harmed by them. Thus just as initiatives of leading firms in newly liberalized markets can involve an ambiguous mixture of welfare-enhancing value creation and the arbitrary wielding of organized market power, so too can initiatives involving the use of states to intervene in markets involve an ambiguous mixture of harmful rent-seeking by special interests and reasonable efforts to offset the negative consequences of powerful firms reworking the organization of production in the markets they dominate.

For US trade policy this means that we should look for politics and for the hand of the state not just in protectionist barriers to free trade but in the way that rules, institutions, and leading firms organize liberalized markets as well. Contrary to the common prevailing separation of markets and politics discussed above, we should expect to see the US government involved in reinforcing the types of rules that arbitrarily promote the interests of leading US firms, as well as negotiating conflicts between winners and losers from market interactions. However, just as with the ambiguity of a firm that uses its production of a wonderful new product to suppress competitors, so too the US government's actions are ambiguous in promoting values that can be portrayed as universally beneficial even as they confer advantages on US firms at the expense of others.

In assessing the involvement of the US government in these ways it is important also to recognize the impact on this of variations in the technological profiles of industries.[3] Some industries, such as the electrical and chemical industries, are highly knowledge-intensive while others, such as apparel and steel, are not. This has profound implications for the organization of the industry and for its relationships with governments. In knowledge-intensive industries leading firms often can maintain their lead by the constant generation of new innovations. Their lead is consolidated not just from the revenues from selling products based on these innovations, but also from their ability to set the technical standards to which other firms must adjust, and from their ability to use one innovation as a platform to create the next. Moreover many key innovations are connected to large-scale modifications in production processes that extend well beyond the originating firm to include suppliers, customers and governments (for instance in providing complementary infrastructure or laws). This can consolidate a firm's position in the industry relative to potential competitors. In knowledge-intensive industries patents and licenses have often been used by leading firms to reinforce their dominance in markets and to consolidate alliances (see Chapter 9 by May in this volume). By contrast, in industries that are not knowledge-intensive the product is commodified: competitors are easily able to learn how to make the product, and competition is intense and price-based.

In knowledge-intensive industries, then, the most important form of government assistance is likely to be support for research and development and legal support for organizational mechanisms suited to the large-scale arrangements needed to launch major new technological systems, including ways to control the dissemination of knowledge, such as the use of patents. By contrast, in industries that are not knowledge-intensive the most likely form of government assistance is to assist domestic firms in retaining their market share by creating barriers to imports, or if the industry is relatively unimportant, simply to create the rules within which conventional arm's length trading can take place.

Key developments in US trade policy

In this section three periods in US trade policy are examined in order to assess the approach towards understanding US trade policy that was developed in the previous section. The first part reviews the arrangements that were established after Second World War. The second part examines the aggressive unilateralism and bilateralism that emerged in the 1970s and 1980s. The third part analyses US trade policy since the completion of the Uruguay Round in 1994. In each case I am looking to see if the policies adopted are best explained as a conflict between free traders committed to the free play of competitive market forces unimpeded by state intervention and protectionists manipulating the state in their own interest, or whether instead, as suggested above, the US state has consistently intervened in ways that confer advantages on leading US firms with variations arising from differences in the technological profiles of targeted industries rather than the relative political influence of free traders and protectionists.

In examining each of these three periods it is important to look not just at what was included in trade negotiations in that period, but also what was excluded in one period but included in another. This includes, especially, investment, competition policy and intellectual property rights, all of which are very relevant to trade and are high on the present trade agenda but were handled outside trade negotiating processes in earlier periods.

The post-Second World War arrangements

In the period immediately following the Second World War a priority for the US government was to consolidate the increased prominence of US firms in the international economy that had been developing in the first half of the century but was threatened by the use of state intervention in the economy by trading partners in Europe and elsewhere. State intervention in social-democratic, communist and fascist forms had developed as a response to the economic dislocations of the interwar period and was being envisioned as a response by countries considering how to deal with the economic problems, such as unemployment and the need for reconstruction that associated with the end of the War. US firms had become more active in the international economy both through exporting and by direct foreign investment abroad, and the US government took measures to support both these types of activities.

On the trade front the most important initiative was the creation, with the US playing a leading role, of the GATT in 1947. In the ensuing 25 years the GATT would sponsor a series of tariff-reducing negotiating rounds that are widely seen as having been hugely successful in contributing to the growth of trade and prosperity. However, from the beginning the GATT was criticized for its failure to address key areas of concern for developing countries. Most seriously, textiles and apparel, the first industry that most industrializing countries develop, was excluded from the GATT's disciplines and instead was handled under a series of short- and long-term agreements that involved state-managed quotas restricting the growth of imports into the US and other industrialized country markets (see Chapter 1 by Wilkinson in this volume). Another serious concern was the failure to include agriculture despite its importance for developing countries (see Chapter 5 by Grant in this volume).

On the investment front there were a number of policy initiatives taken by the US government. Leading US firms have traditionally expanded their productive capacity through the creation of very large oligopolistic corporations built through mergers and acquisitions, often coordinating tacitly through techniques such as price leadership by the top firm. By contrast, other countries, most notably Germany and Japan, had relied much more heavily on cartel arrangements in which many firms collaborated in the domestic and cross-border organization of production and markets, a type of explicit horizontal collaboration that was prohibited by anti-trust law in the United States. During the interwar period international cartels had been a significant alternative form of international economic organization to the US-compatible model of production coordination carried out by a small number of leading firms with vast numbers of wholly owned branches and subsidiaries throughout the world. After the Second World War the US government made the prohibition of cartels in other countries and at the international level a top policy priority, carried out through its influence in international organizations such as the UN, the OECD, and the European Economic Community, and through its military control over Germany and Japan. In this campaign US-style oligopoly was portrayed as associated with free markets while cartels were associated with the most terrible expressions of excessive use of state power – German and Japanese militarism. This was successful in reworking the international legal environment to make it more consistent with that in the United States and with the form of industrial organization characteristic of US firms. However by the late 1960s, when European and developing countries began to call for the use of anti-trust policies against the market domination of US firms, US support for international anti-trust policies was dropped (Porter 1999).

The success of US firms at establishing global networks of branches and subsidiaries was facilitated by a number of other factors as well. For the industrialized countries agreements on permitting cross-border capital flows at the Organization for Economic Cooperation and Development were important. The United States vigorously pursued the international legal principle of the private property rights of foreign investors against a growing tendency of developing country governments to nationalize foreign operations, often without compensation, and to assert their sovereign jurisdiction over their economic resources (Dell 1990). Additionally it used the military and economic power of the US government to support developing country governments that were friendly to US firms, often including some of the most authoritarian ones, and to weaken others. US firms also benefited from their large technological lead in some areas, such as the assembly-line production of automobiles, and by the rapid expansion of demand in many markets, which left room for expanded production by both local firms and US branches and subsidiaries.

Finally, in some areas, most notably semiconductors, the US government's funding of research and development provided an important boost to the knowledge-intensive activities that provided leading firms in most industries with their capacity to dominate markets. Federal government expenditures on research and development were greater than industry expenditures until the 1980s (Office of Technology Competitiveness 1997: 7). As one senior Commerce Department official put it, 'from this base of government research and development arose America's global leadership in computers and electronics, satellite communications, aerospace, and later in pharmaceuticals' (Office of Technology Competitiveness 1997: 1). The US chemical industry was given a major boost by the US government in the 1940s, first by its heavy management and financing of the industry during wartime, and then by its sale, far below cost, of government-owned operations to the large US chemical companies at the end of the war (Chapman 1991: chapter 4).

Aggressive unilateralism in the 1970s and 1980s

By the 1970s key US industries were being seriously challenged by competitors in other countries. This included for instance, automobiles, steel, semiconductors, oil production and petrochemicals. In most cases these challenges were mounted with a greater degree of direct government involvement than was typical in US markets. These government measures ranged from nationalizations (as for instance with steel and oil production facilities) to government support for collaborative research in key technologies (as with the Japanese semiconductor industry). In between, governments experimented with a wide range of policy tools aimed at enhancing the capacity of local workers and firms, including compulsory licensing of technology, export requirements imposed on the local operations of foreign firms, requirements for these firms to source locally, and requiring foreign firms to include local firms in joint venture arrangements. Those supporting these government interventions saw them as a way to use the main institutional resource available locally – the state – to enhance local economic capacity relative to the existing large organization capacity of US-based multinational corporations.

Although the primary justification of initiatives taken by the US government against these challenges was the economic inefficiency of government intervention, it is not clear that all the interventionist measures were harmful or inconsistent with economic efficiency and growth. In many cases the countries using them had enjoyed high growth rates. Moreover some of the measures could be viewed as positive for competitive markets in the degree to which they offset the anti-competitive effect of a foreign subsidiary in a local market.

Additionally, despite its ostensible commitment to free trade, the United States itself stepped up its use of government measures dramatically. This had four main elements. First, the anti-dumping (AD) and countervailing duty (CVD) provisions were used to exclude imports in vulnerable industries. Although supporters of these trade policies claim they are used to offset unfair trading (AD is supposed to target exports sold below the cost of production or below home-country prices and CVD is supposed to target foreign government subsidization of exports), both AD and CVD have been heavily criticized for the way in which they can be used to arbitrarily protect US firms. For instance the data demanded of those targeted is very extensive and must be presented in English in a particular format – and should this not be done data provided by the US firm that has brought the complaint will be used. The data calculations do not take into account various alternative explanations for allegedly unfair pricing, such as exchange rate fluctuations between the time the product is sold in home markets and its sale in US markets. Moreover the calculations do not assess prices in US and other markets with the same methodology, thereby increasing the likelihood of finding a violation when none existed (Krueger 1995: 42–6).

Second, the US government in the 1970s and 1980s negotiated a series of bilateral agreements with trading partners that had been expanding their exports to US markets. Framed as 'voluntary restraint agreements' to remain formally consistent with GATT commitments, these used the threat of AD and CVD actions to get foreign governments to restrain their countries' firms' exports. The most important of these were in the steel, automobile and semiconductor industries. In essence these were government-run market-sharing agreements, much like those that had already been in place in textiles and apparel. Ironically, in the case of semiconductors, the agreement required the Japanese government to engage in much more extensive coordination with its firms than had been the case previously (Flamm 1996).

Third, and relatedly, in some cases bilateral agreements and disputes combined threats of exclusion from US markets with demands for expanded access to a foreign country's market. Japan was a key target, as for instance with the US–Japan agreements on semiconductors, on construction contracts (Krauss 1993), and more generally in the Structural Impediments Initiative launched in 1989 in which the US sought to alter Japan's marketing and financial systems and its government–business relations in order to increase Japanese imports of US products. Sometimes changes were made in response to US threats without formalizing an agreement, as for instance with the modifications the US obtained in Japanese and European financial markets (Bayard and Elliott 1994: chapter 11). These initiatives were accompanied by ambiguity with regard to the question of whether the problem was informal and unfair exclusions of US firms from the Japanese market, or rather a failure on the part of US firms to make the types of efforts and adjustments to enter the Japanese market that the Japanese firms had made on entering the US market. These efforts to gain access to foreign markets were pursued even more systematically through an aggressive use of Section 301 of the 1974 Trade Act, especially when it was strengthened in a 1988 revision of the Act to create 'Super 301', in which the US Trade Representative was required to create a list every year of countries engaging in what it considered to be unfair trading practices, negotiate removal of those practices, and, if the practices were not removed, to place restrictions on imports from the targeted country. 'Special 301' was a similar measure targeted at countries not conforming to US expectations regarding protection of intellectual property. Although supporters have portrayed these as designed to open markets, they have been widely condemned by critics as a type of unilateralism that undermines the GATT (Bayard and Elliott 1994).

Fourth, the United States stepped up its aid to its industries, tailoring it to the particular needs of the industry. In steel the accumulated support was estimated in a 2000 publication to be '$100 billion in trade restraints and corporate welfare' over 30 years (Barringer and Pierce 2000). In semiconductors the government worked with leading firms to create a research and development consortium, SEMATECH, involving 14 leading US producers accounting for 75 per cent of US production, promising to support it with $100 million per year for the first five years (Porter 2002: 118). A 1984 revision of US anti-trust law designed with an eye to foreign competition allowed the types of horizontal collaboration that the US had previously vigorously opposed (Porter 1999: 273).

An important tool used since 1971 by the US government to support its largest multinational corporations is tax breaks for exporters. Originally called the domestic international sales corporation legislation, this was reformulated as the foreign sales corporation legislation in 1985 after the original program was judged to be an illegal export subsidy by the General Agreement on Tariffs and Trade, but the new legislation had a very similar effect. After continual complaints from the EU the legislation was again ruled illegal by the WTO in 2002, and the EU was authorized to impose sanctions equivalent to the estimated value of the subsidy, $4 billion per year, equivalent in value to 20 per cent of US tariffs (*Wall Street Journal* 2003a). An indication of the subsidy's significance is its value to the chemical industry, an estimated $125–$250 million per year (*Chemical Market Reporter* 2002).

The Uruguay Round and beyond

The Uruguay Round and the agreements associated with it are often interpreted as a major victory for free trade at the expense of protectionism. New areas were brought under GATT disciplines, including financial and other services, agriculture, textiles and apparel, trade-related intellectual property rights and trade-related investment measures. Voluntary export restraints were prohibited. Moreover the creation of the WTO, with a remarkably strong legalistic dispute settlement mechanism, promised to move the world significantly closer to a trading system governed by trade rules rather than politics. The United States has been seen as offering crucial support to this expansion of free trade, not just in its participation in the negotiations, but also in the degree to which the aggressive unilateralism discussed above contributed to bringing its partners to the negotiating table. There are two main reasons to question the view that in supporting the Uruguay Round the United States was signalling its commitment to the type of universally beneficial free trade that is counter-posed to protectionism in the free-trade story discussed earlier in this chapter. First, the United States has continued to aggressively use the power of its government to defend the interests of its producers in ways that are more consistent with traditional protectionism than with rule-governed multilateral free trade. Second, the new areas into which the Uruguay Round expanded rule making are ones that are of primary concern to leading US firms. These two areas of activity correspond to sets of firms with quite different technological profiles. The most aggressive use of US protectionism has been in commodified industries with low levels of knowledge intensity while the areas of new multilateral rule making are ones in which the most knowledge-intensive firms have a lot to gain.

The three most extreme cases of persisting protectionism on the part of the US government are with steel, softwood lumber and agriculture: three industries which are among the most commodified.[4] Troubles in the steel industry became severe in the wake of the financial crises of 1997 and 1998 in East Asia and Russia. Steel exports from these areas to the United States began to escalate as collapsing currencies in the exporting countries reduced the prices of the steel exports and as domestic economic troubles led steel firms to search out foreign customers. There was an upswing of US AD and CVD measures against imported steel. In 2001 the Byrd amendment took effect – a law that for the first time gave the money from the AD and CVD duties, that previously would have been directed to the Commerce Department, to those US firms involved in AD and CVD cases, a sum estimated to be $200 million per year (Sheppard 2002: 133). Although ostensibly enacted for all industries, most of the benefits will go to the steel firms, a key industry in Senator Byrd's home state of West Virginia. Critics were angered by the way Byrd slipped his amendment into an unrelated bill, thereby avoiding public debate (Sheppard 2002: 140). Then in March 2002 President George Bush unilaterally imposed a tariff on steel imports of up to 30 per cent, affecting about $8 billion of imports (*Economist* 2002). These measures were met with shock and anger by US trading partners.

In the softwood lumber dispute with Canada the conflict revolved around the question of whether lumber from publicly owned forests in Canada was being sold at unfairly low prices as compared to the mainly privately owned forests in the United States. The dispute dates back to a CVD investigation by the US government in 1982. Despite rulings in its favour from a Canada–US Free Trade Agreement panel, faced with the threat of punitive CVD measures the Canadian government concluded bilateral agreements with the United States designed to control Canadian lumber exports into the United States. Lee (2002: 161), in an analysis of the 1996 agreement concluded after the Uruguay Round had supposedly outlawed voluntary export restraints, comments that 'power politics, rather than economic rationale was the dominant factor in this process'. In 2002 efforts to conclude yet another such agreement broke down and on May 23 the United States unilaterally imposed a 27 per cent tariff on Canadian lumber exports.

In agriculture the Bush government shocked its trading partners by agreeing to a massive agricultural subsidy, again a policy initiative diametrically opposed to the principles that had been codified in the Uruguay Round (see Chapter 5 by Grant in this volume). It raised agricultural subsidies by at least 80 per cent and is estimated to cost as much as $190 billion over ten years (Tyson 2002). As Tyson commented, only six months previously the developing countries had agreed to launch a new trade round in good part because of promises to address subsidies. 'This about-face has dealt a severe blow to American credibility around the world.' (Tyson 2002: 26). US cotton subsidies were roughly $3.4 billion in 2001, about 68 per cent of cotton subsidies worldwide, and the source of up to half of the income of US cotton firms. A fifth of US cotton comes from Texas, which, along with other cotton states, exercises heavy influence in the House and Senate agriculture committees. Cotton is an especially important crop for many poor countries that cannot afford subsidies, and critics have pointed to the damage the US subsidies do to them (*Wall Street Journal* 2002).

The new areas of rule-making established in the Uruguay Round are mostly ones that were of special concern to leading US firms and that are not necessarily consistent with the image of highly competitive and universally beneficial markets associated with free trade ideals. The intellectual property provisions at the WTO were put on the negotiating agenda at the initiative of the largest US pharmaceutical companies (Sell 1999; May, Chapter 9 of this volume). Patent protection confers a monopoly on the patent holder and in the case of the Uruguay Round agreements, this was set at 20 years. Even Bhagwati (2001: 26), one of the best-known economists promoting the benefits of free trade, has criticized the inclusion of intellectual property in the trade agreements, arguing that it is 'pretty close to an unrequited transfer of royalties from the using to the producing countries. In effect, its inclusion turned the WTO into a royalty-collection agency'.

One of the key elements of the agreement at Doha to launch a new round of trade was to ease the Uruguay Round intellectual property rules to allow developing countries to address public health emergencies, such as the AIDS/HIV pandemic (see May, Chapter 9 of this volume). This provoked a flurry of lobbying by pharmaceutical companies, including $50 million put towards helping

Republicans win control of Congress in November 2002. More than two dozen Republicans signed letters opposing the loosening of intellectual property restrictions to help developing countries, including Rep. Nancy Johnson, Senator Orrin Hatch, and Senator Charles Grassley, who had received $204,817, $387,824 and $100,000 respectively in pharmaceutical company donations (*Wall Street Journal* 2003b). As a result the United States reversed its Doha position, and was the only country among the 144 WTO members to block a proposal to provide cheaper patented medicine to developing countries, a move that significantly contributed to the loss of momentum of the Doha Round.

Similarly, financial services liberalization was aggressively promoted by the Clinton administration in response to pressure from Wall Street and is now viewed by many as having been excessively fast, exposing the countries hit by crisis in 1997 and 1998 to destructive waves of exuberance and panic rather than the type of efficiency- and growth-maximizing market competition associated with the free-trade ideal. With regard to investment measures, as noted above it is not clear that all the types of state intervention that are designed to restrict are necessarily incompatible with efficient markets (see Chapter 8 by Wiener in this volume). In some cases they may usefully offset the excessive power of dominant firms. While investment treaties have been enthusiastically embraced by developing country governments, the degree to which this is economically optimal rather than a reflection of their weak bargaining power relative to multinational firms (much like the willingness of competing jurisdictions to offer very large tax concessions to attract foreign investment) remains unclear. Lack of consensus on the desirability of a comprehensive investment component at in the WTO agreements has left unclear the likely nature of any investment negotiations in the Doha Round (Kentin 2002). The dispute resolution mechanism, while greatly strengthened, still relies in the end for sanctions on the ability of the aggrieved country to deny access to its market – an arrangement that favours large important markets like the United States.

While the bringing of textiles and apparel into the Uruguay Round agreement is certainly a shift away from state-managed market sharing agreements to more competitive markets, it is not inconsistent with the current interests of the US industry, since most apparel production relevant to US firms has been shifted offshore while the more knowledge- and capital-intensive textile industry, often closely associated with chemical multinationals such as Dupont, has been more successful than apparel at competing internationally. The voice of the US textile industry, the American Textile Manufacturers Institute (ATMI), has pursued a strategy to respond to competition from East Asia by having the US government reduce tariffs on apparel from the Americas that uses the fabric that ATMI's member firms produce (*Wall Street Journal* 2003c). Moreover, the most important aspects of the commitments to liberalize textiles and apparel in the Uruguay Round were delayed to 2005 (Dickerson 1999).

In general US firms have multiple points of access to the US government, and US trade policy consistently reflects their varying interests rather than an ideological or institution-based struggle between the ideals of globally beneficial free trade and the backwardness of self-interested protectionism. As noted above, both traditional industries such as steel and cotton, and high-tech industries such as pharmaceuticals, work through Congress to achieve their goals, with the former pushing for subsidies or tariffs and the latter to protect their intellectual property. Industries can make use of the more bureaucratic AD and CVD measures administered by the US International Trade Commission an independent, quasi-judicial federal agency or the Foreign Sales Corporation tax measures administered by the Treasury Department. At times, as Cortell (1997) has demonstrated with regard to the 1985 semiconductor trade measures brought about by centralized cabinet-level action, a particular industry can also get effective protective action at the executive level. The Trade Promotion/Fast Track Authority helps reconcile differences between presidents and Congress, because the President's ability to have trade agreements ratified with a simple yes or no vote instead of Congress modifying particular aspects of agreements is only obtained in exchange for close consultation with Congress during the trade negotiations. Moreover each such grant of authority to a president has been preceded by significant concessions to those desiring protection, including the steel and agriculture measures that preceded the 2002 Trade Promotion Authority obtained by President Bush (Bergsten 2002).

Conclusion

Looking back over the past half century of US trade policy, it is apparent that for commodified industries with low levels of knowledge-intensity the US government has consistently used trade policy to shield US firms from foreign competition. By contrast, for the types of knowledge-intensive industries in which most leading US multinational companies are located, the US government has always been eager to use its power to help firms commercialize internationally the technological innovations upon which their market dominance was based, whether through gaining access for branches and subsidiaries in foreign countries or more recently through intellectual property rights.

This latter aspect of US trade policy has always been portrayed as in the world's best interest, whether as a counterforce to the excessive statism associated with fascism or communism, or as an expression of free competitive growth-enhancing markets. Thus this aspect of US trade policy appeared to involve a fortuitous compatibility between global welfare and the interests of US firms. Yet there are numerous ways in which these policies can been seen as arbitrarily tilting the rules in favour of the leading oligopolistic firms that are so prominent in the US economy, whether in the prohibition of cartels but the acceptance of oligopolies created through mergers and acquisitions; in the dropping of anti-trust initiatives when they began to be turned against US firms; in the opening of financial markets to the type of activities in which US firms had excelled even when the rules were not yet in place to ensure that markets operated effectively; in the prohibition of measures that, arguably, could be used to offset excessive market power of leading firms in small countries; and in the strengthening of monopolies in key technologies through the integration of patent rights into the Uruguay Round agreement.

Looking back over the past quarter century, it is remarkable how effectively the US turned back challenges to its competitiveness. In the mid-1970s industry after industry appeared to be collapsing from the onslaught of foreign competition, especially from East Asia. By the 1990s books such as *Comeback: The Fall and Rise of the American Automobile Industry* (Ingrassia and White 1994) and *Steel Phoenix: The Fall and Rise of the US Steel Industry* (Hall 1997) signalled US exuberance at the revitalization of these threatened industries.

The prevailing story is that this restoration of US dominance was due to East Asian mismanagement and US entrepreneurialism. Yet it also involved an aggressive use of US trade policy. Restrictions on foreign imports in key industries gave those industries in which knowledge-intensive production was an option time to reorganize and rework the structure of the global industry. The United States has been able to use its own trade policy as the type of lever that it has sought to deny to other countries in its promotion of rules on trade-related investment measures in trade negotiations. Exports to the United States from Japan and South Korea, two of the top targets of US unilateralism, have declined as a share of their total exports since the 1980s[5] and while there are many factors contributing to this, including the expansion of other markets and currency shifts, the restructuring of the trading relationship facilitated by US trade policy is part of the story.

Overall, then, US trade policy, in both its liberalizing and protectionist variants, has sought to promote the interests of US firms, contradicting the ideal of universally beneficial highly competitive free trade with which supporters of US trade policy often justify it. US trade policy is closer to that of a heavy-handed hegemony than a liberal leader.

Acknowledgement

The research assistance of Diana Cucuz was important in the preparation of this chapter.

Notes

1. An interesting example of the way in which leading firms can manage markets is their capacity to maintain differentials in prices. For instance, in 2002 it was reported that an auto company was planning to prevent 'grey market' sales of cars between Canada and the US. The price differential between the two countries, close to 30 per cent in some cases, can only be explained by a deliberate segmentation of a market that one might otherwise expect to be fluid and competitive given the NAFTA. 'Auto maker alarmed by soaring "grey" sales', *Globe and Mail*, May 21, 2002, pp. A1, A9.
2. Bates *et al.* (1991) discuss the relationship between the risks to which citizens are exposed by trade, and the tendency to use either tariffs or social welfare spending to alleviate these. In the United States, where social protections are relatively weak, it would not be surprising to see an aggressive use of protectionist policies as an alternative.
3. For a more extensive analysis of the significance of technological profiles, see Porter (2002).
4. A fourth case of protectionism in 2002 was the development of energy legislation that would subsidize a gas pipeline through Alaska and prohibit a Canadian alternative, as well as promoting ethanol, which is protected against foreign suppliers (*Oil and Gas Journal* 2002).
5. Based on International Monetary Fund Direction of Trade Statistics, various years.

References

Barringer, W.H. and Pierce, K.J. (2000) 'Paying the Price for Big Steel: $100 billion in Trade Restraints and Corporate Welfare', Washington: American Institute for International Steel.

Bates, R.H., Brock, P. and Tiefenthaler, J. (1991) 'Risk and Trade Regimes: Another Exploration', *International Organization*, 45, 1, Winter: 1–18.

Bayard, T.I. and Elliott, K.A. (1994) *Reciprocity and Retaliation in U.S. Trade Policy*, Washington: Institute for International Economics.

Bergsten, C.F. (2002) 'A Renaissance for U.S. Trade Policy?' *Foreign Affairs*, Nov./Dec.: pp. 86–98.

Bhagwati, J. (2001) 'After Seattle: Free Trade and the WTO', *International Affairs*, 77, 1: pp. 15–29.

Chapman, K. (1991) *The International Petrochemical Industry: Evolution and Location*, Oxford: Blackwell.

Chemical Market Reporter (2002) 'ACC Remains Hopeful on High Stakes Trade Dispute', *Chemical Market Reporter*, 28 January: 1, 24.

Cohen, S.D. (2000) *The Making of United States International Economic Policy: Principles, Problems and Proposals for Reform*, Fifth Edition, Westport: Praeger.

Cortell, A.P. (1997) 'Centralization, Access and Influence: The Reagan Administration and the Semiconductor Industry's Trade Complaints', *Governance*, 10, 3, July: 261–85.

Cronin, B. (2001) 'The Paradox of Hegemony: America's Ambiguous Relationship with the United Nations', *European Journal of International Relations*, 7, 1: 103–30.

Dell, S. (1990) *The United Nations and International Business*, Durham: Duke University Press.

Dickerson, K.G. (1999) *Textiles and Apparel in the Global Economy*, Third Edition, Upper Saddle River: Prentice Hall.

Economist (2002) 'George Bush, Protectionist; Tariffs on Steel', 9 March: p. 13.

Flamm, K. (1996) *Mismanaged Trade? Strategic Policy and the Semiconductor Industry*, Washington: Brookings Institute.

Frieden, J. (1988) 'Sectoral Conflict and U.S. Foreign Policy, 1914–1940' in Ikenberry, G.J., Lake, D.A. and Mastanduno, M. (eds.) *The State and American Foreign Economy Policy*, Ithaca and London: Cornell University Press, pp. 59–90.

Haggard, S. (1988) 'The Institutional Foundations of Hegemony: Explaining the Reciprocal Trade Agreements Act of 1934' in Ikenberry, G.J., Lake, D.A. and Mastanduno, M. (eds) *The State and American Foreign Economy Policy*, Ithaca and London: Cornell University Press: pp. 91–120.

Hall, C.G.L. (1997) *Steel Phoenix: The Fall and Rise of the US Steel Industry*, New York: St. Martins.

Ikenberry, G.J., Lake, D.A. and Mastanduno, M. (eds.) (1988) *The State and American Foreign Economy Policy*, Ithaca and London: Cornell University Press.

Ingrassia, P. and White, J.B. (1994) *Comeback: The Fall and Rise of the American Automobile Industry*, New York: Simon and Schuster.

Kentin, E. (2002) 'Prospects for Rules in Investment in the New WTO Round', *Legal Issues of Economic Integration*, 29, 1: pp. 61–71.

Krauss, E. (1993) 'Negotiations to Open Japan's Construction Markets to US Firms', in Walters, R.S. (ed.) *Talking Trade: US Policy in International Perspective*, Boulder: Westview: pp. 78–104.

Krueger, A.O. (1995) *American Trade Policy: A Tragedy in the Making*, Washington: AEI Press.

Lake, D.A. (1993) 'Leadership, Hegemony, and the International Economy: Naked Emperor or Tattered Monarch with Potential?', *International Studies Quarterly*, 37, 4, December: pp. 459–89.

Lee, Y-S. (2002) 'Revival of Grey-Area Measures: The US–Canada Softwood Lumber Agreement: Conflict with the WTO Agreement on Safeguards', *Journal of World Trade*, 36, 1: pp. 155–65.

Office of Technology Competitiveness (1997) *The Global Context for U.S. Technology Policy*, Washington DC: Office of Technology Competitiveness.

Oil and Gas Journal (2002) 'The New US Protectionism', *Oil and Gas Journal*, 27 May: p. 19.

Porter, T. (2002) *Technology, Governance and Political Conflict in International Industries*, London: Routledge.

Porter, T. (1999) 'Hegemony and the Private Governance of International Industries' in Cutler, A.C., Haufler, V. and Porter, T. (eds.) *Private Authority and International Affairs*, Albany: State University of New York Press, pp. 257–82.

Sell, S. (1999) 'Multinational Corporations as Agents of Change: The Globalization of Intellectual Property Rights' in Cutler, A.C., Haufler, V. and Porter, T. (eds) *Private Authority and International Affairs*, Albany: State University of New York Press: pp. 169–98.

Sheppard, H.E. (2002) 'The Continued Dumping and Subsidy Offset Act (Byrd Amendment); A Defeat Before the WTO May Constitute an Overall Victory for U.S. Trade', *Tulane Journal of International and Comparative Law*, 10, Spring, Lexis-Nexis version.

Shoch, J. (2001) *Trading Blows: Party Competition and U.S. Trade Policy in a Globalizing Era*, Chapel Hill: University of North Carolina Press.

Tyson, Laura D'Andrea (2002) 'The Farm Bill is a $200 Billion Disaster', *Business Week*, Issue 3785, June 3, p. 26.

Wall Street Journal (2003a) 'How to Start a Trade War' [Author: Lawrence B. Lindsey], 25 June, Proquest version.

Wall Street Journal (2003b) 'U.S. Flip on Patents Shows Drug Makers' Growing Clout – Political Donors get Help in Reversing Policy on Poor Nations' Access to Cheaper Medicines' [Author: Tom Hamburger], 6 Feb., Proquest version.

Wall Street Journal (2003c) 'U.S. Offers Cuts in Tariffs to Spur Trade in Americas – Proposal is Silent on Issues of Sugar and Textiles, Key to Securing an Agreement' [Author: Neil King Jr.], 12 February, Proquest version.

Wall Street Journal (2002) 'Hanging by a Thread: In U.S. Cotton Farmers Thrive: In Africa, they Fight to Survive-America's Subsidies Depress World Prices, Undermining its Foreign-Policy Goals-Sowing Seeds of Frustration' [Authors: Roger Thurow and Scott Kilman], 26 June, Proquest version.

12
The Politics of Trade in Brazil

Pedro da Motta Veiga

Throughout the last decade, trade policies and trade policymaking have suffered profound changes in Brazil. Such changes cannot be understood without reference to the specific characteristics of the liberal revision process that affected the Brazilian development model in the 1990s. Compared to the changes that occurred in other large Latin American countries such as Mexico, and even Argentina itself, the distinguishing trait of this particular process is the balanced combination of elements of both disruption and continuity that characterizes the process in Brazil.

In fact, the resistance posed by Brazilian business, union and bureaucratic concerns that had consolidated their positions during the long and relatively successful period of protectionist industrialization acted as a 'moderating' force in the implementation of market-oriented reforms. In both trade and industry policies, the key role of import-competing sectors is widely recognized (in general, the same sectors that had benefited from the microeconomic policies of previous decades: automobile, chemicals, electro-electronic and capital goods, among others).

The major consequence of the 'negotiated' nature of the Brazilian transition was the persistence, after the liberalizing reforms, of protection structures and highly discriminating inter-sectoral incentives, despite the fact that clear business-supporting policies had evolved towards the use of 'horizontal' instruments, over the last decade. Thus, the changes in trade policy and policymaking that occurred during the 1990s can only be understood in the light of a logical reasoning in which both continuity and discontinuity combine. The unilateral trade liberalization that took place early in the decade, Brazil's role in various trade-negotiation processes and the efforts made to improve the export performance of the manufacturing sectors were shaping factors in this process of policy changes.

Two dimensions of Brazil's trade policies in the 1990s fairly illustrate this hypothesis: the participation of Brazil in preferential trade negotiations and the changes in the process of trade policymaking. As far as trade negotiations are concened, Brazil's agenda became increasingly complex in the second half of the 1990s. A widely diversified listing of external negotiations involving other member-states of the Latin American Integration Association (LAIA) as well as developed countries was added to the complex internal agenda of the Mercosur.

In December 1994, the Free Trade Area of the Americas (FTAA) was launched as an initiative spurred largely by the United States, followed by the signature of an Inter-regional Cooperation Agreement in 1995 between Mercosur and the European Union, covering trade and economic cooperation. In both these processes, Mercosur acts as a single economic bloc, which has not been the case in negotiations with other LAIA members, such as the Andean Community nations and Mexico (see Chapter 10 by Phillips, this volume).

In preferential trade negotiations with developed partners, Brazil's prevailing approach has been shaped by caution or, more accurately, by a defensive stance. How can this defensive stance on the part of Brazil be understood, when contrasted with, for instance, the active approach of Mexico when discussing free trade agreements with its partners in North America in 1994, and recently with the European Union? A reason traditionally invoked to justify this stance points to the fact that Brazil is a *global trader*, hence maintaining strong trade relations with different regions of the world and hosting foreign direct investments originating in the United States, the European Union and Japan. The main policy implication of this feature of Brazil's international insertion would be to reduce its interest in participating in preferential trade negotiations.

This is a relevant argument, and there are certainly significant economic risks for Brazil associated with preferential liberalization initiatives involving its relations with the United States or the European Union. However, this does not fully explain the logic of Brazil's negotiating position as Brazil's stance, particularly in its talks with developed countries, is not based on a rational assessment of the economic costs and benefits associated with these negotiations. To be sure, that happens to be the case for most countries. In addition to being shaped by the interests and lobbying capacity of public and private players, the negotiating position of Brazil is grounded on cost/benefit assessments of negotiating processes whose reference framework is the nation's foreign policy – and the paradigm shaping this policy – more than on economic or trade considerations or concerns.

In the field of trade policymaking, the domestic mechanisms of consultation and negotiations in the area of policy were diversified over the 1990s and have produced communication routines characterized by a certain regularity and frequency. In general, these mechanisms became more formal and institutionalized, even if there are varying degrees of institutionalization according to each mechanism. In addition, informal lobbying and practices of direct pressure on public agents continued to be significant in public–private relations, especially in lobbying for protection for specific segments, such as textiles, automobiles and footwear. In general, the dialogue between public sector and private agents in the area of trade (and industrial) policies is still strongly sectoral, maintaining the characteristic traditions of the protectionist development model. Increasingly, however, in the area of trade negotiations this dialogue is being carried on with civil society entities that have the characteristics of 'horizontal' representation (that is, trans-sectoral). This is caused by the typically complex, multiple-issue (that is, not restricted to market-access issues) agendas of such negotiations.

This chapter consists of three sections, in addition to the introduction. In the next section, it analyses the factors shaping the negotiating position of Brazil at the level of Mercosur's foreign relations. This is followed by a section dealing with changes in trade policymaking in Brazil, and a final section presenting the main conclusions of the chapter.

Brazil and preferential trade negotiations with developed countries

Conditioning factors and rationale of Brazil's stance

Accounting for some two-thirds of the total GDP of Mercosur, Brazil's economic performance, domestic policies and negotiating stance within this bloc have marked effects on the overall development of the integration process, its methodology and its negotiating agenda. In the external relationships of Mercosur, and specially as far as relationships with developed partners are concerned, the role of Brazil has also been that of a protagonist and the negotiating stance of Brazil is clearly defensive.

What is the logic of Brazil's negotiating strategy within these processes, and what are the factors shaping it? There are apparently two aspects behind this attitude:

- the first involves the political economy of the liberalization reform in Brazil, particularly the supremacy that the import-competing sectors have managed to maintain over export sectors in the field of trade policy and politics; and
- the second is the four-decades hegemonic paradigm of foreign policy, characterized by competition with the United States and the objective of developing the nation's industrial capacity as a key condition for independent activities within the international system.

As far as the political economy of the liberalization reform is concerned, in late 1994, Brazil was completing a triple-pronged trade liberalization drive: the Customs Union was coming into effect in Mercosur; it was preparing to sign the multilateral commitments resulting from the Uruguay Round; and thanks to the foreign exchange policy of the Real Economic Stabilization Plan, the competitive impacts of the unilateral liberalization completed at the end of the previous year were reaching their full potential.

From 1995 onwards, the liberal guidelines of industrial and foreign trade policies in Brazil began to shift. At least two factors lie at the roots of this change:

- first, Mexico's *Tequila Crisis* in late 1994 was at the origin of an import administration process based largely on tariffs and designed to avoid a sharp deterioration of Brazil's trade balance, which slipped into the red in 1995 after over a decade of significant positive results. The deterioration of the trade balance could have undermined the stabilization strategy based on the nominal exchange rate.

Common External Tariff (CET) rates moved – generally upwards – in order to discourage imports of durable and non-durable consumer goods;

- second, as the exchange rate appreciated after the introduction of the stabilization programme, the impacts of the reduction in the tariff protection introduced between 1990 and 1993 were magnified. Hence, less competitive industrial sectors were severely affected, prompting the reappearance of protectionist pressures from these sectors. Some segments (such as toys and clothing) benefited through the introduction of import quotas, while the Federal Government regulated and implemented new trade protection mechanisms (anti-dumping rules and safeguards) in accordance with the Uruguay Round agreements on these issues.

Hence, the macro- and micro-economic impacts of the exchange rate appreciation and rising doubts about the sustainability of Brazil's stabilization strategy converged to make the Government gradually adopt new policy guidelines in the industrial and export areas. Fresh incentives were introduced for sectors that were being restructured and for attracting producers able to substitute imports (such as telecommunications equipment manufacturers). In the export area, Government support was expanded through public financing and phased out existing export taxes on semi-processed products, in parallel to the introduction of the export credit insurance system.

These new trends confirm that, from 1995 onwards, a neo-activist stance firmed up in the fields of foreign trade and industrial policy that extended beyond the emergency measures justified through the macro- or micro-economic conjunctural rationale. This shift laid down the limits of the liberalizing reforms in Brazil in the fields of trade and industrial policy. With no clear-cut reversal in the liberalization process, trade policy began to reflect to an increasing extent the idea that the negative effects of trade liberalization were significant and had not yet been absorbed by industry. In addition, sizeable risks were foreseen in any new measure that could increase the openess of the domestic goods and services markets.

This meant that the view began to firm up among policymakers that, once the unilateral tariff reduction schedule, the Mercosur transition period and the multilateral negotiation cycle of the Uruguay Round were completed, Brazil should 'digest' this three-track liberalization movement, pruning from its external agenda any initiatives that might result in any additional commitments to further liberalization. The core role played in Brazil's strategy by the perception of the competitive fragility of Brazilian industry – and its consequent potential vulnerability – is compatible with a view of policy shaped mainly by the interest of the import-competing sectors.

This hegemony of import-competing sectors in Brazil's trade policy recalls a distinctive trait in the transformation dynamics sweeping through Brazil during this decade, when compared to changes taking place in other major Latin American nations, such as Mexico and Argentina. In Brazil, resistance among entrepreneurial, trade union, bureaucratic and corporate interests consolidated during the long and reasonably successful period of protectionist industrialization had marked effects on the implementation of reforms slanted towards the market and liberalization.

The main outcome of the negotiated style of the transition in Brazil – whose sole period of exception consists of the 30 months of the Collor Administration – consisted of the survival, even after reforms, of protection structures and discriminatory (inter-sectoral) incentives, both benefiting these same import-competing sectors that were privileged by industrial and export policies over earlier decades (auto-assembly, chemicals, electronics and capital goods sectors).

At the foreign policy level, continuity prevailed with no ambiguity, despite major changes in regulations in the Brazilian economy. The globalistic paradigm that has dominated Brazil's foreign policy since the 1960s remained in position and framed the political logic behind Brazil's participation in Mercosur, as well as in other preferential liberalization initiatives underway.

But what about the 'globalistic paradigm' that has formed the cornerstone of Brazilian foreign policy for the past four decades? This is a view of the Brazilian position in international relationships that results from 'combining ... several different intellectual influences: the nationalistic criticism of the pro-US foreign policy matrix produced under the aegis of the Brazilian Studies Superior Institute (ISEB – *Instituto Superior de Estudos Brasileiros*); the view of the Economic Commission for Latin America and the Caribbean (ECLAC) on the center–periphery relationship; and the tradition of realistic thought in international relations, particularly the concept of the international system as an anarchic context' (Soares de Lima 1994). In this view, the North–South polarization provided the rationale for Brazil's foreign policy, which was supposed to make room for the implementation of an autonomous national industrial strategy. Overall, the paradigm which frames Brazilian foreign policy includes, as its main components, competition with the United States – particularly in the Americas – as the establishment of conditions fostering the nation's industrial development strategy.

Brazil, the FTAA and negotiations with the European Union

In terms of Brazil's trade negotiations with non-Mercosur countries, the convergence (in Brazil) between the prevailing view of foreign policy and the hegemony of the import-competing sectors in national and sub-regional trade policy results in: (1) encouraging the establishment of preferential links with the other countries in South America; and (2) conferring on agreements outside this regional scope the status of initiatives that in principle are not aligned with the core objectives of Brazil's foreign policy.

Within this context framed by a 'political' (more than an economic) foreign policy view, an agreement with the United States is by definition the less desirable option, particularly if it is viewed as a project urged by that country which threatens the survival of the sub-regional political initiative backed by Brazil: Mercosur. Seen from Brasília, this risk is perceived as political more than economic: it is a risk that involves competition for hegemony and not merely markets (see Chapter 11 by Porter, this volume).

The FTAA is often seen as an economic project that could generate huge and long-lasting political consequences: its implementation would permanently shift the balance of power within the Hemisphere and especially in South America. Beyond that, as a former Brazilian ambassador puts it, 'it will expand and legitimate the US preeminence in the Americas, favoring the emergence of an unipolar world. And even if other factors lead to the emergence of a multipolar world, (the FTAA) will place Latin America within the zone under the direct hegemony of the US, thus letting (to LA countries) scarce space for political manoever' (Souto Maior 2001). On the other hand, in this view, an agreement with the European Union gains political functionality, deriving solely from the 'threat' represented by the FTAA. From this standpoint, should this threat cease to exist, the political incentives urging an agreement with the European Union would wilt.

It is interesting to note that, from a 'national industrial strategy' point of view, an agreement with the European Union should not motivate Brazil. Seen from that point of view, the talks with the European Union are basically a North–South bargaining system based on the hypothesis of a trade-off between opening up the agricultural market to exports from Mercosur and opening up the industrial markets of Mercosur countries to European exports. Consequently, the interest shown by the Brazilian authorities in terms of the agreement with Europe is essentially explained through a foreign policy (political) rationale, strengthened by the fact that the European Union – in contrast to the US within the FTAA – explicitly defends bi-regional negotiation between these two blocs, consequently endowing the Mercosur with significant political support, particularly at a time of crisis such as that facing this sub-regional project.

The dominant perception in Brazil with regard to the two negotiation processes highlights the risks associated with them, to the detriment of potential opportunities. From this standpoint the potential costs of Brazil's participation in the FTAA process and negotiations with the European Union are seen as essentially linked to transitional adjustments particularly in the industrial sectors and to the divergences in the priorities of the negotiating agendas of Brazil, on the one hand, and its partners, on the other. For Brazil, the risks of this divergence in the negotiation priorities are linked mainly to the consolidation of arrangements where the issues stressed by the more powerful countries are dealt with adequately, while the same cannot be said for those assigned higher priority by countries with less negotiating clout: the obstacles to dealing with agricultural matters in both negotiating processes, but particularly in the talks with the European Union, is the best illustration of this type of problem.

The core strategy of Brazil in both negotiations has been to protect its national production structure and regulatory regimes as much as possible from the potential adjustment costs triggered by liberalization and negotiation of disciplines, this priority overcoming the objectives of using the agreements as a tool for attracting investments and generating new export flows. The assessment of these agreements in Brazil as a whole consequently tends to be negative, except when one of the talks is perceived as a tool for neutralizing the other one or for increasing the bargaining power of Brazil and Mercosur.

Trade policymaking and trade negotiations – domestic process in the 1990s

Trade (and industrial) policymaking from import substitution to liberalization

During the period of protectionist industrialization, the management of protection extended to local industries against competition from imported goods (especially non-tariff protection) was one of the major mechanisms of industrial policy implementation, together with the use of investment incentive tools. From the 1970s on, active export-promotion activities were added to this set of instruments, supported by tax and credit incentives.

A remarkable characteristic here is that both the design and management of these instruments were essentially sectoral. Hence, the dialogue and consultations between public sector and private agents – in this case, only the companies and sectoral associations directly concerned – were almost entirely restricted to this axis of articulation. Other important characteristics of this period were the lack of transparency of the mechanisms used to manage trade and industry policy and the 'informality' of relations between public and private agents. Both these characteristics relate to the existence of an authoritarian state, with the economic policy instruments under the control of a strong techno-bureaucracy.

As for trade negotiations, they too followed the 'sectoral' model: the bilateral agreements negotiated in the context of the ALADI were based on intra-sectoral concessions. Furthermore, the companies and segments concerned participated actively in the negotiations, defending their particular interests. Consultations between the public sector and the private agents also took place during the negotiation of bilateral or multilateral issues concerning specific sectors (multifibre negotiations / textile sector, VER negotiations with the US / steel sector). The agro-industrial sectors alone monitored closely the evolution of the Uruguay Round, albeit scarcely participating in the definition of the Brazilian positions at the negotiations.

The macroeconomic crisis, which intensified from the second half of the 1980s on, halted the foreign trade negotiations within ALADI. Furthermore, it drastically reduced the state's capacity (both financial and regulatory) to formulate industrial and trade policies. This led to a gradual deterioration of the institutional mechanisms of communication and articulation between public and private sectors, which were then typical of a period of import substitution.

In the second half of the 1980s, several attempts were made to implement industrial policies with a sectoral bias, but none was successful due to internal disagreements within the Federal Government about the importance of such initiatives. The disaggregating effects of the economic crisis on any attempt at coordinated public/private actions also contributed to this failure. One of the few legacies from these experiences has been the gradual shift of industrial policies from a sector to a productive chain emphasis (c.f. Breslin, Chapter 19 in this volume). This shift continued throughout the 1990s, and the 'productive chain' consolidated its position as one of the significant units for industrial and trade policy formulation, as well as for the public/private sector dialogue.

At the same time, there were several attempts to reduce inflation – usually in the form of heterodox shocks. In the succeeding governments, design and implementation of stabilization plans were priorities. In this context, interaction with the private sector was shunned, even more so in view of the growing notion that the major business groups in the various sectors and their class organizations constituted an 'inflationary coalition': as direct beneficiaries of the accelerating inflation rates, they resisted the efforts to achieve stabilization. This notion inspired the disruption policy of the Collor administration, which implemented a program of unilateral reduction of import duties, eliminated a whole series of non-tariff barriers and engaged Brazil in a sub-regional liberalization process in the *Cone Sul* (Southern Cone), breaking away from the sectoral tradition of the ALADI negotiations.

All these measures were part of a strategy of confrontation with the organized business sectors. The trade liberalization and the early years of the Mercosur are usually quoted as a model case of non-participation by the private sector and of Government resistance to private sector attempts at interference. Nevertheless, during the Collor administration the *Grupos Executivos de Política Setorial (GEPS –* Executive Groups of Sectoral Policy) were created. Although the GEPS never succeeded in consolidating their position, they were the inspiration for the Sectoral Chambers, a mechanism created in 1991 for the negotiation of prices and salaries, and which evolved into a forum for the discussion and negotiation of sectoral development and competitiveness issues. A new feature introduced by the Sectoral Chambers was participation by the labour unions in the mechanisms for dialogue between Government and the private sector – in which only the business sector had participated until then. The major – and perhaps the only – practical results of the creation of Sectoral Chambers were the various automobile agreements negotiated between the government, the companies and the unions. The 1995 version of the agreement produced a highly discriminating sectoral trade and investment regime.

The results of such public/private articulation initiatives may have been extremely limited in terms of industrial policy, but the idea of a three-party participation (government, business and workers) 'migrated' to the Mercosur process of negotiations and, via its technical subgroups, was incorporated into the institutional framework of the quadripartite Agreement by the constitution of the Social-Economic Consulting Forum.

On the other hand, the 1994 negotiations of the Mercosur *Tarifa Externa Comum* (Common External Tariff) provided the opportunity to reinstate consultation and negotiation routines between government negotiators and the private sector. As for the labour unions, the foreign trade and international integration issues were introduced into their agenda via the Mercosur discussions. In fact, it was after the Mercosur technical sub-groups were formed, in 1992/1993, that the *Central Única dos Trabalhadores* (CUT) became involved in discussions regarding labour issues and industrial policy (sectoral policies, above all) and foreign trade matters.

'Horizontal' business associations, such as the *Confederação Nacional da Indústria* (CNI), and sectoral entities also joined meetings of the Mercosur technical subgroups, especially those dealing with issues in which they were particularly interested: industrial policy, technical standards, and so on. However, this participation is not institutionalized: business and labour organizations attend the meetings as 'guests', or 'observers'. The articulation between private sector and Government in these subgroups is essentially informal, and seldom promotes the development of routines for coordinating and monitoring the negotiations.

Recent evolution in the trade negotiations policymaking

From 1998, the priority given by the Government to expanding exports, the intensification of the FTAA negotiations and the prospect – finally frustrated in Seattle – of launching a new round of multilateral negotiations caused an important change in the trade policy-management environment in Brazil. The issue of 'trade negotiations' has acquired greater importance in the trade policy agenda in view of Brazilian participation in processes characterized by a large variety of issues, including borderline and 'domestic' issues. This expansion of the agenda imposes a gradual redefinition of the way private sectors organize themselves, and of their dialogue with the Government.

In this field, the FTAA negotiations have been the driving force of a broad reorganization of domestic negotiation and consultation processes. On the business side, the negative experience of the early Mercosur years and the gradual involvement in negotiations from 1994 onwards, provided the incentive for a strong and growing participation in the ALCA (Área de Libre Comercio de las Américas) negotiations. Articulated around the *Confederação Nacional da Indústria* – CNI (National Confederation of Industries), the *Coalizão Empresarial Brasileira* (Brazilian Business Coalition) was founded, bringing together industry, agriculture and the service sector. On the public sector side, the Secretaria Nacional da ALCA – SENALCA (National FTAA Secretariat) was created under the Ministry of Foreign Affairs. This new entity is the forum for debating issues related with the hemispheric negotiations, and is in charge of coordinating the definition of a national position regarding the issues under discussion. There are monthly SENALCA meetings in which representatives from various Ministries, the Foreign Trade Chamber of the Office of the President of the Republic, the Central Bank and other organs of the federal Government participate. The decree that created SENALCA allows for the possible participation, as guests, of entities representing civil society. Some of the national business entities and one labour union-association have gradually joined the SENALCA meetings – as observers invited by the Government, it should be noted – but the scope of the discussions, the agenda of the debates and their limits are clearly defined by the Government coordinators of the forum, that is, representatives of the Ministry of Foreign Affairs.

As the ALCA negotiations evolved, Inter-ministerial (thematic) Groups were organized. These groups are responsible for monitoring the discussions in each of the hemispheric agreement Negotiation Groups. Technical representatives from various ministries and other government organs take part in these groups, while private sector participation is informally admitted in some, but not in others.

There are no express reasons for such exclusions. Apparently, it could be attributed to a set of factors including personal idiosyncrasies and intra-bureaucratic disputes developing in a context where the Government is endeavouring to modify the pattern of its relationship with private agents in trade negotiation processes, although the objectives and methods of this revision are not very clear.

The pace of FTAA negotiations, participation in Negotiation Groups and TNC meetings, etc. defines the work agendas of both SENALCA and the Inter-ministerial Groups. As a rule, each round of meetings is followed by a domestic round to present the results, discuss the issues making up the agenda for the coming meetings and to prepare negotiation proposals. It is interesting to note that the Inter-ministerial Groups, which were originally created to deal with the FTAA negotiations, are increasingly incorporating discussions on other negotiation processes within their respective thematic fields. Hence, a typical agenda of the Services Inter-ministerial Group would comprise, for instance, the FTAA negotiations, recent developments in WTO debates on the built-in agenda of the Uruguay Round, internal Mercosur negotiations and discussions with the EU on this subject. Therefore, there is a clear ongoing process to generate, from FTAA-driven mechanisms, institutional spillovers whose effects on the future evolution of domestic trade policy negotiation and consultation mechanisms are difficult to assess at this point in time.

More recently, the SENALCA model has been adopted to support Brazilian negotiations with the European Union (through Mercosur). In this case, the agency (SENEUROPA) includes, in addition to government representatives, a member of the Brazilian Section of the Mercosur Joint Parliamentary Commission and another from the Brazilian Section of the Economic and Social Consulting Forum, both representing civil society.[1] This first case of fully institutionalized participation of representatives from civil society is being challenged as other entities active in the field of trade negotiations argue that the *Fóro Consultivo Econômico e Social* has no legitimacy as a representative of the business sector.

The design of the institutional model adopted for domestic consultation on trade negotiations seems to be undergoing a transition phase. Clearly, the days when the Foreign Affairs Ministry held a monopoly in the formulation of Brazilian negotiation positions and of the country's 'national interest' are gone. Furthermore, both informal and direct mechanisms of dialogue between the Government and the companies and sectors concerned in bilateral market-access agreements within LAIA (ALADI) have suffered a relative decline in importance, but without disappearing. Nowadays, institutional consultation formats seem to vary according to the items on the agenda and to the progress in the negotiation process. Complex agendas comprising non-border trade issues generate frequent and relatively institutionalized domestic consultation and negotiating mechanisms, with a clearly defined hierarchy, formal convening and result-assessment mechanisms, together with a reasonable amount of transparency vis-à-vis the groups that have access to them (Government, business associations, labour union associations and Congress). In negotiations that become intense, such as is the case with FTAA, these mechanisms tend to consolidate and become more and more sophisticated.

As for negotiations with other LAIA (ALADI) countries, where the items on the agenda are still limited to tariff concession exchanges, there is a rather informal consultation mechanism that is fundamentally driven by the dynamics of negotiations, the latter being far less regular and systematic than FTAA's. In general, the Government asks horizontal entities of the private sector to coordinate the process of consulting the various sectors to prepare lists of liberalization proposals and demands. From then on, a series of meetings between Government and private entities takes place, to establish strategies, criteria and so on. The process is not regular: the Government organizes meetings with businessmen; the private sector may propose meetings with the Government; and the Government can halt consultations with no further explanations offered.

Typically, in the ALADI bilateral negotiations there are normally no pre-defined targets such as the establishment of a Free Trade Zone, and as the Government seldom defines guidelines and rules on minimum levels of liberalization, overall objectives of the negotiations, and so on, they continue to be strongly influenced by sectoral interests, particularly those of import-competing sectors.

A telling example is the negotiation between Brazil and Mexico over recent years. On the one hand, the objective of a broad bilateral trade liberalization agreement was frustrated by pressure from the sectors threatened by import competition, such as the electro-electronic sector. This sector would express its opposition to the agreement in the proper Government consultation forums, but at the same time, unilaterally develop a lobby and pressure strategy to influence various government agencies in Brasília. On the other hand, and in the opposite sense, the automobile sectors of both countries separately negotiated an increase in bilateral interchange quotas, aimed at maximizing their regional production and marketing strategies, which led Brazil and Mexico to leading positions as car-making centres in Latin America.

Final comments

This chapter analysed two dimensions of Brazil's trade policies in the 1990s: the participation of Brazil in preferential trade negotiations and the changes in the process of trade policymaking. A common trait of both dimensions is the coexistence of elements of continuity and rupture, which expresses the 'negotiated' nature of the Brazilian transition from the protectionist industrialization period to a more liberal regime of policies.

In the field of trade negoatiations, the logic of the action employed by national and regional players involved in the talks and the strategies deriving from them are prompted less by a 'rational' assessment of the economic incentives and cost structure theoretically associated with preferential liberalization processes than by the prevailing perceptions regarding the nature and content of national or regional interests, as well as the functionality of the various negotiations to the accomplishment of these interests. The case of Brazil illustrates this hypothesis. In fact, the functionality of the various preferential liberalization projects is assessed in Brazil in the light of their capacity to help strengthen the nations' power – both political and economic (industrial) – in the field of international relations, and particularly its objective of boosting Brazil's negotiating clout when facing the United States within the hemisphere, and particularly in South America.

The specificity of Brazil's trade negotiations strategy does not lie in the fact that it is framed by a political vision. It can be argued that the subordination of trade policy to foreign policy does occur in a large number of countries. Peharps the distinctive feature of Brazil in this field is to be found in the 'close subordination' pattern which relates trade policy to foreign policy and the consequent hegemony of the political motivations over economic considerations when assessing actual and prospective trade negotiations.

As far as trade policymaking is concerned, the mechanisms for consultation and negotiation between public and private sectors in the area of trade have been going through important changes in Brazil. The major distinctive features of these changes are the diverse 'paths' followed and the heterogeneous results, in institutional terms, of the various initiatives.

On the one hand, there is an undeniable and consistent trend towards the diversification and formalization of the channels for consultation and negotiation more frequently used by the public and private agents. These channels follow a 'horizontal' pattern in the FTAA and Mercosur negotiations, and a sectoral/chain bias in policy initiatives in the areas of export and competitiveness promotion. In the case of the latter type of initiative, participation by productive sectors has been formally established and institutionalized since its inception. In contrast, in trade negotiations the public/private dialogue takes place in forums that were originally created as in-government coordination mechanisms, to which business and labour representative entities were later admitted as guests.

Typically, representation of productive sectors in the existing consultation mechanisms is restricted to two large interest groups: industry entities and labour union confederations. Non-Governmental Organizations, Congress and academic institutions may take part in the discussions, seminars and meetings on issues of trade negotiations and policies, but they do not participate in the routine of preparation and assessment of negotiations. On the other hand, less formal and more traditional public/private dialogue practices remain that are unlikely to be absorbed by institutionalized schemes. Among such practices are the sectoral demands for protection and the ALADI negotiations, which are excessively characterized by exchanges of sector-level concessions, with no prior definition of overall objectives by the governments involved.[2]

The FTAA negotiations on the framework inherited from the 1990s had an important effect on the mobilization of civil society sectors – particularly business and labour entities – around trade issues. At the same time, it has fostered the creation of in-government consultation structures organized around the various issues being negotiated, which have gradually incorporated the permanent participation of business and labour entities. These structures are evolving and taking over consultation functions aimed at formulating the negotiating positions for the various negotiation processes (WTO, Mercosur, EU), in addition to the FTAA.

More recently, the issue of hemispheric negotiations seems to be assuming an increasingly relevant portion of the domestic political agenda, which – if the trend were to be confirmed – would mark a break with the tradition of segregation between domestic and foreign issues in the Brazilian political agenda. The recent presidential elections (October 2002) and the start, in the beginning of 2003, of market-access negotiations in the context of FTAA should strengthen this new trend and introduce important changes in the picture described in this work, particularly regarding participation by organized segments and groups of civil society and the mechanisms for consultation between Government and society around trade issues.

Beyond that, a more 'politicized' context may trigger the appearance of one scenario dominated by a trade liberalization cycle based on the preferential negotiations in the FTAA, as well as with the European Union. The question here is: how will the political economy of Brazil's trade negotiations evolve in the next years? It is true that the progress of the negotiations with the European Union and the FTAA seems to contribute to the emergence of a new liberalization cycle. However, the politicization of domestic discussions on these talks will tend to buttress – at least initially – the partisans of the hegemonic paradigm of foreign policy, as the political debates concentrate on highly sensitive issues like the risks associated with US hemispheric hegemony or the asymmetry of the negotiations between Brazil and the developed countries.

Notes

1. It is worth mentioning that, in June 1999, the Inter-ministerial Work Group on the International Trade of Goods and Services was created, under the Foreign Affairs Ministry. This group is in charge of formulating and coordinating the Brazilian position in preparation for the WTO negotiations. The Group had no practical consequence, as a result of the failure to launch the Millennium Round in December of that same year.
2. When a free trade agreement is negotiated, the overall liberalization parameters are defined in accordance with the WTO's generic rules. Hence, the overall guidelines for an agreement of this kind act as a constraint to sectoral demands for protection and exclusions from its scope. When exchanges of bilateral concessions are negotiated with no overall objective defined, the negotiations are much more vulnerable to sectoral pressures and demands. This is what occurs in negotiations in the context of ALADI.

References

Soares de Lima, M.R. (1994) Ejes analiticos y conflictos de paradigmas en la política exterior brasileña, in *America Latina / Internacional*, Autumn–Winter, vol. 1, No. 2.

Souto Maior, L.A. (2001) Integração, coerência e política internacional, in *Carta Internacional*, ano. IX, n. 101, NUPRI/USP.

13

European Union Trade Policy: Domestic Institutions and Systemic Factors

Stephen Woolcock

This chapter discusses the 'how' factors shaping EU (European Union) trade policy and the manner in which they have changed over time. The established literature covers a range of factors that have been seen as shaping trade policy, including systemic factors, domestic factors, ideas or ideology, and so on. This chapter briefly summarizes these explanations, before assessing how useful these are in explaining EU trade policy.

The chapter suggests that systemic factors have influenced European trade policy less than, for example, US policy. In recent years there are indications that this may be changing, with geopolitical aims being reflected in some of the EU's bilateral or regional trade agreements. Indeed, in recent years the EU has begun to articulate more systemic policy objectives for trade policy in terms of support for a multilateral, rules-based system and its contribution to global economic governance.

In general, however, EU trade policy, like trade policies in many other cases, can best be explained by domestic factors. In this respect the institutional framework within which decision-making on and ratification of agreements occurs appears to be relatively more important in the EU than societal or sector interests. This is probably due to the more elaborate institutional structures required to devise common policies among EU member-states. The complexity of EU policymaking in trade policy also means that national and then EU policy preferences are aggregated and defined within bureaucratic or technocratic channels rather than in national or European parliaments, which still have only a limited role.

Finally, the chapter points to the importance of domestic regulatory norms in shaping the trade policies of all countries at a time of a growing internationalization of domestic policies. When trade policy intrudes into policy areas that are shaped by established regulatory norms, themselves shaped by the aggregation of domestic preferences over an extended period, the dynamics of policy cannot easily be understood by competing sector interests alone. Change in domestic regulatory regimes is more complex than adding protection here or market opening there in order to favour this or that sector. In such cases EU trade policy becomes a search for compatibility between the EU 'domestic' regime and the emerging WTO or other regime. Inevitably any analysis of trade policy will be case-dependent, making generalizations on its nature difficult. What this chapter seeks to do is to provide some analysis of how the various explanatory factors, which have usually been developed with single countries (and usually the United States) in mind, apply in the case of the EU. The broad conclusions summarized above must therefore be viewed as tentative.

The factors shaping trade policy

From the established literature the factors shaping EU trade policy can be summarized as covering systemic or strategic factors, domestic factors, including societal and institutional factors, ideas or ideology.

Systemic factors

The classic systemic explanation for trade policy is the role of an economic hegemon in shaping the international trading system. This has been much associated with the debate about US trade policy, both in terms of the role of the United States in shaping the post-1947 GATT system and the impact of the decline of US hegemony on the stability of the GATT system. By the 1970s the United States was looking to Europe and Japan to cooperate in maintaining the international trading system (Keohane 1984). From the 1970s until perhaps the end of the 1990s the trading system can be characterized as a US–EU duopoly. But to what extent can EU trade policy be seen as a reaction to US policy and policy initiatives? Has the EU assumed a shared role in maintaining an open international trading order and if so how has this constrained or shaped EU policy? Is EU trade policy now shaped by more systemic objectives?

Strategic or foreign policy aims may also shape trade policy. For example, the United States made concessions to negotiating partners in trade during the postwar period on foreign policy grounds. The US acceptance of the imbalanced provisions of the Kennedy Round in the 1960s was one example of such a link. Realists argue that countries favour their allies in trade and other economic agreements, because of the positive security externalities trade agreements can offer. But again much of this literature has been shaped by observing US policy. Does the EU favour its allies in trade relations? Has EU trade policy been used as a substitute for a common foreign or security policy? Strengthening trade and investment ties is clearly seen as a means of contributing to the economic and thus the political stability of the EU's trading partners. Perhaps the best example of this is the use of trade and commercial agreements with the EU's near neighbours in eastern and central Europe as well as the Mediterranean and south Eastern Europe (Balkans). But how far is the EU ready to make concessions in trade policy for such foreign policy and security objectives?

Today systemic factors must include questions of 'global governance' as well as realist perceptions of relative power relationships. Since the 1970s, trade policy has become progressively more concerned with rule-making as well as market access issues. With WTO membership increasingly geographically encompassing, rule-making in the organization must be seen as part of global economic governance. In its formative years the EU tended to reflect the views of member-states that were generally antipathetic towards a rules-based system for trade. But the shift towards more rule-making within the EU and a desire – beginning in the mid-1980s – to contain unilateralist policies of the United States, has resulted in EU rhetoric favouring a multilateral rules-based trading system. Furthermore this rhetoric envisages a role for legitimate policy aims apart from liberal market opening. But has this rhetoric this been reflected in reality?

Domestic factors

Domestic factors have traditionally been divided between societal factors, that is, competing protectionist and liberal sector interests, and institutional factors, or the formal and informal institutional framework within which trade policy decisions are taken. With the increased internationalization of domestic policy preferences, it is also important to add a third domestic factor, namely the role of domestic regulatory norms.

Societal factors are generally powerful factors shaping trade policy. British liberal policy in the nineteenth century was shaped by competition between the protectionist agricultural interests favouring the Corn Laws and the liberal manufacturers. US trade policy has often been described by the balance between liberal and protectionist interests. For example, sectors with increasing returns to scale will favour liberalization while declining sectors will seek protection. Rational choice approaches to trade policy have sought to illustrate how the political actors in government seek to maximize their chances of remaining in power by favouring those sector interests that are most likely to be useful in this endeavour. Principal–agent models see national negotiators as agents acting for sector interest principles. These models are often powerful tools and sector interests clearly have an important role in shaping trade negotiations and agreements. But they have often been developed with the United States in mind where decision-making could well be seen as approximating to such a pluralist model. But do they apply as well in Europe? Is the way sector interests are channelled in EU trade policy different in Europe?

Today it is important to consider how civil society fits into the societal model of trade policy formulation. Since the early 1990s civil society NGOs have become more important in trade policymaking. Environmental NGOs first became aware of the potential clash between trade and environmental policies in the early 1990s with the tuna–dolphin case concerning the compatibility of US national legislation on the protection of dolphin and GATT rules on trade. Since the collapse of the Multilateral Agreement on Investment (MAI), which was attributed, at least in part, to the opposition of civil society NGOs, governments have gone out of their way to consult with civil society on trade policy. But does consultation with civil society have any impact on EU policy?

State-centred explanations

This last point about how sector and other interests are channelled draws our attention to the institutional framework of decision-making for trade policy. If sector interests are channelled through a political framework, such as through ministers, the US Congress or national or European parliaments, there will be a tendency for decisions to be influenced by (relatively short-term) political objectives, such as re-election. For this reason most national trade policy decision-making has sought to insulate trade policy from political pressures. In the United States this was thought essential after the disastrous experience of the Smoot–Hawley tariff of the 1930s. The immediate post-war years saw a period in which trade policymakers had a significant degree of freedom to define US policy – a period in which US policy promoted unqualified support for a liberal multilateral trading system. Subsequently the trend has been towards Congress re-establishing its control over policy, and US support for a liberal multilateral order has been progressively qualified.

In Europe the institutional framework for trade policy is more complex because of the need to aggregate 15 national positions. The treaty, in article 133 (TEU), grants exclusive competence to the European Communities for external trade policy. According to the treaty the Commission proposes a mandate to the Council, which it adopts with a qualified majority vote (Woolcock 2000). The Commission then negotiates for the EU in consultation with the member-states and the final agreement is adopted, again by a qualified majority vote, by the Council (General Affairs). But in practice unanimity is the basis for EU trade policy, at least as far as the interests of major sectors or major member-states are concerned. The voting rules also vary for most bilateral and regional agreements, where Article 310 TEU requires unanimity, and for the application of instruments of commercial defence, that is, anti-dumping, where the Council's adoption of definitive anti-dumping duties is made by a simple majority of the member-states. So what are the implications of the multilevel EU institutional setting for trade policymaking? How much scope does it provide EU policymakers, such as the Commission, to pursue its own agenda?

Domestic regulatory norms

While there is considerable literature on the impact of domestic factors on trade policy and the impact of the internationalization of national economies on domestic policymaking, the focus of this work has tended to be on the political impact of sector interests or factors of production (Garret 1998; Keohane and Milner 1996). There has been relatively little attention paid to the impact of specific domestic regulatory regimes. Since the 1970s international trade policy has become progressively more intrusive into national policies and policy preferences. This trend was clearly present in the Uruguay Round (UR) when the provisions on services, intellectual property and sanitary and phytosanitary measures (SPS) included some degree of policy harmonization. Trade policy is becoming less and less about swapping tariff concessions and more and more about reconciling different domestic regulatory norms. Another way of putting this is that trade policy is divided into two broad components, market access negotiations and rule-making, and that rule-making has become more and more important.

The influence of such norms is clearly apparent when one considers the shape of agreements such as the Canada–US Free Trade Agreement or NAFTA, in which the influence of US domestic norms can be clearly seen. For the EU the 'domestic' regulatory norm is, of course, the *acquis communautaire*. As this has been established only after many hours of difficult negotiation between the EU member-states, it must be expected that the EU will be more reluctant to change its domestic norms than other countries. The question is, however, how much does the domestic *acquis* shape EU trade policy? Does the EU seek to export the EU model through bilateral or multilateral negotiations?

Ideas or ideology

The literature also reminds us that these systemic and domestic factors cannot completely explain trade policy outcomes. Ideology will play a role, as has been shown with regard to how national trade policies can remain liberal in the face of protectionist pressures (Goldstein 1993). Ideology and ideas clearly shaped the development of trade policy in the 1970s when it motivated the calls for a New International Economic Order (NIEO) and in the 1980s when the general ideological trend was towards a liberal paradigm.

Events

Finally, one must not forget that events unconnected to trade policy will also shape outcomes and, in particular, influence the ability of governments to conclude agreements and thus the timing of trade negotiations. For example, trade policy in the 1960s and during the Kennedy Round negotiations was shaped by events associated with the creation of the European Economic Community. The Tokyo Round of trade negotiations began in September 1973 and was followed in October by the Yom Kippur war between Israel and its Arab neighbours and then the first oil crisis. In the 1980s EU trade policy was affected by the ending of the Cold War, the fall of the Berlin Wall, the re-unification of Germany and the EU's response to this in terms of two Intergovernmental Conferences on monetary and political union, not to mention the first Gulf War in 1991 and various national electoral cycles. All this occurred at a critical time during the Uruguay Round.

The multilevel nature of international trade policy

Before we can discuss the relative importance of these factors in EU trade policy it is necessary to distinguish between the different levels at which trade policy takes place and the different stages of negotiation. Broadly speaking trade policy in the EU, like that in other countries, happens at different levels. There is the multilateral level of the WTO, but also a range of plurilateral, regional and bilateral trade relationship, such as within the Organisation of Economic Cooperation and Development (OECD), region to region negotiations with Mercosur or in the shape of the European Partnership Agreements (EPAs) with the African Caribbean and Pacific (ACP) states and bilateral agreements with South Africa, Chile, Russia and so on. There is also the day-to-day level of trade policy in the form of the implementation of trade policy instruments, such as anti-dumping and safeguard measures, what one might call the unilateral level, although even here policy is conducted within the framework of multilateral rules. The factors shaping EU policy are likely to differ from level to level. For example, sector interests will have a central role in day-to-day measures to provide import relief in the shape of anti-dumping measures, but may have to compete with foreign policy objectives when the EU is negotiating a regional agreement or, for example, a bilateral agreement with Russia. In multilateral negotiations issues of global governance, relations with the United States, and relations with developing economies will play a more important role.

Different phases of negotiation

To this complex picture we must add one further consideration, namely that the relative impact of factors may differ between phases in any trade negotiation or trade policy action. The *initiation* of negotiations may well be shaped by broad economic and foreign policy aims – for example, the decision to negotiate with the EU's central and east European and Mediterranean neighbours. But when it comes to determining the *agenda and content* of negotiations sector interests, including the defensive interests of import-competing sectors are likely to feature more. In the *negotiations themselves* and the *adoption* of the results institutional factors shaping trade policy within the EU are likely to have a greater relative impact. Clearly, as Putnam made clear some time ago, there is an interplay between the negotiation and adoption or ratification phase in any negotiation (Putnam 1988). Finally the *implementation* of any agreement will be shaped by EU and member-state institutional and legal arrangements.

Systemic factors shaping EU policy

In general terms systemic factors appear to have been less important than domestic factors in shaping European trade policy. Compared to the United States, which saw trade as fulfilling objectives such as the maintenance of an open liberal trading system in the post-1945 period, European trade policy has not had such systemic goals. Indeed, European trade policy was influenced by US policy and for many years the EU tended to respond to US initiatives rather than initiate trade policy in its own right.

The decision to create a European customs union was of course a strategic choice. For some European countries, such as France, this was seen as a means of strengthening European independence from the United States. With Britain still outside the EEC thanks to De Gaulle's veto in January 1963, the strategy of maintaining a tough position in defence of the Common Agricultural Policy (CAP) and the EEC became easier. The creation of the EEC in 1958 and the introduction of the CAP in 1962 had important systemic effects on the trading system (Preeg 1970). It represented, above all, the first major exception to most favoured nation status (MFN) and thus provided a precedent for the preferential agreements that followed. But EU trade policy in the 1950s and 1960s was mostly driven by domestic factors. In the Kennedy Round negotiations between 1963 and 1968, the EU position was dominated by domestic concerns.

During the Tokyo Round, likewise, EU policy was largely shaped by domestic factors. These negotiations were initiated by the United States, with a desire to bring the trading system up to date (Winham 1986). A US trade deficit and the end of the dollar pegged to gold indicated an end to post-war US hegemony. Greater cooperation in the shape of the G7 and on trade issues suggested that US hegemony was in the process of being replaced by some form of cooperation between the major players. With Japan not playing an active role in trade negotiations, the trading system began to assume the form of a US–EU duopoly. But it was still the United States that initiated negotiations, for example on the inclusion of a range of non-tariff measures, such as subsidies, government procurement and technical barriers to trade. In these areas the EU adopted a defensive position because most national governments continued to support national champions and EU rules did not yet limit the scope for national industrial policies. In so far as the EU engaged in discussions on rule-making, therefore, it did so in order to defend European practices against US-inspired international rules.

By the 1980s the support of the EC was clearly necessary for any trade agreement, as was illustrated by the fact that the ambitious Uruguay Round of GATT negotiations could not start until it received EC backing. Indeed, it is fair to say that US–EC cooperation was largely sufficient to ensure progress in the Uruguay Round. Although the positions of Brazil and India were as critical and opposed to new trade negotiations at the beginning of the 1980s as they are at the beginning of the new millennium, divisions among developing countries meant that the US and EU could effectively determine the agenda of the UR. In effect, the Uruguay Round was the result of US and EU agreements that were subsequently 'multilateralised' to include other WTO members. Although the EU entered the 1980s still in a reactive mode, there was an important albeit progressive shift in the EC's position on GATT rules during the 1980s. For example, at the outset of the Uruguay Round the EC had opposed more legalistic dispute settlement and was suspicious of US efforts to extend GATT rules to regulatory policies in services and investment. But by the end of the negotiations the EU fully supported a rules-based system, the creation of strengthened institutional structures for trade in the shape of the World Trade Organisation, and had become more aggressive in pushing for services to be covered than the United States.

The EU supported a more rules-based trading system, because of the shift in its domestic regulatory norms towards a European-wide rules-based system that limited government intervention. It supported multilateral rules because it wanted to contain the growth of US unilateralism, as reflected in the 'fair trade' provisions in the 1988 US Omnibus Trade and Competitiveness Act (Low 1993).

During the 1980s and 1990s the EU also began to use trade policy for geostrategic aims. Indeed, in the absence of a common foreign and security policy, the EU made more and more use of trade as an alternative instrument. This was particularly the case with bilateral or regional negotiations. The promotion of economic and thus political stability in neighbouring countries has clearly been an important factor shaping EU bilateral negotiations. This holds for the Europe Agreements negotiated during the early 1990s with the EU's eastern neighbours, as well as the Euro–Mediterranean agreements with the EU's neighbours in North Africa and the Middle East. Towards the end of the 1990s the bilateral agreements with Mexico, Mecosur and Chile were also in part shaped by a desire to strengthen political relations with these countries, but in part by commercial concerns such as countering the risk of trade diversion as a result of agreements between these countries and the United States (Reiter 2003).

Relations with the United States have been a central feature in EU trade policy for some years. This has taken a number of forms. The EU has been defensive, such as in its resistance to US efforts to control European subsidies and support programmes for industry and agriculture. Competition with the United States is also a factor when it comes to shaping international trade rules. Here the EU has sought to promote its approach to liberalization and market regulation in competition with a US approach. But there have also been efforts to use transatlantic trade and commercial relations as a means of underpinning transatlantic political and diplomatic relations – including the Transatlantic Declaration of 1990 and the New Transatlantic Agenda of 1995 which sought to counter a perception of a drift in US domestic politics towards a more isolationist position in the immediate post-Cold War period.

In the post-Uruguay Round period the EU adopted a more proactive stance, taking the lead in arguing, from 1996, for a comprehensive new (millennium) round of trade negotiations. The EU policy rhetoric also contained more and more references to support for multilateralism. This continued to be the case even after setbacks in multilateral negotiations such as those at Seattle in 1999 and Cancún in 2003. The EU interest in a comprehensive agenda to include the so-called Singapore issues (investment, competition/anti-trust, public procurement and trade facilitation) as well as trade and the environment and, ideally, labour standards, suggests a broad interest in rule-making or global governance. In other words the EU, drawing on its domestic experience in establishing regulatory norms for competing markets, is pursuing a systemic aim of establishing trade rules that correspond to the current global nature of the economy. The alternative interpretation of EU policy is that the proposal for a comprehensive agenda was a negotiating ploy to forestall agricultural liberalization. But there has clearly been a shift in EU trade policies towards greater support for multilateralism and a rules-based system from the mid-1980s, which cannot be explained by such tactical arguments (Woolcock 2003).

'Domestic' factors

Until recently therefore systemic factors have not played a significant role in EU trade policy. Assessing the impact of systemic factors on trade policy is not straightforward. Systemic factors can help to explain general patterns in policy, whereas domestic factors have a more immediate and specific impact. Assessing the relative importance of systemic and domestic factors is something that can therefore only really be done on a case-by-case basis. The following sections now turn to a discussion of the domestic factors shaping EU trade policy.

Societal factors

The key societal factors in the EU as in other countries have been sector interests. European trade policy has been fundamentally shaped by the balance between protectionist and liberal sectors, or between defensive and aggressive interests as it is often put in trade policy. In recent years however, other societal factors, in particular those represented by civil society groups, such as environmental, developmental and consumer lobbies have assumed a more important, though probably still secondary role in trade policy formulation in the EU.

The influence of sector interests varies depending on the level at which trade policy is made. For example, when it comes to the use of trade instruments, such as anti-dumping or less frequently other forms of trade measure such as safeguards, sector interests are almost always the initiator of policy. The institutional framework for handling trade instruments determines just how much sector interests can drive EU policy. In the first instance, an industry which believes it is suffering from dumped imports will approach the Commission and probably a number of key member-states to seek anti-dumping actions. EU anti-dumping provisions, in line with the existing WTO anti-dumping rules are couched in such a fashion that it is generally not too difficult to find dumping. In other words the European Commission, which must assess both the level of dumping margin and whether the industry concerned has been injured, has a good deal of discretion. Unlike the US and other administrations, the EU anti-dumping measures do include a community-interest test. This must consider broader interests in addition to those of the producers affected by any dumping, for example, consumers and the end users if the product concerned is an intermediate product. But it is not clear that the community-interest test has done much to weaken the relatively strong influence of sector interests in anti-dumping actions.

While the Commission can use its discretion to introduce provisional dumping duties or negotiate price undertakings with exporters, it is the Council that must decide on the adoption of definitive dumping duties (Woolcock 2000: 390). Here the institutional structure has been changed to make it easier to adopt anti-dumping duties. In 1995, the voting rules concerning the adoption of anti-dumping rules were modified as a side payment to France and some of the more 'defensive' member-states in order to obtain their approval for the adoption of the Uruguay Round agreements. This change in the voting rules entailed a lowering of the hurdle for adopting anti-dumping duties from a qualified majority vote to a simple majority vote in the Council.

The EU like the United States also provides a channel for aggrieved sector interests to challenge other 'unfair' trade practices of its trading partners. In the United States the adoption of the Super 301 provisions in the 1988 Omnibus Trade and Competitiveness Act, made it almost automatic that the US Trade Representative Office would take action against perceived 'unfair' trade practices of other countries. In 1994 the EU introduced its Trade Barriers Regulation (TBR) modelled on the US Section 301 (Regulation (EC) 3286/94). This could also be used to provide a direct route to trade protection for defensive sector interests, but unlike in the case of anti-dumping, the institutional provisions provide a check on such abuse. First of all the TBR requires the EU to seek remedies within the WTO and only when the EU fails to gain satisfaction from the WTO dispute settlement procedure can the Council, acting by a qualified majority, approve action

(Woolcock 2000: 393). With a solid minority of liberal member-states (including Britain, Sweden, The Netherlands, Denmark and, on most issues, Germany), the EU 'unfair' trade instrument has not been used.

With regard to bilateral or regional level agreements the motivation on the part of the EU for initiating negotiations has often been foreign policy or strategic reasons as discussed above. At this level the Commission will also initiate the negotiation process and work with the 133 Committee of member-states officials to get an agreed mandate. At this stage sector interests will begin to get engaged and lobby their national governments and the Commission. Thus negotiations that start by generously offering access to the EU market can soon become the target of demands for exceptions from liberalization provisions. This was, for example, the case with the Europe agreements negotiated between the EU and the central and east European economies in the wake of the Cold War. After generous political statements of support for the transition economies, the EU position in negotiations became less generous as sectors such as steel and agriculture sought to avoid opening the EU market to competition from the relatively low wage transition economies. Similarly the Partnership and Co-operation Agreement (PCA) with Russia negotiated in 1994 and implemented in 1997, retains exceptions for steel imports from Russia, although these, like the similar restrictions for other transition economies are being removed. The EU agreement with South Africa (Trade and Co-operation Agreement of October 1999) is another example of how a negotiation favoured for broad political objectives and one that had considerable political support, ran into difficulties because of the defensive interests of a few producers. In this case it was the issue of wines and spirits.

The decision-making structure used for bilateral and regional agreements tends to facilitate the inclusion of such exceptions to protect sensitive sectors. Bilateral or regional agreements generally require unanimity in the General Affairs Council, and require the European Parliament to give its assent. Assent in the European Parliament has not been shaped very much by sector interests. When the European Parliament has threatened to withhold support for an agreement it has usually been on political grounds, such as the human rights record of the country concerned. But unanimity in the Council means that a defensive interest only needs to get support from one member state to have an effective veto over a bilateral negotiation that does not account for its interests.

This decision-making process for bilateral agreements contrasts with the rather more complicated position that exists in multilateral negotiations. In multilateral negotiations sector interests, with the exception of agriculture, have tended to have less influence. First of all, in large multilateral negotiations there are a great many potential trade-offs and linkages. This means that the Commission negotiators can more easily neutralize a sector pressing for exceptions or the continuation of protection. This can be done by ensuring that the aggressive interests – those wishing to see an agreement because it offers greater liberalization – neutralize pressure from defensive interests. This is one reason why Director-General (DG) Trade in the European Commission actively seeks the views of manufacturing and service interests in order to be able to put together its list of aggressive demands for improved market access. In the Uruguay Round, the aggressive interests of EU service providers in establishing a liberal framework for trade in services in the WTO helped offset the defensive interests of the textiles and clothing lobbies. Despite this, the latter was still able to have liberalization of textiles and clothing delayed until 2004. Sector interests are also filtered through European and national confederations, in which liberal forces usually balance pressures for protection. In many cases the confederations or federations of industry hold back from supporting specific sector interests and tend to make a general case for further liberalization and thus help to offset the influence of specific sectors.

The decision-making procedures for multilateral negotiations also serve to reduce the role of sector interests and increase the role of institutional factors. This is because the adoption of the results of multilateral negotiations, at least in areas where the European Community has competence, is by a qualified majority vote in the General Affairs Council. This has the effect of weakening the ability of a single member-state to block policy that threatens the interests of an important sector. This remains the case even if the practice within the EU is to seek consensus on major trade issues.

Agriculture is a rather special case in that the EU position on agriculture is in effect determined by the Council of Agricultural Ministers. The Commissioner responsible for agriculture is also often directly involved in negotiations. Normally, the Commissioner responsible for external trade has overall control of negotiations. But he has had to share this with the Commissioner for agriculture.

The discussion so far has centred on sector interests as the only societal factors in trade policy. As noted above, however, since the mid 1990s civil society in the shape of environmental NGOs, development NGOs, consumers and all manner of specialist civil society NGOs has grown to become a further important factor. The EU has had an institutionalized form of representation for civil society for many years in the shape of the Economic and Social Committee (ESC), but this has little influence and can only adopt opinions on proposed trade negotiations. The ESC tends to be seen more as a product of the corporatist past than as a reflection of a current desire for transparency, but it may be more representative than many civil society fora. The European Commission has also moved to provide a direct channel of communication with civil society on trade policy following the collapse of the Multilateral Agreement on Investment in 1998, when it became clear that civil society had to be listened to more intently than had been the practice in trade policy up to that time. The European Commission established 'consultations' on trade policy with European NGOs, including businesses in the same large meetings as civil society (or non-profit-making organizations). Such 'consultations' are held regularly, and although they provide a means for NGOs to express their views, the NGOs have no real input into policy. NGOs have therefore sought to channel their lobbying towards public opinion and as such have had a significant, but indirect impact on EU trade policy preferences. Such lobbying has begun to shape opinion in national parliaments and perhaps in the European Parliament. As these bodies will ultimately have to ratify any major trade round, negotiators will have to bear in mind opinion on such issues as investment (where provisions in multilateral negotiations are opposed by civil society NGOs) and the environment (on which some NGOs want to see rules included in the WTO).

Institutions

The institutional arrangements for decision-making play a particularly important role in EU trade policy. We have indicated above how the institutional structure, and in particular the voting procedures, varies between different levels of trade policy and that these differences are likely to be important in shaping policy outcomes. In addition to providing the channel through which societal factors shape trade policy, the institutional setting also determines the degree of flexibility or discretion for EU negotiators. For example, if the Commission negotiates for 25 member-states how do the member-states control outcomes? In the literature on international economic negotiation, this is what has been termed 'agent slack' (Odell 2000). The institutional framework for decision-making in trade policy also shapes bureaucratic politics, such as the inter-Directorate General discussions within the European Commission or the inter-departmental discussions within the governments of the member-states.

With 25 member-states the procedural and decision-making rules are vital when national positions need to be reconciled before the EU can negotiate effectively with a single voice while at the same time remaining democratically accountable. Decision-making is, in general, more complex than in the United States, for example (Meunier and Nicolaides 1999), but a simple approximation of a two-level process can be made in which the Council or Article 133 Committee represent the 'domestic' level in a two-level negotiation process. The Commission then fulfils the role of chief negotiator and seeks to reconcile the two levels through strategic interaction (Putnam 1988). Although the Council adopts a negotiating mandate and thus authorizes the Commission to negotiate on behalf of the member-states, this falls somewhat short of the kind of authority the USTR has under the US fast-track procedure. The main difference is that the member-states, through the Article 133 Committee and various Councils, maintain constant control over the Commission. In the EU the Commission has probably less scope to define its own tactics than the USTR has in the US system. Both must find an agreement in the international negotiations (level I) that will be ratified at home (level II), but the USTR must 'simply' ensure that there will be sufficient support for the final package in the US Congress. In the EU, the member-states are not willing to allow the Commission the discretion to shape such a package out of fear that it will neglect the specific interests of certain member-states, so they intervene to shape the nature of the package.

One illustration of this is the debate that took place when the Uruguay Round started to expand the domain of trade policy into the area of intellectual property and services. The Commission took the view that these new issues should be dealt with through the well-established Community procedures. However, there was sufficient dissent from member-states for the matter to be referred to the European

Court of Justice for an advisory opinion. Somewhat to the Commission's surprise they took a fairly cautious approach, arguing that in general, competence in non-goods trade was shared between the Community and the member-states. The one exception they were prepared to allow was cross-frontier services that did not involve the movement of persons, typically communication services.

This restrictive interpretation created something of a crisis in the handling of trade policy within the Community, as the contentious and expanding area of services and intellectual property would not be able to be dealt with in what the Commission regarded as an efficient way. The Treaty of Amsterdam introduced a rather unsatisfactory compromise that allowed for the future expansion of exclusive competence by a unanimous vote of the Council. The issue had to be addressed again in the context of the Intergovernmental Conference that led to the Nice Treaty. What had to be found was a compromise between the 'maximalist' position that would make all trade in services a Community matter and the 'minimalist' one that would retain mixed competence except for listed issues. A way forward was found by extending competence for most services issues to the Community level, but retaining unanimous voting. The most important exception was cultural and audio-visual services, a major area of concern for France. This was placed in the new legal category of 'mixed competence' issues. Intellectual property issues were divided into commercial aspects which are a Community matter and all other aspects which are shared.

Bureaucratic politics is also a factor in EU trade policy, both in terms of the inter Directorate discussions within the European Commission and the inter-departmental discussions within the member-state governments. Within the Commission DG Trade leads on trade policy and has tended to assume the role of the proponent of multilateralism and the main promoter of agreement in any given negotiation. DG Trade then interacts with other DGs representing industry, services and agricultural interests. Within the Commission DG Enterprise has come to assume broadly liberal positions, but DG Agriculture has been the brake on all multilateral negotiations in which the EU has been involved. Given the central importance that agriculture has played in GATT and WTO negotiations, one is led to conclude that bureaucratic politics within the Commission have contributed to the ability of agriculture to hold general trade policy hostage by the apparent inability of DG Trade to retain effective control over agricultural aspects of negotiations. Much the same applies for the inter-departmental discussions within the member-states Governments, in which agricultural ministries have held out against the pressure for liberalization from the trade, industry and finance ministries.

EU trade policy is also shaped by bureaucratic politics in the sense that the main interaction between the Commission and the member-states takes place between bureaucrats in the Article 133 Committee. This brings together the Commission officials with the senior trade officials in each member-state. Trade policy is therefore shaped by senior civil servants who often remain in place despite changes of government. With the Commissioner for trade now having a five-year term of office, this brings a good deal of continuity to EU policy and contrasts with the position in the United States where officials are political appointees and have a four-year term in office, which is effectively truncated by the need to get Congressional endorsement for the USTR post.

In the EU as elsewhere trade policy decision-making structures have been designed to limit the role of politicians and politics, because of the bad experience with politically determined trade policy in the interwar years. The mediation and balancing of competing sector interests was to be carried out within the bureaucratic machinery of government rather than by elected members in legislative chambers. Starting with the Tokyo Round in the early 1970s, the more complex and technical nature of trade policy also facilitated a growth in the influence of the expert government officials. This trend continued through into the 1990s with the highly complex Uruguay Round negotiations. In the EU the nature of decision-making with the national representatives effectively deciding policy in the Article 133 Committee and the various Councils made effective scrutiny by national parliaments difficult, with the European Parliament playing only a limited and indirect role in scrutinising EU policy. This meant that national and Commission trade officials had considerable scope to shape EU policy.

But if bureaucrats as the agents have a good deal of agent slack vis-à-vis their principals, who are the principals? Are these the sector and other societal interests within the EU or are they the national governments? The agent slack or degree of insulation of trade policy from societal interests is, with the exception of agriculture, quite considerable. This is due to the fact that EU preferences are aggregated at two levels, first by national governments and then within the Article 133 Committee. This gives trade officials a good deal of discretion to find trade-offs between sectors and member-states. So the agent slack with regard to the principal (societal) interests can be considerable, and is probably more than in the case of, for example, the United States where societal actors have more direct impact on the policy process. This would seem to help explain why private sector interests in the EU have not been very proactive in shaping trade negotiations in the EU and more inclined to leave decision-making up to government (Woolcock 2000).

Agent slack in terms of the relations between the member-states (principals) and European Commission (agent) is, however, another matter all together. Through the Article 133 Committee and if need be the General Affairs Council, member-states retain tight control over the Commission. This enables national governments to ensure that the priorities of national governments are reflected in EU positions. While the principle of a qualified majority vote gives the Commission some leverage vis-à-vis the member-states, the practice of consensus on major issues means that a national government or a group of member-states can have an effective veto over EU policy – as has been the case in agriculture.

The relatively tight control exercised by the member-states over the Commission is perhaps one reason why the EU has consistently maintained tough negotiating positions in trade negotiations, despite the fact that policymaking is fragmented between the member-states. Models of policymaking based on strong or weak states (Katzenstein 1985) predict that fragmented states will be weak. But the history of multilateral trade negotiations suggests that the EU has generally adopted a tougher position and given less ground in negotiations than its main negotiating partner the United States. For example, in the Kennedy Round the EEC refused to include agriculture and held out for tariff concessions that were very much in the EEC's favour vis-à-vis the United States. In the Tokyo Round the EC again refused to make any concessions on agriculture, a position the United States was ultimately forced to accept. Finally in the Uruguay Round the final out-come on agriculture was much closer to the EU's position, as articulated in the McSharry proposals of 1991, than the zero subsidies option which the US admin-istration claimed to be its position.

Is this established pattern of what we might call technocratic decision-making under threat? The debate surrounding the perceived globalization of economic activity has meant that perceptions of trade policy have changed. Civil society is pressing for a greater say in the policy process in order to make it more account-able. To date civil society has been kept at arms length by including NGOs in consultations but not ceding any real control over the policy process. But this could change. Civil society groups have had an impact on public opinion, which could in turn influence national and European Parliaments to seek more immediate control over trade policy. The other major change under way is the enlargement of the EU to 25. Unlike the Scandinavian enlargement, which strengthened the so-called 'northern league' of liberal states, eastern enlargement could provide some support for the less liberal camp in the EU.

Domestic regulatory norms

The discussion of the institutional factors shaping EU policy shows a complex picture but one which provides trade officials and governments with considerable influence over policy. EU trade policy must, however, also reconcile 'domestic' reg-ulatory norms with international agreements or rules. If the domestic norms or *acquis communautaire* are not easily changed, then this will tend to limit the scope for the exercise of policy discretion in negotiations.

Until the Tokyo Round, tariffs were the main instrument of trade policy. This remains the case with agriculture but since then, as other chapters in this book suggest, there has been a progressive deepening of the trade policy agenda to include more and more areas of what were previously considered to be domestic regulatory policies. The Tokyo Round included, for example, provisions on subsi-dies, technical regulations (health and safety) and government procurement. The Uruguay Round took trade policy yet further into domestic regulation with the addition of services, investment, intellectual property and SPS measures. Subsequently we have seen environment, labour and the Singapore issues (com-petition, government procurement, trade facilitation and investment) added to the multilateral trade agenda. Given that these are areas in which the EU has been active in 'domestic' legislation, the established EU regulatory norms are clearly going to influence the EU's approach to trade policy.

This can be seen in the EU's policies on technical barriers to trade, services, gov-ernment procurement and other issues raised in the Uruguay Round. Indeed the

EU position on tariffs could also be seen to be a result of 'domestic' factors in the sense that the formation of a customs union created relatively harmonized tariffs. Thus although EU tariffs were on average higher than US tariffs, there were fewer tariff peaks. As a result, EU policy has always been to reduce tariffs across the board, ideally using a formula that reduces peak tariffs more, whereas the United States has been quick to offer zero tariffs but has retained a number of important exceptions for those sectors that still benefit from the protection of tariff peaks.

This influence of 'domestic' regulatory norms is not peculiar to the EU. Other countries with well-developed regulatory norms also seek to ensure that international rules or norms reflect their own domestic approaches as closely as possible. But in the case of the EU one would expect the existence of an *acquis communautaire* to be more important because it has had to be negotiated by all member-states and could therefore be expected to be more difficult to modify in order to comply with different international norms. The reality is inevitably somewhat more complicated than this. First of all, the tolerance by EU member-states of the loss of sovereignty involved in accepting EU regulation helped facilitate the shift towards greater acceptance of a rules-based multilateral system. If the multilateral rules are compatible with the EU approach then support for multilateral rules is, of course, that much easier to find. In practice while the *acquis* may represent the starting point for an EU position on rule-making issues in negotiations, it has inevitably had to accept shallower integration at the multilateral level.

Second, in its approach to bilateral negotiations the EU has not insisted on the application of the *acquis* to the same degree that one might have expected. The EEA is a clear exception here in that it entails the adoption of the EU *acquis*. In negotiations with other parties the EU has been more flexible and has not insisted on the full adoption of the EU norms (Sampson and Woolcock 2003). In contrast the United States has developed templates or models for bilateral or regional agreements that reflect domestic US norms.

The EU, like other countries in the trading system, runs into difficulties when its domestic norms develop in such a fashion that they are incompatible with international rules. This has been the case in the area of food safety, where the adoption by food safety regulation of the precautionary principle developed in environmental regulation, has pitted the EU against international norms. The food safety field provides a clear example of how the scope for EU trade negotiators is limited when the EU's international commitments clash with domestic regulatory norms.

Conclusions

The preceding sections have argued that systemic factors played little role in EU trade policy through to the 1990s. EU trade policy was initially shaped by the need to establish a customs union and then a single market. As a consequence policy during this period was very largely shaped by domestic factors. If there was a systemic factor shaping EU trade policy it was the proactive policies of the US in trade, with the EU responding to these. By the end of the 1980s there were the beginnings of a shift in EU policy towards a greater consideration of systemic objectives in trade policy. This has continued through the 1990s. EU trade policy during the 1990s was also increasingly shaped by foreign policy/strategic concerns. By the end of the 1990s EU trade policy had become more proactive, with the EU becoming the main proponent of new multilateral negotiations. The EU's approach was also in part influenced by global governance objectives.

If systemic factors have become more important they are probably still less important than domestic factors in shaping EU trade policy. Much the same finding would probably have to be made for the US and other major trading countries. What characterizes EU trade policy is the greater relative importance of institutional factors shaping policy. Although sector interests and other societal factors are present in EU policy they tend to go through a double filter at both national and EU level. This, along with the complex institutional provisions required to ensure that the 25 EU member-states can speak with one voice, has resulted in greater 'bureaucratic control' over trade policy formulation. In other words trade negotiators are relatively well insulated from sector interest pressures compared, for example, to the United States. Sector interests are important but are aggregated at first the national level and then the EU level. Agent slack or the degree of discretion open to EU negotiators vis-à-vis non-state actors is therefore fairly large and certainly larger than in the case of the United States.

The agent slack with regard to the member-states is, however, much less because national governments retain tight control over the negotiating position of the EU taken by the European Commission. This has enabled the EU to maintain consistently tough negotiating positions in trade policy despite its inherently fragmented nature, which would normally suggest weakness in trade negotiations. This control by the member-states and the fact that the EU seeks consensus on major trade issues has enabled individual member-states, and in particular France, to defend its national positions on trade – and in particular agriculture.

Together with these domestic institutional factors, EU policy is, like other countries' policies increasingly shaped by the nature of the domestic regulatory regime. Trade policy is indeed becoming more a question of how to reconcile established domestic regulatory regimes with the emerging international regimes governing and regulating markets.

References

Garret, G. (1998) *Partisan Politics in the Global Economy*, Cambridge: Cambridge University Press.

Goldstein, J. (1993) *Ideas, Interests and American Trade Policy*, Ithaca: Cornell University Press.

Hodges, M. and Woolcock, S. (1996) 'The European Union in the Uruguay Round: The Story behind the Headlines', in Wallace, H. and Wallace, W. (eds) *Policy-Making in the European Union*, third edition. Oxford: Oxford University Press.

Katzenstein, P. (1985) *Small States in World Markets: Industrial Policy in Europe*, Ithaca, New York: Cornell University Press.

Keohane, R. (1984) *After Hegemony: Cooperation and Discord in the World Political Economy*, Princeton: Princeton University Press.

Keohane, R. and Milner, H. (eds) (1996) *Internationalization and Domestic Politics*, Cambridge: Cambridge University Press.

Low, P. (1993) *Trading Free: the GATT and US Trade Policy*, New York: Twentieth Century Fund Press.

Meunier, S. and Nicholaidis, K. (1999) 'Who speaks for Europe? The Delegation of Trade Authority in the EU', *Journal of Common Market Studies*, 37, 3.

Odell, J. (2000) *Negotiating the World Economy*, Ithaca, New York: Cornell University Press.

Preeg, E. (1970) *Traders and Diplomats: An Analysis of the Kennedy Round of Negotiations under the GATT*, Washington: Brookings.

Putnam, R. (1988) 'Diplomacy and Domestic Politics: The Logic of Two-Level Games', *International Organization*, 42, 3: 427–60.

Reiter, J. (2003) 'The EU-Mexico Free Trade Agreement: Assessing the EU approach to Regulatory issues' in Sampson, G. and Woolcock, S. (eds) *Regionalism, Multilateralism and Economic Integration: The Recent Experience*, Tokyo: United Nations University Press.

Sampson, G. and Woolcock, S. (2003) *Regionalism, Multilateralism and Economic Integration: The Recent Experience*, Tokyo: United Nations University Press.

Winham, G.R. (1986) *International Trade and the Tokyo Round Negotiations*, Princeton: Princeton University Press.

Woolcock, S. (2000) 'European Trade Policy; Global Pressures and Domestic Constraints', in Wallace, H. and Wallace, W. (eds) *Policy-Making in the European Union*, fourth edition. Oxford: Oxford University Press.

Woolcock, S. (2003) 'The Singapore Issues in Cancun', *Intereconomics Review of European Economic Policy*, 38, 5: 249–55.

14
German Trade Policy: An Oxymoron?

Andreas Falke

Germany remains one of the leading powers in the world trading system. In 2002, Germany, behind the United States, but ahead of Japan, was the second largest trading nation in the world. The surplus in the German merchandise trade balance in 2001 reached almost € 90 billions (BMWA 2003). Germany is a member of the EU with an enormous interest in trade, but as a member of the EU with a reduced ability to conduct a trade policy of its own. The title of this essay might then apply to the trade policy of any member of the EU. Writing about German trade policy or trade policy of any member-state of the EU confronts every scholar with a dilemma. With trade policy being one of the primary EU responsibilities, there should not be much room for trade policies of the member-states. This is reflected in the dearth of literature about member-states trade policy, which is particularly acute with regard to Germany. Most works on German trade policies are more than ten years old (Bellers 1990; Howell and Hume 1992; Weiss 1989). There has not been a major work or monograph on German trade policy in the past ten years, with the exception of a research project that looked at trade policy as part of the concept of a study of 'civilian powers' (Kirste 1998). Information has to be plucked from various sources and accounts of intergovernmental decision-making within the EU system and interviews with German officials.

The question of the role and nature of German trade policy consequently boils down to an analysis of Germany's strategies and influence on the trade policies pursued by the European Union. Trade policy in Brussels is actually characterized by a close interaction of the Commission with the member-states (see Woolcock, Chapter 13 of this volume). While the Commission devises the basic overall strategy, member-states have to ratify it in ministerial councils, with regard to trade negotiations in terms of giving a mandate and in approving the results of negotiations. There is also constant member-state–Commission interaction through the 133 Committee which is comprised of national trade policy officials, who collectively provide member-state input into everyday Commission decision-making, and thus manage to steer and control the Commission on many details of EU trade policy. So the question of EU member-states' trade policy is not a mute one. Accounts of EU trade policymaking frequently reveal the sharp divergence of national interests in the EU trade policymaking system. This clearly implies that more than a residue of national trade policy orientation remains as a potent force in EU trade policy. However, this fact has not given rise to systematic study of member-state preferences and orientation and to efforts to develop a general framework of national trade policies and positions within the EU system. It is true that some generalizations about the behaviour of member-states' basic traditions on trade policy are frequently used in scholarly and journalistic discourse. The best-known one is the categorization of member-states in a 'liberal' Northern camp, usually with Germany as the leader, and a 'protectionist' Southern camp, with France at the helm. While this may be helpful for the purpose of general orientation, it remains a crude categorization that raises more questions than it answers.

In the past decade trade policy has undergone a dramatic transformation. At-the-border issues (such as tariffs and quotas) have declined in importance, and new issues such as services and intellectual property rights that deeply impinge on domestic regulatory structures have become central issues. The globalization debate has introduced another set of issues, such as trade and labour and trade and the environment, where international policy directly intersects with domestic environmental and social policies. It is unclear whether the Northern–Southern divide can fully capture the differences among member-states with regard to the new set of issues. For instance, the Scandinavian countries are basically free traders, but support the inclusion of new issues such as trade and environment, despite their possible protectionist potential. Last but not least, with the single market programme and the Maastricht Treaty, European integration has made great strides forward and has affected the trade policy orientations and capacities of member-states in unforeseen ways. What is actually needed is a systematic study of how these developments have impacted the domestic line-up for trade policymaking within the member-states and how domestic actors have reacted to the changes. In the process of adapting to change, how has the internal pecking order of institutions and actors changed? And what effect have these changes had for the basic trade policy orientation of a member-state?

Ideally, we would need an account of trade policy making in terms of process and substance 'from the bottom-up' to complement the perspective from Commission policymaking. While this chapter does not profess to develop such a theory, it attempts to lay the empirical groundwork for such a framework by outlining the changes German trade policy has undergone since the beginning of the 1990s. The central thesis with regard to Germany is that there has been a noticeable decline in Germany's capacity and willingness to stake out a distinctive trade policy position to the effect that Germany has lost its capacity to shape trade policy according to the liberal paradigm. Germany does not anymore have a clear trade policy identity, and deference to Commission positions have become the norm. This chapter identifies five basic factors that account for the change:

- The priority German politicians have accorded to pursuing European integration over pursuing national trade preferences.

- The 'French connection', the tendency to support the more restrictive trade policy positions of France in order to prop up the general political relationship which has served as the engine of European integration.
- The dramatic decline of the standing of the Economics Ministry within the inter-agency power structure, coupled with weak trade policy leadership at the ministry and the German economic policy elite in general.
- The impact of the globalization debate, which, with the Greens and the left wing of the Social Democrats serving as conduit, has given new actors a voice that uses trade policy as a means to pursue other goals than market opening, and has swayed the unions to take more protectionist positions.
- The rhetorical persistence of the free trade consensus that, in the light of continuing export success, has led to policy complacency.

The benign neglect of Germany's immediate trade interests must also be seen in the context of the general decline of German competitiveness and the serious structural problems, particularly in the labour and some product markets, as well as the increasing regulatory load with which the economy is burdened (Wurzel 2003). These problems have not really been reflected in Germany's trade performance yet, but the insouciance that the German political class shows towards trade policy is indicative of the same phenomenon, namely the lack of focus on crucial challenges that the German economy faces at the beginning of the millennium. Given these developments, it is useful to recall the liberal heritage of German trade policy.

The liberal heritage: the FRG as the champion of trade liberalization

The standard categorization of Germany's trade policy orientation within the EU/EC System is that of the leader of the free trade block, usually lining up with the Netherlands, Denmark and the UK and since their accession Sweden and Finland. Together these countries form the group of the 'open regionalists' in the EU (Deutsch 1999: 43–47). The historical roots of this orientation go back to the early 1950s, when German trade policies under the leadership of Germany's first Economics Minister Ludwig Erhard opted for a strategy of trade liberalization, thus repudiating the tradition of autarky during the Third Reich. Trade policy was cast deliberately as a strategy of export-led growth that had wide political support in German post-war society and developed almost into a cult (Milward 1992: 147). When joining the GATT in 1951, Germany, pressured by the US, switched from specific to *ad valorem* tariffs and lowered its level of protection across the board in exchange for enjoying full MFN-privileges as a GATT member (Buchheim 1990: 138–40). In 1955, Germany, under leadership of economics minister Ludwig Erhard, lowered unilaterally more than 700 tariff positions. According to Richard Senti, Germany has been the only industrial country that reduced tariffs unilaterally, pursuing Erhard's conviction that unilateral free trade is welfare enhancing (Senti 2003: 5). As a result of this strategy, as Alan Milward has shown, the Federal Republic of Germany was already in its early years of existence the least protectionist country in Western Europe. It had lower tariffs than France, Britain and

Italy and dismantled the post-war quota regime faster than its partners in Europe (Milward 1992: 144).

The clear bent for trade liberalization was evident in the discussions on the economic merits of joining the European Economic Community, when Erhard and the senior staff of the Economics Ministry voiced objections to German membership on the grounds that a customs union with higher external tariffs would impede trade with non-EEC countries and that trade liberalization would be restricted to too small an area. In addition, Erhard feared the closer economic ties with France and its acceptance of inflationary policies. German industry shared these views, but was finally swayed by the lure of the French and Italian markets, access to which had proved exceedingly difficult. In the end all the doubters of the merits of the EEC were overruled by Chancellor Konrad Adenauer on political grounds, specifically that the supranational structure would guarantee foreign policy equality for Germany and firmly establish Germany on the international stage (Milward 1992: 197–201). This episode clearly established that German trade policy was to be firmly anchored in an overarching foreign policy framework, where vital trade policies interests were to play a subordinate role should they conflict with vital foreign policy goals.

From its inception, the Federal Republic of Germany was never an absolute free trader. The German option for trade liberalization was firmly grounded in a mix of industrial policy and protection for weaker sectors. The model of export-led growth was buttressed by close links between industrial and trade policies that functioned on the basis of close cooperation and coordination between business groups, banks, unions and central and state governments, in what has been described as the politics of productivity (Maier 1978). Because of the decentralized nature of the German political system, Germany never adopted central industrial policies along the French or Japanese lines, but developed a highly informal, voluntaristic and at times opaque system that allowed flexible solutions with regard to government's role (Hart 1992: 182–221). As Michael Kreile (1978: 193–5) has argued, Germany developed an 'export mystique' that no social or political grouping called into question. Foreign economic policy was fully directed at developing and expanding export markets for German industry. The political and business elite as well as union leaders rallied around the goal of increasing German competitiveness in foreign trade. Monetary and exchange rate policy by the Bundesbank supported this objective by making price-stability its overriding goal and by maintaining parity of exchange rates. The resulting undervaluation of the DM until the end of the Bretton Woods system was probably the most effective plank of the export promotion programme. The success of this strategy cannot be questioned. The share of German exports of world exports rose from 4.6 per cent in 1953 to 11.2 per cent in 1973, when Germany was the second largest trading nation behind the United States. The ratio of exports to GDP rose during the same period from 8.5 per cent to 23.1 per cent (Kreile 1978: 192). However, despite the impressive export performance, there has always been in Germany a lack of appreciation for the value of imports, in terms of making a contribution to better consumer choice, securing cheaper inputs for German down-stream processors, and for effecting structural changes in the economy through import competition (Interview Mueller, H.J.).

With its heavy emphasis on the benefits of trade liberalization and export-led growth in German foreign trade discourse, it is frequently overlooked that weaker sectors of the German economy were granted substantial protection. From the founding of the Federal Republic, agriculture and textiles enjoyed special protection through high tariffs and a complex system of quotas. In the mid-1950s, these quotas, which affected 18 per cent of all imports, were not dismantled even when their original GATT rationale, restrictions for balance of payments reasons according to Article XII, could not be maintained anymore. Germany obtained a waiver without a sunset provision. However, the protectionist aspects of German trade policy were less salient as competences in agriculture were transferred to Brussels, and textiles protectionism were sanctioned by international agreements, starting with the Cotton Textile Agreement of 1961 (Buchheim 1990: 138, 155–7).

With the EEC/EC assuming full responsibility over trade policymaking, the protectionist elements of Germany's trade policy were folded into the common commercial policy. However, Germany also availed itself of Article 115 exceptions that allowed deviations from the common treatment of imports, although it used these restrictions until their abolition less frequently than any other member-state except Denmark (Weiss 1989: 70). Sectors other than agriculture and textiles that enjoyed effective protection through tariff and non-tariff measures included shipbuilding, coal, iron and steel and aircrafts (Weiss 1989: 79–84). Another more recent deviation from the free trade path was Germany's attempt, at the behest of Volkswagen and the American transplants, to limit the import of Japanese cars in the early 1980s. Although Germany never maintained the same level of restrictions as Italy, Spain and France, which kept Japanese market share to 3 per cent or even less, German economics minister Count Otto Lambsdorff of the Free Democrats, the stalwart of free market economics in the Kohl government, went to Tokyo to request export moderation by the Japanese. Although a formal VER was never signed, it is consensus that an informal agreement kept Japanese market share below 15 per cent (Deutsch 1999: 140 f.). A similar commitment existed with regard to colour TV sets until 1988 (Howell and Hume 1992: 157). It should also be noted that Germany, not unlike many other European countries, maintained fairly closed markets in services, public utilities and public procurement, a situation that only changed with the waves of liberalization in the 1980s and 1990s through the EU single market and the WTO services and telecommunications agreements.

Notwithstanding these past (and partially remaining) residues of protectionism, the basic trade policy discourse in Germany is dominated by a free trade orientation. This orientation supports open markets, a rejection of open state intervention, and the maintenance of a stable and open world trading system. It is shared by most social, political and economic groups, that is, business organizations, unions, the major political parties, federal and state bureaucracies, academia and research institutions and the mainstream media, reflecting the heavy dependence on exports for growth and economic well-being. This has resonated with the mass media and the public at large. Economists, researchers, officials and business journalist subscribe to the neo-classical theory that free trade is beneficial. The only exception here is the agricultural lobby. In many ways, Germany can be described as a trading state (Rosecrance 1986; for Germany see Bellers 1990: 43) that derives part of its international identity, standing and influence from its export performance and its presence in international markets. Because of the success and importance of the export-led growth model, support for free trade is broad and deep. The unchallenged embrace of the free trade dogma has both practical and intellectual bases (Howell and Hume 1992: 156).

The other central element of the German trade policy consensus is the adherence to the multilateral order of the GATT/WTO system. As a middle-sized civilian power, Germany, unlike the United States, has few other levers to assert its trading interests but through the maintenance of an open, rules-based, multilateral trading system. For this reason, Germany has been a staunch advocate for expansion of the GATT/WTO regime. For German policymakers this attitude is primarily grounded in Germany's position as one of the leading trading powers, but because of Germany's size, German policymakers feel an obligation towards the maintenance of the system as a whole (Kirste 1998). Germany early on supported the 'widening and deepening' of the GATT order, objected to Commonwealth and colonial preferences, acted as broker between the United States and the EEC/EC to avoid the break-down of trade talks, and supported the extension of multilateral disciplines to new areas. Above all, it rejected any form of unilateralism and criticized not only American versions such as the section 301 and Super 301 laws, but also did not support the 'New Commercial Policy Instrument' that the EC adopted in the early 1990s. In theory and rhetoric, German policy was geared to strengthening the rules-based aspects of the world trading system and a plea for a further 'juridification' of trade policy and trade conflicts. For this reason, Germany emphatically supported the establishment of the dispute settlement mechanism in the Uruguay Round (Kirste 1998).

As German policymakers ascribe the success of Germany's export performance to the post-war multilateral trading order, the GATT/WTO system thus has almost the same sanctimonious status as the free trade orientation. This again is shared by all political parties, despite the presence of a strong agricultural wing in the CDU and an anti-globalization wing in the Greens and the SPD. When the Uruguay Round stalled in the early 1990s, German parliamentary debates and resolutions always ended with an urgent plea by speakers of all parties to conclude the Round as soon as possible. As Florian Lütticken has shown in a analysis of parliamentary trade discourse over the Uruguay Round in the Bundestag, three lines of argument were dominant: (1) An economic argument: the conclusion of the GATT Round is in the interest of the German export sector; (2) a moral argument: that growing protectionism in the absence of concluding the Round harms above all developing and the emerging market economies in Eastern Europe; (3) A historical argument: the protectionism of the 1920s and 1930s helped pave the way for the Third Reich and Second World War. All speeches were spiced with vehement rejection of protectionism. Only speakers of the Greens and the post-communist

PDS put the emphasis on helping the Third World. But any divisions or dissent regarding the value of the multilateral trading order was conspicuous by its absence. In contrast, for instance, to the debates in the US Congress, there was unanimous support for the GATT/WTO order. Only the occasional references to the need not to burden German farmers disproportionately indicated that there might be a gap between rhetoric and reality (Lütticken 2001: 121–4; for the US see Falke 2001).

The institutional setting of German trade policy

On the government's side, the most prominent actor in German trade policy is the Federal Economics Ministry, since the formation of the Schröder government and the merger with substantial portions of the Labour Ministry now called the Federal Ministry for Economics and Labour affairs. The Economics Ministry has exclusive responsibility for trade policy and has been the bastion of free trade liberalism in the entire post-war period into the 1990s, when it went into decline. With Ludwig Erhard as the founding father of the free trade tradition, this tradition has been carried forward by his successors, who from 1969 to 1998 came from the Free Democratic Party (FDP), the party with the most liberal economic programme of all German parties. While the standing and political influence of the FDP ministers has varied, the flag of trade liberalization has usually been carried by a string of highly experienced and articulate state secretaries from the civil service, who frequently filled the function of a *de facto* trade minister.

However, in the German political system, with the autonomy ministers enjoy in their original area of responsibility, the nature of coalition governments, which allow for specific parties or their wings parties to claim a particular ministry, and the weak every-day coordination performed by the Chancellor's office, the Economics Ministry's free trade stance is frequently compromised if responsibilities of other ministries come into play. This is particularly the case with agriculture, which remains the stronghold of agricultural protectionism and before telecommunication liberalization and privatization also with telecommunications, which was in the hands of the Ministry for Post and Telecommunication. Ministerial primacy is responsible for the inconsistency in Germany's trade policy positions that is liberal for goods trade and protectionist for agricultural trade (Howell and Hume 1992: 154).

As the German Foreign Ministry is the lead agency on EU policy, this situation is to a lesser extent repeated in issues which are dealt with in the General Affairs Council, where the Foreign Ministry represents Germany. For the Foreign Ministry, economic and trade issues are usually subordinate to its general foreign policy objectives toward European integration and thus only a bargaining chip to be traded away to achieve those objectives. This was also true under FDP foreign minister Genscher. On the bureaucratic level, this tendency is reinforced by the generalist nature of the German Foreign Service, which allows only shallow expertise on technically complicated economic issues, by a disdain among diplomats for dealing with 'lowly' business issues and the fact that careers are hardly to be made by representing Germany's economic interests or by developing economic expertise. Genscher's successor, Klaus Kinkel, tried to make economic issues and support for German business more central to the ministry's portfolio and play a more proactive role in trade policy (Falke 1997), but this changed little about the standing of economic issues within the ministry. In general, the Foreign Ministry has been fully focused on promoting European integration and in this regard it has been fully cognizant of the need to take into account French interests, including trade interests. 'How does our position affect France' is a frequently heard refrain of German foreign office staff, when confronted with issues in international trade policy.

The chancellor's office has little trade policy expertise of its own. It has a small subsection for international economics, but this section is mostly concerned with preparing the Chancellor's or other senior chancellery's officials trips to international meetings (G-7/8, European Council meetings etc.). The staff of the chancellery does not develop a trade agenda for the Chancellor, in the way USTR or White House staff does for the American president. The Chancellery is largely dependent on the input of the Economics Ministry and other agencies. As it performs only a weak coordinating function, it does not leave a decisive imprint on conflicting views. Frequently, conflicts are left lingering, which then makes for a very weak or ambiguous German policy position in international fora. The trade interests of the Economics Ministry, however, fully lose out when trade policy affects issues that are of major concern to the Chancellor, particularly issues of European integration. This tendency, however, is dependent on the personal characteristics of the incumbent, particularly his interest in economic affairs. Helmut Schmidt, Chancellor of the social–liberal coalitions 1973–82, a trained economist with a strong interest in, and claim to, managing the world economy, had a clear understanding of the place of German trade policy interests in overall international coordination of economic policy (Putnam and Henning 1989). His successor's approach to economic issues, including international trade, was characterised by a complete disinterest in economic policy (Interview von Dewitz). Although Germany faced major economic challenges particularly following unification in the 1990s, Helmut Kohl paid only scant attention to these challenges.

The most important business organization, with a stake in trade policymaking is the Bundesverband der Deutschen Industry – BDI (Federation of German Industry). The BDI is German Industry's peak organization and is made up of the sectoral industry associations such as the German Steel Association, the German and the German Chemical Association. Companies are not directly members of BDI, although industrialists and CEOs from major corporations traditionally sit on its board and thus guard the influence of the heavyweights of German industry. BDI has a professional full-time executive director, but the Presidency of BDI is an honorary position that is usually given to an industrialist from a publicly held or a major privately held company. BDI cannot unequivocally be described as a force for trade liberalization. The heritage of the dominant position of German heavy industries such as coal and steel, both sectors heavily dependent on protection or subsidies, have retarded the development of a clear free trade orientation. BDI is at best a reluctant or defensive liberalizer that was frequently held back by the sectoral interests of some of its members. Until the beginning of this decade, for instance, BDI was unable to push aggressively liberalizing agricultural trade as some of its members such as the Association of German Food Processors and the Chemical Association, because of its interests in fertilizers, were closely aligned with agricultural interests (Howell and Hume 1992: 188). BDI has made an intense effort to be responsive to the needs of smaller companies, Germany's cherished Mittelstand, and to recruit service sector organizations among its members, which is likely to lead to changes in how BDI operates.

The corporatist heritage of German industrial policymaking also weighs heavily on the BDI's ability to articulate an independent trade policy stance. Corporatist structures rely on the cooperation of the business sector (and the unions) with the government and have led to a dense network of business actors with governmental actors (for a description of the German system see Katzenstein 1987; James 2000). This creates dependencies on these networks and an unwillingness with regard to second-tier issues such as trade policy to risk breaching the consensus with government which may be needed in other, potentially more important policy-arenas. This need to maintain networks with the political classes is buttressed by personal links of senior BDI officials with political parties, particularly the CDU. The highly respected current executive director of BDI, Ludolf von Wartenberg, is a former CDU-member of parliament and a former parliamentary state-secretary in the Economics Ministry in the Kohl government.

This same pattern of behaviour is increasingly evident vis-à-vis the European Commission as Brussels has won enlarged competences in economic and regulatory policy that are of vital interest to German industry (such as corporate governance, energy deregulation, competition and environmental policy). It is therefore unwise to rock the boat on trade policy matters. In return, EU trade commissioner Pascal Lamy, for instance, has made it a habit to cultivate relations with BDI through frequent visits to Berlin headquarters and consultations with BDI officials. BDI's attitude to Berlin as well as Brussels politics is characterized by a degree of deference that serves to safeguard the linkages with the public sector so as to be able to use them when vital interests of German industry are at stake. Trade policy is not necessarily a part of them. Even when a sector has a particular trade policy concern that calls for more aggressive advocacy, BDI may not be ideal vehicle to voice it. BDI is an association of associations, and as an umbrella organization functions as a filter that in the complex decision-making involving more than 30 membership organizations in the Foreign Trade Committee (Aussenwirtschaftsbeirat) is more geared to develop consensus than stake out politically controversial policy positions (Howell and Hume 1992: 160, fn 44).

This all makes BDI less of an independent, proactive advocate on trade policy. In many ways BDI is a follower rather than a leader. This was most evident in a recent paper by two BDI staffers on German industry's interests in the Doha Round. The paper does not really make an effort to define German industry's interests on the basis of empirical findings from member organizations and firms, but posits a certain intellectual framework of comprehensive world economic order (Böhmer and Glania 2003). The chapter lays heavy emphasis on investment and competition issues as the cornerstone of Germany's business interests, which coincides with the strong support for these issues in the Brussels bureaucracy, although the support for these issues on part of German business is shallow, and these issues may rather serve as a stumbling block for multilateral negotiations. The sources for such a positioning derive from a bureaucratic impulse to chart the course for members on the basis of a predetermined conceptual framework instead of developing pragmatically a position based on member input. At the same time it is motivated by a search for convergence with the dominant trends that are developing in EU-Commission. From the BDI's perspective, this behaviour is quite rational as it is consistent with the prevailing free trade doctrine that its primary interlocutor in the government, the Economics Ministry, steadfastly adheres to, German industry's trade policy interests appear to be taken care of a priori. But the general doctrinal adherence to free trade principles usually cannot make up for the need to develop and push specific strategies and be prepared for the many everyday conflicts that the world trading system generates. BDI thus rarely functions as a powerful agenda-setter.

Less constrained than BDI, but also far less influential, is the second major national business organization, der Deutsche Industrie und Handelskammertag (DIHK). DIHK is an umbrella organization of the local chambers of commerce in Germany to which dues-paying membership by every business is mandatory. Because of its much more diversified base (DIHK has smaller service sector businesses such as retailers among its members) it is not beholden to industrial interests and, except for vocational training, not part of industrial policy corporatist networks. It has maintained a consistent free market philosophy and a free trade position. It has been a constant critic of German agricultural protectionism, and supported the opening up of German procurement markets and the liberalization of public utilities in Germany. However, with regard to trade policy, it is only a second-tier player, since it does not represent Germany's producer interests, and as such is not seen by the government as a force to be reckoned with. In addition, it has only a small staff for trade policy that is not very focused. Most of its staff resources are absorbed by following EU regulatory affairs from a domestic perspective and the management of the elaborate network of German chambers of commerce abroad, whose primary role is export promotion and helping German affiliates abroad instead of national trade policy. DIHK is a more credible, but much less effective force in trade policy.

The business organization in Germany that most consistently supports free trade policies is the Bundesverband Groß- und Außenhandel (BGA), the Federation of German Wholesale and Foreign Trade, which primarily organizes German import businesses. Although the BGA also functions as an employer association for its members, by its very nature BGA is a pure trader and free trade theory and practice is its lifeblood. It is the equivalent to what Destler and Odell (1987) have identified as the 'anti-protection forces' in US trade policies. BGA has tried to push the German government to support free trade policies in Brussels, has fought against excessive use of anti-dumping and escape clause instruments, most recently against using defensive measures against Chinese imports, and against escalating trade conflicts with the US such as the Foreign Sales Corporation Case (for a description of the case and its impact on European business see Hocking and McGuire 2002). Since it does not represent German producer interests, its impact is naturally smaller than that of other business organizations. However, German businesses increasingly have to rely on cheap imports to remain competitive, and discount retail chains in particular, which have gained substantial market share and popularity, support open trade policies. In addition, an articulate new President, who knows how to address a wide range of economic issues, a dedicated staff and good press work have established BGA as a credible voice on trade policy.

The strength of the German agricultural lobby organized in the Deutsche Bauernverband (DBV) is undiminished. Ninety per cent of German farmers are members, and DBV has been able to fend off challenges from 'green' farmers to build their own organization. The DBV has in the Agricultural Ministry its client ministry, and the Bavarian sister party of the CDU, the CSU, functions almost as the client party. It is probably the best organized pressure group in German politics, whose influence also extends to the state governments and through them to the Bundesrat, the upper chamber in the German parliamentary system (Howell and Hume 1992: 184–7). Historically, German farmers have been interested primarily in high domestic prices and have been staunch defenders of the system of variable levies. They were less interested in the system of export subsidies, but did support the system as part of the overall community bargain. German farmers have grudgingly supported the MacSharry reforms of 1992, decoupling domestic subsidies from production through direct payments, but because of the addition of the East German farming sector with its large farms, the DBV feels uneasy about the Fischler proposals to switch funds from direct support to rural development and has criticized it as weakening the EU's position in the WTO negotiations. It has been also opposed to the caps foreseen in current EU proposals because of the potential impact on the large farms in East Germany. On farm trade it fully supports the defensive line of the European Commission, and stresses the need to protect high environmental, animal and nature protection standards. The DBV recently loudly criticized the WTO draft for agricultural reform, submitted by the chair of the WTO negotiating group. It may show more flexibility on the abolition or reduction of export subsidies (DBV 2003).

German trade strategy within the EU to the end of the Uruguay Round

Until the 1990s, German trade policy displayed a stable and predictable pattern. It anticipated the danger that Ludwig Erhard had foreseen in signing the Rome treaties, namely that the association with protectionist France (and Italy and Belgium) would have the potential to compromise Germany's liberal trade stance. Since joining the EEC and since the full adoption of trade policy as a community competence in 1968, Germany has been faced with the dilemma of being in a minority position. Among the EEC-six, only the Netherlands was a reliable ally, Britain's accession was balanced by Ireland, and the southern enlargement in the

1980s completed the southern club led by France. Nevertheless, starting with the Tokyo Round until the 1990s, Germany made good on its claim to be the guardian of trade liberalization (outside of agriculture) and the multilateral trading order. Despite the fact that trade policy is a supranational competence, Germany traditionally insisted that it should act as an independent actor that would shape EU trade policy using the intergovernmental mechanisms such as the 113/133 committee (Kirste 1998).

This claim was difficult to fulfil within the EEC/EC system, given the structural dominance of a protectionist block in the EEC and the need to maintain good relations with France. But Germany, since the 1970s, availed itself of external mechanisms to influence EU trade policy such as the G-7 summits, its dominant role in monetary policy in Europe and its close alliance with the United States. During the negotiations over monetary policy following the breakdown of the Bretton Woods system, the Germans managed to prod the French to agree to the conclusion of the Tokyo Round (Winham 1986: 25). Germany in close conjunction with the US also used the 1978 G-7 summit to get France and Italy to agree to complete the Tokyo Round. Germany's action, however, was greatly aided by the subsequent American willingness not to attack basic tenets of the Common Agricultural Policy. Germany, in short, used levers outside the community system to push for expansion of multilateral trade liberalization. It did not maximize its influence from monetary strength, but used cooperation in monetary and exchange rate policy in exchange for cooperation on trade policy by key EEC partners such as France and Italy (Falke 2001: 342–5; Putnam and Henning 1989; Winham 1986: 146–58, 165–7).

That pattern continued through the 1980s, but Germany's approach became less effective, in part because Helmut Schmidt's successor did not master the details of international economic policy coordination as well as his predecessor, nor did he show significant interest in them, and because EU enlargement in the 1980s dramatically increased the protectionist Southern block through the accession of Greece (1981), Portugal and Spain (1986). German trade policy officials became concerned that Germany would become increasingly isolated with its basic push to strengthen multilateral trade liberalization. German trade officials responded under the leadership of then economics minister Lambsdorff, state secretary von Würzen and director for trade policy Lorenz Schomerus to coordinate their activities with the liberal minded member states (Netherlands, the UK, Denmark), although the block remained weak until the Swedish and Finnish accession in the 1990s (interview von Dewitz). In addition, German energies during the early part of the Round were deflected by the challenge of the single European Act and the implementation of the single market programme, which had significant trade aspects through the removal of the Article 115 restrictions (see Hansen 1998).

In the Uruguay Round, however, Germany's ability to pursue multilateral trade liberalization was greatly compromised because of the resistance of the German farm sector. In this context, Chancellor Kohl's ambitions with regard to European integration policies were an additional political factor, militating against liberalization. While most subjects of the Round were ready for completion at the

Brussels ministerial of 1990, agriculture presented a final stumbling block. Germany threw its weight behind French and Irish attempts to block agreement on the liberalization of farm trade. Kohl was reluctant to act against the French, and he therefore refrained from reining in his agricultural minister and refused to play a coordinating role between the Economics and the Agricultural Ministries. In the Agricultural Affairs Council, Germany together with Ireland and France blocked any agreement in the run-up to the Brussels conference. Kohl refused to give the Commission a flexible negotiating mandate, and initiatives by the Economics Ministry to move the Round forward were stymied by Kohl and his closest advisors. A prominent role in this was played by Franz-Josef Feiter, Kohl's agricultural advisor and by Joachim Bitterlich, his foreign policy advisor, both officials with strong links to France. Also G7-summits such as 1992 Munich summit were not used by Germany to reach agreement on the Uruguay Round, Kohl rather tried to keep the subject off the agenda (Lütticken 2001: 71).

While Germany's position at the outset was primarily motivated by protecting its farm sector and winning the farm vote in the 1990 election, this changed with Commission proposals for reforming the CAP, switching to a system of set-asides and direct payments and the American acceptance of these payments as a GATT-consistent subsidy. Germany actually became more forthcoming in giving the Commission more negotiating flexibility, but the political strategy moved from protecting German agriculture to protecting France. Kohl and his closest advisers opted for buttressing the political relationship with France that Kohl needed to further his European agenda.

This motivation was particularly evident, when the Chancellor backed away from the Blair House Agreement, the compromise with which the Commission and the US tried to solve the oil seed conflict and the agricultural impasse in the Uruguay Round. Even after the German agricultural minister had accepted the compromise, and the German government had officially gone on record to oppose any reopening of the hard-won agreement, Kohl supported the French wish for a 'clarification' of the agreement. Germany basically reinforced and made viable France's hard line, which the United States under pressure of the fast-track deadline grudgingly accepted. Germany, against its self-professed role as the leader of the 'Northern liberals', backed France, and in addition to the modifications of the Blair House Agreement, agreed to additional direct payments to French farmers. On trade policy, Germany at the urging of France, sacrificed its long-standing opposition to introducing an instrument against 'unfair' trading practices, and agreed to the strengthening of anti-dumping procedures. Germany also supported the French demand for an exception on audiovisual services. In addition, Germany ratified the principle that voting procedure on trade agreements would *de facto* require unanimity, thereby safeguarding the veto option (Lütticken 2001: 96–106; Meunier 2000: 121–6).

The Uruguay Round was paradigm setting for German trade policymaking in the EC/EU system. It firmly established the 'French connection' as the overriding paradigm (Lütticken and Stahl 2003). This paradigm implies that the political relationship with France, particularly with regard to matters of European integration would be paramount over Germany's trade policy concerns. This pattern would be determining for German trade policy. It motivated German behaviour with regard to the question of creating a transitional regime for Japanese car imports following the termination of Article 115 restrictions (Deutsch 1999: 174). In order not to upset France, Germany also lessened its opposition to the banana regime, which it had first opposed vigorously in early council decision-making and against which it brought an unsuccessful challenge before the ECJ (Rosegrant 1999; Lütticken and Stahl 2003). It should be noted that this paradigm was more characteristic of the Chancellorship of Helmut Kohl, but it did show again in the interactions between Kohl's successor, Gerhard Schröder and President Jacques Chirac over Agenda 2000 and the financing of eastern enlargement in the fall of 2002, although the need to give in to France was the result of conflicting German negotiating objectives and inconsistent strategy (Guerot 2002).

The implication of this paradigm is that the German Economics Ministry 'northern camp' strategy is severely compromised and does not apply to central questions of European trade policy when core issues of European integration are involved or vital interests of France are at stake. The 'northern camp' liberal strategy thus becomes a residual strategy that is only operative on minor issues of market access such as the severity of escape clause restriction against Chinese imports or reaction to American steel restrictions (interview with D. Falke). The consequence of this situation is that Germany's claim to be the leader of the liberal trade block is seriously undermined.

The encounter with globalization and the decline of German trade policy

The globalization debate was a latecomer to Germany. Until the election of the first red–green coalition German trade policy remained amazingly resistant to the issues pushed by globalization critics from the labour and environmental side (interview von Dewitz). Inside the Kohl government there was no force pushing for it, and the Economics Ministry kept social and environmental standards off the agenda. Also the unions had not discovered this issue yet, and continued to maintain their traditional free trade stance. Only in academic policy circles with ties to the union movement such as the unions' foundations did anti-globalization themes resonate (Scherrer *et al.* 1998). It was only the election of the red–green government in 1998, which brought the trade-related anti-globalization subjects such as trade and labour standards and trade and environmental standards to the forefront of the debate in Germany. The Greens were instrumental in pulling in anti-globalization NGOs (particularly environmental and development groups) to the official policy discourse and giving them standing in hearings and channels of informal policy input (interview P. Biesenbach. For the scholarly discussion see Brunnengräber *et al.* 2001). The traditional interest-group base of trade policymaking was changing to include non-traditional trade stakeholders who wanted to push concerns other than the exchange of goods and services. Traditional trade associations such as the BDI and the DIHK were on the defensive, although particularly the BDI was quick in establishing a dialogue with

NGOs. In some contexts, it could be argued that these groups gained privileged status that put them in a new client–bureaucracy relationship that had not existed before. As in many other member states of the European Union, the globalization debate transformed the political base of trade policymaking.

In many ways Germany followed suit in a development that in other industrialized countries such as the US and Canada had already taken hold (Destler and Balint 1999). In Germany one consequence of this development was the increasing influence that other ministries than the Economics and Agricultural Ministries gained on the trade policymaking process. These include the Environmental Ministry, the Aid and Development Ministry and the Labour Ministry. With Renate Künast of the Greens taking over the Agricultural Ministry, which was rechristened the Ministry for Consumer Affairs and Agriculture, the protectionist producer interests were slightly weakened. But this was more than offset by the strengthening of the more trade-restrictive agenda of environmental and food-safety standards. The Economics Ministry now had more than one competitor that in the past had just been the old Agricultural Ministry.

The diminished standing of the Economics Ministry in trade policymaking was part of a secular decline of this ministry that in the 1950s and 1960s had been among the preeminent ministries. With the social democrats coming to power again in 1998, then Finance Minster Oskar Lafontaine stripped the ministry of the economic policy division and the European division, transferring them to the Finance Ministry. Particularly the loss of the European division weakened the Economics Ministry on trade policy as many European issues intersected with trade policy. The capacity for intra-ministerial coordination was lost. The ministry was further weakened by losing the lead role in export credit insurance and export controls to the Foreign Office, run by Green foreign minister Joschka Fischer (interview H.J. Mueller). On trade policy proper, one of the few functions that the ministry kept, the situation was exacerbated by weak political leadership and personnel changes. During his first term, Chancellor Schröder picked an unknown energy manager with no ties to the SPD, Werner Müller, for the post of economics minister – primarily to effect and accelerate the exit from atomic energy, a task he accomplished. Müller showed no interest in foreign economic policy (interview Müller, H.J.). In the inter-ministerial arena that was more competitive than ever, the Economics Ministry slipped to a defensive position, and allowed other ministries to claim the lead for their trade-related agenda (particularly environment and development). For a while, the Development Ministry and Environmental Ministry dominated the discussion on trade policy leading up to a new WTO Round, trying successfully to define the thrust of German trade policy for the entire government (Handelsblatt 2001a; Wieczorek-Zeul 2001). Werner Müller, as a non-partisan, had no backing in the SPD-party caucus. Rather the caucus was the origin of a push to put trade and labour standards on the agenda. In addition, during Müller's tenure (1998–2002), the highly respected state secretary of international economics and the office director for trade policy retired and were replaced by officials who previously served on the administrative side of the ministry and were relatively unfamiliar with the state of play in trade policy.

At the same time, anti-globalization themes began to resonate strongly in the SPD and the Green parliamentary caucuses. Propelled by events and effects of the failure of the WTO ministerial in Seattle, the two caucuses agreed to appoint a parliamentary commission on Globalisierung, the Enquete Kommission Globalisierung, which was dominated by the anti-globalization left-wing of both parties (for themes and recommendations see Höhn 2003). While the party leadership, including the Chancellor's office did not share the thrust of the Commission, it allowed it to operate almost unimpeded, as it came in handy in deflecting the SPD left's criticism of the limited third-way reform agenda (tax and social security reform) that Chancellor Schröder pushed through until 2000. The left in the Bundestag was given free rein in its anti-globalization strategy in exchange for its acquiescence to the Chancellor's domestic reform agenda. The assumption was that such a commission would serve as a vent for the sentiments and concerns of the left wing of both governing parties while the damage could be contained. While there had been a steady decline in trade policy expertise and interest in the German parliament (Interview Müller, H.J.), interest in trade policy was now reactivated from a perspective critical of globalization and liberalization. Particularly the unions and their supporters in the Bundestag seized on the theme of trade and labour standards and demanded an inclusion of these topics for a new WTO Round. The Greens pushed for the inclusion of the precautionary principle in WTO rules (Höhn 2003: 41).

One fallout of the Enquete Kommission Globalisierung was a resolution passed by the Bundestag in October 2001, demanding (aside from environmental standards and incorporation of the precautionary principle in WTO rules) that the German government only support a negotiating mandate for the EU Commission for the Doha WTO Ministerial if it included trade and labour standards as a negotiating item (Deutscher Bundestag 2001; Deutscher Gewerkschaftsbund 2001; Handelsblatt 2001b). The problem for the government with this demand was that the Commission at the time had already rejected it as not realistic (interview with Economics Ministry official and with SPD caucus staffer). The majority caucuses tried to play a 'tying hands' strategy with regard to the government's position in Brussels that the government managed to deflect only by persuading the parliamentary leaders to refer the resolution to committee for further consideration – following the Doha conference (interview with SPD caucus staffer). The line of defence of the government became the call to toe the line of the EU Commission. However, the Globalization Commission Report as well as the parliamentary leaders had results in that it encouraged the unions and their allies in the Bundestag to persuade the government to accept highly restrictive positions for the EU's services offer. The German government accepted the demand not to open up educational, health and audio-visual services (Putzhammer 2002; Scherrer and Fritz 2002; Interview with German Economics Ministry official). This position was shared by France and thus easily became the negotiating position of the EU. It is noteworthy that this new German restrictiveness is happening in a future-oriented sector such as services, where a developed country such as Germany certainly has a significant export potential. This episode underlines that German trade policy under the globalization debate has become more restrictive.

The globalization debate and the decline of the Economics Ministry as the lead agency on trade policy have had a sustained impact on German trade policy. The paradigm of market access-based multilateral liberalization, while still being paraded abstractly as a guidepost by most participants, has been severely eroded. It has become an ideological shell that does not describe the reality and the pluralistic complexity of Germany's trade policy position. As a matter of fact, it may actually be counterproductive as it serves to create complacency about Germany's market access needs and a self-righteousness of Germany in its role as the guardian of a liberal trading order that Germany is increasingly unable to fill anymore. The liberal trade ideology also serves to paper over the fact that German trade policy has lost all focus and influence in Europe. Under the free trade ideology, German trade policy has become a shopping bag of conflicting demands, which range from market opening over consumer protection to animal rights. While this may be expected at the European level, given the heterogeneity of European trade policy cultures and traditions, for a country of the size and interests such as Germany, such an outcome is rather surprising. Germany has lost a trade policy profile of its own, and it thus fails to craft a trade strategy that will make a difference in Brussels.

All the factors identified in this chapter such as Germany's wish to further European integration, the need to take into account the 'French connection', the decline of the Economics Ministry, the loss of an independent monetary policy – with the Maastricht Treaty – as an independent lever to influence trade policy, and the pressures from anti-globalization social forces in Germany, have all contributed to lowering Germany's profile in European trade policy making. Germany's trade policy, for a member state of its size and its substantial trade interests, is characterized by excessive deference toward Brussels. Deference toward Brussels is now the default condition of German trade policy. This is evident in the lack of a proactive agenda, the lack of profile and focus and the failure or reluctance to forge alliances with like-minded member states to influence Commission agenda-setting. The exception to this rule may be if a major foreign policy issue with France is at stake, but in general, deference to Brussels has the effect that French trade policy designs will not be countered by Germany. Aside from factors identified above, one aspect that facilitated the decline of German trade policy is fact that Germany has exported 'itself to death'. Paradoxically, German export success is at the root of the decline of Germany trade policymaking capacity. It helps to create and buttress the assumption that given continuing and growing export surpluses, Germany does not have to have a trade policy. A liberal trade policy is seen by many of the major players in industry and politics as a self-executing strategy or an automatism that does not require special effort (Interview Müller, H.J.). This attitude serves to reinforce the German political class's deference to Brussels.

The implications of deference for Germany's relations with Brussels are ambivalent. On the one hand, it may be welcomed by the Commission in that it creates a reliable a priori supporter for whatever compromise package the Commission comes up with to meet the demands of the 'median' member-state. Germany is the perfect docile member-state. In this sense, the lack of a clear-cut profile in

German trade policy matches the lowest common denominator that inevitably dominates Brussels policymaking. Deference also has its advantages. It can act as a shield against domestic pressures by reference to Brussels' wishes, as in the case of union pressure for the inclusion of labour standards. As a line of defence the government could argue that this position had no support in the Commission. In addition, it relieves the German agencies of the effort to develop a position of their own, which, given the resource constraints that the Economics Ministry experiences in foreign economic policy, is sometimes the only logical strategy.

On the other hand, the Commission may wish at times to have Germany take a much more active position, particularly in cases where elements of the Commission want to pursue a more liberal strategy, and need a counterweight to protectionist forces. In the upcoming negotiations on agriculture and services in the Doha Development Round, EU trade commissioner Pascal Lamy may need more from Germany than a shopping-bag approach to the multilateral Trade Round and the cultivation of the 'French connection', particularly if Germany is needed as an effective counterweight to France. This state of affairs points to another aspect of trade policymaking in the EU: German deference to Brussels and lack of focus disturbs the equilibrium in the diagram of forces in the EU trade policymaking system. When the linchpin of the liberalizing forces among the EU member states drops out, the 'Northern camp' is dramatically weakened. Strategies attached to it can only be revived periodically and selectively. Without a Germany, pushing vigorously its export and market access concerns, EU trade policy will simply be less liberal.

The decline of a liberal German trade policy is of course only a small piece in the larger puzzle of German economic decline, which is rooted in the economic aftermath of German unification and exposed by the severe structural and growth problems of the German economy (von Hagen *et al.* 2002). Coping with internal economic stress and with furthering European integration has made the German economic policy elite much more inward looking. German leadership in the world economy has declined as such and this decline is also noticeable in other arenas such as the G-7/8 meetings and in other international institutions. With the implementation of European monetary integration, one of the principal levers of German foreign economic policy, monetary and exchange rate policy has been lost and this has led to diminished attention to international economics. International economic expertise within the bureaucracy is not so much in demand anymore and Germany's focus on international organizations, including the EU bureaucracy, has declined. The problems that the German government had in 2000 in finding a qualified candidate for the post of managing director of the IMF and getting this candidate accepted, is testimony to this situation (Kahler 2001: 30–42).

However, on trade policy, a note of caution is in order. The impact that the anti-globalization agenda had on German trade policy is not unique, but similar to the experiences of other EU member states. More comparative research on the trade policies of EU member states would allow a sounder basis for judgment as to what degree German trade policy has changed. The anti-globalization agenda clearly has affected the Commission, but it is not clear what role individual member states have played. The impact of the anti-globalization movement is only one factor in changes in German trade policy outlined in this chapter. But given the strength of the free trade tradition in Germany, including the free trade orientation of German unions, one would have expected greater resistance to the anti-globalization agenda within Germany.

What may be the future of German trade policy within the EU system? Chancellor Schroeder after his re-election in 2002 replaced Economics Minister Werner Müeller with the governor of North-Rhine Westphalia, Wolfgang Clement, one of the heavyweights in the Social Democratic Party. He also merged the Economics Ministry with the Labour Ministry, creating a Super Ministry for Clement. Clement's basic focus is the reform of Germany's rigid labour market. Clement is determined to restore the position of the ministry as the lead agency for economic policy and is determined to recover the ground lost to other ministries. With his solid standing in the party he has the political capital to effect such change. So far, Clement has focused on labour market issues. But as the governor of a state that is adjacent to the Netherlands, Clement has an instinctive understanding of the role of trade and competitiveness, and in the need for openness in a globalized world economy. It is quite possible that, should he start to focus on trade policy, he may be able to restore the role of the enlarged Economics Ministry in trade policymaking and revive some of the liberal elements of the German tradition. Even the merger with the Labour Ministry that is traditionally staffed with union-friendly bureaucrats may not make a difference here, as the labour side is fully absorbed by labour market reforms. The decline of the German Economics Ministry seems to have come to an end with positive future implications for a more activist German role.

References

Bellers, J. (1990) Die Außenwirtschaftspolitik der Bundesrepublik Deutschland. Münster: Dampfboot.

BMWA (2003) Bundesministerium für Wirtschaft und Arbeit, Handelsstatisken Außenwirtschaft. (availabe at: http://www.bmwi.de/textonly/Homepage/Politikfelder/Au%Dfenwirtscha)

Böhmer, A. and Glania, G. The Doha Development Round: Reintegrating Business Interests into the Agenda – WTO Negotiations from a German Industry Perspective, Beiträge zum Transnationalen Wirtschaftsrecht, No. 15, June 2003. (available at www.telc.uni-halle.de)

Brunnengräber, A., Klein, A. and Walk, H. (ed.) (2001) NGOs als Legitimationsressource. Zivilgesellschaftliche Partizipationsformen im Globalisierungsprozess. Opladen: Leske & Budrich.

Buchheim, C. (1990) Die Wiedereingliederung Westdeutschlands in die Weltwirtschaft. 1945–1958, Munich: Oldenburg.

DBV (2003) WTO wird nicht an der Landwirtschaft scheitern, Pressemitteilung 3 April 2003, available at http://www.bauernverband.de/pressemitteilung_405.html

Destler, I.M. and Odell, J. (1987) *Anti-Protection: Changing Forces in United States Policy*. Washington DC: Institute for International Economics.

Destler, I.M. and Balint, P.J. (1999) *The New Politics of American Trade: Trade, Labour and the Environment*. Washington: Institute for International Economics.

Deutsch, K.G. (1999) *The Politics of Freer Trade in Europe. Three-level Games in the Common Commercial Policy of the EU, 1985–1997.* Münster: LIT Verlag.

Deutscher Bundestag (2001) Antrag Sicherung eines fairen und nachhaltigen Handels durch eine umfassende Welthandelsrunde, 14. Wahlperiode, Drucksache 14/x

DGB – Deutscher Gewerkschaftsbund (2001) Die nächste WTO Runde muss nachhaltige Entwicklung und soziale Gerechtigkeit auf ihr politische Agenda setzen, Beschluss des DGB Bundesvorstand vom 3. Juli 2001. Mimeographed. Düsseldorf.

Falke, A. (1997) *TAFTA: Eine Perspektive für eine neue transatlantische Wirtschaftsarchitektur?* in Meier-Walser, R. (ed). Transatlantisch Partnerschaft, Munich: Olzog Verlag.

Falke, A. (2001) 'The USA: Why fundamentals do not always matter or it's the politics stupid' in Deutsch, K.G. and Speyer, B. (eds) *The World Trade Organisation Millennium Round.* London: Rouledge, 17–32.

Guerot, U. (2002) 'French-German Food Fight' in *Internationale Politik*, transatlantic edition, 4: 24–7.

Handelsblatt (2001a) Bundesumweltminister Trittin macht Druck, Nov. 8, 5.

Handelsblatt (2001b) Koalition streitet um WTO, Oct. 23, 3.

Hansen, B. (1998) 'What happened to Fortess Europe? External Trade Policy Liberalization in the European Union'. *International Organization*, 52, 1, 55–85.

Hart, J. (1992) *Rival Capitalists. International Competitiveness in the United States, Japan, and Western Europe.* Ithaca and London: Cornell University Press.

Hocking, B. and McGuire, S. (2002) 'Government-Business Strategies in EU-US Relations: The Lessons of the Foreign Sales Corporation Issue'. *Journal of Common Market Studies*, 40 (3), 449–70.

Höhn, H. (ed.) (2003) Globalisierung der Weltwirtschaft – Herausforderungen und Antworten. Eine Dokumentation in Auszuegen aus dem Schlussbericht der Enquete-Kommission des Deutschen Bundestages', *Aus Politik und Zeitgeschichte*, B5, 35–46.

Howell, T. and Hume, G. (1992) 'Conflict among Nations. Trade Policies in the 1990s', in Howel T. (ed.) *Germany*, Boulder: Westview Press, 145–204.

James, H. (2000) Kooperation, Konkurrenz und Konflikt: Wirtschaftsbeziehungen zwischen den USA und der Bundesrepublik 1968–1990, in Junker D. (ed.) *Die USA und Deutschland im Zeitalter des kalten Krieges. Ein Handbuch.* Vol. 2. Deutsche Verlagsanstalt: Stuttgart, 294–316.

Kahler, M. (2001) *Leadership Selection in the Major Multilaterals*, Washington DC: Institute for International Econmics.

Katzenstein, P. (1987) *The Semi-Sovereign State: Policy and Politics in West Germany*, Cornell: Cornell University Press.

Kirste, K. (1998) Internationale Wirtschafts- und Handelsbeziehungen Japans, der USA und der Bundesrepublik Deutschland. Fallstudie, DFG Projekt Zivilmächte', Tier: University of Trier (available at: http://www.deutsche-aussenpolitik.de/resources/conferences/wirt.pdf)

Kreile, M. (1978) 'West Germany: The Dynamics of Expansion', in Katzenstein, P. (ed.) *Between Power and Plenty. Foreign Economic Policies of Advanced Industrial States.* Madison: University of Wisconsin Press, 191–224.

Lütticken, F. (2001) *Deutsche und spanische Außenhandelspolitik im Rahmen der Uruguay-Runde des GATT*, MA thesis, University of Trier. (available at: http://www.politik.uni-trier.de/pubs/ma/index.php)

Lütticken, F. and Stahl, B. (2003) Deutschland im GATT/WTO-System, unpublished manuscript, Lehrstuhl Internationale Beziehungen, University of Trier. (availalbe at: http://www.politik.uni-trier.de/forschung/pafe_gatt.pdf)

Maier, C. (1978) 'The Politics of Productivity. Foundations of American International Economic Policy after World War II', in Katzenstein, P. (ed.) *Between Power and Plenty. Foreign Economic Policies of Advanced Industrial States*, Madison, WI: University of Wisconsin Press, 23–50.

Meunier, S. (2000) 'What Single Voice? European Institutions and EU–U.S. Trade Negotiations'. *International Organization* 54, 1: 103–35.

Milward, A. (1992) *The European Rescue of the Nation State*. Berkeley, CA: University of California Press.

Putnam, R. and Henning, C. (1989) 'The Bonn Summit of 1978: A Case Study in Coordination', in Cooper, R. *et al.* (eds) *Can Nations Agree?*, Washington, DC: Brookings, 12–118.

Putzhammer, H. (2002) Das Bildungswesen darf nicht durch Marktliberalisierung unter die Raeder kommen. Pressekonferenz des DGB-Bundesvorstandes. Berlin (mimeographed)

Rosecrance, R. (1986) *The Rise of the Trading State*, New York: Basic Books.

Rosegrant, S. (1999) Banana Wars: Challenges to the EU's Banana Regime. Harvard University, Kennedy School of Government Case Study, C14-99-1.

Scherrer, C., Frank, V. and Greven, T. (1998) *Sozialklauseln. Schriftenreihe der Hans-Böckler-Stitfung*, Münster: Dampfboot.

Scherrer, C. and Fritz, T. (2002) *GATS 2000. Arbeitnehmerinteressen und die Liberalisierung des Dienstleistungshandel.* Duesseldorf: Hans-Boeckler Stiftung.

Senti, R. (2003) Die Welthandelsordnung im Urteil der Sozialen Marktwirtschaft. Ludwig-Erhard-Gedächtnis-Vorlesung, University Erlangen-Nürnberg, 23 January 2003 (unpublished manuscript).

von Hagen, J. *et al.* (2002) East Germany: Transition with Unification, Experiments and Experiences, ZEI Working Papers, B19–2002, Bonn: Zentrum für Europäische Integrationsforschung. (available at: http://www.zei.de/publications)

Weiss, F. (1989) 'Domestic Dimensions of the Uruguay Round. The Case of West Germany in the European Communities', in Nau, H. (ed.) *Domestic Trade Politics and the Uruguay Round*, 69–90. New York: Columbia University Press.

Winham, Gilbert (1986) *International Trade and the Tokyo Round Negotiation*, Princeton: Princeton University Press.

Wieczorek-Zeul, H. (2001) 'The Next WTO Round will be a Development Round: Germany's Position on the Future Trade Round', *Development and Cooperation*, 5, September/October.

Wurzel, E. (2003) 'Germany: The Case for Reform', *OECD Observer*, 237, 12–14.

Interviews

Biesenbach, Peter, chief of staff, office of the President of BDI, Berlin, 18 February 2003, Berlin.

Falke, Dirk. Trade policy staffer, Federation of German Wholesale and Foreign Trade, 18 February 2003, Berlin.

Mueller, Hans-Juergen. executive director, Federation of German Wholesale and Foreign Trade, 17 February 2003, Berlin.

Von Dewitz, Wedige, former director general for trade policy, German Economics Ministry, 19 December 2002, Bonn.

15
The Political Economy of African Trade in the Twenty-first Century

Mills Soko

That Africa is faced with a serious political and economic crisis is a matter of common cause. The reasons for this crisis are documented extensively in the literature (e.g. Adedeji 1993; Ake 1981; Onimode 1989; Ravenhill 1986; Rodney 1972) and will not be discussed in detail here. Suffice to say that Africa's precarious and marginal position in the global political economy is the consequence of the interplay of internal and external factors including domestic economic mismanagement, a pervasive lack of democracy, perennial inter-state and intra-state conflicts, failed regional integration projects, colonial rule, collapse of commodity trade, unfair trade terms, a foreign debt crisis, endemic corruption, weak states and institutional decay, and ill-conceived structural adjustment policies. Indeed, Africa's position in the international division of labour has deteriorated so badly that even the continent's structural relevance to the present global economic order has become questionable (Hoogvelt 2001: 175).

The facts and figures are alarming. Sub-Saharan Africa accounts for less than 1 per cent of global gross domestic product (GDP), and for about 3 per cent of world investment flows, the majority of which are concentrated in the extractive industries, predominantly oil, in a handful of countries (World Bank 2002a: 64–6). Of the 49 countries currently designated by the United Nations (UN) as the least developed countries (LDCs), the overwhelming majority of them are African. The share of LDCs in total inflows to developing countries decreased from 2.2 per cent during 1986–90 to 2.0 per cent during 1996–99. While overseas development assistance (ODA) has made up the largest proportion of resource flows into LDCs, it has declined in absolute and relative terms; LDCs as a whole received US$11.6 billion of bilateral and multilateral ODA in 1999, compared to US$16.7 billion in 1990 (UNCTAD 2001a: 1–3). Since the onset of the debt crisis in 1982, Africa's foreign debt has skyrocketed from US$84.1 billion to US$235.4 billion (Hoogvelt op cit. 175). Africa represents 33 of the 41 countries classified as heavily indebted in terms of the highly indebted poor countries (HIPC) initiative, and 19 of the 26 countries that have fulfilled the conditions for debt relief under this debt forgiveness scheme. The foreign debt crisis has been deployed as a tool by international financial institutions (IFIs) to foist failed orthodox structural adjustment programmes on African countries. It is Africa's most pressing problem and the 'noose that keeps it articulated to the global capitalist system' (ibid.).

Against this dismal backdrop this chapter sketches an analytical overview of African global and regional trade in the early 2000s. Three interrelated arguments are advanced in this chapter. The first is that the failure of industrialized countries to deliver on the undertakings they made to the least developed countries, most of which are African, during the Uruguay Round of trade negotiations poses a grave threat to the future of the global trade system. The second contention is that a reorientation of African countries' domestic policies is as equally necessary as that of their international policies. Third, it is asserted that regional and sub-regional integration, albeit of a different character, among African countries remains the most essential tool through which they could reverse their subordinate role in world trade and constitutes a key vehicle for their effective integration into the global political economy. The chapter is divided into five sections. The first section analyses Africa's position in the contemporary global trade regime with specific reference to the region's role in the Uruguay and Doha Rounds of multi-lateral trade negotiations. Second, the chapter examines African trade performance in the world economy within the context of initiatives designed to bolster the continent's external trade. Third, it assesses the state of African intra-regional integration efforts and draws attention to the growing centrality of non-state actors, notably private firms and civil society formations, to the evolving integration processes at domestic, sub-regional and regional levels. The fourth section explores the implications of the US-led global war on terrorism for African trade. The chapter concludes by stressing the need for African countries to undertake necessary domestic policy changes to complement their international policy initiatives.

Africa and the contemporary global trading system

A striking feature of African economies today – more than twenty years after the 'lost decade' of the 1980s which marked the nadir of Africa's multidimensional crisis – is their unchanged terms of incorporation into the international division of labour: they remain locked into the role of traditional commodity exporter and importer of capital goods and technologies. Their disarticulation from the global economy is exemplified by the serious deficiencies that characterize their foreign trade. African economies rely excessively on slow growth commodity exports. While East Asian countries succeeded over the past decades to diversify their exports and transform themselves into internationally competitive manufacturing economies, their African counterparts have lagged far behind. Closely tied to high export dependence is the problem of product concentration. Most African economies are undiversified and exports are concentrated in a narrow range of products. Primary commodities still account for about 70 per cent of exports from Sub-Saharan Africa (World Bank op cit.: 59–61).

With the exception of a few countries such as South Africa, Morocco and Mauritius – which have a relatively diversified export base – African external trade continues to revolve around one or two traditional commodities, mainly oil and agricultural exports. This renders African economies vulnerable to external shocks such as volatile swings in commodity prices, which have an adverse impact on their terms of trade and overall growth. Indeed, export instability has been the key factor responsible for chronic current account deficits and balance of payments crises in African countries (Onimode 2000: 82–3). Diversifying Africa's production and exports is vital to the overall success of their trade performance. African countries must eschew their excessive dependence on commodity exports and develop import and export policies that will foster industrialization as well as serve as sources of innovation in the economy. The urgency of carrying out the necessary policy, institutional and administrative reforms to achieve these ends cannot be over-emphasized.

The Uruguay Round

The significance of the Uruguay Round (UR) of trade negotiations rested with its aim to subject trade in agriculture and textiles to GATT rules and disciplines. It was also notable for its introduction of new issues into GATT negotiations – namely trade in services, investment and intellectual property rights. It was largely around these issues that divisions between the developed and developing countries revolved during the pre-negotiation phase of the UR. Most developing countries, including African nations, were opposed to the inclusion of these new issues, fearing that 'the GATT rules developed for the new issues could be used by the industrialised countries to overwhelm their fledgling industries and to undermine domestic policies that the developing countries considered critical to their national economic development' (Spero and Hart 2000: 84). They wanted to ensure that if they were forced to make concessions in these areas, the developed countries would reciprocate by making real concessions on issues of importance to them such as textiles, clothing and agriculture.

For most developing countries, and for African nations in particular, the UR represented a major setback: they gained little or nothing from it, despite assurances made by developed countries to provide them with larger market access for their agricultural products and clothing and textile exports, as well as with the necessary technical assistance to implement their World Trade Organisation (WTO) obligations. According to Raghavan (1990) the UR ushered in a new international division of labour that amounted to the recolonization of Africa and the rest of the developing world, while at the same time reorganizing the global economy in ways that entrenched the position of the United States as a global superpower. Although it is debatable whether the UR occasioned the recolonization of Africa, what is abundantly clear is that it sharply brought into focus the serious marginalization of African countries in the global trade regime. Not only did the UR fall short of delivering meaningful results on issues of interest to Africa such as providing greater market access for its agricultural exports as well as textiles and clothing products, it also failed to deal satisfactorily with systemic issues such as the GATT articles, safeguards, subsidies, multilateral trade negotiation agreements, special and differential treatment, and enforcement of rights and obligations (Onimode op cit.: 185–7). African countries also had to contend with the new trade issues – trade in services, intellectual property rights and investment – which they did not understand and for which they were not adequately prepared to negotiate. In sum, the UR yielded a few winners, predominantly from the economically advanced nations, and many losers, mainly from the developing countries. And it is this faultline that made it difficult for the WTO to agree on an agenda for its Seattle ministerial meeting in 1999.

The Doha Round

The ill-fated WTO ministerial meeting held in Seattle in 1999 took place against the backdrop of circumstances different to those that marked the UR. First, developing countries – which make about two-thirds of the WTO membership – showed that they were increasingly aware that their voice mattered in the WTO. Owing to their numerical preponderance in the WTO, they proved that trade liberalization could not proceed without their agreement: deals cut in secretive 'green room' processes by powerful trading nations were no longer sufficient to win consensus on a new trade round. Second, most developing countries which took part in the UR expressed disappointment and resentment that they had gained little or nothing from it, despite the assurances made by developed countries to provide them with larger market access and technical aid. Third, the Seattle meeting highlighted growing public disaffection with and distrust of the multilateral trade system, prompting the then US Trade Representative, Charlene Barshefsky, to remark that 'the single greatest threat to the multilateral trade system is the absence of public support' (*Financial Times* 11 October 1999).

Since the conclusion of the UR of trade negotiations in 1994, African countries have become active participants in the multilateral trade system. This represents a significant departure from the 1980s when most African nations regarded the GATT as 'a rich man's club' that was concerned exclusively with the interests of developed countries. Two factors account for this departure from the previous stance. First, the realization that special and differential treatment granted to poor countries in the mid-1980s did not improve their economic position significantly. Second, the rise of the newly industrializing countries (NICs) such as Korea, Hong Kong and Taiwan highlighted growing economic differentiation among developing countries, with the NICs showing a clear interest in an open trading system. Over the past eight years the number of Sub-Saharan countries affiliated to the WTO has grown from 15 to 38, with an additional five countries enjoying an observer status.[1] Africa is now the largest regional bloc in the WTO, accounting for 26 per cent of all WTO membership.

The Doha Round (DR) of multilateral trade negotiations was launched in November 2001 in terms of the principle of the 'single undertaking': nothing is agreed until everything is agreed. The decision to initiate the DR flowed from a combination of factors that exerted tremendous pressures on the rules-based global trade system, threatening to imperil the post-war consensus upon which the multilateral trade regime was founded. These include an exponential increase in the membership of the WTO, an ever-expanding trade negotiating agenda, a governance process over-burdened by competing national interests, a burgeoning desire by WTO members to conclude bilateral and regional trade deals, as well as increasing concerns about the social and environmental effects of free trade (Cronin 2003: 369–70). The momentum for initiating the DR also derived from widely shared perceptions that a repeat of the Seattle-type impasse could inflict irrevocable harm to the multilateral trade system. Tied to this concern were mounting fears about the parlous state of the global economy and the implications for the US economy following the terrorist attacks on the World Trade Centre on 11 September 2001 (ibid. 378).

The pre-Doha ministerial meetings were marked by disagreements similar to those that paralyzed the unsuccessful Seattle summit (see Jawara and Kwa 2003: 50–79). These revolved mainly around differences between developed and developing countries over issues to be covered by the Doha negotiating agenda. Pushing aggressively for a broad-based negotiating round was the EU which, together with Japan and South Korea, was keen to see the DR build on a limited set of investment liberalization measures that were agreed to in the UR and 'give their corporations maximum flexibility in managing their operations abroad' (Cronin op cit.: 381). Although the EU's attitude towards the elimination of export subsidies was lukewarm, it nevertheless sought to establish a linkage between trade and the environment in response to demands by environmental lobby groups. Furthermore, the EU pushed for substantial reductions in industrial tariffs by developing countries and the tightening of labour standards in the global trade system (Jawara and Kwa op cit.: 53). For its part the United States wanted the DR to deal with the established issues of agriculture, services and industrial tariffs. The United States also wanted the Round to tackle the issue of transparency in government procurement and trade facilitation. Unlike the Democratic administration under Clinton, which was indebted to labour interests, the Bush administration did not consider it necessary to push for the linking of trade and labour standards. The Republican government also did not see the linking of trade and the environment as a priority (ibid.). Furthermore, the United States refused to enter into any discussions aimed at reviewing the existing anti-dumping rules, which it has employed extensively to protect powerful domestic lobbies (Cronin op cit.: 379).

Most African countries were opposed to a comprehensive round of trade negotiations, especially the inclusion of the 'new issues' – also known as Singapore issues – such as competition, investment and trade facilitation and transparency in government procurement. Opposition to the addition of Singapore issues sprang from the belief on the part of these countries that they had gained little or nothing from the previous UR, notwithstanding pledges made by developed countries to provide them with larger market access for their agricultural products and apparel and textile exports, as well as with the necessary technical assistance to implement their WTO obligations. Driving African efforts to resist the inclusion of the 'new issues' were several African states which had organized themselves in the 'Like-Minded Group (LMG)', a vocal coalition of 15 developing nations within the WTO.[2] Not only were these countries wary of engaging in negotiations about these issues in the DR, they were also concerned about the added weight the new responsibilities entailed in light of the formidable UR implementation challenges they still had to fulfil. For this reason they insisted that the DR negotiations should rather focus on implementing UR agreements on such matters as granting greater market access to agricultural products from the developing world, as well as providing technical assistance to poor countries.

Nonetheless, harmonizing trade negotiating positions among African countries ahead of the 2001 Doha ministerial meeting was not always successful – as was demonstrated by the sharp differences that developed between South Africa, the largest and most developed economy in Africa, and other African countries at the Doha summit. Central to this rupture were differences on how African countries ought to have approached the negotiations in the DR. The initial position of most African countries was to obstruct a new round of WTO negotiations on the grounds that they had given away more than they had got in the UR and were reluctant to support a new round of trade liberalization unless their grievances had been addressed. Although South Africa agreed that Africa's concerns – especially the implementation of UR agreements by developed countries – ought to be prioritized, it argued nevertheless for broad-based negotiations covering the 'new issues'. South Africa did not support the ambitious EU agenda but was prepared to consider a modified, less ambitious and carefully defined agenda.

In adopting this position South Africa was influenced not only by a recognition of rapid changes in the global economy that needed to be accommodated within the WTO but also by a conviction that a wider negotiating agenda would make it possible for developing nations to extract key concessions from industrialized countries in respect of agriculture and industrial tariffs.[3] It could be asserted that South Africa's Doha negotiating posture is in part reflective of the collaborative and bridge-building role which so-called 'middle powers' tend to adopt in multilateral institutions (see Cooper *et al.* 1993). But more specifically it illustrates a dilemma faced by semi-peripheral states such as South Africa in the international political economy (see Chapter 16 Taylor). Partially industrialized, South Africa's economic profile exhibits the traits of both developed and underdeveloped societies. This explains why even though the country has identified with the trade problems faced by its less developed African counterparts – and has actively pushed for their resolution – it has also sought to advance its trade policy objectives in respect of the new WTO issues in which it has a keen interest. This stance has occasionally driven a wedge between South Africa and its African allies.

It is worth placing these differences in perspective. South Africa, unlike most of its African counterparts, is fundamentally a trading nation – over 50 per cent of its national economy is dependent on external trade. Moreover, South Africa has ambitions to become a dynamic manufacturing economy with a diversified export base (Department of Trade Industry 2001: 13–16). It has an interest, therefore, in working for the success of the global trading system and cannot afford to insulate itself from the world economy in the same way as some African countries can. The low level of agricultural development and the problems intrinsic to some African economies has prompted them to focus primarily on the need for technical assistance rather than on expanding their export capacity. It is for this reason that the New Partnership for Africa's Development – discussed in detail later in this chapter – places a special emphasis on agriculture, industrialization and boosting the export capabilities of African nations.

Additionally, South Africa is relatively endowed with technical capabilities – increasingly shared with its SACU (Southern African Customs Union) trade partners – to participate actively in the WTO processes and has not refrained from exploiting its strengths in this regard. These considerations do not, of course, imply that African countries cannot forge coordinated positions on strategic issues; indeed, most of the differences that have arisen between South Africa and its regional trade partners have been about process not substance. What they do underline though is that it is not unusual for countries, even close allies, to hold different positions on trade negotiations. These differences notwithstanding, it is worth emphasizing that the Africa WTO Group (AWG) – a caucus group made up of Geneva-based African trade representatives which meets weekly to synchronize African countries' trade negotiating positions on sectoral and product specific provisions – has made enormous progress in spearheading African trade diplomacy and forging unified African positions within the WTO in recent years.[4] Post-apartheid South Africa has made the pursuit of African economic revitalization the keystone of its foreign economic policy (see Department of Foreign Affairs 2003: 1–2). The extent to which this policy ideal can be realized, however, will depend ultimately on how skilfully South Africa can negotiate the delicate balance between, on the one hand, its global ambitions and, on the other, its domestic and regional commitments.

Despite the misgivings African countries have about the contemporary global trade regime, they still believe that the multilateral trading system provides them with a tool to facilitate the integration of their economies into the global economy and to foster economic development (WTO African Group 2001: 2). And they have identified a number of salient issues for the attention of the WTO. First, market access. Widening access for competitive African exports – agriculture, textiles and clothing – to developed country markets is a crucial goal of most African countries. Of all the issues considered in the UR of trade negotiations, agricultural reform was the most pressing for African governments.[5] The importance of agriculture to Africa is underscored by the fact African countries authored or co-authored about one-third of the 50 proposals on agricultural trade tabled for the DR (United States Trade Representative 2002: 39). Yet agricultural protectionism, especially in the EU, remains an important obstacle to achieving this goal.

Although the subsidization of agriculture in the developed countries is allowed under the Agreement on Agriculture agreed in the UR, it has 'resulted in creating imbalance in the rights and obligations among Members to the detriment of developing countries, as many developing countries are deprived of the financial resources to afford such an export competition policy' (UNCTAD 2001b: 3). Not only does this agreement penalize African countries – whose exports are concentrated in products where market access is highly restricted – but it also fails to acknowledge the critical social and economic significance of the agricultural sector in African countries for their economic development.

Agriculture is the mainstay of African economies and the key to the continent's economic revival. It remains, though, the last citadel of developed country protectionism. Of the US$1.2 trillion that constitutes the value of the global trade in agricultural products, Africa gets only about US$20 billion; about 2 per cent of the total. The Common Agricultural Policy (CAP), the EU's flagship policy, makes up about half of Brussels' US$95.7 billion budget (*International Herald Tribune* 25 October 2002). However, trade protectionism is not the preserve of the European nations. Agricultural subsidy support is also very high in Japan, Switzerland, Iceland, Korea and Norway (see World Bank/IMF 2002b; WTO 2002a).[6] Moreover, in May 2002 the United States, itself a visceral critic of the EU's agricultural regime, enacted legislation that raised farm subsidies substantially. Considered the most generous farm subsidy package in American history, the Farm Security and Rural Investment Act increases federal spending on farm programmes by US$82.6 billion over the next decade, in addition to the US$100 billion Congress was already set to provide to farmers (WTO op cit.: 19).

Nowhere have the deleterious effects of US agricultural subsidies been felt more than in west and central Africa. The International Centre for Trade and Sustainable Development (ICTSD) has stated that the massive subsidies provided by the US government to its 25,000 cotton farmers threaten to wipe out the livelihoods of ten million west and central Africans who rely on cotton production. At US$4 billion, US cotton subsidies alone surpass by 60 per cent the entire GDP of Burkina Faso. The steady collapse in world prices induced by subsidization has reversed the remarkable success that had been achieved by poor west African and central African countries to make their cotton industries among the most competitive in the world. Thanks to US subsidies, in the past four years the region recorded a 31 per cent decrease in export revenue even though its production rose by 14 per cent. The decline in cotton prices costs African cotton farmers about US$1 billion a year in lost exports, three times the whole US aid budget for Africa. It is estimated that the elimination of US cotton subsidies could raise world prices by 26 per cent, which could go a long way towards alleviating poverty in these countries (ICTSD May, 2003). The controversy over cotton subsidies was partly responsible for the failure of the 2003 WTO ministerial meeting in Cancún and several African countries consider its resolution as central to restarting the Doha negotiating process (*Financial Times* 16 September 2003).

These developments do not augur well for the DR of trade negotiations. The DR has been billed as a development round, which implies a greater commitment by industrialized countries to accommodate the sensitivities of poor nations. Protectionism in the OECD countries is harmful to developing countries. Not only does it considerably distort international commodity markets, it also damages the economies of poor countries, the majority of which are African. Dismantling trade barriers is, therefore, central to the economic rejuvenation of Africa: it would enhance agricultural production in countries where food could be produced most efficiently and in a more sustainable fashion, especially in those countries faced with endemic food insecurity. Eliminating trade distortions also has the potential to considerably increase real incomes and reduce poverty in poor countries

(World Bank, 2003).[7] For these reasons it is imperative for industrialized countries to radically overhaul their agricultural policies, especially with regard to the reduction of market subsidies, protectionist tariff barriers and the dumping of surpluses on world markets. On the issue of agricultural trade there remains a yawning gap between the rhetoric of the industrialized countries and what they do in practice. Not only does this undermine the credibility of the global trade system, but it also poses a terminal danger to the Doha negotiation process. Agriculture is not a panacea for Africa's pervasive poverty. Coherent international and domestic policies, and targeted investment are also necessary if economic success is to be generated in the region. Nevertheless, the agricultural sector has the potential to secure food self-sufficiency and expand economic opportunities for growth.

African states have called for a greater commitment to the principle of special and differential treatment. These countries 'continue to be constrained by weak technical and institutional capacities to fully adapt their national laws and obligations as required and take full advantage of the provisions of the multilateral trade agreements' (WTO African Group op cit.: 4). In particular, capacity constraints have severely hampered the ability of the LDCs to understand the new trade issues and to cope with the obligations imposed by the WTO system. At Doha developing countries extracted a concession from industrialized countries on the issue of special and differential treatment: the Doha Declaration (DD) commits rich nations to providing technical assistance to poor countries, although it does not specify the scale of assistance that will be offered and how the needs of individual countries will be determined and fulfilled (WTO 2002b: 33–5). Many LDCs see a direct link between the issues of technical assistance and market access: even if they are granted access to industrialized country markets, their supply-side constraints bar them from taking full advantage of these market openings. Improved technical assistance could play a vital role, therefore, not only in reinforcing the ability of developing nations to assess the advantages and costs of various trade agreements and enabling them to participate more effectively in trade negotiations and dispute settlement, but also in bolstering their manufacturing capabilities.

Furthermore, African nations have drawn attention to the need to address asymmetries and imbalances in WTO rules and agreements, which continue to hinder their growth and development. In particular they have emphasized the need to curtail the abuse by the key industrialized nations, notably the United States, of countervailing measures such as anti-dumping procedures to exclude their exports (ibid. 38–40). They have also raised concerns about the consequences of replacing textile quotas with tariffs, agreed in the UR, which had kept out their products and wanted the arrangement nullified (Jawara and Kwa op cit.: 55). In addition, they have demanded a transparent and inclusive decision-making process in the WTO, which they see as crucial in restoring the credibility of and public support for the multilateral trading system. One of the issues central to the DR has been the matter of trade-related intellectual property rights (TRIPs) and public health (see Chapter 9 by May). African countries secured guarantees from the industrialized nations that existing TRIPs commitments would not obstruct efforts to tackle public health problems faced by poor countries – particularly those induced by epidemics such as HIV/AIDS, malaria and tuberculosis (WTO op cit.: 24–6).

The conclusion of an agreement in August 2003 permitting developing nations faced with public health emergencies to override patents and import copies of life-saving drugs represented a major advance for the developing world, especially given that such an agreement was nearly foiled by the US administration – at the behest of the country's powerful pharmaceutical industry – which had wanted the patent override to be extended only to the LDCs and for a limited number of diseases (*The Guardian* 21 December 2002). Developing countries have rebuffed attempts by the US and EU to include the issues of labour and environmental standards in the Doha negotiating agenda (see Chapter 7 by Haworth and Hughes and Chapter 6 by Newell). Developing country resistance to the incorporation of labour standard dates back to the 1996 Singapore ministerial meeting, but it hardened when former US President Bill Clinton, prior to the start of the failed Seattle meeting in 1999, proposed a linking of trade and labour in response to domestic political pressures. Following a stalemate over the issue, it was decided by the WTO to refer the problem to the International Labour Organisation (ILO) for clarification.

The EU has been under pressure from domestic lobbies to push for an alignment of trade rules with the environment (see Chapter 14 by Falke). Although this EU negotiating stance has generally been opposed by developing countries, the EU secured an agreement at Doha to commence negotiations in three issue areas to: clarify the relationship between existing WTO rules and specific trade commitments outlined in multilateral environmental agreements (MEAs); elaborate procedures for regular information exchange between MEA Secretariats and the relevant WTO committees; and reduce or eliminate tariff and non-tariff barriers to environmental goods and services (WTO op cit.: 13). African nations succeeded to persuade WTO members to set up working groups to examine the relationship between trade, debt and finance, as well as between trade and technology transfer – crucial issues of enormous interest to poor countries. WTO members also committed themselves to the goal of providing duty-free and quota-free access for goods produced by the LDCs (Cronin op cit.: 385). Moreover, the ACP countries secured a waiver of the WTO rule stipulating that any trade deal accorded to one member must be extended to all members. Designed to accommodate the Cotonou Agreement, the waiver will be effective until the preferential market access granted to ACP exports by the EU terminates on 31 December 2007 (WTO op cit.: 51–7).

Trade performance

By all accounts the economic performance of most Sub-Saharan African countries in recent decades has been abysmal. The 1980s marked a precipitous decline in the continent's growth. While the overall growth rate in Africa from 1965 to 1980 averaged as high as 4.2 per cent per annum, it dropped to 1.8 per cent from 1980 to 1990, and averaged 0.9 per cent during the 1990–94 period (Belshaw and

Livingstone 2002: 5). Tied to Africa's poor growth has been its terrible export performance. In value terms, merchandise exports grew at an average rate of 1.5 per cent over the decade up to 1990, rising to 3.4 per cent over the period 1990–97/98. However, over the whole period 'this still meant a fall in value of exports per capita of 19 per cent and of agricultural exports per capita, especially, of 31 per cent' (ibid. 6).

The past few years have seen the launch of initiatives by the US and the EU calculated to bolster African export performance. The EU's 'Everything but Arms' (EBA) scheme and the US African Growth and Opportunity Act (AGOA) are designed to remove trade barriers to and facilitate greater access for African exports to the US and EU markets. Introduced in March 2001, the EBA extends duty-free access for a further 919 tariff lines to the world's 49 LDCs' exports except the arms trade (European Commission 2000a: 3). Market opening, however, will be phased in progressively for three sensitive products – bananas, sugar and rice.[8] The EU is the LDCs' leading export market, accounting for over 50 per cent of their agricultural exports. Nonetheless, while the EBA initiative could yield significant benefits for the LDCs in the long run, its short-term impact is likely to be minimal. This is due to the fact that at present 99 per cent of LDC exports to the EU, which constitute 1 per cent of the latter's imports, are already exempt from customs duties in terms of the Lomé Convention for African, Caribbean and Pacific (ACP) countries and the GSP for non-ACP countries (Resal 1999: 2). Furthermore the LDCs are likely to be constrained by their very limited comparative advantages and production capacity, which might reduce their ability to take advantage of EBA benefits. Another shortcoming of the EBA scheme is the retention by the EU of its prerogative to implement safeguard measures against LDC imports if it deems that such imports are causing or threatening material damage to its competing industries (ibid. 3).

Of the two external trade initiatives, AGOA has attracted more attention. Promulgated in October 2000, AGOA is 'a central element of the Bush Administration's trade and investment policy toward Sub-Saharan Africa, which aims to promote free markets, expand US-African trade and investment, stimulate economic growth, and facilitate Sub-Saharan Africa's integration into the global economy' (United States Trade Representative op cit.: 1). With 35 beneficiaries, AGOA designates over 1800 products from Sub-Saharan Africa for duty-free access to the United States – in addition to the 4650 products already eligible under the General System of Preferences (GSP).[9] Thanks in part to AGOA the US has eclipsed the EU as Sub-Saharan Africa's biggest single market, accounting for 27 per cent of the region's exports in 2000. US imports from Sub-Saharan Africa have risen 61.5 per cent since 2000. The US imported US$8.2 billion of duty-free goods in 2001 under AGOA, representing almost 40 per cent of all its imports from Sub-Saharan Africa. In addition, US exports to Sub-Saharan Africa reached record levels in 2001, growing to nearly US$7 billion, a 17.5 per cent increase from 2000. Even so, Africa accounts for less than 1 per cent of US merchandise exports, and less than 2 per cent of US merchandise imports (ibid. 2–5). Moreover, AGOA trade preferences have benefited only a few countries, with Nigeria, Gabon and South Africa accounting for 92 per cent of duty-free benefits.

On the surface, AGOA seems to have a potential to bolster African external trade. But it has a number of drawbacks. First, like the EBA it is a unilateral and autonomous trade initiative that can be withdrawn arbitrarily by the US administration. In addition, Jagdish Bhagwati has argued that trade preferences such as AGOA, EBA and GSP achieve very little for the poor countries: by their nature such preferences divert trade away from non-preferred countries, thereby playing off poor nations against each other (*The Economist* 20 June 2002). Second, the most contentious aspect of AGOA is the insistence that its benefits be extended only to those countries that have established or are making progress towards meeting specific eligibility criteria including maintaining a market-based economy, establishing the rule of law, eliminating barriers to US goods and investment, protecting intellectual property, fighting corruption, reducing poverty, protecting workers' rights and eliminating child labour (United States Trade Representative op cit.: 15). Eligible countries are required to undergo an annual review of their status and may be added or withdrawn from the list during this review.[10] This provides the United States with the opportunity not only to oblige qualifying countries to embrace its model of democratic governance but also to shape African economies to its own preferences.

Third, while fulfilling some of the AGOA criteria undoubtedly could benefit African countries the overall thrust of the US trade agenda in Africa is not as benign as it is projected. It could be argued that AGOA forms an integral part of a wider strategy deployed by the United States and other industrialized countries to use regional, unilateral and bilateral accords with African countries to introduce issues they have difficulty tabling in the WTO. Through AGOA African countries are enjoined to adopt disciplines pertaining to new trade issues such as intellectual property rights protection, government procurement, electronic commerce, telecommunications, as well as investment and financial liberalization. This strategy finds a wider expression in the recently proposed free trade talks between the United States and SACU – made up of South Africa, Botswana, Lesotho, Swaziland and Namibia – which are mainly geared at prising open African economies to American business interests. The US objectives for these trade talks were explicitly summed up in an open letter sent by Robert Zoellick, the US Trade Representative (USTR), to Senator Robert Byrd, the former leader of the Senate:

> The administration is committed to bringing back trade agreements that open markets to benefit our farmers, workers, businesses and families. With the Congress's continued help, we can move promptly to advance America's trade interests ... In pursuing a negotiation with SACU, we are responding to Congress's direction, as expressed in the African Growth and Opportunity Act, to initiate negotiations with interested beneficiary countries to serve as the catalyst for increasing free trade between the United States and sub-Saharan Africa and for increasing private-sector investment in the region. (Cited in *Mail and Guardian* 21 January 2003).

Intra-regional integration

Regional economic integration has historically constituted a major aspect of African development strategy (see Asante 1997). It has been viewed as a means to overcome the continent's structural deficiencies, including political fragmentation, small intra-regional markets and narrow resource bases. As such, economic integration has been considered not only desirable but also necessary if Africa is to achieve meaningful industrialization, develop intra-African trade, and participate effectively in the evolving global linkages. The regionalization of the world economy has reinforced the vulnerability of Africa in the international political economy and underscored the centrality of intra-regional integration to the continent's development. The economic crisis of the 1980s 'shattered both the illusion of the possibility of independent development by each African country and that of external dependence as the path to African development' (Onimode op cit.: 283). As McCarthy (1999: 18) explains:

> The small size of African economies and the observation that in the long run the prices of many primary commodities tend to decline in relation to those of manufactures have converted African leaders, the Organisation of African Unity (OAU) and the UN Economic Commission for Africa (ECA) to economic integration as the road to development.

Pressing demands for globalization, coupled with the economic setbacks of the past two decades, have exposed the futility of pursuing atomistic nationalistic development and highlighted the necessity of elaborating a collective agenda for African economic recovery (Onimode op cit.: 265). Strengthening regional and sub-regional integration among African states is thus necessary if they are to reverse their marginalization in world trade and facilitate their effective integration into the global political economy.

Yet the record of regional economic integration in Africa has been one of unmitigated failure. Sub-Saharan Africa is replete with over-ambitious, grandiose and overlapping regional integration plans that have failed to materialize. And this failure is reflected predominantly in the low levels of intra-regional trade. According to Hawkins (2002: 3) in 2000 only 2 per cent of African cross-border trade occurred among African states: this compares unfavourably with the fact that by the 1990s about 60 per cent of world trade – jumping from 35 per cent in the 1960s – occurred within regional integration projects. Africa's poor intra-regional trade underscores the dominance of Africa's trade with the EU and the United States, which is locked into a 'hub-and-spoke' pattern: African countries produce primary commodities for developed country markets and import manufactured goods, but very negligible trade takes place among themselves (McCarthy op cit.: 21).

Intra-regional trade in Africa is severely constrained by a plethora of structural factors including the lack of adequate transport and communications infrastructure, the poor implementation of regional trade agreements, the absence of complementarity in production, as well as weak financial sectors (ibid.). Bucking this pattern, however, have been SACU and the *Communauté Economique de l'Afrique de l'Ouest* (CEAO), whose respective shares of intra-regional trade have exceeded 10 per cent of total trade (McCarthy op cit.: 22). Both SACU and CEAO owe their successes to the presence in these regional schemes of relatively prosperous and developed members (South Africa in the case of SACU and Ivory Coast and Senegal in the case of CEAO) which have been willing to bear a bigger share of integration costs (ibid. 22–3).

The generally low levels of African intra-regional trade have, however, masked an intensification of bilateral trade and investments between specific countries, which have come about largely as a result of the normalization of economic relations between South Africa and the wider African region in the early 1990s. Most notable has been the exponential growth in trade and investment between South Africa and Nigeria, Africa's principal regional powers, which rose sharply from US$12 million in 1994 to US$400 million in 2001 (*Business Day* 17 April 2002). The establishment in 1999 of a high-level binational commission between Nigeria and South Africa, chaired by the countries' vice-presidents, testifies to the growing importance of the bilateral trade relationship. Nevertheless, South Africa's overall trade with the rest of the continent remains heavily skewed in its favour: total trade with Africa excluding SACU totalled US$856 million in imports and US$3.7 billion in exports in 2001 (ibid.). South Africa's exports, mostly manufactured goods, to other Sub-Saharan African countries registered a 9 per cent growth in 2002 (US Trade Representative op cit.: 25) – widening an already huge trade imbalance. It is this enormous trade disparity that has been a source of friction between South Africa, which accounts for 40 per cent of Sub-Saharan Africa's total GDP, and its continental trade partners – some of which have described the rapid explosion of South African trade and investment as a new form of colonialism (*New York Times* 17 February 2002).

The proliferation of regional and bilateral trade agreements between industrialized countries and African countries poses a key challenge to African economic integration. This challenge has been heightened recently by the replacement of the Lomé convention – which since 1975 had provided the structure for trade and cooperation between the EU and ACP countries – by the Cotonou Agreement. The agreement provides for the expiry in 2007 of the EU non-reciprocal concessions to exports from ACP countries in line with the commitments made by both the EU and ACP countries to enter into WTO-compatible trade arrangements from 1 January 2008. To this end, ACP countries are required to negotiate reciprocal economic partnership agreements (EPAs) either bilaterally or on a regional basis with the EU (EU Commission 2000b: 1–12). There is a concern that the introduction of reciprocity in trade between unequal economic partners such as the EU and African countries will have adverse effects on most African economies (see Cheru 2003: 29). Furthermore, by inducing a fragmentation of the multilateral trade regime, trade arrangements such as the Cotonou accord threaten to undermine Africa's regional integration efforts and its bargaining power in the WTO.

It is imperative that African countries integrate their economies and engage strategically with the world trading system as a cohesive and coherent regional bloc. Such integration, nevertheless, must jettison the failed, over-ambitious market integration schemes of the past in favour of modest, flexible and function-based models of regional economic cooperation that revolve around specific themes or sectors. The benefits of this regional approach are cogently summed up by McCarthy (op cit.: 39) who notes that:

> Among the advantages of this 'made to order' approach are its flexibility and pragmatism in circumventing the problems posed by nationalism and equity in the distribution of costs and benefits. It is also better suited to deal with the many fiscal, physical and technical barriers to trade that cannot be addressed by trade policy. Since the focus is on specific tasks, issues are depoliticised and thus present less of a challenge to existing power structures. In time a 'culture' of regional co-operation is created, thus laying the foundation for market integration and the acceptance of the loss of sovereignty this entails.

New regionalisms

In contemporary Africa there has been a growing prominence of new regionalisms, of both a formal and an informal character (see Shaw 2002; Shaw and Nyang'oro, 2000; Shaw and van der Westhuizen 1999). These meso-level regionalisms 'vary considerably from de facto informal regional economic arrangements and emerging regional civil societies to embryonic regional security communities' and have 'emerged in response to the new international division of labour and new international division of power, as well as to competitive regional proposals made from inside and outside the continent' (Shaw and Nyang'oro op cit.: 278–9). They involve states, private firms and regional civil society formations, although the rationale for their existence is not necessarily consistent with traditional definitions of regionalism. Local and transnational spatial development initiatives such as the Gauteng SDI, Blyde River Initiative, West Coast Investment Initiative, Maputo Development Corridor, Lubombo Initiative and Walvis Bay Initiative provide good examples where the private sector has taken the lead in developing and managing regional economic projects, while local, provincial, national and regional governments have performed supporting regulatory, technical, facilitative and promotional functions. Multinational corporations, predominantly but not exclusively of South African origin, have employed trade and investment to carve their own distinct regions. Over the past few years a multitude of South African firms have set up business operations throughout the African continent, including the telecommunications giant M-Cell-MTN, the electricity supplier Eskom, South African Airways, Sasol, Spoornet, banking institutions, retail stores such as Shoprite as well as a wide array of joint-venture operations.

Alongside these meso-level interstate regionalisms has been the growth of cross-border linkages among civil society groups. Propelled by regional non-governmental formations, these civil societies are concerned mainly with pursuing alternative, transformative regional agendas and engaging in 'resistance from below' (Söderbaum 2002: 107). Civil society regionalism is dynamic and adaptable, and is organized in interconnected networks that mobilize around a wide range of issues including human rights, trade and globalization, food security as well as debt and structural adjustment (ibid. 104). One such network is the Africa Trade Network (ATN), a coalition of civil society organizations that campaigns around trade and investment policy issues in Africa and facilitates interaction between civil society groups and African governments, especially the annual Conference of African Ministers of Trade. The ATN has 'given training to and provided information on trade policy matters to several civil society organisations, and mobilised African civil society participation on the WTO' (Africa Trade Network, www.twnafrica.org) and enjoys an observer status within the Organisation of African Unity (OAU) and the United Nations Economic Commission for Africa (UNECA). It also spearheaded the campaign and lobby efforts of African civil society groups at the Seattle WTO ministerial meeting in 1999.

Other influential regional networks include the Africa Knowledge Network Forum, a pan-African group dedicated to enhancing interaction between African intellectuals and policy-makers, the African Social Forum, the African Financing for Development Caucus, the African Trade Union Conference, the Rural Development Services Network, the Council for Development and Social Science Research, the South African National NGO Coalition and the African Forum on Debt and Development.

The war on terror and African trade

In its national security strategy (The White House 2002: 10) the US administration asserts that pervasive poverty in Africa 'threatens both a core value of the United States – preserving human dignity – and our strategic priority – combating global terror'. To deal with the problems of global poverty and terrorism, it proposes that the United States will seek to 'ignite a new era of global economic growth through free markets and free trade' and 'bring every nation into an expanding circle of development' (ibid. 17–23). None has been more forceful in positing this liberal internationalist notion of enhanced economic cooperation as a counter-strategy against global terrorism than the USTR Robert Zoellick. In a speech before the Council on Foreign Relations he asserted that:

> Trade is about more than economic efficiency; it reflects a system of values: openness, peaceful exchange, opportunity, inclusiveness and integration, mutual gains through interchange, freedom of choice, appreciation of differences, governance through agreed rules, and a hope for betterment for all peoples and lands. Therefore, just as the Cold War reflected a contest of values, so will this campaign against terrorism. Just as our Cold War strategy recognised the interconnection of security and economics, so must America's strategy against terrorism. (Zoellick 2001: 4)

It is worth observing that the 2002 report of the USTR widens the list of eligibility criteria for AGOA trade benefits to include the provision that beneficiary countries must not engage in activities that undermine US national security or foreign policy interests nor provide support for acts of international terrorism (United States Trade Representative op cit.: 15). This accords neatly with the putative strategy enunciated by Zoellick, which exhorts African countries to embrace liberal political and economic values and to demonstrate unwavering loyalty to the United States in return for the trade preferences extended to them. It could be surmised that in the future US economic engagement with Africa will be more than ever before conditional upon the willingness of African countries to support American security policies in the region. This has profound consequences for unstable and failed African states such as Burkina Faso and Liberia, which have been accused by European intelligence agencies of complicity in an Al-Qaeda conspiracy to channel diamonds through West Africa (*The Guardian* 8 January 2003).

The 'war on terror' has catapulted African oil to the heart of US security concerns. The notion that the United States has no vital interests in Africa has been challenged by two influential Washington insiders, Barry Schutz and Paul Michael Wihbey (2001: 15), who have argued that such a perception 'ignores the reality of US dependence on imported oil'. They point out that:

> As the Persian Gulf becomes increasingly dangerous – one need only think of the recent terrorist attack on the USS Cole in Yemen – the availability of alternative, more reliable sources of oil becomes increasingly attractive. The major African supplier, Nigeria – and growing West African sources from Senegal to Angola – provides the US with alternatives to heavy dependence on the Persian Gulf and on politically sensitive wilderness areas like Alaska. (Ibid.)

Already Africa provides 18 per cent of US crude oil, compared with the 27 per cent the US imports from the Persian Gulf (United States Trade Representative op cit.: 28). The expectation that oil production in Angola and Nigeria, America's leading suppliers, will double or triple in the next decade is destined to make Africa an important actor in international oil politics in the future. An escalation of the Middle East crisis will benefit oil-exporting African nations such as Libya, Nigeria, Angola, Gabon, Congo-Brazzaville, Equatorial Guinea and the Democratic Republic of Congo. But it will also have adverse economic consequences for oil-importing African nations in the form of mounting oil prices and foreign debt. The issue of African oil also raises questions about the proclamations of the United States, in terms of the AGOA scheme, about the need for good governance in Africa. A case in point is the leaked confidential IMF report which shows that US$4.3 billion has vanished from the Angolan public purse in the past five years as a result of irregular bookkeeping at Sonangol, Angola's state-owned oil corporation (*Newsweek* 4 November 2002).[11] Failure to condemn such excesses reinforces the perception that US policy towards Angola is motivated exclusively by its interest in securing Angolan oil.

The international community's preoccupation with terrorism is likely to overshadow the New Partnership for Africa's Development (NEPAD). Conceived by presidents Thabo Mbeki of South Africa, Olusegun Obasanjo of Nigeria, Abdoulaye Wade of Senegal and Abdelaziz Bouteflika of Algeria, Nepad is designed to 'promote accelerated growth and sustainable development, eradicate widespread and severe poverty, and halt the marginalisation of Africa in the globalisation process' (Nepad 2001:1). It is a pledge by African leaders to end poor governance, corruption and conflicts in their countries in return for increased aid, private investment and a reduction of trade barriers by industrialized countries.

Yet Nepad has been excoriated by African scholars and civil society groups. Although some criticisms are merely tangential, two concerns about Nepad have a substantive basis and will be discussed briefly here. First, Nepad has been rejected on the grounds that it is a top-down project 'driven by African political elites and drawn up with the corporate forces and institutional instruments of globalisation, rather than being based on African people's experiences, knowledge and demands' (Africa Trade Network op cit.). The second criticism is that NEPAD is too externally oriented in the sense that it is 'mainly concerned with raising external financial resources, appealing to and relying on external governments and institutions' (ibid.) rather than seriously focusing on internal resource mobilization for its implementation. In this respect Nepad represents a departure from erstwhile African development blueprints such as the Lagos Plan of Action (1980), the African Alternative Framework to Structural Adjustment Programmes (1989) and the Arusha Charter (1990), which placed an accent on strategies of collective self-reliance and popular participation.

The failure of African leaders at the 2002 Group of Eight summit in Kananaskis to convince Western leaders to deliver on their pledges bestows credence on the arguments of Nepad's critics. At the summit industrialized countries refused to commit themselves to significant reductions in the massive agricultural subsidies provided to their farmers and in the high duties levied on African exports in their markets. On the issue of debt relief developed countries pledged only US$1 billion – mainly to make up for falling commodity prices – instead of the US$15–20 billion proposed by heavily indebted African countries. In respect of aid and investment they undertook to earmark US$6 billion a year worth of aid, rather than the US$35 billion requested by African leaders, for Africa by 2006 (*The Guardian* 28 June 2002; *Business Day* 28 June 2002).

All these problems underscore the importance of generating internal resources for Africa's social and economic advancement. Without substantial domestic savings and investment African states will not be able to build a sound public and social infrastructure and tackle the monumental developmental challenges they confront. National savings and investment played a crucial catalytic role in the successes of the East Asian economic tigers, where the saving ratio in most countries was estimated at 50 per cent compared with 18 per cent in Africa (Onimode op cit.: 234). A major problem is that 33 per cent of Africans' savings are held offshore, thanks to anxieties about political and economic instability in many parts of the continent. Creating a political and economic climate conducive to local investment is thus a key test for African governments. African states could take a leaf from the Indian government, which provided an array of incentives for affluent Indians to return their savings to the country, resulting in about US$70 billion being brought back to the country (*The Observer* 10 August 2003).

African governments would be better served if they also tapped into the enormous internal investments that are locked in the 'informal sector', which could contribute considerably towards evolving alternative strategies of accumulation.[12] Furthermore, it is important that Nepad is subjected to democratic scrutiny and popular participation. Development is intrinsically a political matter and therefore a function of democracy in form as well as in content.

Concluding remarks

Domestic policies are equally as important as international policies in addressing Africa's economic concerns. The experience of numerous countries in Sub-Saharan Africa in the 1970s demonstrated unequivocally that a positive international economic environment was not sufficient to guarantee self-sustained growth (UNCTAD 2001c: 49). The investment and growth generated by African countries – by way of positive terms of trade and aid – was not accompanied by efforts to raise domestic savings and diversify exports. This meant that when the external economic environment weakened African growth could not be sustained. Aligning domestic actions with international policy efforts remains, therefore, a key imperative for African governments. To this end greater attention should be given to undertaking appropriate reforms in domestic policy areas including savings and investments, exchange rates, education and training, research and development as well as political and economic institutions.

There is also a compelling need for African states to overcome the political, technical and structural constraints that have hamstrung the development of the region's agriculture and to create the appropriate circumstances for its transformation. The failure of African governments to undertake the necessary agricultural domestic reforms over the past decades has contributed immensely to the continent's dreadful economic performance (Cheru op cit.: 89–120). Despite the preponderance of its agricultural sector, Africa has yet to experience an agricultural revolution. The agricultural sector has the potential to expand economic opportunities for growth in Africa and to propel industrialization and social progress. While a favourable external environment is necessary in advancing Africa's prospects in world trade, the principal duty for creating conditions conducive to sustained development resides with the African countries themselves.

Any attempts to reverse Africa's marginalization in the global political economy will not succeed unless they simultaneously address the crisis of governance in the region. The descent of Zimbabwe, Ivory Coast and Liberia into anarchy and lawlessness has highlighted once again the interconnectedness of the political, economic and social domains in Africa. Economic crises in Africa have engendered political and social crises and collectively they have propelled the downward spiral in the majority of countries (Ghai 2000: 1–4). As the UNDP (2002: 13) points out, 'in Sub-Saharan Africa human development has regressed in recent years, and the lives of its very poor people are getting worse'. It seems highly unlikely, on the basis of current trends, that Africa will fulfil the Millennium Development Goals set by the UN General Assembly in 2000.[13]

Combined with the absence of democratic accountability, the paucity of visionary leadership in Africa has been a major contributor to its multifarious socio-economic and political ills. Although Africa has made remarkable strides towards embracing democracy over the past decade, autocratic and self-serving rule continues to be a defining feature of politics in many parts of the region.[14] African leaders cannot claim to be active champions for reform in global economic governance while domestically induced problems of political misrule, endemic corruption, human rights abuses, high levels of capital flight and gross fiscal mismanagement continue to linger on unchecked. The Nepad peer review mechanism they have adopted to foster political, economic and corporate accountability in their countries could, if stringently implemented, go a long way towards tackling these problems.

Acknowledgements

I am grateful to Tshediso Matona, Chiedu Osakwe, Francis Botchway and Peter Draper for comments on a previous draft. The usual disclaimer applies.

Notes

1. These are Cape Verde, Ethiopia, Sao Tome and Principe, Seychelles and Sudan.
2. The 'Like-Minded Group' of countries are India, Mauritius, Pakistan, Malaysia, Cuba, Zimbabwe, Dominican Republic, Kenya, Egypt, Tanzania, Indonesia, Sri Lanka, Uganda, Honduras and Jamaica.
3. This point was communicated to me by a senior South African trade official.
4. The meetings of the AWG are convened and chaired by participating states on a rotational basis and the incumbent state acts as a general spokesperson of all countries for the duration of its one-year tenure. Although the AWG's status is informal, its views are accorded serious attention within the WTO primarily because they are elaborated in consultation with trade bureaucrats and political principals in the national capitals.
5. Apart from making up 35 per cent of Africa's GDP, agriculture accounts for 70 per cent of the region's employment and 40 per cent of its exports.
6. According to the WTO, in the Republic of Korea, Norway and Switzerland, total agricultural support is close to, or exceeds, the sector's contribution to GDP.
7. The World Bank has calculated that the total benefit of liberalizing global agricultural trade will be in the region of US$250 billion by 2015, of which nearly US$150 billion would accrue to developing countries. It estimates that of the US$150 billion in agricultural related gains to be reaped by developing nations, US$115 billion would come from liberalization in developing countries themselves.
8. Customs duties on bananas will be reduced by 20 per cent per year beginning 1 January 2002 and will be completely removed by 1 January 2006; customs duties on rice will be reduced by 50 per cent on 1 September 2007, by 80 per cent on 1 September 2008, and completely removed on 1 September 2009; customs duties on sugar will be reduced from 20 per cent on 1 July 2006, by 50 per cent on 1 July 2007, by 80 per cent on 1 July 2008, and totally eliminated on 1 July 2009.
9. Benin, Botswana, Cameroon, Cape Verde, Central African Republic, Chad, Congo, Djibouti, Eritrea, Ethiopia, Gabon, Ghana, Guinea, Guinea-Bissau, Kenya, Lesotho, Madagascar, Malawi, Mali, Mauritania, Mauritius, Mozambique, Namibia, Niger, Nigeria, Rwanda, Sao Tome and Principe, Senegal, Seychelles, Sierra Leone, South Africa, Swaziland, Tanzania, Uganda, Zambia.

10. The US administration has previously threatened to suspend the trade privileges of Eritrea and Swaziland unless they improved their human rights records.
11. Oil companies wishing to work with Sonangol Oil Corporation are expected to pay 'signature bonuses' and their executives sit on the board of Angolan president Eduardo dos Santos' charitable foundation.
12. The informal sector refers to the sector(s) of the economy not under state regulation.
13. To be met by 2015, the Millennium Development Goals include the eradication of poverty and hunger, achievement of universal primary education, attainment of gender equality, reduction of child mortality, improvement of maternal health and pursuit of environmental sustainability.
14. The word democracy is used in this context to refer to minimalist liberal democracy rather than substantive participatory democracy (see Grugel 2002: 6–7).

References

Adedeji, A. (1993) *Africa Within the World – Beyond Dispossession and Dependence*, London: Zed Books.
Ake, C. (1981) *A Political Economy of Africa*, London: Longman.
Asante, S.K.B. (1997) *Regionalism and Africa's Development*, Houndmills: Macmillan Press.
Belshaw, D. and Livingstone, I. (eds) (2002) *Renewing Development in Sub-Saharan Africa – Policy, Performance and Prospects*, London: Routledge.
Cheru, F. (2003) *African Renaissance – Roadmaps to the Challenge of Globalisation*, London: Zed Books.
Cooper, A., Higgott, R. and Nossal, K.R. (eds) (1993) *Relocating Middle Powers: Australia and Canada in an Evolving World Order*, Vancouver: University of British Columbia.
Cronin, P. (2003) 'The Doha Round: Prospects for the Rules-Based Trading System', in Goddard, R. C., Cronin, P. and Dash, K. C. (eds) *International Political Economy – State-Market Relations in a Changing Global Order*, Basingstoke: Palgrave.
Department of Foreign Affairs (2003) 'South Africa's International Relations 2002/3', a report presented by the South African Foreign Minister, Dr Nkosazana Dlamini-Zuma, to the South African Parliament, Cape Town, 23 March 2003.
Department of Trade and Industry (2001) *Annual Report 2000/1*, Pretoria: Government Printer.
EU Commission (2000a) *Everything but Arms Proposal – Possible Impacts on the Agricultural Sector*, Brussels: EU Commission.
EU Commission (2000b) *The Cotonou Agreement – General Overview*, Brussels: EU Commission.
Ghai, D. (2000) 'African Development in Retrospect and Prospect', in Ghai, D. (ed.) *Renewing Social and Economic Progress in Africa – Essays in Memory of Philip Ndegwa*, Basingstoke: Palgrave.
Grugel, J. (2002) *Democratisation – A Critical Introduction*, Basingstoke: Palgrave.
Hawkins, T. (2002) 'African Trade', *Policy Brief*, Lausanne: Evian Group.
Hoogvelt, A. (2001) *Globalisation and the Post-Colonial World*, Basingstoke: Palgrave.
ICTSD (The International Centre for Trade and Sustainable Development) (2003) 'Elimination of Cotton Subsidies: A Development Deliverable for Cancún', *Bridges*, no. 4, May 2003.
Jawara, F. and Kwa, A. (2003) *Behind the Scenes at the WTO – The Real World of Trade Negotiations*, London: Zed Books.
McCarthy, C. (1999) 'Regional Integration and Trade Liberalisation in Sub-Saharan Africa', in Oyejide, A., Ndulu, B. and Greenaway, D. (eds) *Regional Integration and Trade Liberalisation in Sub-Saharan Africa*, Basingstoke: Macmillan Press.
Nepad Secretariat (2001) *New Partnerships for Africa's Development*, Midrand: Nepad.
Onimode, B. (1989) *A Political Economy of the African Crisis*, London: Zed Books.

Onimode, B. (2000) *Africa in the World of the 21st Century*, Ibadan: Ibadan University Press.

Raghavan, C. (1990) *Recolonisation: GATT, the Uruguay Round and the Third World*, London: Zed Books.

Ravenhill, J. (1986) *Africa in Economic Crisis*, Basingstoke: Macmillan Press.

Resal (*Réseau Européen de Sécurité Alimentaire*) (1999) 'The "Everything But Arms" Initiative – What are Its Consequences for Resal Countries?' Solagral: Resal.

Rodney, W. (1972) *How Europe Underdeveloped Africa*, Dar es Salaam: Tanzania Publishing House.

Schutz, B.M. and Wihbey, P.M. (2001) 'Perceptions and Realities in US-Africa Policy', *Africa Analysis*, London, 6 April 2001.

Shaw, T.M. and van der Westhuizen, J. (1999) 'Towards a Political Economy of Trade in Africa: States, Companies and Civil Societies', in Hocking, B. and McGuire, S. (eds) *Trade Politics – International, Domestic and Regional Perspectives*, London: Routledge.

Shaw, T.M. and Nyang'oro, J.M. (2000) 'African Renaissance in the New Millennium? From Anarchy to Emerging Markets?', in Stubbs, R. and Underhill, G. R. D. (eds) *Political Economy and the Changing Global Order*, Canada: Oxford University Press.

Shaw, T.M. (2002) 'New Regionalisms in Africa in the New Millennium: Comparative Perspectives on Renaissance, Realisms and/or Regressions', in Breslin, S., Hughes, C.H., Phillips, N. and Rosamond, B. (eds) *New Regionalisms in the Global Political Economy*, London: Routledge.

Söderbaum, F. (2002) *The Political Economy of Regionalism in Southern Africa*, Göteborg: Göteborg University.

Spero, J.E. and Hart, J.A. (2000) *The Politics of International Economic Relations*, New York: St. Martin's Press.

The White House (2002) *The National Security Strategy of the United States of America*, Washington, DC: The White House.

United Nations Conference on Trade and Development (2001a) *FDI in Least Developed Countries at a Glance*, Geneva: United Nations.

United Nations Conference on Trade and Development (2001b) *Current Developments on Issues of Interest to African Countries in the Context of Post-Seattle WTO Trade Negotiations*, Geneva: United Nations.

United Nations Conference on Trade and Development (2001c) *Economic Development in Africa – Performance, Prospects and Policy Issues*, Geneva: United Nations.

United Nations Development Programme (2002) *Human Development Report – Deepening Democracy in a Fragmented World*, New York: United Nations.

United States Trade Representative (2002) *US Trade and Investment Policy Toward Sub-Saharan Africa and Implementation of the African Growth and Opportunity Act*, a report submitted by the President of the United States to the United States Congress, May 2002.

World Bank (2002a) *Global Development Finance*, Washington, DC: World Bank.

World Bank/IMF (2002b) *Market Access for Developing Country Exports – Selected Issues*, Washington, DC: World Bank/IMF.

World Bank (2003) *Global Economic Prospects and the Developing Countries 2003: Investing to Unlock Global Opportunities*, Washington, DC: World Bank.

World Trade Organisation (2002a) *Annual Report*, Geneva: WTO.

World Trade Organisation (2002b) *Doha Declarations*, Geneva: WTO.

WTO African Group (2001) 'Inputs from the WTO African Group for Agenda Item 6 of the Experts Segment of the 4th Ordinary Session of the OAU/AEC Conference of Ministers of Trade – Preparations for the Fourth Ministerial Meeting of the World Trade Organisation', Geneva, 14 September 2001.

Zoellick, R. (2001) 'The WTO and New Global Trade Negotiations: What's at Stake', a speech presented before the Council on Foreign Relations, Washington, DC, 30 October 2001.

16
The Contradictions and Continuities of South African Trade Policy

Ian Taylor

South African trade policy has been undergoing a process of structural reform over the last twenty years (see Baker *et al.* 1993; Padayachee 1997). The current African National Congress (ANC)-led government's trade policy is a reflection of this and resonates continuity with the old apartheid state vis-à-vis policies enacted in order to situate South Africa within the global economy. Any discussion of contemporary South Africa's trade policy has to situate this within its historical context and the tensions and contradictions that were engendered by the transition from apartheid to a non-racial liberal democracy, with particular reference to the evolution of economic policy. The current position of Pretoria regarding its trade policy is marked by a high degree of tension between various constituencies within the ruling party and its coalition partners, the Congress of South African Trade Unions (COSATU) and the South African Communist Party (SACP). This is centred around the essentially neo-liberal Growth, Employment and Redistribution (GEAR) programme currently being pursued by the government.

Indeed, the speed of reform and the neo-liberal direction in which it has been taken in the context of increasing levels of unemployment and extremely high levels of poverty, supply-side difficulties in the economy and increasing frustration at the failure of the North to follow through with its liberalization rhetoric (exemplified by George W. Bush's introduction of protective measures for the American steel industry and increased subsidies for domestic farmers) means that the virtues of trade liberalization within the political debate in South Africa is constantly under attack. In South Africa, like elsewhere economic policy cannot be divorced from its political milieu.

Origins of South African trade policy reform

Pressure from internal and external capital to move the National Party away from national socialist policies were long-standing prior to the eventual dismantling of apartheid, and were an outcome of the conjuncture of forces of increasing globalization and the processes that had been stimulated by the 40 years of National Party rule. The National Party originally found its support base rooted in the Afrikaner working class, but its rule facilitated the entry of Afrikaners into the

295

ranks of corporate South Africa, an area previously controlled by Anglophones (Clark 1994). As a result, the class basis of the National Party changed until the National Party became the organizing and structuring political instrument for capital. The wealthier fraction of Afrikanerdom increasingly came to align itself with the already existing transnationalized class elite within South Africa, represented by the big Anglophone conglomerates and monopolies (see Innes 1984; Tregenna-Piggott 1976). In short:

> The NP's economic vision underwent a dramatic transformation in the late 1970s. Afrikaner firms, benefiting from three decades of government contracts and contacts, developed into large conglomerates with a significant stake in all sectors of the country's economy. Afrikaner businessmen, like their English counterparts, felt confident enough to advocate both political and economic liberalization and socio-economic reform. They also pushed for the gradual liberalization of the South African financial system and (eyeing future markets abroad) for the country's further integration into the world economy. (Habib and Padayachee 1999: 6)

As a result, 'the National Party jettisoned almost every last element of its own, decades-old ethnic programme and world view' (O'Meara 1996: 421). Essentially, the pull of greater capital accumulation that active intercourse with globalizing impulses and the concomitant transnational linkages so visibly witnessed in the Anglophone companies of South Africa was too much to resist for aspiring Afrikaner elites. These conglomerates represented a fraction that established South Africa as the entrée for the rest of the region and were of immense importance to the global capitalist system (Fine and Rustomjee 1996).

It was to this fraction that the emergent and highly influential Afrikaner capitalists aspired. In alliance with their English-speaking counterparts, it was this group in particular that came to push the National Party towards negotiations. This process was spurred on by the deepening contradictions that apartheid dialectically spawned and the resistance that this engendered in the Black working class, first in 1976 and then in the resurgent township revolts of the early 1980s. Such crises convinced the South African capitalist elite, with the urging of their class allies based in the core, that a political solution that involved the preservation of the vital interests of capitalism within the framework of a non-racial democracy was of great urgency. Apartheid became bad for business and the elites at both the national and international level realized this. Pressure was thus intensified on the National Party to open up the political process and by 1984 the Afrikaner establishment had accepted that change was inevitable (Sparks 1994: 74).

Gradually, South Africa's economic crisis came to be seen as a result of market imperfections introduced by external actors, most notably the national socialist – 'volkskapitalisme' – polices of the National Party (O'Meara 1983). An abandonment of such distorting impulses and the call for a move towards 'the market' as the regulator of the economy had been articulated since the mid-1970s, for example, the 'O'Dowd Thesis', which placed South Africa early in the second stage of industrialization and which argued that capitalism created material wealth more efficiently than 'socialism'. However, an acceptance of this at the elite levels only really began to be articulated in the 1980s (see O'Dowd in Leftwich 1974). This in itself reflected the change in the balance of power in South Africa at the elite level from domestic-oriented economic nationalists (upon which apartheid was predicated) to an increasingly transnationalized, globally oriented, neo-liberal fraction. This was to have important ramifications for later South African trade policy.

A key point in the evolution of this trend was the publication of the White Paper on Privatization and Deregulation in the Republic of South Africa in 1987, committing the government to a series of 'radical measures, including systematic privatisation and deregulation and to a process of opening up the economy more fully to "market forces" ' (Lazar 1996: 618). This process was stalled somewhat first by the deepening crises of the mid-1980s and then by the negotiating process surrounding the transition. Nevertheless, such commitments represented a fundamental shift in the economic ideas underpinning the formerly statist National Party and a broad fit between capital and government over trade policy (Fine and Rustomjee 1996). Indeed, by the early 1990s, 'government and (most factions of) big business were at one in respect of policy issues relayed to liberalizing external economic relations', and shared an agenda for the future (Padayachee 1997: 41).

From liberalizing apartheid to neo-liberal non-racialism

Though elements from the Left and COSATU in particular attempted to stem the drift rightwards, by the time of the democratic elections of 1994 the macroeconomic debate had been largely won by those within and outside the ANC who favoured – to varying degrees – orthodox trade policies. Certainly, 'by late 1992 nationalisation was effectively no longer a serious option on the economic agenda of the ANC' (Habib and Padayachee 1999: 8). While it is true that the ANC did not entirely surrender before the incessant demands of capital and some progressive components broadly remained within the ANC's economic propositions, a discernible neo-liberal slant emanated from ANC policy, leading at least one commentator to remark that:

the new government is bending over backwards to send the right signals to the motley crowd of Business SA lobbyists, financiers and financial economists, Anglo-American executives, *Business Day* editorialists and low-grade public relations specialists who regularly pronounce on the progress ANC leaders have made on embracing neo-liberalism. (Bond 1994: 8)

Certainly, the ANC's trade policy became mainly predicated upon the assumed inflow of international investment, with everything hingeing on a supine posture towards international capital and the international financial institutions. Such policies, linked to a more 'flexible' labour market were supposed to encourage a concomitant increase in investment by domestic capital (as opposed to indulging in an investment strike and offshore relocation as many subsequently did). Ironically, this in turn had been facilitated – at the demand of capital – by the effective removal of exchange controls in March 1995 when the dual exchange rate system was unified.

How and why the ANC fundamentally changed its macroeconomic policies is beyond the scope of this chapter (on this, see Bond 2000; Taylor 2001a, Taylor and Vale 2000; Vale and Taylor 1999; Williams and Taylor 2000). However, with the National Party leaving the post-apartheid Government of National Unity (GNU) in June 1996 the notion that conservative non-ANC elements were constraining the liberation movement's economic direction proved to be false: the introduction of GEAR was a product of the ANC elites thinking on economic issues and 'signal[led] the government's acceptance of market-imposed criteria for the conduct of macroeconomic policy' (Blumenfeld 1998: 5). This was manifested through the release of the GEAR document. Released in February 1996 by then Deputy-President Thabo Mbeki, this document ambitiously claimed it would increase annual growth by an average of 4.2 per cent create 1.35 million jobs by 2000, boost exports by an average 8.4 per cent per year and – perhaps crucially – improve social structure.

The ideology contained in the GEAR document is consistent 'with the strong international consensus on the efficiency of the market system' (*Cape Times* 7 May 1997), exhibiting a 'commitment to conservative fiscal policies, trade liberalisation and a shift from consumption to investment spending' (*Business Day* 30 October 1998). While the new framework stunned many on the Left within the ANC alliance, it did finally illustrate 'quite clearly that the "common-sense" orthodoxy of neo-liberal development [was] entrenched' in government thinking (Leysens and Thompson 1994: 56). While the government has been touchy on accusations that its policies are essentially neo-liberal monetarism, a 1996 document sent out by the government openly admitted that 'certain measures in GEAR are similar to many neo-liberal packages' (quoted in Rob Davies, 'Engaging with Gear' (draft), 1997: 3 cited in Marais 1998: 161). One analysis has summed this up by saying that 'to all intents and purposes, the policy that almost replaced the sacred Freedom Charter in its vision of a more equal and progressive order has now been shelved [and a] Thatcherite discourse of fiscal discipline and market forces has taken over' (Adam *et al.* 1997: 161).

Essentially, GEAR (with regard to trade policy) is based on accelerated integration with the global economy. Mbeki confirmed this assertion when he declared soon after the GEAR programme was launched that the GNU was 'determined to ensure that we further open up our economy' (*The Sowetan* 27 March 1996). Yet, recognition by the ANC of the contradictions of neo-liberalism and resistance from the Left within government mean that a tentative tempering effort must be conducted, at least publicly, for while 'as a political party, the alliance (the ANC, COSATU and the SACP) is still Left-wing the ANC government is right of centre' (*Cape Argus* 8 March, 1999). This has had important implications for trade policy-making in post-apartheid South Africa. Pretoria's trade policy is first drawn up by the Department for Trade and Industry (DTI). The DTI then runs trade proposals past the trade unions and representative of business via the National Economic

Development and Labour Council (NEDLAC). Launched in February 1995, NED-LAC is ostensibly an 'inclusive' decision-making body aimed at consensus seeking in the economic realm (see Adler 2000; Monnakgotla 1998). NEDLAC is made up of government, business and labour, as well as a number of organizations representing various community interests. Every year NEDLAC holds an annual summit (with much fanfare) which supposedly receives feedback on its performance.

The formulation of trade policy, in the form of NEDLAC, has been cast as being corporatist in nature. However, it is doubtful whether this is strictly true, particularly as both government and business have, if Pretoria's trade policies are anything to judge by, much greater weight than the trade unions. In fact, it has been argued that NEDLAC's ostensible corporatism is a means by which political opposition to policies that the government thought needed to be implemented could be dissipated while giving trade policy formulation a veneer of legitimacy from union participation (Habib 1997). Yet, as the ANC continues to advance its grip over the commanding heights of the state the balance of power between the government, essentially white capital and the labour movement, is seemingly ever-shifting in favour of the state (Pretorius 1996). It is thus likely that even the pretence of a corporatist 'solution' to South Africa's policymaking over trade and economic issues will be quietly abandoned at some point in the future – although NEDLAC's shelf-life may be extended because of a need by Mbeki's government to continue the pretence that the ANC has not totally given up on the labour movement and its inherent socialist tendencies – despite Mbeki's increasing caricature of such impulses as 'ultra-leftist'. This will then place labour in South Africa in an invidious position regarding South Africa's trade policies since, as Webster (2001) pointed out, the trade union movement will increasingly have to either knuckle under and accept the ANC's neo-liberal turn (and thus face marginalization and opprobrium from their constituencies) or, and this seems to be happening, actively encounter such policies becoming de facto in opposition to their erstwhile partners.

Such tensions will likely increase regarding the formulation of trade policy, particularly as South Africa's position is centred around liberalization of its own economy, alongside pressure for the North to similarly open up. This is especially so with regard to agriculture, explaining South Africa's activist role within the Cairns Group. As it stands, the issue of subsidized agriculture is seen as a major barrier to any substantial increase in South African product's competitiveness. In this, South Africa's trade policies have sought to advance a critique of the North's hypocrisy over supposed global 'free trade' while protecting their own agricultural constituencies. Since the 1980s South Africa's agricultural sector has been progressively weaned off state support and is now among the most globally competitive (in part due to very low labour costs). This has gone hand in hand with a trade policy vis-à-vis agriculture which encourages the sector to look to exports as the main goal. Indeed, very soon after the new ANC government took power the 1995 White Paper on Agriculture clearly pointed in the direction of moving from a quasi-autarkic stance (that had developed under apartheid), to a policy that depended on the international market. In light of this, agricultural tariffs have been reduced or scrapped and marketing boards discarded.

South Africa and the WTO

As one might surmise, Pretoria's policies can only stand a chance of even relative success if the liberalization and free trade project is embarked upon with equal vigour in the developed world. Otherwise, liberalized South African industries will be competing with protected manufacturers in the North, a scenario that can only impact negatively upon exports from Pretoria. It is this that impels Pretoria to engage with initiatives such as the Cairns Group. Similarly, South Africa's position at the World Trade Organisation (WTO) accepts the call for liberalization and restructuring, but turns this rhetoric around to urge the developed world to engage in supposed real free trade, rather than the 'actually existing free trade' situation currently marking international commerce. How Pretoria has reacted to the WTO demonstrates to the observer the fundamental contours of post-apartheid South Africa's engagement with the international political economy.

Essentially, Pretoria's posture towards the WTO is predicated on the position that 'investor friendly' policies are a precursor to investment capital flows and hence growth of the economy (Hirsch 1995). At the same time however, Pretoria's foreign policy must balance the desire to appear as attractive as possible to money capital with its commitment to redistributive goals and soothe the concerns of its Leftist partners and constituency. One way it attempts to strike this balance, however contradictory this may actually be, is to adopt a reformist position.

This policy is based around the 'rules-based' system that the WTO puts forward. Indeed, the director general of the Department of Foreign Affairs has suggested that the promotion of such a global regime is a major plank to South Africa's trade policy and is integral to the government's growth policies as:

> the creation of a rules based international system of interaction between states contributes to our domestic agenda. The setting of international standards and rules, the creation of transparent trading and other systems and ensuring that no single country or group of countries can dominate world affairs creates an environment within which growth and development can take place. (Selebi 1999)

To be sure, Pretoria accepts that it has obligations stemming from its membership of the WTO and broadly accedes to such prescriptions. Yet at the same time, it pursues a policy to turn commitments within the WTO rules into concrete actualities and promote equal treatment for all. This is one way the South African government has decided to interact with the WTO. As Mandela remarked, 'we are firmly of the belief that the existence of the GATT, and now the World Trade Organisation, as a rules-based system provides a solid foundation on which our deliberations can build in order to improve. Rules must be applied without fear or favour' (Mandela 1998).

By putting forward such a position, Pretoria has opened up space for manoeuvrability and has pursued a set of policies that it believes will benefit its local industry – at least in internationally competitive sectors. This is not necessarily in the wider interests of the broader South African population (for such a policy is predicated on the basis of quid pro quo by which non-competitive South African industries – essentially productive capital based and inwardly looking – face collapse); nor indeed may it be in the interests of the region which is replete with non-competitive industrial sectors.

Nonetheless, the government has seized on the declamatory statements of the WTO and the aspiration to craft a rules-based multilateral trading system and taken them at their word. This space is possible because unlike the IMF or the World Bank there is no in-built asymmetry of power between the various member states, and a country like South Africa has the (theoretical) ability to challenge major global players on their policies – something which could never happen in the North-dominated Bretton Woods bodies (Raghavan 1990: 64).

South Africa might be said to have three key objectives underpinning its involvement with the WTO. First, Pretoria seeks to advance movement in the location of global production that is, from the North to the South. Second, South Africa is attempting to level the playing field and reduce the ongoing imbalances in already existing trade agreements within the global system. Third, Pretoria is aiming to enlarge regulations regarding 'special and differential' treatment for the developing world (Department of Trade and Industry 2000).

South Africa's active membership of the WTO is important for the country as it gives a powerful signal to overseas capital that the new South Africa accepts and plays by the hegemonic 'rules of the game' when it comes to trade policy. This is of course directly connected to the move rightwards that the ANC elite performed during and after the transition period. GEAR is, in other words, complementary to the WTO prescriptions. Indeed, a United Nations report has asserted that GEAR 'closely resembled an IMF structural adjustment programme' and in fact 'had embraced liberalisation beyond the WTO's requirements' (*Sunday Independent* 24 May 1998). By engaging with the WTO and advocating that its regulations are applicable to all members, including the North, Pretoria holds up to the world the hypocrisy of much of the rhetoric emanating from the developed countries. From this South Africa not only gains kudos among elements in the South for 'tackling' the North, but also furthers its own money capital's interests as well as its broader export sector. At the same time, negative aspects of globalization and unpopular decisions that the government imposes on its domestic constituency (particularly organized labour and the Left in general) can be cast as 'inevitable' results of South Africa engaging with 'the world' that is, the WTO. This last point should not be underestimated, for as one analyst wrote of the WTO, 'contracting parties externalis[e] the onus for reform. The imposition of GATT/WTO injunctions can be a useful way for governments to sell politically unpopular measures to domestic constituencies' (Higgott in Cooper 1997: 32).

Sprung from a historical compromise and caught among a web of contradictions, this ability to back pedal on its more progressive posturing prior to GEAR (indeed, prior to taking office) and shifting the culpability onto the constraints of 'globalization' in the form of WTO rules and regulations, is a highly useful device for the ANC elite in justifying their stance on such issues to its Left leaning constituency and partners. This lies at the heart of much of its trade policy when it comes to selling more and more liberalization and restructuring in the name of greater competitiveness and adherence to global trading rules.

This seeming accession to the discourse of globalization is balanced however by the desire to play a mediating role between North and South (but one which was essentially tilted in favour of the transnational elites). As a state classified by the WTO as developed but as a country that has chaired organizations such as the United Nations Conference on Trade and Development, as well as the Non-Aligned Movement, this mediating position is perhaps to be expected. This positive engagement with the WTO and appealing to its rules-based regime and attempting to bind the major powers to their commitments, 'engaging globalization and extracting benefits' as Mbeki has called it, can be seen graphically in Pretoria's enthusiastic referral to the organization on matters relating to anti-dumping, which has become the most common trade defence remedy available to state administrations. Since South Africa began to partake in anti-dumping measures in 1994, Pretoria has been consistently among the most regular initiators of dumping cases at the WTO. The ability to do so under the rules-based WTO shows that there has been a reappraisal of the usefulness of anti-dumping measures by countries in the South. Traditionally, anti-dumping measures were viewed by developing nations as a form of disguised protectionism, arguing that it permitted developed economies to discriminate against their cheaper imports (*Financial Times* 6 May 1999). However, the regulations of the WTO have allowed those elites based in the South – who are willing to engage with and use the WTO's mechanisms – to apply them to their rich trading partners. This in itself reflects the changes that have occurred within the global economy and in particular mirrors the dominant ideology that is an integral part of the ongoing order. As one analyst wrote, 'the history of the developing countries in the world trading system reveals initial hostility to a regime that was controlled by advanced and industrialized countries. However it is obvious that the developing countries' attitudes [have changed]' (Kufour 1998: 194).

At the same time, it provides these selfsame elites with a 'safety valve' by which they can protect (or attempt to safeguard) domestic industries against unfair foreign competition. With tariffs largely being taken away, anti-dumping measures can provide a degree of protection. Even if initiated cases are unsuccessful, by launching them an administration that is in the process of opening up its markets can posture itself as having the welfare of domestic interests at heart and be seen to act in its interests, even if the reality is somewhat different and policy is being driven by more externally oriented elite fractions. This, and the policy of advancing a rules-based global regime, may account for Pretoria's enthusiastic engagement of anti-dumping regulations.

South Africa and the Battle of Seattle

South Africa's continued active engagement within the WTO is indicative of a posture that has sought to promote the WTO regime while also putting forward propositions that would aid developing countries to cope with the liberalizing agenda of the organization. Prior to Seattle, South Africa was pushing a campaign to restart negotiations over agriculture, and 'attack' uncompetitive industries in the

North, such as steel (South African Press Agency [Cape Town], 19 August 1999). However, as the process evolved, with mass protests outside and impasse over various issues inside, it soon became apparent that the Seattle Ministerial was doomed, with the South steadfastly refusing labour standards being used as a mechanism to block their exports to the developed world. Though good progress was claimed on agriculture, non-agricultural market access, implementation and trade and investment, all agreements were frozen as the talks collapsed (see Chapter 1 by Wilkinson). Indeed, Pretoria claimed that important concessions had been won.

However, what is problematic about South Africa's role in the Seattle process was its willingness to join a special meeting of developed and developing countries, convened by the United States, to negotiate separately in the fabled 'Green Rooms' (backroom negotiation forums). This was seen as a means to marginalize the rest of the developing world, particularly Africa, and brought Pretoria into some conflict with its African neighbours. One report saw Pretoria 'going alone with the global power brokers rather than the rest of [the Southern African Development Community's] membership' (South African Press Agency [Lagos], 10 December 1999). Ghana's minister of trade and industry, first vice chairman of the Organisation of African Unity (OAU), condemned the blatant lack of transparency in the negotiations and the marginalization of Africa. The OAU expressed particular concern at the declared determination to produce a ministerial text 'at all costs, even at the cost of procedures intended to guarantee participation and consensus'. This stimulated the OAU to block the consensus needed to launch the Millennium Round. Their position was echoed by Caricom (joined by a number of Latin American countries), who also issued a condemnation of the lack of transparency of 'Green Room' proceedings (*Le Monde Diplomatique* January 2000).

South Africa's position, compared to that of the rest of the OAU, was remarkably different, with Pretoria being far more upbeat about the achievements at Seattle than the rest of the continent. Indeed, after the Seattle debacle, Pretoria's trade and industry minister quickly initiated a process aimed at restarting the Seattle round of talks. It rapidly became apparent that post-Seattle, South Africa had been among the most active, in liaison with Brazil, India, Nigeria and Egypt, to formulate a way to reconvene the talks. In consultation also with the United States and the European Union (EU), ministers from the four developing countries pledged to meet to take the initiative further. Pretoria claimed that after Seattle, developing countries had more common ground than before, all now being firm advocates of a rules-based trading system. The contentious issue with the EU over labelling, which continually derailed a trade agreement between South Africa and the EU was given as an example of how a rules-based system helped developing countries, as it was asserted that the EU was unable to use its economic muscle to bully South Africa, due to WTO rules (*Business Day* 22 January 2000).

South Africa's trade policy in perspective

Pretoria's overall trade policies have sought to promote a rules-based neo-liberal regime while also putting forward propositions that would aid developing countries to cope with ongoing liberalization. By doing so, South Africa pursues a bridge-building role aimed at developing 'confidence' in the system, a tactic designed ultimately to strengthen the WTO but along lines that would benefit those elites in the South who stand to gain from a more reciprocal rules-based trading regime that outlawed unilateral behaviour from the North – a scenario where only the developing world would suffer. This role has been criticized by analysts for 'supporting free trade while at the same time insisting that [South Africa] must attempt to change the rules of the system in a non-confrontational manner amounts to a one-way traffic bridge. It accepts that the end of history, or for that matter ideology, has indeed been reached' (Thompson and Leysens 1996: 9).

At the same time, Pretoria also attempts to balance the diverse pressures being exerted on it, on the one hand being seen to concur with the neo-liberal agenda demanded by powerful externally oriented capital; and on the other posturing an ostensibly Southern-oriented position that seeks to ameliorate the more negative effects of globalization and the demands put on the domestic polity by the rules and regulations of the WTO. By doing so, criticism from labour and the Left could be deflected – though most analysts agree that the newly regularized trading regime 'could create exciting possibilities for the big SA clients' (*Financial Mail* 19 December 1997). It is this contradictory behaviour that has marked South African trade policy and which can be witnessed in Pretoria's role in other multilateral bodies, such as the Cairns Group of agricultural nations, a group closely linked to the ongoing process of liberalization (see Taylor 2001a).

However, such manoeuvrings fail to question fundamentally the unequal nature of the South's (and Africa in particular) trading relationship with the developed world. Indeed, by engaging with such bodies, Pretoria affords a high measure of legitimacy to not only the (fundamentally neo-liberal) organizations, but also to the overall international political economy. Such 'problem-solving' behaviour seems to accept the immutability of the current world order and seeks to ameliorate its worse aspects, rather than promote debate regarding the future organizing principles of a more just international political economy. Whether the ANC has accepted totally the 'end of history' thesis as some commentators argue is a moot point (see *Sunday Times* 16 May 1999). Certainly, the balance of forces within the government at present seems to be firmly in favour of those fractions who urge an increased engagement with 'globalization', rather than a more interrogatory position. Such a position would put forward 'progressive' economic policies to counter the destructive features of over-hasty liberalization, and promote equality as well as efficiency. At the moment, however, a concerted progressive agenda in Pretoria's trade policies seem unlikely.

This scenario springs from a conglomeration of interests that emerged out of the 1994 compromise and the ongoing formation of a historic bloc involving external capital and those ANC elites (and their allied constituencies, such as the Black 'patriotic bourgeoisie') who favour free market principles. These factors in themselves coincide with the interests of a wider transnational elite. South Africa often promotes itself as a 'bridge-builder', in effect playing a middle power role, while at the same time, Pretoria is frequently the state that seeks to nudge and cajole others in the South to accept 'global realities'. Indeed, South Africa has often been in advance of others in the developing world in pushing an acceptance of globalization, albeit tempering such calls with a recognition that negative effects of the process do exist and need to be guarded against.

However, the urge for a critical engagement with the North tends to be subsumed under the rhetoric of 'partnership', which Pretoria has been particularly enthusiastic to promote in its dealings with those organizations devoted to development. This has formed a major theme of South Africa's foreign policy, where Pretoria has led the way and, at times, been instrumental in changing 'confrontationist' rhetoric vis-à-vis the North and globalization, to more accommodatory postures that accept what the South African leadership sees as both the positive and negative aspects of the ongoing globalizing process. Though this has meant that Pretoria has been in advance of most of the South, Pretoria's policy has sought to promote a more receptive attitude to the world-wide liberalization thrust, a tactic that not only posits South Africa as a worthy investment destination, whose administrators understand the global 'realities', but also improves Pretoria's overall position with regard to those who hold international power. As a discussion paper asserted, 'judicious multilateral diplomacy will enhance South Africa's international standing' (African National Congress 1994).

Such 'pragmatic' policies have increasingly been transposed to specifically continental institutions, such as the OAU (now African Union) and have recently been concretized in the New Economic Partnership for Africa's Development (NEPAD), launched in Abuja, Nigeria, on 23 October 2001. The NEPAD's message, like South Africa's broader trade strategy, is very much linked to the discourse of globalization and the workings of the 'free market' (see Taylor 2001b). After all, South Africa's finance minister is chairperson of both the IMF and World Bank's Board of Governors. Indeed, commenting on the NEPAD one analyst remarked that:

> Nothing here [in the NEPAD] would dismay the World Bank or the International Monetary Fund, although reform of these institutions is also a priority. The latest buzzword in the corridors of these institutions is 'authorship' – jargon for a hands-off approach to reform. The plan chimes with this new approach by encouraging African governments to claim 'ownership' of reforms which, just a few years ago, foreign lenders were happy to prescribe from Washington. (Ashurst 2002: 37)

In the NEPAD document, it states that Structural Adjustment Programmes 'provided only a partial solution', removing serious price distortions but giving 'inadequate attention to the provision of social services', resulting in a situation where 'only a few countries managed to achieve sustainable higher growth under these programmes'. Pàtrick Bond asks a number of very important questions about such statements, worth repeating here:

- What if structural adjustment represented not 'a partial solution' but instead, reflected local and global power shifts, a profound defeat for genuine African nationalists, workers, peasants, women, children, manufacturing industry and the environment?

- What if promoting reforms really amounted to the IMF and World Bank imposing their cookie-cutter neo-liberal policies on desperately disempowered African societies, without any reference to democratic processes, resistance or diverse local conditions?
- What if the removal of 'price distortions' really meant the repeal of exchange controls (hence allowing massive capital flight), subsidy cuts (hence pushing masses of people below the poverty line) and lowered import tariffs (hence causing widespread de-industrialization)?
- What if 'inadequate attention to the provision of social services' in reality meant the opposite: excessive attention to applying neo-liberalism not just to the macro-economy, but also to health, education, water and other crucial state services?
- And what if the form of IMF/Bank attention included insistence upon greater cost recovery, higher user-fees, lower budgetary allocations, privatization, and even the disconnection of supplies to those too poor to afford them, hence leading to the unnecessary deaths of millions of people? (Bond 2001).

Ignoring such fundamental questions, the NEPAD puts forward an agenda which demands that global integration must be facilitated by a working relationship with transnational capital and corporations, an aggressive liberalization policy and an essentially prostrate attitude towards the international financial institutions (Taylor and Nel 2002). According to one account, 'it is only a small exaggeration to say that the [NEPAD] prescribes for an entire continent the kind of policies already pursued in South Africa' (Ashurst 2002: 37).

That said, Pretoria's trade policy should not be caricatured as being some sort of unquestioning 'disciple' of the West or international capital. Though at a basic level Pretoria's elites have embraced neo-liberalism and see 'no alternative' to globalization, they are cognisant of the downside and pressures that are concurrent with globalization. By engaging with the 'objective' process of globalization rather than challenging it, South Africa sees such a tactical policy as the best way to ameliorate the contrary processes that impact negatively upon Pretoria. This in part springs from a particular understanding of the international political economy, which is seen as exerting powerful constraints on any alternative positions. Hence, this elite has opted for trade policies that exhibit a considerable amount of awareness to what it views as the forces that exact upon the global system, even if this results in an agenda that is at variance with the long-held positions of the ANC.

Such contradictions have been evident in South Africa's trade policies, where it has promoted a reformist agenda aiming to 'improve' the global system while promoting a more rules-based international regime. This policy not only serves the interests of important South African industries (the government believes), but it also acts to flag to its constituency on the Left that the government is attempting to promote the interests of the disempowered. Concurrently, and perhaps more importantly as far as Pretoria is concerned, its policies signal to the global power-holders (both domestically and internationally) that an ANC-run South Africa is trustworthy enough to invest in. In essence, while as a government in office the party complies with the principles of the hegemonic order, as a movement in a political alliance with labour and the Left the state leadership must effect a careful equilibrium, recognizing the divergent social forces acting upon and within the South African and international polity. Pursuing tactical reformism in its trade policies vis-à-vis the global economic order is one way in which this can be satisfied.

Unless the state elites question their understandings of what constitutes globalization and the wisdom of pursuing neo-liberal macroeconomic policies, the trade policy of South Africa will likely remain wedded to a problem-solving approach that seeks to iron out problems in the ongoing order. Hence, Pretoria is likely to continue promoting the ongoing discourse of neo-liberalism and continue playing a middle power role in its foreign policy, serving essentially to legitimize the current world order. This is despite the contradictions this may engender for a country which ostensibly is a leader of the South.

References

Adam, H., Van Zyl Slabbert, F. and Moodley, K. (1997) *Comrades in Business: Post-Liberation Politics in South Africa*, Cape Town: Tafelberg.

Adler, G. (2000) *Engaging the State and Business: The Labour Movement and Co-determination in Contemporary South Africa*, Johannesburg: Witwatersrand University Press.

African National Congress (1994) *Foreign Policy Perspective in a Democratic South Africa*, Johannesburg: African National Congress.

Ashurst, M. (2002) 'Taking the Initiative', BBC Focus on Africa, January–March.

Baker, P., Boraine, A. and Krafchik, W. (1993) *South Africa in the World Economy in the 1990s*, Johannesburg: David Philip.

Blumenfeld, J. (1998) 'Assessing South Africa's Growth Strategy', Briefing Paper no. 49, July 1998, Royal Institute of International Affairs-Southern Africa Study Group.

Bond, P. (1994) 'Economics Diary', *Southern African Review of Books*, issue 33, September/October, pp. 15–17.

Bond, P. (2000) *Elite Transition: From Apartheid to Neo-liberalism in South Africa*, London: Zed Books.

Bond, P. (2001) 'What is Pretoria Planning for Africa?', KABISSA-FAHAMU-SANGONET Newsletter no. 45, December, www4mail@kabissa.org

Clark, N. (1994) *Manufacturing Apartheid: States Corporations in South Africa*, New Haven: Yale University Press.

Department of Trade and Industry (2000) *Note on South Africa's Approach to the WTO and Key Elements of a Negotiating Position*, Pretoria: International Trade and Economic Development Division.

Fine, B. and Rustomjee, Z. (1996) *The Political Economy of South Africa: from Minerals-Energy Complex to Industrialisation*, Johannesburg: Witwatersrand University Press.

Habib, A. (1997) 'From Pluralism to Corporatism: South Africa's Labour Relations in Transition' *Politikon*, 24, 1, pp. 57–74.

Habib, A. and Padayachee, V. (1999) 'Economic Policy and Power Relations in South Africa's Transition to Democracy', unpublished paper.

Higgott, R. (1997) 'Issues, Institutions and Middle-Power Diplomacy: Action and Agendas in the Post-Cold War Era', in Cooper, A. (ed.) *Niche Diplomacy: Middle Powers After the Cold War*, Basingstoke: Macmillan, pp. 25–45.

Hirsch, A. (1995) 'From the GATT to the WTO: The Global Trade Regime and Its Implications for South Africa', in Mills, G., Begg, A. and van Nieuwkerk, A. (eds) *South Africa in the Global Economy*, Johannesburg: South Africa Institute of International Affairs, pp. 41–55.

Innes, D. (1984) *Anglo-American and the Rise of Modern South Africa*, London: Heinemann.

Kufour, K. (1998) 'The Developing Countries and the Shaping of GATT/WTO Antidumping Law', *Journal of World Trade*, 32, 6, December, pp. 167–96.

Lazar, D. (1996) 'Competing Economic Ideologies in South Africa's Economic Debate', *British Journal of Sociology*, 47, 1, December, pp. 599–626.

Leysens, A. and Thompson, L. (1994) 'A Paper Tiger? Political Implications of an Export-Led Growth Strategy for South Africa', *South African Journal of International Affairs*, 1, 2, pp. 21–37.

Mandela, N. (1998) 'Address by President Mandela on the Occasion of the 50th Anniversary of the General Agreement on Tariffs and Trade (GATT)', Geneva, issued by the Office of the President, May 19.

Marais, H. (1998) *South Africa: Limits to Change – The Political Economy of Transformation*, London: Zed Press.

Monnakgotla, M. (1998) The Role of Nedlac in Trade and Industrial Policy Pretoria: TIPS Occasional Paper.

O'Dowd, M. (1974) 'South Africa in the Light of the Stages of Economic Growth', in Leftwich, A. (ed.) *South Africa: Economic Growth and Political Change with Comparative Studies of Chile, Sri Lanka and Malaysia*, New York: St. Martin's Press, pp. 41–62.

O'Meara, D. (1983) *Volkskapitalisme: Class, Capital and Ideology in the Development of Afrikaner Nationalism, 1934–1948*, Johannesburg: Ravan Press.

O'Meara, D. (1996) *Forty Lost Years: The Apartheid State and the Politics of the National Party, 1948–1994*, Randburg: Ravan Press.

Padayachee, V. (1997) 'The Evolution of South Africa's International Financial Relations and Policy: 1985–1995', in Michie, J. and Padayachee, V. (eds) *The Political Economy of South Africa's Transition*, London: Dryden Press, pp. 27–54.

Pretorius, L. (1996) 'Relations Between State, Capital And Labour In South Africa: Towards Corporatism?' *Journal of Theoretical Politics*, 8, 2, pp. 255–81.

Raghavan, C. (1990) *Recolonization: GATT, the Uruguay Round and the Third World*, London: Zed Books.

Selebi, J. (1999) 'Multilateralism and South Africa's Foreign Policy' Paper presented to Department of Political Science, University of Stellenbosch, 26 February.

Sparks, A. (1994) *Tomorrow is Another Country: The Inside Story of South Africa's Negotiated Settlement*, Johannesburg: Struik.

Taylor, I. (2001a) *Stuck in Middle GEAR: South Africa's Post-Apartheid Foreign Relations*, Westport, CT: Praeger.

Taylor, I. (2001b) 'The "Mbeki Initiative": Towards a Post-Orthodox New International Order?' in Nel, P., Taylor, I. and van der Westhuizen, J. (eds) *Promoting Change? Aspects of Reformism in South Africa's Multilateral Diplomacy*, Aldershot: Ashgate, pp. 59–75.

Taylor, I. and Vale, P. (2000) 'South Africa's Transition Revisited: Globalisation as Vision and Virtue', *Global Society*, 14, 3, July, pp. 399–414.

Taylor, I. and Nel, P. (2002) ' "Getting the Rhetoric Right", Getting the Strategy Wrong: "New Africa", Globalisation and the Confines of Elite Reformism', *Third World Quarterly*, 23, 1, February, pp. 163–80.

Thompson, L. and Leysens, A. (1996) 'Comments: South African Foreign Policy Discussion Document', unpublished paper, August.

Tregenna-Piggott, J. (1976) 'Concentration and South African Industry' Studies in Economics and Econometrics Paper no. 5, Economic Research Unit, University of Natal.

Vale, P. and Taylor, I. (1999) 'South Africa's Post-Apartheid Foreign Policy Five Years On-From Pariah State to "Just Another Country"?', Round Table: Commonwealth Journal of International Relations, 352, October, pp. 629–34.

Webster, E. (2001) 'The Alliance Under Stress: Governing in a Globalizing World', *Democratization*, 8, 1, pp. 255–74.

Williams, P. and Taylor, I. (2000) 'Neo-liberalism and the Political Economy of the "New" South Africa', *New Political Economy*, 5, 1, March, pp. 21–40.

17

From APEC to ASEAN+3?: The United States–China–Japan Triangle and the Geopolitical Economy of Trade in the Asia-Pacific

Mark T. Berger

The collapse of the Soviet Union at the end of the 1980s signalled the start of a new global era. In the Asia-Pacific, meanwhile, the end of the Cold War was also the end to the 'Golden Age of the US-China-Japan Triangle' (Vogel *et al.* 2002). The waning of Soviet power altered the dynamics of the US–China relationship and Washington's relationship with Tokyo. Despite the establishment of the Asia Pacific Economic Cooperation (APEC) forum in 1989, ostensibly committed to the promotion of free trade in the region, there were major differences between Washington and the Chinese, Japanese and other governments on how best to promote regional economic integration and security in the 1990s.[1] Things came to a head with the Asian crisis in 1997–98. In particular, the crisis facilitated US efforts to more directly wind back protectionist trade and investment practices in countries such as South Korea, Thailand and Indonesia, rather than trying to achieve these goals via the unwieldy and non-binding arrangements that underpinned APEC.

At the same time, it became increasingly clear that the Asian financial crisis had significantly, even fatally, weakened APEC in favour of more exclusive forms of Pan-Asian regionalism of the sort long advocated by the Prime Minister of Malaysia, Mahathir Mohamad. However, such Pan-Asian initiatives continued to be constrained by the wider US-centred world order of the post-Cold War and post-9/11 era (Beeson 2003). The vicissitudes of regionalism in the Asia-Pacific are reflected in the way in which the definition of the region itself remains highly contested and is a far more incompletely realized project than European regionalism (Berger 1998; Dirlik 1992; Soesastro 1994). In fact, the term 'Asia-Pacific' only gained widespread currency in the 1990s (parallelling the emergence of APEC) and it continues to be used alongside (and may eventually even be displaced by) the more long-standing usage of, and emphasis on, 'East Asia' or 'Asia'.[2] Since the end of the Cold War these terminological differences have been directly linked to the rise and decline of APEC as a regional economic organization and its partial, but far from straightforward displacement by ASEAN+3 (the Association of Southeast Asian Nations plus China, Japan and South Korea).[3]

The question of economic cooperation in the Asia-Pacific generally, and trade cooperation and/or the pursuit of freer trade more specifically, clearly needs to be set against the backdrop of the wider geopolitical economy of the region: central to that geopolitical economy is the complex and changing dynamics of the US–China–Japan Triangle. This chapter begins by looking at Asia in the final decades of the Cold War with a focus on the overall changes in this period. It then turns to a discussion of Japan and then China's relationship to various regional initiatives in the Asia-Pacific. The second part of the chapter turns to an examination of post-Cold War regional trends particularly inter-state struggles over economic and security issues and the countervailing trend towards the strengthening of established, or the consolidation of new, regional organizations. This is followed by a discussion of the Japanese and Chinese trajectories in the post-Cold War era and their significance for Asia-Pacific regionalism generally and US hegemony more specifically. These are particularly important nation-states and their present circumstances and future directions have major regional and global implications for trade and investment flows and economic development and stability. The ongoing processes of national economic and political reorientation and even crisis in Japan and China in the post-Cold War era are closely connected to the continued and/or increased potential for both intra-state and inter-state conflict and to a shift towards new or reconfigured regional economic and political groupings of nation-states in Asia and elsewhere.

Asian regionalism in a Cold War context

The passing of, or dramatic weakening of state-mediated national development, ostensibly grounded in both inclusive social goals (the record of which was exceedingly uneven in Asia and elsewhere) and in highly protectionist approaches to trade and investment, has important implications for intra- and inter-state conflict. At the same time, although APEC appears to have been partially displaced by a strengthened ASEAN+3, and by recent plans to create an ASEAN Economic Community (and an ASEAN Security Community) centred on the ten member governments of ASEAN (with links to Japan, China, South Korea and India), looming inter-state conflicts and current and worsening intra-state conflicts cannot necessarily be ameliorated by regional trade and security organizations, in the context of uneven economic development, high and growing levels of social inequality, not to mention the presence of a number of particularly weak states such as Indonesia, Burma and the Philippines.

The geopolitical and economic policies of the administration of President Richard Nixon (1969–74) have a particular significance in relation to East Asia, insofar as the Vietnam War and US relations with China were central to the dramatic reorientation in US policy in the early 1970s. The Nixon administration's decision to normalize relations with China in 1972, which became known in Japan as the second 'Nixon Shock' (the first 'Nixon Shock' was the end of the Bretton Woods arrangements the previous year), had surprised the Japanese government. Washington's geopolitical *demarché* fuelled resentment in Tokyo over the

United States' continuing lack of consultation with its main ally in the region. In fact, by the late 1960s, Washington had already become wary of Japan and West Germany's successful post-1945 exercises in state-guided national development, a factor that contributed to the first Nixon Shock. By the time of Washington's geopolitical and economic re-orientation in the 1970s, the United States had been eclipsed by Japan as Asia's most significant source of foreign aid and investment. Between the 1940s and the 1970s, the Japanese government and Japan-based corporations, with US sponsorship, had gradually re-built their linkages with Northeast and Southeast Asia (Kelly 2002: 67–105).

Japan

The growing regional economic significance of Japan, against the backdrop of the country's post-1945 economic boom, was complemented by renewed efforts on the part of Japanese officials and commentators to encourage regional integration and the creation of a 'Pacific Community'. It was the promulgation of an 'Asia-Pacific policy' by the Japanese Foreign Ministry in late 1966 (in the wake of the establishment earlier in the year of the Asian Development Bank under the auspices of the Japanese government with support from the United States) that is seen to have signalled the start of Japan's effort to build a regional trade organization. Against the backdrop of its new Asia-Pacific policy the Japanese government put forward a proposal for a 'Pacific Free Trade Area'. This represented an explicit reaction to the emergence of the European Economic Community (EEC) now the European Union (EU).

This initiative did not gain widespread support, but it did ease the way for the Pacific Basin Economic Council (PBEC) in April 1967, which is comprised of nationally based business organizations. Meanwhile, at the beginning of 1968 a regional organization for economists, the Pacific Trade and Development Conference (PAFTAD), had its first meeting in Tokyo (Terada 1998). During the 1970s, the Japanese government, with Australian support, floated the idea of a pan-Pacific trade organization made up of as many of the governments in the region as possible. This led to the formation of the Pacific Economic Cooperation Conference (PECC), later Council, which had its first meeting in Canberra in late 1980, and included representatives from the United States, Japan, Canada, Australia, New Zealand, Korea, Malaysia, Thailand, Indonesia, Singapore and the Philippines. During the 1980s the governments of China, Taiwan, Brunei and the South Pacific Forum also began sending delegates to the PECC. While the PECC brought together academics, business and government officials, a key characteristic of its operation was the unofficial role played by governments. Although the PECC has produced a host of reports and recommendations over the years they are not binding.

Meanwhile, following the lifting of a number of restrictions on the export of capital in the late 1960s, foreign direct investment (FDI) from Japan moved into manufacturing in Taiwan and South Korea and into raw material extraction and shipment in Southeast Asia. By the first half of the 1970s, four times as much FDI was going to South Korea from Japan as from the United States. From the mid-1970s to the mid-1980s, investment by Japanese corporations in Northeast and Southeast Asia continued to increase at a steady rate, as Japanese manufacturers continued to expand their activities in South Korea, Taiwan, Singapore, and Hong Kong and beyond, and corporations involved in 'resource-extraction' dramatically increased their involvement in Indonesia. Then, in the second half of the 1980s, the amount of Japanese FDI spreading around the region underwent a dramatic increase. Within three years of the ratification of the Plaza Accord in September 1985 – which represented a successful Washington-led effort to wind back a growing US trade deficit with Japan by getting the major G-5 central banks to increase the value of the Japanese yen against the US dollar – the value of the yen in relation to the dollar went from 238 to 128.

This encouraged a growing number of Japanese corporations to move their operations offshore. At the outset, Taiwan and South Korea were the main destinations for FDI from Japan, but, following the appreciation of the Taiwanese and South Korean currencies, the appeal of Southeast Asia to Japanese investors also increased. Southeast Asia's proximity to Japan, along with the economic downturn of the mid-1980s which had encouraged greater interest in FDI on the part of many governments in Southeast Asia, and the fact that Japanese corporations perceived countries such as Thailand, Malaysia and Singapore as being in possession of the requisite infrastructure, work-forces and generally stable and efficient administration with a commitment to export-oriented industrialization, all combined to bring about a dramatic rise in Japanese investment into Southeast Asia in the second half of the 1980s.

In the early 1980s Japanese investment in the ASEAN countries was about $900 million annually. Then, following a slight drop, the figure rose to $4.6 billion for 1989 and $15 billion for the period from 1988–91. While Thailand and Singapore were the initial foci, Japanese manufacturers subsequently turned to Malaysia and Indonesia. Meanwhile, South Korean and Taiwan-based companies also expanded into Southeast Asia and coastal China. In 1990 and 1991 Taiwanese investments in Malaysia exceeded those from Japan. Meanwhile Hong Kong-based investors also directed attention at Malaysia and Thailand, and of course southern China (Stubbs 1994: 371–2).

The rising Japanese investment in South Korea and Taiwan in the 1960s was bolstered by Japanese government aid (Yasutomo 1986). The subsequent arrival of a growing number of Japanese investors in China and Southeast Asia in the 1970s also coincided with the transfer from Tokyo of large quantities of development aid to the region. In this period the governments of Thailand, the Philippines, Malaysia and Indonesia were given approximately one-third of all Japanese bilateral aid. In the wake of the dramatic rise of Japanese investment in Southeast Asia the total amount of Japanese aid going to the region also rose dramatically going from $914 million in 1986 to $2.3 billion in 1990. For China the figures were $497 million in 1986 and $832 million in 1989 (Shiraishi 1997: 187–8).

The spread of Japanese corporations to South Korea and Taiwan, and subsequently to Southeast Asia and China, resulted in the regionalization of certain structural aspects of Japanese industry. It represented an attempt, which was only ever partially realized, to build a 'regional production alliance' which would mirror the domestic political economy of Japan, and was grounded in the use of an array of flexible medium and small subcontractors (Hatch and Yamamura 1996). Trade within the Asian region also increased dramatically. For example, in 1986 the nation-states of ASEAN exported $15.2 billion worth of goods to Japan (13.75 per cent of these were manufactured goods), but by 1991 the figure was $30.26 billion (31.7 per cent of which were manufactures) (Stubbs 1994: 373).

By the 1980s East Asia generally had become a major site for the relocation of manufacturing, particularly from Japan, but also from North America and Western Europe. This geographical restructuring of the world economy was directly linked to the rise of the US-led globalization project and the passing of the high period of national development in North America, Western Europe and Japan (Wallerstein 1999: 36–7). It was also linked, however, to the countervailing trend towards selective industrial protectionism in the 1980s aimed at curbing the expansion of Japanese manufactures into the markets of North America and Western Europe. This latter trend led to the continued deepening of economic and political ties between the various nation-states of Asia and Japan.

The deepening of regional economic integration centred on Japan was directly linked to the end of almost two decades of 'high-speed' economic growth and an important shift in the Japanese economy in the 1970s. With the end of the US occupation of Japan in 1952 the foundation for a resurgent capitalist nation-state had been laid. Between the mid-1950s and the early 1970s the Japanese economy boomed, growing at an average of 10 per cent a year in the 1960s (Tipton 1998: 412). Up to the 1970s and beyond two key aspects of the post-1945 global order facilitated the Japanese boom. First, Japanese exports had relatively open access to world markets in the context of the wider GATT. In this situation, Japanese manufacturers targeted a small number of important markets selling manufactured goods at prices only a little above, and even on occasion on a par with production costs. At the same time, assured access to low priced foodstuffs and raw materials, and particularly energy, was crucial to the boom up to the 1970s. Between 1945 and the beginning of the 1970s, the prices for commodities remained very low in comparison to the prices for manufactured goods.

During much of the 1970s and 1980s Japan's economy expanded at a rate of about 4 per cent per year (Tipton 1998: 415). In this period, Japanese companies started to shift their efforts towards technology-intensive production. The labour-intensive industries, as well as iron and steel and shipbuilding that had been central to the 1950s and 1960s were usually moved from Japan to elsewhere in Asia (although they were still characterized by Japanese ownership and/or involvement). By the early 1980s, Japan was exporting technology-intensive merchandise (computers, office machines, telecommunications equipment and electrical goods) around the world (Morris-Suzuki 1994: 161–208). At the same time, as already noted, the country's spectacular export-driven industrial expansion had been grounded in access to world markets and to inexpensive sources of raw materials and energy. During the 1970s, both of these preconditions came under a cloud. The dramatic rise in world oil prices was a serious threat to a nation-state that had no oil reserves.

Also threatening were the protectionist initiatives of the 1970s and the early 1980s emanating from North America and Western Europe (that coincided ironically with the rise of neo-liberalism). By the 1980s, the EEC later the EU had introduced selective barriers to Japanese imports, while US-based producers of video equipment, as well as televisions and automobiles, succeeded in exerting pressure in Washington that resulted in the Japanese government agreeing to 'voluntary export restraints'.

The Japanese government sought to compensate by broadening and deepening the various economic connections with the nation-states of Asia in particular (although Latin America also became a growing focus of trade and investment from Japan). As we have seen, the Japanese government increasingly directed large quantities of foreign aid to key nation-states in Asia as part of a wider strategy to encourage economic cooperation in the region. Japanese corporations followed Tokyo's lead as direct investments flowed into petroleum and mining in Southeast Asia (and Australia) in an effort to secure access to fossil fuels and minerals and open up new markets for Japanese manufactured goods to counter the possibility of increased protectionism emanating from North America and Western Europe. Japanese corporations also shifted labour-intensive manufacturing from Japan to a number of nation-states in Asia where wages were considerably lower, ensuring access to markets for a variety of low-priced manufactures in the region and beyond. During the 1980s the Japanese government sought, with some success, to ameliorate the suspicions many people had in the region as a result of the Second World War. A number of nation-states in Asia, such as Malaysia, not only accepted Japan as a major source of investment and trade, but they also viewed it as a state-led development model to be emulated (Terry 2002).

In Japan the 1980s is now described as the era of the 'bubble economy' (referring to the incredible asset price inflation of this period) during which the Japanese government, in the view of some commentators, 'lost control of the economy'. Deregulation in the financial sector by the 1980s had permitted a number of major Japanese corporations to alter the way in which they raised funds. In the past Japanese companies had procured capital primarily by taking out loans from banks; however, with the changes of the 1970s, they increasingly raised funds by selling warrants and convertible bonds to investors. The corporations then put some of the money raised this way into 'high-yielding financial assets' (these were often also high risk). At the same time, the banks required new clients to fill the gap left by the decline in borrowing on the part of the big corporations. This role was increasingly assumed by land investors, which contributed to the dramatic inflation of real estate prices. The Japanese government attempted, but failed, to curb this trend. The property boom was also aggravated by other developments. For example, the Japanese government had begun running budget deficits in the mid-1960s to cover the rising cost of various subsidies and its commitment to spending initiatives aimed at stimulating economic growth. With the oil crisis of the 1970s this trend increased.

By the end of the 1970s the Japanese government had one of the largest public debts of any government in the world. The Ministry of Finance pushed for reduced government spending, especially on infrastructure, and for tax increases. The government's income from taxes also went up as a result of the property boom, leading to declining public debt and budget surpluses. As the government also became a less significant absorber of new loans, the banks redoubled their loans to the real estate industry. Real estate and share prices boomed and Japan-based investors became increasingly reckless in their purchases of real estate and other trophy investments inside and outside of Japan (Tipton 1998: 418–19). This trend was symbolized by the purchase of the Rockefeller Center in New York by Mitsubishi Real Estate for US$850 million in the late 1980s. By the end of the 1980s it was calculated that one-third of all commercial real estate in Los Angeles was owned by Japan-based investors (Arrighi 1994: 17–18; Hartcher 1997: 63).

China

By the 1980s, meanwhile, China had become a major focus of economic activity as it increasingly emerged as the new 'workshop of the world', in contrast to Japan's assumption of the role of 'banker to the world'. Coastal China in particular began to experience a light-manufacturing boom that effectively continues to this day (and is discussed more fully in Chapter 19 by Breslin).

It should be noted that the post-1978 state-guided national development project in China was distinct from earlier East Asian developmental states in important ways. First, unlike the Japanese and South Korean trajectories, the Chinese leadership emphasized the need for large enterprises in the 'national team' to continue to be primarily publicly owned. The central government was wary of large Chinese corporations becoming too resistant to bureaucratic intervention. Second, the state structures that the Chinese leadership were using to carry out an industrial policy centred on the creation of large globally competitive firms were far larger, in relative and absolute terms, than South Korea and Japan, and lacked the intensity of the commitment to national development that had characterized the leadership in South Korea (in the context of its position as a front-line state in the Cold War) and Japan (in the wake of a traumatic military defeat) in an earlier period. Third, the effort to initiate China's capitalist national development project and encourage the emergence of large corporations that would be globally competitive coincided with dramatic changes in the practices of the increasingly large oligopolistic transnational corporations with which the Chinese firms were expected to compete. In contrast to the early Cold War era, when the Japanese and South Korean states had promoted the interests of large corporations, the global context had been very different. After 20 years of effort, beginning in the late Cold War era and extending into the post-Cold War era, against the backdrop of the elaboration of the US-led globalization project, the large Chinese companies that have been singled out as potential global competitors are 'painfully weak', particularly in areas such as aerospace and pharmaceuticals (Nolan 2001: 15–20, 93–4, 155, 186–8).

Post-Cold War regional trends

The steady, albeit uneven, elaboration of the US-led globalization project also saw the emergence in the post-Cold War era of new or reinvigorated regional economic and politico-military organizations in various parts of the world. This trend was manifested in Asia by the establishment of the APEC in 1989 (Ravenhill 2001). In the context of the rise of neo-liberalism in the 1980s, influential member-governments of APEC, such as the United States and Australia, ensured that APEC was oriented from the outset towards trade liberalization and globalization. This contrasted with the emphasis placed on trade cooperation in the 1980s by the Japanese government, which as we have seen was a long-standing proponent of some form of regional organization.

While the Japanese government, which played a key role in the establishment of APEC, conceded to the neo-liberal agenda, the organization was vigorously challenged by Prime Minister Mahathir. As an alternative to APEC, Mahathir proposed the establishment of a trading bloc, initially called the East Asian Economic Bloc (EAEB), which would exclude the United States, Australia and New Zealand and all other 'non-Asian' nation-states. To underline his opposition to APEC, Mahathir refused to attend the organization's first heads of government meeting in Seattle in 1993. However, by the time of the annual summit in November 1998, which was held in Kuala Lumpur (KL), he was the presiding host, and his East Asian Economic Bloc, under the guise of the East Asian Economic Caucus (EAEC), had been folded into APEC (Berger 1999).

APEC emerged at the start of the 1990s out of the geopolitical and economic complexities of the transition from Cold War Asia to post-Cold War Asia as the major institutional expression of the idea of a Pacific Century that had taken hold in this period (Aikman 1986; Gibney 1992; Linder 1986; McCord 1991; Winchester 1991). It initially represented the main forum for the articulation and accommodation of a revised and reconfigured version of various long-standing geopolitical and geo-economic visions for the region (Berger 1998). As the Cold War came to an end, elites in Northeast and Southeast Asia had become increasingly concerned that the post-Cold War international political economy was shifting towards economic blocs centred on Western Europe (EU) and North America (NAFTA). Concerns were also being expressed about changes in the US approach to security issues in the post-Cold War era. At the outset Washington was preoccupied with the situation in Europe, but in a 1991 visit to East Asia, George Bush's Secretary of State, James Baker reaffirmed a US commitment to the region emphasizing the continued importance of Washington's bilateral security arrangements.

These arrangements maintained, in a somewhat revised fashion, the basic bilateral politico-military architecture of the Cold War (Yamakage 1997: 291–2). This did not necessarily mean that the United States actively opposed regional and multinational initiatives; however, it was the Australian government that had taken the lead, with Japanese encouragement, in the establishment of APEC less than two years before. As already noted, although the Japanese government was more interested in trade cooperation than trade liberalization, APEC quickly emerged as a forum for the latter. From the outset APEC was portrayed by its officials and its supporters as being committed to 'open regionalism' in contrast to the preferential trading practices that characterize the EU and North American

Free Trade Agreement (NAFTA).[4] The Eminent Persons Group (EPG), which laid down much of the early organizational framework for APEC, made it clear that APEC would 'not be a community' like the EU, which is 'characterized by acceptance of the transfer of sovereignty, deep integration and extensive institutionalization'. By contrast it emphasized that APEC would 'be a community in the popular sense of a "big family" of like minded economies' that are 'committed to friendship, cooperation and the removal of barriers to economic exchange among members in the interest of all' (Beeson and Jayasuriya 1998: 327).

At the same time, C. Fred Bergsten (former chair of the EPG and Director of the Washington-based Institute for International Economics) emphasized that the organization should not only play a central role in regional trade liberalization, but it should also act as a 'force for world-wide liberalisation' (1994). This perspective reflected a wider elite-driven view that APEC could play a key role in the international diffusion of economic liberalism. This vision was readily apparent at the first major meeting in Seattle in late 1993, and the second major meeting in Bogor, Indonesia in November 1994. In retrospect this was APEC's golden age. On the final day of the Bogor meeting the leaders from the 18 member countries agreed in principle to the virtual elimination of tariff barriers and obstacles to capital flows within the APEC region by the year 2020 (2010 for developed nations and 2020 for developing nations) (*The Economist* 1994: 29–30; Walsh 1993: 22–7).

On the eve of the Bogor summit President Clinton emphasized his 'vision of a new Asia-Pacific community with no artificial dividing line down the middle of the Pacific'. This meshed with an increasingly influential strand of the Pacific Century narrative that was grounded in the idea of a synthesis between East and West. The public articulation of synthetic visions of the region's future by prominent politicians and intellectuals facilitated consensus building aimed at easing tensions in and around APEC (see Anwar 1996; Borthwick 1992). Regardless of the alleged antipathy between East and West, APEC had emerged as a site for a wider process of elite integration in the Asia-Pacific, and this was facilitated by the domestication of influential East Asian narratives of progress to the dominant neo-liberal discourses in the name of a new East–West synthesis. Despite the continued prevalence of conflicting ideas about Eastern versus Western modes of capitalist development, rising elites also sought to merge vague and ostensibly culturally specific formulations with the dominant international neo-liberal discourses. In this sense, the establishment of APEC was indicative of the post-Cold War transition to a reconfigured form of neo-liberalism that accommodated ostensibly Asian ideas and practices against the backdrop of the continued resilience of US hegemony.

In the post-Cold War era the dominant interpretations of the East Asian Miracle and the coming of the Pacific Century were promoted, and the APEC process unfolded, in the context of an international political economy in which the United States was the hegemonic power. Furthermore, despite the efforts at elite consensus building and the emerging East–West synthesis, the end of the Cold War and the continued spread of economic liberalism, contributed to considerable tension. For example, in the post-Cold War era, relations between the

United States and Japanese governments, the key axis of the new East–West synthesis and the wider APEC process continued to be beset by friction on a range of economic issues especially related to trading practices (see Chapter 18 by Kelly).

At the same time, the ostensibly consensual character of agreements made at APEC meetings also pointed to the real limitations of such an organization, as no enforcement mechanisms were set up and no legally binding commitments were made. Prior to 1997 the dominant neo-liberal narratives on the Pacific Century rested on the assumption that the rise of East Asia and the end of the Cold War had produced increased opportunities for greater regional integration and the spreading and deepening of economic prosperity and political stability. APEC was grounded in these optimistic visions and directly implicated in the view that the economic trends that were carrying the region forward were going to continue indefinitely, delivering prosperity to an ever-growing number of people. This celebratory view of the Pacific Century specifically, and the history of capitalism more generally, was dramatically challenged as the financial crisis which began in Thailand in July 1997 rapidly engulfed the region.

Within months of the fall of the Thai baht in July 1997 commentators, such as Kishore Mahbubani (a prominent advocate of the new East–West synthesis), were warning that the crisis could 'split' the Pacific Ocean 'down the middle' and create 'an east-west divide'. As long as the various leaders who attended APEC's annual summits were only being called upon to agree to relatively distant trade liberalization targets the meetings had proceeded with few serious problems. By the time of the meeting in Vancouver in November 1997, however, the East Asian crisis presented APEC leaders with a serious and immediate problem, and, not surprisingly, the 1997 APEC meeting produced little of substance.

In fact, by the time of the Vancouver summit, the organization had already become irrelevant. The prominent role the International Monetary Fund (IMF) began to play in the management of the crisis provided the United States with the opportunity to pursue economic liberalization and deregulation far more effectively than could ever have occurred with APEC. In the second half of 1997 as APEC drifted to the sidelines, the IMF embarked on major efforts to restore financial stability to the region via loan packages to the governments of Thailand, Indonesia and South Korea. IMF loans were conditional on the implementation of a range of austerity measures and liberal economic reforms. The IMF set out to remake the financial systems of the various countries. This included allowing foreign capital to embark on hostile acquisitions and mergers. The IMF's solution to the crisis also resulted in an extended period of deflation and an ongoing region-wide liquidity crisis because it insisted on tight restrictions on public expenditure and high interest rates for domestic borrowers. The overall approach taken by the IMF reflected the dominant neo-liberal perspective that the crisis flowed from the inefficiencies and distortions that were characteristic of the various state-centred approaches to capitalist development that prevailed in East Asia ('crony capitalism') (International Monetary Fund 1997).

Of course, this view was challenged at the outset from a number of quarters. These critiques were linked to the rising Pan-Asianism that interpreted the Pacific

Century in terms of a New Asian renaissance in which Asia would return to centre stage in world affairs unfettered by the West generally and the United States more specifically (Berger 2003). Mahathir reaffirmed this view at the first Asia–Europe Summit (ASEM) in Bangkok in early March 1996, when he reversed the dominant tendency to universalize 'Western' liberalism and asserted that 'Asian values are universal values', while 'European values are European values'. The idea of a New Asian Renaissance and the resurgence of Pan-Asianism had provided an important backdrop to Mahathir's promotion of an EAEB in the immediate post-Cold War period.

In post-crisis Asia, APEC has drifted to the sidelines and ASEAN+3 has emerged as the potential organizational realization of Mahathir's long-standing Pan-Asian vision. At the most recent ASEAN meeting in October 2003 in Bali (Indonesia), the member governments signed what has been characterized as a 'watershed agreement' committing the organization to the creation of an 'ASEAN Economic Community' by 2020 (the same year that had been set as the deadline for the realization of APEC's free trade goals). Under this agreement the ten member nation-states of ASEAN are to move towards becoming a free-trade zone, at the same time as it is anticipated that their commitment to an Economic Community will strengthen efforts to negotiate free trade arrangements between ASEAN and China, Japan, South Korea (ASEAN+3) and India. While the ASEAN+3 meeting that followed this year's ASEAN meeting included the government of India, the Australian government, a key player in APEC, was excluded despite its requests to attend as an observer. At this juncture, however, there are numerous obstacles to the actual realization of the ASEAN Economic Community (not to mention strengthened links between the ASEAN Economic Community and other major national economies in Asia). Proclaiming a commitment to free trade across ASEAN may eventually prove to be as dubious a goal as the aspirations to Asia-Pacific free trade laid down by APEC at the beginning of the 1990s.

The ASEAN Economic Community initiative is hobbled by the fact that the members of ASEAN are committed to consensus and non-intervention in each other's affairs and the ASEAN Economic Community is no more binding than APEC was. Furthermore, political instability in nation-states such as Burma, Indonesia and the Philippines may ensure that political and security questions increasingly over-ride trade and economic issues in future ASEAN meetings. In this context, movement towards more liberal trading and investment arrangements is as much a destabilizing as stabilizing factor. At the same time, an Economic Community centred on Southeast Asia still puts China and Japan (and ASEAN+3 more generally) in a secondary position despite their overall economic significance and the fact that successful economic regionalism, such as the EU and NAFTA has been anchored and led by particularly large national economies (France and Germany in the former case and the United States in the latter case). Despite the significance of the ASEAN Economic Community its implications for Northeast Asia remain particularly unclear, nor are Japan or China (or both) in a position to play the kind of role that the leading powers in Europe and North America have played in the emergence of coherent regional economic groupings.

Japan and regional trajectories

For example, there continue to be important constraints on Japan's ability to become a leading or hegemonic power in East Asia. Although, as we have seen, in the early 1990s influential narratives continued to generate an image of Japan as a rising capitalist developmental state that represented a challenge to, or a model for, the United States and beyond, this perception was already misleading well before the onset of the East Asian crisis at the end of the 1990s. The end of the Cold War coincided with, and reinforced, a growing array of economic problems linked to the decrepit character of Japanese politics. In fact, the relative inertia of domestic politics and the waning of the Japanese 'economic miracle' often over-shadowed wider concerns in Japan about its position in post-Cold War Asia (Fukui and Fukai 1997).

Up to the end of the Cold War the long-term implications of the rise of the US-led globalization project for the Japanese trajectory (not to mention for Asia more generally) were not clear. At the end of the 1980s, interest rates were driven up causing a dramatic drop in the stock market at the beginning of 1990. Some banks collapsed and a number of bank mergers were arranged in an effort to keep the financial system afloat in the context of a vigorous political debate in the early 1990s about how to address the economic malaise. Throughout the 1990s various government efforts to kick-start the Japanese economy via lower interest rates, tax cuts and public spending continued to be unsuccessful. With a political system driven by money and a commitment to the status quo, the prospects for a Japanese economic resurgence prior to 1997, without major political and social change, were already limited. Of course, some commentators continue to believe that Ministry of International Trade and Industry (MITI) and the Ministry of Finance (MOF) would have the resilience and acumen to bring about a reverse course, and it was hoped that the long-established patterns of cooperation between business, government and organized labour could still provide the framework for a Japanese economic resurgence and expansion into Asia and beyond (Tipton 1998: 415–20).

With the onset of a full-scale economic crisis in the region in 1997, the Japanese economy came under increased pressure. While six of the top ten companies in the world (measured by market capitalization) were based in Japan in 1990, by 1998 there were no Japanese companies in the top ten. By 1998 the Japanese share of global stock market value had dropped to 10.5 per cent from 41.5 per cent in 1990. By 1998, 18 of the top 50 companies in the world (measured by total sales) were in Japan, but only 1 Japanese company was in the top 50 on the basis of profits. By 1999 there was some suggestion that restructuring was beginning to occur in Japan's major companies. A number of corporations began to carry out significant downsizing. Meanwhile, a number of large mergers occurred in the country's banking system in response to similar mergers in the banking systems in North America and Western Europe. There have also been some important mergers and/or takeovers between Japanese and foreign companies. The most well known was the purchase of a controlling share of Nissan by Renault, an acquisition that has resulted in major organizational changes at Nissan under Carlos Ghosn, the new CEO appointed by Renault.

By the end of the twentieth century the *keiretsu* system and the wider Japanese political economy was undergoing a major reorientation, although the role of the Japanese state has certainly been wound back and Japanese corporations have undergone significant changes the process is very uneven (Nolan 2001: 129–31). And as in China, the banking system in Japan is in a chronic state of crisis. Estimates of the size of non-performing loans in relation to total assets held by Japan-based banks range up to a figure of almost 40 per cent contained in a report prepared by Goldman Sachs at the end of 2001 (Holland 2001: 66–9).

The ongoing economic malaise, centred on the banking system, has meant that the Japanese government and Japanese corporations have been unable to play as significant a role in the region in the post-Cold War era as many had anticipated or intended. The prevailing view in Japan prior to 1997 was that the end of the Cold War, combined with the economic dynamism of much of the rest of the region (if not of Japan itself), made it possible for the Japanese government to be 'internationalist' and 'Asianist' simultaneously (Shiraishi 1997: 191–4). Then, in the aftermath of the Asian crisis, the new Koizumi government sought to combine an appeal to conservative and populist neo-nationalist ideas with a far more significant commitment to the neo-liberal restructuring of the Japanese developmental state and the strengthening of its alliance with the United States (Campbell 2001: 29). However, it was soon apparent that the Koizumi's planned reforms for the Japanese banking system and other areas of the economy would proceed at a slow pace (*The Economist* 2001a: 29–30).

In geopolitics, the Japanese government was quick to support the United States in its effort to build a global coalition to carry out its 'war on terrorism'. However, the exact character of that support was relatively minimal and it did not involve an actual Japanese military commitment (*The Economist* 2001b: 32). At the same time, Japan's general acquiescence to the United States and the maintenance of the bilateral ally–client relationship of the Cold War era remains in place. Against the backdrop of the economic decline and crisis of the 1990s, there is an inability on the part of the Japanese government (as well as virtually all other leaders in the region) to stand up to the United States and create an economic (or a politico-military) framework aimed at greater regional integration and autonomy vis-à-vis Washington.

Although the 'Asia-first' approach emphasized by Mahathir certainly meshed with the views of some influential members of the Japanese elite, in the post-Cold War era it was widely assumed amongst Japanese policymakers that the Japanese economic presence could be extended ever more deeply into the region, without challenging either the US–Japan alliance or the far more liberal forms of economic regionalism represented by APEC and advocated by the United States. Up to the mid-1990s, this view meshed with the version of the coming Pacific Century being promoted in North America. However, with the onset of the East Asian crisis it became apparent that this was a somewhat fanciful view of the future of the Asia-Pacific. Writing before the onset of the crisis, Takashi Shiraishi argued that in the face of these sorts of crises it would be 'better' for the Japanese government to address them 'collectively with the United States as the senior partner rather than making it an "imperial" issue to be resolved by Japan alone' (Shiraishi 1997: 193–4). Certainly, this was more or less what Tokyo did, allowing the IMF to take the lead, notwithstanding early efforts by the Japanese government to play a more significant role.

In particular, the Asian Monetary Fund (AMF) proposal was notable in that there were to be no conditions attached. It would have maintained the restrictions on foreign ownership of financial institutions and sustained the economic practices that East Asian elites associate with rapid capitalist development. However, the idea of an AMF was defeated at the November 1997 APEC Finance Minister's meeting in Manila and the end result of the ASEAN summit in Kuala Lumpur, the following month, was a weak endorsement of the IMF's plan for the crisis. Despite this trend, Mahathir did not seem to abandon the pan-Asian idea. With the Malaysian government in the lead, a number of governments appeared to be drifting in the direction of capital controls by the end of 1998. In India and China, which had capital controls before the crisis started, and in a number of countries beyond Asia political support for controls on capital flows was on the rise (Wade and Veneroso 1998a: 20–1, 30, 41–2).

Prominent advocates of neo-liberalism were also continuing to worry about the rise of protectionist trade practices as a global recession loomed (*The Economist* 1998c: 15–16). There was evidence, however, that support for protectionism (at least among elites), even in many East Asian countries remained weak, even though the popularity of capital controls was rising worldwide (*The Economist* 1999: 53–4). In the immediate aftermath of the Asian crisis renovated versions of neo-liberalism continued to provide the dominant narratives on economic development and no alternative to the IMF approach has gained a position of influence regionally or internationally. In fact the IMF has become a key instrument in the wider promotion of the US-led globalization project (Wade and Veneroso 1998b: 18–19).

Meanwhile, the November 1998 APEC meeting produced even less of substance than in previous years, signalling to all that events would unfold despite, rather than because of APEC (*The Economist* 1998a: 41; Sanger 1998: 5). Nor did an important ASEAN meeting in December 1998 result in any significant initiatives to address the crisis (*The Economist* 1998b: 29–30). ASEAN did not have the institutional capability or the stature to react to the crisis in an effective fashion. The organization's founding principle of non-intervention in relation to the domestic issues of member governments prevented a 'comprehensive collective response', with or without Japanese support (Funabashi 1998: 28).

All this points to the fact that the United States remains the only truly world power in military and economic terms, at the same time as it exercises a broad and diffuse political and cultural influence. US hegemony is mediated through an array of complex power relations, economic arrangements, social structures and cultural practices; however, Washington maintains effective control over the important aspects of the international political economy. In East Asia, US hegemony continues to rest on the alliance conditions and arrangements that the Japanese and South Korean states accepted during the Cold War era (and which also constrain virtually all other states in the region). Nor, at this juncture, does

China represent a serious politico-military or economic threat to US hegemony and the likelihood of China achieving economic superpower status (and thus becoming a politico-military 'threat' to the United States) needs to be set against the complex centrifugal forces that confront the present Chinese leadership's pursuit of national and regional greatness.

China and regional trajectories

The Chinese leadership's pursuit of national development and/or regional hegemony continues to be profoundly constrained by looming political, social, environmental and economic crises grounded in rapid and uneven capitalist development and characterized by increasingly stark divisions between the booming coastal regions and the impoverished interior. In urban centres as well there are now millions of disgruntled workers who have lost their formerly secure jobs at state-owned enterprises that have begun to respond to market pressures to be more competitive. As this process unfolds the re-employment rate has declined steadily from 50 per cent in 1998 to 9 per cent for the first part of 2002 (Murphy 2002: 30–3). Meanwhile, the crisis in the banking system in China, centred on the four large state-owned institutions, which are said to be currently presiding over non-performing loans worth 28 per cent of their total assets (independent observers put the figure at 50 per cent or more), suggests the prospects for the successful emergence of a 'national team' of large globally competitive companies is not great (Lague 2001: 70–2; 2002: 32–5). This is all set against the backdrop of the Chinese state's domestication to, and resistance against, the US-led globalization project as manifested by Beijing's induction into the World Trade Organisation (WTO) in September 2001 on the one hand and its growing involvement in ASEAN+3 on the other hand (Hongyi 2001: 237–55).

US–China relations are at the centre of any equation regarding the geopolitical economy of regionalism in the Asia-Pacific. For almost two decades from the early 1970s until 1989 US–China relations rested on what observers such as Lampton have called a 'Grand Bargain'. The explicit and implicit elements of this 'Grand Bargain' included an agreement by both sides that the issue of the status of Taiwan was to be set aside and dealt with at some unspecified time in the future. Second, because the Chinese government was primarily concerned with gaining US support against the USSR, policymakers in Beijing also tended to avoid the question of Japan, even seeing the US–Japan security alliance as central to the wider containment of the USSR. At the same time, while both sides wanted improved trade relations, as long as a mutual concern about the Soviet Union prevailed questions about any imbalances or problems in trade relations were relegated to the background. The end of the Cold War, which coincided with improving relations between Beijing and Moscow, meant the disappearance of the main reason (the Soviet threat) both China and the United States had for ignoring or downplaying areas of contention between them. The brutal repression of protestors in Tiananmen Square in 1989 also undermined the 'Grand Bargain'.

Simultaneously, a range of other trends ensured by the beginning of the 1990s that the US–China relationship entered a new and more difficult era than the previous two decades. First, as already suggested, the PRC had emerged by the late 1980s as a particularly successful economic modernizer, resulting in more economic friction between Beijing and Washington than had been anticipated when the initial Chinese turn to the market had been executed. Second, in the case of Taiwan, the island had made a transition from authoritarian military rule in the 1970s to parliamentary democracy by the late 1980s and politicians on Taiwan increasingly began to intrude into US–China relations, challenging Beijing's continued claims to the island and/or US equivocation on the issue. Third, in the post-Vietnam era, the US Congress has sought to scrutinize and examine US foreign policy in Asia generally and towards China more particularly, making US–China relations an important concern for domestic politics in the United States. Fourth, the growing flow of information and news across the Pacific and around the world, as a result of the technological and economic changes of the previous decades has meant that the communication and information flows associated with globalization had added a whole new dimension to US–China relations. Fifth, the Gulf War highlighted the so-called 'revolution in military affairs' at the beginning of the 1990s and the Chinese leadership increasingly sought to come to grips with these changes by increased defence spending, military reorientation and upgrading resulting in changes to the military balance in the region (Lampton 2001: 2–4).

In the 1990s, with the end of the Cold War and the wider demise of the 'Grand Bargain', China-watchers increasingly drew attention to Beijing's effort to inherit the mantle of state-guided capitalist developmentalism earlier exemplified by Japan and South Korea (e.g. Bernstein and Munro 1997). However, the Clinton administration, not always consistently, sought to pursue a policy of 'engagement' and 'enlargement' rather than 'containment' towards China and the world (Office of the President of the United States 1996). During Clinton's years in office, however, US–China relations were punctuated by major ups and downs. 'Engagement' and 'enlargement' were reflected in Clinton's elimination of the connection between Most Favoured Nation (MFN) trading status for China and its record on human rights, a link that his administration had insisted upon the previous year. By 1995–96, Washington and Beijing were drifting towards the brink of military and naval confrontation in the Taiwan straits, as Beijing sought to use live-fire military manoeuvres off Taiwan to influence elections on the island. By the late 1990s relations had improved and there was considerable discussion of the establishment of a 'constructive strategic partnership'. The second half of 1999 again saw a downturn in relations, beginning with the failure to reach agreement in April of that year about China's entry into the WTO. This was followed by the US bombing of Beijing's embassy in Belgrade, a US Congressional report detailing a wide-ranging series of espionage activities in the United States by Chinese agents, at the same time as the issue of Taiwan continued to simmer (Lampton 2001: 15–16, 30–1, 39–45, 46, 55, 62–3).

Under these circumstances, and in the context of the growing political debate in the United States about China by the second half of the 1990s, and particularly in the lead up to the 2000 election, the Clinton administration was not always as committed to 'engagement' and 'enlargement' as its original pronouncements on the subject might suggest (Betts 1993/94: 34–77; Nye 1998; Ross 1997: 33–44; Shambaugh 1996: 180–209). Nevertheless, the administration continued to argue that engaging rather than containing Beijing would enhance security.

In the lead up to, and immediately following, his election as president at the end of 2000, George W. Bush emphasized that China was a long-term military threat in the wider context of the new administration's efforts to reassert Washington's regional and global military power, at the same time as he initially sought to avoid the entanglements that had ostensibly characterized the Clinton era. During its first six months in office, the Bush administration explicitly identified the Chinese state (which has been regarded by US China-watchers and strategic planners as *the* major military threat to the United States and its interests in the Asia-Pacific for a number of years) as a major focus of a reoriented US military effort (*The Economist* 2001a: 13; 2001b: 21–6, 31–2; Achcar 1998: 102–5, 115–26).

Meanwhile, the initial commitment of the Bush administration to focus more on containing China, rather than engaging China now appears to have also been tempered by the somewhat improved US–China relations that followed the resolution of the US spy plane incident earlier in 2001 and the shift in US foreign policy to Central Asia and the Middle East. As a China specialist at the Rand Corporation observed: the 'war on terrorism' has 'encouraged a shift toward the notion of tactical cooperation with China', but no one is 'talking about a strategic shift'. This is reinforced by the deputy director of the Institute of American Studies at the Chinese Academy of Social Sciences who emphasized that: 'the parameters of the relationship haven't changed'.

Conclusion: from APEC to ASEAN+3?

The 1990s saw the rise and the decline of APEC, while post-crisis Asia has been characterized by the strengthening of ASEAN+3 and recent plans for an ASEAN Economic Community. Despite renewed Pan-Asian regionalism, however, neither Beijing nor Tokyo has sought to provide the kind of regional leadership in trade, finance or monetary affairs that has been characteristic of more successful efforts at economic or political regionalism in North America and Western Europe. Financial and monetary questions were central to the Asian crisis and are also of as much, if not more importance than trade, in advancing regional economic integration. Tokyo and Beijing, despite all the expectations or fears about their respective potential as regional leaders and major challengers to US hegemony, remain focused on their national monetary and financial interests and this is a brake on any move in the near future towards regional monetary cooperation, which in turn constrains trade and economic integration more generally. This situation also flows to a considerable degree from the limits of the wider global order centred on US power. Central to the post-Cold War order has been an increasingly global economic framework that involves a growing disjuncture between a deregulated international financial system on the one hand and the 'real' economy of the production of, and trade in, goods and services on the other hand.

In this situation, unless there is a systematic and region-wide effort to introduce capital controls (such as was pursued for a while in Malaysia during the Asian crisis) even the political elites presiding over the largest and most independent national economies are profoundly limited in their ability to prevent the conflation of the interests of 'Wall Street' and the financial markets on the one hand with the macroeconomic policy settings of governments around the world on the other. US power, therefore, mediated through key financial sector institutions, such as the IMF, continues to impose limits on specific national trajectories in East Asia and on regional integration as a whole. While the Chinese leadership is seeking to manage its integration into the global capitalist economy via membership of the WTO, and the government of Japan remains focused on the country's ongoing economic difficulties, the prospects for major advances in regional economic and political integration centred on Beijing or Tokyo or both, in a fashion that would challenge US hegemony seems remote.

In fact, the rise of bilateral trade arrangements in the region and beyond points not only to the passing of APEC, but the relative weakness of economic multilateralism in the region more generally. It is far too soon to view the recent declaration on the formation of an ASEAN Economic Community as having any prospect of actually becoming an organization of genuine substance by the target date of 2020. This weakness is also apparent in the primarily bilateral politico-military alliances and other defence arrangements that were laid down during the Cold War. And the Bush administration's vigorous pursuit of unassailable global military supremacy in the context of the increased emphasis on security and the ongoing 'war on terrorism', while contributing to a military build-up in the Asian region generally also serves to further underwrite US hegemony in the region even as it contributes in important ways to regional instability. As far as Northeast and Southeast Asia are concerned, it is possible that, as the post-Cold War and post-9/11 order takes shape regional elites may increasingly turn to ASEAN and ASEAN+3 to try and overcome intra-regional tensions and to challenge US hegemony. However, in the context of the ongoing crisis centred on North Korea, and political and economic instability in Indonesia, the Philippines, Burma and elsewhere, there is considerable uncertainty about the future of regionalism in Asia and the Asia-Pacific.

Acknowledgements

I would like to thank Dominic Kelly for his helpful comments on earlier drafts of this chapter. Thanks also to Mark Beeson for input and Kerstin Calley for her impeccable research assistance.

Notes

1. The founding member nation-states of APEC were Australia, Brunei, Canada, Indonesia, Japan, Malaysia, New Zealand, the Philippines, Singapore, South Korea, Thailand and the United States. Hong Kong, the People's Republic of China and Taiwan joined in 1991, followed by Mexico and Papua New Guinea in 1993. In 1994 Chile was admitted, while

Peru, Russia and Vietnam became members in the late 1990s. For a good overview of APEC see Ravenhill 2001.

2. East Asia, which is often used to refer to Northeast Asia, is also increasingly used to refer to Northeast and Southeast Asia. The latter usage will be followed in this article. Meanwhile, 'Asia' is widely used to refer to all of South Asia, Southeast Asia and Northeast Asia. However, in some instances Asia is also used to refer to East Asia. In this chapter this latter usage will be followed and when it is not the meaning will be clear from the context.

3. The Association of Southeast Asian Nations (ASEAN) was set up on 8 August 1967 by the governments of Thailand, Singapore, the Philippines, Malaysia and Indonesia. Brunei joined in January 1984, while the end of the Cold War saw the entry of Vietnam (July 1995), Burma (July 1997), Laos (July 1997) and Cambodia (April 1999). While East Timor gained independence from Indonesia in 2001 and initially sought early entry into ASEAN, it has met opposition on this score from the government of Burma and its entry into ASEAN has not only been postponed, apparently indefinitely, but as of mid-2003 it was still being refused entry to the much larger, 23-member, ASEAN Regional Forum (ARF). ASEAN+3 was a relatively recent innovation, which involves regular meetings and negotiations between the members of ASEAN, along with China, Japan and South Korea, while India has also recently begun participating in this grouping.

4. 'Open regionalism' is a much debated term. It is most commonly, and narrowly, defined as a concerted and unilateral process of trade liberalization along MFN – most favoured nation – lines. (See Drysdale *et al.* 1998: 6–9.)

References

Achcar, G. (1998) 'The Strategic Triad: The United States, Russia, and China', *New Left Review (I)*, 228, pp. 91–127.

Aikman, D. (1986) *Pacific Rim: Area of Change, Area of Opportunity*, Boston: Little Brown.

Anwar, I. (1996) *The Asian Renaissance*, Singapore: Times Books International.

Arrighi, G. (1994) *The Long Twentieth Century: Money, Power, and the Origins of Our Times*, London: Verso.

Beeson, M. (2003) 'ASEAN Plus Three and the Rise of Reactionary Regionalism', *Contemporary Southeast Asia*, 25, 2, pp. 251–68.

Beeson, M. and Jayasuriya, K. (1998) 'The Political Rationalities of Regionalism: APEC and the EU in Comparative Perspective', *The Pacific Review*, 11, 3, pp. 311–36.

Berger, M.T. (1998) 'A New East–West Synthesis? APEC and Competing Narratives of Regional Integration in the Post-Cold War Asia-Pacific', *Alternatives: Social Transformation and Humane Governance*, 23, 1, pp. 1–28.

Berger, M.T. (1999) 'APEC And Its Enemies: The Failure of the New Regionalism in the Asia-Pacific' *Third World Quarterly: Journal of Emerging Areas*, 20, 5, pp. 1013–30.

Berger, M.T. (2003) 'The New Asian Renaissance and Its Discontents: National Narratives, Pan-Asian Visions and the Changing Post-Cold War Order' *International Politics: A Journal of Transnational Issues and Global Problems*, 40, 2, pp. 195–221.

Bergsten, C.F. (1994) 'APEC and the World Economy: A Force for Worldwide Liberalisation', *Foreign Affairs*, 73, 3, pp. 20–6.

Bernstein, R. and Munro, R.H. (1997) *The Coming Conflict With China*, New York: Alfred A. Knopf.

Betts, R.K. (1993/94) 'Wealth, Power, and Instability: East Asia and the United States after the Cold War', *International Security*, 18, 3, Winter, pp. 34–77.

Borthwick, M. (1992) (with contributions by selected scholars), *Pacific Century: The Emergence of Modern Pacific Asia*, Boulder, CT: Westview Press.

Campbell, K.M. (2001) 'Koizumi as Japan's Reagan', *Far Eastern Economic Review*, 23 August.

Dirlik, A. (1992) 'The Asia-Pacific Idea: Reality and Representation in the Invention of Regional Structure', *Journal of World History*, 3, 1, pp. 55–79.

Drysdale, P., Vines, D. and House, B. (1998) 'Europe and Asia: a Shared Global Agenda?', in Drysdale, P. and Vines, D. (eds) *Europe, East Asia and APEC: a Shared Global Agenda?* Cambridge: Cambridge University Press.

The Economist 25 November (1994), 'A Dream of Free Trade'.

The Economist, 21 November (1998a), 'APEC's family feud'.

The Economist 19 December (1998b), 'Asean Looks to the New Year'.

The Economist, 19 December (1998c), 'A Bad Time to be an Ostrich'.

The Economist 2 January (1999), 'Liberalism Lives'.

The Economist 8 September (2001a), 'Japan's Reform on Hold'.

The Economist 22 September (2001b), 'Japan and the United States: on Board?'

Fukui, H. and Fukai, S.N. (1997) 'The End of the Miracle: Japanese Politics in the Post-Cold War Era' in Berger, Mark T. and Borer, Douglas A. (eds) *The Rise of East Asia: Critical Visions of the Pacific Century*, London: Routledge.

Funabashi, Y. (1998) 'Tokyo's Depression Diplomacy' *Foreign Affairs*, 77, 6, pp. 26–36.

Gibney, F. (1992) *The Pacific Century: America and Asia in a Changing World*, New York: Macmillan.

Hartcher, P. (1997) *The Ministry*, New York: Harper Collins.

Hatch, W. and Yamamura, K. (1996) *Asia in Japan's Embrace: Building a Regional Production Alliance*, Cambridge: Cambridge University Press.

Holland, T. (2001) 'Banking in Asia: Japan' *Far Eastern Economic Review*, 4 October.

Hongyi, H.L. (2001) 'Behind China's World Trade Organization Agreement with the USA', *Third World Quarterly*, 22, 2: 237–55.

International Monetary Fund (1997) *Interim Assessment of the World Economic Outlook*, Washington: International Monetary Fund, December.

Kelly, D. (2002) *Japan and the Reconstruction of East Asia*, Basingstoke: Palgrave.

Lague, D. (2001) 'Banking in Asia: China' *Far Eastern Economic Review*, 4 October.

Lague, D. (2002) 'China: On the Road to Ruin', *Far Eastern Economic Review*, 14 November.

Lampton, D.M. (2001) *Same Bed, Different Dreams: Managing US–China Relations 1989–2000*, Berkeley, CA: University of California Press.

Linder, S.B. (1986) *The Pacific Century: Economic and Political Consequences of Asian-Pacific Dynamism*, Stanford, CA: Stanford University Press.

McCord, W. (1991) *The Dawn of the Pacific Century: Implications for Three Worlds of Development*, New Brunswick: Transaction Publishers.

Morris-Suzuki, T. (1994) *The Technological Transformation of Japan: From the Seventeenth to the Twenty-first Century*, Cambridge: Cambridge University Press.

Murphy, D. (2002) 'Urban Poverty: Nothing More to Lose', *Far Eastern Economic Review*, 7 November.

Nolan, P. (2001) *China and the Global Economy*, Basingstoke: Palgrave.

Nye Jr., J. (1998) 'The Case Against Containment: Treat China Like an Enemy and That's What It Will Be', *Global Beat* 22 June (www.nyu.edu/globalbeat/asia/china/ 06221998nye.html)

Office of the President of the United States (1996) *A National Security Strategy of Engagement and Enlargement*, Washington: US Government Printing Office, www.fas.org/spp/military/docops/national/1996stra.htm

Ravenhill, J. (2001) *APEC and the Construction of Pacific Rim Regionalism*, Cambridge: Cambridge University Press.

Ross, R.S. (1997) 'Beijing as a Conservative Power', *Foreign Affairs*, March–April 76, 2: 33–44.

Sanger, D.E. (1998) 'Tongue-Lashings and Backlashes', *The New York Times*, 22 November.

Shambaugh, D. (1996) 'Containment or Engagement of China? Calculating Beijing's Responses', *International Security*, 21, 2 Fall, pp. 180–209.

Shiraishi, T. (1997) 'Japan and Southeast Asia', in Katzenstein, Peter J. and Takashi Shiraishi (eds) *Network Power: Japan and Asia*, Ithaca, NY: Cornell University Press.

Soesastro, H. (1994) 'Pacific Economic Cooperation: The History of an Idea', in Garnaut, Ross and Drysdale, Peter (eds) *Asia Pacific Regionalism: Readings in International Economic Relations*, Sydney: Harper Collins.

Stubbs, R. (1994) 'The Political Economy of the Asia-Pacific Region', in Stubbs, Richard and Underhill, Geoffrey R.D. (eds) *Political Economy and the Changing Global Order*, London: Macmillan.

Terada, T. (1998) 'The Origins of Japan's APEC Policy: Foreign Minister Takeo Miki's Asia-Pacific Policy and Current Implications', *The Pacific Review*, 11, 3, pp. 337–63.

Terry, E. (2002) *How Asia Got Rich: Japan, China and the Asian Miracle*, Armonk, NY: M. E. Sharpe.

Tipton, F.B. (1998) *The Rise of Asia: Economics, Society and Politics in Contemporary Asia*, London: Macmillan.

Vogel, E., Yuan, M. and Akihiko, T. (eds) (2002) *The Golden Age of the USA–China–Japan Triangle 1972–1989*, Cambridge, MA: Harvard University Press.

Wade, R. and Veneroso, F. (1998a) 'The Gathering World Slump and the Battle Over Capital Controls', *New Left Review (I)*, 231, pp. 13–42.

Wade, R. and Veneroso, F. (1998b) 'The Asian Crisis: The High Debt Model Versus the Wall Street–Treasury–IMF Complex', *New Left Review (I)*, 228, pp. 3–23.

Wallerstein, I. (1999) 'The Rise of East Asia, or the World-System in the Twenty-First Century', in Wallerstein, I. (ed.) *The End of the World As We Know It: Social Science for the Twenty-First Century*, Minneapolis, MN: University of Minnesota Press.

Walsh, J. (1993) 'Toward the Pacific Age', *Time: International*, 22 November.

Winchester, S. (1991) *Pacific Rising: The Emergence of a New World Culture*, New York: Prentice Hall.

Yamakage, S. (1997) 'Japan's National Security and Asia-Pacific's Regional Institutions in the Post-Cold War Era', in Katzenstein, P.J. and Takashi Shiraishi (eds) *Network Power: Japan and Asia*, Ithaca, NY: Cornell University Press.

Yasutomo, D. (1986) *The Manner of Giving: Strategic Aid and Japanese Foreign Policy*, New York: D.C. Heath.

18
The Political Economy of Japanese Trade Policy

Dominic Kelly

Japan is a relative 'latecomer' amongst the ranks of the leading industrial nations. This late arrival has had many consequences three of which are particularly relevant here. The first is that Japan's socio-economic development has apparently followed a trajectory at a tangent to those travelled by its continental European cousins, and by the United Kingdom and the United States. In the latter countries the principle of *laissez faire* is said to hold back government intervention in the market, while in the former close ties clearly exist between government, business and labour but are directed towards broadly social goals (Albert 1993; Hart 1992; Zysman 1983). In Japan, by contrast, the 'iron triangle' formed by relations between government, bureaucracy and big business has seemingly resulted in the adoption of (neo)mercantilist economic policies aimed at enriching the nation as a whole and big business in particular at the expense of Japanese workers and consumers and, significantly, workers and consumers in the United States, Europe and elsewhere (Nester 1991).

The second consequence is that Japanese trade policy has been more visibly linked to economic policy in general and industrial policy in particular than appears to be the case in the United States, United Kingdom and on mainland Europe (Johnson 1982, 1995; Okimoto 1988; Pempel 1978). The third consequence is that Japanese industrial and trade policy have been linked to Japan's efforts at carving out two empires – one a 'visible' empire that came to an end in 1945 (Beasley 1987; Calman 1992; Marshall 1967), and the other an 'invisible' empire built not on physical conquest but upon the development of production, trade and investment networks that now cover the globe (Hatch and Yamamura 1996; Katzenstein and Shiraishi 1997; Kelly 2002; Steven 1990).

The aim of this chapter is to explore the consequences of Japan's status as both latecomer and 'outlier' for its foreign economic policy in general and its trade policy in particular. It analyses the origins of the 'iron triangle' formed by close relations between government, bureaucracy and big business, and the characterization of Japanese industrial relations as 'corporatism without labour' (Pempel and Tsunekawa 1979). It analyses the links between industrial policy and trade policy, and it traces the connections between these and the building of a visible and an invisible 'empire'. Finally, it analyses the transformation of Japan's foreign economic and trade policy since reaching 'maturity', and the pressures that brought this about.

The chapter proceeds as follows. The first section considers the legacy of Japanese colonialism and participation in the Second World War as these fed into post-war occupation and reconstruction, and into the relationship with the United States during the Cold War. This section begins by suggesting that although the US occupation of Japan (1945–52) points to a major rupture between pre- and post-war Japanese society there are a sufficient number of continuities – institutional as well as philosophical – to warrant a comparison of the two (Dower 1999; Gordon 1993; Johnson 1982; van Wolferen 1993). It continues with the story of post-war recovery and focuses in particular on the complexities of Japan–US relations, as security issues constantly impinged upon the economic relationship – and vice versa – to the extent that the alliance itself sometimes appeared under threat.

The second section examines contemporary Japanese trade policy and its consequences in Japan, East Asia and the wider world. This section focuses first on the changing nature of the domestic economy and society and how this has impacted directly upon the economies and societies of East Asia through the various regional initiatives that have been set in motion, and second on the impact of all this on the wider world and of Japan's place in it.

Japanese industrial and trade policy within the US alliance system

Paradoxically, and perversely, defeat in the Second World War may well have been the best thing that has happened to modern Japan. It left the country physically wounded and psychologically damaged but wide open to the forces of change (Tsuru 1993). These forces, Japanese and American in origin, did their utmost to re-orient Japan so that it might more closely reflect – and more vigorously defend – contemporary visions of a just, equitable and progressive society. This required that a democratic polity be set in place, and that this be attended by a market economy.[1]

On the face of it, the occupation of Japan between 1945 and 1952 accomplished these two goals. The new Constitution removed political power from the emperor and vested it instead in the Diet. It also contained the infamous 'peace clause' renouncing for ever Japan's sovereign right to wage war. Universal suffrage was introduced and restrictions on civil participation through trades unions and political parties were abolished. The education system was revised so as to remove all traces of reverence for the emperor system. The leaders of the former regime – particularly the military, government and big business – were purged and many faced execution. The bureaucracy was subject to the same purge (albeit to a lesser degree), its structure decentralized and some of its key institutions broken up. The economy was thoroughly overhauled so that the concentration of economic power in the hands of the *zaibatsu* (family-owned conglomerates) was ended (Hadley 1970), while land reform broke the rural peasantry free from the powerful hold of the landlord class (Dore 1959). In other words the occupation destroyed the system that had brought about Japanese imperialism in the first place, and replaced it with one that would guarantee a peaceful future for Japan and its neighbours.

Or so it was hoped. In reality several factors combined to slow, prevent or reverse many of these changes. On the domestic side reform was hampered by stiff resistance from reactionary forces – a resistance strengthened by the necessity of using Japanese bureaucrats to implement the process.[2] Indeed, the power of the bureaucracy was actually strengthened during the occupation since former bureaucrats moved into the void left in the ranks of the political parties and big business.

On the international side, the onset of the Cold War – and in particular the 'loss' of China to communism and the subsequent outbreak of the Korean War in 1950 – convinced US planners that Japan's location off mainland Asia was of vital strategic importance in the ongoing war against communism. Moreover, Japan and its people could play an important role as a junior partner to the United States in the waging of this war. As a consequence, from about 1948 the speedy reconstruction of the Japanese economy was to take precedence over political democratization and economic de-concentration.

This had little effect on the writing of the new Constitution or the programme of land reform. It did, however, ensure that the more radical political agendas associated with some of the newly liberated social forces – the labour movement in particular – were quickly, and brutally, squashed (Moore 1983). It was the right-wing that was to dominate the post-war political scene – characterized by conservatism with a big and a small 'c' and embodied by the dominance of electoral politics by the Liberal Democratic Party (LDP).[3] Similarly, the de-concentration of the economy never really happened. The *zaibatsu* were threatened but survived in their new guise as *keiretsu* – the key difference being that the latter had at their core not a family but a 'main bank'. Thus the economy retained the 'dual structure' that had been one of its major characteristics since the late Meiji era – and was dominated by a few huge export-oriented conglomerates linked by cross-shareholding and by membership of the peak business associations, and by sub-contracting relationships built up over many years. The remainder, constituting the bulk of all business activity and employment in Japan, enjoyed none of the privileges accruing to the favoured few – acting instead as a 'shock absorber' in times of economic downturn such as that following the oil price rises of the 1970s.[4]

In combination the suppression of left-wing politics, the survival of the huge conglomerates and the enhanced power of the bureaucracy served to close off any opportunities for Japan to embrace the kind of social market politics that was taking shape in Europe (see Pempel 1998). The bureaucracy was firmly in control, and had been given a mandate to deliver speedy economic growth. Given the history of the country and the social norms in play, there was never any doubt about who they would turn to: that is, big business. Just as they had in the Meiji era, big business, the bureaucracy and the government set out to plan and implement economic recovery. Safe beneath the US military umbrella, they succeeded beyond even their wildest dreams.

Trade politics within the 'American Greenhouse'[5]

If post-war, post-occupation Japan remained in important respects wedded to its pre-war past, it is also the case that it faced the same set of 'situational imperatives' that had pushed it down the road to imperialism. These included 'late development, a lack of natural resources, a large population, the need to trade and the constraints of the international balance of payments' (Johnson 1982: 307). This time, however, Japan faced a very different strategic environment (Yahuda 1996). On its doorstep sat three hostile communist powers, two of whom – the People's Republic of China (PRC), and the Democratic People's Republic of Korea – had played vital roles in the Japanese empire, and the third of which – the Soviet Union – had proved a hostile neighbour in the past. It also faced two former colonies – the Republic of China (Taiwan) and the Republic of Korea – both capitalist countries and fellow members of the US alliance structure but who shared a deep suspicion of all things Japanese. Thus, Japan found itself cut off from its 'natural' markets in Korea (South and North) the PRC and Taiwan. It was also cut off, initially at least, from its secondary markets in Southeast Asia. This left Japan in a situation where it was extraordinarily dependent on one country, the United States, for military protection, trade and investment.[6]

Fortunately for Japan the United States proved to be both a generous victor and a willing recipient of Japanese goods. Through the 1950s and 1960s Japanese manufacturers made steady inroads into the US economy, taking significant market shares in a variety of sectors. By 1955, for example, Japan was exporting 140 million square yards of cotton to the United States, which was up from a total of only 2 million square yards in 1951 (Argy and Stein 1997: 204–23). In response, the United States quickly persuaded Japan to agree to impose a voluntary export restraint (VER) on cotton from December 1955.

At the same time, however, the United States continued to support Japan in its efforts at domestic reconstruction and to encourage its rehabilitation within the family of states. This included toleration of Japanese protectionism, and sponsorship of Japan's entry into the General Agreement on Tariffs and Trade (GATT) as well as membership of other key global institutions such as the United Nations, the World Bank, the International Monetary Fund and the Organization for Economic Cooperation and Development (OECD).

The quid pro quo demanded for this largesse was Japan's agreement to sign a security treaty with the United States in 1960.[7] The provisions of this treaty allowed for the stationing of US troops in Japan and committed the United States to defend its ally in the event of a military threat, but did not commit Japanese forces to a similar defence of US forces or its territory. On the face of it this was a good deal for the Japanese since it allowed at least a pretence of adherence to constitutional requirements. In the long run, however, it became a major controversy in Japanese domestic politics and a huge thorn in the side of US–Japan bilateral relations in general and trade relations in particular.

The security treaty became an issue in domestic politics because it meant that Japan played a role – albeit passive – in the waging of the Cold War. This ranged from provision of matériel for the Korean and Vietnam wars, to the use of Japanese territory as a base of US operations, to the unacknowledged introduction of US nuclear weapons into Japan, and to the payment by the Japanese government of the basing costs incurred by US forces (Hook 1996). It also meant that Japan has been labelled an accomplice to US foreign policy. This has had some disastrous effects – including the oil price rises and embargo imposed on Japan in the 1970s as a consequence of its tacit support for the state of Israel, and the prevention of the normalization of relations between the PRC and Japan until after the reversal of US policy towards China during the 1970s.

It has remained an issue in domestic politics since the end of the Cold War because it has been seen to have contributed to Japan taking a more active role in military affairs. This includes participation in the Rim of the Pacific exercises with US forces, the patrolling of Japan's sea lanes out to a distance of 1000 nautical miles and the revision of the Guidelines for Japan–US Defence Cooperation (Kelly 2002: ch. 7). It also includes the despatch of Japanese troops on UN-mandated peace-keeping operations around the world, as well as to the Gulf in 1991 (after hostilities had ended) and their proposed despatch in 2003.

The security treaty has become a thorn in the side of US–Japan economic and trade relations for two main reasons. First, it has perpetuated the memory of Japanese imperialism in Asia, and thus contributed to hostility towards Japanese investment in and trade with the region which grew at a phenomenal pace through the post-war years (Kelly 2002; Manglapus 1976; Sudo 1992). Second, the unbalanced burden it places on its signatories has resulted in US charges that Japan is enjoying a 'free ride' on defence at US expense (Islam 1993). This free ride on defence has arguably allowed the Japanese government to plough more money into economic development – through tax breaks and subsidies for example – than would have been the case if it had been forced to divert money into defence spending.

Thus, while the United States was busy defending Japan and the free world, Japanese manufacturers were able to seize market share first in textiles then in steel, television sets, automobiles and semiconductors.[8] Since the mid-1960s this has resulted in a persistent Japanese trade surplus with the US which reached US$81 billion in 2000 (Cohen *et al.* 2003: 238). This trade surplus has been accompanied by persistent current account surpluses, which reached $150 billion in 1994. To this day the US economy continues to absorb approximately one-third of all Japanese exports, while the Japanese economy absorbs only about a quarter of US exports. Moreover, the composition of exports from Japan to the United States (almost wholly manufactured goods, and chiefly automobiles and electronics) as against imports from the United States (mainly agricultural products and raw materials) provides further evidence of the imbalance in the relationship.

Escalating trade conflict and 'unfair' trade practices

This, then was the backdrop against which US–Japan trade relations played out through the 1960s, 1970s and 1980s. From small beginnings constant trade frictions throughout these years slowly but steadily eroded the confidence of each side in the US–Japan alliance (Bergsten and Noland 1993; Cohen 1998; Destler and

Sato 1982). Combined with the ups-and-downs associated with the unbalanced political and strategic partnership between the two countries, these tensions reached a point where some of the more excitable commentators saw the end of the Cold War as an opportunity for the United States to begin an economic war with Japan (Friedman and LeBard 1991; Olsen 1992).

By this time, however, the 'war' had arguably been under way for some time.[9] In a repeat of a pattern established in 1955, VERs had already been instituted on Japanese exports to the US of steel (1972), television sets (1977), automobiles (1981) and semiconductors (1986). By the late 1980s the US Trade Representative (USTR) was increasingly resorting to use of the 'super 301' clause of the Omnibus Trade and Competitiveness Act of 1988 as a means of bringing 'unfair' Japanese trade practices to an end.[10] Unilateral measures of this sort undercut the limited progress achieved in bilateral trade talks between the two countries launched from the mid-1980s, such as the Market Oriented Sector Specific Talks and the Structural Impediments Initiative. This led to a switch in emphasis by the Clinton administration when a results-oriented approach was adopted for the US–Japan Framework Talks on Bilateral Trade. This aimed to establish market opening by setting numerical targets (or 'voluntary import expansion') in a number of key sectors such as semiconductors, automobiles and auto-parts. So incensed were the Japanese by this high-handed – and essentially unilateralist – approach that for the first time they refused to negotiate further (Maswood 1997).

What is apparent from the steady escalation of trade conflicts and the negotiations that attended them is that US negotiators were slowly zeroing in on what they perceived as the key issue. This was the need to eradicate the source of unfair Japanese trading practices – which in effect meant breaking the close and enduring relationship, or 'iron triangle', between the bureaucracy, big business and the government that, arguably, had existed at least since the Meiji era (Hall *et al.* 1981). This relationship – encapsulated by a variety of commentators as 'Japan Inc.' (Kaplan 1972), the 'capitalist developmental state' (Johnson 1982), 'patterned pluralism' (Muramatsu and Krauss 1987), 'reciprocal consent' (Samuels 1987), 'truncated pyramid' (van Wolferen 1993) and 'crisis and compensation' (Calder 1988a) amongst others – was apparently the disease of which the Japanese trade surplus was the major symptom. As befitted its neomercantilist origins, the disease itself was multifaceted. It combined a one-party state with bureaucratic dominance; big business with small sub-contractors; high productivity with (relatively) low wages; parachuting (*amakudari*) with administrative guidance; import protection with export promotion; subsidies with tax breaks; high savings with low interest rates; a current account surplus with official development assistance (ODA); and pacifism with free-riding.[11] What is more, it worked under both a fixed (1949–70) and a floating exchange rate regime.

From the US perspective the fact that this 'system' was widely perceived to be the source of the Japanese economic 'miracle' of the 1950s and 1960s was less important than the eradication of the US trade deficit with Japan. From the Japanese perspective, however, US efforts to dismantle this winning combination met with resistance from the iron triangle itself and howls of protest from other sections of Japanese society and beyond (Ishihara 1991; Mahathir and Ishihara 1996). Less predictably, it also met with quiet words of encouragement from within Japan. This signalled two things: first that the iron triangle is not and never has been a monolithic entity (Stockwin 1999); and second, that the horse had already bolted.

Contemporary Japanese political economy: between regionalism and globalism

Since the early 1970s, following the Nixon (dollar devaluation, US recognition of China) and oil 'shocks', many Japanese have recognized the need to look beyond their own shores for solutions to the economic dilemmas posed by the 'situational imperatives' faced by their country. Moreover, almost three decades of high speed growth combined with the pressures associated with membership of the US alliance had begun to severely strain the domestic political settlement and the security partnership with the United States. On the domestic scene these strains showed themselves in protests against environmental pollution, poor living conditions, government corruption and Japan's role in the Vietnam war. On the international scene they pointed to a gradual divergence of Japanese and US interests and the pursuit of a more proactive Japanese foreign policy (Kelly 2002: ch. 4). These tensions were exacerbated by the end of double digit growth that coincided with (but was not reducible to) the Nixon and oil shocks.

As a consequence, a series of broad movements within the Japanese political economy can be detected. First, Japanese workers have been forced to raise productivity while accepting a falling rate of return on their labour. On the one hand this is associated with the adoption of new working practices under 'lean production'. On the other it is associated with falling union membership as a consequence of new contractual arrangements, the employment of non-unionized staff, intimidation of individual enterprise unions, and privatization of public sector industries including the militant rail industry. By 1994, these pressures had led to the first fall in average earnings in the private sector for 44 years and to unprecedented levels of unemployment. Combined with the ageing of the Japanese population, this points to a long-term fall in the savings rate in Japan and thus to a fall in both the current account and trade surpluses (Itoh 1999).

Second, the dynamic, export-oriented manufacturers have moved much of their operations offshore – mainly to Asia and the United States but also to Europe. This movement is the result of both push and pull factors (which are, of course, related). Push factors include the shift to a system of floating exchange rates (and the dramatic realignment in currency values following the Plaza Accords in particular), high wages and other costs associated with a mature industrial economy such as the anti-pollution legislation passed in the late 1970s. Pull factors include access to capital, low wages, less regulation, proximity to raw materials and, of course, the avoidance of tariff barriers. Moreover, the Japanese economy as a whole continues to move up the value-added ladder, and has become predominantly service-based. In combination, these developments have shifted the traditionally inward orientation of business outwards towards the global market. Thus, protectionist sentiments remain – especially in agriculture – but have become more muted.

Third, the Japanese bureaucracy has taken steps to mitigate the domestic effects of high speed economic growth through introduction of new legislation on pollution, for example, and publication of a number of reports on the state of Japanese society. The recommendations contained within these reports are designed to move the country away from images associated with 'Japan Inc.' and towards a vision for Japan as a 'lifestyle power'. Similar plans and reports took a wider focus, and envisaged an integrated Asian economy with Japan at its centre (Hatch and Yamamura 1996; Kelly 2002: ch. 8). Moreover, the stifling regulatory framework has been partially dismantled so as to promote innovation, and the vast array of visible barriers to trade has been completely done away with. By the late 1980s Japan arguably had the lowest tariff barriers of all the leading industrial countries (Komiya and Itoh 1988: 214–16). Finally, the whole bureaucratic structure was overhauled in 2001. The infamous Ministry of International Trade and Industry was renamed the Ministry of Economy, Trade and Industry and given an even wider mandate – and arguably even more power (Elder 2003).

Fourth, the fortunes of the traditional party of government, the LDP, have taken a turn for the worse as a series of corruption scandals, perceived mishandling of the economy and factional in-fighting led to its ousting from power in 1993. It has since returned to power but primarily as part of a series of coalition governments and only on the promise of genuine electoral and economic reform (Curtis 1999; Stockwin 1999).

Fifth, the Japanese government has taken a (slightly) more independent line on foreign policy. This is evident in, for example, Japan's early diplomatic re-engagement with the PRC following the events in Tiananmen Square in 1984, its handling of relations with North Korea and its refusal to ostracize the government of Myanmar. It is also evident in Japan's sponsorship of a concept of 'comprehensive security' which places economics alongside strategic issues in importance as both cause and solution to a range of conflicts. This has fed into a number of issues including Japanese attempts to gain a seat at the UN Security Council (UNSC), its sponsorship of the infamous *East Asian Miracle* report by the World Bank (1993), the Asian Monetary Fund proposal, the creation of the ASEAN Regional Forum (ARF), participation in the ASEAN + 3 meetings and other similar initiatives (Chapter 17 by Berger; Kelly 2002).

In combination these movements leave Japan very much more exposed to the vagaries of the global political economy than has been the case since 1945 and very much more willing to engage proactively with it. In other words, it is in the process of casting aside its former hesitancy and distancing itself from its former reputation as a 'reactive' state (Calder 1988b). This has clearly had both positive and negative effects for the country.

On the negative side the historically weak position of labour within Japan has been weakened still further. Significantly, even the traditionally cosseted 'salaryman' has felt the cold winds of economic rationalization. In the short term this has fed into the trade imbalance between Japan and the rest of the world – and therefore into US–Japan trade conflict – since Japanese manufacturing produces far more goods than can be absorbed by domestic demand. Thus, even though there has been a fundamental shift away from the philosophy of neomercantilism in Japan's industrial and trade policy, Japan's trade surplus has remained. Nevertheless, as noted above, the long-term trend will be towards lower trade surpluses and therefore, presumably, less trade conflict with the United States.[12] In addition, there is no question that Japan's 'bubble' economy of the late 1980s and the subsequent banking crisis and 'lost decade' of the 1990s was a result of ill-advised speculation facilitated by relaxation of formerly strict regulations in the financial sector (Cerny 2001). The Japanese economy is still a long way from over-coming the effects of this crisis, and has been further hampered by the fall-out from the East Asian economic crisis of 1997 (Yamamura 1997).

On the positive side Japan can bask in the glory of being the world's biggest aid donor and a major prop to the US economy through its huge public and private investments in that country. It is a major player on the world stage through its par-ticipation in the International Monetary Fund and the World Bank, and in East Asia in particular through such mechanisms as the Asian Development Bank and the ASEAN+3 grouping. It is, moreover, no longer quite so reliant on the US economy, having diversified both its investments and its trade into Asia and Europe.

Japan's trade policy: between regionalism and globalism

All this has impacted on Japanese trade policy in three main ways. First, it has highlighted the potential benefits of membership of the World Trade Organization (WTO). Second, it has highlighted the potential benefits of regional trade agree-ments; and third, it has highlighted the benefits of linkage between Japanese trade and global security and development.

Taking these in reverse order, as part of its promotion of the concept of com-prehensive security it is clear that Japan has compensated for its inability to make a direct contribution to the resolution of military and other conflicts by flexing its huge financial muscles. Through the 1970s, 1980s and 1990s this saddled Japan with a reputation for 'cheque book diplomacy' which left its hands clean but its pockets dirty – as Japanese troops remained tucked up in their barracks while other soldiers (mainly from the United States) fought and died on their behalf. Moreover, most of the ODA money apparently found its way back to Japan in the form of (tied) purchases of Japanese goods and services (Yasutomo 1995). These long-standing criticisms combined with US and other complaints concerning Japan's merely financial contribution to the Gulf War of 1991 to spur a change in policy (Kelly 2002: 81–8). Hereafter, Japan would trade with and supply aid to countries only under certain conditions. In each case the target country would be examined for:

(1) the trends of its military expenditures;
(2) the trends of its development and production of weapons of mass destruction and delivery systems;

(3) its export and import of arms;

(4) its efforts at promoting democratization, basic human rights and freedoms and the introduction of market-oriented economic policies (MOFA 1994).

There are a host of problems associated with these criteria and their application, not least of which is the potential effects strict application of them would have in the case of both the PRC and the United States. Nevertheless, the Japanese government is making an effort to stress both the market- and WTO-conforming nature of these criteria and their potential contribution to reducing conflict.

The concept of comprehensive security also lies behind Japan's advocacy of a 'new development strategy', which was endorsed by the OECD in 1996. This advocates a 'comprehensive approach' to development moving beyond its former reliance on ODA to include greater emphasis on trade, market access, institutions and social capital. In concrete terms this has manifested in the TICAD process – a series of conferences deriving their acronym from the first Tokyo International Conference on African Development, held in 1993.

Turning to the second theme identified above, in common with other countries and regions (see Chapter 10 by Phillips) Japan has finally embraced the 'wisdom' of bilateral regional trade agreements (RTAs). It became the first Northeast Asian country to sign an RTA in 2002 when its Economic Partnership Agreement with Singapore came into effect. This has been followed by proposals for other such agreements between Japan and Korea, Japan and Mexico and Japan and ASEAN (Krauss 2003), and even for a Northeast Asia Free Trade Area with South Korea and the PRC.

The avowed aim of these moves is to promote closer economic partnership with Asian countries (METI 2002). This is no doubt true. The recovery of the Asian economies from the effects of the crisis of 1997 is well under way, and continued strong growth in the PRC as well as its accession to the WTO suggests a continuation of this broad trend, even given the problems noted by Breslin (Chapter 19). Moreover, Japan and the PRC are now effectively competing with one another for economic leadership of the region and RTAs are seen as one way in which Japan can continue to compete with its giant neighbour. One (other) form this competition might take may be in the relationships Japan seeks to build with developing countries. The implications for the politics of international trade of the 'rise' of the G20/21 are not yet clear (see Narlikar 2003). However, both China and Japan are likely to try to take advantage of it in some way or another. Finally, the content of the Japan–Singapore agreement is illuminating since it deals chiefly with trade in high value-added goods and specifically leaves out trade in agricultural products. This ties in with Japan's promotion of its high-tech industries and services sector.

There are, however, other motivations. The promotion of RTAs between Japan and other countries and groupings plays into a wider policy of regional multilateralism that has been underway for some time (Kelly 2002; Krauss 2003). This has seen Japan heavily involved in the creation of the Asia Pacific Economic Cooperation (APEC) grouping and, in the strategic sphere, the ARF. More recently, the stalling of the APEC process has played a part in its participation in the ASEAN + 3 arrangement (see Chapter 17 by Berger). In a sense, therefore, Japan's pursuit of RTAs must be seen as a 'natural' outgrowth of its outward-oriented economic policies and as part of its efforts to promote free trade at multiple levels.

Finally, Japanese participation in RTAs is a response to similar moves by the United States and Europe. The European Union (EU) continues to expand eastward, and has launched an ambitious initiative – the Asia-Europe Meeting – designed to tap into East Asian economic dynamism (Gilson 2000). It is no secret, moreover, that the United States is using such agreements to put pressure on its major trading partners to push ahead with the agenda of the WTO. By playing its part in this 'competition in liberalization' (Gordon 2003: 105) Japan is reaffirming its free-trading credentials, keeping up with its major allies and competing against them.

Turning to the third and final theme identified above, Japan is making use of the WTO and its dispute settlement mechanism in particular. Membership of and leadership in the WTO is an important part of Japan's wider mission to be seen as a major player on the world stage. Again, lacking a key military role and a seat on the UNSC Japan has to make the most of its membership in the key global economic institutions such as the WTO. This will become more difficult now that the PRC has joined the organization.

Be that as it may, in stark contrast to its former reluctance to use the mechanisms available to it under the GATT Japan has frequently resorted to the dispute settlement mechanism of the WTO. The reasons for this are complex but can be summarized as a desire on behalf of Japan to use the WTO as both a 'sword' and a 'shield' in the conduct of its trade diplomacy – and particularly that with the United States (Pekkanen 2003a). In this way Japan has sought to gain legal backing, and therefore legitimacy, for both its domestic economic arrangements and its challenges to the 'unfair' trade practices of its trading partners (Pekkanen 2001, 2003b).

Conclusion

In policy terms Japan's trade strategy appears, at first glance, to be converging towards the 'norm' set by its major trading partners in Europe and North America. Domestic pressures for reform have joined long-standing demands by the United States in particular that Japan open its economy to foreign competition and jettison the restrictive practices associated with the operation of the 'iron triangle'. This points to the end of Japan's (neo)mercantilism as it embarks upon a brighter future as an outward-oriented global player fully compliant with and active within the WTO. More widely, it implies that Japan has finally 'caught up' with the leading industrial countries and has thrown off the double stigma of being both a 'latecomer' to and an 'outlier' in the global economy.

Two things are certain. First there has been a significant – though not total – move away from the protectionist mindset and towards acceptance of the benefits of freer if not free trade. Second, despite this changing mindset conflict and cooperation over the future direction of the Japanese political economy continue to characterize relations between the government, bureaucracy and business. This leads to the conclusion that Japanese capitalism may well be converging with its Anglo-Saxon rival but that it has not yet fully done so.

The flip side of this argument is also interesting. There has been significant movement by Japan's trading partners, and particularly the United States, towards protectionism. Under the fig leaf of such concepts as 'fair' and 'managed' trade, as well as the development of new trade theories defending strategic trade policy and industrial policy (Krugman 1995) Japan's major rivals, and the United States in particular, have effectively moved onto Japan's traditional ground. This situation is replete with ironies. It does, however, provide further explanation for both Japan's greater activism at the WTO and its successful use of the dispute settlement mechanism. Moreover, it paints the US strategy of 'competition in liberalization' through proliferating RTAs in a particularly bad light. This may mean that the future of the trading system and of the WTO is a gloomy one. What it certainly means is that Japan will be playing a more active role in global trade politics for the foreseeable future.

In terms of theoretical considerations the foregoing analysis suggests the following conclusions. First, the iron triangle that forms the centrepiece of the majority of analyses of Japan's industrial and trade policies is both an outgrowth and descendant of other institutions (both narrowly and broadly conceived) that were themselves, arguably, forged in the transition from a feudal to a capitalist society. As such, the erosion of its cohesion and power are to be expected, as is the emergence of other institutions and patterns of authority with power over the trade policymaking process. Indeed, the Koizumi reforms confirm that patterns of authority within Japan extend far beyond the boundaries of the Japanese state as traditionally conceived (see Neary 2002). It is not just the big ministries and institutions that are being re-shaped but regional, local and sectoral institutions as well – some of which have only tenuous formal links with Tokyo.

Second, the debate over free trade versus protectionism is far from over. Rather, a middle ground is forming around several philosophical and conceptual positions. The United States is defending 'fair', 'managed' or 'strategic' trade on the basis of the existing 'unfairness' of the trading practices and policies of its major trading partners. Free trade is still the eventual (yet increasingly rhetorical) aim, but in the meantime the United States has adopted a position from which it can both defend its own economy and strike out at others. Europe resolutely defends its 'social market' orientation, even in the face of serious internal tensions and dissent. Japan, on the other hand, is moving away from its mercantile past while at the same time continuing to protect certain politically sensitive industries and chiefly agriculture. It is, moreover, promoting its 'brand' of capitalism and particular concepts of security and development in such a way as to undercut the US position. In so doing it is playing to national, regional and global galleries.

Third, trade and trade policy are nested within a wider policy framework that must be historically sensitive and take into account events and movements at the domestic, international and global levels in the economic, political, social and strategic spheres. In other words a narrow focus on the institutions of trade policymaking, on the economic sphere, or on hegemonic states will not provide comprehensive understanding of the politics of international trade.

Fourth, and finally, it is now necessary to look beyond the state as the only actor in international politics. In attempting to sketch the 'big picture' this chapter has not focused in much detail on the minutiae of the trading relationships established by Japanese firms over the years. What is clear, however, is that the kind of tie-ups elaborated by Breslin (Chapter 19) increasingly characterize the Japanese economy as well. Berger (Chapter 17) alludes to the most famous of these – the purchase by Renault of a controlling stake in Nissan and the radical shake-up that followed. Many more examples could be cited (see Kelly 2002). It is also worth recalling the huge shift of Japan's productive capacity to Southeast Asia, North America and Europe from the 1980s onwards, and the complex network of relationships that has built up between Japanese and 'foreign' firms as a result (Hatch and Yamamura 1996; Katzenstein and Shiraishi 1997).

As Breslin points out, this fragmentation of the production structure makes a mockery of trade statistics. The important point here, however, is that not only does this signal the end of the 'national champion' and the beginning of a 'global web' of production based on technological change and the search for value-added (Reich 1991), but also that understanding trade politics demands a more nuanced understanding of the identity, place and role of the key actors in policymaking. The image of an 'iron triangle' dominating Japanese politics is no longer appropriate; not only because the 'triangle' began to break apart as long ago as the 1970s but also because even though the state as traditionally conceived remains central the 'governance' of Japan is conducted from beyond as well as from within its shores – by global institutions and by a global capitalist class acting upon, within and through the 'traditional' mechanisms of Japanese government (Gill and Law 1989; Murphy 2000). As other contributions to this book make clear, in this Japan is not alone.

Notes

1. On what follows see amongst others Cohen (1973), Dower (1999) and Kelly (2002).
2. This was due to a lack of language skills amongst the US forces of occupation and an unfamiliarity with the structures and processes (both formal and informal) at work within Japanese society.
3. The LDP was the party of government between 1955 and 1993. After a brief hiatus it returned to power in the mid-1990s and has remained there ever since – albeit for most of that time in coalition with other parties.
4. The chief link – and transmission belt – between these 'two' economies was the subcontracting system. In times of trouble the *keiretsu* simply instructed sub-contractors to cut costs and/or to accept deferred payment. One outcome of all this was, of course, unemployment.
5. See Hellmann (1988).
6. For good surveys of this period see Komiya and Itoh (1988) and Okimoto (1988).
7. This Treaty of Mutual Cooperation between the United States and Japan was a revision of the 1951 Security Treaty between the United States and Japan. For the texts of these treaties see Hook *et al.* (2001: 469–73).

8. Japanese manufacturers were also using US technology illegally and more importantly, to aid the enemy – as exemplified by Toshiba's infamous sale of milling machines to the Soviet Union in the early 1980s. These machines enabled the Soviets to produce much quieter propellers for their submarines and thus avoid detection by their US counterparts.
9. For extended discussions see Cohen (1998), and Cohen *et al.* (2003: 230–44).
10. This clause allows the USTR to name countries engaged in 'unfair' trade practices, and to raise tariff barriers against all exports from that country if the unfair practices are still in place after 18 months. By 1992 Japan had been cited 13 times under this clause and its predecessor (which only allowed individual products/sectors to be so targeted).
11. *Amakudari* (literally 'descent from heaven') is a Japanese term that refers to the (common) practice of civil servants moving to the boards of companies or other organizations on retirement. See Schaede (1995).
12. As Cohen *et al.* note (2003: 243–4) there are other reasons for this, chief amongst which is the complete reversal in economic fortunes of the two countries in the 1990s. The new focus by both countries on the PRC is also particularly significant.

References

Albert, M. (1993) *Capitalism vs. Capitalism*, New York: Four Walls, Eight Windows.

Argy, V. and Stein, L. (1997) *The Japanese Economy*, Basingstoke: Macmillan.

Beasley, W.G. (1987) *Japanese Imperialism 1894–1945*, London: Oxford University Press.

Bergsten, C.F. and Noland, M. (1993) *Reconcilable Differences? United States–Japan Economic Conflict*, Washington, DC: Institute for International Economics.

Calder, K.E. (1988a) *Crisis and Compensation: Public Policy and Political Stability in Japan, 1949–1986*, Princeton, NJ: Princeton University Press.

Calder, K.E. (1988b) 'Japanese Foreign Economic Policy Formation: Explaining the Reactive State', *World Politics*, 40, 4: 517–41.

Calman, D. (1992) *The Nature and Origins of Japanese Imperialism*, London: Routledge.

Cerny, P.G. (2001) 'Financial Globalization and the Unravelling of the Japanese Model', in Hook, Glenn D. and Hasegawa Harukiyo (eds) *The Political Economy of Japanese Globalization*, London: Sheffield Centre for Japanese Studies/Routledge.

Cohen, J.B. (1973) *Japan's Economy in War and Reconstruction*, Westport, CT: Greenwood Press.

Cohen, S.D. (1998) *An Ocean Apart: Explaining Three Decades of U.S.–Japan Trade Frictions*, Westport, CT: Praeger.

Cohen, S.D., Blecker, R.A. and Whitney, P.D. (2003) *Fundamentals of US Foreign Trade Policy: Economics, Politics, Laws and Issues*, Boulder, CO.: Westview Press, 2nd edition.

Curtis, G.L. (1999) *The Logic of Japanese Politics: Leaders, Institutions, and the Limits of Change*, New York: Columbia University Press.

Destler, I.M. and Hideo Sato (1982) *Coping with US–Japanese Economic Conflicts*, Lexington, MA.: Lexington Books.

Dore, R.P. (1959) *Land Reform in Japan*, Oxford: Oxford University Press.

Dower, J. (1999) *Embracing Defeat: Japan in the Aftermath of World War II*, London: Allen Lane.

Elder, M. (2003) 'METI and Industrial Policy in Japan: Change and Continuity', in Schaede Ulrike and Grimes William (eds) *Japan's Managed Globalization: Adapting to the Twenty-first Century*, Armonk, NY: M.E. Sharpe, pp. 159–90.

Friedman, G. and LeBard, M. (1991) *The Coming War with Japan*, New York: St. Martin's Press.

Gill, S. and Law, D. (1989) 'Global Hegemony and the Structural Power of Capital', *International Studies Quarterly*, 33: 475–99.

Gilson, J. (2000) *Japan and the European Union: A Partnership for the 21st Century?*, Basingstoke: Macmillan.

Gordon, A. (ed.) (1993) *Postwar Japan as History*, Berkeley, CA: University of California Press.

Gordon, B.K. (2003) 'A High-Risk Trade Policy', *Foreign Affairs*, 82, 4: 105–18.

Hadley, E.M. (1970) *Antitrust in Japan*, Princeton, NJ: Princeton University Press.

Hall, J.W. *et al.* (eds) (1981) *Japan Before Tokugawa: Political Consolidation and Economic Growth, 1500–1650*, Princeton, NJ: Princeton University Press.

Hart, J.A. (1992) *Rival Capitalists: International Competitiveness in the United States, Japan, and Western Europe*, Ithaca and London: Cornell University Press.

Hatch, W. and Kozo Yamamura (1996) *Asia in Japan's Embrace: Building A Regional Production Alliance*, Cambridge: Cambridge University Press.

Hellmann, D.C. (1988) 'Japanese Politics and Foreign Policy: Elitist Democracy Within an American Greenhouse', in Takashi Inoguchi and Okimoto Daniel I. (eds) *The Political Economy of Japan Volume Two*, Stanford: Stanford University Press, pp. 345–78.

Hook, G. (1996) *Militarization and Demilitarization in Contemporary Japan*, London: Routledge.

Hook, G., Gilson, J., Hughes, C.W. and Dobson, H. (2001) *Japan's International Relations: Politics, Economics and Security*, London: Sheffield Centre for Japanese Studies/Routledge.

Ishihara, S. (1991) *The Japan That Can Say No*, London: Simon and Schuster.

Islam, S. (1993) 'Foreign Aid and Burdensharing: Is Japan Free Riding to a Coprosperity Sphere in Pacific Asia?', in Frankel Jeffrey and Kahler Miles (eds) *Regionalism and Rivalry*, Chicago: The University of Chicago Press, pp. 321–89.

Itoh, M. (1999) 'Trade Imbalance, Trade Frictions and Maintaining a Liberal Trade Regime in the Asia-Pacific: Recent Trends in Japanese Trade Policies', *The Pacific Review*, 12, 2: 319–31.

Johnson, C. (1982) *MITI and the Japanese Miracle: The Growth of Industrial Policy, 1925–1975*, Stanford, CA: Stanford University Press.

Johnson, C. (1995) *Japan: Who Governs? The Rise of the Developmental State*, London and New York: W.W. Norton and Co.

Kaplan, E. (1972) *Japan: The Government–Business Relationship*, Washington, DC: US Department of Commerce.

Katzenstein, P.J. and Takashi Shiraishi (eds) (1997) *Network Power*, Ithaca, NY: Cornell University Press.

Kelly, D. (2002) *Japan and the Reconstruction of East Asia*, Basingstoke: Palgrave.

Komiya, R. and Motoshige Itoh (1988) 'Japan's International Trade and Trade Policy, 1955–1984', in Takashi Inoguchi and Okimoto Daniel I. (eds) *The Political Economy of Japan Volume Two*, Stanford, CA: Stanford University Press, pp. 173–224.

Krauss, E.S. (2003) 'The US, Japan, and Trade Liberalization: From Bilateralism to Regional Multilateralism to Regionalism', *The Pacific Review*, 16, 3: 307–29.

Krugman, P.R. (ed.) (1995) *Strategic Trade Policy and the New International Economics*, Cambridge, MA: MIT Press.

Mahathir, M. and Ishihara, Shintaro (1996) *The Voice of Asia: Two Leaders Discuss the Coming Century*, Tokyo: Kōdansha International.

Manglapus, R. (1976) *Japan in Southeast Asia*, New York: Carnegie Endowment for International Peace.

Marshall, B.K. (1967) *Capitalism and Nationalism in Prewar Japan: The Ideology of the Business Elite, 1868–1941*, Stanford, CA: Stanford University Press.

Maswood, S.J. (1997) 'Does Revisionism Work? US Trade Strategy and the 1995 US–Japan Auto Dispute', *Pacific Affairs*, 70, 4: 533–54.

METI (Ministry of Economy, Trade, and Industry) (2002) *2002 Report on the WTO Consistency of Trade Policies by Major Trading Partners*, Tokyo: METI.

MOFA (Ministry of Foreign Affairs) (1994) *Japan's Official Development Assistance*, Tokyo: Association for Promotion of International Cooperation.

Moore, J. (1983) *Japanese Workers and the Struggle for Power, 1945–1947*, Wisconsin: The University of Wisconsin Press.

Muramatsu, M. and Krauss, E. (1987) 'The Conservative Party Line and the Development of Patterned Pluralism', in Kozo Yamamura and Yasukichi Yasuba (eds) *The Political Economy of Japan*, Stanford, CA: Stanford University Press, pp. 263–88.

Murphy, C.N. (2000) 'Global Governance: Poorly Done and Poorly Understood', *International Affairs*, 74, 4: 789–803.

Narlikar, A. (2003) *International Trade and Developing Countries: Bargaining Coalitions in the WTO*, London: Routledge.

Neary, I. (2002) *The State and Politics in Japan*, Cambridge: Polity.

Nester, W.R. (1991) *Japanese Industrial Targeting: The Neomercantilist Path to Economic Superpower*, New York: St. Martin's Press.

Okimoto, D.I. (1988) 'Political Inclusivity: The Domestic Structure of Trade', in Takashi Inoguchi and Okimoto Daniel, I. (eds) *The Political Economy of Japan Volume Two*, Stanford, CA: Stanford University Press, pp. 305–44.

Olsen, E. (1992) 'Target Japan as America's Economic Foe', *Orbis: A Journal of World Affairs*, 36, 3, 441–503.

Pekkanen, S.M. (2001) 'Aggressive Legalism: The Rules of the WTO and Japan's Emerging Trade Strategy', *The World Economy*, 24, 5: 707–37.

Pekkanen, S.M. (2003a) 'Sword and Shield: The WTO Dispute Settlement System and Japan', in Schaede Ulrike and Grimes William (eds) *Japan's Managed Globalization: Adapting to the Twenty-first Century*, Armonk, NY: M.E. Sharpe, pp. 77–100.

Pekkanen, S.M. (2003b) 'International Law, Industry and the State: Explaining Japan's Complainant Activities at the WTO', *The Pacific Review*, 16, 3: 285–306.

Pempel, T.J. (1978) 'Japanese Foreign Economic Policy: The Domestic Bases for International Behavior', in Katzenstein, Peter J. (ed.), *Between Power and Plenty: Foreign Economic Policies of Advanced Industrial States*, Madison, WI: University of Wisconsin Press, pp. 139–90.

Pempel, T.J. (1998) *Regime Shift: Comparative Dynamics of the Japanese Political Economy*, Ithaca and London: Cornell University Press.

Pempel, T.J. and Tsunekawa, Keiichi (1979) 'Corporatism without Labour? The Japanese Anomaly', in Schmitter Philippe, C. and Lehmbruch Gerhard (eds) *Trends Toward Corporatist Intermediation*, Beverly Hills, CA: Sage.

Reich, R. (1991) *The Work of Nations: Preparing Ourselves for 21st Century Capitalism*, New York: Knopf.

Samuels, R.J. (1987) *The Business of the Japanese State: Energy Markets in Comparative and Historical Perspective*, Ithaca and London: Cornell University Press.

Schaede, U. (1995) 'The "Old Boy" Network and Government-Business Relationships in Japan', *Journal of Japanese Studies*, 21, 2: 293–317.

Steven, R. (1990) *Japan's New Imperialism*, London: Macmillan.

Stockwin, J.A.A. (1999) *Governing Japan: Divided Politics in a Major Economy*, Oxford: Blackwell, 3rd edition.

Sudo, S. (1992) *The Fukuda Doctrine and ASEAN*, Singapore: Institute of Southeast Asian Studies.

Tsuru, S. (1993) *Japan's Capitalism: Creative Defeat and Beyond*, Cambridge: Cambridge University Press.

van Wolferen, K. (1993) *The Enigma of Japanese Power: People and Politics in a Stateless Nation*, Tokyo: Charles E. Tuttle.

World Bank (1993) *The East Asian Miracle*, Oxford: Oxford University Press for the World Bank.

Yahuda, M. (1996) *The International Politics of the Asia-Pacific, 1945–1995*, London: Routledge.

Yamamura, K. (1997) 'The Japanese Political Economy after the "Bubble": Plus Ça Change?', *Journal of Japanese Studies*, 23, 2: 291–331.

Yasutomo, D.T. (1995) *The New Multilateralism in Japan's Foreign Policy*, New York: St. Martin's Press.

Zysman, J. (1983) *Governments, Markets, and Growth: Financial Systems and the Politics of Industrial Change*, Ithaca and London: Cornell University Press.

19
China's Trade Policy
Shaun Breslin

When China embarked on a process of economic reform in 1978, it was rare to find Chinese-made goods on sale in the West. China was not a major trading nation, and what it did trade was overwhelmingly in primary produce with other developing nations. Today, the 'Made in China' stamp is common throughout the world, China's trade surplus with the United States is greater than the entire US trade deficit in 1996, and China was the world's biggest holder of foreign exchange reserves in 2003. Indeed, the growth of Chinese exports is raising serious concerns in many countries over the impact on domestic employment:

> From Tokyo to Milan, from Mexico City to Chicago, everyone is wondering whether China can continue to grow so fast and how their own jobs and businesses will be affected if it does. (Sala-I-Martin 2003: 11)

In overseeing this transition from relative isolation to engagement, the Chinese leadership pursued a very simple and logical strategy – trade was encouraged where it was deemed beneficial, and resisted where it was perceived to threaten domestic Chinese producers. This resulted in a dualistic structure with a relatively closed domestic economy alongside a relatively open 'processed' trade, centred along China's coastal provinces. But by the end of the 1990s, the policy of defending domestic producers whilst promoting export industries was facing considerable challenges – both domestic and external. These challenges, best epitomized by the protracted negotiations over China's World Trade Organisation (WTO) entry, are not only significant in themselves, but also highlight key tensions over strategy for the liberalization of the Chinese economy. As such, while this chapter focuses on explaining the growth of Chinese trade in the post-Mao era, it also considers what the WTO entry debate tells us about the trajectory of the Chinese reform process, the domestic context of internationalization and the implications for future state–society relations in China.

Opening China

There is a tendency to describe China in the Maoist period as a 'closed economy'. This popular perception rather exaggerates the level of isolation, and is primarily a product of equating the capitalist world with the international economy. As Zhang (1998: 26–31) has demonstrated, while China did look to self-reliance where possible in economic development, foreign trade did play a role 'as a balancing sector' of the Chinese economy. Nevertheless, despite the fact that trade increased after 1949, it is fair to say that China was not a significant player in the global economy during the Maoist era. After China's break from the Soviet Union and the gradual and moderate programme of re-engagement with the West in the 1970s, trade did increase, but trade volumes remained relatively low. Total Chinese trade was a meagre US$4.8 billion in 1971, and even after an almost five-fold expansion in trade, still only totalled US$20.6 billion in 1978 (Howell 1993).

But 1978 marked a watershed in Chinese economic policy. The initial moderate reforms initiated in 1978 gave only a strictly limited role for international economic interaction, and China's re-integration into the global economy was initially a slow and gradual affair. Indeed, in many respects, China's re-engagement with the global economy only really takes off in earnest in the early 1990s. But whilst rather modest compared with later changes, the adoption of a more open policy towards the global economy in 1978 marked a fundamental ideological shift that was a prerequisite for all that was to follow.

At the risk of oversimplification, we can divide the opening of China into four stages. The first, from 1978 to 1986 marked the gradual opening of parts of China to the global economy. Following the Third Plenum of the 11th Central Committee in 1978, China opened four Special Economic Zones (SEZs) with the (limited) freedom to conduct international economic relations.[1] At the Fifth National People's Congress in July 1979, the government passed a supporting law which provided a legal basis for the existence of joint ventures and foreign investment. These SEZs were conceived as 'windows on the world' for China – allowing international economic contacts to grow, but limiting them to specific areas to allay fears from political conservatives that such contacts would lead to 'bourgeois spiritual pollution' (Bachman 1988). The initial success of these SEZs in attracting investment resulted in considerable lobbying from other coastal cities to be allowed the same access to the global economy. In 1984, the government decided to open 5 more cities to trade, but as a result of lobbying from local leaders, a total of 14 cities were instead 'opened up' (Hamrin 1990: 83).

The second key change came in 1986, with what has now come to be known as the 'twenty-two regulations'. These regulations created a more beneficial environment for foreign investors including lower fees for labour and rent, tax rebates for exporters and made it possible for foreign companies to convert the Renminbi (RMB)[2] into foreign exchange and repatriate profits. It also extended the joint venture contracts beyond the original 50-year limit, and created a legal basis for wholly foreign owned enterprises (rather than investors having to sign a joint venture with a Chinese partner). This move considerably increased the attraction of investing in China to produce exports for other markets. While foreign invested enterprises only accounted for 2 per cent of exports and 6 per cent of imports before 1986, the figure increased to 48 per cent and 52 per cent respectively by 2000 (Braunstein and Epstein 2002: 23).

The third key change came in 1992. From 1989, Premier Li Peng instituted a retrenchment policy with a limited reversal of reform in an attempt to bring inflation under control. China's international image was also somewhat tarnished (to say the least) by the 1989 Tiananmen incident, and the resulting 'conservative' wind in policy. In a tour of southern China in 1992 Deng Xiaoping effectively set policy in an ad hoc manner praising the emergence of proto-capitalist practices in open areas and calling for a new policy of rapid economic reform and further opening. Following Deng's exhortations, the Party Congress in October 1992 formally declared that China now had a 'socialist market economy'. As with the original decision taken to open China at the 1978 Third Plenum, the key issue here is the ideational change promoted by key leaders to pursue a more open and marketized strategy rather than specific legal changes.

In many respects, it was only in 1993 that China began to emerge as a global trading power. From 1993, exports increased by 60 per cent in two years (53 per cent in real terms), and doubled in the space of five years.[3] In the process, a US$12.2 billion trade deficit in 1993 was transformed into a US$5.4 billion surplus the following year, with the trade surplus rising to US$40.3 billion in 1997. And it is no coincidence that 1993 also marked the emergence of China as a major recipient of Foreign Direct Investment (FDI) – indeed there was more FDI into China in 1993 than in the entire preceding 14 years of reform put together. China constructed a remarkably liberal internationalized export regime built on encouraging FDI to produce exports for external markets – indeed, as China joined the WTO, some 60 per cent of all imports came into China tariff free in the form of components that were processed and subsequently re-exported as finished goods.[4] But this liberal export regime sat alongside a relatively closed and protected domestic trading regime designed to protect domestic producers from competition. As such, any analyses of Chinese trade should start by following Naughton (2000) and dividing the focus of analyses into two.

The fourth and to date unfinished stage began with China's entry into the WTO at the Doha Ministerial round of 2001. Whilst China's attempts to join the WTO (previously GATT) had been ongoing since 1986, the final terms on which China joined marked a key turning point. For much of the negotiating period, Chinese aims had been to defend the dualistic trade regime outlined above. But the terms of the agreement signed in 2001 mark yet another key ideational change, backed up with the force of an international agreement. Far from protecting domestic producers, the agreement should enforce change and reform on domestic producers, ending the system of promoting exporting industries while protecting the domestic. Whether the terms of the agreement will be fully implemented however, remains to be seen.

Chinese export growth – who benefits?

In assessing China's re-engagement with the global economy, we should recognize that uneven regional development has been a key characteristic of the Chinese reform process. FDI into China and exports from China are concentrated in

Table 19.1 Provincial share of national FIE exports

Guangdong	44
Shanghai	12
Jiangsu	11
Fujian	7
Shandong	7
Tianjin	5
Liaoning	5
Zhejiang	4
Coastal 8	95

nine coastal provinces accounting for roughly 80 per cent of the total of both investment and exports. Even this does not tell the full story as Guangdong Province alone accounts for roughly 40 per cent of national exports. If we put investment and exports together, then Table 19.1 shows the regional imbalance in exports by foreign invested enterprises.

'Domestic' Chinese exports and protectionism

Chinese state actors at both national and local levels have taken a proactive role in promoting export industries. National and local authorities have introduced a number of measures to support exporters, and to protect domestic enterprises from international competition (particularly those in the state owned and collective sectors). For example, they have eased access to investment capital by providing loans through the creation of specialist banks, and provided a number of tax exemptions and other incentives for exporters.

The government has also protected key domestic sectors by using import plans, licenses and quotas and retained some of the highest import tariffs in the world (though these have been steadily reduced). In 1995, the Office of the United States Trade Representative (USTR) drew up the 'November Roadmap' outlining the areas in which the US government thought China was 'unfairly' protecting domestic producers, and where changes would have to be made before WTO entry could be considered. In addition to 'normal' trade issues such as tariffs, trading rights and access to 'closed' sectors of the Chinese economy, USTR pressed for a number of other reforms. For example, incomplete currency convertibility resulted in restricted access to foreign currency and also meant that converting and repatriating profits is difficult if not impossible; the lack of transparency in China's policymaking (and in particular, the monopoly of the state news-agency, Xinhua, in the dissemination of economic information) placed outsiders at a disadvantage; intellectual and property right infringement was costing millions to copyright owners; and the differential application of the fiscal system where local companies typically negotiated tax free deals with the local government, effectively provided a hidden fiscal tariff for foreign companies.

Furthermore, US trade officials claimed that the lack of full price reform in China also acted as a hidden state subsidy for those Chinese producers in the state sector, or private enterprises that retained close and warm links with the state administration. They paid cheap state set prices, while external actors were forced to pay the higher market rate (Barshefsky 1999). Chinese enterprises were also supported through massive subsidies, which often took the form of 'loans' from government or the banking system that will never be repaid.

Another key area of controversy was the 'restructuring' of China's foreign exchange rate system in 1994. The Chinese currency, RMB, is not fully convertible on international markets, and exchange rates remain under central government management and control. However, in the early 1990s, a market rate of sorts appeared as the government relaxed regulations on currency exchanges. To facilitate increased international economic contacts, a number of 'swap shops' were established where individuals could trade RMB for foreign currency. Although the official exchange rate at the time was RMB5.7 to the dollar, the swap shop rate was influenced by supply and demand, and was closer to RMB9 to the dollar.

Faced with this disparity, and a record trade deficit in 1993, the government 'unified' the two rates in 1994. This essentially entailed moving to the swap shop rate, with the new exchange rate of RMB8.7 to the dollar apparently representing a 50 per cent devaluation. For some observers, this devaluation was the starting point for regional financial chaos that resulted in the financial crises of 1997 (Bergsten 1997; Makin 1997). But in reality, the headline figure of a 50 per cent devaluation misses the point that most companies were already using the market rate for the majority of their foreign currency trading. As such, the headline 50 per cent devaluation was probably nearer 20–30 per cent for most exporters – and Fernald *et al.* (1998: 2–3) put the figure at a mere 7 per cent.

Nevertheless, combined with the other incentives offered to exporters, by 1994 China was an increasingly important source of exports. And while it is not the case that trade relationships in Asia represent a zero-sum game, it is true that China was increasingly competing with other export oriented states for foreign investment, and competed with the same states for access to the key lucrative markets of the United States, Japan and the European Union (EU). Fernald *et al.* (1998) argue that the date shows that the growth of Chinese trade did not impact on exports from other regional states. However, the Japan External Trade Organization has disaggregated overall figures and suggested that there is a correlation with the rise of Chinese exports to the United States and Japan of specific goods, and the decline in exports of those same goods from regional states.

In addition, calculations by World Bank economists (Kawai and Bhattasali 2001) suggest that China's entry into the WTO imply that Southeast and South Asian nations will suffer as investment and trade is further diverted into China. In essence, the closer the export profile to that of China, the more the state is expected to lose. Indonesia alone is expected to lose US$73 million as a result of China's WTO accession. The impact on certain sectors – notably textiles – will be even more dramatic. In short, these figures question how much room there is in the 'market place' for so many countries searching for the same FDI to produce the same goods for export to the same markets. The potential problem for late developing states emphasizing low costs as a means of attracting investment to spur export led growth is that an even later developer with even lower costs might erode their comparative advantage.

Re-exports and the processing trade

Those companies who primarily invest in China to access the huge potential domestic market do have an important impact on China's trade profile. In establishing operations in China, the investors often bring with them equipment for their new factories. The desire to encourage such technology imports was one of the main reasons that the Chinese authorities encouraged FDI at the very start of the reform process. As such, these investors have been granted tax exemptions on high-tech imports that the Chinese authorities feel will strengthen the technological base of the Chinese economy.

In addition to technology imports, this type of market-based investment has also generated increased exports from China. By restricting licenses to produce in China, the Chinese authorities have a firm bargaining position with potential investors. They have control over something that the investors want (i.e. access to the Chinese market) and can play off rival bidders against each other. Thus, many investors have been forced to sign agreements to export a proportion of whatever they produce in China – in an admittedly extreme case, Sony agreed to export 70 per cent of their production in China.

Whilst market-based investment has increased China's foreign trade profile – both in terms of the volume and quality of traded goods – the implications of the growth of 'export-based investment' has been even more significant, and has had a profound impact on both the growth and structure of Chinese trade. While the Chinese authorities may have hoped that FDI would help reinvigorate the domestic Chinese economy by using domestically produced components, investors have frequently complained about the poor quality and unreliability of Chinese supplies. Thus, the majority of these investors choose to import key components from existing plants overseas, with the Chinese sites typically only concentrating on labour intensive component assembly.

Thus, export-based investment in China has resulted in a significant growth of both imports (in the form of components) and exports (of finished goods). From being an almost insignificant element of Chinese trade in the 1980s, it accounts for over half of all trade today. This transition is reflected in the structure of Chinese trade. The majority of investors source their components from other production sites in Asia, and sell their finished goods in the developed markets of the West. This has contributed to the situation where China now runs massive trade surplus with the primary destination for processed exports, the United States, and trade deficits with those Asian states that are the source of component imports (notably South Korea and Taiwan).

This brings into question how best to classify the 'nationality' of exports. If components are simply being assembled in China, are the resulting goods really Chinese? Jin Bei (1997), from the Chinese Academy of Social Sciences, argues that we should distinguish between those exports that are produced by 'the national industry' and those that are 'non-domestically manufactured goods'. To count as real Chinese exports, the goods must be produced by Chinese enterprises or by companies where Chinese interests control share ownership. They should be produced with equipment and technology operated by Chinese technicians and with a 'certain figure' of Chinese components. Finally, for Jin Bei, brand-naming is the key to identifying the real 'country of origin'. It 'serves as an important indicator of the "nationality" of a product', and only those goods carrying Chinese trademarks should count as Chinese exports.

Those goods that meet most, but not all, of these requirements, should be called 'para-domestically manufactured goods'. Those exports carrying foreign brand names produced with foreign materials and/or controlled by foreign managers and/or technicians should simply not be considered to be Chinese, as they contribute little to the development of the national economy. He illustrates his argument with a case study of Pierre Cardin shirts produced at the Beijing Shirt Factory. These shirts retailed (at the time) at the equivalent of RMB300 in the West, yet the Beijing shirt factory only received RMB3 to RMB4 for each unit in processing fees. As such, while China was benefiting through jobs and income, the main beneficiaries of Chinese trade in this case was the foreign producer itself.

A more often cited example is the case of Barbie dolls. The case study was first reported in the United States itself in a Los Angeles Times article (Tempest 1996). The fact that the issue was raised in an American source has been seized on by the Chinese authorities, who cited the paper liberally in the State Council (1997) White Paper 'On Sino-US Trade Balance'.[5] Barbie dolls retailed in the US at the time at around US$10 each, even though the unit import cost of each was a mere US$2. Although trade figures show a US$2 import from China, the argument here is that this US$2 exaggerates the value of the dolls to the Chinese economy. The raw materials for the plastics were imported into Taiwan from the Middle East, and the hair similarly exported to Taiwan from Japan. The goods were semi-finished in Taiwan, and only then exported to China for the final stages of production. The real value to the Chinese economy was a mere 35 cents, with the remainder of the US$2 either already accounted for in production costs outside China (65 cents) or in transportation costs (US$1).

The suggestion in this report was that the United States should not calculate China's trade surplus based on the value of the good that leaves China. Rather it should factor in the value of the good as it is imported into China, and consider the other elements to be part of its trade relationship with Taiwan, Japan and the Middle East. In other words, it is unfair, not to say wrong, to simply count the last country in a production chain as the country that you have a trade relationship with for that commodity. In particular, the diffused nature of production means that the final stage in the production chain is usually labour intensive component assembly and/or finishing semi-finished produce – in other words, areas with low value added.

What the report on Barbie dolls did not go on to mention is that Barbie is produced by the Mattel Company which has its headquarters in El Segundo in California. Mattel, (which also produces Fisher Price, Matchbox, Cabbage-patch dolls, Disney, Pooh, Sesame Street, Nickelodeon and others) is only one of a number of US based toy companies that have at least part of their production process located in China. It was the US toy industry that took the lead in trying to instigate a consumer boycott of cheap Chinese imports in the United States. Yet these US based corporations are now making so much use of cheap labour in China to boost corporate profits.

All this does not suggest that China has not benefited from the export of assembled goods. It has created jobs – although typically low wage and low skilled jobs – and generated income. But it does suggest that China has not gained as much as simply looking at bilateral figures for export growth initially suggests. Rather, we need to take a more holistic view of trade figures, and consider the value added, rather than the nominal value, of exports. Indeed, perhaps we need to ignore nationally based statistics altogether, and consider inter- and intra-company trade instead of national trade. Neither should we forget that major western corporations are also benefiting greatly – and perhaps most – from the expansion of the Chinese processing trade.

It should be noted that it is not always easy to identify the extent of the involvement of United States and other western firms in the Chinese economy. As noted above, components are often routed through Hong Kong and/or Taiwan, or are produced by subcontractors in other parts of Asia. In addition, FDI is also often 'routed' through subcontractors in Asia. For example, the biggest shoe factory in the world is in Guangdong Province. This factory is a joint venture with Yu Yuan in Taiwan, and produces sports shoes carrying Reebok, Nike and Adidas labels (Chan 1996). FDI and import statistics indicate the importance of relations with the rest of Asia, and export figures show another Chinese export to Japan and the West – yet the brand names on the goods are associated with major Western corporations.

There are many more examples. When Dr Martins transferred their shoe production to China, they worked through two Taiwanese intermediary companies. Taiwanese computer companies which invest in China almost all produce on Original Equipment Manufacturing (OEM) contracts with US or Japanese firms. And Singapore Flextronics works on behalf of Microsoft, Motorola, Dell, Palm and Sony Erickson in China. In all these cases, the 'Made in China' brand will appear on the good – a good which carries a non-Chinese brand name, but the investment and trade figures will show inter-Asian trade and investment.

Given the size of the Chinese trade surplus with the United States, it is perhaps not surprising that many in the United States are identifying China as the source of unemployment in US industries facing cheap Chinese imports. In calling for the introduction of restrictions on textile imports from China, Lindsey Graham, Republican Senator for South Carolina justified his calls by saying that:

> I have long maintained that China cheats on trade agreements. The practices of Chinese companies and the policies of the Chinese government are illegal and give them an unfair advantage. (Barboza 2003)

I would not suggest that all that is done in China conforms with principles of free trade, or even with what China signed up to when it joined the WTO. But I do suggest that if people like Graham did not just look at bilateral figures based on the nation state as the unit of analysis, and instead considered the real origin of Chinese imports, they might realise that it is US investors that are actually behind at least some of the Chinese exports that are threatening US jobs.

Export growth, employment and social stability

Protecting domestic producers whilst promoting exports was an important tool in the government's strategy to implement what Lau *et al.* (2000) call 'reform without losers'. It not only protected inefficient loss making state owned enterprises (SOEs) from international competition, but it was also an important policy for rural China. On one level, keeping the rural sector protected from international competition ensured relatively stable incomes for agricultural producers. On another level, Zweig (2001: 160) has shown how small scale Township and Village Enterprises (TVEs) 'swapped access to China's domestic markets in return for international capital and access to international markets'. Such TVEs accounted for around half of all Chinese exports in 1996 – though again we should note the uneven geographic impact of this process with rural TVEs in coastal provinces being the main engine of rural export growth.

It is difficult to overestimate how seriously the Chinese government takes the threat to social instability from any increase in urban unemployment. Sporadic and uncoordinated cases of social disorder increased in the late 1990s and into the new century. The majority of these appear to have been demonstrations against the ad hoc nature of taxation in the countryside, but some were responses to proposed closures and mergers of enterprises, to unpaid welfare payments to laid off workers, or to unpaid pensions from closed or loss-making enterprises. With no recourse through the political system, the only way to express a grievance is to take to the streets.

The government is officially committed to keeping urban unemployment below 4 per cent. In reality, Chinese researchers claim the urban unemployment rate is probably already nearer 15 per cent, as workers can be 'laid off' from their jobs for up to three years before they are officially classified as 'unemployed'. Furthermore, a national figure of less than 4 per cent hides significant regional variations. While coastal regions that have attracted FDI have been able to create new jobs for both local workers and migrants from other parts of China, the unemployment problem is more acute in North East China and central provinces such as Hunan. It is suggested that as many as a third of all state employees are surplus to requirements, and perhaps as many as 200 million rural workers are without a job for most of the year. When you simply consider that in 2001, China had a potential workforce of 719 million, with 10 million new entrants into the job market every year, then it is not difficult to see why the issue of employment is so important for the Chinese leadership.

There are a number of explanations for the growth of unemployment (Hu 1999). While the structural causes of unemployment are deep seated and long term, two elements of the economic reforms associated with Zhu Rongji in the second half of the 1990s accelerated unemployment growth. First, Zhu reconfirmed his commitment to restructuring loss-making state owned enterprises in 1997. In addition to resulting in around 10 million laid off workers in two years, fears of potential job losses also dampened domestic demand. This leads us to the second factor. From 1994, Zhu Rongji instituted a deflationary strategy. This programme was highly successful in its own terms. Inflation was brought under control while real GDP growth only fell from 12.6 per cent to 7.8 per cent.

But a key problem here was that the deflationary drive overshot its target. From a high point of over 20 per cent in 1994, the retail price index went into negative figures in 1998. To make matters worse, continued interest rate reductions and other attempts to stimulate demand failed to have any real impact at all (Yu 1999: 11). What is more, the profitability of the TVE sector as a whole began to decline after 1997, with over 70 per cent of all TVEs falling into debt by 1999.

China and the WTO

In many ways, the Chinese experience of reintegration with the global economy provides a positive example for other developing states of how to manage international economic contacts as a means of generating employment and maintaining social stability. It is particularly notable that the maintenance of a relatively closed financial system provided a bulwark against speculative capital flows. As Yu (1999: 15) put it (ironically, just prior to the announcement of an agreement between Zhu Rongji and the United States) in 1999:

> For many years, observers have criticized China's slowness in developing financial markets and liberalizing its capital account. The Chinese government itself was also worried by the slow progress. Rather theatrically, the disadvantage has turned into advantage. Owing to capital controls and the underdevelopment of financial markets and the lack of sophisticated financial instruments, such as stock futures and foreign exchange forwards, RMB escaped the attack by international speculators.

In foreign trade too, China's relative lack of openness has allowed the government to defend perceived national interests by protecting domestic producers and supporting exporters. Perhaps even more than the first generation of late developing states in East Asia, China's re-engagement with the global economy appeared to be a great example of how to reap the benefits of the global market-place whilst maintaining strong defences against the dangers of globalization.

It came as something of a surprise to many (not least many within China itself) that the government moved to end years of at times rather bitter negotiations by signing an agreement with the US government in November 1999 with the aim of facilitating China's entry into the WTO. The Chinese leadership formally notified General Agreement on Tariffs and Trade (GATT) of its decision to seek resumption of its status as a contracting party in July 1986, and negotiations proceeded with the establishment of a GATT working party on China's accession in May 1987. At the outset, the Chinese negotiators attempted to maintain a dualistic approach of defending domestic producers while gaining access to key overseas markets as far as possible. In order to achieve this, the original negotiations were dominated by two issues of not quite semantics.

The first related to whether China was joining or re-joining GATT/WTO. China could, at the onset, have requested to join GATT as a new member as long as two-thirds of members voted in favour. But the Chinese approach was to 'resume' the original membership that was held by the Taiwanese leadership under the name of the Republic of China, which was terminated in 1950. At that time, the Guomindang regime on Taiwan was (largely) recognized as the sole legitimate government of all of China by the international community. Beijing's argument was that as there is only one political entity called China, then the People's Republic of China was entitled to simply resume the original Chinese membership, irrespective of the fact that original membership was signed and terminated by a different (rival) regime. On the other hand, the United States argued that 'members' of the GATT were 'contracting parties' to an international agreement that participants signed on to after an open-ended accession process. As such, there were no country seats as in the UN, and the concept of a 'China Seat' in the GATT was fundamentally misconceived.[6]

An explanation for this semantic and diplomatic juggling is found in the responsibilities of existing WTO members to new signatories – which since the establishment of the WTO, is now laid down in Article XIII of the Marrakesh agreement. In short, existing members do not have to extend full national treatment to new members, including the automatic right to Most Favoured Nation (MFN) status by the United States (in the same way that the Japanese were denied some benefits in 1955). Thus, if China acceded as an 'old' member rejoining, then the United States would have been obliged to automatically extend MFN status to China. If China acceded as a new member, then everything was up for grabs during the negotiation process, including the possible retention of restrictions on Chinese exports.

The question of China's entry or re-entry was essentially solved by a fudge which resulted in China formally requesting resumption of membership, but being treated in practice as a new member. A second, more problematic, question of semantics was over China's position as a 'developing' or a 'developed' nation. The Chinese placed great emphasis on being classified as a developing nation, which they insisted meant that the criteria for membership in terms of domestic economic liberalization would not be as extensive as those required of developed nations. In particular, they argued that as a developing nation China would be subject to the generalized system of preferences, which essentially allows special consideration for exports from developing states. It would also allow China to retain some import restrictions (to protect agriculture and young industries) and to provide limited subsidies for exporters.

By May 1996, the Chinese authorities claimed that they had already reached the criteria for membership as a developing nation (China News Digest 1996). But in reality, there were no such criteria – it is not simply a case of ticking off the boxes when certain criteria have been met until all the boxes have been ticked as those boxes simply do not exist. Indeed, both the concept of developing nation and the criteria for joining the WTO are, to say the least, vague. As Jackson (1989) puts it in if anything an understated manner, 'the whole legal system is one of extraordinary ambiguity'.

Within the WTO constitution, there is a tight definition of 'least developed country' which uses the definitions established by United Nations Conference on Trade and Development (UNCTAD) (2001). But while many of the WTO's regulations refer explicitly to the specific position of developing country members, the classification actually has no legal status under WTO provisions. As the WTO itself states:

> There are no WTO definitions of 'developed' and 'developing' countries. Members announce for themselves whether they are 'developed' or 'developing' countries. However, other members can challenge the decision of a member to make use of provisions available to developing countries.

In providing a legal basis for the 'generalized system of preferences', it was agreed that this must take the form of a waiver to the then GATT MFN clause. But as Jackson (1989: 279) notes, 'it was left to each industrial country to define what was a "developing country" ' and 'a great deal of individual discretion was left to each of the sovereign industrial nations implementing it'.

If anything, the legal basis of negotiating membership to the GATT/WTO is even more vague, and the legal provisions in the WTO constitution for negotiating membership are remarkably short. There are no set patterns or processes. Instead, not only the terms of the agreement, but also decisions on how these terms should be negotiated, are developed on a case by case basis. Article XII of the WTO Marrakesh agreement places the process in the hands of the WTO's working party on individual countries accession, and through bilateral negotiations between the prospective member and any existing member that requests a bilateral agreement (or in the case of individual EU states, through the EU as a bilateral partner). So irrespective of China's level of development, and how it wanted to classify itself, the real question is what the negotiating partners insist on in drawing up an accession package. Rather than the process consisting of crossing clear and identifiable hurdles, it is instead an issue of negotiation and (economic) diplomacy based on the interests of the negotiating parties. So while the WTO is a multilateral organization, negotiating entry proceeds through multiple bilateral negotiations. As there is no set criterion for what should be discussed, or how it should be discussed, this can generate considerable confusion as each set of bilateral negotiations is conducted in isolation from other bilateral negotiations.

Time and again through the years of negotiation, China's entry bid stalled over disputes over its status. It can be argued that the ambiguity in the WTO's legal framework for new members and the lack of a clear concept of what a 'developing nation' actually is made this conflict all but inevitable. But in many respects, it was also a pointless debate, as all that really mattered was the specifics of the bilateral deals that China negotiated. Indeed, as the then acting US Trade Representative Charlene Barshefsky put it in 1996, the issue was 'a red herring and largely irrelevant to the discussions', and that developed, developing or whatever, China should only be allowed to join on what she called a 'commercially meaningful basis'.[7]

Notably, there is no mention of the words 'developing country' at all in the official accession document presented to the ministerial meeting on 10 November (WTO 2001) and pragmatism prevailed in the negotiations. For example, despite reported long protracted arguments over whether China would limit agricultural subsidies to 5 per cent as a developed country or 10 per cent as a developing country, the final agreement was for subsidies for agricultural production at 8.5 per cent of the value of farm output. In addition, China agreed to adhere to Article 6.2 of the WTO's Agriculture Agreement, which, according to the US Department of Agriculture Foreign Agricultural Service, means that 'China agreed to forego the developing country exemption'.[8]

In reality, China's accession protocol entailed significant concessions that far exceed the obligations of previous 'developing country' members. For example, existing WTO members do not have to gradually phase out transitional safeguard measures during the first 12 years of Chinese entry which is normally the case for new members. In addition, importing countries can impose anti-dumping measures on goods from China for 15 years after entry 'if the producers under investigation cannot clearly show that market economy conditions prevail in the industry producing the like product with regard to manufacture, production and sale of that product'. In addition, in passing legislation to approve China's entry into the WTO (US–China Relations Act of 2000) the United States amended the 1974 Trade Act by adding Section 421 which provides a 'transitional bilateral safeguard' agreement allowing US domestic producers to obtain relief if the USITC finds that Chinese products are imported into the United States in such increased quantities as to cause a market disruption.

Argentina, the EU, Hungary, Poland, the Slovak Republic and Turkey also negotiated specific reservations whereby they reserve the right to maintain controls on imports of specific goods. These reservations were largely related to textiles, clothing, footwear (though not sporting footwear – much of which is produced by large MNCs operating in China), toys, ceramics and cigarette lighters.[9] Mexico did not reach a bilateral agreement with China at all, but agreed not to block accession by keeping 21 items on its reserved list which are not subject to normal WTO rules.

Far from being a great success in negotiation, the Chinese deal appears to be one of, if not the, most restrictive of all new entry deals. As Kawai and Bhattasali (2001: 2) from the World Bank argue, 'In many areas, the range of liberalization measures agreed surpasses efforts made in many developing and developed countries'. Indeed, Jeffrey Garten (2001), Dean of the Yale School of Management, argues that Chinese concessions have gone so far, that the United States should accept that it will be politically and economically difficult for the Chinese government to implement all the agreements.

Opposition to entry

Throughout the negotiation process, there was considerable unease, not to say down right opposition, within China over the wisdom of pursuing WTO membership.

Opposition was partly based on ideological considerations. Some leaders such as Deng Liqun continue to complain against the influence of the West, spiritual pollution and bourgeois liberalization. Much more important were voices of opposition to US domination of the international system. A number of highly successful books published in the mid- to late 1990s by a generation of young journalists caught something of the popular mood in favour of resisting unfair international pressure on China to conform to Western-centric norms.[10]

Even louder voices of concern were heard from those who had more pragmatic fears over the implications of WTO entry for key sectors of the Chinese economy, and indeed perhaps for social stability in China. For the sceptics, an existing fragile system could potentially become unstable if WTO commitments made it impossible to continue providing the support for vulnerable groups noted above. Agricultural incomes could fall through a reduction of subsidies and an influx of cheaper grain from the international markets; loss-making enterprises could go to the wall, and even those that were operating at a profit might fall into the red in the face of increased international competition; exporters – particularly from the state sector – might suffer through the eradication of government support such as tax exemptions and the cheap state-set price of industrial inputs. As a Chinese Academy of Social Sciences research report argued, 'structural unemployment may be China's chief adjustment cost for WTO accession' (Yu *et al.* 2000: 1–2). Whether this comes true or not is in some ways irrelevant – in politics perceptions, combined with uncertain futures, are often more important than realities. Why then, risk all this in pursuit of WTO membership?

Explaining Chinese entry

The first answer to this question is found in a desire to become involved in the negotiations on the WTO's future. As the then General Secretary of the WTO, Renato Ruggiero (1997), suggested, 'Only inside the system can China take part in writing the trade rules of the twenty-first century'. Whilst there is an extensive literature on the might of the Quad in the WTO and the opaque nature of WTO power processes (see Chapter 1 by Wilkinson), membership at least allows China to participate in discussions and negotiations. Better to accept the current set of criteria than face a possibly more stringent set of conditions in the future, and try to mobilize support against the power of the Quad.

A second and more important explanation lies in the need to stabilize China's access to major markets in the West – and particularly the United States. Although access to the US market was facilitated by the annual renewal of MFN status, there was considerable unease in China over the lack of certainty. On one level, the size (and growth) of China's trade surplus with the United States was used as an example of the dangers of engaging China by those whose economic interests are at stake (most notably, US toy and textile producers). On another, those who opposed China's human rights record, Tibetan independence supporters, critics of China's one-child policy, opponents of nuclear technology transfer to Pakistan, and critics of Chinese arms sales, call for political conditionalities to be placed on any economic deals with China. WTO entry, then, was seen as a means of depoliticizing market access issues, and of providing access to WTO dispute resolution mechanisms.

But to truly understand the importance of export markets for Chinese development, it is essential to consider the relationship between export growth and 'domestic' growth. China's desire to join the WTO peaked twice – once in 1989 and again at the end of the 1990s. At both times, the domestic Chinese economy was in deflation, leaving export growth as essentially the only means of generating growth, and in turn minimizing the impact of deflation on unemployment. In 1989, this was fired by a real fear that the EU and North American Free Trade Agreement (NAFTA) might become economic fortresses that developing countries outside the global trading organization would be unable to penetrate. In the 1990s, continued export growth was seen as providing the breathing space required to tackle domestic inflation, and to close down the high proportion of loss-making SOEs.

In combination, these dynamics help explain why sections of the Chinese leadership felt the need to push for WTO membership during 1999. But what they do not do is explain the timing – nor the acceptance that the benefits of WTO membership at this stage outweigh the drawbacks resulting from opening the Chinese economy to real competition. Here, I suggest we need to look to a third explanation which combines a consideration of the internal politics of China with the interests of key external actors.

During his period as premier, Zhu Rongji effectively re-defined China's national economic interest. Rather than seeing this interest served by protecting existing domestic producers – particularly the SOEs – Zhu instead perceived that breaking the link with the old system once and for all was the only way to achieve financial stability and guarantee future growth. Faced with considerable opposition from within China to his proposals for reform, I suggest that he instead turned to the international community, and the United States in particular, for external support and validation. As Fewsmith (2001: 574) argues:

> Frustrated by bureaucratic obstruction to fundamental reform, Zhu was willing to avail himself of foreign competitive pressures to force restructuring. As Zhu put it in his report to the recent meeting of the NPC, 'China's economy has reached the point where it cannot further develop without being restructured'.

Thus, by November 1999, Zhu was looking for external support and pressure in his battle with other members of the Chinese party-state elites. At the same time, a liberal international relations agenda was influencing policy in Washington, which promoted the idea of protecting US interest by locking China into the world system and to supporting Zhu's liberalization agenda. This is not to suggest that the United States would have signed any deal whatever the concessions on offer. The two years of intense negotiations after the signing of the November 1999 deal between China and the United States go a long way in proving this. Nevertheless, US and EU policy towards Chinese entry was informed by an understanding that in the long term, it should lock China in to 'international norms' of trade that have been established by the advanced industrialized democracies. In short, as Deng and Wang (1999: 7) put it in what could almost be a definition of liberal international relations theory:

> International enmeshment facilitates China's social learning in terms of the values, norms and principles, and rules of the international system and adds China's stakes in the existing institutions and order. China's worldview and definition of national interests can be transformed toward greater compatibility with the rest of the world through transnational activities and networks, including tourism, academic and cultural exchanges, and commercial ties.

It will take a long time for the real implications of WTO membership to become clear. And of course, there is no guarantee that China will implement all of its obligations. In the first year of Chinese membership external observers were initially relatively happy with the record of compliance. To be sure, there were calls for China to do more, but while the glass was not full, most portrayed it as being half full rather than half empty.[11] Subsequently, however, criticisms of China's compliance became louder and fiercer. In July 2003, US Secretary of Commerce Donald Evans issued a stinging attack on China's compliance record, complaining about the slow pace of reduction of trade barriers and government subsidies to domestic producers, and lack of action over copyright infringement (*Taipei Times* 2003). In addition, a new area of concern has emerged relating to the pegging of the RMB to the US dollar. With the RMB pegged to a depreciating dollar, there have been complaints in the United States that this acts as a quasi-devaluation of the RMB. If, as I suggested, one of the reasons that China wanted to join the WTO was to reduce the politicization of trade issues with the United States (particularly related to the annual MFN vote), then its objectives have only been partially met. It is true that trade issues are now less often linked to domestic Chinese political issues such as human rights. But domestic US issues still very much provide a political context to US–China trade relations.

The question of compliance is not unique to China. All countries, even those in the developed world, face problems in fully liberalizing in keeping with WTO requirements. But for those who suggest that compliance will be even more difficult for China, three re-occurring themes can be identified. The first relates to the isolation of Chinese negotiators from their own colleagues in China. Time and again, interviewees have argued that China's chief negotiator, Long Yongtu, was isolated from other political elites within China. Long and his fellow negotiators did not discuss their negotiations with other interested parties in China other than the top leadership and instead became embroiled in the process of finding agreement with their foreign counterparts. In effect, the process became a 'one-level game', with the need to come to an agreement with negotiating partners – the international game – overriding the need to ensure that domestic Chinese constituents were happy with any concessions – the domestic game. As a result, there was a huge amount of ignorance amongst party-state bureaucrats in China over what the entry requirements actually meant for them.

The second, related, theme is that policymakers have become increasingly aware of the potential destabilizing impact of WTO membership. Indeed, a survey of US companies operating in China found that most expected that the social costs of implementing the requirements would be so great that the Chinese would find it extremely difficult to implement all obligations – this was not so much a complaint as a statement of fact.[12] In theory, joining the WTO was to ensure that leadership changes could not alter the general orientation of policy. But the early evidence of the post-Zhu Rongji leadership suggests some changes in policy, if not a reversal of overall trends. Wen Jiabao and Hu Jintao appear to be placing a greater emphasis on helping those who have lost out during the transition from socialism than their predecessors, and this might have to include protecting those who stand to lose in the wake of WTO entry.

The third theme is that neither the WTO negotiators nor the Chinese national leadership have the ability to force through reform. On one level, Kynge (2002) argues that 'the regulatory agencies who often regard themselves as the protector of domestic companies rather than the regulator' have played a particularly important role in 'interpreting' WTO agreements in ways that allow more protection for domestic producers than was originally intended. This has resulted in 'a dense web of Chinese regulations' which in some cases has undermined the liberalizing logic of the WTO agreement (Dougherty 2002).[13]

On another level:

> Corruption and local protectionism are rampant in China, and gaining the cooperation of local officials and government bureaucrats that oversee various affected industries could prove difficult in the short run. (Morrison 2002)

The fragmentation of power in China makes it all but impossible for the central government to ensure compliance in the provinces. Despite attempts to give Beijing more control over the national economy since 1994, local authorities retain significant local control over their economic affairs – indeed, after 20 years of reform, the Chinese economy has done more to open to the outside world than it has to open to itself.

Conclusions: the politics of Chinese trade and China's WTO entry

It is far too early to know what the impact of WTO entry will be on Chinese trade and China's domestic political economy. Most models suggest that WTO membership will lead to an aggregate increase in Chinese growth of between 0.5 per cent and 1.5 per cent per annum. But even if this is the case, a key issue for China's leaders will be dealing with the uneven distribution of this growth – in terms of both the differential impact by sector, and the differential impact by location. For example, a World Bank paper (Kawai and Bhattasali 2001: 11) which posited a very rosy 'win-win' future as a result of WTO entry noted that those who face the biggest risk are 'rural farmers on marginal land resulting in greater poverty'. It also noted that the impact on agriculture will 'vary by province'. Furthermore, 'the export intensive coastal provinces will gain, while the inland provinces – which contain the bulk of grain production and capital-intensive SOEs – may not gain much or lose'.

Those industries and sectors that stand to lose most, even under rosy assumptions, are those where the hand of the state – or the hand of the old style of state control – still dominates. Those that stand to gain most – particularly in clothing and textiles – are sectors where the new quasi-private sector and foreign ownership dominate. For example, attempts to calculate the impact of WTO entry on China's share of world markets suggest that Chinese exports of clothing will rise from 19.5 per cent of world exports in 1995 to 42.2 per cent in 2005 (Ianchovichina *et al.* 2000). The new opportunities in the service industry will likewise favour those who are not under old-style state control. To call it a quasi-privatization of the Chinese economy is perhaps pushing it too far – not least because current party-state officials (the party-state bourgeoisie) are key actors in the new non-state economy. But WTO membership will further facilitate the ownership basis of the Chinese economy and the class basis of CCP rule that has been ongoing since 1994.

What this suggests, at the most basic level, is that the evolution of China's trade regime in general, and relations with the WTO in particular, can only be explained by accepting the most basic tenets of International Political Economy (IPE) – that the politics and economics and the domestic and the international are inextricably linked. Domestic political interests and bargaining – not just in China, but in the United States and other developed countries – have influenced the negotiation of international trade relationships; and international agreements and transnational alliances are a key determinant of the future evolution of China's domestic political economy.

In the Chinese case, a key sea-change was the changing conception of what is in China's national interests by those who Sklair (1995: 135–36) terms 'globalizing state bureaucrats'. This group, epitomized by the policies of Zhu Rongji, became engaged in a process of making the investment regime within China more and more liberalized and 'attractive' to international capital, and reforming the domestic economic structure. It is going too far to say that China has wholly adopted the neo-liberal paradigm. And it is also going too far to say that domestic politicians have ceded control of the Chinese economy to external actors. Nevertheless, in asserting that neo-liberalism was now hegemonic, Robert Cox's (1999: 12) understanding of world order does help us understand the processes of change that are ongoing in China:

> States now by and large play the role of agencies of the global political economy, with the task of adjusting national economic policies and practices to the perceived exigencies of global economic liberalism. This structure of power is sustained from outside the state through a global policy consensus and the influence of global finance over state policy, and from inside the state from those social forces that benefit from globalization (the segment of society that is integrated into the world economy).

Notes

1. Zhuhai, Shantou, Xiamen and Shenzhen. Hainan Island was later added as the fifth.
2. The Chinese currency is officially the Renminbi Yuan. Renminbi is the name of the currency – the equivalent of saying sterling – while Yuan is the denomination – the equivalent of saying Pound. Just to confuse matters, virtually nobody in China uses the official term 'Yuan' preferring instead the colloquial 'kuai'.
3. Unless indicated to the contrary, all the trade data used in this chapter originates from sources that use figures from the PRC General Administration of Customs. These figures are lower than those estimates of non-Chinese agencies due to different accounting methods. While these figures might deflate the real value of exports by western standards, they are the only way of ensuring the use of common figures, and therefore making like-to-like comparisons.
4. See Lardy (1998, 2002).
5. The example was also repeated on Chinese television on a number of occasions during Zhu Rongji's visit to the United States in March 1999.
6. Discussions with Bill Abnett, USTR official. Note that as the WTO is open to all entities that have 'full autonomy in the conduct of its external commercial relations' (i.e. economic entities, not 'states') Taiwan also joined the WTO after the PRC's accession. Indeed, there are now four Chinese economic entities in the WTO – the People's Republic of China (2001), Hong Kong (1986), Macao (1991) and the rather inelegantly titled Separate Customs Territory of Taiwan, Penghu, Kinmen and Matsu (2002).
7. Reuters via China News Digest, 10 December 1996.
8. http://www.fas.usda.gov/itp/china/accession.html
9. These are broad headings which are then broken down by specific items in keeping with specific HS codes. Thus, within the broad heading of Textiles and Clothing, there are 83 HS code items on the Argentine's list of reservations.
10. See, for example, Chen *et al.* (1996) and Liu and Liu (1997).
11. See, for example, United States–China Business Council (2002),United States General Accounting Office (2002) and Dong Liu (2002). With thanks to Bill Abnett.
12. United States General Accounting Office (2002).
13. According to Stratford (2002), this process of overturning original intentions takes three forms – 'legitimate (though unwelcome) exploitations of "loopholes"', 'China's aggressive interpretations of ambiguous language', and 'blatant disregard for clear-cut obligations'.

References

Bachman, D. (1988) 'Varieties of Chinese Conservatism and the Fall of Hu Yaobang', *Journal of Northeast Asian Studies*, Spring: 22–46.

Barboza, D. (2003) 'Textile Industry Seeks Trade Limits on Chinese', *New York Times*, 25 July.

Barshefsky, C. (1999) 'Statement of Ambassador Charlene Barshefsky Regarding Broad Market Access Gains Resulting from China WTO Negotiations,' Office Of The United States Trade Representative: Washington DC, 8 April.

Bergsten, C.F. (1997) 'The Asian Monetary Crisis: Proposed Remedies,' prepared remarks to the U.S. House of Representatives Committee on Banking and Financial Services, 13 November.

Braunstein, E. and Epstein, G. (2002) 'Bargaining Power and Foreign Direct Investment in China: Can 1.3 Billion Consumers Tame the Multinationals?', CEPA Working Papers 2002–13, Center for Economic Policy Analysis (CEPA), New School University.

Chan, A. (1996) 'Boot Camp at the Show Factory: Regimented Workers in China's Free Labour Market', The Washington Post, 3 November.

Chen Feng, Zhao Xingyuan, Huang Jiaoyu, Yang Mingjie and Yuan Xixing (1996) Zhongmei Jialian Caxiezheng (A History of Sino-American Rivalry), Beijing: Zhongguo Renshi Publishers.

China News Digest (1996), 7 May.

Cox, R. (1999) 'Civil Society at the Turn of the Millennium: Prospects for an Alternative', *Review of International Studies*, 25 (1), pp. 3–28.

Deng Yong and Fei-ling Wang (eds) (1999) *In the Eyes of the Dragon: China Views the World*, Lanham: Rowman and Littlefield.

Dong Liu (2002) 'China under scrutiny over WTO commitments', *China News Digest*, 28 September.

Dougherty, C. (2002) 'Chinese Fall Short on WTO Promises', *The Washington Times*, 5 July.

Fernald, J., Edison, H. and Loungani, P. (1998) 'Was China the First Domino? Assessing Links between China and the Rest of Emerging Asia', Board of Governors of the Federal Reserve System International Finance Discussion Paper No. 604, March 1998.

Fewsmith, J. (2001) 'The Political and Social Implications of China's Accession to the WTO' *The China Quarterly*, 167.

Garten, J. (2001) 'China in the WTO: Let's Cut It Some Slack', *Business Week*, 8 October.

Hamrin, C. (1990) *China and the Challenge of the Future*, Boulder, CO: Westview.

Howell, J. (1993) *China Opens Its Doors – The Politics Of Economic Transition*, Boulder, CO: Harvester Wheatsheaf.

Hu Angang (1999) 'Unemployment and Development: China's Employment Problem and Employment Strategy' *World Economy and China*, 7 (5–6): 34–48.

Ianchovichina, E., Martin, W. and Fukase, E. (2000) 'Comparative Study of Trade Liberalization Regimes: The Case of China's Accession to the WTO' Third Annual Conference on Global Economic Analysis, Monash, Melbourne, June. http://www.monash.edu.au/policy/conf/75Martin.pdf

Jackson, J. (1989) 'The World Trading System: Law and Policy of International Relations', Cambridge, MA: MIT Press.

Jin Bei (1997) 'The International Competition Facing Domestically Produced Goods and the Nation's Industry', *Social Sciences in China*, 18, 1.

Kawai, Masahiro and Bhattasali, Deepak (2001) 'The Implications of China's Accession to the World Trade Organisation', paper presented at Japan and China: Economic Relations in Transition Jan 2001 Tokyo. Cited with authors' permission.

Kynge, J. (2002) 'Survey – China & The World Trade Organisation' *Financial Times*, 15 March.

Lardy, N. (1998) *China's Unfinished Economic Revolution*, Washington, DC: Brookings.

Lardy, N. (2002) *Integrating China Into the Global Economy*, Washington, DC: Brookings.

Lau, L., Qian Yingyi and Roland, G. (2000) 'Reform without Losers: An Interpretation of China's Dual-Track Approach to Transition', *Journal of Political Economy*, 108, 1: 120–43.

Liu Xiguang and Liu Kang (1997) *Yaomo Fa Zhongguo de Beihou* (Behind the Demonisation of China), Beijing: Social Science Publishers.

Makin, J. (1997) 'Two New Paradigms', *Economic Outlook*, American Enterprise Institute, 1 October.

Morrison, W. (2002) 'Issue Brief for Congress Received through the CRS Web' Order Code IB9921 China–U.S. Trade Issues 2002. With thanks to Bill Abnett.

Naughton, B. (2000) 'China's Trade Regime at the end of the 1990s', in Carpenter, T. and Dorn, J. (eds) *China's Future: Constructive Partner or Emerging Threat?* (Washington, DC: Cato Institute), pp. 235–60.

Ruggiero, R. (1997) 'China and the World Trading System', Speech at Beijing University, 21 April.

Sala-I-Martin, X. (2003) *Global Competitiveness Report Executive Summary*, Geneva: World Economic Forum.

Sklair, L. (1995) *Sociology of the Global System*, Harvester Wheatsheaf [2nd edition].

Stratford, T. (2002) Testimony to The Office of the United States Trade Representative Regarding China's Implementation of its WTO Commitments, 18 September 2002. With thanks to Bill Abnett.

Taipei Times (2003) 'Evans Warns China to Comply with its WTO Commitments', 9 July, p. 3.

Tempest, R. (1996) 'Barbie and the World Economy', *Los Angeles Times*, 22 September.

UNCTAD (2001) Statistical Profiles Of LDCs, 2001 (available on-line on http://www. unctad.org/en/pub/ldcprofiles2001.en.htm)

United States-China Business Council (2002), 'China's WTO Implementation Efforts: An Assessment of the First Nine Months of China's WTO Membership', Written Testimony by the United States-China Business Council, Prepared on 3 September.

United States General Accounting Office (2002) 'World Trade Organization: Selected U.S. Company Views about China's Membership', Report to Congressional Committees, September 2002.

WTO (2001) 'Protocol On The Accession Of The People's Republic Of China', WTO Document No WT/L/432, 23 November.

Yu Yongding (1999) 'China's Macroeconomic Situation and Future Prospect' *World Economy and China*, 8, 3–4, pp. 3–17.

Yu Yongding, Zheng Bingwen, and Song Hong (eds) (2000) Zhongguo 'RuShi' Yanjiu Baogu: Jinru WTO de Zhongguo Chanye (Research Report on China's Entry into WTO: The Analysis of China's Industries) (Beijing: Social Sciences Documentation Publishers).

Zhang Yongjin (1998) *China in International Society Since 1949: Alienation and Beyond*, Basingstoke: Macmillan.

Index